Microsoft®
Visual C#
2005

UNLEASHED

800 East 96th Street, Indianapolis, Indiana 46240

Microsoft® Visual C# 2005 Unleashed

International Standard Book Number: 0-672-32776-7

Library of Congress Catalog Card Number: 2006901231

Printed in the United States of America

Second Printing June 2006

09   08   07   06   4   3   2

Trademarks

Warning and Disclaimer

Bulk Sales

Sams Publishing offers excellent discounts on this book when ordered in quantity for bulk purchases or special sales. For more information, please contact

U.S. Corporate and Government Sales
1-800-382-3419
corpsales@pearsontechgroup.com

For sales outside the United States, please contact

International Sales
international@pearsoned.com

Publisher	Paul Boger
Acquisitions Editor	Neil Rowe
Development Editor	Mark Renfrow
Project Editor	Tonya Simpson
Copy Editor	Margaret Berson
Indexer	Ken Johnson
Proofreader	Susan Eldridge
Technical Editor	J. Boyd Nolan
Publishing Coordinator	Cindy Teeters
Interior Designer	Gary Adair
Cover Designer	Alan Clements

This Book Is Safari Enabled

The Safari® Enabled icon on the cover of your favorite technology book means the book is available through Safari Bookshelf. When you buy this book, you get free access to the online edition for 45 days.

Safari Bookshelf is an electronic reference library that lets you easily search thousands of technical books, find code samples, download chapters, and access technical information whenever and wherever you need it.

To gain 45-day Safari Enabled access to this book:

- Go to http://www.samspublishing.com/safarienabled
- Complete the brief registration form
- Enter the coupon code 69HV-6HSH-YGZT-X8H5-ACFJ

If you have difficulty registering on Safari Bookshelf or accessing the online edition, please email customer-service@safaribooksonline.com.

Contents at a Glance

Table of Contents

About the Author

Kevin Hoffman has been programming for more than 20 years. He got started when his grandfather repaired a discarded Commodore VIC-20 and he got right to work creating text-based role-playing games in BASIC. Since then, he has dedicated himself to learning all there is to know about programming, and using every programming language he could find, including Pascal, C, C++, Scheme, LISP, ADA, Perl, Python, Java, and many others. When he first saw a pre-beta release of C# 1.0, he was hooked. He knew at that moment that the .NET Framework would revolutionize how developers created software and how people designed software, and would enable new types of applications and new functionality that either used to be impossible or too cost-prohibitive to even attempt. As a result of his passion for the .NET Framework, he has dubbed himself the ".NET Addict."

Dedication

Writing a technical book involves just as much creativity and inspiration as writing a fantasy or a science fiction novel; it's just a different kind of inspiration. I would like to dedicate this book to my inspiration: my wonderful wife, Connie.

Regardless of where the inspiration comes from or what it produces, it's still a highly creative process that is subject to writer's block and fits of irritability, crankiness, defeatism, and being so absorbed in a particular topic that the world around me ceases to exist until I have conquered that topic.

It truly is a battle, "me vs. the technology." The problem is that this battle requires a huge time investment. Somehow my wife has managed to tolerate me being in the same room but simply "not being there" while I type away in order to defeat the chapters that loom before me, daring me to take them on. My daughter, Jerrah, has her own keyboard so that she can pretend to "be busy" just like Daddy. There's something bittersweet about the fact that she wants to be like me, but that her impression of me is one of being busy and typing all the time.

My wife's patience, love, caring, and support have been invaluable. Without her support, I would've given up on writing before I even got started. And certainly without her I never would have been able to write this book, the single largest and most time-consuming book I've ever written.

Regardless of which deity you believe in, or whether you believe in one, you must concede the existence of angels. After all, I am married to one.

We Want to Hear from You!

As the reader of this book, *you* are our most important critic and commentator. We value your opinion and want to know what we're doing right, what we could do better, what areas you'd like to see us publish in, and any other words of wisdom you're willing to pass our way.

As a publisher for Sams Publishing, I welcome your comments. You can email or write me directly to let me know what you did or didn't like about this book—as well as what we can do to make our books better.

Please note that I cannot help you with technical problems related to the topic of this book. We do have a User Services group, however, where I will forward specific technical questions related to the book.

When you write, please be sure to include this book's title and author as well as your name, email address, and phone number. I will carefully review your comments and share them with the author and editors who worked on the book.

Email: feedback@samspublishing.com

Mail: Paul Boger
           Publisher
           Sams Publishing
           800 East 96th Street
           Indianapolis, IN 46240 USA

Reader Services

Visit our website and register this book at www.samspublishing.com/register for convenient access to any updates, downloads, or errata that might be available for this book.

Introduction

If you can force yourself to think back 10 years, think about the proliferation of technology in just that short period of time. Back in the "good ole" days, you could walk down a busy city street, and you probably wouldn't see anyone talking on a cell phone. You wouldn't see people busily tapping at their PDAs. You definitely didn't see anyone sitting in an Internet café using a Tablet PC to send hand-sketched application designs halfway around the world to a remote development team.

Connectivity between applications and application components used to be something that required the use of extremely skilled, highly expensive development efforts. Sure, we had technologies like CORBA, but they had limited use.

Today, connectivity itself has become so ubiquitous that it is *demanded*. When people turn on their PDA in an Internet-enabled coffee shop, they fully expect that they will be able to connect to the Internet from there. If they don't—they will complain to the owner. When people flip open their brand new cellular phone, not only do they expect it to take photographs, but they expect to be able to upload their photos to a central location to be shared with friends, family, or the entire Internet. They expect that they can download ringtones, games, even music and videos. If they can't—they want their money back.

This same demand for connectivity, performance, and modern features can be found in desktop software and web software as well. People want their applications to follow the "It Just Works" principle. They should be able to beat on and otherwise abuse that application without fear of retribution in the form of lost or corrupted data. Users want their Windows applications to work properly whether they're connected to the Internet or not. They want their web applications to be more responsive than they used to be, they want them to look great, and they want them to run fast, and they want them to remember what they like, what they don't like, and who they are.

In short, the demands modern users are placing on the quality, features, and functionality of the applications they use have never been more strict. Programmers today must create some of the most powerful applications ever written, and they need to do it quickly, reliably, and cheaply.

This book will take the developer through an in-depth exploration of the features, power, and capabilities of Visual C# .NET 2005, the latest and most powerful version of the C# language running on the .NET Framework 2.0.

Among many other things, by reading this book you will

- Learn the fundamentals of the C# language and the core features of the .NET Framework 2.0, such as object-oriented programming, generics, and other basics such as delegates and event-driven programming.

- Learn how to work with data in many forms from many sources using ADO.NET 2.0, even how to write stored procedures for SQL Server 2005 in C#!

- Create Windows Forms applications with rich, highly responsive user interfaces.

- Deploy Windows Forms applications from the web or anywhere else with the click of a button.

- Create Windows Forms applications that *update themselves* automatically over the Internet by checking for new releases and patches.

- Learn how to create ASP.NET 2.0 applications and the new features that come with them.

- Utilize master pages, themes, and skins to create a consistent look and feel throughout your site and even provide the ability for users to select their own style theme.

- Use Web Parts and Web Part Pages to create dynamic, user-controllable content pages that contain information and functionality targeted to the specific user or the user's security level.

- Use the new Provider model in ASP.NET to create an application that can authenticate users, store user role membership, store user profile data, and user personalization information (such as Web Part preferences) in SQL Server 2005 *in 15 minutes or less!*

- Use client callbacks to create highly interactive, Ajax-style interfaces in ASP.NET 2.0.

- Learn how to create custom, reusable ASP.NET controls.

- Learn how to create and consume web services.

- Use remoting and/or COM+ to create distributed, connected applications.

This book is crammed full of information on how to get you up to speed on the newest technology. It also provides you with practical application of the technology. As we all know, applying a technology just because it's new or interesting isn't necessarily the right thing to do. As you read this book, you will be introduced to the new technology from the ground up (learning to walk before you can run), as well as learning where that technology makes sense and when it should be applied.

You might find some of the earlier chapters to be somewhat of a review if you have already been working with C# 2005. However, many of the later chapters in the book build on technologies and techniques introduced in earlier chapters, making this book ideally suited to being read from start to finish.

PART I

C# 2.0 Fundamentals

IN THIS PART

Introduction to C# 2.0

This chapter provides a brief introduction to the world of C#. As you will see, the syntax of the language itself is fairly easy to learn. The thing that takes the most time is learning how to program on the .NET Framework using the C# language. You will see the basic syntax of the C# language, including how to declare variables, create code blocks, and of course, create your first "Hello World" application.

If you already have a working knowledge of the C# language from your experience with previous versions (either 1.0 or 1.1), you can skip this chapter and move on. Take care not to skip too many of the early chapters, as there have been enhancements to the language that are covered early on in the book, such as generics and anonymous methods. This chapter also skips over some details that you may not be aware of if you have very little exposure to programming. If you have never written software on the Windows platform (either Windows or Web-based), this is the wrong chapter, and perhaps the wrong book, for you.

What Is the .NET Framework?

Before you learn the mechanics of the C# language itself, it is important that you learn the evolution of technologies that created the need for a language like C#. This section takes you on a quick tour of the history of C#, followed by an explanation of the Common Language Runtime, the Common Type System, and concluding with an overview of garbage-collected environments.

The Evolution of .NET

Before the .NET Framework was released to the public, the majority of component-oriented development for the Windows platform took the form of COM objects. Component Object Model (COM), a binary standard for creating reusable components, allowed developers to write code that solved smaller problems in smaller problem domains. By breaking down the problem into components, the solution often became easier and the components used to solve the problem could be reused to solve other similar problems.

COM offered many advantages and disadvantages. One of the most common problems with the COM standard was appropriately dubbed "DLL hell." DLL hell arose when COM interfaces were indexed in the registry and then newer versions of those components were released. Versioning often caused developers headaches due to the tightly coupled, binary nature of the standard. In addition, if a DLL's location changed on the file system without the information in the registry being modified, the COM interfaces contained within that DLL would become inaccessible. You could see examples of this when a new application was installed with a different version of some shared component, and it would not only break the new application, but all other applications using that component as well.

Other problems with development at the time included things like difficulty managing memory, slow development times, GUI controls that were typically insufficient for many tasks, as well as a lack of interoperability between languages such as C++ and Visual Basic.

As a solution to this and countless other problems with development at the time, Microsoft began working on what was then referred to as *COM+ 2.0*. The solution would provide a managed environment in which code would be executed that would provide for enhanced type safety, security, and an incredibly extensive library of useful classes and functions to make the lives of developers much easier. Eventually this solution became what is now the .NET Framework. Versions 1.0 and 1.1 have been released and now version 2.0 is available. In the next few sections, some of the key aspects of the .NET Framework will be discussed: the Common Language Runtime, the Common Type System, and the concept of garbage-collected managed code.

The Common Language Runtime

Before talking about the basics of C#, you need to know a little bit about how C# (and all other .NET languages) works and where it sits in relation to the various components that make the entire .NET Framework run.

One such component is the *Common Language Runtime* (almost exclusively referred to as the CLR). Unlike previous versions of C++ and similar languages, C# runs in a managed environment. Code that you write in C# runs inside the context of the Common Language Runtime. The runtime is responsible for managing things like memory and security and isolating your code from other code so that malicious or poorly written code can't interfere with the normal operation of your application.

Figure 1.1 illustrates the layers of .NET.

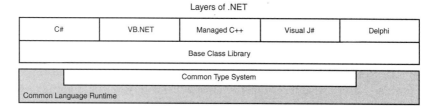

FIGURE 1.1   The layers of .NET.

At the top layer you have the various .NET languages (this figure only includes a few of the languages that run under the CLR). Beneath those languages you have the Base Class Library. The BCL (Base Class Library) is the collection of classes and utilities written in the .NET Framework that provide you with the fundamentals you need in order to create your applications, such as code to allow you to deal with encryption, data access, file I/O, web applications, Windows applications, and much more. As you will see throughout the book, much of the task of learning C# isn't learning the language syntax; it's learning about the vast library of the BCL. In short, the CLR is the managed execution engine that drives the code written in the BCL and any applications you create.

Don Box has written an excellent book on the Common Language Runtime that gives all the detail you can possibly imagine on what the CLR is and how it works. The book is called *Essential .NET Volume I: The Common Language Runtime* (ISBN 0201734117, Addison-Wesley Professional).

The Common Type System

A common problem in many programming languages is the inability to exchange data between programs written in different languages. For example, you have to take special precautions when invoking C methods from Pascal, and Pascal methods from C because of parameter ordering. In addition, strings in C consist of an array of characters that are terminated with the ASCII NULL (typically represented as \0). In Pascal, the first byte of a string actually contains the length of the string. These problems are just the tip of the iceberg. As you can tell, getting different languages to communicate with each other can be a nightmarish task (and, historically, it has been).

A solution to this is to allow all of the languages to share a common representation for data types. The Common Type System provides for a common set of data types. For example, if you refer to a string in VB.NET, C#, J#, Delphi (.NET), managed C++, or any other .NET language, you are guaranteed to be referring to the same entity. This is because the type string is actually defined within the .NET Framework itself, not the language. Removing the data type definition from the languages creates an environment where VB.NET and C# code can coexist side by side without any communication issues.

Taking Out the Trash: Coding in a Garbage-Collected Environment

As I mentioned earlier in this section, the CLR does quite a bit of memory management on your behalf. If you have used C# 1.0 or 1.1, you will be familiar with this concept.

One of the components of the CLR is the *Garbage Collector*. When you declare new variables (we'll get to that in the next section) in C#, they are managed by the Garbage Collector. When a collection cycle takes place, the Garbage Collector examines your variables and if they are no longer in use, it will dispose of them (referred to as a *collection*). In Chapter 16, "Optimizing your .NET 2.0 Code," you will learn more about the Garbage Collector (GC) and how awareness of its presence while coding and designing can improve the speed of your applications. For now, it is good enough to know that the GC is there managing your memory and cleaning up after you and your variables.

Working with Variables in C# 2.0

My favorite analogy for explaining variables is the "bucket" analogy. Think of a variable as a bucket. Into that bucket, you can place data. Some buckets don't care what kind of data you place in them, and other buckets have specific requirements on the type of data you can place in them. You can move data from one bucket to another. Unfortunately, the bucket analogy gets a little confusing when you take into account that one bucket can contain a little note inside that reads "see Bucket B for actual data" (you'll read about reference types shortly in the section "Value Types vs. Reference Types").

To declare a variable in C#, you can use the following syntax:

```
type variable_name;
```

You can initialize a variable on the same line:

```
type variable_name = initialization expression;
```

where *type* is a .NET type. The next section lists some of the core .NET types.

Common .NET Types

Table 1.1 shows some of the basic .NET data types. As you will see in later chapters, this is just the beginning. When you start using classes, the variety of types available to you will be virtually unlimited.

TABLE 1.1   Core .NET Data Types

Data Type	Description
System.Boolean	Provides a way to store true/false data.
System.Byte	Represents a single byte of data.
System.Char	A single character. Unlike other languages, this character is a 2-byte Unicode character.
System.Decimal	A decimal value with 28 to 29 significant digits in the range $\pm1.0 \times 10^{-28}$ to $\pm7.9 \times 10^{28}$.
System.Double	A double-precision value that represents a 64-bit floating-point value with 15 to 16 significant digits in the range $\pm5.0 \times 10^{-324}$ to $\pm1.7 \times10^{308}$.
System.Single	A single-precision value that represents a 32-bit floating point number in the range $\pm1.5 \times 10^{-45}$ to $\pm3.4 \times 10^{38}$.

TABLE 1.1   Continued

Data Type	Description
System.Int32	Represents a 32-bit signed integer in the range –2,147,483,648 to 2,147,483,647.
System.Int64	Represents a 64-bit signed integer in the range –9,223,372,036,854,775,808 to 9,223,372,036,854,775,807.
System.SByte	A signed 8-bit integer.
System.Int16	A signed 16-bit integer.
System.UInt32	An unsigned 32-bit integer.
System.UInt64	An unsigned 64-bit integer.
System.UInt16	An unsigned 16-bit integer.
System.String	An arbitrary-length character string that can contain Unicode strings.

If you aren't familiar with .NET or C#, you may be wondering what the "System" is in the data types listed in Table 1.1. .NET organizes all types into *namespaces*. A namespace is a logical container that provides name distinction for data types. These core data types all exist in the "System" namespace. You'll see more namespaces throughout the book as you learn about more specific aspects of .NET.

Type Shortcuts

C# provides you with some shortcuts to make declaring some of the core data types easier. These shortcuts are simple one-word lowercase aliases that, when compiled, will still represent a core .NET type. Table 1.2 lists some data type shortcuts and their corresponding .NET types.

TABLE 1.2   C# Aliases for .NET Data Types

Shortcut	.NET Type
bool	System.Boolean
byte	System.Byte
char	System.Char
decimal	System.Decimal
double	System.Double
float	System.Single
int	System.Int32
long	System.Int64
sbyte	System.SByte
short	System.Int16
uint	System.UInt32
ulong	System.UInt64
ushort	System.UInt16

Value Types vs. Reference Types

Up to this point, this chapter has just been illustrating data types in one category. Earlier in the chapter, I mentioned a "bucket" analogy where data in one bucket could actually refer to data contained in some other bucket. This is actually the core point to illustrate the difference between *value types* and *reference types*.

A *value type* is a type whose data is contained with the variable on the stack. Value types are generally fast and lightweight because they reside on the stack (you will read about the exceptions in Chapter 16, "Optimizing your .NET 2.0 Code").

A *reference type* is a type whose data does not reside on the stack, but instead resides on the heap. When the data contained in a reference type is accessed, the contents of the variable are examined on the stack. That data then references (or *points to*, for those of you with traditional C and C++ experience) the *actual* data contained in the heap. Reference types are generally larger and slower than value types. Learning when to use a reference type and when to use a value type is something that comes with practice and experience.

Your code often needs to pass very large objects as parameters to methods. If these large parameters were passed on the stack as value types, the performance of the application would degrade horribly. Using reference types allows your code to pass a "reference" to the large object rather than the large object itself. Value types allow your code to pass small data in an optimized way directly on the stack.

C# Basic Syntax

You will learn a lot of C# syntax tricks as you progress through the book. This section introduces you to the most basic concepts required to create the simplest C# application—the canonical "Hello World" sample.

Code Blocks

As you know, all programming languages work on the same basic principle: individual instructions are executed in sequence to produce some result. Instructions can be anything from defining a class to printing information to the Console output.

In C#, multiple lines of code are grouped together into a logical execution block by wrapping the lines of code with the "curly brackets" or braces: the { and } symbols.

The Canonical "Hello World" Sample

It seems as though virtually every book on a programming language starts off with a program that prints the phrase "Hello World" to the console. Rather than risk horrible karma and unknown repercussions from breaking with tradition, I am going to inflict my own version of "Hello World" upon you.

To start, open up whatever 2005 IDE you have (C# Express 2005, or any of the Visual Studio 2005 editions) and create a new Console Application (make sure you select C# if you have multiple languages installed) called HelloWorld. Make sure that your code looks the same as the code shown in Listing 1.1.

LISTING 1.1   The Hello World Application

```
using System;
using System.Collections.Generic;
using System.Text;

namespace HelloWorld
{
  class Program
  {
    static void Main(string[] args)
    {
      Console.BackgroundColor = ConsoleColor.DarkBlue;
      Console.ForegroundColor = ConsoleColor.White;
      Console.WriteLine("---   Visual C# 2005 Unleashed   ---");
      Console.BackgroundColor = ConsoleColor.Black;
      Console.ForegroundColor = ConsoleColor.Yellow;
      Console.Write("Hello ");
      Console.ForegroundColor = ConsoleColor.Magenta;
      Console.WriteLine("World");
    }
  }
}
```

The Console class (you'll learn about classes in Chapter 5, "Objects and Components") provides a set of methods for dealing with the console. In previous versions of .NET, you could not do anything with colors in the Console class. With .NET 2.0, you now have the ability to change the foreground and background colors of the console.

Press Ctrl+F5 or choose Debug and then Start without Debugging. Figure 1.2 shows the output of the application, including the newly added color features of the 2.0 Console.

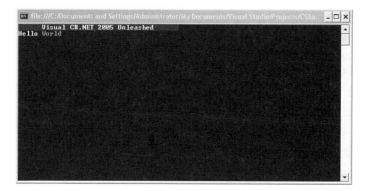

FIGURE 1.2   The Hello World Application, in full color.

What You Can Do with C#

As you will see throughout this book, you can produce all kinds of applications using C#. The C# language, and the .NET Framework underneath it, allow you to create

- Windows applications—Create compelling, fast, powerful desktop applications that can do amazing things, including update themselves over the web automatically.

- Web applications—Create amazingly powerful, rich, full-featured web applications in the shortest amount of time ever, taking advantage of new features like Web Parts, Master Pages, Themes, and much more.

- Web services—Get on board with Service-Oriented Architecture by exposing business logic and data over industry-standard protocols.

- Data-driven applications—Consume data from a wide variety of sources, aggregate data from multiple sources, and expose that data to end users through Web or Windows interfaces.

- Mobile applications—Create web applications that automatically recognize mobile platforms and adapt to the small form factor and limited capacity of PocketPCs and cellular phones.

- Mobile clients—Create applications that target the PocketPC platform and can not only communicate with other desktop applications, but can also communicate with the Internet, consume web services, and interact with SQL databases.

- SQL Server 2005—Create stored procedures, functions, and user-defined data types that reside directly inside the SQL Server 2005 database engine for unprecedented productivity, performance, and reliability.

- Integration applications—Take advantage of COM Interoperability as well as .NET-based APIs to integrate your own code with other applications such as Office 2003, SharePoint Portal Server 2003, and much, much more.

Summary

This chapter provided you with a brief introduction to the world of the .NET Framework and C# 2.0. You read about how the .NET Framework evolved as well as what it is now. In addition, you were introduced to the Common Language Runtime, the Garbage Collector, the Common Type System, and finally a very small introductory application.

This chapter has provided you with the basic foundation that you will need in order to continue learning about C# 2005 by progressing through this book.

CHAPTER 2

Expressions and Control Structures

At the core of every language is the ability to perform two different types of tasks: repetition and conditional logic. Repetition involves using language constructs called *loops* to perform the same task multiple times. Conditional logic involves writing code that will only execute certain code based on specified conditions. This chapter introduces you to the basics of how to accomplish both of these types of tasks using the C# language.

If you have any familiarity with programming languages at all, the concepts discussed in this chapter should seem familiar and will be easy for you to pick up the C# syntax. If you have already been using C# for some time, you should be able to skim this chapter briefly as a refresher before continuing on through the rest of the book.

Branching and Conditional Logic

Every modern programming language supports the notion of branching and conditional logic. This gives your applications the ability to do different things based on current input, events, error conditions, or any condition that can be expressed logically. This section first shows you how C# allows you to form logical expressions and how to create code blocks that are executed conditionally based on those expressions. Then you'll see a couple of shortcuts and extras that C# contains to make using certain types of common logic statements even easier.

Introduction to Boolean Expressions

A Boolean expression is a code statement that will eventually evaluate to either true or false. At the most basic level, all Boolean expressions, no matter how long or complex, are still going to evaluate to either `true` or `false`.

The simplest of all Boolean expressions is *equality*. This expression is used to test whether or not one value is equivalent to another value. This can be something simple, such as

```
2 == 4
```

This expression will evaluate to `false` because 2 is not equal to 4. It can also be something complex, such as

```
MyObject.MyProperty == YourObject.YourProperty
```

This expression could evaluate to anything, and would be determined at runtime. If you are familiar with C, C++, or even C#, you know that the == (double-equals) is a logical Boolean operator, and the = (single equals) is an assignment operator used to set values. A common source of runtime and compile-time errors revolves around using these operators in the wrong place.

Table 2.1 shows the logical operators available in the C# language and provides a brief description of their purpose.

TABLE 2.1   C# Logical Operators

Operator	Description
&&	A Boolean AND operator. Expressions involving this operator will evaluate to `true` if *both* the expression on the left side of the operator *and* the expression on the right side of the operator evaluate to `true`.
||	A Boolean OR operator. Expressions using this operator will evaluate to `true` if *either* the *left* expression or the *right* expression are true, or if *both* expressions are true.
!	The NOT operator. It negates the Boolean value of whatever expression it is applied to. So, if ! is applied to a true expression, the expression will become false. Likewise, if ! is applied to a false expression, the expression will become true.
^	The exclusive OR operator (often referred to as XOR in many languages). This functions the same way as the standard OR (||) operator, with the exception that if *both* sides of the expression are true, this operator will return `false`.
~	This operator performs a bitwise complement on its operand. This means that it will reverse every single bit in whatever operand is supplied. On a single-bit value, it is the same as the ! operator. However, on numbers such as integers, decimals, and so on, it has a more profound effect.
&	The bitwise AND operator. Instead of performing an AND against two Boolean expressions, it performs it against two numeric values. The numbers are lined up, and the AND is performed against each bit. The result of this operation is a new number. Bitwise logic has very specific uses, often when storing long lists of Boolean values as numbers.
|	The bitwise OR operator. As with the bitwise AND operator, it performs an OR operation against each bit of the two operands supplied for the expression, the result being returned as a numeric value.

Using Basic Conditional Statements

In the preceding section you were introduced to the tools you need in order to form Boolean expressions. These will allow you to assert whether or not an expression is true. When you have such an assertion, you need to be able to provide some conditional statements in your code to allow you to do something meaningful based on the results of a Boolean expression. This section will show you the basic conditional statements that are at the heart of almost all logic code in C#.

Using If/Else Statements

The format of an if statement is as follows:

```
if ( expression )
    code_block
else if ( expression_1 )
    code_block
else if ( expression_2 )
    code_block
else
    code_block
```

Both the else if and else sections are optional, and are only required if you want your code to perform alternate tasks when the original Boolean expression evaluates to false.

Because each of the code blocks in the preceding example can also contain their own if statements, you can nest your conditional code nearly as deep as you like. However, good style and etiquette recommend that you avoid deep nesting because it makes your code difficult to read and analyze.

The following sample if statements illustrate using if simply, nested, and with else statements:

```
if ( strInput == "Hello" )
   Console.WriteLine("You said Hello");


if ( strInput2 == "Goodbye" )
   Console.WriteLine("You said Goodbye");
else if ( strInput2 == "Later" )
   Console.WriteLine("You didn't say goodbye, you said Later.")
else
{
   if (strInput3 == "Hola")
      if (strInput4 == "Senor")
         Console.WriteLine("Hello!");
}
```

Using the `Switch` **Statement**

If you want to test a single variable against a list of possible values using just the standard `if/else` keywords, you will end up with code that looks like the following:

```
if (val == 1)
   ...
else if (val == 2)
   ...
else if (val == 3)
   ...
else if (val == 4)
   ...
else
   ...
```

Although this may get the job done, it's not the most elegant or the most easily readable block of code. For this situation, C# has the `switch` statement, which allows you to combine several logic tests into a single expression, as shown in the following example:

```
switch (val)
{
    case 1:
       ...
       break;
    case 2:
       ...
       break;
    case 3:
       ...
       break;
    default:
       ...
}
```

Using the `Goto` **Statement**

The goto statement has two main uses; one is to transfer control from one `case` within a switch statement, and the other is to break out of loops. You will see more on loops later in this chapter.

The following is a sample of a `switch` statement that utilizes the goto keyword for transferring control:

```
switch (val)
{
    case 1:
       ...
       break;
```

```
   case 2:
      ...
      goto case 1;
      break;
   case 3:
      ...
      goto case 1;
      break;
   default:
      ...
}
```

Using Advanced Conditional Statements

One of the most common uses for an `if`/`else` statement is to conditionally print something or render something through Windows Forms or Web Forms. For example, suppose that you want to print the word "Good" if the profit margin is greater than 20, or "Bad" if the profit margin is less than or equal to 20. You might use an `if`/`else` that looks like the following:

```
if (profitMargin > 20)
   Console.WriteLine("The profit margin is Good!");
else
   Console.WriteLine("The profit margin is Bad!");
```

This is perfectly fine, but C# includes a ternary operator called the `conditional` operator that allows you to embed an `if`/`else` combination in a single line. You can rewrite the preceding code segment in a single line as follows:

```
Console.WriteLine("The profit margin is " + (profitMargin > 20) ? "Good" : "Bad");
```

The ternary conditional operator has the following format:

```
expression ? return_when_true : return_when_false
```

Looping and Repetition

In addition to conditional logic and branching, looping is one of the most common tasks performed by all applications, regardless of the application type. It is impossible to find a production-quality application written in .NET today that does not include some use of loops.

A loop is a repetition of a code block a certain number of times. The number of times is determined by the type of loop being used. This section will show you the basics of creating and using loops in C#.

Using the `for` Loop

Each `for` loop has three sections:

1. The initializer. This is a block of code that is executed once at the beginning of the `for` loop. Variables declared in this section are available for the scope and duration of the loop but will not remain outside the loop. This section is typically used to initialize the counter variable or variables.

2. The exit condition. This section defines a Boolean expression that is used to determine how long the `for` loop keeps running. As long as the Boolean expression continues to evaluate to `true`, the loop keeps running. This expression is tested at the *beginning* of each loop execution.

3. The iterative code. This section is arbitrary, and can contain any code that you want to execute at the end of each iteration through the loop. This is typically where the loop counter variables are incremented.

The format of the `for` loop is as follows:

```
for ( initializer; exit condition; iterative code )
{
    ...
}
```

So, to create a `for` loop that will execute a block of code five times, you would write the following:

```
for ( int x = 0; x < 5; x ++)
    Console.WriteLine("The value is " + x.ToString() );
```

This will print the following output:

```
0
1
2
3
4
```

Using the `while` Loop

Whereas the `for` loop is typically used to provide an indexed (a counter variable) loop, the `while` loop will continually perform the same action over and over again so long as a given Boolean expression evaluates to `true`. The format of this loop is as follows:

```
while ( expression ) { ... }
```

If you wanted to perform an action until some flag indicated that you could not perform it any more, your `while` loop might look something like the following:

```
bool canContinue = true;
while (canContinue)
{
    ... perform action ...
    canContinue = ...
}
```

The expression is evaluated at the beginning of each loop execution, and if the evaluation is false, the code within the loop will not be executed. A common mistake when using `while` loops is neglecting to set the exit condition for the loop. In the preceding example, this is the `canContinue` variable. If you don't set the exit condition for the `while` loop, it will run forever (or until you shut the application down forcefully).

Using the do Loop

The `do` loop is similar to the `while` loop, except that the Boolean expression is evaluated at the end of the loop execution instead of at the beginning of the loop. The format of the do loop is as follows:

```
do
{
    ...
} while ( expression );
```

The use of the do loop always guarantees that the code inside the loop will execute at least once. All the other loop types have the ability to execute 0 times if the entry condition fails. Here is a sample do loop:

```
int x = 1;
do
{
    Console.WriteLine(x);
    x++;
} while ( x < 10 );
```

Summary

Whether you're working with a database, 3D graphics, a console application, a Windows Forms application, or a Web Forms application, there are a few types of tasks that need to be performed: looping and branching.

Looping and branching are at the core of any language's definition. This chapter has shown you how you can use C# to create complex branching using Boolean expressions as well as multiple ways to perform iterative programming tasks by using loops.

This chapter has presented some information that, on its own, may not appear to be entirely useful. However, when you look at virtually every programming problem you will ever face in the future, you will be hard-pressed to find a scenario that does not involve looping and branching in some respect.

CHAPTER 3

Strings and Regular Expressions

Regardless of what type of data you're working with or what kind of application you're creating, you will undoubtedly need to work with strings. No matter how the data is stored, the end user always deals in human-readable text. As such, knowing how to work with strings is part of the essential knowledge that any .NET developer needs to make rich and compelling applications.

In addition to showing you how to work with strings in the .NET Framework, this chapter will also introduce you to regular expressions. Regular expressions are format codes that not only allow you to verify that a particular string matches a given format, but you can also use regular expressions to extract meaningful information from what otherwise might be considered free-form text, such as extracting the first name from user input, or the area code from a phone number input, or the server name from a URL.

Working with Strings

Being able to work with strings is an essential skill in creating high-quality applications. Even if you are working with numeric or image data, end users need textual feedback. This section of the chapter will introduce you to .NET strings, how to format them, manipulate them and compare them, as well as other useful operations.

Introduction to the .NET String

Before the .NET Framework and the Common Language Runtime (CLR), developers used to have to spend considerable amount of effort working with strings. A reusable library of string routines was a part of virtually every C and C++ programmer's toolbox. It was also difficult to write code that exchanged string data between different programming languages. For example, Pascal stores strings as an in-memory character array, where the first element of the array indicated the length of the string. C stores strings as an in-memory array of characters with a variable length. The end of the string was indicated by the ASCII null character (represented in C as \0).

In the .NET Framework, strings are stored as immutable values. This means that when you create a string in C# (or any other .NET language), that string is stored in memory in a fixed size to make certain aspects of the CLR run faster (you will learn more about this in Chapter 16, "Optimizing Your NET 2.0 Code"). As a result, when you do things such as concatenate strings or modify individual characters in a string, the CLR is actually creating multiple copies of your string.

Strings in C# are declared in the same way as other value types such as integer or float, as shown in the following examples:

```
string x = "Hello World";
string y;
string z = x;
```

Formatting Strings

One of the most common tasks when working with strings is formatting them. When displaying information to users, you often display things like dates, times, numeric values, decimal values, monetary values, or even things like hexadecimal numbers. C# strings all have the ability to display these types of information and much more. Another powerful feature is that when you use the standard formatting tools, the output of the formatting will be localization-aware. For example, if you display the current date in short form to a user in England, the current date in short form will appear different to a user in the United States.

To create a formatted string, all you have to do is invoke the Format method of the string class and pass it a format string, as shown in the following code:

```
string formatted = string.Format("The value is {0}", value);
```

The {0} placeholder indicates where a value should be inserted. In addition to specifying where a value should be inserted, you can also specify the format for the value.

Other data types also support being converted into strings via custom format specifiers, such as the DateTime data type, which can produce a custom-formatted output using

```
DateTime.ToString("format specifiers");
```

Table 3.1 illustrates some of the most commonly used format strings for formatting dates, times, numeric values, and more.

TABLE 3.1   Custom `DateTime` Format Specifiers

Specifier	Description
d	Displays the current day of the month.
dd	Displays the current day of the month, where values < 10 have a leading zero.
ddd	Displays the three-letter abbreviation of the name of the day of the week.
dddd(+)	Displays the full name of the day of the week represented by the given `DateTime` value.
f(+)	Displays the x most significant digits of the seconds value. The more f's in the format specifier, the more significant digits. This is *total* seconds, not the number of seconds passed since the last minute.
F(+)	Same as f(+), except trailing zeros are not displayed.
g	Displays the era for a given `DateTime` (for example, "A.D.")
h	Displays the hour, in range 1–12.
hh	Displays the hour, in range 1–12, where values < 10 have a leading zero.
H	Displays the hour in range 0–23.
HH	Displays the hour in range 0–23, where values < 10 have a leading zero.
m	Displays the minute, range 0–59.
mm	Displays the minute, range 0–59, where values < 10 have a leading zero.
M	Displays the month as a value ranging from 1–12.
MM	Displays the month as a value ranging from 1–12 where values < 10 have a leading zero.
MMM	Displays the three-character abbreviated name of the month.
MMMM	Displays the full name of the month.
s	Displays the number of seconds in range 0–59.
ss(+)	Displays the number of seconds in range 0–59, where values < 10 have a leading 0.
t	Displays the first character of the AM/PM indicator for the given time.
tt(+)	Displays the full AM/PM indicator for the given time.
y/yy/yyyy	Displays the year for the given time.
z/zz/zzz(+)	Displays the timezone offset for the given time.

Take a look at the following lines of code, which demonstrate using string format specifiers to create custom-formatted date and time strings:

```
DateTime dt = DateTime.Now;

Console.WriteLine(string.Format("Default format: {0}", dt.ToString()));
Console.WriteLine(dt.ToString("dddd dd MMMM, yyyy g"));
Console.WriteLine(string.Format("Custom Format 1: {0:MM/dd/yy hh:mm:sstt}", dt));
Console.WriteLine(string.Format("Custom Format 2: {0:hh:mm:sstt G\\MT zz}", dt));
```

Here is the output from the preceding code:

```
Default format: 9/24/2005 12:59:49 PM
Saturday 24 September, 2005 A.D.
```

```
Custom Format 1: 09/24/05 12:59:49PM
Custom Format 2: 12:59:49PM GMT -06
```

You can also provide custom format specifiers for numeric values as well. Table 3.2 describes the custom format specifiers available for numeric values.

TABLE 3.2   Numeric Custom Format Specifiers

Specifier	Description
0	The zero placeholder.
#	The digit placeholder. If the given value has a digit in the position indicated by the # specifier, that digit is displayed in the formatted output.
.	Decimal point.
,	Thousands separator.
%	Percentage specifier. The value being formatted will be multiplied by 100 before being included in the formatted output.
E0/E+0/e/e+0/e-0/E	Scientific notation.
'XX' or "XX"	Literal strings. These are included literally in the formatted output without translation in their relative positions.
;	Section separator for conditional formatting of negative, zero, and positive values.

If multiple format sections are defined, conditional behavior can be implemented for even more fine-grained control of the numeric formatting:

- Two sections—If you have two formatting sections, the first section applies to all positive (including 0) values. The second section applies to negative values. This is extremely handy when you want to enclose negative values in parentheses as is done in many accounting software packages.

- Three sections—If you have three formatting sections, the first section applies to all positive (*not* including 0) values. The second section applies to negative values, and the third section applies to zero.

The following few lines of code illustrate how to use custom numeric format specifiers.

```
double dVal = 59.99;
double dNeg = -569.99;
double zeroVal = 0.0;
double pct = 0.23;

string formatString = "{0:$#,###0.00;($#,###0.00);nuttin}";
Console.WriteLine(string.Format(formatString, dVal));
Console.WriteLine(string.Format(formatString, dNeg));
Console.WriteLine(string.Format(formatString, zeroVal));
Console.WriteLine(pct.ToString("00%"));
```

The output generated by the preceding code is shown in the following code:

```
$59.99
($569.99)
nuttin
23%
```

Manipulating and Comparing Strings

In addition to displaying strings that contain all kinds of formatted data, other common string-related tasks are string manipulation and comparison. An important thing to keep in mind is that the string is actually a class in the underlying Base Class Library of the .NET Framework. Because it is a class, you can actually invoke methods on a string, just as you can invoke methods on any other class.

You can invoke these methods both on string literals or on string variables, as shown in the following code:

```
int x = string.Length();
int y = "Hello World".Length();
```

Table 3.3 is a short list of some of the most commonly used methods that you can use on a string for obtaining information about the string or manipulating it.

TABLE 3.3   Commonly Used String Instance Methods

Method	Description
CompareTo	Compares this string instance with another string instance.
Contains	Returns a Boolean indicating whether the current string instance contains the given substring.
CopyTo	Copies a substring from within the string instance to a specified location within an array of characters.
EndsWith	Returns a Boolean value indicating whether the string ends with a given substring.
Equals	Indicates whether the string is equal to another string. You can use the '==' operator as well.
IndexOf	Returns the index of a substring within the string instance.
IndexOfAny	Returns the first index occurrence of any character in the substring within the string instance.
PadLeft	Pads the string with the specified number of spaces or another Unicode character, effectively right-justifying the string.
PadRight	Appends a specified number of spaces or other Unicode character to the end of the string, creating a left-justification.
Remove	Deletes a given number of characters from the string.
Replace	Replaces all occurrences of a given character or string within the string instance with the specified replacement.
Split	Splits the current string into an array of strings, using the specified character as the splitting point.

TABLE 3.3   Continued

Method	Description
StartsWith	Returns a Boolean value indicating whether the string instance starts with the specified string.
SubString	Returns a specified portion of the string, given a starting point and length.
ToCharArray	Converts the string into an array of characters.
ToLower	Converts the string into all lowercase characters.
ToUpper	Converts the string into all uppercase characters.
Trim	Removes all occurrences of a given set of characters from the beginning and end of the string.
TrimStart	Performs the Trim function, but only on the beginning of the string.
TrimEnd	Performs the Trim function, but only on the end of the string.

Take a look at the following code, which illustrates some of the things you can do with strings to further query and manipulate them:

```
string sourceString = "Mary Had a Little Lamb";
string sourceString2 = "   Mary Had a Little Lamb        ";
Console.WriteLine(sourceString.ToLower());
Console.WriteLine(string.Format("The string '{0}' is {1} chars long.",
    sourceString,sourceString.Length));
Console.WriteLine(string.Format("Fourth word in sentence is : {0}",
    sourceString.Split(' ')[3]));
Console.WriteLine(sourceString2.Trim());
Console.WriteLine("Two strings equal? " + (sourceString == sourceString2.Trim()));
```

The output of the preceding code looks as follows:

```
mary had a little lamb
The string 'Mary Had a Little Lamb' is 22 chars long.
Fourth word in sentence is : Little
Mary Had a Little Lamb
Two strings equal? True
```

Introduction to the StringBuilder

As mentioned earlier, strings are immutable. This means that when you concatenate two strings to form a third string, there will be a short period of time where the CLR will actually have all three strings in memory. So, for example, when you concatenate as shown in the following code:

```
string a = "Hello";
string b = "World";
string c = a + " " + c;
```

You actually end up with four strings in memory, including the space. To alleviate this performance issue with string concatenation as well as to provide you with a tool to make concatenation easier, the .NET Framework comes with a class called the `StringBuilder`.

By using a `StringBuilder` to dynamically create strings of variable length, you get around the immutable string fact of CLR strings and the code can often become more readable as a result. Take a look at the `StringBuilder` in action in the following code:

```
StringBuilder sb = new StringBuilder();
sb.Append("Greetings!\n");
formatString = "{0:$#,###0.00;($#,###0.00);Zero}";
dVal = 129.99;
sb.AppendFormat(formatString, dVal);
sb.Append("\nThis is a big concatenated string.");
Console.WriteLine(sb.ToString());
```

The output of the preceding code looks like the following:

```
Greetings!
$129.99
This is a big concatenated string.
```

Note that the \n from the preceding code inserts a newline character into the string.

Working with Regular Expressions

Regular expressions allow the fast, efficient processing of text. The text being processed can be something as small as an email address or as large as a multiline input box. The use of regular expressions not only allows you to validate text against a defined pattern, but it also allows you to extract data from text that matches a given pattern.

You can think of a regular expression as an extremely powerful wildcard. Most of us are familiar enough with wildcards to know that when we see an expression like "SAMS *", everything that begins with the word SAMS is a match for that expression. Regular expressions give you additional power, control, and functionality above and beyond simple wildcards.

This section provides you with a brief introduction to the classes in the .NET Framework that support the use of regular expressions. For more information on regular expressions themselves, you might want to check out *Regular Expression Pocket Reference* (O'Reilly Media, ISBN: 059600415X) or *Mastering Regular Expressions, 2nd Edition* (O'Reilly Media, ISBN: 0596002890). These books will give you the information you need in order to create your own regular expressions as well as a list of commonly used expressions. Regular expressions themselves are beyond the scope of this chapter.

Validating Input

One extremely common use of regular expressions is to validate user input against some predefined format. For example, rules are often enforced to ensure that passwords have certain characteristics that make them harder to break. These rules are typically defined as regular expressions. Regular expressions are also often used to validate simple input such as email addresses and phone numbers.

The key class provided by the .NET Framework for working with regular expressions is the RegEx class. This class provides a static method called IsMatch that returns a Boolean indicating whether the specified input string matches a given regular expression.

In the following code, a common regular expression used to test for valid email addresses is used:

```
string emailPattern =
@"^([\w-\.]+)@((\[[0-9]{1,3}\.[0-9]{1,3}\.[0-9]{1,3}\.)¦[ccc]
(([\w-]+\.)+))([a-zA-Z]{2,4}¦[0-9]{1,3})(\]?)$";
Console.Write("Enter an e-mail address:");
string emailInput = Console.ReadLine();
bool match = Regex.IsMatch(emailInput, emailPattern);
if (match)
    Console.WriteLine("E-mail address is valid.");
else
    Console.WriteLine("Supplied input is not a valid e-mail address.");
```

Don't worry if this regular expression doesn't make much sense to you. The basic idea behind the email pattern is that it requires some alphanumeric characters, then an @-sign, and then some combination of characters followed by a ".", and at least two characters following that. Try out the preceding code on different inputs and see what results you get. Even if you don't understand the regular expressions themselves, knowing that they exist and that you can use them to validate input is going to be extremely helpful in the creation of your applications.

Extracting Data from Input

The other common use for regular expressions is in parsing text according to the expression and using that to extract data (called Group matches) from user input.

Regular expressions include a particular feature called *groups*. A group allows you to put a named identifier on a particular section of the regular expression. When you call Match() to compare input data against the pattern, the results actually separate the matches by group, allowing you to extract the portion of the input that matched each group.

For example, in the preceding example we could have created a group called username that would have allowed us to extract all of the data that precedes the @ symbol in an email address. Then, when performing a match, we could have extracted the username from the input using the regular expression's named group.

Take a look at the following code, which illustrates how to extract both the protocol name and the port number from a URL entered by the user at the console. The great thing about regular expressions is that they are their own language, so they don't have a particular affinity toward C, C++, C#, VB.NET, or any other language. This makes it easy to borrow regular expressions from samples and reference guides on the Internet and in publications. In the following code, the regular expression was borrowed from an MSDN example:

```
string urlPattern = @"^(?<proto>\w+)://[^/]+?(?<port>:\d+)?/";
Console.WriteLine();
Console.Write("Enter a URL for data parsing: ");
string url = Console.ReadLine();
Regex urlExpression = new Regex(urlPattern, RegexOptions.Compiled);
Match urlMatch = urlExpression.Match(url);
Console.WriteLine("The Protocol you entered was " +
  urlMatch.Groups["proto"].Value);
Console.WriteLine("The Port Number you entered was " +
  urlMatch.Groups["port"].Value);
```

When you run the preceding code against a URL without a port number, you will notice that you don't get any group values. This is because the input doesn't actually match the regular expression at all. When there are no matches, you obviously can't extract meaningful data from the named groups. When you run the preceding code against a URL with port numbers that match the regular expression, you will get output that looks like the following text:

```
Enter a URL for data parsing: http://server.com:2100/home.aspx
The Protocol you entered was http
The Port Number you entered was :2100
```

Summary

In this chapter you have seen that the days of having to carry around your own library of string routines like a portable life preserver are long gone. With C# and the .NET Framework, strings are a native part of the library of base classes, and as such provide you with a full host of utility methods for comparison, manipulation, formatting, and much more. You also saw that the `StringBuilder` class provides you with an easy-to-use set of utility methods for dynamically building strings without the performance penalty of native string concatenation.

Finally, this chapter gave you a brief introduction into the power of regular expressions and how that power can be harnessed with the `Regex` class. After reading through this chapter and testing out the sample code, you should be familiar with some of the things that you can do with strings and regular expressions to make your applications more powerful.

CHAPTER 4

Arrays and Collections

Even if you are writing an application that works with ADO.NET and relational databases, you will still encounter situations where you need to know how to manage lists of information. Even if you aren't the one who created the lists, you should still know how to use them. For example, there are many controls available in Windows Forms and Web Forms that expose lists or collections to allow you to manipulate their data.

This chapter introduces you to the basics of working with arrays and collections. You will learn the differences between the two types of data and the situations in which both are used.

Working with Arrays

Arrays are basically lists of sequentially accessible data. They provide a means of accessing and storing data in a way that allows multiple related elements to be manipulated via numeric index. This section shows you how to declare and use arrays within your code, including using multidimensional arrays and nested or jagged arrays.

Declaring and Initializing Arrays

To differentiate between a single value and an array value, the *array indexer notation* is used. This notation is represented by the square brackets [and]. To properly declare an array, you need to indicate the data type of the individual elements of the array. This data type is what precedes the [] notation in the sample array declarations that follow:

```
byte[] byteValues;
int[] counts;
string[] words;
```

```
Object[] objList;
Customer[] customers;
```

Unlike with some other languages, in C# you don't specify the size of the array in the declaration portion. So, to specify an array of 12 elements, you cannot declare that as follows:

```
byte[12] byteArray;
```

Initializing the array is what provides C# with the boundary information on the array. Because arrays are essentially just specialized classes, you initialize them with the new keyword, as shown in the following samples:

```
byte[] byteArray = new byte[21];
int[] counters = new int[99];
string[] wordList = new string[21];
```

The preceding code initializes empty arrays out to a given length. These can then be populated programmatically from any number of sources, such as user input, XML files, or a relational database. Keep in mind that if you attempt to use an array that has not been initialized, you will get an error.

If you know the data that will be in the arrays at design time, you can pre-initialize the arrays with data as shown in the following samples:

```
byte[] byteArray = new byte[] { 1, 2, 3 };
byte[] byteArray2 = { 1, 2, 3 };
string[] wordList = { "The", "Quick", "Brown", "Fox" };
```

Using One-Dimensional Arrays

You can do many different things with a one-dimensional array. Because arrays are classes, you can press the "." key at the end of any array variable to bring up IntelliSense and get a list of operations that are available to you for a given array, as shown in Figure 4.1.

FIGURE 4.1   IntelliSense for an *Array* object.

Tables 4.1 and 4.2 describe some of the properties and methods that are provided by the Array class.

TABLE 4.1   Array Properties

Property	Description
IsFixedSize	Indicates whether the array is fixed size
IsReadOnly	Indicates whether the array is read-only
Length	Returns the total number of elements in the array
Rank	Returns the number of dimensions of the array

TABLE 4.2   Array Methods

Method	Description
Clear	Clears out all array elements and sets them to the default value for the data type (for example, 0 for integers, null for object types, and so on).
ConvertAll	Converts all elements within the array from one type to another.
Exists	Determines if an element exists in the array based on a Boolean test function.
Find	Searches the array for an element that is matched based on a Boolean test function. Static.
FindAll	Returns a list of all matches where the Boolean test function returns true. Static.
FindLast	Returns the last occurrence of an array element where the Boolean test function returns true. Static.
Initialize	Invokes the default constructor of the type of the array to initialize each element.
Resize	Static method used to resize a given array.

Take a look at the code in Listing 4.1, which illustrates how to make use of some of the methods and properties listed in Tables 4.1 and 4.2.

LISTING 4.1   One-Dimensional Array Manipulation

```
using System;
using System.Collections.Generic;
using System.Text;

namespace Array1D
{
  class Program
  {
    static void Main(string[] args)
    {
      string[] daysOfWeek = {"Mon", "Tue", "Wed",
        "Thu", "Fri", "Sat"};
```

LISTING 4.1   Continued

```
    string[] productNames = {
      "Blue Pen",
      "Red Pen",
      "Blue Eraser",
      "Red Eraser"};

    Console.WriteLine("Days of the Week:");
    for (int x = 0; x < daysOfWeek.Length - 1; x++)
    {
      Console.Write(string.Format("{0}\t", daysOfWeek[x]));
    }
    Console.WriteLine();

    string[] blueProducts = Array.FindAll(productNames, IsBlueProduct);
    Console.WriteLine("All blue products:");
    foreach (string product in blueProducts)
    {
      Console.Write(string.Format("{0}\t", product));
    }
    Console.WriteLine();
    Array.ForEach(productNames, UpperCaseString);

    Console.ReadLine();
  }

  static bool IsBlueProduct(string productName)
  {
    if (productName.ToUpper().Contains("BLUE"))
      return true;
    else
      return false;
  }

  static void UpperCaseString(string productName)
  {
    Console.WriteLine(productName.ToUpper());
  }
 }
}
```

The code for the FindAll and ForEach methods might appear to be a little odd if you are used to working with C# 1.1. Underneath those methods lies the power of Generics, which you will be introduced to in Chapter 6, "Introduction to Generics." You don't need to know every detail about how it works now because it will become clearer as you continue through the book. The good thing to know is that working with arrays in C# 2.0 is even easier than it was in the previous release.

Using Multidimensional Arrays

Multidimensional arrays are, as the name states, arrays with more than one dimension. This means that these arrays require multiple indices when accessing data contained within the array. Before taking a look at code that utilizes multidimensional arrays, you should be familiar with *why* you might want to use arrays with two, three, or even more dimensions.

One of the most common uses for 2D arrays is the storage of data in a Cartesian coordinate system (data that has an X and a Y coordinate location). These coordinates are found virtually everywhere you look in Windows Forms application because all controls have an X and a Y location.

So, assume that you had a grid that contained controls. You might access the control in the third column of the second row with the following code:

```
Control myControl = controlArray[2, 1];
```

Note that I used [2,1] to access the data instead of [3,2]. This is because arrays are zero-indexed, so the first element is at index 0, the second element is at index 1, and the third element is at index 2.

You can use two-dimensional arrays for any kind of data that can be expressed as a matrix (rectangular grid of data), such as the game board for a game of checkers or tic-tac-toe, or a spreadsheet containing sales values of various products organized by month.

Three-dimensional arrays are typically used to represent cube-shaped data. For example, you can use three-dimensional arrays to supply the information for Excel-style pivot tables, or you can use a 3D array to support three-dimensional location coordinates that include an X, Y, and Z location value.

Arrays with four or more dimensions can quickly become extremely difficult to maintain and are often extremely confusing when someone is attempting to read code involving arrays with four or more dimensions. These types of arrays are usually reserved for data with very specific requirements that are beyond the scope of this book. The rules for four-dimensional arrays are the same as the rules for two- and three-dimensional arrays, so your code will look similar.

You declare a multidimensional array by using a comma to indicate the presence of multiple dimensions in the array, as shown in the following example:

```
byte[,] twoDByteArray;      // two-dimensional array of bytes
SpaceShip[,,] objectsInSpace;   // stores ships that exist in various coordinates
PlayerPiece[,] checkerBoard;  // stores pieces on a checkerboard
```

The number of commas indicates the number of dimensions. As with single-dimension arrays, you cannot specify the maximum bounds of each dimension in the declaration;

you can only specify it in the initialization. In addition, you may have noticed that there is no way to specify the minimum bounds. This is because in C#, all arrays start with the 0 index.

In the sample shown in Listing 4.2, you will see some code that works with two-dimensional arrays as well as one-dimensional arrays. The sample creates an array of month names and an array of product names. These arrays will be used as the labels for the rows and columns in a spreadsheet-style output that shows total product sales for each month. The product names will run vertically down the left side, and the month names run horizontally along the top. In the middle of the spreadsheet, the product sales values will be displayed using a two-dimensional array as the source.

LISTING 4.2   Two-Dimensional Array Sample

```
using System;
using System.Collections.Generic;
using System.Text;

namespace ArrayDemo
{
  class Program
  {
    static void Main(string[] args)
    {
      string[] months = {"Jan", "Feb", "Mar",
                "Apr", "May", "Jun", "Jul", "Aug",
                "Sep", "Oct", "Nov", "Dec" };

      string[] products = {"PROD1",
        "PROD2",
        "PROD3",
        "PROD4",
        "PROD5" };

      int[,] productCounts = new int[12,5];

      // set the product counts for each product for each month
      for (int x = 0; x < 12; x++)
      {
        for (int y = 0; y < 5; y++)
        {
          productCounts[x, y] = x + y; // some arbitrary number
        }
      }
```

LISTING 4.2   Continued

```
      Console.Write("\t");
      for (int month = 0; month < 12; month++)
      {
        Console.Write(string.Format("{0}\t¦ ", months[month]));
      }
      Console.WriteLine();

      for (int product = 0; product < 5; product++)
      {
        Console.Write(string.Format("{0}:\t", products[product]));
        for (int month = 0; month < 12; month++)
        {
          Console.Write(string.Format("{0}\t¦ ",
            productCounts[month, product]));
        }
        Console.WriteLine();
      }

      Console.ReadLine();
    }
  }
}
```

The output of the preceding code looks as follows (with a few months cut out to make the display fit on a page):

```
        ¦ Jan ¦ Feb ¦ Mar ¦ Apr ¦ May
PROD1:    0  ¦  1  ¦  2  ¦  3  ¦  4
PROD2:    1  ¦  2  ¦  3  ¦  4  ¦  5
PROD3:    2  ¦  3  ¦  4  ¦  5  ¦  6
PROD4:    3  ¦  4  ¦  5  ¦  6  ¦  7
PROD5:    4  ¦  6  ¦  6  ¦  7  ¦  8
```

Using Jagged Arrays

The preceding section dealt with rectangular arrays, in which the number of columns (elements) would be the same for each row, giving you data that is shaped like a matrix. Jagged arrays are arrays whose elements are also arrays.

A *jagged array* (also referred to as an array of arrays) is an array (single-dimension or multi-dimensional) in which the elements are themselves arrays. This allows each element of the array to be an array with a different size.

There are many ways to declare jagged arrays, some of which take advantage of the same initializer shortcuts that are available for other array types. The following few lines of code declare a jagged array without doing any initialization:

```
string[][] jaggedStrings;
int[][] jaggedInts;
Customer[][] jaggedCustomers;
```

Note that instead of declaring it with the comma notation indicating a multidimensional array, the "Array of Arrays" notation is used, which is two array bracket symbols: [][].

The following lines of code illustrate a few of the ways in which you can initialize jagged arrays, including some of the shortcuts that allow you to omit the new keyword when providing the initial values for the array:

```
int[][] jaggedInts = new int[2][];
jaggedInts[0] = new int[10];
jaggedInts[1] = new int[20];

int[][] ji2 = new int[2][];
ji2[0] = new int[] { 1, 3, 5, 7, 9 };
ji2[1] = new int[] { 2, 4, 6 };

// doesn't need the initial 'new int[][]' ,
// compiler can infer it
int[][] ji3 =
{
    new int[] { 1, 3, 5, 7, 9 },
    new int[] { 2, 4, 6 }
};

// 'new int[][]' used explicitly, though it isn't
// needed.
int[][] ji4 = new int[][]
{
    new int[] { 1, 3, 5, 7, 9 },
    new int[] { 2, 4, 6 }
};
```

As confusing as it might seem, you can mix jagged and rectangular arrays to create some powerful (and often difficult to decipher) structures. Take a look at the following code, which creates a jagged array in which each element is a different-size two-dimensional array:

```
int[][,] mixedJagged = new int[][,]
{
    new int[,] { {0,1}, {2,3}, {4,5} },
```

```
    new int[,] { {9,8}, {7,6}, {5,4}, {3,2}, {1,0} }
};

Console.WriteLine(mixedJagged[1][1, 1]);
Console.ReadLine();
```

The preceding code declares the jagged array of two-dimensional arrays and will print the value 6. By accessing element 1 in the first dimension, the code is referencing the second multidimensional array. Then, the indexer [1,1] indicates the second pair of numbers, and the second number within that pair: 6.

The code in Listing 4.3 uses jagged arrays to display the list of the top-selling products during each month. The data here is fabricated, but real data would come from a relational data source such as SQL Server or an XML file (or XML from a web service) in a production application.

LISTING 4.3   Jagged Array Demonstration

```
using System;
using System.Collections.Generic;
using System.Text;

namespace JaggedArrays2
{
  class Program
  {
  static void Main(string[] args)
  {
    string[][] productSales =
    {
      new string[] { "Rubber Band", "Bouncy Ball", "Sticky Goo" },
      new string[] { "Rock Candy", "Rubber Band", "Bouncy Ball", "Sticky Goo"},
      new string[] { "Little Giant Dynamite Stick", "ACME Inferno Ball of Flame",
                     "Portable Detonator Caps" }
    };
    string[] saleMonths = { "April", "May", "June" };

    Console.WriteLine("Happy Toy Company Top Sellers By Month");

    for (int month = 0; month < saleMonths.Length; month++)
    {
      Console.WriteLine(string.Format("{0}:\n---------", saleMonths[month]));
      for (int product = 0; product < productSales[month].Length; product++)
      {
         Console.WriteLine(string.Format("\t{0}",
```

LISTING 4.3   Continued

```
            productSales[month][product]));
      }
    }
    Console.ReadLine();
  }
 }
}
```

One of the most important pieces of the preceding code is the looping through the arrays. Note that we don't actually know the size of the array in each element of the first dimension of the jagged array. We have to obtain that length dynamically by checking:

`productSales[month].Length`

The other thing is that the preceding code won't work if one of the elements in the first dimension is null, so your production code should have additional safety checks to prevent Null Reference exceptions. The output of the preceding code is as follows:

```
Happy Toy Company Top Sellers By Month
April:
- - - - - - - - - -
    Rubber Band
    Bouncy Ball
    Sticky Goo
May:
- - - - - - - - - -
    Rock Candy
    Rubber Band
    Bouncy Ball
    Sticky Goo
June:
- - - - - - - - - -
    Little Giant Dynamite Stick
    ACME Inferno Ball of Flame
    Portable Detonator Caps
```

Working with Collections

Collections are lists of data that don't necessarily need to be accessed by numerical index. In many cases, collections have custom index types and some collections, such as the Queue and Stack, don't support indexed access at all.

This section begins by comparing and contrasting the various features of arrays and collections and offers some advice on how to decide between the two. Then you will get an overview of some of the collections provided by the .NET Framework. This section will not cover `Generic` collections, as those will be addressed in Chapter 6, "Introduction to Generics."

Comparing Arrays and Collections

All arrays are indexed with integers, regardless of whether they are jagged arrays, rectangular arrays, or one-dimensional arrays. One main deciding factor is that arrays are generally faster to use. The main reason for this is that arrays are designed to be fixed-length and they are also all numerically indexed. A numerically indexed list of data is much faster at sequential access than a list of data that is accessed by a long string key such as a GUID. Some collections can use arbitrary objects as their keys. The tradeoff is performance versus functionality. If the data you need to store can possibly be stored as an array of fixed length (meaning the length doesn't change after initialization, not that you need to know the length at design time), that is definitely the way to go. However, you may need additional functionality provided by some of the classes described in the rest of the chapter. Collections are designed to store dynamic lists of data that can grow or shrink at runtime that may or may not be indexed numerically. If one of the `Collection` classes suits your needs, you may decide that it would be better to use that collection than to try to fit your data into an array.

One final point of comparison is the ability to resize. Although all arrays can be resized by invoking `Array.Resize`, the performance penalty is pretty high. When you invoke that method, a new array of the appropriate size is created, and then each element from the existing array is copied into the new array. Although it's faster than doing this yourself manually, it still has a fairly high overhead, especially if you plan on resizing your array often. In short, arrays are generally of a fixed length while collections are designed to have a variable size.

Using the `ArrayList`

The `ArrayList` functions much like an array, with a few extremely powerful exceptions. The most notable of these is the fact that you can dynamically add and remove items from the list at runtime without incurring the fairly large penalty for regular array resizing. `ArrayList`s, just like regular arrays, are accessed via a zero-based integer index. When you create a new `ArrayList`, it starts with a capacity of 0 and 0 items in the list. You then dynamically add and remove items programmatically via methods on the `ArrayList` class. One other thing to keep in mind before diving into the code for the `ArrayList` class is that the `ArrayList` considers nulls valid (so you can add a null to the list), and you can add the same value more than once.

Before getting into the code, let's take a look at some of the properties and methods of the `ArrayList` class in Tables 4.3 and 4.4.

TABLE 4.3   ArrayList Properties

Property	Description
Capacity	Indicates (or sets) the size of the ArrayList.
Count	Returns the number of items contained in the list.
IsFixedSize	Indicates whether the ArrayList is a fixed size.
IsReadOnly	Indicates whether the ArrayList is read-only.
Item	Provides access to an individual item within the ArrayList. C# uses indexer [ ] notation.

TABLE 4.4   ArrayList Methods

Method	Description
Add	Adds an item to the end of the list
AddRange	Adds a list of items to the end of the ArrayList
Clear	Empties the list
Contains	Indicates whether the specified item is in the list
GetRange	Returns a subset of the ArrayList
IndexOf	Returns the index within the list where the specified item resides
Remove	Removes an item from the list
RemoveAt	Removes the item at a given index
Reverse	Reverses the order of the elements in the list
Sort	Sorts some or all of the ArrayList
ToArray	Converts the ArrayList into a fixed-length array of a given type

Listing 4.4 illustrates the use of the ArrayList using strings as the element type.

LISTING 4.4   ArrayList Demo

```
using System;
using System.Collections;

namespace AlDemo
{
  class Program
  {
    static void Main(string[] args)
    {
      ArrayList al = new ArrayList();

      al.Add("Every good boy deserves fudge");
      al.Add("The quick brown fox...");
      al.Add("A stitch in time saves nine.");
      al.Add("A penny saved a day is 7 cents a week.");
      Console.WriteLine("First item " + (string)al[0]);
      Console.WriteLine(string.Format(
```

LISTING 4.4   Continued

```
        "List has {0} elements, capacity of {1}, is fixed size? {2}",
        al.Count, al.Capacity, al.IsFixedSize));

    Console.WriteLine(string.Format(
        "Index of 'The quick brown fox...' within the list is {0}\n",
        al.IndexOf("The quick brown fox...")));

    al.Sort();
    Console.WriteLine("Sorted list:");
    foreach (string s in al)
    {
        Console.WriteLine(s);
    }
    Console.ReadLine();
    }
  }
}
```

The output from this demo looks like this:

```
First item Every good boy deserves fudge
List has 4 elements, capacity of 4, is fixed size? False
Index of 'The quick brown fox...' within the list is 1

Sorted list:
A penny saved a day is 7 cents a week.
A stitch in time saves nine.
Every good boy deserves fudge
The quick brown fox...
```

Using the Hashtable

The Hashtable is a special form of collection that stores name-value pair combinations like a traditional dictionary. The Hashtable is optimized, however, in that the object used as the indexer is *hashed* for more efficient access. What that all boils down to is that the Hashtable is extremely efficient at retrieving single values with keys of arbitrary data types, but is only as efficient as the other collection classes at being enumerated. Although the Hashtable accepts any kind of object as the key, one of the most common uses of the Hashtable is using strings as indices for data, as shown in the example in Listing 4.5. The code in Listing 4.5 shows you two different ways to iterate through the values and keys stored in the Hashtable, as well as how to directly access the data, add new data, and query Hashtable properties.

LISTING 4.5   Hashtable Demo

```
using System;
using System.Collections;
using System.Text;

namespace HashtableDemo
{
  class Program
  {
  static void Main(string[] args)
  {
    Hashtable ht = new Hashtable();

    // store favorite color of each
    // user
    ht.Add("kevin", "Green");
    ht.Add("joe", "White");
    ht.Add("bob", "Red");
    ht.Add("Mary", "Pink");
    ht.Add("Jane", "Yellow");

    Console.WriteLine(
      string.Format("There are {0} items in the hashtable.", ht.Count));

    foreach (string user in ht.Keys)
    {
      Console.WriteLine(string.Format("{0}'s favorite color is {1}",
        user, ht[user]));
    }

    Console.WriteLine("Stored colors:");
    foreach (DictionaryEntry de in ht)
    {
      Console.WriteLine(string.Format("{0}:{1}", de.Key, de.Value));
    }

    Console.ReadLine();
  }
 }
}
```

Using the `Queue`

The `Queue` is a special kind of collection. Unlike with most other collections, in Visual C#
you don't have direct access to all of the items within the `Queue`. The `Queue` is a first-in,

first-out collection of items. You *enqueue* an item when you place it in the collection and you *dequeue* an item when you obtain the first item in the collection.

In several scenarios, the Queue class can be quite useful. If you are working with data that is handled in the order in which it was received, the Queue is the class to use.

You cannot access individual items in a Queue through an index, but you can obtain the number of items in the Queue with the Count property. Table 4.5 is a list of some common methods of the Queue class.

TABLE 4.5   Queue Methods

Method	Description
Clear	Removes all items from the Queue
Enqueue	Adds an item to the end of the Queue
Dequeue	Returns and takes an item off the beginning of the Queue
Peek	Returns the item at the beginning of the Queue without removing it
ToArray	Converts the contents of the Queue to a fixed-length array of a given type

Listing 4.6 illustrates the use of the Queue collection.

LISTING 4.6   Queue Demo

```
using System;
using System.Collections;
using System.Text;

namespace QueueDemo
{
 struct Message
 {
   public string Text;
   public string To;
   public string From;
 }
 class Program
 {
  static void Main(string[] args)
  {
   Queue mq = new Queue();
   Message m = new Message();
   m.Text = "Sample Text";
   m.To = "user1";
   m.From = "user2";

   mq.Enqueue(m);
   m = new Message();
```

LISTING 4.6   Continued

```
    m.Text = "Other Text";
    m.To = "user3";
    m.From = "user2";
    mq.Enqueue(m);

    Console.WriteLine(
     string.Format("{0} messages to be processed.", mq.Count));

    m = (Message)mq.Dequeue();
    Console.WriteLine(
     string.Format("De-queued message '{0}', {1} items remaining.",
       m.Text, mq.Count));
    m = (Message)mq.Dequeue();
    Console.WriteLine(
     string.Format("De-queued message '{0}', {1} items remaining.",
       m.Text, mq.Count));

    Console.ReadLine();
  }
 }
}
```

Using the Stack

The Stack class is a simple last-in first-out (LIFO) collection of objects. It works very much like the queue, except that the last item to be added to the Stack is going to be the next item that will come off the stack. Listing 4.7 provides a quick demonstration of the features of the Stack class.

LISTING 4.7   Stack Demo

```
using System;
using System.Collections;
using System.Text;

namespace StackDemo
{
 class Program
 {
  static void Main(string[] args)
  {
    Stack s = new Stack();
    s.Push("Houston");
```

LISTING 4.7   Continued

```
      s.Push("New York");
      s.Push("Los Angeles");

      Console.WriteLine(s.Count.ToString());

      foreach (String str in s)
      {
        Console.WriteLine(str);
      }

      string city = (string)s.Pop();
      Console.WriteLine(city);
      string city2 = (string)s.Peek();
      Console.WriteLine(city2);
      Console.ReadLine();
    }
  }
}
```

Using the SortedList

The SortedList is a name/value collection where the items are sorted by the keys, and you can access the data within the collection both by the object key and by numerical index. When you add an item to the collection, it is then sorted based on the key of the item, as shown in the following example:

```
SortedList sl = new SortedList();

sl.Add("Zippy Firecrackers", 24.99d);
sl.Add("Aardvaark Candy", 52.99d);
sl.Add("Mighty Bomb", 21.99d);
sl.Add("Really Big Bomb", 33.99d);

Console.WriteLine("Sorted List of Products:");
foreach (DictionaryEntry de in sl)
{
  Console.WriteLine(
    string.Format("{0} costs {1:c}", de.Key, de.Value));
}
Console.ReadLine();
```

The output from the preceding code shows how the items have been reordered to be properly sorted:

```
Sorted List of Products:

Aardvaark Candy costs $52.99

Mighty Bomb costs $21.99

Really Big Bomb costs $33.99

Zippy Firecrackers costs $24.99
```

The SortedList class provides a simple, easy-to-use means by which you can sort a list of items. A lot of user interface controls for both Web and Windows provide their own sorting code, but knowing that you can rely on the SortedList class for your own sorting can come in handy.

Summary

This chapter has provided coverage of both arrays and collections. You should have a good idea of how to utilize single-dimension arrays, multidimensional arrays, and jagged arrays. In addition, you should be able to compare and contrast the features and drawbacks of using arrays or collections. This chapter also provided an overview of some of the stock collection classes that are included with the .NET Framework, such as the ArrayList, SortedList, Queue, Stack, and more. As you continue through the book, you will be able to use the information in this chapter to utilize the powerful features of both arrays and collections in creating professional applications.

CHAPTER 5

Object-Oriented Programming in C#

Object-oriented programming is a fundamental part of the .NET Framework. The entire framework is built in an object-oriented fashion. Whether you are creating a game, a Windows Forms application, a Web Forms application, a web service, or anything else—if you're using .NET, you're using objects and classes.

Before you move through the rest of the book learning about Windows Forms and Web Forms, you should spend some time familiarizing yourself with object-oriented design (OOD) and object-oriented programming (OOP) concepts, as well as how to implement classes, inheritance, and interfaces in C#.

This chapter provides you with an introduction to the design and implementation of classes, interfaces, inheritance, and polymorphism.

Object-Oriented Design

The technical details of using C# to create classes and interfaces are fairly easy to master. The difficult thing to master is good design of those objects. This section gives you an introduction to object-oriented design (OOD), class design, and interface design.

Introduction to Object-Oriented Design

Object-oriented design isn't just about designing objects— it's about designing objects *properly*. When you are designing objects, two distinct areas of thinking are involved. You can either design an object that performs a specific, discrete task that is done when creating tools, or you can design an object that is a model or representation of a concept within the problem domain of the application. For example, you can create a class called `CustomerManager`, which is a *tool-type* object, or you can create a class called `Customer`, which models the real-world attributes and behaviors associated with a customer. The reality is that a little of each pattern is often used in commercial applications. This section illustrates some of the principles and concepts associated with designing classes and interfaces.

Designing Classes

Before the advent of object-oriented programming environments and languages such as C++, Java, and the .NET Framework, programming was *procedural*. In other words, your program started at some fixed point, and then invoked a series of subroutines in sequence to produce the desired result. More robust programs could be written by adding logic, looping, and conditional operators to the procedural code, but the code never actually modeled any real-world scenarios.

Classes are abstractions of real-world concepts used to allow developers to think in terms of the problem at hand rather than having to translate the problem into a series of convoluted procedures.

A class has *attributes*, which are essentially discrete pieces of information about the class. An attribute can either affect the class itself (referred to as a *static member* in C#) or it can affect instances of the class (*instance members*). An example of an attribute would be a field or a property of a class, such as `ID`, or members that are specific to a certain problem domain, such as `Density`, `Volume`, `Price`, or `Age`.

A class also has *operations* (referred to as "methods" in C#), which are the tasks that a class (or an instance of that class) can perform. These operations can range from simple constructors for initializing data, to complex operations that can consume valuable resources such as CPU time, memory, and so on.

When you design a class, you decide which attributes and operations the class will provide, as well as the *accessibility* of those attributes and operations. Accessibility refers to whether the class member can be accessed by other class members, by members of descendant classes, by code outside the class definition, or by code outside the assembly in which the class is defined.

This chapter does not discuss what constitutes good class design. The purpose of this chapter is to give you the knowledge you need to start writing object-oriented code with C#. If you want to do some further reading about object-oriented design, you should consult *Object-Oriented Analysis and Design with Applications* (2nd edition), ISBN 0805353402, Addison-Wesley Professional.

Visual Studio 2005 includes a tool that allows you to do class design within the IDE. You can create class diagrams from classes that you have already coded, and you can also generate classes from the diagrams you have drawn.

Figure 5.1 illustrates a class design in progress. It is an incomplete design of an object hierarchy representing vehicles. An object hierarchy like this could be used for various kinds of business problems—anything from selling cars to performing intense analysis of crash test results.

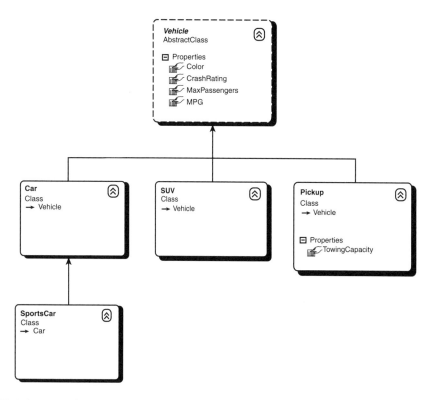

FIGURE 5.1   A work-in-progress class design.

In the next section of this chapter, you will see how to take your class designs and turn them into code written in C#.

Designing Interfaces

The difference between an interface and a class is one that might not be immediately obvious if you're new to object-oriented programming. A class is an encapsulation of attributes and operations that may or may not inherit from another base class (the CLR does not support multiple inheritance). An *interface* is a contract that defines the attributes and operations that a class *must* implement in order to satisfy the conditions of the interface.

For example, you can have a class that exposes a property called Color that might indicate the color of the object. You can also create an interface called IColorable. Any class that then implements that interface *must* define a property called Color. So, the essential difference between classes and interfaces is that classes are the definitions of abstractions of real-world entities, and interfaces are *requirements* and *constraints* to which all classes bound to the interfaces must conform. You will see more of how this works in the next section, where we get into some real object-oriented code.

Naming Conventions for Interfaces and Classes

By convention, as well as by recommendation of many designers, interface names typically begin with a capital "I" and are often descriptive words. Classes should not begin with any set prefix character and are almost always nouns. Both class and interface names should have their first letter capitalized, and the first letter of each word if there are multiple words joined in a class or interface name, for example, `SportsCar`, `Customer`, `CustomerManager`, `Account`, `AccountsPayable`.

Object-Oriented Programming

As stated in the preceding section, it is beyond the scope of this chapter to teach you all there is to know about good class design and OOD. The goal of this chapter is to show you how to implement your class hierarchies in C#. This section shows you how to create simple classes, how to implement the appropriate member security, how to create an inheritance tree, how to use polymorphism, and finally how to implement interfaces.

Creating Simple Classes

All classes begin with the basic class declaration, which defines the name of the class, as shown in the following snippet:

```
public class Vehicle
{
}
```

This is the most basic class definition. It will create a new class named `Vehicle` with no members and no methods. The class will be visible and available to be instantiated by any other .NET code because of the use of the `public` keyword.

Within the class definition itself, you can declare members that belong to the class itself, such as private members for storing internal data, properties, or methods. If you are following along inside Visual Studio, add a few member declarations for storing private data, as shown in the following example:

```
public class Vehicle
{
    private int numWheels;
    private int mpg;
}
```

Now you've got two members: one for storing the number of wheels on the vehicle, and one for storing the miles-per-gallon (mpg) rating of the vehicle. You'll see how to handle member visibility (private, public, and so on) in the next section.

Next, let's add an operation, or method, to the class:

```
public void PrintWheels()
{
  Console.WriteLine(
    string.Format("This vehicle has {0} wheels.", numWheels));
}
```

This method will display the number of wheels on the vehicle when the method is invoked. You invoke this method on an object instance as shown in the following example:

```
myVehicle.PrintWheels();
```

There are also special types of methods called `Constructors`, which are automatically invoked when the class is instantiated. For example, you can create a class that will automatically set the number of wheels to four whenever an instance of that class is created by using the following constructor:

```
public Vehicle()
{
    numWheels = 4;
}
```

This will set the private member `numWheels` to 4 whenever an instance of the `Vehicle` class is instantiated.

Finally, you can add some properties that allow code to access the private members `numWheels` and `mpg`, as shown in the following example:

```
public int Wheels
{
  get { return numWheels; }
  set { numWheels = value; }
}

public int MPG
{
  get { return mpg; }
  set { mpg = value; }
}
```

This is nowhere near a complete coverage of class building in C#. You can learn quite a bit about classes and object-oriented programming within C# simply by reading through this book.

Handling Member Visibility

C# enables you to control the visibility and access of classes and their members. You can prevent code from another assembly from seeing your code, or you can even limit the visibility so that only descendants (you will learn more about inheritance in the next subsection, "Using Object Inheritance") can access specific members. Also, new to C#, you can individually control the accessibility level of the get and set accessors of individual class properties.

You control the accessibility of members through accessibility keywords, such as public, private, and so on. Table 5.1 gives you a complete listing of accessibility keywords and their meanings, as well as the types of code entities to which the keywords apply.

TABLE 5.1   Member Visibility Levels

Visibility Keyword	Description
public	This member is accessible from both inside the assembly and outside the assembly, as well as by members inside and outside the class.
private	This member is accessible only from code within the class definition itself.
protected	This member is accessible only to derived types, both inside and outside the assembly.
internal	This member is accessible by any code within the assembly.
public protected	This member is accessible by all code within the assembly, but only by derived types outside the assembly.
private protected	This member is protected within the assembly (accessible only to derived types), but is inaccessible outside the assembly.

The following lines of code are examples of the various ways in which accessibility keywords can be applied to classes and individual members:

```
using System;
using System.Collections.Generic;
using System.Text;

namespace Classes
{
    // this class is only accessible to code within the assembly
    internal class Accessibility
    {
        // accessible to derivative classes, inside and outside
        // this assembly
        protected int someNumber;

        // accessible only to this class
        private int anotherNumber;
```

```
        // accessible to all code, inside and outside
        // this assembly
        public string SomeString; // will appear as a public field on the class

        public int SomeNumber
        {
            get { return someNumber; }
            protected set { someNumber = value; }
        }
    }
}
```

With the table of accessibility levels in hand, the preceding code should make perfect sense. One thing to note, however, is the use of the keyword protected on the public property SomeNumber. This is a new feature in C# 2.0, and it allows you to differentiate the accessibility of one property accessor from another. For instance, in the preceding example, all code is allowed to retrieve the value of SomeNumber, but only derivative classes (inside or outside the assembly) are allowed to use the property to modify the value. This allows finer-grained control over what other code (possibly even code you or your team didn't write) can do with your classes.

Using Object Inheritance

Object inheritance is the concept that allows one class to *inherit* attributes and operations from a parent class. In the case of the .NET Framework, a class can only have one parent. This is referred to as *single inheritance*. Languages such as C++ allow for *multiple inheritance*, which allows a single child class to inherit from multiple parents at the same time.

Inheritance is an extremely useful and powerful concept within the .NET Framework and within C# itself. You see inheritance used over and over in the base classes provided with the .NET Framework. For example, in Windows Forms, a ListBox control inherits from the ListControl class, which in turn inherits from the Control class, which in turn inherits from the Component class, which in turn inherits from the MarshalByRefObject class, which in turn inherits from the class from which all classes in the .NET Framework are derived, System.Object.

By allowing for rich object hierarchies, developers can realistically model business, data, and user interface scenarios in a truly object-oriented fashion, giving them rapid development ability and high code reuse.

The code in Listing 5.1 illustrates the use of inheritance and how the different members of classes in an object hierarchy are handled. There are two keywords that you need to familiarize yourself with when dealing with inheritance:

- new—This keyword indicates to the compiler that the member you are defining on a derived class provides a new, alternate implementation than the member defined on the base class.

- override—This keyword also indicates to the compiler that the member being defined provides a new implementation. The difference between override and new is that override no longer allows access to the inherited implementation. This difference will become clearer in the discussion on polymorphism.

LISTING 5.1   The Animal, Cat, and Lion Classes Illustrating Object Inheritance

```
using System;
using System.Collections.Generic;
using System.Text;

namespace Inheritance
{
    public abstract class Animal
    {
        private string color;

        public Animal()
        {
            color = "Blue";
        }

        public virtual void MakeNoise()
        {
            Console.WriteLine("Like, Roar, or something!");
        }

        public string Color
        {
            get { return color; }
            set { color = value; }
        }
    }

    public class Cat : Animal
    {
        public Cat()
            : base()
        {
            Color = "Black";
        }

        public new void MakeNoise()
        {
```

LISTING 5.1 Continued

```
            Console.WriteLine("Meow, already.");
        }
    }

    public class Lion : Cat
    {
        public Lion()
            : base()
        {
            Color = "Yellow";
        }

        public new void MakeNoise()
        {
            Console.WriteLine("ROOooWWRrrrRR!!");
        }
    }
}
```

The first thing you see is an abstract class. An abstract class is essentially the concept of a class. It provides a standard set of code from which child classes can inherit. The difference between an abstract class and a regular parent class is that an abstract class *cannot be instantiated*. It is there purely to provide inheritable code. The Animal class sets up a default color for all child classes, as well as providing a default noise that child classes will inherit if they don't modify it. The virtual keyword allows that method to be superseded by child classes if the creator of the child class so decides.

The Cat class inherits from the Animal class as indicated by the following line:

```
public class Cat : Animal
```

The Cat class sets its own color in the constructor, and provides its own implementation of MakeNoise without completely hiding the original parent's implementation.

The Lion class inherits from the Cat class, providing its own color and its own implementation of MakeNoise. If we execute the following lines of code:

```
Cat c = new Cat();
c.MakeNoise();

Lion l = new Lion();
l.MakeNoise();
```

The output will be as follows:

```
Meow, already.
ROOooWWRrrrRR!!
```

The other thing to note is that all of the derivative classes have access to the members of the parent, so long as those members are `protected` or even more accessible.

Introduction to Polymorphism

Polymorphism is the ability to treat one object instance as if it were an instance of a different member of the inheritance tree. For example, using polymorphism and explicit typecasting, you can treat a `Lion` class as though it were a `Cat` class (because `Lion` inherits from `Cat`), and you can treat a `Lion` class as though it were an `Animal` class (because `Lion` inherits from `Cat`, which in turn inherits from `Animal`).

The real power of polymorphism comes from the fact that, through various keywords, you can control what members are used by which classes in the object hierarchy, even if the object is typecast to an ancestor. For example, we can create a class called `ReallyBigLion` that uses the `override` keyword that will provide its own implementation of `MakeNoise()`, even if the object is typecast to `Lion` instead of `ReallyBigLion`:

```
public class ReallyBigLion : Lion
{
    public ReallyBigLion()
        : base()
    {
        Color = "BrightRed";
    }

    public override void MakeNoise()
    {
        Console.WriteLine("REALLY BIG ROAR.");
    }
}
```

Now, when we run the following code to demonstrate polymorphism:

```
Cat polyCat = (Cat)l;
polyCat.MakeNoise();

ReallyBigLion rbl = new ReallyBigLion();
rbl.MakeNoise();
Lion polyLion = (Lion)rbl;
polyLion.MakeNoise();
polyCat = (Cat)rbl;
polyCat.MakeNoise();
```

We will get the following output:

```
Meow, already.
REALLY BIG ROAR.
REALLY BIG ROAR.
Meow, already.
```

What's interesting to note here is that when you typecast ReallyBigLion to Lion, the MakeNoise() method that is invoked is the one from ReallyBigLion because Lion used the virtual keyword and ReallyBigLion used the override keyword. However, when you typecast ReallyBigLion to Cat, the MakeNoise() implementation that is invoked belongs to the Cat class because the Cat class did not allow its method definition to be superseded with a keyword. This also illustrates how you can create a class and guarantee that no one will tamper with your implementation of a method if you don't want them to.

Implementing Interfaces

As you read earlier in this chapter, interfaces are essentially contracts that define required attributes and operations for classes that implement those interfaces. Rather than being a hierarchical inheritance model, interfaces function more as a list of requirements to be enforced on a class. However, one interface can inherit from another interface, the end result being that the class that implements the child interface must adhere to *all* requirements as defined by *both* the child interface and the parent interface.

The following interface defines a list of requirements to which all implementing classes must conform:

```
interface ICreature
{
  int NumLegs { get; set; }
  string Color { get; set; }

  void MakeNoise();
}
```

Note that there are no accessibility keywords. Interfaces do not define the accessibility of a member, only the member's presence. The interface defined in the preceding example requires that implementing classes define both the get and set accessors for the NumLegs and Color properties, as well as a void method called MakeNoise().

Thankfully, Visual Studio makes it extremely easy to implement interfaces. To see this in action, create a new class file called Creature, and then type the following:

```
public class Creature : ICreature
```

After you type ICreature, you will be able to use the related smart tag to automatically implement empty stubs that implement the interface as defined. For big interfaces, this can save you a lot of typing and reduce a lot of typo-related errors. The resulting class is shown in Listing 5.2.

LISTING 5.2   The Creature Class, Autofilled with Empty ICreature Implementation Stubs

```
using System;
using System.Collections.Generic;
using System.Text;

namespace Inheritance
{
class Creature : ICreature
{
#region ICreature Members

public int NumLegs
{
    get
    {
        throw new Exception("The method or operation is not implemented.");
    }
    set
    {
        throw new Exception("The method or operation is not implemented.");
    }
}

public string Color
{
    get
    {
        throw new Exception("The method or operation is not implemented.");
    }
    set
    {
        throw new Exception("The method or operation is not implemented.");
    }
}

public void MakeNoise()
{
    throw new Exception("The method or operation is not implemented.");
}

#endregion
}
}
```

With the empty stubs in place, all you have to do is remove the exceptions created by Visual Studio and replace them with real code, and your class will have satisfied the requirements of the interface.

Note that one of the basic reasons for an interface is that it provides one common type to which you can typecast a variety of object instances. For example, you might have 10 different object hierarchies that consist of Predators, Omnivores, Herbivores, and so on. However, all of these object hierarchies all implement the ICreature interface, so you can create methods that look like this:

```
public void DisplayCreature(ICreature creature)
{
    Console.WriteLine("The creature has " + creature.NumLegs.ToString() + "legs.");
}
```

You can also typecast an object instance to any interface that the object implements with the C# typecast operator, as shown in the following example :

```
SnowOwl owl = new SnowOwl();
ICreature creature = (ICreature)owl;
DisplayCreature(creature);
```

You can also pass the object instance to a method that is expecting just the interface, and C# will do the type conversion for you:

```
SnowOwl owl = new SnowOwl();
DisplayCreature(owl);
```

The only time this will cause a problem is if you pass the method an object that doesn't implement the required interface. In this case you will get a type conversion exception.

Summary

This chapter has provided you with some of the basics of how C# has implemented object-oriented programming. You saw how to create basic classes that expose fields, properties, and methods. In addition, you saw how to create object hierarchies using object inheritance, abstract classes, and polymorphism. Finally, this chapter provided a quick overview of creating and implementing interfaces. This chapter is far from the ultimate reference on object-oriented programming. However, it should give you enough basic information that you will be familiar with the OOP concepts and code used throughout the remainder of this book.

CHAPTER **6**

Introduction to Generics

Generics are a feature new to C# 2.0 that adds a tremendous amount of power and flexibility to object-oriented programming using the language. Many definitions of generics start off with a comparison of template-based programming in C++, but I feel that does generics an injustice.

Generics allow class designers to defer the specification of types within a class definition until such time as that class is instantiated. This chapter not only shows you how to use generics, but gives you a good idea of *when* you should use generics and how they can create drastic performance improvements and make code reuse significantly easier.

This chapter is by no means the definitive and complete guide for generics-based programming in C# 2.0. However, it will provide you with the information you need to know in order to quickly start using generics in your everyday coding as well as to understand the use of generics throughout the rest of the framework such as ASP.NET, ADO.NET, and so on.

Overview of Generics

Generics are a feature of C# 2.0 that allow you to defer the specification of an actual data type until your code creates an instance of the generic type. This section introduces you to some of the benefits of using generics, as well as illustrating how to use type parameters and how to implement constraints on a type parameter.

Benefits of Generics

Generics provide the developer with an extremely high-performance way of programming as well as increasing code reuse and allowing for extremely elegant solutions.

Before you see how generics make the world a better place, you need to see an example of the problem they address. Consider the following class:

```
public class Customer
{
    public void AddDetailItem( object detailItem )
    {
        if (detailItem is OrderItem)
            PerformAction( (OrderItem)detailItem );

        if (detailItem is CalendarEvent)
            AddCalendarEvent( (CalendarEvent)detailItem);


        ...
    }
}
```

When writing complex code, especially in multitiered applications or when using code written by other developers or third-party companies, it is often necessary to deal with things in the abstract. We often use interfaces so that we can guarantee that parameters will conform to a specific contract, or we will use the object class to allow for a lot of runtime flexibility.

The problem is that this runtime flexibility comes at a price. In the preceding code, there is a lot of typecasting going on and some implicit Reflection operations (the is operator).

Using type parameters and generics, you could specify at the time of instantiation whether you want the Customer class to work with CalendarEvent detail items or OrderItem detail items, as shown in the following code:

```
public class Customer<T>
{
    public void AddDetailItem( T detailItem )
    {
      ...
    }
}
```

While the preceding class is a Customer, it should be pointed out that the most common use of generics is to create and use specialized collection classes. You will see how to use some of the new Generic collection classes provided with the .NET Framework 2.0 later in this chapter.

Introduction to Type Parameters

As you can see in the preceding sample, the code is far simpler. The data type `object` has been replaced with the type parameter `T`. What this means is that C# will actually defer the definition of that type until runtime. When a generic class is instantiated, it is instantiated with a type parameter, binding the incomplete amorphous class implementation with a real type, creating a concrete generic class instance, as shown in the following example:

```
Customer<OrderItem> customer = new Customer<OrderItem>();
```

Type parameters are always specified using the new generics operator <>.

Although you can name your type parameters whatever you like, a convention exists that defines the letter "T" as the standard name for the first type parameter. If your class requires additional type parameters, convention dictates that you continue with the alphabet starting at the capital letter "U" and proceeding from there. If you manage to make it to "Z" with type parameters, you may have a fairly large design problem that generics simply can't fix.

Another convention that is far more friendly is to only use single letters when the purpose of the type parameter is extremely obvious, such as defining `MyList<T>`. For situations where the purpose of the type parameter isn't self-explanatory, Microsoft actually recommends that you use a descriptive name for the type parameter that is prefixed with a capital T, as shown in the following code:

```
public class MyGenerics<TDataAccessClass>
```

To specify multiple type parameters in a class definition, simply separate them with commas:

```
public class MyGenerics<T, U, V>
```

And to instantiate a class that requires multiple type parameters, you separate the types with commas as well:

```
MyGenerics<int, string, object> x = new MyGenerics<int, string, object>();
```

Constraining Type Parameters

When you have a type parameter specified in your class definition, there is actually very little you can do with it by default. For example, how do you create a new instance of that object? You might think that the following code should compile error-free:

```
public class Customer<T>
{
    public void AddDetailItem(string itemName)
    {
        T newItem = new T();
```

```
        items.Add(newItem);
    }
}
```

Unfortunately C# has no way of knowing whether the data type specified by the parameter T has a default constructor, so the compiler will not allow you to use that type in a new statement with no parameters.

To get around this, you can use *constraints* on type parameters. These constraints specify certain requirements of the type parameter that must be met. For example, you can specify that any type parameter passed to your Generic class implementation must implement a default (parameterless) constructor.

All constraints on Generic classes are indicated with the where keyword, and you can specify multiple constraints on the same parameter by separating the constraints with a comma.

A sample of specifying a constraint is shown in the following code:

```
public class Customer<TDetailItem> where TDetailItem : new()
```

The preceding constraint indicates that the type parameter specified by TDetailItem must implement a default constructor. The following few lines show a few more complex ways of specifying constraints:

```
public class CustomList<T> where T: class, IListItem
public class Customer<T,U> where T: new() where U: ICustomerData
```

Table 6.1 shows all of the constraints that you can apply to generic type parameters.

TABLE 6.1   Generic Type Parameter Constraints

Constraint	Description
where T:struct	Indicates that T must be a value type (except Nullable).
where T:class	Indicates that T must be a reference type, including any class, delegate, or interface.
where T:new()	Indicates that T must implement a default constructor. The new() constraint must be specified last if it is used with multiple constraints on the same type.
where T: (base class)	Indicates that T must either be or derive from the base class indicated.
where T: (interface)	Indicates that T must either be or implement the interface indicated.

An extremely common design pattern in object-oriented programming is the factory pattern. In this pattern, code requests new instances of a given type from that type's factory rather than instantiating them directly. This gives the factory complete control over the instantiation process, as well as the ability to do things like cache preinstantiated types, perform transparent Remoting or Web Services calls to obtain support data, and much more.

To prevent the factory from having to do excessive typecasting, the pattern often calls for the development of a single factory for each class. So, if you have a `Customer` class, you will also have a `CustomerFactory` class. This model is also used in things like Container-Managed Persistence and Object-Relational Mapping.

To see how you can make quick use of generics and type parameter constraints, take a look at the following code, which creates a factory class that can serve up both the `Customer` type as well as the `SpecialCustomer` type:

```
public class CustomerFactory<TCustomer, U> where TCustomer : Customer, new()
{
   public TCustomer GetCustomer()
   {
     return new TCustomer();
   }
}
```

The preceding sample constrains the `TCustomer` type by requiring the `TCustomer` parameter to be or derive from the `Customer` type as well as implement a default constructor. Because the `TCustomer` argument has been constrained with the `new()` constraint, the code can explicitly create a new instance of that type. Through the power of generics, this new instance is *never* anything but the exact type specified. There is no typecasting required in the preceding factory class, which is a huge boon to object-oriented developers.

Building Generic Types

A generic type is any C# type that accepts a type parameter, as described in the preceding section. The hardest part of building generic types isn't the technical details behind the syntax implementation; it is in the design of the types themselves. Although generics are an incredibly powerful tool, the use of generics purely for the sake of using generics can cause its own unique set of problems. The next section of this chapter will cover the basics of working with generic classes, Interfaces, and methods.

Creating Generic Classes

You have seen several examples of how to create and consume generic classes. Generic classes are designed to encapsulate operations and provide models that are not specific to a single data type. The operations encapsulated by generic classes can either apply to all data types, or specific data types such as all derivatives of a certain base class or all classes that implement a specific interface. To recap the preceding section, you use the type parameter operator (<>) to indicate the use of a generic type parameter within your class definition. In places where there used to be a concrete type reference such as `int`, `string`, or `object`, you can then use the type parameter to allow your generic class to defer the specification of the actual type until the class is instantiated.

Creating Generic Methods

In addition to supplying type parameters for the class itself, you can also supply type parameters for individual methods that belong to a class. A generic method is just a method that takes a type parameter. The important thing to keep in mind is that the type parameter that is accepted by a method is *unrelated* to any type parameter accepted by the class in which the method is defined. This generic method can make use of the class type parameter, but it isn't necessary.

Listing 6.1 provides an illustration of both writing and consuming generic methods.

LISTING 6.1   Creating and Consuming Generic Methods

```
using System;
using System.Collections.Generic;
using System.Text;

namespace Generics1
{
    public class MethodTest
    {
        public static bool IsGreater<TOperand>(TOperand op1,
            TOperand op2) where TOperand : IComparable
        {
            return (op1.CompareTo(op2) > 0);
        }
    }

    public class MethodTest2<TItem> where TItem : IComparable
    {
        public bool IsGreater(TItem op1, TItem op2)
        {
            return MethodTest.IsGreater<TItem>(op1, op2);
        }
    }
}
```

The first class, `MethodTest`, defines a static generic method that takes a single type argument, `TOperand`, that must implement the `IComparable` interface. The `IsGreater` method returns whether op1 is greater than op2, where both op1 and op2 will be of the type indicated by `TOperand` when the generic method is *closed* (closing is the process by which an open generic definition is bound to a concrete type during the instantiation or method invocation process).

Next, the generic class `MethodTest2` takes a single Parameter Type `TItem` that also must implement the `IComparable` interface. This class has a single instance method that invokes the static method `IsGreater` on the `MethodTest` class. The preceding code sample not only illustrates how to create and consume generic methods, but it also shows you how the class-level type parameters are completely unrelated to the method-level type parameters, though you can use a class-level type parameter within a generic method if you choose. The following few lines of code show how to use both the MethodTest and the MethodTest2 classes:

```
Console.WriteLine(
    string.Format("Is 2 greater than 3? : {0}",
    MethodTest.IsGreater<int>(2, 3)));

MethodTest2<string> m2 = new MethodTest2<string>();
Console.WriteLine(
    string.Format("Is Z greater than A? : {0}",
    m2.IsGreater("Z", "A")));
```

One distinct advantage of generic methods is that the compiler can create shortcuts for you. For example, if you pass two integer arguments to the IsGreater method, you don't need to explicitly tell the compiler that the method is being invoked with integers, as shown in the following code:

```
Console.WriteLine(
            string.Format("Implicit Type Parameter test, 2 > 3 : {0}",
            MethodTest.IsGreater(2, 3)));
```

Creating Generic Interfaces

A generic interface functions in much the same way as a generic class. The interface itself accepts one or more type parameters in the same fashion as the generic class. Instead of utilizing the type parameter in the class definition, the type parameter is then utilized in the member declaration statements that make up the interface.

A huge benefit of allowing generic type parameters to be present in interfaces is that the classes that implement those Interfaces will not need to perform any unnecessary boxing/unboxing or typecasting. You will learn about boxing and unboxing in Chapter 16, "Optimizing your .NET 2.0 Code." For now, it should suffice to know that boxing and unboxing are operations done to switch between value and reference types, and the operation is costly. The code in Listing 6.2 illustrates a generic interface.

LISTING 6.2   A Generic Interface

```
using System;
using System.Collections.Generic;
using System.Text;

namespace Generics1
{
  public interface IDataHandler<TRowType> where TRowType : new()
  {
```

LISTING 6.2   Continued

```
        void AddRecord(TRowType record);
        void DeleteRecord(TRowType record);
        void UpdateRecord(TRowType record);
        void SelectRecord(TRowType record);
        List<TRowType> SelectRecords();
    }
}
```

What the preceding interface accomplishes is indicating that any class that implements IDataHandler<TRowType> will provide the standard Add, Delete, Update, and Select methods typically associated with a data access object regardless of the underlying type of the data being stored. This is an extremely useful interface to have as it allows a lot of flexibility when working with the data tier.

Using Generic Collections

So far you have seen the basics of how you can implement generics in your own code as you develop solutions in C# 2.0. One of the most common uses of generics is in the implementation and manipulation of strongly typed collections. This section of the chapter gives you samples of how to work with some of the most common generic collection types available in version 2.0 of the .NET Framework: the Dictionary<> class, the List<> class, the Queue<> class, and the Stack<> class.

Using the Dictionary Class

The Dictionary class is designed to store values keyed to a lookup value. Traditionally programmers have used this class to store values associated with strings such as names, keywords, or GUIDs, but you can use an object of any type as the key and an object of any type as the value.

Adding generics to the picture allows you to avoid the use of costly System.Object instances as both the key and value, and you can specify the type of the key and the type of the value at the time of instantiation using type parameters, as shown in the following sample snippet:

```
// Test a Dictionary
Dictionary<string, int> monthDays = new Dictionary<string, int>();
monthDays["January"] = 31;
monthDays["February"] = 28;
monthDays["March"] = 31;
Console.WriteLine("March has " + monthDays["March"].ToString() + " days.");
```

The preceding sample creates and manipulates a Dictionary<> class where all of the keys are strings, and all of the values are numbers, storing the number of days in each month.

Using the `List` Class

The `List<>` class is fairly self-explanatory. Its sole purpose is the storage of a list of items. Without generics, Lists were responsible for storing a list of `System.Object` types, and whenever the developer needed a true data type out of the list, it would involve type-casting operations and potentially convoluted code. As you can see in the following example, creating and using arbitrary lists of strongly typed data has never been easier:

```
// Using the List class
List<Customer> custList = new List<Customer>();
Customer newCust = new Customer();
newCust.LastName = "Hoffman";
newCust.FirstName = "Kevin";
newCust.CustomerID = 1;
custList.Add(newCust);
Console.WriteLine(
    string.Format("There are {0} customers, the first one is {1} {2}",
    custList.Count, custList[0].FirstName, custList[0].LastName));
```

The preceding code produces the following output:

```
There are 1 customers, the first one is Kevin Hoffman
```

Something to pay attention to is the fact that you can now write code like the following without having to write any of your own custom classes:

```
custList[0].FirstName
```

To get a list to work as shown in the preceding line of code, developers used to have to spend countless hours creating their own strongly typed collection classes. Now you can create strongly typed collections at runtime with no performance loss and no typecasting required in a way that makes your code easier to read and reuse.

Using the `Queue` Class

As you saw in Chapter 4, "Arrays and Collections," the `Queue` class is designed as a FIFO (First-In First-Out) collection. When you *enqueue* an item, it remains at the front of the Queue. As you add more items to the Queue, they stack up at the end the same as people would while waiting in line to get into a movie or to reach that elusive bank teller. Each time you *dequeue* an item from the Queue, you remove an item from the beginning of the collection and can then process it. The generic `Queue<>` class allows you to specify the data type of the items in the queue at the time of instantiation, as shown in the following sample:

```
Queue<Customer> custQ = new Queue<Customer>();
custQ.Enqueue(newCust);
Customer dqCust = custQ.Dequeue();
```

```
Console.WriteLine(
    string.Format("Dequeued  the following customer: {0} {1}",
    dqCust.FirstName,  dqCust.LastName));
```

Using the Stack Class

In contrast to the Queue<> class, the Stack<> class is a LIFO (Last-in First-out) collection. If you think of a pile of items sitting on the floor representing a stack, you know that in order to get to the item on the bottom of the stack, you have to remove all of the items on top first. The same goes for the Stack<> class; when you *push* an item onto a stack, it goes on top, and when you *pop* an item off the stack, you take the topmost item. You can also *peek* at the item currently sitting on top of the stack without removing it. The following code illustrates pushing items onto a generic stack and popping them off. To be sure you know how stacks work, you can play with the order in which items are *push*ed to see the results:

```
Stack<Customer> custStack = new Stack<Customer>();
Customer cust1 = new Customer();
cust1.FirstName = "John";
cust1.LastName = "Doe";
cust1.CustomerID = 99;
custStack.Push(newCust);
custStack.Push(cust1);
Customer popCust = custStack.Pop();
Console.WriteLine(
    string.Format("Customer popped off the stack was {0} {1}",
    popCust.FirstName, popCust. LastName));
```

Summary

This chapter has given you a glimpse at the incredible power that a developer can wield using generics. Generics are a tool that allow developers to maximize performance and code reuse as well as create a robust object-oriented programming environment by not having to resort to repetitive typecasting and the overuse of parameters of type System.Object. Using generics, developers can defer the specification of data types until such time as their class is instantiated, but still reap the benefits of strong data types. After reading this chapter, you should be able to continue learning all that C# 2.0 has to offer and feel comfortable when you see generics being used by the .NET Framework and in your own sample code.

PART II

.NET Framework 2.0 Fundamentals

IN THIS PART

I/O and Persistence

In this day and age of enterprise applications and smart clients that get their data from large relational databases like SQL Server and Oracle, it is often easy to overlook the fact that we still use the underlying file system for something other than storing shortcuts and documents.

We use files for numerous tasks, including storing configuration settings, images, icons, textual data (such as comma-delimited files from other sources like mainframes), file-based databases such as Microsoft Access, Excel spreadsheets, and even XML data.

This chapter shows you the basics of working with files using the .NET Framework, including how to work with streams, the basic unit of input/output (I/O) used throughout the entire framework. Finally, you'll see some more advanced file I/O techniques such as asynchronous I/O and the use of isolated storage to provide a secure, isolated location for your application's data.

Introduction to Streams

A *stream* is an object that essentially connects data between two endpoints with a narrow access window. Streams allow you to write and read small portions of data at a time, providing for an extremely efficient means of access. For example, using a stream, you can read data in small portions from a file that is several hundred megabytes in size without actually consuming several hundred megabytes of memory. The same is true of writing to streams. You can place small amounts of data on a stream without having to have all of the data in memory at any given time.

In addition to the performance benefit, streams also provide a unified model for reading and writing data, regardless of the format or location of the underlying data. For example, you can access data from a disk file using a stream and you can access data from a relational database or from a web service in a stream as well.

Streams can also be connected through a process referred to as *composition*. By composing streams, you can attach various types of reader and writer classes to the end of the stream to make data access easier. As you will see in Chapter 15, "Cryptography and Data Protection," you can even attach specially encrypted streams so that data is encrypted as soon as it is placed on the stream. Streams can also be used for network communication in addition to file I/O.

Using Memory Streams

Streams are the basic unit of I/O in the .NET Framework and you will find them used everywhere. Before getting into working with physical files on disk, this section will illustrate the basics of opening streams and reading and writing from streams using the MemoryStream class as an example. When you know how to manipulate a MemoryStream, you will find that you will be able to use all of the other types of streams exposed by .NET Framework classes with little difficulty.

As mentioned earlier, streams provide a narrow window of access. This often causes developers trouble. For example, when you write to a stream, the Position of the pointer in the stream advances. When you read from a stream, the read *always starts from the current pointer position within the stream*. A common source of problems when reading from streams is not setting the pointer position properly with the Seek method.

Before taking a look at the MemoryStream sample code, take a look at Tables 7.1 and 7.2, which list the methods and properties that belong to all Stream classes, regardless of the underlying data store.

TABLE 7.1 Stream Properties

Property	Description
CanRead	This property is used by deriving classes (such as MemoryStream) to indicate whether the stream supports read operations.
CanWrite	Indicates whether the stream supports write operations.
CanSeek	Indicates whether the stream supports seek operations. Some streams are forward-only and do not allow seeking to specific positions.
Length	Indicates the length, or size, of the stream in bytes.
Position	Indicates the current pointer position of the stream.

TABLE 7.2 Stream Methods

Method	Description
BeginRead	Starts an asynchronous (multithreaded) read operation
BeginWrite	Starts an asynchronous write operation
Close	Closes the current stream and releases associated resources (such as underlying database resources, network sockets, OS-level file handles, and so on)

TABLE 7.2   Continued

Method	Description
EndRead	Completes an asynchronous read operation
EndWrite	Completes an asynchronous write operation
Flush	Clears any buffers in the stream and stores any uncommitted data in the underlying backing store
Read	Reads an array of bytes from the stream
ReadByte	Reads a single byte from the stream
Seek	Moves the pointer to the indicated position, relative to the beginning, end, or current position of the stream
SetLength	Expands or contracts the stream, if supported
Write	Writes an array of bytes to the stream
WriteByte	Writes a single byte to the stream

The code shown in Listing 7.1 illustrates how to instantiate a stream, as well as how to read and write information from that stream.

LISTING 7.1   MemoryStream Sample

```
using System;
using System.IO;
using System.Collections.Generic;
using System.Text;

namespace MemStream
{
    class Program
    {
        static void Main(string[] args)
        {
            string sourceString = "Mary had a little lamb.";
            MemoryStream ms = new MemoryStream(100) ;

            // put some data on the stream
            ms.Write(ASCIIEncoding.ASCII.GetBytes(sourceString),
              0, sourceString.Length);

            Console.WriteLine("After initial write:");
            Console.WriteLine(string.Format(
                "Capacity: {0}\nLength: {1}\nPosition: {2}",
                ms.Capacity, ms.Length, ms.Position));

            ms.Seek(0, SeekOrigin.Begin);
            // read the first 4 bytes of the stream
```

LISTING 7.1   Continued

```
        byte[] tempBytes = new byte[sourceString.Length];
        ms.Read(tempBytes, 0, 4);

        Console.WriteLine(ASCIIEncoding.ASCII.GetString(tempBytes));

        // get the word 'lamb'
        ms.Seek(-5, SeekOrigin.End);
        ms.Read(tempBytes, 0, 4) ;
        Console.WriteLine(ASCIIEncoding.ASCII.GetString(tempBytes));

        // write some bytes
        ms.Seek(11, SeekOrigin.Begin);
        ms.Write(ASCIIEncoding.ASCII.GetBytes("really"), 0, 6);

        // now get the whole stream
        ms.Seek(0, SeekOrigin.Begin);
        ms.Read(tempBytes, 0, (int)ms.Length);
        Console.WriteLine(ASCIIEncoding.ASCII.GetString(tempBytes));

        ms.Close();

        Console.ReadLine();
      }
    }
}
```

Before running this code, see if you can predict the output. The code that retrieves the first four bytes of the stream should be fairly obvious; the output will be the word *Mary*.

Working with Unicode

When working with streams that contain textual data, knowing the size of your characters is paramount. For example, when working with traditional ASCII characters, the size of each character is exactly one byte. This makes math easy. However, when working with Unicode when dealing with foreign languages, you need to remember that each character requires two bytes. Therefore, when you convert byte arrays into strings, you need to use the UnicodeEncoding class, and you need to allocate twice the number of characters in bytes when initializing your byte arrays.

Next, the code seeks to a position five bytes before the end of the stream and then grabs the next four bytes, producing the word "lamb."

The next few lines of code are typically where a lot of developers get confused. When you write to a stream, you overwrite whatever bytes might lie underneath. So, when writing "really" to the stream, you don't get "Mary had a really little lamb." as one might expect. Rather, your stream contains "Mary had a really lamb.". If your goal is truly to insert data at a certain point in the stream, and have the remainder of the stream remain intact, you will need to do it the "old-fashioned way." This involves using two streams and copying the old into the new, making sure to insert the new data in the right place in the new stream.

Introduction to Basic File I/O

In the .NET Framework, file I/O is accomplished using streams. Although some classes may make certain aspects of reading and writing to text files easier, those classes still make use of streams for the final read and write operations on operating system files. This section shows you how to create, append to, read from, and query information about files. You will also see how the framework provides utility classes for common file operations, such as the StreamWriter class that is used in conjunction with the File class to make working with plain text files easy.

Creating and Appending Files

When working with files using the Stream pattern, the majority of the work is done in the constructor for the FileStream class. This constructor allows you to specify the file-name (or a classic Win32 file handle), as well as access modes, sharing modes, and much more. Using the constructor, you indicate whether you want to create a new file or open an existing file, or open an existing file for appending.

The following few lines of code create a new file and write some text to it:

```
string origString =
    "I never saw an author who was aware that there is any " +
    "dimensional difference between a fact and a surmise.\n" +
    " - Mark Twain";

// create the file, write to it, save it.
FileStream fs = new FileStream("quote.txt", FileMode.Create);
fs.Write(ASCIIEncoding.ASCII.GetBytes(origString), 0,
    origString.Length);
fs.Close();
```

Note that you need to close the FileStream in order for the contents of the Stream to be written to disk. As mentioned in the description for the Stream class, the Close method releases all resources and flushes the remaining contents of the buffer to whatever under-lying media backs the stream, such as a disk file.

You can use a different option in the constructor to obtain a FileStream for the same file, but this time you can use the Stream to append additional data to the file:

```
string addString =
    "\n\nGood friends, good books and a sleepy conscience: " +
```

```
    "this is the ideal life.\n" +
    " - Mark Twain";

fs = new FileStream("quote.txt", FileMode.Append);
fs.Write(ASCIIEncoding.ASCII.GetBytes(addString), 0, addString.Length);
fs.Close();
```

The preceding code uses the `FileMode.Append` enumeration item to indicate how the file should be opened. Table 7.3 contains a description of each of the possible file modes.

TABLE 7.3   File Mode Enumeration Values

File Mode	Description
Append	Opens the file if it exists and seeks to the end of the file. If the file does not exist, a new file is created.
Create	Creates a new file. If a file already exists with the indicated name, the file is over-written.
CreateNew	Creates a new file. If the file already exists, an `IOException` error will be thrown.
Open	Opens an existing file. A `FileNotFoundException` exception will be thrown if the file does not exist.
OpenOrCreate	Opens an existing file. If the file does not exist, it will be created.
Truncate	Opens an existing file. After the file is opened, its size will be reduced to 0 bytes and all data contained within it will be lost.

Now that you have seen the low-level way of creating basic files, whether they are binary files or text files, let's take a look at a quicker and easier way of working with text files.

You can replace the preceding code where you have to work with arrays of bytes with the following code, making the code easier to read and simpler to write:

```
StreamWriter sw = File.CreateText("quote2.txt");
sw.Write(origString);
sw.Write(addString);
sw.Close();
```

As you can see, the code is a lot simpler than the previous examples. The reason this chapter started off showing you how to work with arrays of bytes is that this knowledge will help you if you need to work with files that don't contain simple text, such as image files or binary files containing fixed data structures.

Reading from Existing Files

Reading from files using streams works just like all other I/O that has been discussed in this chapter up to this point. You obtain a reference to the file either using the `FileStream` class constructor or using the `File` class.

When you have a reference to the file from which you want to read, you can read that data using the stream's `Read` or `ReadByte` methods.

The following code uses a `FileStream` class to open an existing file, read an array of bytes from it, and display the resulting array of bytes as an ASCII string:

```
byte[] fileBytes = new byte[origString.Length + addString.Length];
fs = new FileStream("quote.txt", FileMode.Open);
fs.Read(fileBytes, 0, (int)fs.Length);
Console.WriteLine("Quote from the file:");
Console.WriteLine(ASCIIEncoding.ASCII.GetString(fileBytes));
```

And now take a look at the same effect using the `OpenText` method of the `File` class to create an instance of the `StreamReader` class:

```
StreamReader sr = File.OpenText("quote2.txt");
Console.WriteLine("Entire file: \n" + sr.ReadToEnd());
sr.Close();
```

Using Directories and the File System

In all the previous examples, the filename of the file with which we were working was known and fixed. This isn't exactly a good model of reality. In most commercial applications that deal with files, you need to do things like check to make sure that a file exists, or check to see if a specific directory exists. If the directory doesn't exist when you need to create the file, you need to create the directory as well.

To help developers deal with this, the `System.IO` namespace provides the following classes:

- `File`—A static class that provides methods for testing for the existence of a file, copying files, deleting files, moving files, as well as the opening of files and, as shown in the preceding example, the creation of streams from files.

- `FileInfo`—An instance class that provides information about a specific file. Also contains instance methods for performing copy, move, delete and related operations.

- `Directory`—Static class that provides methods for determining the existence of directories, creating directories, and much more.

- `DirectoryInfo`—Provides instance methods for operating on a specific directory, including renaming, obtaining the list of files within the directory, and so on.

- `Path`—A utility class for parsing and building path strings.

For more information on each of these individual classes, you can refer to the MSDN documentation online at http://msdn.microsoft.com. The example in Listing 7.2 illustrates how to test and see if a file exists, and if it does, create a subdirectory, copy the file there, and then display some operating system-level information about the file itself.

LISTING 7.2   File Manipulation and Query

```
using System;
using System.Security;
using System.Security.Principal;
using System.Security.AccessControl;
using System.IO;
using System.Collections.Generic;
using System.Text;

namespace DirManip
{
class Program
{
static void Main(string[] args)
{
    if (File.Exists("quote.txt"))
    {
        if (!Directory.Exists("quotedir"))
        {
            Directory.CreateDirectory("quotedir");
        }
        FileInfo f = new FileInfo("quote.txt");
        if (!File.Exists(@"quotedir\quote.txt"))
            f.CopyTo(@"quotedir\quote.txt");
        Console.WriteLine("File: " + f.FullName);
        Console.WriteLine("Location: " + f.Directory.FullName);
        Console.WriteLine("Created: " + f.CreationTime.ToShortDateString());

        FileSecurity fs = f.GetAccessControl();
        Console.WriteLine("Owner: {0}", fs.GetOwner(typeof(NTAccount)));
        AuthorizationRuleCollection arc =
            fs.GetAccessRules(true, true, typeof(NTAccount));
        foreach (FileSystemAccessRule ar in arc)
        {
            Console.WriteLine(ar.ToString());
            Console.WriteLine("User: {0}", ar.IdentityReference);
            Console.WriteLine("Type: {0}", ar.AccessControlType);
        }
        Console.ReadLine();
    }
}
}
}
```

The core of the code starts with the instantiation of a new `FileInfo` object, from which you can perform many different operations (such as a copy) as well as query detailed information about the file itself.

Developers who are familiar with file-level programming in previous versions of C# may start to get a little giddy when they notice that you can now obtain an ACL (Access Control List) starting with the `FileInfo` object. Previously, obtaining the list of access rights associated with a file was a painful and tedious task that involved invoking the Win32 API using a technique (discussed in Chapter 13, "COM and Windows Interoperability") called "Platform Invoke."

The output of the preceding code looks as follows:

```
File: D:\SAMS\C# Unleashed 2005\Chapters\07\Code\
➥DirManip\DirManip\bin\Debug\quote.txt
Location: D:\SAMS\C# Unleashed 2005\Chapters\07\Code\DirManip\DirManip\bin\Debug
Created: 11/7/2005
Owner: Everyone
User: Everyone
Type: Allow
```

Using Asynchronous File I/O

By default, when you read data from a file or write data to a file, the operation is synchronous. A *synchronous* operation is one where the code will attempt to complete the operation before continuing on to the next line of code. So, if it takes your code 20 minutes to perform a read operation of an entire file, the next line of code in your application will have to wait 20 minutes before executing.

This kind of waiting behavior is usually frowned upon by end users: No one wants to sit and twiddle their thumbs while an application locks everything up to complete an incredibly long operation.

This chapter does not go into too much detail on how to accomplish multithreaded programming, as more will be discussed on that topic later in the book. However, you will see that asynchronous file I/O is not only possible, but easy if you plan ahead. Take a look at the sample in Listing 7.3.

LISTING 7.3   Asynchronous File I/O

```
using System;
using System.IO;
using System.Collections.Generic;
using System.Text;

namespace AsyncFile
{
```

LISTING 7.3 Continued

```
class Program
{
static bool fileDone = false;
static FileStream fs = null;
static void Main(string[] args)
{
    fs = new FileStream("quote.txt", FileMode.Open);
    byte[] fileBytes = new byte[fs.Length];
    fs.BeginRead(fileBytes, 0, (int)fs.Length, new AsyncCallback(ReadEnd), null);
    while (!fileDone)
    {
        Console.WriteLine("Waiting for file read to finish...");
    }

    Console.ReadLine();
}

static void ReadEnd(IAsyncResult ar)
{
    int bytesRead = fs.EndRead(ar);
    Console.WriteLine("Read {0} bytes.", bytesRead);
    fs.Close();
    fileDone = true;
}
}
}
```

A fairly large `quote.txt` file was created for this example. If you run it with that file, you should see that the message "Waiting for file read to finish…" appears several times before the operation is complete. This illustrates that the `while` loop immediately after the `BeginRead` method began executing even before the entire file had been read. This gives your application the ability to continue processing and providing the user with a rich experience while the data is being loaded in the background.

The concepts behind the `AsyncCallback` class and the `IAsyncResult` interface are covered more in depth throughout this book as the topics become more complex and you explore event-based programming and using multithreaded techniques to improve your application.

Working with Isolated Storage

Isolated storage is the solution to a unique problem that has arisen recently due to the increased security of users' desktops as well as the security enforced by the Common Language Runtime itself. All managed applications run within a security "sandbox" and this sandbox often prevents an application from creating files or accessing the user's hard disk at all. This security is highly desired, especially for applications obtained through the Internet to prevent malicious code from having unrestrained access to the user's hard disk.

However, for every malicious application for which the security is absolutely required, there are many more innocent applications that just want to use the disk storage to store things like user preferences. User preferences can be anything from the last position of a recently opened window to highly complex workflow and business rule options specific to the user. Also, components written by the same vendor may need to access shared data but might lack the security clearance necessary to access such data.

Isolated storage provides an area in which applications can store private information, such as user preferences, that is under the complete control of the end user. This gives the application the ability to read and write from a safe location to store information and gives the user the peace of mind of knowing that even if an application can save data, it can't do damage to any files other than the ones created by the application.

When you open an isolated storage location, your code must specify a *scope* for this store. This allows you to separate stores by user, by application, by domain, and even allows you to store the data within a user's roaming profile.

The code in Listing 7.4 shows an example of an application that stores and retrieves the user's favorite color. This preference will follow the user in his roaming profile if applicable.

LISTING 7.4   Example of Isolated Storage

```
using System;
using System.IO;
using System.IO.IsolatedStorage;
using System.Collections.Generic;
using System.Text;

namespace IsoSample
{
class Program
{
static void Main(string[] args)
{
    IsolatedStorageFile isoFile =
        IsolatedStorageFile.GetStore(IsolatedStorageScope.Assembly ¦
        IsolatedStorageScope.User ¦
        IsolatedStorageScope.Roaming,null, null) ;

    string curColor = "(none)";
```

LISTING 7.4   Continued

```
IsolatedStorageFileStream isoFs =
    new IsolatedStorageFileStream("favColor.txt", FileMode.OpenOrCreate,
    FileAccess.ReadWrite);
if (isoFs.Length > 0)
{
    byte[] fileBytes = new byte[isoFs.Length];
    isoFs.Read(fileBytes, 0, (int)isoFs.Length);
    curColor = ASCIIEncoding.ASCII.GetString(fileBytes);
}
isoFs.Close();

Console.WriteLine("Current Favorite Color: {0}", curColor);
Console.Write("New favorite color: ");
string newColor = Console.ReadLine();

IsolatedStorageFileStream newFs =
    new IsolatedStorageFileStream("favColor.txt", FileMode.Create);
newFs.Write(ASCIIEncoding.ASCII.GetBytes(newColor), 0, newColor.Length);
newFs.Close();
}
}
}
```

The first time you run the preceding application, it will indicate that the user's current favorite color is "(none)". The next time you start the application, it will show you the color that you entered on the previous run. The data is being stored in the isolated storage area, an area that won't allow the application to do damage to the hard disk or important files.

When you store data in isolated storage on Windows XP for a user, it will be located in <drive>\Documents and Settings\<User>\Application Data for a roaming-enabled profile, and <drive>\Documents and Settings\<User>\Local Settings\Application Data for a non-roaming-enabled profile.

Summary

When most people think of reading and writing application data, they almost instinctively think about large relational databases such as SQL Server or Oracle, or flat-file databases like Microsoft Access. Even when surrounded by all of that database power, applications still need to read and write data from regular files on disk.

This chapter introduced you to the concept of streams, the basic unit of I/O used throughout the .NET Framework. You can use streams to access data for virtually any underlying source, even if that source is entirely in memory as in the case of the MemoryStream class.

Finally, this chapter showed you how to work with the operating system itself to manipulate directories and files, as well as obtain detailed information about files on disk. In addition, you saw how to use isolated storage to allow your application to store user data in a way that is easy to use and doesn't violate CLR security policy for untrusted applications.

Whether you are creating large or small applications, Windows or web, you will undoubtedly find that the information in this chapter on streams and basic I/O is useful and applicable.

CHAPTER 8

Working with XML

The eXtensible Markup Language (XML) has seen widespread adoption throughout almost every industry in recent years. Its ability to allow applications to exchange data in a standardized format through web services and XML documents, and its adoption by SQL Server 2005 and most of Microsoft's new and upcoming applications, make the use of XML almost compulsory when creating applications in the .NET Framework. Whether you're using XML in your application's configuration file, consuming or exposing web services, working with XML in SQL Server, or working with datasets, knowing how to work with XML programmatically with the .NET Framework is an essential skill for any C# developer. This chapter does not cover the basics of XML itself or other standards such as XPath and XSLT. Instead, you will see how to work with XML, XPath, and XSLT using C# 2.0.

Reading and Writing XML Documents

One of the most basic tasks that you can perform with XML is manipulating the contents of an XML document. This includes traversing the list of nodes in the document, setting and querying attribute values, and manipulating the tree itself by creating and inserting new nodes.

This section shows you how to read XML documents using the Document Object Model (DOM)) modeled by the XmlDocument class in the System.Xml namespace. The DOM is recursive, meaning that each node has the same properties and methods as every other node in the document. Tables 8.1 and 8.2 provide a brief overview of many of the properties and methods of the XmlNode class before getting into the code sample. The XML node is the most basic unit of abstraction within a DOM-modeled document.

TABLE 8.1   Commonly Used `XmlNode` Properties

Property	Method
`Attributes`	The attributes of the node (`XmlAttributeCollection`).
`ChildNodes`	The list of child nodes of the current node (`XmlNodeList`).
`FirstChild`	Returns the first child of the XML node (first being first in document order).
`HasChildNodes`	A Boolean that indicates whether the node has child nodes.
`InnerText`	Gets or sets the text inside the node.
`InnerXml`	Gets or sets the XML within the node.
`LastChild`	Returns the last child (document order relative) of the node.
`Name`	The name of the node.
`NodeType`	Indicates the type of the node. This can be several things, including (but not limited to): `Document`, `DocumentFragment`, `Element`, `EndElement`, `Entity`, `Notation`, `Text`, `Whitespace`, or `XmlDeclaration`.
`OuterXml`	The XML representing the current node and all its child nodes.
`OwnerDocument`	The document to which the current node belongs.
`ParentNode`	The parent node of the current node, if any.
`PreviousSibling`	Gets the node immediately preceding the current node in document order.
`Value`	Gets or sets the value of the current node.

TABLE 8.2   Commonly Used `XmlNode` Methods

Method	Description
`AppendChild`	Adds a child node to the end of the current list of child nodes
`Clone`	Creates a duplicate of the node
`CreateNavigator`	Creates an `XPathNavigator` for this node
`InsertAfter`	Inserts the given node immediately after the current node
`InsertBefore`	Inserts the given node immediately before the current node
`PrependChild`	Adds the given child node at the beginning of the child node list
`RemoveAll`	Removes all child nodes
`RemoveChild`	Removes the given child from the current node
`SelectNodes`	Selects a list of nodes matching the `XPath` expression (discussed in the following section)
`SelectSingleNode`	Selects a single node that matches the `XPath` expression

The `XmlDocument` class, which deals with the entire document, is also itself an `XmlNode`. If you look at the documentation for the `XmlDocument` class, you'll see that it inherits from `XmlNode`. This fits with the DOM pattern in that the document is a node that can have child nodes. The methods in Table 8.3 show some of the additional methods available to the `XmlDocument` that aren't part of a standard node class.

TABLE 8.3   `XmlDocument` Class Methods

Method	Description
`CreateAttribute`	Creates an `XmlAttribute` with the given name
`CreateCDataSection`	Creates a `CData` section with the given data
`CreateComment`	Creates an `XmlComment`
`CreateDocumentFragment`	Creates a document fragment
`CreateElement`	Creates an `XmlElement`, an `XmlNode` with element-specific functionality
`CreateNode`	Creates an `XmlNode`
`CreateTextNode`	Creates an `XmlText` node
`CreateWhitespace`	Creates whitespace for insertion into the document
`ImportNode`	Imports a node from another document
`Load`	Loads the XML from the given file
`LoadXml`	Loads the XML from the given XML string
`Save`	Saves the XML document
`Validate`	Validates the XML document against a schema

To show off the code for manipulating an XML document, we need a document. For the rest of this chapter, we will be working with a document called `items.xml`, which contains a list of items from a fictitious role-playing game and the various aspects of those items. The contents of this file are shown in Listing 8.1.

LISTING 8.1   `Items.xml`

```
<?xml version="1.0" encoding="utf-8"?>
<items>
  <item id="1" name="Flaming Sword of Doom"
        description=
"This sword will vanquish all of your foes with a single swipe">
    <attribute name="attack" value="10"/>
    <attribute name="weight" value="21" />
  </item>
  <item id="2" name="Bag of Really Big Stuff"
        description="This bag can hold a lot of stuff.">
    <attribute name="weight" value="1" />
    <attribute name="capacity" value="80" />
  </item>
  <item id="3" name="Broach of Bug Smashing"
        description="This broach will kill any bug. Instantly.">
    <attribute name="weight" value="1" />
    <attribute name="attack" value="11" />
    <specials>
      <special name="killbug" description="This thing kills any bug instantly."/>
    </specials>
  </item>
```

8

LISTING 8.1 Continued

```
  <item id="4" name="Wand of Traffic Vanquish"
        description=
"A single wave of this wand will part the highway before you.">
    <attribute name="weight" value="5" />
    <attribute name="attack" value="20" />
    <specials>
      <special name="parttraffic"
description="All nearby vehicles move out of your way." />
    </specials>
  </item>
</items>
```

Although XML allows you to freely mix freeform text with markup, for the purposes of the code in this chapter, the examples use XML documents as pure data storage.

The code in Listing 8.2 shows the use of the XmlNode class and its associated properties and methods for traversing an XML document and displaying its contents to the console.

LISTING 8.2 XML Document Display Sample

```
using System;
using System.Xml;
using System.Collections.Generic;
using System.Text;

namespace ReadWriteXml
{
class Program
{
static void Main(string[] args)
{
XmlDocument itemDoc = new XmlDocument();
itemDoc.Load(@"..\..\..\..\items.xml");
Console.WriteLine("DocumentElement has {0} children.",
    itemDoc.DocumentElement.ChildNodes.Count);

// iterate through top-level elements
foreach (XmlNode itemNode in itemDoc.DocumentElement.ChildNodes)
{
    // because we know that the node is an element, we can do this:
    XmlElement itemElement = (XmlElement)itemNode;
    Console.WriteLine("\n[Item]: {0}\n{1}", itemElement.Attributes["name"].Value,
        itemElement.Attributes["description"].Value);
    if (itemNode.ChildNodes.Count == 0)
        Console.WriteLine("(No additional Information)\n");
```

LISTING 8.2 Continued

```
    else
    {
        foreach (XmlNode childNode in itemNode.ChildNodes)
        {
            if (childNode.Name.ToUpper() == "ATTRIBUTE")
            {
                Console.WriteLine("{0} : {1}",
                    childNode.Attributes["name"].Value,
                    childNode.Attributes["value"].Value);
            }
            else if (childNode.Name.ToUpper() == "SPECIALS")
            {
                foreach (XmlNode specialNode in childNode.ChildNodes)
                {
                    Console.WriteLine("*{0}:{1}",
                        specialNode.Attributes["name"].Value,
                        specialNode.Attributes["description"].Value);
                }
            }
        }
    }
}
Console.ReadLine();
}
}
}
```

Querying XML with XPath

XPath is a language used for querying information contained within XML documents. An explanation of the XPath language itself is outside the scope of this chapter. If you're looking for a tutorial on XPath, you might try http://www.w3schools.com/xpath. Several other extremely good tutorials are also found at this site.

The basic premise behind XPath is that an XPath expression is essentially a description of the result set. More specifically, anything in the source document that satisfies the XPath expression will be returned when the expression is used to select nodes. Hierarchy levels within an XML document are represented in an XPath expression using the forward slash (/). If the double slash (//) is used, it indicates that position within the document tree is irrelevant to whether or not a node satisfies the expression. This is often referred to as a "deep" search.

During filtering and selecting, attributes are specified using the @ prefix, and predicates (conditions that must be satisfied) on a node are specified within square brackets ([]).

The simplest thing you can do with XPath is to select a list of nodes without filtering the results. To do that, you simply specify the nodes you want, as shown in the following XPath statement:

```
/items/item
```

This will select all item nodes that have the items node as a parent. If you want to select just the items node, you can use the XPath expression /items. To select all item nodes without regard to their location within the hierarchy, you can use the expression //item.

Using the square bracket ([]) notation, you can also select nodes based on their position within the current context. So, to select the second item beneath the items parent, you would use the following expression:

```
/items/item[1]
```

Note the zero-based indexing when using the square bracket notation.

Before getting into the more complex XPath statements, let's take the simple expressions and execute them in some .NET code, as shown in Listing 8.3.

LISTING 8.3   Simple XPath Expressions

```
using System;
using System.Xml;
using System.Collections.Generic;
using System.Text;

namespace XpathDemo
{
class Program
{
static void Main(string[] args)
{
    XmlDocument docItems = new XmlDocument();
    docItems.Load(@"..\..\..\..\items.xml");

    XmlNodeList allItems = docItems.SelectNodes("/items/item");
    Console.WriteLine("Found {0} items", allItems.Count);

    XmlNode thirdItem = docItems.SelectSingleNode("/items/item[2]");
    Console.WriteLine("Third node is {0}", thirdItem.Attributes["name"].Value);

    Console.ReadLine();
}
}
}
```

And now take a look at some code that uses some more advanced XPath expressions:

```
// return a list of all attributes where the weight is > 10...
XmlNodeList heavyAttribs = docItems.SelectNodes(
    "/items/item/attribute[@value > 10 and @name='weight']");
Console.WriteLine("Heavy items:");
foreach (XmlNode heavyAttrib in heavyAttribs)
{
    Console.WriteLine(heavyAttrib.ParentNode.Attributes["name"].Value);
}


// return all capacities and weights of all items
XmlNodeList cw = docItems.SelectNodes(
    "//attribute[@name='capacity'] ¦ //attribute[@name='weight']");
// do something with the list of capacities and weights...

Console.WriteLine("Heavy Items (descendant axis predicate):");
XmlNodeList heavyItems = docItems.SelectNodes(
    "//items/item[descendant::attribute[@name='weight' and @value > 10]]");
foreach (XmlNode heavyItem in heavyItems)
{
    Console.WriteLine(heavyItem.Attributes["name"].Value);
}
```

Transforming Documents with XSLT

An XSL Transformation (XSLT) essentially combines the XPath language for searching XML nodes and returning node lists with a set of functions designed specifically for converting a source XML document into a destination XML document. This destination document can be another XML document that simply contains the data in a different format, or it can be in the form of XHTML, an XML-compliant HTML document.

Converting XML into XHTML is probably the most common use for XSLT, though it is frequently used for converting document formats and facilitating data exchange between disparate systems.

To transform an XML document, you need an XSLT document. Listing 8.4 shows you an XSLT document for transforming the items.xml document shown earlier in the chapter. If you want more information on XSLT, there are several books available, as well as many online references, such as http://www.w3schools.com/xsl.

LISTING 8.4   itemsTransform.xslt

```
<?xml version="1.0" encoding="utf-8"?>

<xsl:stylesheet version="1.0"
    xmlns:xsl="http://www.w3.org/1999/XSL/Transform">
```

LISTING 8.4   Continued

```xsl
<xsl:template match="/">
    <html>
      <head>
        <title>List of Game Items</title>
      </head>
    <body bgcolor="#c0c0c0">
      <table width="100%" border="0" cellspacing="2" cellpadding="2">
        <tr>
          <th align="left">ID</th>
          <th align="left">Name</th>
        </tr>
        <xsl:for-each select="/items/item">
          <tr>
            <td>
              <xsl:value-of select="@id"/>
            </td>
            <td>
              <xsl:value-of select="@name"/>
            </td>
          </tr>
          <xsl:for-each select="attribute">
            <tr>
              <td colspan="2">
                <b>
                  <xsl:value-of select="@name"/>
                </b>
                :
                <xsl:value-of select="@value"/>
              </td>
            </tr>
          </xsl:for-each>
          <xsl:for-each select="specials">
            <xsl:for-each select="special">
              <tr>
                <td colspan="2">
                  <b>
                    <xsl:value-of select="@name"/>
                  </b>:
                  <xsl:value-of select="@description"/>
                </td>
              </tr>
            </xsl:for-each>
          </xsl:for-each>
          <tr>
```

LISTING 8.4   Continued

```
            <td colspan="2">
              <hr size="1" color="#880000"></hr>
            </td>
          </tr>
        </xsl:for-each>
      </table>
    </body>
    </html>
</xsl:template>
</xsl:stylesheet>
```

The actual transformation is accomplished using the `XslCompiledTransform` class, as shown in the following code snippet:

```
XslCompiledTransform xct = new XslCompiledTransform();
xct.Load(@"..\..\..\itemsTransform.xslt");
xct.Transform(@"..\..\..\..\items.xml", "items.html");
```

The preceding code results in an HTML page that looks like the one shown in Figure 8.1.

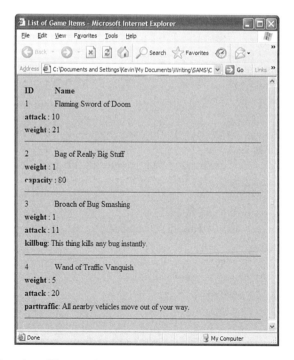

FIGURE 8.1   Results of an XSL transformation of the *items.xml* document.

Validating Documents with XSD

XML Schema Definition (XSD) is an XML dialect that describes the format, data types, and constraints of the information contained in an XML file. Countless online references on the XSD specification itself are available, as well as many publications.

This section shows you how to validate an XML document based on an existing XSD. To show this, we will create an XSD that defines the format of the items.xml document. Without knowing all that much about XSD, you can still easily create schemas by inferring them from instance documents such as items.xml with a command-line utility that ships with the .NET Framework SDK: XSD.EXE.

You can execute XSD.EXE against your instance document, and then modify it using the designer inside Visual Studio to change data types and relationships. The visual designer included with Visual Studio 2005 is an excellent tool for designing XML schemas.

Listing 8.5 contains the results of executing XSD.EXE as well as a modification to indicate that the ID of an item is an integer.

LISTING 8.5   items.xsd

```
<?xml version="1.0" encoding="utf-8"?>
<xs:schema id="items" xmlns=""
xmlns:xs="http://www.w3.org/2001/XMLSchema"
xmlns:msdata="urn:schemas-microsoft-com:xml-msdata">
  <xs:element name="items" msdata:IsDataSet="true" msdata:UseCurrentLocale="true">
    <xs:complexType>
      <xs:choice minOccurs="0" maxOccurs="unbounded">
        <xs:element name="item">
          <xs:complexType>
            <xs:sequence>
              <xs:element name="attribute" minOccurs="0" maxOccurs="unbounded">
                <xs:complexType>
                  <xs:attribute name="name" type="xs:string" />
                  <xs:attribute name="value" type="xs:string" />
                </xs:complexType>
              </xs:element>
              <xs:element name="specials" minOccurs="0" maxOccurs="unbounded">
                <xs:complexType>
                  <xs:sequence>
                    <xs:element name="special"
minOccurs="0" maxOccurs="unbounded">
                      <xs:complexType>
                        <xs:attribute name="name" type="xs:string" />
                        <xs:attribute name="description" type="xs:string" />
                      </xs:complexType>
                    </xs:element>
```

LISTING 8.5   Continued

```
                </xs:sequence>
              </xs:complexType>
            </xs:element>
          </xs:sequence>
          <xs:attribute name="id" type="xs:integer" />
          <xs:attribute name="name" type="xs:string" />
          <xs:attribute name="description" type="xs:string" />
        </xs:complexType>
      </xs:element>
    </xs:choice>
  </xs:complexType>
</xs:element>
</xs:schema>
```

Now take a look at the code that validates an instance document against a schema:

```
static void Main(string[] args)
{
    XmlDocument items = new XmlDocument();
    items.Load(@"..\..\..\..\items.xml");
    XmlSchema schema = XmlSchema.Read(
        new FileStream(@"..\..\..\..\items.xsd",FileMode.Open),
new ValidationEventHandler(OnSchemaValidate));
    items.Schemas.Add(schema);
    items.Validate(new ValidationEventHandler(OnValidate));
    Console.ReadLine();
}

static void OnValidate(object sender, ValidationEventArgs vargs)
{
    Console.WriteLine(vargs.Message);
}

static void OnSchemaValidate(object sender, ValidationEventArgs vargs)
{
    Console.WriteLine(vargs.Message);
}
```

The preceding code adds an `XmlSchema` instance to the document itself. When the
`Validate` method is called, the validation takes place in the background, and each time a
validation error occurs, the `OnValidate` method is invoked. To test this code, go back to
the original `items.xml` code and change one of the item IDs from a number to something
with letters in it. When you run the code, you'll see the following error message:

```
The 'id' attribute is invalid - The value 'abc' is invalid according to its data
type
'http://www.w3.org/2001/XMLSchema:integer' -
The string 'abc' is not a valid Integer value.
```

Summary

This chapter has shown you how you can make use of your existing XML skills in C#. You saw how to manipulate the nodes of an XML document using the DOM class XmlDocument, and you saw how to query XML documents using XPath statements. Finally, you saw how to transform XML documents using XSL transformations.

This chapter didn't go into much detail on the individual standards such as XSL and XPath. If you need to know more about those, many references are readily available.

Now that you have completed this chapter, you should feel comfortable working with XML in any of its forms whether you're working on an ASP.NET application or a Windows Forms application.

CHAPTER 9

Events and Delegates

Delegates and events are a key part of developing applications in C#. Developers often mistakenly assume that event-based programming is the sole domain of Windows Forms programming. The truth is that you can add a lot of power and value to your applications by making use of events and delegates, regardless of whether you're creating a Windows Forms application, an ASP.NET application, or even an application with no user interface at all.

This chapter shows you how to start developing with delegates, anonymous methods, multicast delegates, and events. At the end of the chapter, you will be able to start adding event-based programming patterns to your applications as you continue throughout this book.

Introduction to Delegates

A *delegate* is a special type that maintains a reference to a method. After a delegate has been assigned to an actual method that matches the signature defined by the delegate itself, the delegate can be used the same way the real method can be used. You can execute the method by executing the delegate, pass parameters, and so on.

As long as the method's signature matches the signature defined by the delegate, the method and associated parameters can be assigned to the delegate. This allows you to programmatically change methods and add additional methods to existing classes.

Delegates can also be passed as parameters, making them perfect for *callback* solutions. A *callback* is where a method is passed a delegate parameter indicating a method that should be *called back* periodically. For example, you could have a long-running method invoke the callback method periodically to update a progress bar.

Delegate declarations look much like a method signature, preceded by the keyword dele-gate, as shown in the following examples:

```
delegate void MessagePrintDelegate(string msg);
delegate int GetCountDelegate(object obj1, object obj2);
delegate void LongRunningDelegate(MessagePrintDelegate mpCallBack);
```

A delegate can have scope just like any other member variable; however, you cannot apply the static keyword to a delegate. As such, you can rewrite the preceding declarations as shown in the following example:

```
public delegate void MessagePrintDelegate(string msg);
private delegate int GetCountDelegate(object obj1, object obj2);
internal delegate void LongRunningDelegate(MessagePrintDelegate mpCallBack);
```

When you have a delegate defined, you can create an instance of the delegate, assign a method to it (as long as the signature matches), and pass it as a parameter to other methods. The code in Listing 9.1 illustrates some basic techniques for working with delegates.

Naming Conventions for Delegates

When creating delegates, it is standard convention to postfix the name of the delegate with the word "Delegate" (capitalization is intentional). For example, a delegate that prints a message should be called PrintMessageDelegate. Because delegates are so syntactically similar to regular data types, the use of the postfix is designed to make reading and maintaining event-based code easier.

LISTING 9.1   Basic Delegate Manipulation

```
using System;
using System.Collections.Generic;
using System.Text;

namespace DelegateSimple
{
class Program
{
public delegate void MessagePrintDelegate(string msg);
private delegate int GetCountDelegate(Person obj1, Person obj2);
protected delegate void LongRunningDelegate(MessagePrintDelegate mpCallBack);

static void Main(string[] args)
{
    MessagePrintDelegate mpDel = new MessagePrintDelegate(PrintMessage);
    GetCountDelegate gcd = new GetCountDelegate(GetCount);
    int count = gcd( new Person(), new Person());
```

LISTING 9.1   Continued

```
    Console.WriteLine("Count received {0}", count);
    LongRunningDelegate lrd = new LongRunningDelegate(LongRunningMethod);
    lrd(mpDel);
    Console.ReadLine();
}

static void LongRunningMethod(MessagePrintDelegate mpd)
{
    for (int i = 0; i < 99; i++)
    {
        if (i % 10 == 0)
        {
            mpd(string.Format(
                "Making progress. {0}% Complete.", i));
        }
    }
}

static int GetCount(object obj1, object obj2)
{
    // perform some processing
    Random rnd = new Random();
    return rnd.Next();
}

static void PrintMessage(string msg)
{
    Console.WriteLine("[{0}] {1}", DateTime.Now.ToShortTimeString(), msg);
}
}

class Person
{
}

class Contact : Person
{
}
}
```

When you run the preceding code, you get the output shown in Figure 9.1.

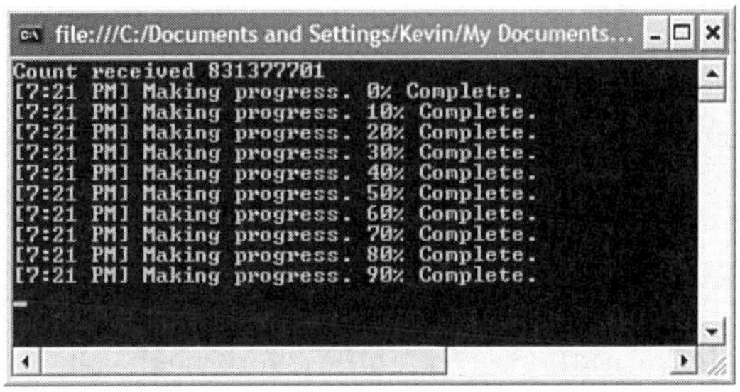

FIGURE 9.1   Output of simple delegate demo.

Covariance and Contravariance

Covariance and contravariance might seem like pretty complex words, but they represent some fairly easy-to-understand concepts. *Covariance* refers to the ability of a delegate method to return derivative data types. In the preceding example, you'll notice that the Contact class derives from Person. Suppose that you have a delegate defined as follows:

```
delegate Person GetPersonDelegate();
```

Then covariance allows for the following lines of code to work properly:

```
GetPersonDelegate gpd = new GetPersonDelegate(GetPerson);
GetPersonDelegate gpd2 = new GetPersonDelegate(GetContact);
```

This sample shows that covariance allows you to create an instance of the GetPersonDelegate for a method that returns a Person instance as well as a method that returns a Contact instance.

Contravariance refers to the ability of a delegate method to take derivative classes as parameters. In Listing 9.1 you saw the delegate GetCountDelegate, which takes two parameters of type Person. Contravariance allows you to pass parameters of derivative types to delegate methods, as shown in the following example:

```
Contact c = new Contact();
Person p = new Person();
int x = gcd(p, p);
int y = gcd(c, c);
```

Using Anonymous Methods

In the example in Listing 9.1, there is a method defined on the class for each delegate. In other words, when an instance of the delegate is created, the name of the method is passed to the constructor, as shown following:

```
MessagePrintDelegate mpDel = new MessagePrintDelegate(PrintMessage);
```

Here, `PrintMessage` is the name of a method that has been defined on the class. Depending on your needs and the type of programming you are doing, it could become extremely tedious and inefficient to code a separate method for each delegate instance that you create.

Anonymous methods allow you to essentially define your method "on the fly" at the same time that you are instantiating the delegate. Anonymous methods are also referred to as "inline methods" by other programming languages.

Another advantage of anonymous methods that sets them apart from using fixed method definitions is that the code written inside your anonymous method *has access to variables in the same scope as the definition*. This is extremely powerful because it eliminates the need to pass unnecessary or redundant data into the fixed method itself (thereby needlessly bloating the delegate's definition) by allowing the anonymous method to access the data directly.

Listing 9.2 illustrates the use of anonymous methods compared with the use of a fixed method.

LISTING 9.2   Anonymous Methods Sample

```
using System;
using System.Collections.Generic;
using System.Text;

namespace AnonMethods
{
class Program
{
delegate void MessagePrintDelegate(string msg);

static void Main(string[] args)
{
    // named-delegate invocation
    MessagePrintDelegate mpd = new MessagePrintDelegate(PrintMessage);
    LongRunningMethod(mpd);

    // anonymous method
    MessagePrintDelegate mpd2 = delegate(string msg)
    {
        Console.WriteLine("[Anonymous] {0}", msg);
    };
    LongRunningMethod(mpd2);

    // use of 'outer variable' in anonymous method
    string source = "Outer";
    MessagePrintDelegate mpd3 = delegate(string msg)
    {
```

LISTING 9.2 Continued

```
        Console.WriteLine("[{0}] {1}", source, msg);
    };
    LongRunningMethod(mpd3);

    Console.ReadLine();
}

static void LongRunningMethod(MessagePrintDelegate mpd)
{
    for (int i = 0; i < 99; i++)
    {
        if (i % 25 == 0)
        {
            mpd(
                string.Format("Progress Made. {0}% complete.", i));
        }
    }
}

static void PrintMessage(string msg)
{
    Console.WriteLine("[PrintMessage] {0}", msg);
}
}
}
```

Figure 9.2 shows the output of the anonymous method sample.

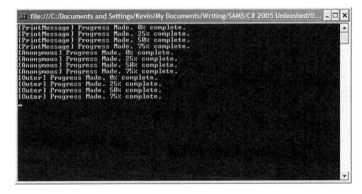

FIGURE 9.2 Output of anonymous method sample.

Creating Multicast Delegates

A multicast delegate is a delegate that can invoke multiple methods, so long as the methods all have the same signature as the delegate's definition. Multicast delegates are the steppingstone between standard delegates and the use of events. When you understand both delegates and multicast delegates, you will be ready to start working with events.

You create a multicast delegate through composition. Composing multiple delegates is accomplished with the +, -, +=, and -= operators. To make a delegate invoke multiple methods, you simply add the method to an existing delegate using + or +=. To remove a method from a multicast delegate, you use the – or the -= overloaded operators.

The code in Listing 9.3 provides an illustration of how to create and invoke multicast delegates. In addition, the sample also shows creating a multicast delegate from both named and anonymous methods, and how to iterate through the list of methods that will be invoked by a multicast delegate.

LISTING 9.3   Multicast Delegate Sample

```
using System;
using System.Collections.Generic;
using System.Text;

namespace MulticastDemo
{
class Program
{
delegate void MessagePrintDelegate(string s);

static void Main(string[] args)
{
    MessagePrintDelegate mpd1, mpd2, mpd3, mpd4;

    mpd1 = PrintMessage;
    mpd2 = PrintStampedMessage;

    // create a multicast by composing two delegates
    mpd3 = mpd1 + mpd2;
    mpd3("Hello World");

    mpd4 = PrintMessage;
    mpd4 += mpd3;
    mpd4("Multicasted!");
```

LISTING 9.3   Continued

```
    // you can also remove a delegate from a composition
    mpd3 -= mpd1;
    mpd3("Hello World (again)");

    // you can compose 2 multicasts
    mpd4 += mpd3;
    mpd4("Really multicasted");

    // you can even add an anonymous method to the multicast
    mpd3 += delegate(string s)
    {
        Console.WriteLine("[Anonymous] {0}", s);
    };
    mpd3("Hello!");

    // you can inspect the list of methods
    // in any given multicast
    Console.WriteLine("Methods in the mpd3 multicast:");
    foreach (Delegate d in mpd3.GetInvocationList())
    {
        Console.WriteLine("\t{0}", d.Method.Name);
    }

    Console.ReadLine();
}

static void PrintMessage(string s)
{
    Console.WriteLine(s);
}

static void PrintStampedMessage(string s)
{
    Console.WriteLine("[{0}] {1}", DateTime.Now.ToShortTimeString(),
        s);
}
}
}
```

When you run the preceding code, the output looks as follows, illustrating how a single invocation to a multicast delegate can invoke the target of that delegate multiple times:

```
Hello World
[8:50 PM] Hello World
Multicasted!
Multicasted!
[8:50 PM] Multicasted!
[8:50 PM] Hello World (again)
Really multicasted
Really multicasted
[8:50 PM] Really multicasted
[8:50 PM] Really multicasted
[8:50 PM] Hello!
[Anonymous] Hello!
Methods in the mpd3 multicast:
        PrintStampedMessage
        <Main>b__0
```

As you can see, multicast delegates are an extremely powerful feature with virtually unlimited applications. Events, which are one of those applications, are discussed next. It is also worth noting that in the preceding output, the anonymous method has been assigned a name by the CLR: <Main>b__0. All methods must be identified by a name, even anonymous methods, so the CLR generates a name dynamically based on the scope and sequence of the method.

Introduction to Events

Events are a way to allow a class to send a signal indicating that an event of some importance has taken place. Events are most commonly used in the Windows Forms user interface, sending signals indicating that the user has clicked on a button, typed characters, moved the mouse, or any number of other events.

Events can also be used to indicate other important events that don't have anything to do with a user interface, such as indicating that an object's internal state has changed, that data in a list has changed, and so on.

Events are created from delegates using the event keyword. First, you declare the delegate:

```
delegate void StateChangedDelegate(object state);
```

Then you declare the event as a member of a class:

```
public event StateChangedDelegate OnStateChanged;
```

Finally, the class interested in the event can subscribe to the event in a syntax that should look familiar to you given your recent exposure to multicast delegates:

```
otherClass.OnStateChanged += new StateChangedDelegate(OtherClass_StateChanged);
```

Now the subscribing class will be notified every time the other class's state changes.

The sample in Listing 9.4 shows a class called `LongTask`. This class has a method called `PerformTask`. This method simulates a long-running process. The class exposes an event called `OnProgress` that allows a subscribing class to be notified when progress on the long-running task has been made. This example also makes use of event arguments to show good design patterns that will look very familiar to you when you start working with Windows Forms.

LISTING 9.4   Event Publishing and Subscribing Sample

```
using System;
using System.Collections.Generic;
using System.Text;

namespace EventSample
{
class Program
{
static void Main(string[] args)
{
    LongTask lt = new LongTask();
    lt.OnNotifyProgress += new
LongTask.NotifyProgressDelegate(lt_OnNotifyProgress);

    lt.PerformTask();

    Console.ReadLine();
}

static void lt_OnNotifyProgress(ProgressArgs pa)
{
    Console.WriteLine("Progress on Long Task Completed. {0}% Complete.",
pa.PercentComplete);
}
}

class LongTask
{
public delegate void NotifyProgressDelegate(ProgressArgs pa);

public event NotifyProgressDelegate OnNotifyProgress;

public void PerformTask()
{
    for (int i = 0; i < 10000; i++)
    {
```

LISTING 9.4 Continued

```
        // perform some processing
        // ...

        // notify subscribers that progress was made
        if (i % 100 == 0)
        {
            OnNotifyProgress(new ProgressArgs( (int) i / 100));;
        }
    }
}
}


class ProgressArgs
{
public ProgressArgs(int pctComplete)
{
    PercentComplete = pctComplete;
}
public int PercentComplete;
}
}
```

When you run the preceding code, you will see 100 lines of text, each one reporting that another percentage point of work has been completed on the simulated long-running task.

One point about event-based programming that can't be stressed enough is that by using events, you allow a loose coupling of classes and maximize your code reuse.

> **TIP**
>
> A *bad* way to create the code in Listing 9.3 would be to write the code that performs the task directly in a Windows Form so that the code could interact directly with the user interface to indicate progress made by possibly changing the properties of a ProgressBar control. The problem that arises from that design is that the long-running task can then never be used anywhere but within that one form. If you want to perform that same task in a Web Service, a console application, a Windows Service, or even in another Windows Forms application, you will have to cut and paste code and perform some tedious tasks to get it to work.

By using events, you can then have one piece of code that is responsible for performing the task, and you could have the user interface environment subscribe to the progress event. This loose coupling allows you to reuse your code without any modification in any GUI environment.

Advanced Event-Based Programming

At this point, if the discussion of programming ended with events, you would have enough information to continue through the rest of the book and nothing that Windows Forms or ASP.NET do related to events would seem unfamiliar to you.

Many techniques that can be applied to event programming will produce some pretty amazing results. For example, one such technique is the use of the `add` and `remove` accessors on an event. Just as properties have a `get` and `set` accessor, events have their own accessors that allow you to write code that will be executed when a client subscribes to an event and when a client unsubscribes from the event. The power that these accessors give your code is incredible. For example, if you have written some code that exposes events over a network using Remoting, you can write code inside the "add" accessor that allows you to detect when a network client subscribes to an event. Likewise, you can detect when a network client unsubscribes, giving you immediate access to that information.

There also may be scenarios when you don't want an event to be fired to all subscribing clients. Take the hypothetical scenario where you have created an event-driven application. The application consists of a central server and multiple clients. Each client subscribes to an event that indicates some data has changed. However, this data is secured at the row level, and not all clients should be able to see it. To maximize security, your application is not even allowed to transmit data over a wire that the client cannot see. To accomplish this using event-based programming, you need to be able to programmatically filter which event targets receive the event and which targets do not.

Each delegate has a `Target` property, which indicates the object that houses the method that will be invoked by the delegate. A trick that I find extremely helpful is that if the code knows the data type of the subscribing class, it can use that information to determine if the delegate should be invoked on that object or not, as shown in the following snippet of code:

```
if (  ((Customer)myDelegate.Target).CustomerID == 12)
    // invoke method
```

The code in Listing 9.5 is a complete sample that demonstrates the use of the `add` and `remove` accessors, as well as the selective invocation of methods on event subscribers.

LISTING 9.5   Advanced Event Programming Sample

```
using System;
using System.Collections.Generic;
using System.Text;

namespace AdvancedEvent
{
delegate void NameChangedDelegate(string name, string newValue);
```

LISTING 9.5   Continued

```
class Program
{
static void Main(string[] args)
{
    Customer c = new Customer();
    Subscriber s1 = new Subscriber(c, "subscriber-A");
    Subscriber s2 = new Subscriber(c, "subscriber-B");
    Subscriber s3 = new Subscriber(c, "subscriber-C");

    c.FirstName = "Kevin";
    c.LastName = "Hoffman";

    s2.Unsubscribe();

    c.FirstName = "Joe";

    c.MiddleName = "Scott";

    Console.ReadLine();
}


}

class Subscriber
{
private string subscriberId = "new subscriber";
private Customer myCustomer = null;
private NameChangedDelegate ncDel = null;

public Subscriber(Customer c, string subId)
{
    subscriberId = subId;
    ncDel = new NameChangedDelegate(myCustomer_OnNameChanged);
    myCustomer = c;
    myCustomer.OnNameChanged += ncDel;
}

void myCustomer_OnNameChanged(string name, string newValue)
{
    Console.WriteLine("[{0}] Customer {1} changed to {2}.", subscriberId,
        name, newValue);
}
```

LISTING 9.5   Continued

```
public void Unsubscribe()
{
    myCustomer.OnNameChanged -= ncDel;
}

public string SubscriberID
{
    get
    {
        return subscriberId;
    }
    set
    {
        subscriberId = value;
    }
}
}

class Customer
{
private string firstName;
private string lastName;
private string middleName;
private event NameChangedDelegate onNameChange;

public event NameChangedDelegate OnNameChanged
{
    add
    {
        onNameChange += value;
        if (value.Target is Subscriber)
        {
            Console.WriteLine(
"Subscriber '{0}' just subscribed to OnNameChanged.",
                ((Subscriber)value.Target).SubscriberID);
        }
    }
    remove
    {
        onNameChange -= value;
        if (value.Target is Subscriber)
        {
            Console.WriteLine(
```

LISTING 9.5   Continued

```
"Subscriber '{0}' just un-subscribed from OnNameChanged.",
            ((Subscriber)value.Target).SubscriberID);
        }
    }
}

public string FirstName
{
    get { return firstName; }
    set
    {
        firstName = value;
        onNameChange("firstname", value);
    }
}

public string LastName
{
    get { return lastName; }
    set
    {
        lastName = value;
        onNameChange("lastname", value);
    }
}

public string MiddleName
{
    get { return MiddleName; }
    set
    {
        middleName = value;
        NotifyAllBut("subscriber-C", "middlename", value);
    }
}

private void NotifyAllBut(string subId, string name, string value)
{
    foreach (NameChangedDelegate d in onNameChange.GetInvocationList())
    {
        if (((Subscriber)d.Target).SubscriberID.ToUpper() != subId.ToUpper())
        {
```

LISTING 9.5   Continued

```
            d(name, value);
        }
    }
}
}
}
```

The first thing that should be noted about the preceding code is that the add and remove accessors are used to print out some informative messages indicating when a class subscribes or unsubscribes from the event. Also note that in these accessors, the Target property is used to print out the SubscriberID of the class subscribing to or unsubscribing from the event.

Next, the NotifyAllBut method will invoke all the subscribing methods to an event *except* the event handler hosted by a Subscriber class whose subscriber ID is 'subscriber-C'. This is proven in the console output of the program shown in the following lines:

```
Subscriber 'subscriber-A' just subscribed to OnNameChanged.
Subscriber 'subscriber-B' just subscribed to OnNameChanged.
Subscriber 'subscriber-C' just subscribed to OnNameChanged.
[subscriber-A] Customer firstname changed to Kevin.
[subscriber-B] Customer firstname changed to Kevin.
[subscriber-C] Customer firstname changed to Kevin.
[subscriber-A] Customer lastname changed to Hoffman.
[subscriber-B] Customer lastname changed to Hoffman.
[subscriber-C] Customer lastname changed to Hoffman.
Subscriber 'subscriber-B' just un-subscribed from OnNameChanged.
[subscriber-A] Customer firstname changed to Joe.
[subscriber-C] Customer firstname changed to Joe.
[subscriber-A] Customer middlename changed to Scott.
```

As you can see from this output, all three subscribers subscribe to the OnNameChanged event. All three of them receive a notification indicating that the first name and last name changed. Then, after subscriber B unsubscribes, only subscribers A and C receive the notification that the first name was changed. Finally, only subscriber A receives notification that the middle name changed because subscriber C was specifically prevented from receiving the event.

Summary

This chapter has introduced you to some of the basic concepts around event-based programming as well as many advanced topics. Delegates are type-safe references to methods that can be invoked in the same manner as methods and they can also be used as parameters to other methods.

Events are special multicast delegates that provide a mechanism by which classes can notify other classes when events of significance take place, whether those events are related to the user interface, to data sources, or to object state.

In the last section of the chapter you saw that event programming can be extremely powerful by allowing developers to write their own code for the add and remove accessors for an event and allowing an event to selectively choose which targets receive the event notification.

When you consider all of this information and add to it the fact that events can be transmitted between GUI controls, between logical tiers or layers, and even between different applications separated by the Internet or an intranet, the idea of adopting and using events in your everyday programming tasks becomes extremely appealing.

CHAPTER **10**

Multithreaded Programming

When considering multithreaded techniques for an application, many developers assume that the only place where multithreaded techniques are valuable is in Windows Forms applications. In reality, the use of threading to increase performance and responsiveness is applicable to all kinds of applications, whether you're creating an ASP.NET application, a web service, a Windows Forms application, or even a Windows service. This chapter introduces you to the concepts and concerns related to programming in a multithreaded environment, and then gradually leads you on a tour of the various techniques involved in utilizing the .NET Framework's powerful multithreading systems to their fullest.

Throughout this chapter you will see examples of where threads are useful, and how to work with them properly. The topic of multithreaded programming is long and often complex, and extremely hard to pack into a small chapter in a compendium book such as this. Using the guidelines in this chapter, you should be able to intelligently discuss the topic of multithreaded programming as well as put it into practice in any of the applications you write as you progress through this book.

The Basics of Threaded Programming

Threads are units of work that are created by a parent process to perform some task. By utilizing multiple threads, an application can delegate the work to multiple workers to reduce the time it takes to complete a relatively long task.

In addition, a background task can be used to perform some long-running or expensive processing in the background while the foreground remains responsive. This allows web applications to process extremely lengthy requests while not blocking out small, lightweight requests in the meantime. It also allows the user interface in a Windows Forms application to remain responsive while large amounts of data are downloaded or processed in the background. Threading has a virtually unlimited number of applications.

However, using threads just because you think they will make your application run faster can often backfire. In fact, using too many threads can actually cause your application to run slower. For example, you could have so many threads running that your application is spending more time swapping context between the threads than it is performing the tasks within the threads. In this case, your application will actually run slower than if it had no threading support whatsoever.

No matter what task you're performing in a multithreaded environment, you will be working with the Thread class in one form or another. Tables 10.1 and 10.2 show some of the commonly used methods and properties of the Thread class.

TABLE 10.1   Thread Properties

Property	Description
ApartmentState	Indicates the Apartment State of the thread. Can be MTA (Multithreaded Apartment), STA (Single-Threaded Apartment), or Unknown (not set).
CurrentContext	Static property that obtains the current threading context in which the thread is running.
CurrentCulture	The current culture for the thread. This becomes important when creating localized/globalized applications.
CurrentPrincipal	The user security context that owns/created the current thread.
IsAlive	Indicates whether the thread is currently active.
IsBackground	Indicates whether the thread is a background thread. Active background threads cannot prevent an application from terminating but foreground threads can.
IsThreadPoolThread	Indicates whether the thread belongs to the thread pool. The thread pool will be discussed later in this chapter, in the section "Using the Threadpool Class."
ManagedThreadId	A unique identifier for this thread.
Name	Gets or sets the name of the thread. Useful for distinguishing one thread from another without relying on thread IDs.
Priority	Indicates the thread's priority with regard to the execution scheduler. Values can be AboveNormal, BelowNormal, Highest, Lowest, and Normal. Default is normal.
ThreadState	Indicates the current state of the thread. Can be Aborted, AbortRequested, Background, Running, Stopped, StopRequested, Suspended, SuspendRequested, Unstarted, or WaitSleepJoin (blocked).

TABLE 10.2   Thread Methods

Method	Description
Abort	Aborts the current thread, requesting that all active work be stopped
AllocateDataSlot	Static method that allocates an unnamed slot for storing data shared among all threads
AllocateNamedDataSlot	Static method that creates a named data slot shared among all threads
BeginCriticalRegion	Indicates that the following section of code is "critical," meaning aborts and unhandled exceptions could put the code in an unstable state
EndCriticalRegion	Indicates that the preceding section of code is to be treated as "critical"
FreeNamedDataSlot	Removes the space previously allocated for a named thread-shared data slot
GetData	Retrieves the data stored in a thread-local data slot
GetDomain	Returns the currently active thread domain
GetNamedDataSlot	Returns a thread-shared named data slot
Interrupt	Interrupts the current thread if it is blocked
Join	Blocks the current thread until another thread completes (explained later in the section "Joining a Thread")
Resume	Resumes the previously suspended thread
SetData	Sets data stored in a thread-local data slot
Sleep	Causes the thread to block and wait for the specified number of milliseconds
Start	Indicates to the scheduler that the thread is ready for execution

Don't worry if some of the properties or methods of the Thread class don't make much sense yet. By the time you've finished this chapter, it should all be clear.

Essentially, two main concepts are involved in creating any good multithreaded application:

- Thread scheduling—You will need to know how to start, stop, suspend, pause, and terminate threads in your applications.

- Thread contention— With multiple threads running at the same time, you will need to learn the techniques required to ensure that you don't have multiple threads modifying the same piece of data at the same time, or that you end up with incomplete modifications of shared data.

Writing Your First Multithreaded Application

For your first multithreaded application, you will learn the basic techniques of working with the scheduler. This means that you will learn the syntax to create, terminate, suspend, sleep, and join threads, as well as what the uses are for each of those operations.

10

Creating and Running a Thread

When creating a thread, you need to use a special delegate called ThreadStart. This delegate will contain a reference to the method that contains the work you want to be performed in the thread. As explained in Chapter 9, delegates are really nothing more than special types that contain methods with specific signatures. You can invoke delegates the same way you invoke methods, and you can pass delegates as parameters to other methods, which is exactly what needs to be done when creating a thread.

To create a thread, you pass a ThreadStart delegate to the constructor of the Thread class, as shown in the following example:

```
ThreadStart myThreadDelegate = new ThreadStart(MyWork);
Thread workerThread = new Thread(myThreadDelegate);
```

What you will often see in many code samples is the preceding two lines of code consolidated into the following:

```
Thread workerThread = new Thread(new ThreadStart(MyWork));
```

In this line of code, MyWork is the name of the method that matches the signature defined by the ThreadStart delegate. All ThreadStart delegates must be void methods.

The code in Listing 10.1 shows how to create and start a thread, as well as how to continuously poll the status of a thread as a crude way of checking to see if it's finished. You'll see a more elegant solution later.

LISTING 10.1   Starting and Running a Thread

```
using System;
using System.Threading;
using System.Collections.Generic;
using System.Text;

namespace RunThreads
{
class Program
{
static void Main(string[] args)
{
    Thread.CurrentThread.Name = "MAIN";
    Console.WriteLine("[{0}] Hello.", Thread.CurrentThread.Name);
    Thread workerThread = new Thread(new ThreadStart(WorkerMethod));
    workerThread.Name = "WORKER";
    Console.WriteLine("[{0}] Created the new worker thread, {1}",
        Thread.CurrentThread.Name, workerThread.Name);
    workerThread.Start();
    while (workerThread.IsAlive)
    {
```

LISTING 10.1   Continued

```
        // do nothing until it's finished
    }
    Console.WriteLine("Looks like the worker thread finished its job.");

    Console.ReadLine();
}

static void WorkerMethod()
{
    for (int i = 0; i < 20; i++)
    {
        Console.WriteLine("[{0}] Doing some work.", Thread.CurrentThread.Name);
    }
}
}
}
```

Figure 10.1 shows the output of this sample.

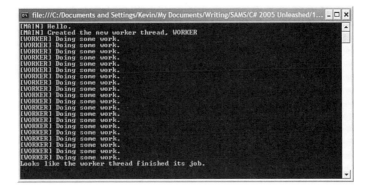

FIGURE 10.1   Starting and running a thread—sample output.

Terminating a Thread

Terminating a thread involves using the Abort method on the thread. Abort can either be called on the thread instance by the block of code that initially created it, or it can be called by the running thread itself.

When a thread is aborted, a ThreadAbortException is thrown. As you will find out in various samples throughout this book, you can trap and suppress most exceptions. The ThreadAbortException is the one exception in the .NET Framework that cannot be ignored—with good reason. This exception must be allowed to travel up the chain of exceptions in order for aborted threads to know to stop working. You can manually suppress this exception with the `Thread.ResetAbort()` method, as shown in Listing 10.2, which illustrates aborting a running thread.

LISTING 10.2   Aborting a Running Thread

```
using System;
using System.Threading;
using System.Collections.Generic;
using System.Text;

namespace AbortThreads
{
class Program
{
static void Main(string[] args)
{
    Thread.CurrentThread.Name = "MAIN";
    PrintMessage("Application Started.");
    Thread worker = new Thread(new ThreadStart(DoWork));
    worker.Name = "WORKER";
    worker.Start();
    Console.WriteLine("Press Enter to Abort the Thread!");
    Console.ReadLine();
    worker.Abort();
    Console.WriteLine("Thread abort signal sent.");
    Console.ReadLine();
}

static void PrintMessage(string msg)
{
    Console.WriteLine("[{0}] {1}", Thread.CurrentThread.Name, msg);
}

static void DoWork()
{
    try
    {
        while (true)
        {
            Console.Write("...");
            Thread.Sleep(100); // small time delay to simulate real work
        }
    }
    catch (Exception e)
    {
```

LISTING 10.2   Continued

```
        PrintMessage("Trapped: " + e.ToString());
    }
}
}
}
```

Figure 10.2 shows a screenshot of the console output of this program. As soon as the user presses Enter, the thread abort signal is sent, and the worker thread catches (and suppresses) the `ThreadAbortException` exception. If the worker method didn't suppress this, the exception would "bubble up" and eventually cause the main application to stop—typically an undesired result.

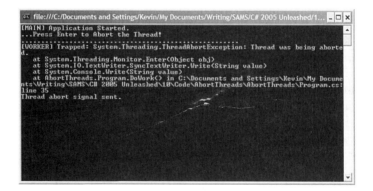

FIGURE 10.2   Thread abort demo output.

Suspending a Thread

When you suspend a thread, you tell the scheduler that the thread no longer needs to be swapped to the foreground for execution. What this means is that as soon as the thread stops executing to give time to another thread, the thread will *not* continue until it has been resumed.

You suspend a thread with the `Suspend` method. It takes no arguments and works fairly simply. To resume the thread at will, you can simply call the `Resume` method on that same thread.

Sleeping a Thread

You saw in Listing 10.2 that there is a method called `Sleep` that does exactly what it sounds like: causes the thread to sleep. By supplying a time interval in milliseconds, the thread will stop executing at that line for the specified duration. You can also pass a `0` as the argument, which will cause the thread to be suspended. If you specify `System.Threading.Timeout.Infinite` as the value, the thread will block indefinitely.

Joining a Thread

The Join method serves as a way to block the current thread until the specified thread has completed. This essentially allows the thread to wait for the completion of another method. This is where the term *join* comes from, where the current thread will wait for another thread to "catch up." Listing 10.3 illustrates the use of the Join method.

LISTING 10.3   Joining a Thread

```
using System;
using System.Threading;
using System.Collections.Generic;
using System.Text;

namespace JoinTest
{
class Program
{
static void Main(string[] args)
{
    Thread worker = new Thread(new ThreadStart(DoWork));
    worker.Start();

    // now do a 'join' to block this thread until worker
    // has completed
    worker.Join();
    Console.WriteLine("This line will not execute until 'worker' is complete.");
    Console.ReadLine();
}

static void DoWork()
{
    for (int i = 0; i < 100; i++)
    {
        Thread.Sleep(100);
        Console.Write(".");
    }
}

}
}
}
```

The use of Join replaces the loop seen in an earlier example where the code executed a while loop that continuously looped until the IsAlive property of the executing thread was false. As mentioned earlier, using Join is a far more elegant (and thread-safe) solution.

Dealing with Thread Synchronization and Contention

All current versions of Microsoft Windows utilize something called *pre-emptive multitasking*. This means that any currently running thread can be interrupted (pre-empted) in order to allow another thread to execute. This type of multitasking environment is far more reliable than previous versions of Windows (16-bit) and drastically reduces the number of times the operating system will hang or freeze unexpectedly due to poorly behaved applications.

The downside to pre-emptive multitasking is that if you want to make your application aware of this, you need to be aware of the fact that your application is executing in a multithreaded environment, and you need to be aware of the consequences. The key thing to remember when building multithreaded applications is synchronization.

Synchronization refers to conditions that arise from having multiple threads attempt to perform the same task or access the same data at the same time, or where a thread may stop unexpectedly and potentially leave data in an indeterminate state.

Various facilities are available within the .NET Framework's core threading library that allow you to manage contention for shared resources within a multithreaded application as well as timing and synchronization issues. Table 10.3 provides an overview of these. Each one will be discussed in more detail in the following subsections.

TABLE 10.3   Synchronization Handling Facilities

Facility	Description	.NET Classes
Mutex	A mutex prevents more than one thread from accessing a shared resource at a time.	`Mutex`
Critical Section	A critical section is similar to a mutex, but it is not cross-process aware.	`lock`, `Monitor`, `Interlocked`, `ReaderWriterLock`
Semaphore	A semaphore limits the number of threads that can access the same shared resource.	`Semaphore`
Event	Event synchronizations raise signals to alert other threads of important state changes.	`AutoResetEvent`, `ManualResetEvent`, `WaitHandle`

Using the `lock` Keyword

The `lock` keyword is one of the simpler synchronization facilities available to you. When you wrap a code block inside a `lock` statement, the code block is guaranteed to allow only one thread at a time to access it. This means that any code written inside that block is thread-safe and you can be sure that there won't be indeterminate or inconsistent data within that block.

When you create a `lock` block, you pass the `lock` keyword an object as a parameter. This object is used to determine the scope of re-entrance around which to build the critical section, as shown in the following code:

```
lock(this)
{
    // thread-safe code
}
```

Using Mutexes

The `Mutex` class is a special type of class that is an extremely powerful thread synchronization tool. A `Mutex` not only provides the ability to synchronize multiple threads, but it can also synchronize those threads across multiple processes. The purpose of the `Mutex` is to prevent unwanted simultaneous access by multiple threads on a single shared resource.

When the first thread to access a shared resource acquires a `Mutex`, all subsequent threads that want to access that shared resource must wait until the first one has released the resource. The release of the resource is signified by the release of the `Mutex`. The `Mutex` class enforces thread identity. This means that only the thread that requested the `Mutex` to begin with can release it. In contrast, the `Semaphore` class can be modified by any thread.

As mentioned before, a `Mutex` can actually be used to synchronize cross-process activities as well as multithreaded activities within the same application. When you create a new instance of a `Mutex`, you can choose to create a local mutex (visible only to the process under which it was created) or a named system mutex (visible to all processes so long as each process knows the name of the mutex).

Be extremely careful when using cross-process mutexes. Because the scope of the mutex is at the operating system level, it is possible that logic failures or unexpected application crashes can cause the mutex to be in an unpredictable state.

When protecting resources with a `Mutex`, the first step is to call `WaitOne`, which will wait until the `Mutex` receives a signal. After the call to `WaitOne`, you can access the shared resources without fear of synchronization problems. Finally, when the method is complete, you must call `ReleaseMutex()`. If a thread stops before a `Mutex` is released, the `Mutex` will be considered abandoned. If you encounter an abandoned `Mutex`, the protected data could be in an inconsistent state. In other words, an abandoned `Mutex` constitutes a coding error that needs to be corrected, *especially* if that `Mutex` is a system-level global `Mutex`.

Listing 10.4 shows both uses of a `Mutex`. First, a global mutex is created. This actually allows the application to tell if another instance of itself is already running (a task that is fairly common, yet often considered difficult). The second `Mutex` is a local `Mutex` used to protect access to a specific shared resource. As you will see when you run the output, the protection of the shared resource by the `Mutex` block is actually forcing the threads to access the data serially (one item after another), instead of simultaneously, thereby ensuring that the calculations on that shared resource will result in consistent and predictable values.

LISTING 10.4   System and Local Mutexes

```
using System;
using System.Threading;
using System.Collections.Generic;
using System.Text;

namespace MutexSample
{
class Program
{
static int sharedNumber = 42;
static Mutex localMut = new Mutex();
static bool isNew;
static Mutex globalMut = new Mutex(true, "Mutex Demo Global Mutex", out isNew);
static void Main(string[] args)
{
    if (!isNew)
    {
      Console.WriteLine("This application is already running, shutting additional
      ➥instance down.");
        return;
    }
    // spin off a bunch of threads to perform
    // processing on a shared resource
    Thread[] workers = new Thread[20];
    for (int i = 0; i < 20; i++)
    {
        Thread worker = new Thread(new ThreadStart(DoWork));
        workers[i] = worker;
        worker.Start();
    }

    foreach (Thread workerThread in workers)
        workerThread.Join();
    Console.WriteLine("All work finished, new value of shared resource is {0}",
sharedNumber);
    Console.ReadLine();
    globalMut.ReleaseMutex();
}

static void DoWork()
{
    // sit and wait until it's OK to access
```

10

LISTING 10.4   Continued

```
    // the shared resource
    localMut.WaitOne();

    // modify shared resource
    // multiple lines of code to modify
    // to show consistent state of data
    // within Mutex-protected block
    Console.WriteLine("Accessing protected resource...");
    sharedNumber += 2;
    sharedNumber -= 1;

    localMut.ReleaseMutex();
}
}
}
```

Synchronized Methods

Often you will want to synchronize (lock out multithreaded access via the `lock` keyword or the `Monitor` class or the `Mutex` class) an entire method. To make this easier and to save you the trouble of obtaining and releasing shared locks for each method, you can use the `MethodImplAttribute` code attribute to mark an entire method as synchronized, as shown in the following example:

```
[MethodImpl(MethodImplOptions.Synchronized)]
public void SynchronizedMethod { ... }
```

Using this attribute can save you some time and effort if you plan on synchronizing access to the entire method rather than just a small portion.

Using Monitors

At first glance, the `Monitor` class might appear to function very much like the `lock` keyword. You use `Monitor.Enter` in much the same way you use `lock(object)`, and `Monitor.Exit` marks the end of a *critical section* the same way that the last curly brace marks the end of a `lock` block, as shown in the following example:

```
Monitor.Enter(this);
// thread-safe code
Monitor.Exit(this);
```

Unlike the `lock` keyword, however, the `Monitor` class implements some other methods that give it some added functionality. The following is a list of the methods that set the `Monitor` class apart from the `lock` keyword:

- TryEnter—You can specify a time period in milliseconds, or pass a TimeSpan instance to this method. This method will then wait for that time period to acquire an exclusive lock on the protected resource. If the timeout period expires, the code will return false and allow the thread to continue execution. This is an invaluable technique for preventing an application from hanging while waiting on one "stuck" thread or a stale/abandoned Mutex.

- Wait—Releases the current lock on the resource (if any) and then waits to reacquire the lock. If the timeout period expires, this method will return a false, allowing your code to respond appropriately to a failed attempt to obtain a thread-safe lock on the shared resource.

- Pulse—Sends a signal to the next waiting thread to start up. This allows the thread to start working before the acquisition of the lock held by the current thread. This is a way that allows your synchronized block of code to signal the next thread in line that your code is about to release the lock.

- PulseAll—Works just like Pulse, except that it sends the signal to *all* waiting threads.

Using the Interlocked Class

As you've probably guessed by now, the more synchronized code blocks you have in your application, the more bottleneck points you create for your background threads because they all have to queue up in line and wait nicely for their turn to access the shared resource.

This means that one of the things you want to watch out for in your code is excessive or unnecessary use of synchronized blocks. Quite often, developers will create a synchronized block just so that they can increment or decrement some shared value safely.

This is where the Interlocked class comes in. This class provides methods that allow you to increment, decrement, or exchange values in a synchronized, thread-safe manner without burdening your application by having to waste a synchronized block on a simple operation.

The following code snippet shows the Interlocked class in action:

```
Interlocked.Increment(ref sharedInteger);
Interlocked.Decrement(ref sharedInteger2);
int origValue = Interlocked.Exchange(ref sharedInteger, ref sharedInterger2) ;
```

10

Using the ReaderWriterLock Class

So far you've seen quite a few ways to protect a block of code in such a way that multiple write operations to the same data cannot happen at the same time. If a piece of code just wants to read from a shared location instead of writing to it, using the methods already discussed would be an unnecessary performance hit and a waste of shared resources (especially if you're using system-level Mutexes).

To get around this problem, the ReaderWriterLock class allows you to read shared data from a thread without having to create a synchronized section that blocks all requests. Instead, the ReaderWriterLock allows us to block *only* if the thread needs to update, and to not bother locking if the thread wants to perform a simple read operation.

Listing 10.5 shows the use of the ReaderWriterLock to acquire locks for reading and locks for writing. It also illustrates the use of the timeout value. The code in Listing 10.5 generates between one and two timeouts when attempting to acquire locks when run on my laptop. Feel free to play with the number of threads and the timeout period to see the results of increasing the number of timeouts. One obvious result is that every time the writer lock fails to acquire, you don't increment the shared resource value, so the more timeouts you end up with, the smaller the final result number will be a the more timeouts you end up with.

LISTING 10.5   Using the ReaderWriterLock Class

```
using System;
using System.Threading;
using System.Collections.Generic;
using System.Text;

namespace ReadWriteLockDemo
{
class Program
{
// shared resource here is a simple int
static int sharedResource = 42;
static int numTimeouts = 0;
static ReaderWriterLock rwl = new ReaderWriterLock();

static void Main(string[] args)
{
    // Create 10 threads that want write access
    Thread[] writers = new Thread[10];
    for (int i = 0; i < 10; i++)
    {
        Thread writeThread = new Thread(new ThreadStart(DoWrite));
        writers[i] = writeThread;
        writers[i].Start();
    }

    // Create 40 threads that want read access
    Thread[] readers = new Thread[40];
    for (int j = 0; j < 40; j++)
    {
        Thread readThread = new Thread(new ThreadStart(DoRead));
        readers[j] = readThread;
```

LISTING 10.5 Continued

```
        readers[j].Start();
    }

    // wait till they're all done
    foreach (Thread writer in writers)
        writer.Join();
    foreach (Thread reader in readers)
        reader.Join();

    Console.WriteLine("All work finished, only {0} timeouts.", numTimeouts);
    Console.ReadLine();
}

static void DoWrite()
{
    try
    {
        rwl.AcquireWriterLock(100);
        try
        {
            Interlocked.Increment(ref sharedResource);
            Thread.Sleep(15);
        }
        finally
        {
            rwl.ReleaseWriterLock();
        }
    }
    catch (ApplicationException ae)
    {
        Interlocked.Increment(ref numTimeouts);
    }
}

static void DoRead()
{
    try
    {
        rwl.AcquireReaderLock(100);
        try
        {

            Console.WriteLine("Inspecting shared value {0}", sharedResource);
        }
```

LISTING 10.5   Continued

```
        finally
        {
            rwl.ReleaseReaderLock();
        }
    }
    catch (ApplicationException ae)
    {
        Interlocked.Increment(ref numTimeouts);
    }
}
}
}
```

Working with Manual and Auto Reset Events

You can create synchronized blocks of code in many ways, including ways to protect shared resources against multiple inconsistent writes. As you saw with the `Mutex` class and others, there are ways to acquire locks and then write code within a thread that waits for the lock to be released, for example, with the `Wait` method.

Reset events are even more tightly controlled synchronization techniques. The basic premise is that you create an instance of a reset event. Then, in a thread, you call the `Wait` method on that event. Instead of waiting for a lock to be released, your code will then wait until *another* thread sends a signal on that same wait event.

Two kinds of reset events are available to you: Manual and Automatic reset events. In almost all aspects they are identical. The two differ only in that an Automatic reset event will set the event's signaled state to unsignaled when a waiting thread is released.

Listing 10.6 shows how to use a `ManualResetEvent` to line up several threads that are all waiting for the last thread to execute before they can continue. This allows you to tightly control the order in which tasks are completed, regardless of when the thread was started or what its execution priority is. This kind of cascading scheduling is important in many multithreaded applications where progress milestones need to be reached before other tasks can be completed. For example, suppose that you are writing a multithreaded application that processes data, writes that data to a file, and then e-mails the file to someone. You might create reset events so that the thread responsible for e-mailing the file can't do anything until the thread(s) responsible for data processing signal that the file is ready for reading, even if the threads themselves might not be complete.

LISTING 10.6   Using Reset Events to Force Execution Order

```
using System;
using System.Threading;
using System.Collections.Generic;
```

LISTING 10.6   Continued

```
using System.Text;

namespace ThreadEvents
{
class Program
{
static ManualResetEvent mre = new ManualResetEvent(false);
static string sharedResource = "Shared.";

static void Main(string[] args)
{
    Thread[] workers = new Thread[10];
    Console.WriteLine("Queueing up threads...");
    for (int i = 0; i < 10; i++)
    {
        Thread worker = new Thread(new ThreadStart(DoWork));
        workers[i] = worker;
        worker.Start();
    }
    // give all the other workers time to line up
    // behind the reset event
    Thread.Sleep(TimeSpan.FromSeconds(2));
    Console.WriteLine("Threads should be lined up, about to signal them to go.");
    mre.Set();
    foreach (Thread worker in workers)
        worker.Join();
    Console.WriteLine("Work's all done, work result: {0}", sharedResource);
    Console.ReadLine();
}

static void DoWork()
{
    mre.WaitOne();
    lock (sharedResource)
    {
        Console.WriteLine("Work was able to be performed.");
        sharedResource += " modified.";
    }

}
}
}
```

10

You can think of reset events like the childhood game of "red light/green light." The threads are all lined up and ready to go, but they're waiting for the signal. You can set these staggering points anywhere you like to gain a lot of tight control over what can be done in what order. When you combine the ability to signal threads in this way with the ability to create thread-safe locked synchronized code blocks, Mutexes, the Monitor class that allows timeout periods when requesting exclusive locks, and the vast array of other tools available, writing multithreaded code looks extremely promising, powerful, and far less intimidating than it does in other languages and platforms.

Using the ThreadPool Class

When it boils down to it, one of the most common states of any application is the "idle" state. Applications spend a lot of time sitting around waiting for something to happen. They're either waiting for a user to click something on a form, or they're waiting for a request to come in on a network port like HTTP or a custom service port. Using full-fledged foreground threads when sitting around waiting for something to happen is more expensive than necessary.

To allow you to create tasks that will operate in the background, but consume the smallest amount of resources possible, the .NET Framework has the *thread pool*.

The thread pool uses a WaitCallback delegate instead of a ThreadStart delegate to indicate the work that should be done in the background. In addition, the thread pool makes it easy to queue up a work item and let it run. You can also pass in a state object so that you can supply a worker thread with the data it needs to perform its task without having to rely on static members or complicated scope management techniques. Without the state object being passed to a worker thread, the worker thread would need to pull its information from global or static objects. When this happens, the thread needs to worry about synchronization of that data. Using the private state object that is scoped at the thread level, there is no need for synchronization since the data belongs only to the current thread.

Listing 10.7 provides a quick illustration of how to queue a user work item. Note that you don't have to explicitly Start the background thread from the pool. The upside of the thread pool is its ease of use. However, if you need complex synchronization techniques such as events, or if you need to call Join on a list of threads as shown in preceding examples, you may find the thread pool insufficient for your needs.

LISTING 10.7   Using the ThreadPool

```
using System;
using System.Threading;
using System.Collections.Generic;
using System.Text;

namespace ThreadPoolDemo
{
```

LISTING 10.7   Continued

```
class Program
{
static void Main(string[] args)
{
    for (int i = 0; i < 20; i++)
    {
        ThreadPool.QueueUserWorkItem(
            new WaitCallback(DoWork), i);
    }

    Console.ReadLine();

}

static void DoWork(object state)
{
    int threadNumber = (int)state;
    Console.WriteLine("Thread {0} reporting for duty.", state);
}
}
}
```

Summary

Threading is a topic that many people avoid because on the surface it seems intimidating. There are a lot of terms like mutex, semaphore, synchronization, and so on that might be unfamiliar to developers. Hopefully, this chapter has demystified multithreaded programming to the point where it is no longer intimidating.

The key to developing high-quality multithreaded applications lies in knowing when you should create thread-safe synchronized blocks and when you can get by with a ReaderWriterLock, and to make use of mutexes, monitors, semaphores, and the various properties and methods of the Thread class itself to create an application that remains responsive and reliable even while performing complex, resource-intensive tasks.

Throughout this book, you will learn many techniques for working with data, working with ASP.NET web applications, working with Windows Forms applications, and much more. As you learn these new techniques, you may want to return to this chapter and see how you can apply your new knowledge of the .NET Framework's multithreading capabilities to increase the performance and responsiveness of your application.

10

CHAPTER **11**

Reflection Fundamentals

Reflection is a runtime facility that allows you to write code that can interrogate data types at runtime. This means that you can obtain information about the data type of variables. More than that, it means that you can obtain information about class members, properties, methods, fields, constructors, and much more.

This chapter introduces you to the basics of reflection: what it is and how it works. Then, you will see how to use reflection to work with methods, members (fields, properties, and so on), events and more. Finally, you will see how reflection works to allow you to create and consume custom attributes that can be used to decorate your class with metadata that can be read at runtime.

Introduction to Reflection

Reflection is what allows code to interrogate type information and metadata at runtime. One core fact allows this to happen: *In the .NET Framework, data types are objects*. This means that every data type—whether it is a class you wrote or a part of the base class library—has methods you can invoke and properties you can examine. This allows you to do things like obtain the list of methods exposed by a class, or determine the data type of a property, or even iterate through the list of parameters to a given method. You can even do things like obtain references to resources embedded with an assembly, though assemblies will be covered in Chapter 12.

In unmanaged languages, such as unmanaged C++, memory is just a collection of bytes. If you declare an array that will consume 32 bytes of memory, C++ has absolutely no idea what is contained in that 32 bytes. In contrast, the Common Language Runtime (CLR) knows exactly what is contained in every piece of memory consumed. Not only does it know where the data starts and stops, but it knows what kind of data it is. Without having access to the source code, you can use reflection to find out the data type of something in memory, and then use additional reflection tools to interrogate that type to find out its parent classes, the interfaces it implements, the methods it exposes, the properties it contains, and even the events it hosts.

A great deal of work with reflection begins by getting a reference to the data type of a particular variable in memory. This is done by calling the `GetType()` method on an object. This returns an object of type `System.Type`. As mentioned earlier, all data types within the .NET Framework are objects. Table 11.1 lists some of the most commonly used methods and properties of the `Type` class, the core of the `Reflection` functionality in the .NET Framework.

TABLE 11.1   `System.Type` Members

Property/Method	Description
Assembly	Gets the assembly in which the type has been defined.
Attributes	Gets the list of attributes associated with the type.
BaseType	The parent type of the current type. Not to be confused with an ancestor, this is the type of the immediate parent only. You can recursively use this property to travel up the inheritance tree.
FullName	Gets the full name of the type, including namespace. Not associated with the assembly name.
GenericParameterPosition	Gets the position of the type parameter in the type parameter list when the type is a generic type.
IsAbstract	Indicates whether the type is an abstract type that must be overridden.
IsArray	Indicates whether the type is an array.
IsByRef	Indicates whether the type is a reference type.
IsGenericParameter	Indicates whether the type is a generic parameter.
IsGenericType	Indicates whether the type accepts generic parameters.
IsInterface	Indicates whether the type is an interface.
Module	Gets the module (compiled output file) in which the type is defined. Only varies from assembly when the assembly is a multifile assembly.
Namespace	Gets the containing namespace of the type.
GetArrayRank()	Gets the number of dimensions in the array if the type is an array type.
GetConstructor()	Gets a specific constructor for the type.
GetConstructors()	Gets all of the constructors for the type.
GetEvents()	Gets a list of events within the type.
GetMember/GetMembers()	Gets member information on the type.
GetMethod/GetMethods()	Gets method information on the type.
GetProperty()/ GetProperties()	Gets information on properties on the type.
MakeGenericType()	Supplies the given array of type parameters to an open generic type and binds it to the parameters, creating a constructed generic type.

Using this table of properties and methods, you can now start to work with specific aspects of reflection, as discussed throughout the remainder of this chapter.

Working with Method Information

Method information centers on the `MethodInfo` class. You can obtain an instance of this through the `GetMethod` or `GetMethods` methods on the `Type` object, as shown in the following example:

```
Type t = cust.GetType();
MethodInfo method = t.GetMethod("DoSomething");
```

Before diving into a code example, let's take a look at Table 11.2, which lists some of the common properties and methods available for the `MethodInfo` class.

TABLE 11.2   `MethodInfo` Properties and Methods

Property/Method	Description
`Attributes`	Gets the list of attributes attached to the method.
`IsAbstract`	Indicates whether the method is abstract.
`IsAssembly`	Indicates whether the method can be called by other classes contained within the assembly.
`IsConstructor`	Indicates whether the method is a constructor.
`IsFinal`	Indicates whether the method has been sealed and made final.
`Name`	Gets the name of the method.
`ReturnType`	Indicates the return type of the method.
`GetMethodBody()`	Obtains information about the inside of the method itself, such as the type and amount of local variables, exception-handling blocks, and so on.
`GetParameters()`	Gets the list of parameters for the method.
`MakeGenericMethod`	Replaces the open generic parameters for the method with the supplied array of types, binding the method to the types at runtime and returning a method that can then be executed.

Now let's see some of these methods and properties in action, as shown in the sample code in Listing 11.1.

LISTING 11.1   Reflecting on Methods and Parameters

```
using System;
using System.Reflection;
using System.Collections.Generic;
using System.Text;

namespace ReflectMethods
{
class Program
{
```

LISTING 11.1   Continued

```
static void Main(string[] args)
{
    Customer<string> cust = new Customer<string>();
    Type t = cust.GetType();

    MethodInfo method = t.GetMethod("DoSomething");
    Console.WriteLine(method.Name);
    Console.WriteLine("-------------------------");
    Console.WriteLine("Abstract: {0}, Visible to Assembly: {1}, Constructor:
    ➥ {2}, Sealed: {3}",
        method.IsAbstract, method.IsAssembly,
method.IsConstructor, method.IsFinal);
    Console.WriteLine("Generic: {0}, Virtual: {1}, Static: {2}",
        method.IsGenericMethod, method.IsVirtual, method.IsStatic);
    Console.WriteLine("{0} returns {1}",
        method.Name, method.ReturnType.ToString());
    Console.WriteLine("Parameters:");
    foreach (ParameterInfo p in method.GetParameters())
    {
        Console.WriteLine("\t{0} : {1} [{2}]{3}",
            p.Name, p.ParameterType.ToString(),
            p.IsOut ? "Out" : "In",
            p.ParameterType.IsGenericParameter ? "* Generic" : "");
    }
    Console.WriteLine("Local variables within method:");
    foreach (LocalVariableInfo lvi in method.GetMethodBody().LocalVariables)
    {
        Console.WriteLine(lvi.ToString());
    }

    Console.ReadLine();
}
}
}
```

The output of the preceding code looks as follows:

```
DoSomething
-------------------------
Abstract: False, Visible to Assembly: False, Constructor: False, Sealed: False
Generic: True, Virtual: False, Static: False
DoSomething returns System.String
Parameters:
        input : U [In]* Generic
```

```
        otherCustomer : ReflectMethods.Customer`1[System.String]& [In]
        newCustomer : ReflectMethods.Customer`1[System.String]& [Out]
        anotherInput : System.Int32 [In]
Local variables within method:
System.Int32 (0)
System.String (1)
System.String (2)
```

The Customer class on which the preceding code is reflecting is shown here:

```
using System;
using System.Collections.Generic;
using System.Text;

namespace ReflectMethods
{
class Customer<T>
{
private int privData = 12;


public int PubData
{
    get { return privData; }
    set { privData = value; }
}

public string DoSomething<U>(U input, ref Customer<T> otherCustomer,
    out Customer<T> newCustomer,
    int anotherInput)
{
    int z = 21;
    string localString = "local";

    newCustomer = new Customer<T>();
    return input.ToString();
}
}
}
```

One thing that might be somewhat surprising for developers who have prior experience with reflection is that *generics are completely compatible with reflection*. Using reflection, you can obtain all information about a method, even information related to generic type parameters. Also, if you look back at the otherCustomer and newCustomer parameters in the console output, you can see that those parameters aren't indicated as being generic.

In fact, you can see that as far as the runtime is concerned, those parameters are of type `Customer<string>`.

Working with Member Information

Working with members is slightly different than working with methods. The reason for this is that there are many different member types, including properties, fields, methods, constructors, and so on. When you obtain a `MemberInfo` instance, you can take a look at the `MemberType` property to determine which kind of member you're looking at.

Table 11.3 gives you a quick overview of some of the more common properties and methods of the `MemberInfo` class.

TABLE 11.3   `MemberInfo` Properties and Methods

Property/Method	Description
`MemberType`	Indicates the type of the member. Can be: `Constructor`, `Custom`, `Event`, `Field`, `Method`, `NestedType`, `Property`, or `TypeInfo`.
`Name`	Name of the member.
`Module`	Module in which the member was defined.
`GetCustomAttributes()`	Gets a list of custom attributes that belong to the member. Attributes are discussed later in the section "Creating and Examining Custom Code Attributes."

When dealing with members of a specific type, you can obtain more detailed information about that member using the appropriate class. For example, you can get more detailed information about a property from the `PropertyInfo` class. Similar classes are available, such as `ConstructorInfo`, `MethodInfo`, `FieldInfo`, `EventInfo`, and `ParameterInfo`. Each of these classes has a corresponding `Getxxxx` method on the containing type. For instance, to obtain a specific field, you would use the `GetField` method on the type itself, which returns a `FieldInfo` instance.

In some cases, when you attempt to retrieve a member, you can pass a `BindingFlags` value. This value is a bitwise-OR'd list of scope items that tell reflection what types of items you want to search for when attempting to locate a member.

Table 11.4 shows a brief summary of some of the different values that you can use for the `BindingFlags` enumeration when locating type members. This isn't the entire list. For the entire list, you can look up the `BindingFlags` enumeration in the online MSDN documentation.

TABLE 11.4   `BindingFlags` Enumeration Members

Value	Description
`IgnoreCase`	Indicates that the case of the member name should be ignored when locating.
`Instance`	Indicates that instance members are to be included in the member search.

TABLE 11.4   Continued

Value	Description
NonPublic	Indicates that nonpublic members should be included in the search. Without this flag, nonpublic members will not be located.
Public	Indicates that public members should be included in the search.
Static	Indicates that static members should be included in the search.

Listing 11.2 shows an example of accessing member information through `Reflection`. Note that for simplicity, the `Customer` class from the preceding sample was reused.

LISTING 11.2   Reflecting on Member Information

```
using System;
using System.Reflection;
using System.Collections.Generic;
using System.Text;

namespace ReflectMembers
{
class Program
{
static void Main(string[] args)
{

ReflectMethods.Customer<string> cust = new ReflectMethods.Customer<string>();
Type t = cust.GetType();
MemberInfo[] members = t.GetMembers(BindingFlags.NonPublic ¦ BindingFlags.Public ¦
    BindingFlags.GetProperty ¦ BindingFlags.SetProperty ¦ BindingFlags.Instance);
foreach (MemberInfo member in members)
{
    Console.WriteLine("{0} ({1})", member.Name, member.MemberType.ToString());
    if (member.MemberType == MemberTypes.Property)
    {
        Console.WriteLine("\tProperty");
        PropertyInfo pi = t.GetProperty(member.Name);
        Console.WriteLine("\t\tData Type : {0}", pi.PropertyType.ToString());
        Console.WriteLine("\t\tCurrent Value: {0}", pi.GetValue(cust, null));
    }
    if (member.MemberType == MemberTypes.Field)
    {
        Console.WriteLine("\tField");
        FieldInfo fi = t.GetField(member.Name,
BindingFlags.NonPublic ¦ BindingFlags.Public ¦ BindingFlags.Instance);
```

LISTING 11.2   Continued

```
        Console.WriteLine("\t\tData Type: {0}", fi.FieldType.ToString());
        Console.WriteLine("\t\tCurrent Value: {0}", fi.GetValue(cust));


    }
}

Console.ReadLine();

}
}
}
```

The keen (or suspicious) eye may have already noticed that the preceding code can actually read data from a private member, even on a class that is completely unrelated to the one making the Reflection calls. This is always a concern, and as such you should never assume that even your in-memory data is secure. You will see some ways in which you can protect your data in-memory in Chapter 15, "Cryptography and Data Protection."

The output from the preceding sample produces text that looks like the following:

```
DoSomething (Method)
get_PubData (Method)
set_PubData (Method)
GetType (Method)
MemberwiseClone (Method)
ToString (Method)
Equals (Method)
GetHashCode (Method)
Finalize (Method)
.ctor (Constructor)
PubData (Property)
        Property
                Data Type : System.Int32
                Current Value: 12
privData (Field)
        Field
                Data Type: System.Int32
                Current Value: 12
```

Examining Events

As you saw in Chapter 9, "Events and Delegates," events are an extremely powerful feature that work with delegates that match a specific method signature to signal important events. You can then "add" your delegate to an event hosted by another class. When that event is triggered, your delegate will be among those methods invoked as a result. In this way, you can write code that will subscribe to be notified when important changes take place or important events need to be signaled.

Using reflection, you can dynamically obtain information about an event at runtime.

The code in Listing 11.3 shows how to use the `EventInfo` class to obtain detailed information about an event, as well as add and remove event handlers. A new delegate and an event called `OnPropertyChanged` were added to the original `Customer` class used in the first sample for the purpose of this demonstration.

LISTING 11.3   Reflecting on Events

```
using System;
using System.Reflection;
using System.Collections.Generic;
using System.Text;

namespace EventInfoDemo
{
class Program
{
static void Main(string[] args)
{
    ReflectMethods.Customer<string> cust = new ReflectMethods.Customer<string>();
    ReflectMethods.PropertyChangedDelegate propDel =
new ReflectMethods.PropertyChangedDelegate(cust_OnPropertyChanged);
    cust.OnPropertyChanged += propDel;

    EventInfo evt = cust.GetType().GetEvent("OnPropertyChanged");
    Console.WriteLine("Event {0}:", evt.Name);
    Console.WriteLine("\tMulticast?: {0}", evt.IsMulticast);
    Console.WriteLine("\tModule: {0}", evt.Module.Name);

    MethodInfo addMethod = evt.GetAddMethod();
    Console.WriteLine("\tAdd Method: {0}", addMethod.ToString());
    Console.WriteLine("\tRemove Method: {0}", evt.GetRemoveMethod().ToString());

    cust.PubData = 99;

    evt.RemoveEventHandler(cust, propDel) ;
    cust.PubData = 42;

    evt.AddEventHandler(cust, propDel);
    evt.AddEventHandler(cust, propDel);
    cust.PubData = 150;
```

LISTING 11.3   Continued

```
    Console.ReadLine();


}

static void cust_OnPropertyChanged(string propName, int value)
{
    Console.WriteLine("Customer Property changed : {0}, {1}", propName, value);
}
}
}
```

Creating and Examining Custom Code Attributes

Creating custom attributes is actually a pretty simple process. A custom code attribute is really just a class that inherits from System.Attribute. After you create a class based on the Attribute class, you can then decorate additional classes with that attribute to serve as metadata that can be read at runtime.

There are many reasons why you would want to associate custom attributes with your code. Some of the attributes that are already part of the framework allow you to control the transactional behavior of classes, the serialization behavior, the COM visibility of other classes, and much more.

Listing 11.4 shows an example of a class that inherits from Attribute. You use private members, constructors, and properties for providing access to the metadata information that will be supplied to the class at runtime through attribute parameters.

LISTING 11.4   Custom Code Attributes: The DataColumnAttribute Class

```
using System;
using System.Data;
using System.Collections.Generic;
using System.Text;

namespace CodeAttributeDemo
{
[AttributeUsage(AttributeTargets.Property | AttributeTargets.Field)]
class DataColumnAttribute : Attribute
{
private string columnName = "Column";
private System.Data.DbType dataType = DbType.String;
```

LISTING 11.4   Continued

```
public DataColumnAttribute()
{
}

public DataColumnAttribute(string column, DbType dbtype)
{
    columnName = column;
    dataType = dbtype;
}

public string ColumnName
{
    get { return columnName; }
    set
    {
        columnName = value;
    }
}

public DbType DataType
{
    get { return dataType; }
    set { dataType = value; }
}
}
}
```

It looks like a fairly simple class. In fact, it is quite simple. All it's maintaining is a couple of bits of information about how to relate a property on a class to a column in a database, a common data access task. Listing 11.5 shows a class called Shape that has attributes that show what it looks like when you associate custom code attributes with a class.

LISTING 11.5   Custom Code Attributes: The Shape Class (Attribute Decoration Sample)

```
using System;
using System.Collections.Generic;
using System.Text;

namespace CodeAttributeDemo
{
[DataTable("tblShapes")]
```

LISTING 11.5   Continued

```
class Shape
{
    private string name = "Square";

    [DataColumn("Name", System.Data.DbType.String)]
    public string Name
    {
        get { return name; }
        set { name = value; }
    }
}
}
```

Finally, Listing 11.6 shows how you can use reflection to obtain references to the custom code attributes on a class instance at runtime.

LISTING 11.6   Using Reflection to Query Custom Attributes at Runtime

```
using System;
using System.Reflection;
using System.Collections.Generic;
using System.Text;

namespace CodeAttributeDemo
{
class Program
{
static void Main(string[] args)
{
    Type t = typeof(Shape);
    DataTableAttribute[] attribs = (DataTableAttribute[])
t.GetCustomAttributes(typeof(DataTableAttribute), true);
    DataTableAttribute attrib = attribs[0];

    Console.WriteLine("The Shape class is persisted via the {0} table in
    ➥a database.", attrib.TableName);

    DataColumnAttribute[] cols =
(DataColumnAttribute[])
        t.GetProperty("Name").GetCustomAttributes(
typeof(DataColumnAttribute), true);
```

LISTING 11.6 Continued

```
Console.WriteLine("The 'Name' property, when persisted to a database,
is called {0}, and is of type {1}",
    cols[0].ColumnName, cols[0].DataType.ToString());

Console.ReadLine();
}
}
}
```

Summary

This chapter has shown you the power of reflection. As you read through this chapter, you learned that in the .NET Framework, data types are also objects that can be treated just like any other object. Data types have methods and properties that can be accessed the same way you access normal object methods and properties. These members allow you to utilize reflection to find out information about methods, members, events, data types, and much more.

Using reflection isn't just a way to find out information about your own code. Having the ability to inspect data types at runtime is an extremely valuable tool. When you find a need for reflection in your own application, you will wonder how you ever managed to write code without it.

CHAPTER **12**

Assemblies and AppDomains

W hether you're building Web Forms applications, web services, Windows applications, applications for PDAs, or even console applications, you are working with assemblies and AppDomains. Regardless of whether you're aware of it, assemblies and AppDomains are at the core of all .NET applications.

This chapter provides you with an introduction to assemblies, as well as a detailed view of what they are, how they work, and how they're built and used by applications. Next, this chapter covers the AppDomain and how knowledge of the existence of AppDomains can make your applications more powerful and more reliable.

Introduction to Assemblies

The assembly is the core unit of *logical* deployment within the .NET Framework. Whenever you compile your code, it must eventually end up in an assembly. When your application is executed after deployment, its assemblies are loaded by the Common Language Runtime. As you will see in the next section, there is a lot more to the assembly than meets the eye. A lot of developers take it for granted that an assembly is just another word for "DLL," but that couldn't be further from the truth.

An assembly is a logical container that stores not only compiled code, but also metadata and resources. Assemblies serve the following purposes:

- Assemblies are containers for compiled code that will be executed by the CLR.

- Assemblies are a logical unit of security. When code permissions are granted or denied, they are often done so at the assembly level.

- Assemblies serve as a logical unit of version control. Every type and resource contained within a given assembly shares the same version number (and other identifying information, such as public key and culture).

- As mentioned, assemblies are a logical unit of deployment. When you deploy your application, it is deployed at the assembly level.

Some of this might not make much sense at the moment, but it will become much clearer in the next section, where we take a look at the internals of assemblies in the .NET Framework.

Assemblies Under the Hood

Many developers assume that an assembly is just a simple DLL or an EXE file; simply the output produced by compilation. On the surface, this appears to be true, but there is a lot more to an assembly than just storing the compiled code.

Inside the assembly, there is far more than just the compiled code. As mentioned earlier, when the compiler creates an assembly, it stores compiled code as well as metadata.

Figure 12.1 illustrates the contents of a .NET assembly. There is a *manifest*, a list of the types contained within the assembly, assembly-level metadata, and finally the MSIL code created by the compiler.

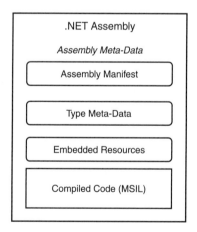

FIGURE 12.1   Contents of a .NET assembly.

When you build an assembly (discussed in the next section), the compiler does a lot of things for you. It stores the list of types contained in that assembly, a list of dependencies (referenced assemblies that are required for the assembly to function properly), resources such as multilingual strings and images, and finally the compiled MSIL code.

An assembly can actually be a *multifile* assembly. In a multifile assembly, you can separate blocks of MSIL code and types into multiple modules. When you create the assembly, you then link the multiple modules via the assembly manifest of the primary assembly. This allows you to create a single logical assembly that can actually contain 20 different files. The beauty of this is that when the CLR attempts to load the primary assembly, it will automatically load all of the multiple files that make up the assembly. If one of the files is missing, the assembly will not load.

Introducing the Assembly Manifest

The assembly manifest is a collection of metadata that describes the contents of the assembly. It contains metadata about the assembly itself such as the version number, the public key, and so on. In addition, it contains a list of dependencies. These dependencies are checked when the assembly is loaded. If one of the dependencies fails to load, so too does the assembly. The manifest also contains a list of the resources used by the assembly.

To take a look at what the CLR sees when it loads an assembly manifest, you can use the ILDASM.EXE tool that comes with the .NET Framework SDK. To use this, you can open up a Visual Studio 2005 Command Prompt from the Visual Studio Tools group on your Start menu. Then type **ILDASM** and a new window will appear. Select File, then Open, and then browse to \Windows\Microsoft.NET\Framework\v2.0.50727\ and select System.Data.dll. You'll see a plethora of information about the types, resources, and metadata contained within the assembly appear in a useful tree structure. Double-click the MANIFEST node and you will see a window that looks like the one shown in Figure 12.2.

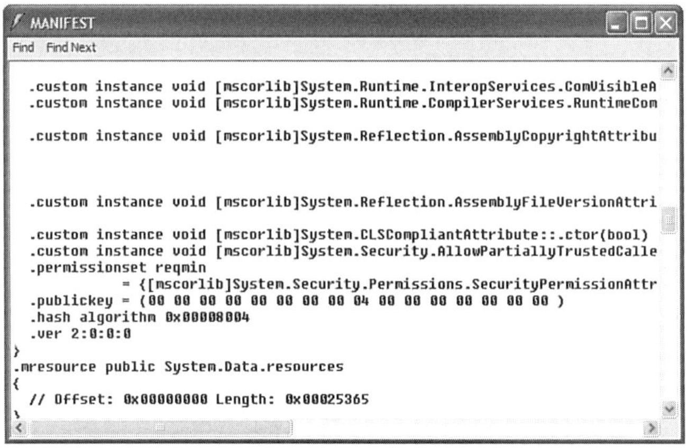

FIGURE 12.2   An assembly manifest, as seen by the ILDASM tool.

You don't need to understand the language of the statements contained in the manifest, but it should be pretty easy to recognize a lot of the elements being discussed here. When browsing through the manifest, you can see the list of dependencies when you see the .assembly extern statements. The list of resources contained within the assembly is also stored within the manifest.

Building and Using Assemblies

There are several ways to go about creating an assembly. The first method, using Visual Studio, you should already be quite familiar with. Every time you have created a solution so far in this book, you have created an assembly. When you create a "Class Library" project within Visual Studio, the output of that Class Library is an assembly with the .DLL extension.

The other way to create an assembly is to use the Assembly Linker tool, AL.EXE. This tool provides a command-line interface to linking multiple compiled modules into an assembly. In fact, this is the only way for you to create a multimodule assembly in C#, as opposed to VB.NET, which allows for the creation of multiple modules per assembly directly within Visual Studio.

You can also use; Reflection to obtain information about an assembly. Listing 12.1 shows how you can retrieve some basic information from the assembly's manifest using the Assembly class.

LISTING 12.1   Using the Assembly Class

```
using System;
using System.Reflection;
using System.Resources;
using System.Collections.Generic;
using System.Text;

namespace AssemblyDemo1
{
class Program
{
static void Main(string[] args)
{
    Assembly a = Assembly.GetExecutingAssembly();
    Console.WriteLine("Current Assembly {0} loaded from {1}",
a.GetName().Name, a.Location);
    Console.WriteLine("\nLoaded from the Global Assembly Cache? {0}",
a.GlobalAssemblyCache);
    Console.WriteLine("This Assembly requires version {0} of the runtime",
 a.ImageRuntimeVersion) ;

    Console.WriteLine("Assembly's entry point {0}.", a.EntryPoint.ToString());

    Console.WriteLine("Types contained in this Assembly:");
    foreach (Type t in a.GetTypes())
    {
        Console.WriteLine("\t{0} contained in {1}",
```

LISTING 12.1 Continued

```
t.Name, t.Assembly.GetName().Name);
    }

    Console.ReadLine();
}
}
}
```

You can also use the Assembly class to load and obtain information from other assemblies. If you add a "Class Library" project to the preceding sample, you can modify the code so it reads information from the compiled DLL in addition to the executable file. This is illustrated in Listing 12.2.

LISTING 12.2 Loading an External Assembly

```
using System;
using System.Reflection;
using System.Resources;
using System.Collections.Generic;
using System.Text;

namespace AssemblyDemo1
{
class Program
{
static void Main(string[] args)
{
    Assembly a = Assembly.GetExecutingAssembly();
    Console.WriteLine("Current Assembly {0} loaded from {1}",
a.GetName().Name, a.Location);
    Console.WriteLine("\nLoaded from the Global Assembly Cache? {0}",
a.GlobalAssemblyCache);
    Console.WriteLine("This Assembly requires version {0} of the runtime",
a.ImageRuntimeVersion);

    Assembly otherAssembly = Assembly.LoadFile(
      AppDomain.CurrentDomain.BaseDirectory + "\\SampleAssembly.DLL");
    Console.WriteLine("Other Assembly: {0}", otherAssembly.GetName().Name);
    Console.WriteLine("Types contained in {0}", otherAssembly.GetName().Name);
    foreach (Type t in otherAssembly.GetTypes())
    {
```

LISTING 12.2   Continued

```
        Console.WriteLine(t.Name) ;
    }



    Console.ReadLine();
}
}
}
```

When you run this application, after having created an empty class library called
SampleAssembly and adding a reference to that project from the main project, you get the
following output:

```
Current Assembly AssemblyDemo1 loaded from C:\Documents and Settings\Kevin\My Do
cuments\Writing\SAMS\C# 2005 Unleashed\12\Code\AssemblyDemo1\AssemblyDemo1\bin\D
ebug\AssemblyDemo1.exe

Loaded from the Global Assembly Cache? False
This Assembly requires version v2.0.50727 of the runtime
Other Assembly: SampleAssembly
Types contained in SampleAssembly
Class1
```

Storing and Retrieving Assembly Resources

If you have experience with storing and retrieving resources in assemblies from previous
versions of the .NET Framework, you'll be pleasantly surprised at how easy it is to do in
C# 2.0.

Many applications need resources. These resources can be things like images, icons, files,
or strings that can be displayed in multiple languages. Developers often embed these
resources in their assemblies so that they are easy to find, easy to use, and won't acciden-
tally be deleted from the disk. The resources are often so critical to the deployment of the
application that, by embedding them within an assembly, they become a fixed part of the
deployment and can't be removed.

The process of adding resources to a project is quite simple in Visual Studio 2005. The
new resource manager is extremely easy to use and allows you to organize all of your
resources quickly and easily.

The first step is to add a resource file to your project. To add a resource to the project,
right-click your project and choose Add and then select New Item. Find the Resources
File item template and choose a name for the resources. By having multiple resource files
in your project, you can organize resources categorically and make things easier to find.

A feature new to Visual Studio 2005 is the addition of a wrapper class that provides strongly typed members that expose the resources you create in your resource file. Each resource file in your project (it has a `.resx` extension) is converted into a class at compile time by Visual Studio.

In this way, if you create a resource file called `StringMessages.resx` in your project, and then create a string resource named `Hello`, you will be able to use the following line of code:

```
Console.WriteLine(StringMessages.Hello);
```

And the type of the resource will be a string, not an object. This is an extremely powerful new feature that dramatically increases productivity for developers working with resources.

The demo in Listing 12.3 consists of a console application called `ResourceDemo`, and a resources file called `DemoResources`. To that resource file, a string called `Greeting` has been added, shown in Figure 12.3.

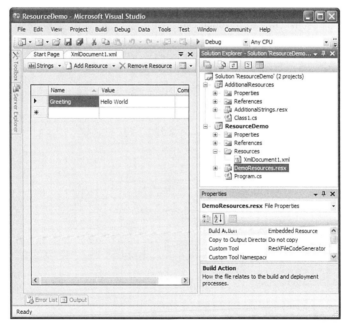

FIGURE 12.3   Adding a string to a resource file using the Resource Editor.

A class library called `AdditionalResources` was then created, and a resource file was added to that project in order to illustrate the right pattern for sharing resources between assemblies. Finally, an XML document was added as a file-type resource to the `DemoResources` resource file. The code in Listing 12.3 shows how to make use of the strongly typed class wrapper that is generated at compile time for access to embedded resources.

LISTING 12.3   Accessing Resources Using the Strongly Typed Wrappers

```
using System;
using System.Xml;
using System.Resources;

using System.Collections.Generic;
using System.Text;

namespace ResourceDemo
{
class Program
{
static void Main(string[] args)
{
    Console.WriteLine(DemoResources.Greeting);
    Console.WriteLine(AdditionalResources.Class1.WelcomeParagraph) ;

    XmlDocument doc = new XmlDocument();
    doc.LoadXml(DemoResources.XmlDocument1);

    foreach (XmlNode order in doc.SelectNodes("//Order"))
    {
        Console.WriteLine("Order id {0}, Total ${1}",
         order.Attributes["id"].Value, order.Attributes["total"].Value);
    }

    Console.ReadLine();
}
}
}
```

The `WelcomeParagraph` string resource in the `AdditionalResources` class library is exposed as a static property as shown in the following example:

```
namespace AdditionalResources
{
public class Class1
{
public static string WelcomeParagraph
{
    get { return AdditionalStrings.WelcomeParagraph; }
}
}
}
```

This illustrates a good design pattern: Each assembly should be responsible for determining to what resources it should provide external access. Although it is still possible using `Reflection` to get these resources, if you control the encapsulation you can control how your resources are used properly.

Localization and Satellite Assemblies

Satellite assemblies are a special kind of assembly that allows you to store resources for multiple languages in an easy-to-access format. You can create a satellite assembly, which is basically just a resource-only assembly, to contain resources for one specific language. This provides you with a lot of flexibility because you could create your application with support for a single language, and then deploy additional languages as satellite assemblies without having to recompile any of your main application code.

Creating applications with localization and globalization in mind is becoming a far more common task. In fact, it is becoming the norm for many application developers. With the use of satellite assemblies, it becomes even easier as you can hire contracted translators to supply you with XML files containing translations that you can then use to build a satellite assembly.

The .NET Framework uses a hub-and-spoke model for locating multilingual resources. If a resource is not available for the locale-specific culture in which the user resides (or claims to reside), the CLR will look for locale-neutral resources for the user's language. Finally, if none of those can be found, the CLR will use the default resources found in the main assembly. An illustration of the hub-and-spoke model for resource localization is shown in Figure 12.4.

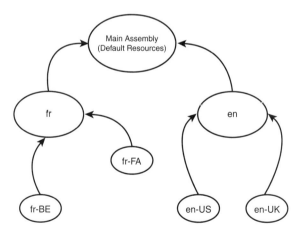

FIGURE 12.4   Resource location model.

As you can see from Figure 12.4, the resource location starts at the most specific possible: the combination of language and locale. Then, if there is no match found, the locale is dropped and an attempt is made to find general resources for a specific language. If that attempt fails, the resources will be used directly from the main assembly in the default language of the application, which is often English.

When you add a resources file to your application, by default you just use a regular filename, such as MyStrings.resx. However, to supply resources (including images, icons, files, and so on) for a different culture, all you have to do is append the locale ID to the end of the filename, such as MyStrings.fr.resx and MyStrings.fr-CA.resx, and so on. Your application will still only create one strongly typed wrapper class called MyStrings, but instead of serving up the default content only, it will automatically detect the culture of the thread making the request for the resource and hand out the appropriate value. This removes the burden of conditional programming from you and makes it easier to support multiple languages.

The code in Listing 12.4 shows what it looks like to print out a value (the phrase for "the weekend") in multiple cultures by setting the current UI culture.

LISTING 12.4   Displaying Localized Strings

```
using System;
using System.Threading;
using System.Collections.Generic;
using System.Text;

namespace Localization
{
class Program
{
static void Main(string[] args)
{

    Console.WriteLine(ApplicationText.Welcome) ;

    Thread.CurrentThread.CurrentUICulture =
new System.Globalization.CultureInfo("fr-CA");
    Console.WriteLine(ApplicationText.Welcome);

    // this displays the french-canadian way of saying "the weekend"
    Console.WriteLine(ApplicationText.weekend);

    // this displays the french-neutral way of saying "the weekend"
    // because there are no localized resources for fr-BE in this app,
    // so it drops down to fr-neutral.
    Thread.CurrentThread.CurrentUICulture =
new System.Globalization.CultureInfo("fr-BE");
    Console.WriteLine(ApplicationText.weekend);
```

LISTING 12.4   Continued

```
    // this displays the neutral (default) way of saying "the weekend" (english)
    // because there are no localized resources for hi-IN.
    Thread.CurrentThread.CurrentUICulture =
new System.Globalization.CultureInfo("hi-IN");
    Console.WriteLine(ApplicationText.weekend);

    Console.ReadLine();
}
}
}
```

Introduction to AppDomains

Whereas the assembly is a logical unit of deployment, the AppDomain is a logical unit of execution. The AppDomain is a sandbox in which .NET code runs. The AppDomain provides a container in which code can execute safely, knowing that code running outside the AppDomain cannot negatively impact it. As you will see throughout this book, cross-process communication done with Remoting is actually the process of passing information between AppDomains, whether they are on the same machine or different machines.

Throughout the course of an application, your code may load a lot of assemblies creating instances of other classes. Without the use of the AppDomain class, all of those assemblies will remain in memory for the lifespan of your application. If you are coding a long-running server application, this is unacceptable. Using the AppDomain class, however, you can manually control the loading and unloading of assemblies, as well as create an isolated environment to run potentially volatile tasks.

The AppDomain class represents the properties and functionalities of this memory sandbox, as shown in Table 12.1.

TABLE 12.1   AppDomain Properties and Methods

Property/Method	Description
ApplicationIdentity	Gets the identity of the application in the AppDomain, containing information such as the location and full name.
BaseDirectory	The base directory that will be used to look for dependent assemblies.
CurrentDomain	Gets an instance of the AppDomain class, indicating the current AppDomain.
FriendlyName	Gets the friendly name of the application domain.
SetupInformation	Gets an AppDomainSetup instance containing application and configuration binding data.
CreateCOMInstanceFrom()	Creates an instance of a COM object. You will learn more about this in Chapter 13.
CreateDomain()	Creates a new named AppDomain.
CreateInstance()	Creates an instance of a specified type in the specified assembly.

TABLE 12.1   Continued

Property/Method	Description
CreateInstanceFrom()	Creates an instance of the specified type in the specified assembly file (requires the .dll or .exe extension).
ExecuteAssembly()	Executes the assembly file specified, such as another .exe.
GetAssemblies()	Obtains the list of assemblies loaded within the AppDomain.
GetData()	Gets data contained in a named slot visible to all assemblies in the AppDomain.
Load()	Loads an assembly into the AppDomain.
SetData()	Sets data contained in a named slot visible to all assemblies in the AppDomain.
SetThreadPrincipal()	Sets the principal (security user) that will be presented when a thread is queried for the security context.
Unload()	Unloads an AppDomain and releases all loaded assemblies.

Programming with AppDomains

To illustrate how to program with AppDomains, we are going to create a solution that has a console application and a class library. The code in the console application is going to create a new AppDomain and use that new AppDomain to execute code within the class library. When that secondary code is finished executing, the code in the console application will then unload the temporary AppDomain, illustrating how you can gain tight control over the memory consumption of your application by manually loading and unloading certain AppDomains. The code for the class library is shown in Listing 12.5.

LISTING 12.5   A Class Library with Simple Code for Displaying the AppDomain's Loaded Assembly List

```
using System;
using System.Reflection;
using System.Collections.Generic;
using System.Text;

namespace SecondaryCode
{
public class Class1 : MarshalByRefObject
{
public void DoWork()
{
    Console.WriteLine("[{0}] Doing some work.",
        AppDomain.CurrentDomain.FriendlyName);
    Console.WriteLine("[{0}] Domain-Wide value is {1}",
        AppDomain.CurrentDomain.FriendlyName,
        AppDomain.CurrentDomain.GetData("THEVALUE"));
```

LISTING 12.5   Continued

```
    Console.WriteLine("This domain currently has {0} Assemblies loaded.",
        AppDomain.CurrentDomain.GetAssemblies().Length.ToString());
    foreach (Assembly a in AppDomain.CurrentDomain.GetAssemblies())
    {
        Console.WriteLine("\t{0}", a.GetName().Name);
    }
}
}
}
```

Listing 12.6 shows the code that creates a new `AppDomain` and executes code within it.

LISTING 12.6   Creating and Unloading an AppDomain

```
using System;
using System.Reflection;
using System.Collections.Generic;
using System.Text;

namespace AppDomainSample
{
class Program
{
static void Main(string[] args)
{
    Console.WriteLine("[{0}] Main Application starting.",
AppDomain.CurrentDomain.FriendlyName) ;
    Console.WriteLine("Main AppDomain has {0} Assemblies Loaded.",
        AppDomain.CurrentDomain.GetAssemblies().Length.ToString());

    AppDomain ad = AppDomain.CreateDomain("WorkerDomain");
    ad.SetData("THEVALUE", "How much wood could a woodchuck chuck...");
    SecondaryCode.Class1 remoteType =
        (SecondaryCode.Class1)ad.CreateInstanceFromAndUnwrap("SecondaryCode.dll",
        "SecondaryCode.Class1");

    remoteType.DoWork();
    AppDomain.Unload(ad);

    Console.ReadLine();

}
}
}
```

To prove that the work is being executed in a separate AppDomain, the output of the preceding code looks as follows:

```
[AppDomainSample.vshost.exe] Main Application starting.
Main AppDomain has 11 Assemblies Loaded.
[WorkerDomain] Doing some work.
[WorkerDomain] Domain-Wide value is How much wood could a woodchuck chuck...
This domain currently has 3 Assemblies loaded.
        mscorlib
        Microsoft.VisualStudio.HostingProcess.Utilities
        SecondaryCode
```

Working with AppDomains may not be something that you do every day as a .NET developer, but being armed with the knowledge of how they work and how they fit into the overall architecture of the framework will help you create better applications.

Summary

In this chapter, you learned about two core concepts within the .NET Framework: the assembly and the AppDomain. The assembly is the most basic logical unit of deployment in the framework. It contains a manifest that stores metadata about the assembly and its dependencies, as well as information about resources and types contained within the assembly. In addition, the assembly contains compiled MSIL code. Lastly, you learned about the AppDomain, the core logical unit of execution within the framework. All code runs within an AppDomain. By being aware of the AppDomain's presence, you can create code that exerts tight control over which assemblies are loaded and unloaded and how they are executed.

The combined knowledge of how both assemblies and AppDomains work as well as interoperate will give you a tremendous advantage as you move forward to learn about more complex aspects of the .NET Framework and C# 2.0.

CHAPTER **13**

COM and Windows Interoperability

Interoperability refers to the ability of managed and unmanaged code to invoke each other and exchange data in an organized and reproducible fashion. This chapter introduces you to the basic concepts behind code and data interoperability in C# and provides you with code samples for communicating with unmanaged code via COM or using Platform Invoke for accessing unmanaged DLLs such as the Win32 API.

Introduction to Interoperability in C#

Interoperability enables you to leverage your existing investment in unmanaged code going forward with the .NET Framework. Unmanaged code consists of all code that is not managed and executed within the Common Language Runtime (CLR). This includes COM objects, C++ DLLs, ActiveX controls, COM+ components, and any other code that is not compiled.

As you will find out, there are two different kinds of interoperability in C#, interoperability with unmanaged DLLs and interoperability with binary COM objects. Each is accomplished using a different technology, but some aspects of interoperability remain the same regardless of whether you're working with unmanaged DLLs or COM objects.

One of the things that remain the same is the need for reliable transfer of data. A common problem among developers before managed code was not being able to write code in one language that could communicate with code written in another language. For example, a C string was stored in memory as an array of bytes terminated by the ASCII null (\0) character. What is called a "Pascal string" is an array of bytes where the length of the string is stored in the 0th element of that array. As you can imagine, you can't simply pass a string from Pascal to C or from C to Pascal without modification.

The same is true of managed and unmanaged code. The process by which data is transferred between managed and unmanaged environments is called *marshaling*. This process is what converts .NET types into types that will be recognizable by unmanaged code and vice versa. As you'll see in the code samples that follow, there are tools that can determine how to marshal data from one environment to the other when reading and writing things like COM type libraries, but you still may need to know ahead of time how the data will need to be marshaled in order to consume unmanaged code from within .NET.

Using COM Objects from the .NET Framework

A COM object identifiesall of the interfaces, methods, and code that are exposed to outside code through the use of a type library. In order to use a COM object from within the .NET Framework, you need access to the type library so that the framework can create an appropriate wrapper around the COM object itself.

This wrapper is called a Runtime Callable Wrapper. These wrapper objects serve as proxies between the actual COM object and the C# client code. When you make a call on the wrapper, the call is to purely managed code and you send standard managed parameters like System.String, System.Int32, and so on. The wrapper then takes care of the marshaling of data between your managed code and the COM object and back again in order to process the results.

When you add a reference from within your project in Visual Studio 2005, a tab appears in the Add Reference dialog called COM, as shown in Figure 13.1.

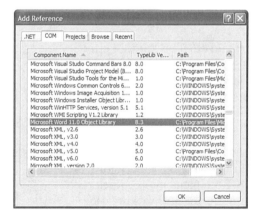

FIGURE 13.1   The COM tab in the Add Reference dialog.

When you add a reference to a COM object, Visual Studio will extract the type library and then create a pure managed class that interfaces directly with the COM code. This enables you to be insulated from the painful and repetitive details of things like reference counting and querying the interface list. You don't even really need to know what a vtable is to consume COM code from C#.

If you don't use Visual Studio to create the Runtime Callable Wrapper (RCW) around the intended COM object, you can use a command-line tool to exert more fine-grained control over the creation of the type library. This tool is called TLBIMP.EXE, and it is part of the .NET Framework SDK.

TLBIMP allows you to specify the namespace of the COM objects contained within the type library, as well as to indicate things like the output filename, the strong-name key pair with which to sign the wrapper Assembly, and whether or not the Assembly will be a Primary InterOp Assembly (discussed in the next section).

The following is an example that takes the Microsoft Fax control from a COM type library and imports it into a DLL called Microsoft.Fax.dll:

```
tlbimp fxsocm.dll /namespace:Microsoft.Fax /out:Microsoft.Fax.dll
```

For a complete list of all the options available in the TLBIMP tool, consult the .NET Framework SDK, or you can simply type TLBIMP in your Visual Studio Command Prompt with no arguments and the list of all options will be displayed.

Using Primary InterOp Assemblies

When consuming a vendor's COM objects, they will often have created Primary InterOp Assemblies. What this means is that the vendor has already done the work of creating the wrapper around the type library, and could possibly have done some extra work to make the library easier to use such as defining custom marshaling rules, and so on. When using a Primary InterOp Assembly (PIA), you reference the PIA the same way you would reference any other managed assembly (for example, you either browse to the file or you find it in the .NET tab of your Add Reference dialog).

Typically, a component or application vendor will install the PIAs when the application is installed to allow developers immediate access to the exposed components whether they're using COM or .NET. For example, when you install Microsoft Office 2003, you can include the .NET Programmability option for each of the Office products like Microsoft Word or Microsoft Outlook.

To create an application that consumes a PIA (or any other COM object, for that matter), first create your project. In this case, we'll be creating a console application because we haven't covered working with Windows Forms yet.

After you've created your project, right-click the project, choose References, and then add a reference. The Primary InterOp Assemblies for Microsoft Office are located in the Global Assembly Cache. You cannot reference Assemblies directly from the GAC; instead you have to reference them from their home directories and the system will use the GAC Assembly at runtime. The same is true for the PIAs.

In the COM tab, browse all the way down to the `Microsoft Word 11.0 Type Library` (assuming you have Office 2003 installed on your PC). Select it and click OK to add the reference to your application.

If there is a PIA for that type library in the GAC, Visual Studio will automatically reference that PIA and will not generate its own private Runtime Callable Wrapper Assembly. Because there is a PIA for Word, the reference in your application is a PIA reference to the assembly in the GAC. You can prove this by hovering the mouse over the `Path` property in the `Word` reference. You will see that it's pointing to a path beneath the `\windows\Assembly` directory, which is where all of the GAC Assemblies are stored.

When you have a reference to Microsoft Word, you can feel free to use the Word object model to manipulate Word documents, as shown in Listing 13.1.

LISTING 13.1   Creating a Word Document Using a COM PIA

```
using System;
using System.Runtime.InteropServices;
using System.Collections.Generic;
using System.Text;
using Microsoft.Office;
using Microsoft.Office.Core;
using Microsoft.Office.Interop;

using Microsoft.Office.Interop.Word;

namespace ComSample
{
class Program
{
static void Main(string[] args)
{
    try
    {
        object missing = Type.Missing;
        object fileName = @"C:\output.doc";
        string textToInsert =
"COM InterOp Using Primary InterOp Assemblies is Easy!";
        Document doc = new Document();

        object startPosition=0;
        object endPosition = 0;
        Range range = doc.Range(ref startPosition, ref endPosition);
        range.Text = textToInsert;
        doc.SaveAs(ref fileName,
ref missing, ref missing, ref missing, ref missing,
            ref missing, ref missing, ref missing, ref missing, ref missing,
```

LISTING 13.1   Continued

```
            ref missing, ref missing, ref missing, ref missing,
ref missing, ref missing);

    }
    catch (COMException ex)
    {
        Console.WriteLine("Failed to insert text into word document: " +
ex.ToString());
    }
}
}
}
```

When you run the preceding application, assuming Office 2003 is installed properly, you will get a Word document like the one shown in Figure 13.2.

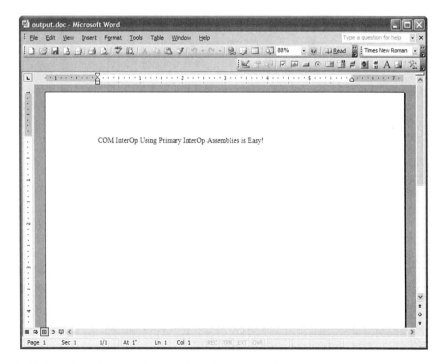

FIGURE 13.2   Word document created via COM InterOp.

What you might notice from the preceding sample is that there are a lot of object references and very little strong typing. This kind of code is typical of COM programming where the original COM API wasn't strictly typed and used a lot of open object references.

The idea behind this sample is that the mechanics of creating the Runtime Callable Wrapper around a COM type library aren't the difficult part: the difficult part is using the code exposed by the COM object to begin with.

Using .NET Classes from COM

Exposing your .NET classes to COM is easy. All you have to do is decorate the class, member, or assembly with the `ComVisible` attribute and that will be enough for the registration tool to determine what information to include in the type library when it is created. To follow along with the samples you are about to see, just create a new class library called `ComVisibleLibrary`.

The easiest way to expose your code to COM is to expose your entire assembly to COM. You can do this by manually editing your `AssemblyInfo.cs` file, or you can right-click your project, choose Properties, and then click the Assembly Information button. You will see a dialog like the one shown in Figure 13.3. Just check the checkbox indicating that the assembly is visible to COM.

FIGURE 13.3   Exposing an entire assembly to COM.

To test this out, change the `Class1.cs` class definition in the `ComVisibleLibrary` class library from the stock definition to the following:

```
using System;
using System.Runtime.InteropServices;
using System.Collections.Generic;
using System.Text;

namespace ComVisibleLibrary
{
[ComVisible(true)]
```

```
public class ComVisibleClass
{
public void DoSomething()
{
    Console.WriteLine("Hello from within a COM object");
}
}
}
```

After you have compiled an assembly that is visible to COM, it isn't automatically made available to COM clients. To make your code available to COM clients, you need to register your COM objects in the registry in a method similar to the way you would register your unmanaged C++ or VB6 COM objects. To register a .NET-hosted COM object, you use the regasm command-line SDK tool, as shown in the following example:

```
regasm ComVisibleLibrary.dll /tlb:ComVisibleLibrary.tlb
```

This will not only register your library with all the other COM objects on the machine, but it will also export a usable type library based on your assembly.

You might think that when you have a .NET COM object registered, you can consume that .NET COM object from managed code. If you try to reference your own COM object from within .NET, as shown in Figure 13.4, you will receive an error message indicating that you cannot create a COM reference to a .NET assembly. This is, of course, for a good reason. If there is a .NET assembly available, there is no need for managed code to use COM, as it would add a lot of unnecessary overhead.

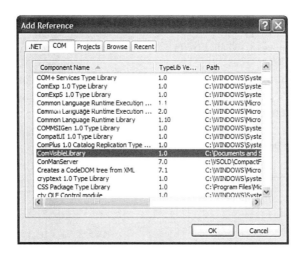

FIGURE 13.4   Referencing a COM object from a .NET project.

To reference your .NET-hosted COM object from an unmanaged language, simply use whatever tools you would normally use to consume unmanaged COM components to reference the .NET-hosted component. The COM-Callable Wrapper that .NET places between the unmanaged COM code and your managed code abstracts the fact that it is a .NET object. The benefit of this is that unmanaged COM clients can use .NET-hosted COM objects and regular/legacy COM objects interchangeably without having to do any additional work.

Accessing Code in Unmanaged DLLs

Accessing code in unmanaged DLLs is similar to accessing code using COM InterOp in that your code is reaching across AppDomain boundaries and from managed to unmanaged code. This type of access requires the SecurityPermission of UnmanagedCode. Don't confuse the phrase "unmanaged DLLs" with "COM DLLs." There is a distinct difference. The contents of a COM DLL conform to a specific binary format with specific functions used to query the list of interfaces exposed by the components contained within that DLL. A standard unmanaged DLL has no such standard.

A normal unmanaged DLL has no way of telling consuming clients what functions are available, so clients need to know ahead of time what functions they can use and the size, type, and direction of all function parameters.

You might remember way back in the days when you couldn't expose true object-oriented components—the best you could do was export functions within a DLL.

To tell the CLR that you are using a method from an unmanaged DLL instead of a native managed method, you decorate a method declaration with the DllImport attribute. This attribute takes the name of the DLL in which the CLR can find the associated extern function, which is declared right under the DllImport attribute, as shown in the following example:

```
[DllImport("myFuncs.dll")]
public static extern void MyFunction();
```

One of the most common uses for consuming functions from unmanaged DLLs is to gain direct access to the Win32 API functions. The code in Listing 13.2 shows you a common way of consuming unmanaged code in the Win32 API.

LISTING 13.2   Using DllImport

```
using System;
using System.Runtime.InteropServices;
using System.Collections.Generic;
using System.Text;

namespace Pinvoke1
{
class Program
{
```

LISTING 13.2 Continued

```
    [DllImport("user32.dll")]
    public static extern int MessageBox(IntPtr hwnd, String text,
String caption, uint type);

    static void Main(string[] args)
    {
        MessageBox(new IntPtr(0) ,
"Greetings from Platform Invoke", "Platform Invoke", 0);
    }
}
}
```

Before you decide to use unmanaged code directly, make sure that the same functionality is not already available within the .NET Framework. As mentioned earlier, the cost of marshaling data and invoking unmanaged code via wrappers is expensive.

You can also use some functionality that is new to .NET 2.0 to create an instance of a delegate that is really a function pointer to unmanaged code. You can then invoke that delegate instance just as you would any other managed delegate, as shown in Listing 13.3. This provides a far easier interface to calling unmanaged code such as the Win32 API than trying to do it "the hard way."

LISTING 13.3 Obtaining and Invoking Unmanaged Function Pointers

```
using System;
using System.Threading;
using System.Runtime.InteropServices;
using System.Collections.Generic;
using System.Text;

namespace PInvoke2
{
class Program
{
[DllImport("kernel32.dll")]
static extern IntPtr LoadLibrary(string dllName);

[DllImport("kernel32.dll")]
static extern IntPtr GetProcAddress(IntPtr hModule, string procName);

delegate int MessageBoxDelegate(IntPtr hwnd,
    [MarshalAs(UnmanagedType.LPWStr)]string text,
    [MarshalAs(UnmanagedType.LPWStr)]string caption,
    int type);
```

LISTING 13.3   Continued

```
static void Main(string[] args)
{
    IntPtr userApi = LoadLibrary("user32.dll");
    IntPtr msgBoxAddress = GetProcAddress(userApi,
"MessageBoxW"); // unicode (wide) message box
    MessageBoxDelegate mbd = (MessageBoxDelegate)
Marshal.GetDelegateForFunctionPointer(msgBoxAddress,
        typeof(MessageBoxDelegate));
    mbd(IntPtr.Zero, "Hello from Platform Invoke", "Platform Invoke", 0);

    DoSomething(mbd);
}

static void DoSomething(MessageBoxDelegate mbd)
{
    Thread.Sleep(200);
    mbd(IntPtr.Zero, "Work completed.", "Work Progress", 0) ;
}
}
}
```

There are a couple of new things in the preceding code. The first is the use of the
`Marshal.GetDelegateFromFunctionPointer()` method. This method is incredibly powerful. It allows you to take any function pointer represented by an `IntPtr` retrieved using
the `GetProcAddress` function from the `kernel32` library and turn that function pointer
into a *managed* delegate. After you've obtained the delegate from the function pointer,
you can create events based on that delegate, you can pass the delegate as a parameter to
other functions, and you can invoke the delegate directly.

There is also a new attribute in the preceding code, `MarshalAs`. This attribute allows you
to define, for any method parameter, how that data type should be marshaled. For
example, if you know that the function you want to call using a managed delegate takes
an `LPWSTR` (long-pointer to a wide Unicode string), you can marshal a managed string as
an `UnmanagedType.LPWStr`. The marshaler will then take care of the details of converting a
managed string into a `LPWSTR`.

Summary

Now that the .NET Framework has been around for over four years, the need to mix
managed and unmanaged code has greatly diminished. However, there are still plenty of
cases where developers need to access COM objects from within the .NET Framework as
well as a need to access .NET components from COM clients. In addition to COM

InterOperability, this chapter covered some of the details involved in working with unmanaged DLLs using the Platform Invoke features such as the DllImport attribute and the Marshal.GetDelegateFromFunctionPointer method that enable easy and straightforward access to unmanaged APIs such as the Win32 API. This chapter isn't the complete source of information on COM and Windows InterOp; however, after completing this chapter you should feel comfortable enough with the concepts and code surrounding Interoperability that you can make use of it in your own projects.

CHAPTER **14**

Code Access Security

Introduction to Code Access Security (CAS)

Code Access Security (hereafter referred to as CAS) is a feature of the CLR that protects resources from unauthorized access. Not too long ago, there was a lot of concern about ActiveX controls because when you trusted such a control, you trusted it *completely* and *implicitly*. That meant that if you downloaded and trusted an ActiveX control, that control could then access your hard drive, delete important files, or otherwise wreak havoc with your computer. Even worse, innocent ActiveX controls could be used as security holes through which malicious code could be injected onto your computer.

CAS provides a stock set of permissions and permission groups that can be used to restrict access to protected resources, giving the end user peace of mind knowing that no .NET code can ever access anything on his machine without his explicit permission. In addition, CAS includes the underlying plumbing that makes all of this possible. CAS is built directly into the .NET Framework so that it is impossible to write managed code that exists outside the boundaries defined by CAS. As you will see later in this chapter, end users and IT administrators alike can create and manage security policy for their computers or for an entire enterprise, choosing exactly which resources specific applications can access.

Permissions are enforced in such a way that code with limited security cannot make use of code with unrestricted security to gain access to protected resources. When the code demands a permission (illustrated in the Imperative and Declarative Security sections), the CLR walks backward along the call stack, examining the permission levels of each assembly in the stack. If the CLR finds an assembly that does not have the permission being requested by the code, the CLR will deny permission to everything on the call stack. This is illustrated in Figure 14.1.

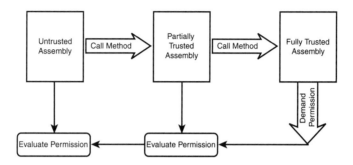

FIGURE 14.1   Using the call stack to ensure secure access to resources.

In this hypothetical scenario, untrusted code makes a call to an assembly that is partially trusted, which then in turn makes a call into a fully trusted assembly. In other scenarios, this could turn into a huge security hole and allow the untrusted code to do things like delete files in the system directory or make damaging changes to the registry. However, when the fully trusted assembly indicates that it needs a specific permission in order to continue, the CLR then walks backward along the call stack and examines the permission levels of all calling assemblies. If any of them have been denied the permission in question, so too will the fully trusted assembly, even though that assembly has the permission. This prevents exploiting fully trusted code for malicious purposes.

Using and Administering Security Policy

Before getting too deep into a discussion on how to use and administer the security policy, you should know what kinds of permissions can be granted and denied to your code and the code of other developers. Table 14.1 lists the various permission classes available within the .NET Framework. CAS is implemented in such a way that each permission is actually a class. You will see more about permission classes in the section on Imperative Security. Don't worry if you don't understand the purpose of each permission, as that will become clear when you work with the technology related to each permission, such as ASP.NET, networking, and so on.

TABLE 14.1   Code Access Permissions

Permission Class	Code Right or Privilege Granted
AspNetHostingPermission	Access to resources within ASP.NET applications.
DirectoryServicesPermission	Access information contained within Active Directory (System.DirectoryServices namespace).
DnsPermission	Ability to resolve host names using DNS.
EnvironmentPermission	Ability to read or write environment variables.

TABLE 14.1   Continued

Permission Class	Code Right or Privilege Granted
EventLogPermission	Ability to write entries to the system event log.
FileDialogPermission	Ability to access the file(s) indicated by a user in a File | Open dialog box.
FileIOPermission	Ability to read/write files or directories.
IsolatedStorageFilePermission	Ability to access Isolated Storage.
MessageQueuePermission	Ability to access MSMQ Queues.
OdbcPermission	Ability to access data sources via ODBC.
OleDbPermission	Ability to access data sources via OLE DB.
OraclePermission	Ability to access an Oracle database.
PerformanceCounterPermission	Ability to read/write system-level performance counters.
PrintingPermission	Ability to communicate with printers.
ReflectionPermission	Ability to obtain run-time type information via Reflection. Never give this permission to suspect or untrusted code.
RegistryPermission	Ability to access the system registry.
SecurityPermission	Ability to execute, assert permissions, call unmanaged code, and other security-related activities.
ServiceControllerPermission	Ability to start/stop/pause system services.
SocketPermission	Ability to communicate over the network using sockets.
SqlClientPermission	Ability to access SQL databases.
UIPermission	Ability to access user interface functionality, such as creating a Windows Form, and so on.
WebPermission	Ability to make or accept web connections.

In addition to the Code Access Security permissions shown in Table 14.1, there are also Identity Permissions and Role-Based Security Permissions. Identity permissions allow code to restrict the callers based on their identity rather than by permissions that have been explicitly granted. For example, you could choose to build an assembly that can only be invoked by other code that you have developed, or you can build an assembly that can only be invoked by code written by Microsoft.

Table 14.2 shows the list of Identity Permissions with which you can work.

TABLE 14.2   Identity Permissions

Permission	Identity Aspect
PublisherIdentityPermission	Refers to the publisher's digital signature.
SiteIdentityPermission	The site from which the code was downloaded.
StrongNameIdentityPermission	The strong-name identity of the assembly. A strong name consists of name, culture, version, and public key token.
URLIdentityPermission	The URL from which the code was downloaded.
ZoneIdentityPermission	The zone from which the code was downloaded.

One identity that is missing from the list in Table 14.2 is the identity of the *user* who is running the code. This is an extremely important aspect because the code needs to know the user who invoked it in order to determine if the user can access certain protected resources such as system files, files owned by other users, or even the network.

You can also write code that restricts the identity of the user who invoked the code based on that user's name or even his domain group/role membership using the `PrincipalPermission` class.

Code Access Security Administration

The .NET security policy is configured through the use of very specific XML files in certain locations. Although it might be useful for you to know the location and the format of these XML files, such information is beyond the scope of this chapter.

Instead, you can make use of some tools that ship with the .NET Framework that allow you to modify the security policy using a easy-to-use, friendly user interface.

The main tool for administering the .NET Framework security policy (as well as many other settings) can be found in your Administrative Tools control panel menu. It is called .NET Framework 2.0 Configuration. This application is displayed in Figure 14.2.

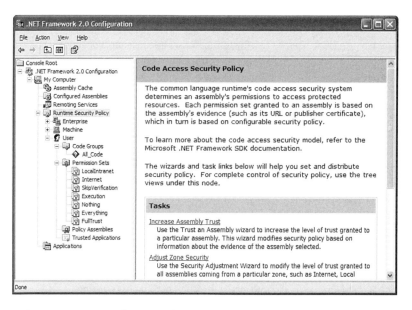

FIGURE 14.2   .NET Framework 2.0 configuration.

To administer the runtime security policy, click the Runtime Security Policy node. You will see the following task list in the right-hand content panel:

- Increase Assembly Trust—Allows you to browse for a specific assembly and increase the trust level of either that specific assembly, or all assemblies with the same public key (all assemblies produced by the same company).

- Adjust Zone Security—Modifies the security settings for each of the zones (Internet, Local Intranet, Trusted, My Computer, and so on).

- Evaluate Assembly—Examines an assembly and displays that assembly's effective permission levels, including permissions inherited from enterprise-level policies.

- Create Deployment Package—Takes an existing security policy level and places it in a Windows Installer (msi) package that can then be used to distribute the policy via Group Policy or Systems Management Server (SMS).

- Reset All Policy Levels—Restores the security policy for the computer to the original settings created by the .NET Framework 2.0's installation. This will remove all changes made since the framework was installed.

You will make use of this administration tool when creating some of the sample applications shown in the following two sections of the chapter dealing with Imperative and Declarative security.

Using Imperative Security

Imperative security is where you create instances of permissions and then use those instances to Demand() or Assert() those permissions, and much more. A demand is used when you want to tell the CLR that if there is code on the call stack that does not have the indicated permission level, a SecurityException will be thrown. An Assert is where your code asserts a specific permission level. All code on the stack *after* the assert will actually have the permission your code asserted, regardless of the assembly's original permission level. You must be *very* careful when asserting permissions because permission assertions can be used to create holes and exploits in CAS.

Creating an instance of a permission works just like creating an instance of any other class, as shown in the following code:

```
FileIOPermission filePerm = new FileIOPermission(FileIOPermissionAccess.Write,
    AppDomain.CurrentDomain.BaseDirectory);
```

The interesting thing to note here is that in order to create an instance of the permission, *the code itself must have that permission*. In other words, you must have a permission before you can demand that all callers on the stack prior to your code have that permission.

To create a sample that illustrates both Imperative Security programming as well as the demand of permissions on a call stack, start off by creating a new console application. In VS 2005, right-click the project, choose Properties, and then choose the Signing tab. Click the Sign This Assembly checkbox, and then choose New from the drop-down box to create a new strong name key pair. Then, create a Class Library project and perform the same steps to create a new SNK (strong-name key) file and sign the class library. Add a reference from the console application to the class library.

With this in place, you can go into the .NET Framework 2.0 Configuration tool in the Runtime Security Policy area. Create a code group that contains only the strong name for the console application, and a code group for the class library. The console application should have just Internet trust, whereas the class library should be fully trusted. Make sure that the console application's code group has a check next to "This policy level will only have the permissions from the permission set associated with this code group"; otherwise, the code group will not enforce any restrictions.

At this point, you should have two code groups at the machine level beneath the `All_Code` parent group. This is an excellent simulation of a partially trusted assembly attempting to call a fully trusted assembly. By default, the .NET Framework does *not* allow partially trusted assemblies to call code from fully trusted assemblies. To counteract this, you can add the assembly-level attribute `AllowPartiallyTrustedCallers` to the assembly as shown in the following code:

```
[assembly:AllowPartiallyTrustedCallers()]
```

Allowing Partially Trusted Callers

You should take extreme care when allowing partially trusted callers into your assembly. If your assembly is fully trusted, and you allow partially trusted callers without making the appropriate permission demands, your assembly can be used as a security exploit or hole. If you can't think of a reason why you would want a partially trusted caller to use your assembly, leave things as they are and don't worry about checking permissions explicitly, because your assembly can't be called without a fully trusted client. On the other hand, if you are creating an API that does high-permission things on behalf of low-permission clients (creating and manipulating proprietary files, for instance), you will need to allow partially trusted callers, and then *explicitly demand every permission you require* of calling clients either imperatively or declaratively.

With all this in place, change the `Class1` definition in your class library to the following code in Listing 14.1.

LISTING 14.1 `Class1.cs`

```csharp
using System;
using System.IO;
using System.Security;
using System.Security.Permissions;
using System.Collections.Generic;
using System.Text;

namespace MoreTrustedAssembly
{
public class Class1
{
public void CreateFile ()
{
```

LISTING 14.1   Continued

```
    try
    {
        FileIOPermission filePerm = new FileIOPermission(
FileIOPermissionAccess.Write,
        AppDomain.CurrentDomain.BaseDirectory);

        filePerm.Demand();

        FileStream fs = new FileStream("myfile.txt", FileMode.Create);
        fs.Write(ASCIIEncoding.ASCII.GetBytes("Hello World"), 0, 11);
        fs.Close();
    }
    catch (SecurityException e)
    {
        Console.WriteLine("Security exception occurred, {0}", e.ToString());
    }
}
}
}
```

The preceding code will create a text file. Without the permission demand, then the partially trusted caller would be able to create the file, even if the caller had no File I/O permission. Now modify the Program.cs from your console application to look like the code shown in Listing 14.2.

LISTING 14.2   Program.cs

```
using System;
using System.Security;
using System.Security.Permissions;
using System.Collections.Generic;
using System.Text;

namespace ImperativeSecurity
{
class Program
{
    static void Main(string[] args)
    {
        MoreTrustedAssembly.Class1 cls = new MoreTrustedAssembly.Class1();
        cls.CreateFile();
    }
}
}
```

With the current security settings, we get the following output when executing the code:

```
Security exception occurred, System.Security.SecurityException: Request for the
permission of type 'System.Security.Permissions.FileIOPermission, mscorlib, Vers
ion=2.0.0.0, Culture=neutral, PublicKeyToken=b77a5c561934e089' failed.
    at System.Security.CodeAccessSecurityEngine.Check(Object demand, StackCrawlMa
rk& stackMark, Boolean isPermSet)
    at System.Security.CodeAccessPermission.Demand()
    at System.AppDomainSetup.VerifyDir(String dir, Boolean normalize)
    at System.AppDomain.get_BaseDirectory()
    at MoreTrustedAssembly.Class1.CreateFile() in C:\Documents and Settings\Kevin
\My Documents\Writing\SAMS\C# 2005 Unleashed\14\Code\ImperativeSecurity\MoreTrus
tedAssembly\Class1.cs:line 17
The action that failed was:
Demand
The type of the first permission that failed was:
System.Security.Permissions.FileIOPermission
The Zone of the assembly that failed was:

MyComputer
```

Now all you need to do is go back to the code group you created for the console application and change the trust level from `Internet` to `FullTrust`. This will result in no output, and you'll see that the file `myfile.txt` has been created.

Enforcing Identity Imperatively

You can use the `PrincipalPermission` class to enforce identity constraints on the user. It is *extremely* important to remember that the user comes directly from `System.Threading.Thread.CurrentPrincipal`. You may notice that this value isn't set by default in a console application, so you have to do it manually. The code shown in Listing 14.3 shows how you can use the `PrincipalPermission` class not only to enforce specific constraints, but also to use it to create a union or intersection of multiple identity constraints, such as requiring that the caller be both part of the Administrators group and the Users group.

LISTING 14.3   Imperative Identity Enforcement

```
using System;
using System.Threading;
using System.Security;
using System.Security.Permissions;
using System.Collections.Generic;
using System.Text;

namespace ImperativeIdentity
{
```

LISTING 14.3 Continued

```
class Program
{
static void Main(string[] args)
{
    System.Security.Principal.WindowsIdentity wi =
 System.Security.Principal.WindowsIdentity.GetCurrent();
    Thread.CurrentPrincipal = new System.Security.Principal.WindowsPrincipal(wi);
    Console.WriteLine(wi.Name);
    Console.WriteLine(Thread.CurrentPrincipal.Identity.Name);
    PrincipalPermission pp = new PrincipalPermission(null, "Administrators", true);
    pp.Demand();

    PrincipalPermission pp2 = new PrincipalPermission(null, "Users", true);
    pp.Union(pp2).Demand();

    // now demand that the user be part of a fictitious group,
    ➥to cause a security exception
    try
    {
        PrincipalPermission pp3 = new PrincipalPermission(null,
"Secret Club Members");
        pp3.Demand();
    }
    catch (SecurityException e)
    {
        Console.WriteLine("You do not have access to the secret club.");
    }

    Console.ReadLine();
}
}
]
```

If you pass a `null` to the name parameter of the `PrincipalPermission` constructor, the permission will not require anything of the user's name. Note that this name requires the domain or computer name prefix. Additionally, if you pass a `null` to the Role parameter, the permission will not require any explicit role membership. If you pass a null to both name and role parameters and just pass `true` to the third parameter, the permission will indicate that the calling user simply needs to be authenticated.

Using Declarative Security

Imperative security involves manually creating an instance of a permission within a method to protect the entire method using that permission and declarative security involves the use of code attributes. Declarative security also allows the CLR and other developers to interrogate an application's security needs even if it's not running by examining the security attributes using Reflection.

When you apply a permission attribute to a method, the code within the method cannot be executed unless the stack-walk check performed by the CLR for the security permission evaluates to true.

The code in Listing 14.4 illustrates the use of a code attribute in declarative security. You can follow the routine from the previous imperative samples to restrict the trust level of this code so that the permission demand will fail.

LISTING 14.4   Declarative Security

```
using System;
using System.IO;
using System.Security;
using System.Security.Permissions;
using System.Collections.Generic;
using System.Text;

namespace DeclarativeDemo
{
class Program
{
[FileIOPermission(SecurityAction.Demand,
AllLocalFiles=FileIOPermissionAccess.Write)]
static void Main(string[] args)
{
    FileStream fs = new FileStream("myfile.txt", FileMode.Create);
    fs.WriteByte(65);
    fs.Close();
}
}
}
```

Refer to the list of permissions earlier in this chapter for the list of permission attributes that you can apply to methods and classes. Also note that you can apply the `PrincipalPermission` attribute to a method, effectively preventing anyone who does not pass the identity check from executing that method.

The first edition of this book showed you how you can create code that will block unwanted callers from using your public classes by using the `StrongNameIdentityPermissionAttribute` class declaratively. The idea is that you restrict the list of potential callers to only those callers that have that public key.

This works just fine in .NET 1.0 and .NET 1.1. However, in .NET 2.0, *any fully trusted assembly will satisfy **any** demand, including link demands for strong name identity permissions.*

In other words, if you decorate your method with a `StrongNameIdentityPermission` attribute like the one in the following code, you will *only be protecting yourself against partially trusted callers*.

```
[StrongNameIdentityPermission(SecurityAction.LinkDemand, PublicKey =
"00240000048000009400000006020000002400005253413100040000010001000D353D6DE2BE4BC" +
"60048A198B5509CF4DF479CBD614EB9FBE3FCDF68937E711630B6F21FA2E7C153F319D213
➥42B1C8C" +
"272647939816EEE90D011D8A17FDF6AA220B4C6F2043496277C1BC392EAD8F0BDEB9046
➥5A7EB9C47" +
"0E1C699ECD1A8E83C670CD74440B0033D7D4C74F7F6C9392F83DCD95054A8DAA57
➥5390CFC1FCF586BF")]
public class Class1
{
    public Class1() { }

    public string GetSecretWord()
    {
        return "SAMSPress";
    }
}
```

If you try to access this code from another C# application that you created on your own hard drive, it would work just fine, completely allowing access to the `GetSecretWord()` method, because code you create on your own machine is fully trusted by default.

If you *really* need to limit the access to your code, you can create an internal method, which will only be visible to code within your *assembly*, and then use the `InternalsVisibleToAttribute` class to indicate to what *assembly* you want to expose internal members and essentially create a "friend" *assembly*. The use of that attribute, however, is beyond the scope of this chapter.

Summary

This chapter has provided you with coverage of one of the core pieces of the .NET Framework: Code Access Security. CAS provides a mechanism for restricting access to protected and potentially dangerous resources like system files, regular files, network sockets, web sites, registry settings, and much more. CAS works intelligently to prevent the situation where an untrusted caller can exploit a fully trusted *assembly* to create a security hole. Although it is difficult to create this scenario, you can leave yourself open to attack and exploitation through the misuse of permission assertions and allowing partially trusted callers. Through the use of both imperative and declarative coding with CAS in mind, you can create secure applications that can access the resources they need while preventing malicious code from exploiting that same access.

CHAPTER 15

Cryptography and Data Protection

Protecting the data used and generated by your application has become exceedingly important in this day and age. The spread of viruses throughout the Internet is so commonplace that most consumers with PCs own some form of virus protection. When designing and building applications that will be exposed to the Internet, one of the primary concerns is security: preventing theft of valuable data as well as controlling damage from malicious attackers.

If you send data over a clear channel that anyone else can read, you can bet that someone is trying to glean some useful information out of the data you're sending. This chapter introduces you to the concepts and programming techniques that you will need to prevent people from reading your private data, as well as techniques that you can use to validate whether data has changed and whether data was sent from a legitimate source. All of this is possible with cryptography and data protection.

Introduction to Cryptography

Cryptography is the science of hiding information from prying eyes. A lot of people think that cryptography is a fairly new science, when in truth it has been around for a long time. As long as people have needed to send secret messages, people have needed cryptography. For example, Julius Caesar used a very simple cipher of shifting letters 19 characters to the right that eventually became known as the *Caesar cipher*. Encrypted information is no good to anyone if the intended recipient of the data doesn't know how to decrypt it. The balancing act of many cryptographic problems is that the sender of encrypted information needs to be able to allow the recipient to decrypt the data without allowing anyone else who might intercept the message to decrypt it as well.

This section discusses the various types of cryptographic tasks that are commonly performed. There is a mythos surrounding much of the science of cryptography that often intimidates developers into developing less secure applications. Hopefully this section will illustrate that you don't need a degree in applied mathematics to utilize the cryptographic tools available to you in the .NET Framework. The next few sections discuss different types of encryption. In a real-world scenario, the different types of encryption are often used in conjunction with each other to maximize data integrity.

Secret-Key Encryption

Secret-key encryption is a symmetric form of encryption. When using secret-key encryption, the same key that is used to encrypt the data is used to decrypt the data. This type of encryption is the fastest form of encryption, and is extremely efficient at encrypting large streams of data such as files, documents, long conversations, and so on.

Secret-key algorithms are also referred to as *block ciphers*. This is because the encryption is done one block at a time. The algorithm determines the size of the block (8, 16, 24, or 32 bytes). Block ciphers can potentially be reversed, however, because a block cipher will encrypt the same block of data the same way every time. So, for example, the same unencrypted block of 8 bytes will produce the same encrypted output every time. This consistency in output can allow a potential hacker to determine the encryption key. This is resolved through the use of an *initialization vector* (IV). The IV is used to help encrypt the first block of the stream, and then a portion of the first block is used to encrypt the second. This blending of blocks will prevent the same 8-byte block from creating predictable encryption results because each time that block is encrypted, it is being encrypted with a portion of the preceding block in the stream.

The downside to secret-key encryption is that both parties need to have access to the secret key.

Public-Key Encryption

Public-key encryption is an asymmetric encryption algorithm because the key used to encrypt the data is *not* the key used to decrypt the data. To exchange data between parties using public-key encryption, the sender will encrypt the data with the receiver's public key. Then the receiver can decrypt the data with her private key. The reverse also applies for sending a message in the other direction. In this way, the public key can be transmitted over any channel, regardless of how secure the channel might be.

Take a look at Figure 15.1. It shows how Joe's public key is used to encrypt messages sent *to* Joe, and Jane's public key is used to encrypt messages sent *to* Jane.

FIGURE 15.1   Public-key encryption.

The problem here is that public-key encryption is fairly slow, and is optimized for encrypting and decrypting small amounts of data. It doesn't work on large streams of data the way block ciphers (secret-key encryption) work, so using public-key encryption to send message after message would be impractical. A real-world scenario would involve Joe using Public Key Cryptography Standards (PKCS) to send Jane a shared secret that was generated for just that one conversation. Jane could then use her private key to decrypt the shared secret. When both parties have the shared secret, they can converse securely and efficiently without fear of anyone intercepting and decrypting their messages. This scenario is illustrated in the sequence diagram shown in Figure 15.2.

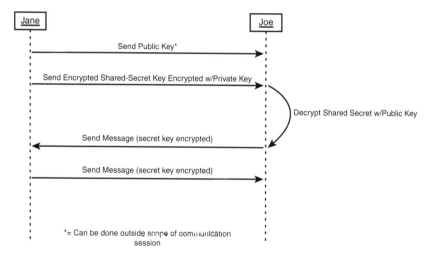

FIGURE 15.2   Real-world scenario combining PKCS with secret-key encryption.

Hashing

A *hash* is a reduced representation of a large amount of binary data. When a set of data is hashed, it is reduced to a fixed-length set of bytes. The benefit of a hash is that, when using an appropriate hashing algorithm, it is statistically impossible to have two sources of data produce the same hash value. This means that for any arbitrarily long set of data, there is only one unique hash value that represents that set of data.

You can detect if data has been tampered with using hashes. If you send someone a message as well as the hash of that message, she can then hash that message on her end using the same hashing algorithm, and compare it against the transmitted hash. If the two hash values are identical, you can be assured that the message has not been tampered with. However, if the hashes don't match, the message has been modified since it was transmitted.

This isn't all that secure. If someone intercepts the original message, they could just as easily rehash the altered message and send it along to the recipient who will validate the message as unmodified. In reality, the hash is usually encrypted using PKCS such that only the recipient can decrypt the hash using his private key. This prevents the message (and the hash) from being tampered with.

The encryption of hashes leads me to another extremely common task in cryptography: digital signatures.

Digital Signatures

Forgery aside, a human signature is evidence that a document was signed by the person who claims to be the originator. So, when the document ends with "Sincerely, Kevin Hoffman," and is followed by my signature, that is reasonable proof that I am indeed the one who wrote the document.

The same can be said of an electronic document or message. You can "sign" that message with a digital signature that serves as proof that you are the one who created that document.

When you digitally sign a message, the first thing you do is create a hash of the message. This hash is then encrypted using your *private key*. This allows anyone with your public key to decrypt the hash, rehash the message on their machine, and compare the two to validate the authenticity of the signature. You encrypt the hash using your private key because you do not want to restrict the list of people who can verify the authenticity of your signature. Therefore, anyone with your public key should be able to verify that a message came from you. Likewise, you should be able to verify the authenticity of any messages sent by people for whom you have public keys.

Using Secret-Key Encryption

Secret-key encryption, also referred to as *symmetric encryption,* is designed to work on large amounts of data. As such, symmetric encryption code works on streams of data as opposed to arrays of bytes. When you wrap a stream of regular data inside a specialized encryption stream called a `CryptoStream`, data is encrypted on the fly as it is placed into the stream. The same is true of decryption; data is decrypted on the fly as it is read from the stream.

As mentioned earlier, in symmetric encryption the key used to encrypt the data is the same key that is used to decrypt the data. As a result, the safety of the key is paramount. If someone were to obtain your key, not only could he decrypt your private data, but he could encrypt his own data as if he were you.

Also, remember that to properly encrypt blocks of data using symmetric encryption, you need an Initialization Vector (IV) to allow the encryption algorithm to encrypt blocks with partial data from previous blocks to reduce the predictability of output.

The code in Listing 15.1 shows the use of symmetric encryption and decryption to encrypt a message into a binary file on disk and then use another CryptoStream to read from the encrypted file.

LISTING 15.1   Symmetric Encryption and Decryption

```
using System;
using System.IO;
using System.Security;
using System.Security.Cryptography;
using System.Collections.Generic;
using System.Text;

namespace SymmetricEncryption
{
class Program
{
static void Main(string[] args)
{
    RijndaelManaged rmCrypto = new RijndaelManaged();
    // these keys are completely artificial. In a real-world scenario,
    // your key and IV will be far less obivous :)
    byte[] key = { 0x01, 0x02, 0x03, 0x04, 0x05, 0x06, 0x07, 0x08,
        0x09, 0x10, 0x11, 0x12, 0x13, 0x14, 0x15, 0x16 };
    byte[] IV = { 0x01, 0x02, 0x03, 0x04, 0x05, 0x06, 0x07, 0x08,
        0x09, 0x10, 0x11, 0x12, 0x13, 0x14, 0x15, 0x16 };

    string clearMessage =
"This string will be encrypted symmetrically and decrypted " +
        "using the same key.";

    FileStream fs = new FileStream("encrypted.dat", FileMode.Create);
    CryptoStream cs = new CryptoStream(
        fs, rmCrypto.CreateEncryptor(key, IV), CryptoStreamMode.Write);
    cs.Write(System.Text.ASCIIEncoding.ASCII.GetBytes(clearMessage),
        0, clearMessage.Length);
    cs.Close();
    fs.Close();

    // open the encrypted file using a different stream to show
    // the symmetric decryption.
```

15

LISTING 15.1   Continued

```
FileStream fs2 = new FileStream("encrypted.dat", FileMode.Open);
CryptoStream cs2 = new CryptoStream(
    fs2, rmCrypto.CreateDecryptor(key, IV), CryptoStreamMode.Read);
byte[] decryptedData = new byte[fs2.Length];
cs2.Read(decryptedData, 0, (int)fs2.Length);
cs2.Close();
fs2.Close();
Console.WriteLine("Decrypted Message:\n{0}",
    System.Text.ASCIIEncoding.ASCII.GetString(decryptedData));

Console.ReadLine();
}
}
}
```

Using Public-Key Encryption

Working with public-key encryption isn't quite as hard as it seems. The task of encrypting and decrypting data in a PKCS environment all boils down to one thing: *key management*. You need to know where your keys are, and you need to make sure that they are protected before you can reliably use public-key encryption.

One of the most common tasks in PKCS encryption is the generation and storage of new keys. Fortunately, the RSA cryptographic service provider will create the public/private key pair automatically for you if you don't supply one. RSA is named for the three people who invented the cryptographic algorithm: Ron **R**ivest, Adi **S**hamir, and Leonard **A**dleman.

You definitely don't want your private key lying around in a simple file on your hard drive, because then all data encrypted with that key becomes just as vulnerable as your hard drive (which is pretty vulnerable).

To solve this problem, Windows allows you to make use of *key containers*. A key container is a secure place to store your key, and you are the only one who has access to that container. Even an administrator with full access to the hard drive will be unable to obtain the key from your key container (unless they have your login and password, of course).

To store your key pair in a container, you need to make use of the `CspParameters` class. This class maintains a list of parameters that are passed to a cryptographic service provider upon instantiation. One of these parameters is a property called `KeyContainerName`. This name can be anything you choose, but make sure it's something that your application can reproduce, because if you forget the container name, you will lose the key pair.

The following few lines of code will create an instance of the `CspParameters` class, indicate the name of the key container, and instantiate the RSA crypto provider. If this is the first time these lines of code have been executed, a new key pair will be generated and placed in the container:

```
CspParameters csp = new CspParameters();
csp.KeyContainerName = "SAMSContainer";

RSACryptoServiceProvider rsa = new RSACryptoServiceProvider(csp);

// perform encryption/decryption operations
```

Each time the code instantiates an RSA crypto provider with the same container name, the code will reuse the existing key pair. Note that another application, logged on under another user, will *not* be able to read the key information, even if the container name matches. For more information about Windows key containers, you can look up the Cryptography topic in the MSDN documentation at http://msdn.microsoft.com.

To demonstrate how to send an encrypted message from one person (or application) to another, I'll start with Jane and John Doe. Jane creates an instance of the RSA provider, and saves her key in an XML file using the `ToXmlString()` method on the `RSACryptoServiceProvider` class. The contents of this XML file aren't all that pretty to look at, but if you're interested you can see the `JanesKey.xml` file with the code accompanying this book.

As mentioned before, to send a message *to* Jane, you need to encrypt it with Jane's public key. So, to create an application that simulates this process, the application will read Jane's public key from the `JanesKey.xml` file, and use that information to encrypt a message to her, as shown in the following example:

```
RSACryptoServiceProvider rsa = new RSACryptoServiceProvider();
StreamReader sr = File.OpenText(@"..\..\..\..\JanesKey.xml");
string rsaXml = sr.ReadToEnd();
sr.Close();
rsa.FromXmlString(rsaXml);

string messageToJane = "Hey Jane, this is John. How are things?";

byte[] encrypted = rsa.Encrypt(
System.Text.ASCIIEncoding.ASCII.GetBytes(messageToJane), false);

FileStream fs = new FileStream(@"..\..\..\..\MessageToJane.dat", FileMode.Create);
fs.Write(encrypted, 0, encrypted.Length);
fs.Close();
```

The code in this sample creates an RSA provider, which loads Jane's public key using the `FromXmlString` method. Then the message is encrypted into an array of bytes, which is then stored in a file called `MessageToJane.dat`. If you run this sample on your own, you'll

15

see that the encrypted file takes up 128 bytes, far more than the plain text version of the message.

To continue the sample, we need to switch to Jane's perspective. She will be attempting to decrypt John's message with her *private* key. So she'll need to load her key either from a container or from an XML file with the FromXmlString method. For simplicity in this sample, she'll load it from XML, as shown in the following example:

```
StreamReader sr = File.OpenText(@"..\..\..\..\JanesKey.xml");
string janesKey = sr.ReadToEnd();
sr.Close();

RSACryptoServiceProvider rsa = new RSACryptoServiceProvider();
rsa.FromXmlString(janesKey);

FileStream fs = new FileStream(@"..\..\..\..\MessageToJane.dat", FileMode.Open);
byte[] encrypted = new byte[fs.Length];
fs.Read(encrypted, 0, (int)fs.Length);
byte[] decrypted = rsa.Decrypt(encrypted, false);
fs.Close();
Console.WriteLine(System.Text.ASCIIEncoding.ASCII.GetString(decrypted));
Console.ReadLine();
```

There are only a few steps in the preceding code. First, Jane's key pair is loaded from the XML file (this is ordinarily a *bad* practice...use key containers for safe storage of key pairs) and then John's encrypted message is loaded into a byte array. That byte array is then decrypted using Jane's private key, and the decrypted message is displayed on the console.

Working with Hashes and Digital Signatures

Hashes and digital signatures work hand in hand in order to give your code the ability to sign data as well as verify that the data has not been tampered with.

The sequence of events typically works like this:

- Your application produces data that needs to be transmitted to another location or to be read by another application.

- Using your private key, your application creates an encrypted signature from a hash of the data to be transmitted.

- The data payload, containing both the data and the encrypted signature, is transmitted to a remote location and/or read by another application.

- The other application decrypts the hashed signature using the sender's public key, and then compares the decrypted hash against a hash that the other application computed on its own using the same hash algorithm. If the computed hash matches the decrypted hash, the other application can be sure that the data has not been tampered with.

Let's take a look at the first half of the process, the hashing of data and the creation of a signature from that hash:

```
string verifiableMesage = "It was the best of times, it was the worst of times.";
SHA1Managed sha = new SHA1Managed();
byte[] hashValue =
    sha.ComputeHash(System.Text.ASCIIEncoding.ASCII.GetBytes(verifiableMesage));

// now that we have a hash, create a signature based on the hash
// re-use Jane's key.
StreamReader sr = File.OpenText(@"..\..\..\..\JanesKey.xml");
string janesKey = sr.ReadToEnd();

RSACryptoServiceProvider rsa = new RSACryptoServiceProvider();
rsa.FromXmlString(janesKey);

RSAPKCS1SignatureFormatter sigFormatter = new RSAPKCS1SignatureFormatter(rsa);
sigFormatter.SetHashAlgorithm("SHA1");
byte[] signedHash = sigFormatter.CreateSignature(hashValue);

// write the signed hash to disk
FileStream fs = new FileStream(@"..\..\..\..\signedHash.dat", FileMode.Create);
fs.Write(signedHash, 0, signedHash.Length) ;
fs.Close();
```

Next, we'll need to write some code that reads the signed hash from the data file, computes its own hash, and does a comparison to verify the authenticity of the data. The following is the code contained in a console application that does this:

```
string verifiableMesage = "It was the best of times, it was the worst of times.";
string wrongMessage = "It was the best of times it was the worst of times";

SHA1Managed sha = new SHA1Managed();
byte[] verifiableMessageHash = sha.ComputeHash(
    System.Text.ASCIIEncoding.ASCII.GetBytes(verifiableMesage));
byte[] wrongMessageHash = sha.ComputeHash(
    System.Text.ASCIIEncoding.ASCII.GetBytes(wrongMessage));

// note that we never manually decrypt the sig, that's done by the sig verifier
FileStream fs = new FileStream(@"..\..\..\..\signedHash.dat", FileMode.Open);
byte[] fileHash = new byte[fs.Length];
fs.Read(fileHash, 0, (int)fs.Length) ;
fs.Close();

// get jane's key so we can decrypt the hash
StreamReader sr = File.OpenText(@"..\..\..\..\JanesKey.xml");
```

```
string janesKey = sr.ReadToEnd();
sr.Close();


RSACryptoServiceProvider rsa = new RSACryptoServiceProvider();
rsa.FromXmlString(janesKey);


RSAPKCS1SignatureDeformatter sigDeformatter =
new RSAPKCS1SignatureDeformatter(rsa);
sigDeformatter.SetHashAlgorithm("SHA1");
if (sigDeformatter.VerifySignature(verifiableMessageHash, fileHash))
{
    Console.WriteLine("The real message is verified as untampered.") ;
}
if (sigDeformatter.VerifySignature(wrongMessageHash, fileHash) == false)
{
    Console.WriteLine("The fake message is verified as fake.");
}
else
{
    Console.WriteLine("This should statistically never happen.");
}


Console.ReadLine();
```

The first thing that this code does is create hashes from two different strings. One string is the original and valid data, whereas the other string is missing a comma. If all that I've said about hashing and signatures is true, the missing comma should cause a signed hash validation to fail, simulating data that has been tampered with.

Next the key is loaded from the XML file (in a real-world scenario, the key would probably be coming from an OS-level key container). A signature deformatter is then loaded based on the SHA-1 hashing algorithm.

Finally, two comparisons are made: one comparison against the legitimate hash, and one against the hash that simulates tampered data. When we run the application, the output confirms that the digital signature is doing its job:

```
The real message is verified as untampered.
The fake message is verified as fake.
```

Using the Data Protection API (DPAPI)

A fairly common technique among teachers is to show the student how to do something the hard way, to make sure they understand the mechanics of what is going on, and then when they understand that, show them an easier way of doing things.

The Data Protection API (DPAPI) is no different. It provides a simplified API for protecting and unprotecting your data while removing the burden of explicitly generating and managing encryption keys from the developer.

When working with data protection, you need three things:

- Data—The data that you want to encrypt or decrypt.

- Entropy—Put simply, this is a random set of bytes used to add a measure of unpredictability to the encrypted output of your protected data. This is not required, but can come in handy.

- Protection Scope—When working directly with the cryptographic service providers, there is no sense of scope. With DPAPI, you can choose the scope in which you want the data protected. This means that you can choose to allow only a specific user to decrypt encrypted data or anyone on the machine. The following is a list of possible values for the protection scope:

     CurrentUser—Data is associated with the user. Only code being executed by or on behalf of the user can decrypt the data.

     LocalMachine—The data is protected at the machine level. Remote attempts to access the data will fail. This option is common in server-side enterprise applications.

One thing to keep in mind about the data protection API is that it is not designed for sending secure data from a source to a specific destination. It is designed to allow your application to encrypt data so that the data stored by your application will not be compromised. If you protect data using DPAPI, and then send the data to someone else, they will have no way of decrypting that data.

Both PKCS and DPAPI are extremely powerful encryption tools, but each one has a specific purpose. Knowing when to use PKCS and when to use DPAPI can save you countless hours of rewriting and troubleshooting.

Listing 15.1 is an illustration of how to encrypt and decrypt information using the Data Protection API. Run the code several times to convince yourself that the protection isn't session based and will work every time the protection scope matches the scope of the protected data.

When writing code with the Data Protection API, there are two different kinds of protection that you can use. You can choose to work with protected memory, which turns any array whose length is a multiple of 16 bytes into unreadable gibberish. When you lift the protection on that array, it becomes readable again. The main benefit of this is that when the array is protected, there is nowhere in memory that contains a decrypted copy of that data. This means that malicious attackers examining the memory used by your application or even trying to reverse engineer your application will not be able to locate the protected data in memory.

15

The second mode of working with the Data Protection API is more traditional. You pass it an array that you want encrypted, an entropy array, and a protection scope. As a return value, you are given an encrypted array of bytes. This method is more suitable for encrypting streams of data, files, and other longer strings. There is also no restriction that the protected data's size be a multiple of 16 as there is with memory protection.

The code in Listing 15.2 illustrates both memory protection and data protection using the Data Protection API.

LISTING 15.2 Memory and Data Protection Using DPAPI

```
using System;
using System.Security;
using System.Security.Cryptography;
using System.Collections.Generic;
using System.Text;

namespace DPAPIDemo
{
class Program
{
static void Main(string[] args)
{
    string messageToProtect = "aaaabbbbccccdddd";
    byte[] messageArray =
System.Text.ASCIIEncoding.ASCII.GetBytes(messageToProtect);

    ProtectedMemory.Protect(messageArray, MemoryProtectionScope.SameLogon);

    // this should print out 16 bytes of garbage
    Console.WriteLine(System.Text.ASCIIEncoding.ASCII.GetString(messageArray)) ;

    ProtectedMemory.Unprotect(messageArray, MemoryProtectionScope.SameLogon);

    // now it should print just fine
    Console.WriteLine(System.Text.ASCIIEncoding.ASCII.GetString(messageArray));

    // protect data that will be used in a stream, in a file, etc
    string fileMessage = "The purple turtle flies coach at dawn...";
    byte[] fileMsgArray = System.Text.ASCIIEncoding.ASCII.GetBytes(fileMessage);

    // some array of bytes for introduced entropy
    byte[] entropy = { 0, 1, 3, 5, 7, 9 };
    byte[] protectedMessage = ProtectedData.Protect(
        fileMsgArray, entropy, DataProtectionScope.CurrentUser);
```

LISTING 15.2   Continued

```
    Console.WriteLine("Protected byte array:") ;
    Console.WriteLine(
System.Text.ASCIIEncoding.ASCII.GetString(protectedMessage));

    byte[] clearMessage = ProtectedData.Unprotect(
        protectedMessage, entropy, DataProtectionScope.CurrentUser);
    Console.WriteLine("Unprotected/Decrypted Data:");
    Console.WriteLine(ASCIIEncoding.ASCII.GetString(clearMessage));


    Console.ReadLine();
}
}
}
```

Make sure that when you create this application, you also add a reference to the
System.Security assembly; otherwise, you won't be able to use the ProtectedMemory class
or the DataProtection class.

When you compile and run the application, you will get output that looks like the output
shown in Figure 15.3.

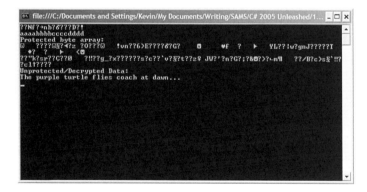

FIGURE 15.3   Output from the data protection sample.

Summary

Today, virtually all application developers have to worry about the security of their data
in some fashion. This chapter provided you with an introduction into the world of cryptography as it applies to protecting valuable data within your applications. This chapter
covered the concepts behind public-key encryption, secret-key encryption, hashing,
digital signatures, and using the Data Protection API to protect in-memory structures as
well as large amounts of data like streams.

15

After reading this chapter, you should now be able discuss the various benefits and drawbacks of each type of encryption, when those types should be used in real-world examples, and you should have enough information to be able to create the code for your own secure data solution.

CHAPTER 16

Optimizing Your .NET 2.0 Code

As you will see throughout this book, you can increase the performance and scalability of Windows Forms, Web Forms, and web services in many ways. This chapter focuses on the things that you can do at the Framework level that can help optimize any code that you write, regardless of the target platform. You will see some habits that are easy to adopt that will help keep your application running smoothly and quickly, as well as a tool that can be used to speed up the application launch process and a tool that can be used to analyze an existing code base and point out a wide variety of potential performance problems.

Understanding Boxing and Unboxing

Early in this book, you learned about the difference between value types and reference types. A *value type* is a type in which the corresponding data is always contained within the variable of that type and is passed as method parameters on the stack. A *reference type* corresponds to what developers of unmanaged code might refer to as a pointer. A variable that represents an instance of a reference type doesn't contain the raw data. Rather, it contains information about where to find the raw data within the managed heap.

Every time a method is invoked, the stack is built and then deconstructed in order to get at the parameter data. As a result of this, as a general rule, developers should avoid creating value types that are very large, to keep stack operations running as quickly as possible.

One aspect of value and reference types that hasn't been mentioned yet is the concept of boxing and unboxing. When a value type needs to be treated as though it were a reference type, the value type is Boxed.

Boxing is the process by which the data for a value type is placed on the managed heap and then a pointer to that data is used as the contents of the newly created reference type instance. For example, the following lines of code illustrate the use of boxing:

```
object o = 21; // boxing operation occurs, "21" becomes reference
int z = 42; // no boxing here, all value type operations
object y = z; // boxing operation occurs, "z" becomes reference
```

The process of boxing a variable takes time because new space needs to be allocated on the managed heap for the variable that would otherwise remain in the relatively fast stack. Then, when the boxed variable is no longer needed, that same space needs to be reclaimed by the garbage collector, further reducing performance.

Conversely, when a boxed value type (value contained in a reference) needs to again be treated as a value type, the value needs to be retrieved from the managed heap and placed on the stack. This process is called *unboxing* and also incurs an overhead cost.

If you write your code in such a way that you avoid boxing and unboxing, *especially* within loops, you will find that your code performs faster. Although the occasional use of boxing or unboxing won't drag your application down, large loops that use boxing inside frequently invoked methods in large, multiuser applications can definitely have a negative impact on performance.

The code in Listing 16.1 uses the Ticks property of a DateTime instance to show the difference in execution time for a 300,000-iteration loop with and without boxing. On the author's machine, the boxing loop took 156,250 ticks, whereas the loop that did not use boxing took place in less than 1 tick. Although that still is a small amount of time on its own, when you attempt to scale that out to a method that is being invoked thousands of times per minute by thousands of users on a large application, the difference in time will become quite noticeable.

LISTING 16.1   Timing Boxing Operations

```
using System;
using System.Collections.Generic;
using System.Text;

namespace ConsoleApplication1
{
class Program
{
static void Main(string[] args)
{
    // boxing loop
```

LISTING 16.1 Continued

```
long before = System.DateTime.Now.Ticks;
for (int x = 0; x < 300000; x++)
{
    // boxing incurred
    object o = x;
}
long after = System.DateTime.Now.Ticks;
Console.WriteLine("Ticks for boxing loop : " +
    (after - before).ToString());


// loop with no boxing
before = System.DateTime.Now.Ticks;
for (int y = 0; y < 300000; y++)
{
    // no boxing incurred
    int z = y;
}
after = System.DateTime.Now.Ticks;
Console.WriteLine("Ticks for non-boxing loop : " +
    (after-before).ToString());

Console.ReadLine();
}
}
}
```

The general rule of thumb is to treat value types as value types unless you absolutely cannot avoid it. In previous versions of the .NET Framework, there were many scenarios where an int would have to be passed as an object in order for a class to be able to work with multiple data types. You can use generics in these situations so that, at runtime, the value type will be treated as a value type and will not incur the boxing overhead.

Using Proper String Manipulation Techniques

Within the .NET Framework, strings are immutable. This means that a string cannot be changed after it has been created. For example, suppose you create a string as follows:

```
String x = "Hello World";
```

The string "Hello World" appears on the managed heap and x contains a reference to that string. To optimize the CLR, strings were made immutable. Examine the following three lines of code:

```
String x = "Hello World";
x += " from ";
x += " C# 2005 Unleashed by SAMS Publishing";
```

Developers with experience in other languages might expect that the x variable is initialized with "Hello World" and then is dynamically expanded twice to first add " from " and then add the remaining string literal.

Here's what actually happens: Three different strings are created on the managed heap, and each time a new one is created, the x variable shifts to point to the newly created string. Because strings are immutable, any change to an existing string creates a new string stored on the heap. Interim strings that are out of scope (such as " from ") will *eventually* be collected by the garbage collector. Figure 16.1 illustrates what happens to the managed heap as a string is concatenated using the += operator.

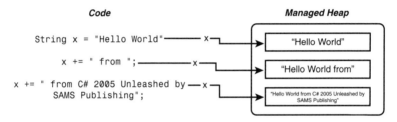

FIGURE 16.1   String concatenation on the managed heap.

To avoid the problems that arise from repeated string concatenation using the += operator, you should instead use the StringBuilder class, as shown in the following example:

```
StringBuilder sb = new StringBuilder();
sb.Append("Hello World");
sb.Append(" from ");
sb.Append("C# 2005 Unleashed by SAMS Publishing");
```

The StringBuilder class also has an AppendFormat method that allows you to format a string at the same time it is being appended, which comes in handy. To access the string within the StringBuilder, simply use the ToString() method as shown:

```
Console.WriteLine(sb.ToString());
```

Efficient Loop Construction

Performance problems that might appear small or insignificant can swell to application-crippling sizes when those problems are executed within a loop or are executed by hundreds or thousands of users simultaneously. Loops act like a magnifying glass for small performance problems and can make them considerably larger.

One of the most common loop mistakes is in invoking an additional cost during loop iterations. Take the following loop for example:

```
for (int x=0; x < myObject.GetItems().Count; x++)
{
    // perform task
}
```

There are two main problems with the preceding loop:

- The maximum bound of the loop could be changed by the code within the loop, creating unpredictable results. For example, if the code within the loop adds an item to the list of items returned by myObject.GetItems(), the loop could end up being infinite or running for longer than expected.

- The call to GetItems() could potentially take a long time. Placing this call within the for statement invokes this method during every single loop iteration. If GetItems() not only takes a long time to execute but returns a large number of items, the loop could take an extremely long time to execute.

A better way to rewrite the preceding loop would be to place the GetItems() call at the beginning of the loop to guarantee consistency in the list of items as well as to incur the overhead cost of the method only once rather than once per iteration:

```
List<CustomObject> list = myObject.GetItems();
int maxBound = list.Count;
for (int x=0; x < maxBound; x++)
{
    // perform task on 'list' variable
}
```

Even accessing the Count property of a list still costs more than accessing a previously defined int variable. The preceding code might have more lines than the first example, but this code runs faster. By pulling expensive calculations out of the loop and performing them before the loop begins, you incur the cost only once instead of once per iteration. In terms of computer science notation, the cost of the GetItems() method is "O(N)" (operational cost is directly related to the number of items in the loop) when placed inside the loop, and "O(1)" (operational cost only incurred once) when placed before the loop.

Speeding Up Application Start Times

When a .NET application is first loaded, the JIT (Just-in-Time) compiler takes the MSIL (Microsoft Intermediate Language) code that is contained within the assembly and compiles that code into a native image. That native image is then stored in the native image cache to be used for subsequent application executions so that the JIT step can be skipped.

When you use the Microsoft CLR Native Image Generator tool (`NGen.exe`), it will manually perform the initial native image generation so that the application will load faster the first time it is executed. When you run the Ngen tool against a .NET application, you get output that looks something like this:

```
Microsoft (R) CLR Native Image Generator - Version 2.0.50727.42
Copyright (C) Microsoft Corporation 1998-2002. All rights reserved.
Installing assembly C:\Documents and Settings\Kevin\My Documents\Writing\SAMS\C#
 2005 Unleashed\16\Code\ProfileDemo\ProfileDemo\bin\Debug\profiledemo.exe
Compiling 1 assembly:
    Compiling assembly C:\Documents and Settings\Kevin\My Documents\Writing\SAMS
\C# 2005 Unleashed\16\Code\ProfileDemo\ProfileDemo\bin\Debug\profiledemo.exe ...
ProfileDemo, Version=1.0.0.0, Culture=neutral, PublicKeyToken=null <debug>
```

Application developers often include execution of `Ngen.exe` upon initial installation to generate the native image and place it in the native image cache so that the application will start more quickly.

Code Profiling Using the Performance Wizard

Code profilers are an often-underrated tool when in fact they can be one of the most powerful tools a developer can possess. Profilers sift through the code and record thousands of data points that are then turned into useful information for the developer. For example, code profilers can show you which method took the most time to execute within the entire application, what variable consumed the most memory, and which operations were the most costly. When developers get into the habit of running a profiler on their code, they will be able to find and correct many performance problems that might not otherwise be immediately obvious.

Visual Studio 2005 has several editions that come with a built-in code performance analyzer. You can get to this performance analyzer by launching the Performance Wizard from the Performance Tools menu under the Tools menu.

To see the Performance Wizard in action, first create some code that does something that is quite obviously a performance problem. The code in Listing 16.2 represents a quick console application that will definitely cause some blatant results in a code profiler.

LISTING 16.2   Inefficient Use of String Concatenation and Looping

```
using System;
using System.Collections.Generic;
using System.Text;

namespace ProfileDemo
{
class Program
{
```

LISTING 16.2   Continued

```
static void Main(string[] args)
{
    // load up a large sample set of data.
    List<string> strList = new List<string>();
    for (int x = 0; x < 10000; x++)
    {
        // inefficiently use string contact
        string entry = "Hello";
        entry += " ";
        entry += x.ToString();
        strList.Add("Hello " + x.ToString());
    }

    // perform a fairly inefficient loop
    string src = string.Empty;
    for (int y = 0; y < strList.Count; y++)
    {
        // really bad string concatenation
        src += strList[y];
    }
}
}
}
```

You have already seen that string concatenation within a loop can cause a massive waste of space on the heap. After running the profiler, you will see *exactly* how much space is wasted. To launch the profiler, first build the application and then launch the Performance Wizard from the Performance Tools menu. At the prompt, select the default project for the target (the project you created for this sample) and choose the Sampling method of analysis. This will create a new performance session. To run the analysis and get results, click the Launch button in the Performance Explorer panel that appeared after creating the session.

When the analysis is complete, a new file with the extension .vsp will be added to your solution. This file is a report that contains several tabs.

Click on the Call Tree tab. From this tab, shown in Figure 16.2, you can see that string concatenation accounted for roughly 96% of the work done by the application.

Next, click on the Allocation tab and you will see a list of the bytes allocated for every single type used in the application, as shown in Figure 16.3. Something really troubling in this figure is that the results of string concatenation were responsible for 99.93% of all allocation within the application; 930MB worth. Even though there were only 10,000 strings in the list, 40,002 instances of strings were created as a result of string concatenation.

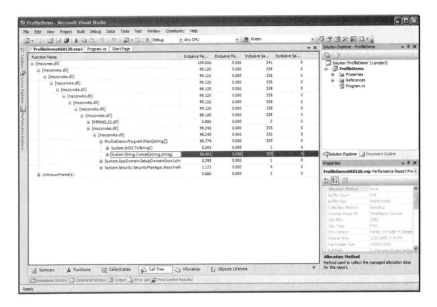

FIGURE 16.2   The Call Tree tab of a performance report.

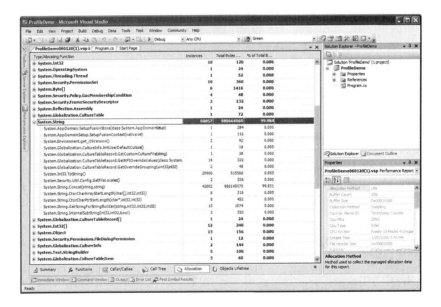

FIGURE 16.3   The Allocation tab of a performance report.

Finally, click the Objects Lifetime tab of the report. This shows you how long objects resided in memory categorized by what the garbage collector refers to as generations. A *generation* is a group of objects with similar uncollected lifetimes. When the garbage collector does a pass through the heap looking for objects to dispose, Generation 0 objects will be disposed immediately. Objects that could not be disposed will be moved to Generation 1 to be disposed later. Finally, if an object cannot be disposed from within Generation 1, it is moved to Generation 2. In order to keep the performance of the garbage collector at a maximum, you want to aim to keep as many of your objects as possible in Generation 0. Figure 16.4 shows that roughly 44,000 strings were Generation 0 objects, 159 lasted long enough to make it into Generation 2, and 5,633 objects were considered "large objects" by the garbage collector.

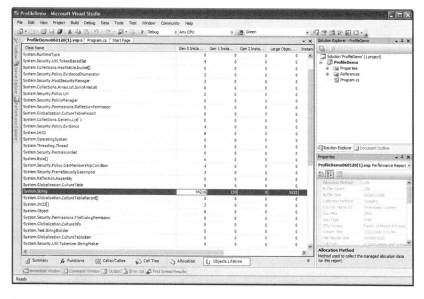

FIGURE 16.4   The Objects Lifetime tab of a performance report.

In addition to performance profiling, you can also use another tool provided by Microsoft that actually validates your code against more than 200 rules of design dictated by the .NET Framework design guidelines. This tool is called FxCop and you can download it from Microsoft. Figure 16.5 shows a screenshot of FxCop after analyzing the preceding code for failures to comply with standard .NET Framework application design guidelines.

Using FxCop and the Visual Studio Performance Wizard, you can get a blueprint of how your application is performing and how well it conforms to accepted .NET Framework design guidelines and best practice rules. Both of these tools should be used regularly by developers to maximize the efficiency and design guideline conformance of their applications.

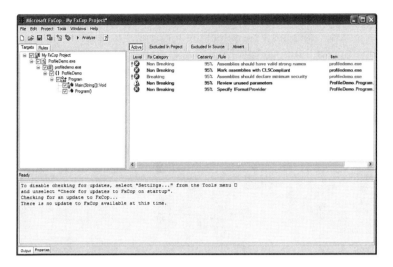

FIGURE 16.5   FxCop in action.

Summary

This chapter has provided you with an overview of some of the techniques that you can use to increase the performance of your code regardless of whether you are building Windows Forms, Web Forms, or even console applications. This chapter discussed the concepts of boxing and unboxing as well as the proper techniques to be used when looping and manipulating strings. This chapter also contained an overview of some tools that you can use to speed up your application, such as NGen.exe, and tools that can recommend ways to increase performance and enhance conformance to design guidelines, such as the Visual Studio Performance Wizard and FxCop.

PART III

Data Access with .NET 2.0

IN THIS PART

ADO.NET Fundamentals

ADO.NET is the set of classes and tools built into the .NET Framework that allow you to create powerful, scalable, and reliable data-driven applications. Using ADO.NET, you can connect to databases of all sorts including SQL Server, Oracle, Microsoft Access, and even some other less common database formats. When connected to a database, you can query and manipulate data in a wide variety of ways.

ADO.NET is an extremely large topic. As such, this one chapter won't cover all of it. This chapter focuses on the fundamentals of ADO.NET programming: using the data providers, connecting to a database, and performing data query and manipulation operations. Other chapters (such as Chapters 18, "Advanced ADO.NET Techniques," and 19, "Working with ADO.NET Data Providers") will show you some more advanced features of ADO.NET, and Chapter 20, "Strongly Typed DataSets," will give you a look at programming with SQL Server 2005 using C#.

Introduction to ADO.NET

ADO.NET is a collection of objects designed to present the developer with a unified, object-oriented interface to relational data stores such as SQL Server, Oracle, and Microsoft Access. ADO.NET consists of several classes that are shared among all data providers such as the DataSet class and base classes such as the DbConnection class and the DbDataReader class. The other portion of ADO.NET is the portion supplied by each data provider. For each data provider, there is a set of classes that interface directly with that data type. For example, there are classes that are specific to SQL Server, to Oracle, to OLE DB data sources, and to ODBC data sources. However, because each of these classes all inherit from common base classes and implement standard interfaces, your experience with one data provider can be reused in working with a different provider.

Establishing a Connection

In most cases when working with data and ADO.NET, you will need to establish a connection to the data source. This data source can be SQL Server 2000, SQL Server 2005, Oracle, Microsoft Access, or any number of other types of data including file-type sources such as Paradox files or even Microsoft Excel documents.

This section provides you with a basic overview of what ADO.NET is and how it works. After that, the discussion will move on to connection strings, what they are, and how you can construct them programmatically. Finally, you will see how to connect to a database and use that connection to query schema and metadata information.

Building a Connection String

Connection strings are often semicolon-delimited strings and contain the information that tells an ADO.NET data provider how to establish a link to the database. Take a look at the following connection string:

```
Initial Catalog=Northwind; Server=localhost; User Id=sa; Password=password;
```

That connection string will open the Northwind sample database on the default SQL Server instance running on the local computer, and will authenticate as the system administrator (sa).

If you have been programming with the same database server for a long time, you can probably construct valid connection strings in your sleep. However, if you're working with a new data provider that has a different connection string format, or you want an easy way to programmatically construct connection strings, there is a new tool in ADO.NET 2.0 to make that task easy.

That tool is the System.Data.Common.DbConnectionStringBuilder class and the classes that descend from it. At its core, it is a dictionary that stores the list of name/value pairs that make up a connection string. Individual providers can then create classes that inherit from DbConnectionStringBuilder to expose strongly typed properties for connection string elements that are specific to that particular provider.

You can either use the base class as a general tool for building connection strings, or you can use the derivative classes for creating connection strings specific to a particular data provider.

For example, if you want to use the basic DbConnectionStringBuilder class, you can simply use the Add method to build the dictionary of connection settings, as shown in the following example:

```
DbConnectionStringBuilder connBuilder = new DbConnectionStringBuilder();
connBuilder.Add("server", @".\SQLExpress");
connBuilder.Add("Initial Catalog", "TestDB");
connBuilder.Add("Integrated Security", "SSPI");
```

The preceding lines of code set up the name/value pairs necessary to connect to a SQL Express database named TestDB on the local server using integrated Windows authentication. To access the formatted connection string, you can use the ConnectionString property of the DbConnectionStringBuilder class.

To make use of a connection string builder class that is specific to a provider, you can use the derivative class, as in this example:

```
SqlConnectionStringBuilder sqlBuilder = new SqlConnectionStringBuilder();
sqlBuilder.DataSource = @".\SQLExpress";
sqlBuilder.InitialCatalog = "TestDB";
sqlBuilder.IntegratedSecurity = true;
```

As you can see, the manually added name/value pairs from the basic DbConnectionStringBuilder class have been replaced by strongly typed properties. This is a huge benefit because the developer no longer has to remember exactly how to format all the different properties of the connection string. In addition, IntelliSense will automatically give the developer a list of all the connection string options available. If you are using a full SQL Server instance instead of just SQL Express, you would use the server name (or its IP address) for the DataSource property.

Using the DbConnection Classes

When you have a connection string, you're ready to connect to your data source. A connection represents a live connection to the data source. In most cases that connection is a network connection between the ADO.NET data provider and the RDBMS server such as SQL Server or Oracle, but it could just as well be a connection to a file on disk, such as an Excel document.

Before seeing the code to establish a database connection, you should be aware of the cost of connections. As a general rule of thumb, database connections are expensive, and acquiring new connections can be costly both in terms of time and resources.

To help alleviate this, many data providers support the notion of *connection pooling*. When pooling is used, connections are placed in a pool when they are first created. When a pooled connection is closed, it is returned to the pool instead of being completely destroyed. The next time your application requests a database connection with the same connection string, the data provider can then retrieve the previously created connection from the pool at a much lower cost than creating one from scratch. Connection pooling is typically enabled in the connection string itself, so if you aren't sure if your provider supports pooling, you can take a look at the provider-specific DbConnectionStringBuilder to see if there are any pooling-related options.

17

Before wading into the code for creating and using a connection, take a look at Tables 17.1 and 17.2, which detail the methods and properties exposed by classes that derive from DbConnection.

TABLE 17.1   DbConnection Methods

Method	Description
BeginTransaction	Establishes and starts a new transaction.
ChangeDatabase	If the connection supports it, this will change databases within the same server using the existing credentials.
Close	Closes the connection to the database.
CreateCommand	Creates an instance of DbCommand specific to the current provider.
EnlistTransaction	Enlists the connection in a previously existing transaction.
GetSchema	Obtains schema information from various schema collections exposed by the provider.
Open	Opens a connection to the database.

TABLE 17.2   DbConnection Properties

Property	Description
ConnectionString	String containing the name-value pairs that describe the connection properties.
ConnectionTimeout	The maximum amount of time that can elapse before a live connection is established.
Database	The name of the database to which the connection is attached.
DataSource	The network identifier for the source of data; can be a network name or IP address.
ServerVersion	The version of the database server software of the server to which the connection is attached.
State	The state of the connection. It can be any of: Broken, Closed, Connecting, Executing, Fetching, or Open.

To experiment with creating a connection, opening that connection, and then obtaining information that can only be obtained when the connection is open, create a new Console application. The code in Program.cs should be as shown in Listing 17.1. If you installed VS.NET 2005 with SQL Express, you should be able to run this sample on your machine. If not, you can modify the connection string to point to the location of a SQL Server 2000 or 2005 instance elsewhere.

LISTING 17.1   Program.cs for a Console Application Verifying a SQL Connection

```
using System;
using System.Data;
using System.Data.Common;
using System.Data.SqlClient;
```

LISTING 17.1   Continued

```
using System.Collections.Generic;
using System.Text;

namespace ConnectionTest
{
  class Program
  {
  static void Main(string[] args)
  {
    SqlConnectionStringBuilder connBuilder =
      new SqlConnectionStringBuilder();
    connBuilder.InitialCatalog = "TestDB";
    connBuilder.DataSource = @".\SQLExpress";
    connBuilder.IntegratedSecurity = true;
    SqlConnection conn = new SqlConnection(connBuilder.ConnectionString);

    conn.Open();
    Console.WriteLine("Connected to SQL Server v" + conn.ServerVersion);
    conn.Close();
    Console.ReadLine();
  }
}
}
```

The `ServerVersion` property of the `SqlConnection` object is a property that cannot be accessed unless a valid connection has been established. When you run this application you should see a valid version number for SQL Server (version 9 and higher for SQL Server 2005). Remember that `Console.ReadLine()` waits for the user to press Enter before continuing processing. A lot of commercial applications will attempt to make a "ping"-type connection to a database before allowing the user to enter any data to verify that there is a valid, running data source. If no database connection can be established, many applications will display an error message and halt processing.

Communicating with the Data Source

This section shows you how to communicate with a data source when you have an open connection. Communication with the data source typically takes the form of executing commands and retrieving data, and now with ADO.NET 2.0 you can query schema and metadata information.

Executing Commands

The command is the basic unit of work when communicating with a data source. Commands are used to execute simple SQL statements like the following:

```
SELECT * From Customers
```

Commands are also used to execute stored procedures, update or delete data, and retrieve complex result sets. All commands inherit from the DbCommand class, whether they are for SQL Server, Oracle, or any other ADO.NET data provider.

The sequence of code when working with a DbCommand is as follows:

1. Create an instance of a DbCommand derivative.

2. Create command parameters and populate parameter values.

3. Execute the command.

4. Handle the output and/or results of the command.

The code in Listing 17.2 illustrates how to execute a SQL statement using parameters against a SQL Server database.

LISTING 17.2   Executing a Parameterized SQL Statement Using a SqlCommand

```
using System;
using System.Data;
using System.Data.Common;
using System.Data.SqlClient;
using System.Collections.Generic;
using System.Text;

namespace Command1
{
class Program
{
  static void Main(string[] args)
  {
    SqlConnectionStringBuilder cb = new SqlConnectionStringBuilder();
    cb.IntegratedSecurity = true;
    cb.DataSource = @".\SQLExpress";
    cb.InitialCatalog = "TestDB";
    SqlConnection conn = new SqlConnection(cb.ConnectionString);
    conn.Open();

    SqlCommand cmd = conn.CreateCommand();
    cmd.CommandText =
      "INSERT INTO Users(UserName, FirstName, LastName) " +
```

LISTING 17.2   Continued

```
       "VALUES(@UserName, @FirstName, @LastName)";
    cmd.CommandType = CommandType.Text;

    cmd.Parameters.Add(
      new SqlParameter("@UserName", "Joe2"));
    cmd.Parameters.AddWithValue("@FirstName", "Joe2");
    cmd.Parameters.AddWithValue("@LastName", "User2");
    cmd.ExecuteNonQuery();
  }
}
}
```

The preceding code uses two different methods for adding new SqlParameter instances. The first method, Add, takes a SqlParameter instance as an argument. The second method, AddWithValue, is a shortcut that lets you supply the parameter name and an object value. You can also use commands to execute stored procedures, as illustrated in Listing 17.3.

LISTING 17.3   Executing a Stored Procedure Using a SqlCommand Object

```
using System;
using System.Data;
using System.Data.Common;
using System.Data.SqlClient;
using System.Collections.Generic;
using System.Text;

namespace Command2
{
class Program
{
static void Main(string[] args)
{
   SqlConnectionStringBuilder sb = new SqlConnectionStringBuilder();
   sb.IntegratedSecurity = true;
   sb.InitialCatalog = "TestDB";
   sb.DataSource = @".\SQLExpress";
   SqlConnection conn = new SqlConnection(sb.ConnectionString);
   conn.Open();

   SqlCommand cmd = conn.CreateCommand();
   cmd.CommandText = "sp_Create_User";
   cmd.CommandType = CommandType.StoredProcedure;
   cmd.Parameters.Add(new SqlParameter("@UserName", "Jane"));
```

17

LISTING 17.3   Continued

```
  cmd.Parameters.Add(new SqlParameter("@FirstName", "Jane"));
  cmd.Parameters.Add(new SqlParameter("@LastName", "Doe"));
  cmd.ExecuteNonQuery();
  }
}
}
```

The preceding code executes a stored procedure named sp_Create_User that contains an INSERT statement that looks similar to the one from the previous listing (17.2). Just as you can supply input parameters to a stored procedure, you can also obtain output parameters when executing stored procedures. This comes in handy when you have stored procedures that perform calculations or provide valuable data in output parameters. The code in Listing 17.4 shows the execution of a stored procedure called sp_Get_UserCount that returns the number of users stored in the database.

LISTING 17.4   Using a Stored Procedure with Output Parameters

```
using System;
using System.Data;
using System.Data.Common;
using System.Data.SqlClient;
using System.Collections.Generic;
using System.Text;

namespace Command3
{
class Program
{
static void Main(string[] args)
{
  SqlConnectionStringBuilder sb = new SqlConnectionStringBuilder();
  sb.IntegratedSecurity = true;
  sb.InitialCatalog = "TestDB";
  sb.DataSource = @".\SQLExpress";
  SqlConnection conn = new SqlConnection(sb.ConnectionString);
  conn.Open();

  SqlCommand cmd = conn.CreateCommand();
  cmd.CommandText = "sp_Query_UserCount";
  cmd.CommandType = CommandType.StoredProcedure;
  cmd.Parameters.Add(new SqlParameter("@UserCount", SqlDbType.Int));
  cmd.Parameters[0].Direction = ParameterDirection.Output;
  cmd.ExecuteNonQuery();
  Console.WriteLine(
```

LISTING 17.4   Continued

```
    string.Format("There are {0} users in the database.",
      cmd.Parameters[0].Value));
  Console.ReadLine();
  }
 }
}
```

Using `DataReaders`

So far you've seen how to use commands to execute SQL statements that take input para-meters and return output parameters. What you haven't yet seen is how to use commands to obtain multiple rows of data, one of the most common uses for commands.

Result sets are obtained through the use of `DataReaders`. A data reader is a highly efficient object that traverses data in a forward-only fashion and is optimized for reading results of queries. There are many different kinds of data readers, all of which inherit from the `DbDataReader` class. The following is a list of the data readers that inherit directly from `DbDataReader`:

- `DataTableReader`—A forward-only reader that traverses a `DataTable`.

- `OdbcDataReader`, `OracleDataReader`, `SqlDataReader`, `SqlCeDataReader`—These are all data readers specific to their respective data providers.

To use a data reader, you must use one of the `Execute` methods of a command that returns a data reader. For example, the `SqlCommand` class provides the following methods that return various data readers:

- `ExecuteReader`—Executes the command and returns a `SqlDataReader` instance.

- `ExecuteXmlReader`—Executes the command and returns an `XmlReader` instance.

The code in Listing 17.5 illustrates the use of a simple data reader. The data reader allows you to access the columns in a result set either ordinarily (by numeric index), or by the field name itself. As you will see in Listing 17.5, there is a `GetXXX` method for each possi-ble data type, as well as a `GetObject` if one of the other data types won't suffice.

LISTING 17.5   Using a `DataReader`

```
using System;
using System.Data;
using System.Data.SqlClient;
using System.Collections.Generic;
using System.Text;
```

LISTING 17.5   Continued

```
namespace DataReader
{
class Program
{
static void Main(string[] args)
{
  SqlConnectionStringBuilder scb = new SqlConnectionStringBuilder();
  scb.DataSource = @".\SQLExpress";
  scb.InitialCatalog = "TestDB";
  scb.IntegratedSecurity = true;
  SqlConnection conn = new SqlConnection(scb.ConnectionString);
  conn.Open();

  SqlCommand cmd = conn.CreateCommand();
  cmd.CommandText = "SELECT * From Users";
  SqlDataReader rdr = cmd.ExecuteReader();
  while (rdr.Read())
  {
    Console.WriteLine(
      string.Format(
      "User {0}, Full Name {1} {2}",
      rdr.GetString(rdr.GetOrdinal("UserName")),
      (string)rdr["FirstName"],
      rdr.GetString(rdr.GetOrdinal("LastName"))));
  }
  rdr.Close();
  conn.Close();
  Console.ReadLine();
}
}
}
```

In the preceding code, you can see that the GetString method will obtain the string in the column indicated by an ordinal position. To determine a named column's ordinal position, you can use the GetOrdinal method. Also, if you want direct object access to the columns of the reader, you can use array-indexing notation to access columns by name or by ordinal value. All DataReaders operate on a single row of data at any given time. This is what makes them so fast and memory efficient. To advance a reader from one record to the next, you can call the Read() method. This will fetch the next row from the data source. If the reader is at the end of the record set, the Read() method will return false. After you have advanced beyond a given row, you cannot go back to that row again. All DataReaders are forward-only and will dispose of all information regarding previous rows after they are advanced.

There are many reasons to use a `DataReader` in an application. For example, you might need to read through several thousand rows of data in order to arrive at some conclusion in your application. If you were to load all of those rows into a single `DataSet` at once, it would consume a lot of memory. The `DataReader` allows your application to work with a single row at a time, providing a fast, forward-only means of reading through large numbers of rows. If the data you're working with is smaller in nature, you can use the overhead of a `DataSet` without too much worry about impacting the performance of your application.

Using Schema Discovery

Schema Discovery is a new feature of ADO.NET introduced in version 2.0. Schema Discovery adds new functionality to the basic `DbConnection` class that provides for discovering detailed information about the database connection as well as the metadata stored on the server.

For example, using Schema Discovery, you can now easily obtain a list of all tables in the system, stored procedures, users, functions, and much more depending on what features the particular data provider supports.

Schema Discovery all takes place within the new method `GetSchema`. If you invoke this method with no arguments, you will receive in return a table that contains a list of all the possible arguments for the `GetSchema` method. This way, you can interrogate the connection to see what information you can obtain via `GetSchema`.

When you invoke `GetSchema` on a SQL 2005 database, you will receive a table that looks similar to the one in Table 17.3.

TABLE 17.3   Results of Invoking `GetSchema()` with No Arguments on SQL Server 2005

Collection Name	Number of Restrictions	Number of Identifier Parts
MetaDataCollections	0	0
DataSourceInformation	0	0
DataTypes	0	0
Restrictions	0	0
ReservedWords	0	0
Users	1	1
Databases	1	1
Tables	4	3
Columns	4	4
Views	3	3
ViewColumns	4	4
ProcedureParameters	4	1
Procedures	4	3
ForeignKeys	4	3
IndexColumns	5	4
Indexes	4	3
UserDefinedTypes	2	1

The number of restrictions and identifier parts is useful to an extent, but the really important information is the name of the collection. This string can be passed to GetSchema as an argument to retrieve information.

The NumberOfRestrictions column indicates the number of restrictions that appear in the Restrictions collection for the indicated collection. So, from Table 17.3, you can tell that there are two defined restrictions for the UserDefinedTypes collection, and both of those will appear in the results if you call GetSchema("Restrictions").

The NumberOfIdentifierParts column that you receive when you invoke GetSchema() with no arguments indicates the number of columns in the table that uniquely identify an entity. For example, when you call GetSchema on the Columns collection, you receive quite a bit of information. The first four columns (TABLE_CATALOG, TABLE_SCHEMA, TABLE_NAME, and COLUMN_NAME) are the four pieces of information that uniquely identify a single column within that table. If you look at Table 17.3, you'll see that for the Columns collection, the number of identifier parts is indeed 4.

Table 17.4 shows all of the columns for each collection when invoking GetSchema. Keep in mind that this varies depending on your data provider. The information in Table 17.4 was obtained from SQL Express 2005.

TABLE 17.4   Columns Provided for Each Schema Collection Used with GetSchema()

Collection	Columns
MetaDataCollections	CollectionName, NumberOfRestrictions, NumberOfIdentifierParts (this is the default collection).
DataSourceInformation	Columns describing the data source itself, such as DataSourceProductName, DataSourceProductVersion, and many others indicating various behaviors. Contains one row.
DataTypes	TypeName, ProviderDbType, ColumnSize, CreateFormat, CreateParameters, DataType, IsAutoIncrementable, IsBestMatch, IsCaseSensitive, IsNullable, IsSearchable, and many more. One row per data type.
Restrictions	CollectionName, RestrictionName, RestrictionDefault, RestrictionNumber. One row per restriction—indicates a restriction on schema information.
ReservedWords	ReservedWord. One row per reserved word.
Users	uid, user_name, createdate, updatedate. One row per user.
Databases	database_name, dbid, create_date.
Tables	TABLE_CATALOG, TABLE_SCHEMA, TABLE_NAME, TABLE_TYPE. One row per table; all four columns indicate the uniqueness of a row.
Columns	TABLE_CATALOG, TABLE_SCHEMA, TABLE_NAME, COLUMN_NAME, ORDINAL_POSITION, COLUMN_DEFAULT, IS_NULLABLE, and so on. The first four columns indicate the uniqueness for a row.
Views	TABLE_CATALOG, TABLE_SCHEMA, TABLE_NAME, CHECK_OPTION, IS_UPDATABLE.

Working with the Data

In the preceding sections you have learned how to connect to a data source. In addition, you have learned how to communicate with that source for data retrieval, manipulation, and schema queries. Armed with that knowledge, you can begin writing applications that interact with and manipulate data. A wide variety of tools are available to you for doing this. In later chapters, you will see how to work with data on specific platforms such as Windows Forms and ASP.NET. This section illustrates tools that are common to all platforms and are central to ADO.NET: the DataSet and the DataAdapter.

Introduction to the DataSet

The DataSet is an extremely powerful class. Essentially this class is an in-memory database. It can contain tables made up of multiple columns of varying data types. Each table can contain multiple rows, and those rows can be related to each other through foreign keys as well as complex relationships that enforce parent/child data constraints. DataTables can assign new, unique, numeric identifiers to rows as they are added to the table. DataSets can also persist their data in various formats such as XML and even a newly added binary format for ADO.NET 2.0.

When a DataSet contains data, you can use various methods to search the contents of the tables contained within it. You can even treat a DataSet as if it was an XML document and perform XPath queries against it.

As shown in Figure 17.1, the DataSet is extremely powerful and flexible and really does have many of the features of a server-hosted database, but contained in a compact, flexible, object-oriented form.

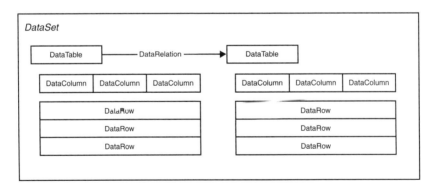

FIGURE 17.1   The DataSet hierarchy.

The code in Listing 17.6 illustrates a few basic tasks that can be accomplished with the DataSet, including dynamically creating a data structure, adding and deleting rows, and querying information contained in a DataTable.

LISTING 17.6   Working with a DataSet

```csharp
using System;
using System.Data;
using System.Collections.Generic;
using System.Text;

namespace DataSet1
{
class Program
{
static void Main(string[] args)
{
// create an empty data set with new structure
  DataSet ds = new DataSet();
  DataTable customers = new DataTable("Customers");
  customers.Columns.Add(new DataColumn("CustomerId", typeof(int)));
  customers.Columns[0].AutoIncrement = true;
  customers.Columns[0].AutoIncrementSeed = 1;
  customers.PrimaryKey = new DataColumn[] { customers.Columns[0] };
  customers.Columns.Add(new DataColumn("CustomerName", typeof(string)));
  customers.Columns.Add(new DataColumn("Email", typeof(string)));
  customers.Constraints.Add(new UniqueConstraint(customers.Columns["Email"]));
  ds.Tables.Add(customers);

  DataRow newCustomer = customers.NewRow();
  newCustomer["CustomerName"] = "John Doe";
  newCustomer["Email"] = "johndoe@someplace.com";
  customers.Rows.Add(newCustomer);

  newCustomer = customers.NewRow();
  newCustomer["CustomerName"] = "Jane Doe";
  newCustomer["Email"] = "janedoe@someplace.com";
  customers.Rows.Add(newCustomer);

  // perform a search on the customers table
  DataRow[] custMatch = customers.Select("Email = 'janedoe@someplace.com'");
  foreach (DataRow customer in custMatch)
  {
  Console.WriteLine(
      string.Format("Customer {0}({1}) matched search with e-mail {2}",
      customer["CustomerName"], customer["CustomerId"], customer["Email"]));
  }
  Console.ReadLine();
```

LISTING 17.6   Continued

```
   }
}
}
```

The preceding code creates a new DataSet with a single table. The Customers table consists of three columns: a unique identifier that autoincrements, a user name, and an email address. There is also a unique constraint placed on the email address column so that users in this table cannot share the same email address. Finally, the code utilizes the Select method to retrieve a list of users that have a given email address.

When the code is executed, the following line is output to the console:

```
Customer Jane Doe(2) matched search with e-mail janedoe@someplace.com
```

Using a DataAdapter

The DataAdapter class functions very much like an electrical plug. An electrical plug connects an appliance to a power source. The DataAdapter connects a DataSet (or DataTable) to a data source. This "plug" has four prongs, one for each type of connection that can take place:

- InsertCommand—This command is executed when an item in an associated DataTable is ready to be inserted into the data source.

- DeleteCommand—This command is executed when an item in an associated DataTable is ready to be deleted from the data source.

- UpdateCommand—This command is executed to commit pending changes to an item in a DataTable.

- SelectCommand—This command is executed to populate the DataTable or DataSet with the information retrieved from the data source.

The best way to see how a DataAdapter works is to look at an example in action. The code in Listing 17.7 illustrates the creation of a DataAdapter as well as several commands. These commands are then executed when the DataSet invokes the Update() method. The sample in Listing 17.7 shows how users can be updated, deleted, inserted, and queried in a DataSet, and then have all of those changes persisted to a data source by the DataAdapter.

To follow along with this sample, you should have a SQL Express (or SQL Server; you'll have to modify the data source property) database called "TestDB." In that database, there is a table called Users with the following columns: FirstName, LastName, UserName, and UserID. You can discern the data type and size of these columns from the stored procedure being invoked in the code in Listing 17.7.

17

LISTING 17.7   Using a DataAdapter to Connect a DataSet to a Data Source

```
using System;
using System.Data;
using System.Data.SqlClient;
using System.Collections.Generic;
using System.Text;

namespace DataAdapter
{
class Program
{
static void Main(string[] args)
{
  SqlConnectionStringBuilder scb = new SqlConnectionStringBuilder();
  scb.DataSource = @".\SQLExpress";
  scb.InitialCatalog = "TestDB";
  scb.IntegratedSecurity = true;
  SqlConnection conn = new SqlConnection(scb.ConnectionString);
  conn.Open();

  SqlCommand selectCommand = conn.CreateCommand();
  selectCommand.CommandText = "SELECT * FROM Users";

  SqlCommand updateCommand = conn.CreateCommand();
  updateCommand.CommandText =
   "UPDATE Users SET UserName=@UserName, FirstName=@FirstName " +
   ",LastName=@LastName WHERE UserID = @UserID";
  updateCommand.Parameters.Add(
    new SqlParameter("@UserName", SqlDbType.VarChar, 50, "UserName"));
  updateCommand.Parameters.Add(
    new SqlParameter("@FirstName", SqlDbType.VarChar, 50, "FirstName"));
  updateCommand.Parameters.Add(
    new SqlParameter("@LastName", SqlDbType.VarChar, 50, "LastName"));
  updateCommand.Parameters.Add(
    new SqlParameter("@UserId", SqlDbType.Int, 4, "UserId"));

  SqlCommand deleteCommand = conn.CreateCommand();
  deleteCommand.CommandText = "DELETE Users WHERE UserID = @UserID";
  deleteCommand.Parameters.Add(new SqlParameter("@UserId",
    SqlDbType.Int, 4, "UserId"));

  SqlCommand insertCommand = conn.CreateCommand();
  insertCommand.CommandText =
    "INSERT INTO Users(UserName, FirstName, LastName) " +
    "VALUES(@UserName, @FirstName, @LastName)";
```

LISTING 17.7   Continued

```
insertCommand.Parameters.Add(
  new SqlParameter("@UserName", SqlDbType.VarChar, 50, "UserName"));
insertCommand.Parameters.Add(
  new SqlParameter("@FirstName", SqlDbType.VarChar, 50, "FirstName"));
insertCommand.Parameters.Add(
  new SqlParameter("@LastName", SqlDbType.VarChar, 50, "LastName"));
insertCommand.Parameters.Add(
  new SqlParameter("@UserId", SqlDbType.Int, 4, "UserId"));

DataSet ds = new DataSet();
SqlDataAdapter sqlDa = new SqlDataAdapter(selectCommand);
sqlDa.UpdateCommand = updateCommand;
sqlDa.DeleteCommand = deleteCommand;
sqlDa.InsertCommand = insertCommand;
sqlDa.Fill(ds);

// update an existing row
DataTable users = ds.Tables[0];
users.Rows[0]["FirstName"] = "Kevin_Modified";

// delete an existing row
users.Rows[1].Delete();

// create a new row
DataRow newUser = users.NewRow();
newUser["UserName"] = "added";
newUser["FirstName"] = "Brand";
newUser["LastName"] = "New";
users.Rows.Add(newUser);

// call Update to invoke the Update command,
// the Delete command, and the Insert command
// on the associated datasource via the dataadapter
sqlDa.Update(ds);
Console.WriteLine("Update Complete");
Console.ReadLine();

}
}
}
```

[handwritten annotation: This Sets the "Frame"]

As you can see from Figure 17.2, the second user (originally called "SecondUser") has been removed from my database. The first user was modified so that the first name was set to "Kevin_Modified". Finally, you can also see that a new user was created. All of this was accomplished by invoking a single Update() method on the DataAdapter.

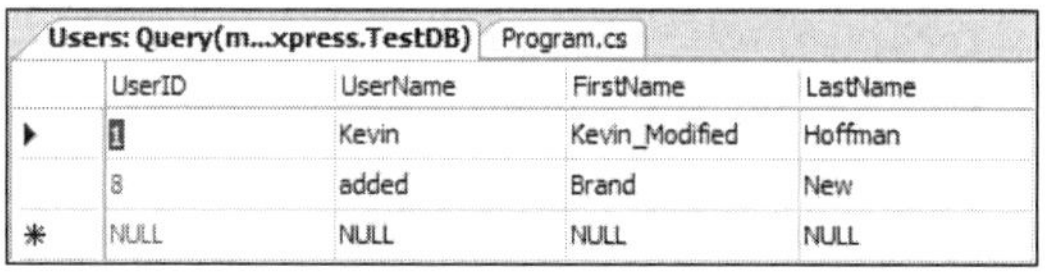

FIGURE 17.2   View of data after being modified by the SqlDataAdapter.

These modifications were made possible because each time you modify anything in a DataSet, you modify the RowState of the row. The RowState indicates whether the row is supposed to be deleted, brand new, or needs to be updated. When the Update() method is invoked, the DataAdapter will iterate through all of the rows that have been inserted, deleted, or modified, and will invoke the corresponding InsertCommand, UpdateCommand, or DeleteCommand, using that row's columns to feed the parameters for the command.

Summary

This chapter has provided you with a basic overview of what ADO.NET 2.0 is and what you can accomplish with it. At this point you should be comfortable with the idea behind data-driven applications and you should feel ready to start experimenting with your own data access applications using the information presented in this chapter. You should be able to start using your own DataSets, DataAdapters, and Connections now, and hopefully you will be able to make use of some of the new features of ADO.NET 2.0 such as Schema Discovery.

This chapter is not designed to be a complete reference for ADO.NET. Rather, it is intended that this chapter will provide you with enough background information that you will be able to follow along in subsequent chapters where data access technology and code becomes more complex and intricate.

CHAPTER **18**

Advanced ADO.NET Techniques

Undoubtedly, ADO.NET has made life a lot easier for developers. It provided a unified means for communicating with relational data sources, whether the source was SQL Server, Oracle, Access, or even XML. In this chapter, you will see some extremely powerful techniques that you can use in your ADO.NET 2.0 programming. You will see some of the improvements made to the `DataTable` class, as well as how to access data asynchronously, update data in batches, and even how to use the new unified transaction model provided by the `System.Transactions` namespace.

Working with the New Improved `DataTable`

The `DataSet` has always been at the core of previous versions of ADO.NET, providing an in-memory representation of relational data including keys, constraints, data relations, and even limited querying capability. The problem many developers had with the `DataSet` is that quite often they only needed to work with a single table at a time. In these situations, the `DataSet` provided too much functionality. The problem with this was that quite often, developers couldn't get around the fact that they needed to use the `DataSet`; the `DataTable` class didn't work very well outside the context of a `DataSet`.

The new version of ADO.NET takes this into consideration by promoting the `DataTable` to a first-class citizen. The `DataTable` can read and write its own data to files without having to reside within a `DataSet`. In addition, you can create a `DataReader` on top of the data contained within a single table.

Loading and Saving DataTables Using XML

With ADO.NET 2.0, you can now read and write the contents of a DataTable using XML. In previous versions of ADO.NET, you had to place a table in a DataSet and then call the ReadXml() and WriteXml() methods on the DataSet to get XML persistence.

Now the DataTable class has its own ReadXml() and WriteXml() methods. One thing you might have to watch out for is that although the current documentation on MSDN indicates that schema inference is possible on a DataTable from XML data, attempting to infer schema at runtime from XML throws an exception indicating that it is not supported on the DataTable class. To get around this, the sample shown in Listing 18.1 uses the XmlWriteMode.WriteSchema option to include the schema in the top of the document.

LISTING 18.1   Reading and Writing XML DataTable Contents

```
using System;
using System.Data;
using System.IO;
using System.Collections.Generic;
using System.Text;

namespace TableXml
{
class Program
{
static DataTable dt;
static void Main(string[] args)
{
    dt = new DataTable("Customers");
    if (File.Exists("Customers.xml"))
    {
        dt.ReadXml("Customers.xml");
        Console.WriteLine("{0} Customers Found", dt.Rows.Count);
        foreach (DataRow row in dt.Rows)
        {
            Console.WriteLine("[{0}] {1} {2}", row["CustomerID"],
row["FirstName"], row["LastName"]);
        }
    }
    else
        CreateCustomers();

    Console.Write("New Customer:");
    string custName = Console.ReadLine();
    if (custName == string.Empty) return;
    string[] cust = custName.Split(' ');
```

LISTING 18.1   Continued

```
    dt.Rows.Add(new object[] { dt.Rows.Count + 1, cust[0], cust[1] });
    dt.WriteXml("Customers.xml", XmlWriteMode.WriteSchema);
    Console.ReadLine();
}
public static void CreateCustomers()
{
    dt.Columns.Add("CustomerID", typeof(int));
    dt.Columns.Add("FirstName", typeof(string));
    dt.Columns.Add("LastName", typeof(string));
    dt.Rows.Add(new object[] { 1, "Kevin", "Hoffman" });
    dt.Rows.Add(new object[] { 2, "John", "Doe" });
}
}
}
```

The preceding code looks for the `Customers.xml` file. If it finds the file, it loads the contents into a `DataTable`; otherwise, it creates a new file with a couple of sample rows. Then the code prompts the user for a new customer, adds that customer as a row, and saves the data back out to the `Customers.xml` file with the schema information included. If you have any experience using the `WriteXml()` and `ReadXml()` methods on the `DataSet` class, the preceding code should seem pretty straightforward. It produces XML in the following format:

```
<?xml version="1.0" standalone="yes"?>
<NewDataSet>
  <xs:schema id="NewDataSet" xmlns=""
    xmlns:xs="http://www.w3.org/2001/XMLSchema"
    xmlns:msdata="urn:schemas-microsoft-com:xml-msdata">
    <xs:element name="NewDataSet" msdata:IsDataSet="true"
      msdata:MainDataTable="Customers" msdata:UseCurrentLocale="true">
    <xs:complexType>
      <xs:choice minOccurs="0" maxOccurs="unbounded">
        <xs:element name="Customers">
          <xs:complexType>
            <xs:sequence>
              <xs:element name="CustomerID" type="xs:int" minOccurs="0" />
              <xs:element name="FirstName" type="xs:string" minOccurs="0" />
              <xs:element name="LastName" type="xs:string" minOccurs="0" />
            </xs:sequence>
          </xs:complexType>
        </xs:element>
      </xs:choice>
    </xs:complexType>
  </xs:element>
```

18

```
  </xs:schema>
  <Customers>
    <CustomerID>1</CustomerID>
    <FirstName>Kevin</FirstName>
    <LastName>Hoffman</LastName>
  </Customers>
  <Customers>
    <CustomerID>2</CustomerID>
    <FirstName>John</FirstName>
    <LastName>Doe</LastName>
  </Customers>
  <Customers>
    <CustomerID>3</CustomerID>
    <FirstName>Bobby</FirstName>
    <LastName>John</LastName>
  </Customers>
</NewDataSet>
```

Using the New DataTableReader Class

The new DataTableReader class works just like any of the other DataReader classes that are available in ADO.NET. Like a SqlDataReader, the DataTableReader exposes fast, forward-only, read-only access to the underlying data. Whereas the SqlDataReader exposes data from a SQL Server database, the DataTableReader simply exposes data from an underlying DataTable.

The code in Listing 18.2 is a quick illustration of how to use a DataTableReader. Fortunately, if you know how to use any of the data readers provided by ADO.NET, you will be familiar with how to use the DataTableReader class.

LISTING 18.2   Using the DataTableReader

```
using System;
using System.Data;
using System.Collections.Generic;
using System.Text;

namespace TableReaderDemo
{
class Program
{
static void Main(string[] args)
{
    DataTable dt = new DataTable("Customers");
    // load data from previous demo
    dt.ReadXml(@"..\..\..\..\TableXml\TableXml\bin\debug\Customers.xml");
```

LISTING 18.2   Continued

```
    DataTableReader dtr = dt.CreateDataReader();
    while (dtr.Read())
    {
        Console.WriteLine("[{0}] {1} {2}",
            (int)dtr["CustomerID"],
(string)dtr["FirstName"], (String)dtr["LastName"]);
    }
    Console.ReadLine();
}
}
}
```

Accessing Data Asynchronously

One of the biggest problems with ADO.NET in previous versions is that no matter how responsive your application was, everything still had to wait for a command to execute. In other words, all command executions were done synchronously, whether the command took .2 or 200 seconds to execute.

Most developers got around this by wrapping the command execution in a method that was spawned in a background thread to allow the execution to take place while the rest of the application remained responsive.

With ADO.NET 2.0, that workaround is no longer necessary. You can use the standard `Begin`/`End` asynchronous method pattern that is prevalent throughout the .NET Framework. The `SqlCommand` class now has a corresponding `Begin`/`End` pair for some of its execute methods: `ExecuteNonQuery()`, `ExecuteReader()`, and `ExecuteXmlReader()`.

Using these new methods, you can initiate an asynchronous command and then continue responding to events from the rest of the application. When the results are available, they will be returned to your application using one of the appropriate `End` methods, as shown in Listing 18.3.

18

LISTING 18.3   Asynchronous Command Execution

```
using System;
using System.Threading;
using System.Data;
using System.Data.SqlClient;
using System.Collections.Generic;
using System.Text;

namespace AsyncCommandDemo
{
```

LISTING 18.3   Continued

```
class Program
{
static void Main(string[] args)
{
    SqlConnection conn = new SqlConnection(
        "data source=localhost; initial catalog=SampleDB;
        ➥Integrated Security=SSPI;Asynchronous Processing=true;");
    conn.Open();
    SqlCommand cmd = conn.CreateCommand();

    cmd.CommandText = "SELECT * FROM Customers";
    cmd.BeginExecuteReader(new AsyncCallback(ExecuteAsync), cmd);
    Console.WriteLine("Asynchronous execution of command has begun...");
    Console.ReadLine();
}

public static void ExecuteAsync(IAsyncResult ar)
{
    Thread.Sleep(3000); // simulate a longer query
    SqlCommand originalCommand = (SqlCommand)ar.AsyncState;
    SqlDataReader dr = originalCommand.EndExecuteReader(ar);
    while (dr.Read())
    {
        Console.WriteLine("[{0}] {1}, {2} {3}", dr["ID"],
            dr["LastName"], dr["FirstName"], dr["MiddleInitial"]);
    }
}
}
}
```

Note that you have to include the Asynchronous Processing=true option in the connection string in order to enable asynchronous command execution in SQL Server. Also keep in mind that asynchronous processing is not part of the DbCommand abstract base class; it is part of the SqlCommand class only.

Updating Data in Batches

In previous versions of ADO.NET, batch updates using DataSets weren't very efficient. The sequence of events using previous versions was as follows:

1. Retrieve data from the database into a DataSet using the adapter's Fill method.

2. Data in existing rows is modified, new rows are added, and yet other rows might be deleted.

3. The adapter's `Update()` method is called. The adapter then runs through the entire list of rows in the given table(s). For each row that has been inserted, deleted, or updated since the last time the `DataSet`'s `AcceptChanges()` method was called (or since creation), a single SQL statement is executed to perform the change on the server.

The problem with this scenario is in the case where there are large numbers of changed records in a `DataSet`. When this happens, the process of creating a new SQL statement, executing it, and then moving to the next updated record in the list adds unnecessary overhead to the update operation.

With the new ADO.NET 2.0 data adapters, you can specify the size of the command batch. If you specify a size of 0, the new data adapter will use the maximum batch size available. If you specify a value greater than 1, the data adapter will perform its update in batches containing the number of statements you indicated.

The only tricky thing to remember about batch updating is that you need to specify `UpdateRowSource.None` for the `UpdatedRowSource` property on all batch-involved commands, as shown in Listing 18.4.

LISTING 18.4   Performing Batch Updates using a `SqlDataAdapter`

```
using System;
using System.Data;
using System.Data.SqlClient;
using System.Collections.Generic;
using System.Text;

namespace BatchUpdate
{
class Program
{
static void Main(string[] args)
{
    SqlConnection conn = new SqlConnection(
        "data source=localhost; initial catalog=SampleDB;
        ➥Integrated Security=SSPI;");
    conn.Open();
    SqlCommand selectCmd = conn.CreateCommand();
    selectCmd.CommandText = "SELECT ID, FirstName,
    ➥LastName, MiddleInitial FROM Customers";

    SqlCommand updateCmd = conn.CreateCommand();
    updateCmd.CommandText = "UPDATE Customers SET FirstName = @FirstName,
    ➥LastName = @LastName " +
        ", MiddleInitial = @MiddleInitial WHERE ID = @ID";
    updateCmd.Parameters.Add(new SqlParameter("@FirstName",
```

LISTING 18.4 Continued

```
SqlDbType.VarChar, 50, "FirstName"));
    updateCmd.Parameters.Add(new SqlParameter("@LastName",
SqlDbType.VarChar, 50, "LastName"));
    updateCmd.Parameters.Add(new SqlParameter("@MiddleInitial",
SqlDbType.NChar, 1, "MiddleInitial"));
    updateCmd.Parameters.Add(new SqlParameter("@ID", SqlDbType.Int, 4, "ID"));
    updateCmd.UpdatedRowSource = UpdateRowSource.None;

    SqlCommand insertCommand = conn.CreateCommand();
    insertCommand.CommandText = "INSERT INTO Customers(FirstName, LastName,
    ➥MiddleInitial) " +
        "VALUES(@FirstName, @LastName, @MiddleInitial)";
    insertCommand.Parameters.Add(new SqlParameter("@FirstName",
SqlDbType.VarChar, 50, "FirstName"));
    insertCommand.Parameters.Add(new SqlParameter("@LastName",
SqlDbType.VarChar, 50, "LastName"));
    insertCommand.Parameters.Add(new SqlParameter("@MiddleInitial",
SqlDbType.NChar, 1, "MiddleInitial"));
    insertCommand.UpdatedRowSource = UpdateRowSource.None; // required for batching


    SqlDataAdapter da = new SqlDataAdapter(selectCmd) ;
    da.UpdateCommand = updateCmd;
    da.InsertCommand = insertCommand;
    da.UpdateBatchSize = 10;

    DataSet ds = new DataSet();
    da.Fill(ds, "Customers");

    // change the first customer
    ds.Tables[0].Rows[0]["FirstName"] = "Modified!";

    // add a couple customers
    DataRow newCust = ds.Tables[0].NewRow();
    newCust["FirstName"] = "Batch1";
    newCust["LastName"] = "Batch";
    newCust["MiddleInitial"] = 'Q';
    ds.Tables[0].Rows.Add(newCust);
    newCust = ds.Tables[0].NewRow();
    newCust["FirstName"] = "Batch2";
    newCust["LastName"] = "Batch";
```

LISTING 18.4 Continued

```
    newCust["MiddleInitial"] = 'J';
    ds.Tables[0].Rows.Add(newCust);

    da.Update(ds, "Customers");

    Console.WriteLine("Batch update performed.");
    Console.ReadLine();
  }
 }
}
```

The preceding code modifies an existing row and then creates two additional rows. In previous versions of ADO.NET, this would generate three separate command executions, including the latency involved with starting and finishing each command. In ADO.NET 2.0, the preceding code will only issue one command to SQL Server. The command issued to SQL Server will contain one UPDATE statement and two INSERT statements. If you want to see how this works, you can easily watch how the statements are sent to SQL Server using SQL administration tools.

Using the New System.Transactions Namespace

The new System.Transactions namespace provides a single, unified means by which your code can take advantage of transactional resources, such as SQL Server databases and Microsoft Message Queues (MSMQ). In addition to providing a new way of consuming transactions as a client, the System.Transactions namespace also allows you to create your own resource manager, allowing other developers and code to take advantage of your proprietary resources in a transactional manner using the same client code that they would use for SQL, DTC, ADO.NET, or MSMQ transactions.

The new transaction manager automatically takes care of transaction escalation. Before System.Transactions, developers had to decide at design time if they needed their transactions to be local or distributed. The new transaction manager can automatically escalate local transactions to distributed transactions based on the resources being consumed and the resource managers involved in the transaction. What this means is that without having to change your code, your application can use low-cost local transactions during one execution, and then autoescalate to using distributed transactions the next time it is run, based on which resources the end user is accessing. The benefits of having a single set of transactional code to write that can be applied to any supported resource manager are too numerous to count.

The new transaction system provides two ways of making use of transactions as a consumer: explicitly using derivates of the Transaction class, and implicitly using transaction scopes.

18

Using Explicit Transactions

When you explicitly create a transaction, you need to manually enlist resource managers in that transaction. In the example shown in Listing 18.5, the resource manager being enlisted is a `SqlConnection` instance. The `CommittableTransaction` hosts the `Commit()` and `Rollback()` methods. This makes it so that whether you're working with MSMQ, DTC, SQL, or any other resource manager, your transactional code can remain identical.

LISTING 18.5   Using Explicit Transactions

```
using System;
using System.Data;
using System.Data.SqlClient;
using System.Transactions;
using System.Collections.Generic;
using System.Text;

namespace ExplicitTransaction
{
class Program
{
static void Main(string[] args)
{
    CommittableTransaction tx = new CommittableTransaction();

    SqlConnection conn = new SqlConnection(
        "data source=localhost; initial catalog=SampleDB;
        ➥integrated security=SSPI;");
    conn.Open();

    SqlCommand updateCommand = conn.CreateCommand();
    updateCommand.CommandText = "DELETE Customers WHERE ID > 3";

    conn.EnlistTransaction(tx);

    updateCommand.ExecuteNonQuery();

    tx.Rollback();

    conn.Close();
    Console.ReadLine();


}
}
}
```

The preceding sample is reusing the SampleDB database used in many chapters throughout this book. It's a simple database with a Customers table that contains a few columns and an ID column. When you run the preceding code, no changes to the table should be visible because the transaction was explicitly rolled back. If you change the Rollback() in the preceding code to Commit(), the transaction will complete and the changes made within the context of the transaction will be saved to the database, effectively deleting all customers with an ID greater than 3. Also note that you need to add a reference to the System.Transactions.dll assembly for the code in Listing 18.5 to work properly.

Using Implicit Transactions

Implicit transactions are much easier to manage by their very nature. As such, Microsoft actually recommends that you use implicit transactions for all of your transactional code unless you really need the explicit transactions shown in the preceding example. The main reason for this is that when using implicit transactions, transactions from multiple resource managers can coexist and operate with each other according to some predefined rules. For example, if you use implicit transactions, your code can simply automatically enlist in a parent transaction if one exists, or your code can create a new transaction if necessary. Even more useful is that if your code invokes other code that is also using implicit transactions, your implicit transaction may not commit until all nested transactions have *voted* to commit as well. This type of transaction nesting and the notion of submitting a vote on whether the transaction commits should be very familiar to anyone who has worked with COM+ before. In fact, System.Transactions transactions can actually interoperate with COM+ transactions, as you'll see in Chapter 40, "Using Enterprise Services."

Implicit transactions are accomplished through the use of the TransactionScope class, which has a usage very similar to the using keyword. Code that resides within a transaction scope is inherently transactional, and access to any supported resource managers (such as SQL 2005) from within a transaction scope will use transactions implicitly. If your code doesn't get to the line where the Complete() method is called on a TransactionScope, any transactions created within the scope will be rolled back, and any parent or ambient transactions utilized through nesting will receive a vote to roll back.

The code in Listing 18.6 illustrates the simple use of implicit transactions using transaction scopes.

LISTING 18.6   Using Implicit Transactions

```
using System;
using System.Data;
using System.Data.SqlClient;
using System.Transactions;
using System.Collections.Generic;
using System.Text;

namespace ImplicitTransaction
{
```

18

LISTING 18.6   Continued

```
class Program
{
static void Main(string[] args)
{
    using (TransactionScope scope = new TransactionScope())
    {
        using (SqlConnection conn = new SqlConnection(
            "data source=localhost; initial catalog=SampleDB;
            ➥Integrated Security=SSPI;"))
        {
            conn.Open();
            SqlCommand cmd = conn.CreateCommand();
            cmd.CommandText = "DELETE Customers";

            cmd.ExecuteNonQuery();

            // this will give us a divide-by-zero exception
            // preventing scope.complete from being called.
            int z = 12;
            int y = 1;
            y -= 1;
            Console.WriteLine("{0}", z / y);

        }
        scope.Complete();
    }
}
}
}
```

The preceding code tricks the compiler into allowing the programmer to create a divide-by-zero situation. Division by zero is never good and is guaranteed to throw an exception. As mentioned earlier, if your code can't execute the scope.Complete() line, the transaction won't be committed. If the scope created the transaction, it will be rolled back immediately. If the scope is part of a parent scope, it will vote to roll back the parent scope by virtue of its inability to complete. If you remove the four lines of code that create the divide-by-zero exception from Listing 18.6, the transaction will commit and the Customers table will be emptied.

Take a look at the code in Listing 18.7. It shows how you can nest TransactionScope instances and have the Complete() method affect the parent scope. The main thing to remember is this: *Every time a scope finishes without the* Complete() *method being called, a* TransactionAbortedException *is thrown.*

LISTING 18.7   Using Nested Transaction Scopes

```
using System;
using System.Data;
using System.Data.SqlClient;
using System.Transactions;
using System.Collections.Generic;
using System.Text;

namespace NestedImplicit
{
class Program
{
static SqlConnection conn;
static void Main(string[] args)
{
    try
    {
        using (TransactionScope scope = new TransactionScope())
        {
            using (conn = new SqlConnection(
             "data source=localhost; initial catalog=SampleDB;
             ➥Integrated Security=SSPI;"))
            {
                conn.Open();
                for (int x = 1; x < 8; x++)
                {
                    DeleteCustomer(x);
                }
            }
            scope.Complete();
        }
    }
    catch (TransactionAbortedException )
    {
        Console.WriteLine(
"One or more of the child scopes voted to abort the transaction.");
    }

    Console.ReadLine();
}

static void DeleteCustomer(int custId)
{
    using (TransactionScope scope = new TransactionScope())
    {
```

18

LISTING 18.7 Continued

```
        SqlCommand cmd = conn.CreateCommand();
        cmd.CommandText = "DELETE Customers WHERE ID = " + custId.ToString();
        cmd.ExecuteNonQuery();

        if (custId < 7)
            scope.Complete();
    }
}
}
}
```

The preceding code creates a parent scope. Inside the scope, a loop is iterated seven times; each iteration attempts to delete a customer. The DeleteCustomer() method will properly delete all customers, except those with an ID of seven or greater. This simulates a potential problem with the database, showing that six out of seven loop iterations called the Complete() method on their respective transaction scopes. The seventh iteration fails to call the Complete() method, and this is the iteration that causes the TransactionAbortedException to be thrown. The presence of this exception causes the parent transaction scope block to stop—its Complete() method is never called.

Summary

This chapter has shown you some of the more powerful things that you can accomplish with ADO.NET and with the System.Transactions namespace. The chapter started out by showing you some of the powerful new features that have been added to the ADO.NET DataTable class, such as the ability to read and write XML and to create a DataTableReader. Next, you saw how to update data in batches and how to perform asynchronous data updates using the appropriate Begin/End methods on the SqlCommand class. Finally, the chapter concluded with a discussion of how to use the System.Transactions namespace to create transactional code that will work with any supported resource manager, such as SQL 2005, MSMQ, DTC, and so on. Having read and understood this chapter, you should feel pretty good about your ADO.NET skills and your ability to access and manipulate data using C# 2.0.

CHAPTER 19

Working with ADO.NET Data Providers

This chapter gives you an in-depth look at the power and functionality provided by the ADO.NET data providers. You'll see how to use provider factories and the factory pattern to create provider-agnostic code. This chapter also provides you with samples of additional functionality exposed by data providers such as data source enumeration, as well as features exposed by the ADO.NET SQL provider specifically.

Introduction to ADO.NET Data Providers

Throughout the last two chapters, you have been using data providers but might not have known it. A data provider is a collection of classes that implement standard interfaces and inherit from predefined abstract base classes to provide a standard means by which a developer can access relational data. For example, ADO.NET comes with a SQL provider, an Oracle provider, an OLE DB provider, and an ODBC provider. All of them, by virtue of their compliance to data provider standards, have a similar list of classes, methods, and properties. This allows developers to reuse their knowledge of one provider to develop against a different provider.

These providers all contain connections, commands, command parameters, various data readers, and data adapters, all of which are specialized to their specific back end. So, although both the Oracle provider and the SQL provider have connections, each one uses a different means for communicating with their respective databases.

As you will see throughout the course of this chapter, data providers are easy to use, flexible, and extremely powerful.

Using Provider Factories

One of the problems of working with data providers is that they are not all the same. Prior to version 2.0 of ADO.NET, developers often had to do a lot of work on their own to get their applications to work with an OLE DB data source as well as a SQL Server data source without having to create two different data layers. In these situations, developers often created their own provider-agnostic wrappers that abstracted the work of allowing code to access both data sources seamlessly.

With ADO.NET 2.0, such wrappers are no longer necessary. The .NET Framework provides several classes that allow you to use a factory pattern to access data providers without specifically tying your code to a single implementation such as the `DbProviderFactories` class and the `DbProviderFactory` class. Using the factory pattern, you can create code that will execute commands on multiple providers without having to create complex conditional logic or multiple layers of abstraction.

Data providers are a lot more powerful under ADO.NET 2.0 than they were in previous versions. For example, when a data provider is installed, it can modify a computer's `machine.config` file to indicate that it has installed a provider factory. This allows developers to query the list of installed provider factories and handle different situations accordingly. In addition, new ADO.NET providers have the ability to provide multiple types of metadata to further assist developers in coding generically against multiple types of data without excessive or redundant code.

Obtaining the List of Installed Provider Factories

You can use the `ProviderFactories` class to obtain a list of installed factories. The list of installed factories comes in the form of a `DataTable` that contains the provider name, its invariant name (fully qualified namespace), a long description, and the fully qualified assembly strong name.

The code in Listing 19.1 iterates through the list of installed provider factories and displays their names and invariant names. You will need a provider's invariant name to create an instance of that provider's factory.

LISTING 19.1   Enumerating the List of Installed Provider Factories

```
using System;
using System.Data;
using System.Data.Common;
using System.Collections.Generic;
using System.Text;

namespace EnumFactories
{
class Program
{
```

LISTING 19.1 Continued

```
static void Main(string[] args)
{
    DataTable tbl = DbProviderFactories.GetFactoryClasses();
    Console.WriteLine("The following data provider factories are available:");
    foreach (DataRow row in tbl.Rows)
    {
        Console.WriteLine("{0} ({1})", row["Name"], row["InvariantName"]);
    }
    Console.ReadLine();
}
}
}
```

The preceding code produces the following output on the author's machine:

```
The following data provider factories are available:
Odbc Data Provider (System.Data.Odbc)
OleDb Data Provider (System.Data.OleDb)
OracleClient Data Provider (System.Data.OracleClient)
SqlClient Data Provider (System.Data.SqlClient)
SQL Server CE Data Provider (Microsoft.SqlServerCe.Client)
```

Using a Provider Factory to Establish a Connection

Using a data provider factory to establish a connection is actually a pretty simple task. First, you create an instance of a specific factory using the DbDataFactories.GetFactory() method. When you have an instance of the factory, you can use any of the following DbProviderFactory methods to create a provider-agnostic instance of an object:

- CreateConnection—Creates a new connection instance. Under the hood, this connection will be specific to the provider you chose at the factory level, but you will receive a basic DbConnection instance in return.

- CreateCommand—Creates an instance of a new command.

- CreateCommandBuilder—Creates a new command builder.

- CreateConnectionStringBuilder—Creates an instance of a connection string builder (covered in the next section).

- CreateDataAdapter—Creates a new data adapter.

- CreateDataSourceEnumerator—If the underlying provider supports it, this will create a new data source enumerator.

- CreateParameter—Creates a new DbParameter instance.

19

Take a look at the code in Listing 19.2, as it provides an illustration of how to establish a connection to a data source and execute a command without ever hard-coding a reference to a `SqlConnection` instance or an `OleDbConnection` instance.

LISTING 19.2   Establishing a Provider-Agnostic Connection

```
using System;
using System.Data;
using System.Data.Common;
using System.Collections.Generic;
using System.Text;

namespace FactoryConnect
{
class Program
{
static void Main(string[] args)
{
    DbProviderFactory factory =
DbProviderFactories.GetFactory("System.Data.SqlClient");
    using (DbConnection conn = factory.CreateConnection())
    {
        conn.ConnectionString =
"data source=localhost; initial catalog=SampleDB; Integrated Security=SSPI;";
        conn.Open();

        DbCommand cmd = factory.CreateCommand();
        cmd.CommandText = "SELECT * FROM Customers";
        cmd.Connection = conn;
        DbDataReader rdr = cmd.ExecuteReader();
        while (rdr.Read())
        {
            Console.WriteLine("{0}, {1} {2}",
rdr["LastName"], rdr["FirstName"], rdr["MiddleInitial"]);
        }
    }
    Console.ReadLine();
}
}
}
```

The important thing to note about the preceding code is that the only indications of the underlying provider are the connection string, and the invariant name of the provider. Both of those pieces of information could have come from a configuration file, from user input, or from another data source. The preceding code will work just as well on any underlying data provider that has a `Customers` table with the `"LastName"`, `"FirstName"`, and `"MiddleInitial"` columns.

Working with Connection Strings

Connection strings are typically specific to the provider for which they are intended. This makes it difficult to create a truly provider-agnostic application, as you'll have to have multiple connection string formats to manage all of the different types of providers to which your application can connect.

This dilemma is partially solved by the `DbConnectionStringBuilder` class. Each provider has its own specific connection string builder class that provides the developer with a standardized interface for creating a connection string. When the `ConnectionString` property is accessed, the output is specific to the underlying provider. The `DbConnectionStringBuilder` class provides the basic mechanism for adding name/value pairs of information to a connection string. Classes like `SqlConnectionStringBuilder` provide additional methods and properties that allow you to configure settings specific to the provider.

When you add a key and value to a connection string builder, it takes the key and interprets it in a way that is specific to the underlying provider. When you examine the connection string property of the builder, the key name might have been changed to reflect the needs of the provider. For example, if you set the "server" key on the SQL client connection string builder, it won't include that key in the output. But the same key on an ODBC or an OLE DB connection string builder will be included in the connection string.

The code in Listing 19.3 illustrates using `DbConnectionStringBuilder` to use provider-agnostic keywords to create connection strings and output them.

LISTING 19.3   Using the `DbConnectionStringBuilder`

```
using System;
using System.Data;
using System.Data.Common;
using System.Collections.Generic;
using System.Text;

namespace ConnBuilder
{
class Program
{
static void Main(string[] args)
{
    DataTable factories = DbProviderFactories.GetFactoryClasses();
    foreach (DataRow row in factories.Rows)
    {
```

LISTING 19.3   Continued

```
        if ((string)row["InvariantName"] != "Microsoft.SqlServerCe.Client")
        {
            DbProviderFactory factory =
DbProviderFactories.GetFactory((string)row["InvariantName"]);
            DbConnectionStringBuilder connBuilder =
factory.CreateConnectionStringBuilder();
            connBuilder.Add("server", "localhost");
            connBuilder.Add("user", "sa");
            connBuilder.Add("password", "secret");
            connBuilder.Add("data source", "SampleDB");
            Console.WriteLine("[{0}] {1}",
                row["InvariantName"],
                connBuilder.ConnectionString);
        }
    }
    Console.ReadLine();
}
}
}
```

The output from the preceding code is as follows:

```
[System.Data.Odbc] server=localhost;user=sa;password=secret;data source=SampleDB
[System.Data.OleDb] Data Source=SampleDB;server=localhost;user=sa;password=secret
[System.Data.OracleClient] Data Source=SampleDB;User ID=sa;Password=secret
[System.Data.SqlClient] Data Source=SampleDB;User ID=sa;Password=secret
```

As you can see, the connection string builder for each data provider produced a connection string specific to the needs of that particular provider.

Enumerating Data Sources

Some data providers now give you the ability to enumerate a list of data sources. For the SQL Server provider, this is a list of available SQL servers. Each data provider will return a DataTable containing different information about the available data sources.

The code in Listing 19.4 shows sample code to determine whether a data provider supports the ability to enumerate data sources and how to examine that list of data sources.

LISTING 19.4   Enumerating Data Sources

```
using System;
using System.Data;
using System.Data.Common;
```

LISTING 19.4 Continued

```
using System.Collections.Generic;
using System.Text;

namespace EnumDS
{
class Program
{
static void Main(string[] args)
{
    DbProviderFactory factory =
DbProviderFactories.GetFactory("System.Data.SqlClient");
    DbConnection conn = factory.CreateConnection();
    conn.ConnectionString =
"data source=localhost; initial catalog=SampleDB; Integrated Security=SSPI;";
    conn.Open();

    if (factory.CanCreateDataSourceEnumerator)
    {
        DbDataSourceEnumerator dsEnum = factory.CreateDataSourceEnumerator();
        DataTable sources = dsEnum.GetDataSources();
        foreach (DataRow dataSource in sources.Rows)
        {
            Console.WriteLine(dataSource["ServerName"]);
        }
    }
    Console.ReadLine();
}
}
}
```

The preceding code takes a few seconds to start, as the GetDataSources() method is fairly lengthy. After it completes, however, you will have a fully populated DataTable containing a list of data sources available for the given data provider (in this case, System.Data.SqlClient).

Obtaining Additional Provider Information

Many of the data providers expose additional information that might be useful for debugging, tracing, and diagnosing purposes. Depending on the provider, you might be able to get information about the database server version or any number of other pieces of useful information, even metadata about columns, tables, and databases contained within the server.

19

Using the `RetrieveStatistics` Method

One of the useful methods exposed by the `SqlConnection` class for debugging, tracing, and diagnosing purposes is the `RetrieveStatistics()` method. This method returns a name/value pair collection of statistics about the connection itself. You can use this information to obtain statistics before and after executing commands to compare and examine the impact of each of your commands. The code in Listing 19.5 illustrates how to use this method.

LISTING 19.5   Using the `RetrieveStatistics` Method

```
using System;
using System.Data;
using System.Data.SqlClient;
using System.Collections.Generic;
using System.Text;
using System.Collections;

namespace SqlStatistics
{
class Program
{
static void Main(string[] args)
{
    SqlConnection conn = new SqlConnection(
        "data source=localhost; initial catalog=SampleDB;
        ➥Integrated Security=SSPI;");
    conn.StatisticsEnabled = true;
    conn.Open();

    Hashtable ht = (Hashtable)conn.RetrieveStatistics();
    foreach (string key in ht.Keys)
    {
        Console.WriteLine("{0} : {1}", key, ht[key]);
    }
    Console.ReadLine();
}
}
}
```

Note that the connection won't gather statistics unless indicated by the `StatisticsEnabled` property due to the overhead involved in maintaining metrics. The output from the preceding code on a freshly created connection is as follows:

```
NetworkServerTime : 0
BytesReceived : 0
UnpreparedExecs : 0
```

```
SumResultSets : 0
SelectCount : 0
PreparedExecs : 0
ConnectionTime : 0
ExecutionTime : 109
Prepares : 0
BuffersSent : 0
SelectRows : 0
ServerRoundtrips : 0
CursorOpens : 0
Transactions : 0
BytesSent : 0
BuffersReceived : 0
IduRows : 0
IduCount : 0
```

Obtaining Schema Information from Data Providers

Another extremely valuable piece of information that you can get from a data provider is a schema. The GetSchema() method of a DbConnection class is the means by which you can interrogate a data provider of an enormous amount of valuable data.

When you invoke this method with no arguments, it provides you with the list of schemas that you can query. For example, when you call GetSchema() on a SQL Server 2005 connection, you get the following list of schemas contained in a table called MetaDataCollections:

```
MetaDataCollections
DataSourceInformation
DataTypes
Restrictions
ReservedWords
Users
Databases
Tables
Columns
Views
ViewColumns
ProcedureParameters
Procedures
ForeignKeys
IndexColumns
Indexes
UserDefinedTypes
```

You can experiment with the results for querying each of the above metadata collections. For example, a query to the data provider for the `Databases` metadata collection resulted in the following list of databases:

```
master
tempdb
model
msdb
ReportServer
ReportServerTempDB
SampleDB
```

The database list also included the database creation date and the `dbid` of the database.

Creating a Custom ADO.NET Data Provider

Creating a custom ADO.NET data provider is definitely a long process that needs to be designed thoroughly before proceeding. However, the use of standard interfaces and base classes makes the task slightly easier.

There aren't all that many reasons to create your own custom ADO.NET data provider. If you find that you need to access data that you want to expose through the connection/command/reader pattern, there is an extremely good chance that the underlying data can be accessed using either ODBC or OLE DB. Remember that you can use OLE DB to access data sources like Excel spreadsheets and even text files. However, if the data is proprietary, or can't be accessed through ODBC, OLE DB, Oracle, or SQL Server, you might find yourself in a situation where you want to create a data provider to expose your data to the .NET Framework in a relational manner.

To do this, you'll need to create a class library that contains implementations of several interfaces. To create a minimal data provider, you will need to create the following:

- A connection—To expose data via a data provider, the data provider must follow a connection model. A connection represents some live connection with a source of data, whether that connection is a reserved file handle, a network socket, or some other representation of a database connection.

- A data reader—You will need to create a class that provides a read-only, forward-only traversal over the underlying data contained within your provider

- A data adapter—Data adapters are responsible for executing commands in order to exchange data between the underlying data source and `DataSets`.

- A command—The command is a unit of instruction sent to the underlying data source. Traditional commands are typically in the form of stored procedures or SQL statements, but your data source can take any type of parameterized command that you feel appropriate. Commands can return both scalar data and data readers.

In the past, some example data providers have been created for ADO.NET that provide exposure for Microsoft Message Queues (MSMQ), Active Directory (AD), and even runtime type information provided by a `Reflection` data provider.

It's beyond the scope of this chapter to walk you through the implementation of a custom provider. In addition to providing implementations of a command, a data reader, a connection, and a data adapter, your data provider would also have to take into account things like transactional support and whether or not you want your provider to register itself with the list of data provider factories.

Summary

This chapter has provided you with a guide to some of the extra features that are exposed by the ADO.NET data providers that come with the .NET Framework. You saw how to create provider-agnostic code using provider factory lists and provider factories. In addition, you saw how you can use the `DbConnectionStringBuilder` class to create connection strings without knowing the specifics of the underlying provider at compile time. Finally, you saw how to squeeze a lot of extra functionality out of the data providers by enumerating data sources, querying metadata collections, and obtaining tracing and monitoring statistics for a given connection.

19

CHAPTER **20**

Strongly Typed DataSets

So far in this book you have been exposed to many different aspects of data access using ADO.NET. One of the core pieces of ADO.NET is the DataSet, an in-memory representation of relational data that can contain multiple related tables, each with primary and foreign keys. DataSets also let you perform queries on the data contained within them, as well persisting that data in XML format. Using a DataAdapter, you can synchronize data contained in a DataSet with data stored in a back-end data source such as SQL Server or Oracle.

This chapter introduces you to a special kind of DataSet, the typed DataSet. You will learn the basics of working with typed DataSets, as well as how to use functionality new to Visual Studio 2005 and .NET 2.0 to connect those DataSets to live data sources using TableAdapter classes. Finally, you'll see how to tailor the member and method names of your typed DataSets to increase their readability and ease of use as well as how to extend the DataSet functionality using the new C# 2.0 partial classes.

Introduction to the Typed DataSet

A typed DataSet is a DataSet whose data structure is known at compile time, allowing Visual Studio to create strongly typed wrappers for the tables, rows, columns, and relationships contained within the DataSet.

You can create a typed DataSet in several ways. The easiest, of course, is to use the designer provided by Visual Studio. The schema (metadata including columns, tables, keys, and relationships) for the typed DataSet is dictated using a dialect of XML called XSD (XML Schema

Definition). You can also create a typed `DataSet` by supplying an XSD file as input to the `XSD.EXE` command-line tool.

In this section you'll see the various ways in which you can produce a typed `DataSet` and how you can use that `DataSet` to work with your data.

Using an XSD Schema to Create a Typed `DataSet`

The format and language of XSD itself is beyond the scope of this chapter. If you want to know all about the XSD standard, you can check out the XML Schema home page at http://www.w3.org/XML/Schema. The important thing to note here is that XML Schema is used for many purposes above and beyond the typing of `DataSets`. XML Schema has numerous uses, and Microsoft has utilized various extensions to the XSD Schema to provide additional features for typed `DataSets`.

Take a look at the following sample schema, which defines a table called `Books` that contains columns describing individual titles:

```
<?xml version="1.0" encoding="utf-8"?>
<xs:schema id="Books" xmlns=""
 xmlns:xs="http://www.w3.org/2001/XMLSchema"
 xmlns:msdata="urn:schemas-microsoft-com:xml-msdata">
  <xs:element name="Books" msdata:IsDataSet="true" msdata:UseCurrentLocale="true">
    <xs:complexType>
      <xs:choice minOccurs="0" maxOccurs="unbounded">
        <xs:element name="Book">
          <xs:complexType>
            <xs:attribute name="id" type="xs:string" />
            <xs:attribute name="author" type="xs:string" />
            <xs:attribute name="title" type="xs:string" />
            <xs:attribute name="price" type="xs:string" />
          </xs:complexType>
        </xs:element>
      </xs:choice>
    </xs:complexType>
  </xs:element>
</xs:schema>
```

This schema defines the structure of a `DataSet`, and you can use the `XSD` command-line tool to create a C# class that inherits from `System.Data.DataSet` that provides strongly typed members specific to the preceding schema, as shown in the following code:

```
xsd books.xsd /d /namespace:SAMS.DataSets
```

This creates a class named `SAMS.DataSets.Books` and places it in a file named `books.cs`. This class inherits from `System.Data.DataSet`, and exposes strongly typed members on each of its rows such as id, author, title, and price. You don't need to access members using the indexer notation as in the following example:

```
myDataSet.Tables["Books"].Rows[0]["author"]
```

Instead, you can use the far more friendly (and strongly typed) member accessors provided by the SAMS.DataSets.Books class:

```
myDataSet.Books[0].author
```

If you don't know enough about XSD to create a schema from scratch, you can also use the XSD tool to infer a schema from an instance document. An instance document is just an XML document that contains data rather than metadata. For example, an instance document that produces the book schema is shown in the following code:

```
<Books>
  <Book id="1" author="Bob Smith" title="Life Demystified" price="99.99" />
  <Book id="2" author="Joe Author" title="How to Get Rich Quick" price="8999.99" />
  <Book id="3" author="Bob Author" title="Minimalism Explained, Volume 29 of 50" />
</Books>
```

To infer an XSD schema from your source data without having to know all of the intricacies of the XSD language, you can issue the following XSD command:

```
xsd books.xml
```

This will create the books.xsd file, which you can then use to create a typed DataSet.

Using the Designer to Build a Typed DataSet

Now that you've seen how to build a typed DataSet the "hard" way, this section will walk you through creating one visually, using the Visual Studio designer. It seems as though using raw XSD to create DataSets is not as common as it was with the first iterations of the .NET Framework and Visual Studio. In fact, support for viewing the XSD source for a DataSet created with Visual Studio has been completely removed from the product, you have to open an XSD file as if it were an XML file to get to the source view.

To get started, create any project type you like, but a console project will do just fine for this exercise. Next, right-click the project and choose Add, and then New Item. Select the DataSet template from the list of options presented to you and give it a suitable name.

You will be presented with a blank design surface onto which you can drag items from the Toolbox or even directly from the Server Explorer. This means that you can accomplish some pretty amazing things just by dragging a table from your source database onto your DataSet's design surface.

For now we'll keep it simple and just drag a DataTable onto the design surface. You can call it whatever you like. Right-click the table and choose Add, and then Column. You can choose the column name, its data type, whether it autoincrements, and much more. You can then right-click your key column and choose Set Primary Key. The interface looks

20

and feels very much like the table creation screens in the SQL Server Management Studio application for SQL Server 2005.

Create a second table and give it a column that matches the primary key column in the first table. Drag a `DataRelation` from the Toolbox onto the design surface, and you can easily and visually set up a parent-child relationship between the two tables, as illustrated in Figure 20.1.

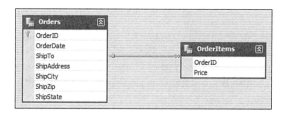

FIGURE 20.1   A simple `DataSet` with a parent table and a child table.

The design surface is an extremely powerful tool because it not only distances you from the low-level XSD generation, but it provides you with a user interface that lets you see the relationships between all of the tables in your `DataSet` at a quick glance, as well as the columns in each table.

Programming with a Typed `DataSet`

Writing code that uses typed `DataSet`s is the easiest part of all. As you saw earlier, with a typed `DataSet` you don't need the string- or ordinal-based member access as shown in the following example:

```
myDataSet.Tables["Books"].Rows[0]["author"]
```

Instead, you can access the members in a more user-friendly fashion because the class that derives from `DataSet` has exposed strongly typed members:

```
myDataSet.Books[0].author
```

After you have added a `DataSet` to your project and configured it using the designer, you can create an instance of it and begin working with it just as you would any other `DataSet`. Listing 20.1 provides an illustration of how to populate a typed `DataSet` using its strongly typed members.

LISTING 20.1   Populating a Typed `DataSet` Programmatically

```
using System;
using System.Data;
using System.Collections.Generic;
using System.Text;
```

LISTING 20.1   Continued

```
namespace DataSet1
{
class Program
{
static void Main(string[] args)
{
    OrderDataSet orderData = new OrderDataSet();
    OrderDataSet.OrdersRow order = orderData.Orders.NewOrdersRow();
    order.OrderDate = DateTime.Now;
    order.ShipTo = "Kevin Hoffman";
    order.ShipAddress = "1 Somewhere Lane";
    order.ShipCity = "Somewhereville";
    order.ShipState = "NY";
    order.ShipZip = "99999";
    orderData.Orders.AddOrdersRow(order);
    orderData.WriteXml("orders.xml");
}
}
}
```

For those of us who prefer business objects with meaningful and appropriately typed members over the generic nature of the traditional DataSet, the typed DataSet is an extremely powerful tool, providing developers with the power and flexibility of the standard DataSet coupled with the easy-to-read and easy-to-maintain strongly typed members. Using a typed DataSet's strongly typed members, you can actually catch type mismatch errors at compile time that might have otherwise taken hours or days to track down using a standard DataSet.

Connecting Typed DataSets to Live Data

DataSets on their own are a pretty powerful tool, but a DataSet doesn't do anyone any good without any data. This section shows you the basics of using a DataAdapter to populate a typed DataSet as well as how to use some of the new features of ADO.NET 2.0, such as the TableAdapter component.

Filling a DataSet Manually Using a DataAdapter

If you are familiar with working with standard DataSets and DataAdapters, the material in this section should be very familiar to you. A typed DataSet is really just a class that derives from System.Data.DataSet in order to provide a developer with a DataSet that is specific to one schema. As a result of this, any existing code that works on standard DataSets will also work on a typed DataSet, including the DataAdapter. The code in Listing 20.2 shows that you can use a DataAdapter to populate a typed DataSet the same way you would have used one to populate a basic DataSet.

20

LISTING 20.2   Populating a Typed `DataSet` using a Standard `DataAdapter`

```
using System;
using System.Data;
using System.Data.SqlClient;
using System.Collections.Generic;
using System.Text;

namespace PopulateTypedDS
{
class Program
{
static void Main(string[] args)
{
    OrderDataSet orders = new OrderDataSet();
    using (SqlConnection conn = new SqlConnection(
        "data source=localhost; initial catalog=SampleDB;
        ➥Integrated Security=SSPI;"))
    {
        conn.Open();
        SqlCommand orderCmd = conn.CreateCommand();
        orderCmd.CommandText = "SELECT * FROM Orders";
        SqlDataAdapter da = new SqlDataAdapter(orderCmd);
        da.Fill(orders, "Orders");
    }

}
}
}
```

Filling Typed `DataSets` Using `TableAdapters`

A `TableAdapter` can be thought of as a strongly typed `DataAdapter` that specializes in synchronizing one table between a typed `DataSet` and the relational back-end database. With previous versions of ADO.NET, Microsoft realized that one of the most common tasks that people performed on `DataSets` was exchanging data between the `DataSet` and the database. Using a `DataAdapter` such as `SqlDataAdapter` can accomplish this, but the regular `DataAdapters` are not designed to work with specific types. When you create a `TableAdapter` using the `DataSet` designer, that `TableAdapter` is designed according to your rules for how data should be loaded into the indicated table.

To create a `TableAdapter`, drag one from the Toolbox onto a blank area of the design surface. Though you might initially think so, you can't drag a `TableAdapter` onto an existing table within your `DataSet` designer. The reason for this is that the act of dragging a `TableAdapter` onto the design surface brings up a wizard that prompts you for information on how the adapter can connect to the database, whether it should use stored procedures or SQL statements, and a host of other options. This also will read the schema information from the database and use that to generate the actual table in the DataSet.

After being created by the wizard, each TableAdapter starts off with two very important methods:

- Fill—This method populates only the table for which the adapter was created. When you call this method, the adapter will read the connection string information obtained by the wizard from inside the DataSet's XSD file, as well as the query information you indicated, and use that to select data from the database table and place it in the strongly typed DataTable.

- GetData—This method performs the same function as Fill(), except that instead of filling a destination table, this method returns a new instance of the strongly typed table, prepopulated with the results from the default SELECT query specified during the TableAdapter configuration wizard.

Figure 20.2 shows the design surface after creating two TableAdapters (and, as a result, two strongly typed DataTables) by indicating to the configuration wizard the location of the tables in the database and the queries that should be run by the adapter.

FIGURE 20.2   Connected TableAdapters and their corresponding tables.

TableAdapters, despite their direct association with a single strongly typed table, do not appear as nested classes within a typed DataSet. Instead, they show up in their own unique namespace related to the DataSet itself.

For example, the DataSet in Figure 20.2 is called ConnectedOrderDataSet. All of the table adapter classes created for that DataSet will appear in a namespace called ConnectedOrderDataSetTableAdapters.

The code in Listing 20.3 shows how to use the Fill() methods on TableAdapters to populate a typed DataSet with data retrieved directly from the database.

LISTING 20.3   Populating a Typed DataSet with TableAdapters

```
using System;
using System.Collections.Generic;
using System.Text;
```

LISTING 20.3   Continued

```
namespace ConnectedDataSet
{
class Program
{
static void Main(string[] args)
{
    ConnectedOrderDataSetTableAdapters.OrdersTableAdapter orderTa =
        new ConnectedOrderDataSetTableAdapters.OrdersTableAdapter();
    ConnectedOrderDataSetTableAdapters.OrderItemsTableAdapter orderItemsTa =
        new ConnectedOrderDataSetTableAdapters.OrderItemsTableAdapter();

    ConnectedOrderDataSet orderData = new ConnectedOrderDataSet();
    orderTa.Fill(orderData.Orders);
    orderItemsTa.Fill(orderData.OrderItems) ;

    foreach (ConnectedOrderDataSet.OrdersRow order in orderData.Orders)
    {
        Console.WriteLine("Order {0} Purchased by {1} on {2}", order.OrderID,
            order.ShipTo, order.OrderDate.ToShortDateString());
        foreach (ConnectedOrderDataSet.OrderItemsRow orderItem in
order.GetOrderItemsRows())
        {
            Console.WriteLine("\t{0} - {1} for ${2:00.00}",
                orderItem.SKU, orderItem.ItemDescription, orderItem.Price);
        }
    }

    Console.ReadLine();
}
}
}
```

One thing that may seem to be missing from the preceding code is the use of a connection string or a connection at all. This is because when you configured the TableAdapter using the wizard, you specified the connection to use and you also specified the query to use when retrieving data from the table. Other options you can choose during the wizard include giving the TableAdapter the ability to directly send INSERT, UPDATE, and DELETE statements to the database.

At the end of the wizard creation, you will see a summary of the actions taken. This typically includes the creation of INSERT, UPDATE, DELETE, and SELECT statements to be used in synchronizing data between the table and the database. This allows you to do things like change a row, call `Update()` on the `TableAdapter`, and have the change automatically propagated to the database:

```
orderData.Orders[0].ShipTo = "Modified User";
orderTa.Update(orderData.Orders);
```

Unfortunately, some of the queries that the wizard generates on your behalf aren't the most efficient. You can easily remedy this by supplying your own manually written query to provide the most optimal update experience possible.

Take a look at the screenshot of the Query Builder that is integrated directly into Visual Studio in Figure 20.3. As you can see, the query used for the `TableAdapter`'s `UpdateCommand` property is pretty inefficient.

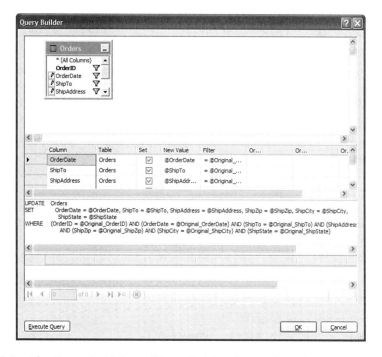

FIGURE 20.3   The `QueryBuilder` editing a `TableAdapter`'s `UpdateCommand`.

The power at your fingertips with the combination of typed `DataSets`, the `TableAdapter`, and the integrated Query Builder is pretty impressive. You can visually design and edit all of the SQL statements (or stored procedures) that will be used when updating and querying the underlying data source. You can combine all of this with the new ability of data adapters to update in batches to create some extremely powerful data access mechanisms with just a few lines of C#.

20

Adding Additional Queries to a Typed `DataSet`

One of the limitations of the `DataAdapter` is that it only has room for four commands: `INSERT`, `UPDATE`, `SELECT`, and `DELETE`. The new `TableAdapter` recognizes the fact that there may be five or six different ways in which you want to retrieve data with the same schema. For example, at one point in your application you might want only the orders that belong to a specific user, and at another point in the application you might want just the orders placed on a specific date. At the same time, you want to be able to maintain the parent/child relationship between orders and order items. You can do this by creating additional queries and placing them inside the `TableAdapter`.

To add an additional query to an existing `TableAdapter`, just right-click the `TableAdapter` on the design surface and choose Add Query. This brings up the query configuration wizard, which first asks if you want to create a new SQL statement, a new stored procedure, or attach your query to an existing stored procedure. You don't have to re-enter any connection information because that is already stored as part of the `TableAdapter` itself.

You will see a dialog prompting you to enter a SQL statement that will be used to populate the data table. You can click the Query Builder button to get a more interactive dialog. You can create a parameterized query here, which will, in turn, create a method on the table that accepts that parameter. In this example, the following query was entered into the dialog:

```
SELECT    OrderID, OrderDate, ShipTo, ShipAddress, ShipZip, ShipCity, ShipState
FROM      Orders
WHERE     (ShipCity = @City)
```

This query will be used in order to selectively fill the table with orders that were shipped to a specific city. When prompted for the method names for the `fill` and `getdata` operations, select something that describes the nature of the operation. In this case, `FillByCity` and `GetDataByCity` are descriptive and appropriate.

After you add the query to your `TableAdapter`, you can call that method the same way you would call any other method and pass the filter parameter:

```
orderTa.ClearBeforeFill = true;
orderTa.FillByCity(orderData.Orders, "Somewhere");
Console.WriteLine("Orders filtered by city: Somewhere");
foreach (ConnectedOrderDataSet.OrdersRow order in orderData.Orders)
{
    Console.WriteLine("Order {0} Purchased by {1} on {2} with {3} order items.",
        order.OrderID, order.ShipTo,
        order.OrderDate.ToShortDateString(),
        order.GetOrderItemsRows().Length);
}
```

The power of being able to create additional parameterized queries exposed as methods on a `TableAdapter` is something that just hasn't been available to developers until

ADO.NET 2.0. The preceding code also demonstrates that the parent-child relationships remain intact when the parent table has been filtered using a custom query.

Annotating a Typed DataSet

When you create a typed DataSet, the XSD tool that generates the C# class provides default names for all of the members, including properties, methods for obtaining child rows, table class names, and row class names. For example, if you were to create a table called Customers, the default class name for a customer would be CustomersRow, not Customer. To access the customer's order history, you would have to use the GetOrderHistoryRows() method rather than something more appropriate like GetOrderHistory().

You can solve this problem by annotating your DataSet. In previous versions of Visual Studio, you could access the XSD text for a typed DataSet directly from within the IDE. For some unknown (and highly aggravating) reason, that feature is no longer present in Visual Studio 2005 by default. To get at the XML view of an XSD file, right-click it in the Solution Explorer and choose Open With and then select the XML Editor option.

When you look at the inside of the XSD file, you will notice that there are a lot of attributes that begin with msprop:Generator_. These are all customizable annotation attributes. By changing these attributes, you can directly control the names of the classes, members, and methods created when the DataSet class is built.

Table 20.1 shows the various annotation attributes and what effect they have on the typed DataSet.

TABLE 20.1 Annotation Attributes (All Prefixed by msprop:Generator_ Unless Otherwise Specified)

Attribute	Effect
DataSetName	Controls the name of the typed DataSet class.
TableClassName	The name of the class produced for a given table, for example, CustomerTable.
RowChangedName	Name of the RowChanged event fired for row changes on the given table, for example, CustomerChanged.
RowClassName	The name of the class generated to encapsulate one row of the table. By default, this has a Row postfix, such as CustomersRow. This is often one of the first attributes changed when annotating.
RowChangingName	The name of the RowChanging event.
RowEvArgName	The name of the RowChanged event argument class.
RowEvHandlerName	Name of the RowChanged event handler.
TablePropName	Name of the property representing this table within the DataSet, for example, "Customers" or "Orders".
TableVarName	Name of the variable that holds the table inside the class.
ColumnPropNameInRow	Name of the property that represents the given column on a row.
ColumnVarNameInTable	Name of the variable that provides access to the column from within the table class.

TABLE 20.1   Continued

Attribute	Effect
ColumnPropNameInTable	The name of the column property in the table. Typically has a "Column" postfix.
rel_Generator_ParentPropName	The name of the parent when accessed from the parent; defaults to the class name of the row. Can be set to things like "Customer" or "Order".
rel_Generator_ChildPropName	The name of the method used to obtain child rows from a parent row. Defaults to Get(childtable)Rows. Often set to names like "GetOrderItems" or "GetChildItems", and so on.

With several of the preceding annotations applied to a typed DataSet containing customer data with a Customers table and an OrderHistory table, you can write code that looks much cleaner and is far more readable than code generated with no annotations:

```
using System;
using System.Collections.Generic;
using System.Text;

namespace AnnotateDS
{
class Program
{
static void Main(string[] args)
{
    CustomerDataSet custData = new CustomerDataSet();

    // populate data from some location...

    foreach (CustomerDataSet.Customer cust in custData.Customers)
    {
        Console.WriteLine("Customer {0} {1}", cust.FirstName, cust.LastName);
        Console.WriteLine("Order History:");
        foreach (CustomerDataSet.OrderHistoryItem histItem in
cust.GetOrderHistory())
        {
            Console.WriteLine("\t{0} - ${1:00.00}", histItem.OrderID,
                histItem.TotalPrice);
        }
    }

}
}
}
```

Because the contents of an XSD file can get fairly bloated, I will only show you the anno-tated "Customers" element from the preceding typed DataSet:

```
<xs:element name="Customers"
  msprop:Generator_UserTableName="Customers"
  msprop:Generator_RowDeletedName="CustomerDeleted"
            msprop:Generator_TableClassName="CustomerTable"
  msprop:Generator_RowChangedName="CustomerChanged"


          msprop:Generator_RowClassName="Customer"
              msprop:Generator_RowChangingName="CustomerChanging"
              msprop:Generator_RowEvArgName="CustomerChangeEvent"
    msprop:Generator_RowEvHandlerName="CustomerChangeEventHandler"
    msprop:Generator_TablePropName="Customers"
    msprop:Generator_TableVarName="tableCustomers"
    msprop:Generator_RowDeletingName="CustomerDeleting">
    <xs:complexType>
      <xs:sequence>
        <xs:element name="ID" msdata:AutoIncrement="true"
msprop:Generator_UserColumnName="ID"
msprop:Generator_ColumnPropNameInRow="ID"
msprop:Generator_ColumnVarNameInTable="columnID"
 msprop:Generator_ColumnPropNameInTable="IDColumn" type="xs:int" />
        <xs:element name="FirstName" msprop:Generator_
UserColumnName="FirstName" msprop:Generator_ColumnPropNameInRow="FirstName"
msprop:Generator_ColumnVarNameInTable="columnFirstName"
msprop:Generator_ColumnPropNameInTable="FirstNameColumn"
type="xs:string" minOccurs="0" />
        <xs:element name="LastName" msprop:Generator_UserColumnName="LastName"
 msprop:Generator_ColumnPropNameInRow="LastName"
msprop:Generator_ColumnVarNameInTable="columnLastName"
msprop:Generator_ColumnPropNameInTable="LastNameColumn"
type="xs:string" minOccurs="0" />
      </xs:sequence>
    </xs:complexType>
  </xs:element>
```

Extending a Typed DataSet Using Partial Classes

After you have created your typed DataSet and configured all of your TableAdapters to run all of the queries that you need and annotated it so that all of the members have appropriate names, you still may find that you want to extend the functionality of your typed DataSet. For example, you may decide that you have several operations that will be performed frequently on the data, such as summing the total price of all orders within the DataSet. Rather than creating a separate utility class that takes a ConnectedOrderDataSet as a parameter, you can actually extend the class itself through the use of partial classes in C#.

To do this, you can either right-click the DataSet in the Solution Explorer and choose View Code, or you can right-click the design surface of the DataSet designer and choose View Code. If this is the first time you have done this, you'll see an empty partial class implementation like the one that follows:

```
namespace ConnectedDataSet {



    partial class ConnectedOrderDataSet
    {
    }
}
```

To add your own custom functionality, all you have to do is add the methods you want, such as the method shown in the following code:

```
namespace ConnectedDataSet {

partial class ConnectedOrderDataSet
{
public decimal SumAllOrders()
{
    decimal totalValue = 0.0M;
    foreach (OrdersRow order in Orders)
    {
        foreach (OrderItemsRow orderItem in order.GetOrderItemsRows())
        {
            totalValue += orderItem.Price;
        }
    }
    return totalValue;
}
}
}
```

With this method in place, you can call this method on the DataSet just like any other method:

```
Console.WriteLine("Total sum of all purchases in DataSet: ${0:00.00}",
    orderData.SumAllOrders());
```

Summary

This chapter started with a basic introduction to the typed `DataSet` including the various ways in which you can create one. In addition, this chapter covered how to connect a typed `DataSet` to live data sources using conventional `DataAdapter`s as well as the new `TableAdapter` component. Finally, you saw how to extend the functionality already provided by a typed `DataSet` by adding additional queries to a `TableAdapter` and by adding code to the partial class provided by the typed `DataSet`.

After reading this chapter, you should have a firm grasp of how you can use typed `DataSet`s in your application to increase productivity, code reuse, and ease of maintenance.

CHAPTER 21

Programming with SQL Server 2005

SQL Server 2005 adds a wealth of new features for developers and DBAs alike. One of the biggest new features of SQL Server 2005 of interest to C# developers is the integration of the CLR directly into the server. This gives SQL Server 2005 the ability to host stored procedures, user-defined functions, user-defined types, and much more—all written in managed code.

The ability to reuse your existing .NET and C# skills from within SQL Server 2005, as well as have access to the entire library of .NET Framework classes, creates an incredible new opportunity for both efficiency and productivity.

This chapter shows you how you can get started writing managed code for SQL Server 2005 both within SQL Server and on the client side, with an eye toward making intelligent decisions about when to utilize the new technology and when to avoid it.

Introduction to the SQL Server 2005 CLR Host

SQL Server 2005 is integrated with the Common Language Runtime (CLR), giving the database access to all of the features and benefits of managed code. Developing in C# is a rich, object-oriented environment that allows for faster time to production and more reliable, more scalable code. The code written in C# still works within the confines of Code Access Security (CAS), which provides enhanced security for all managed code executed by SQL Server 2005. In addition to the ability to write stored procedures in C#, the integration of the CLR into SQL Server 2005 also provides you with the ability to write user-defined data types, functions, and aggregates. One of the other benefits of being able to write C# code for SQL Server 2005 is the ability to use the highly productive IDE native to Visual Studio 2005. Finally, the use of C# can potentially provide dramatic performance increases when applied in the appropriate manner. The following sections will show you how all this and more can be accomplished.

Building C# Stored Procedures

When creating managed code that will reside within SQL Server as a stored procedure, you are basically creating a static method on a class. That static method is then decorated with the `Microsoft.SqlServer.Server.SqlProcedure` attribute. When your assembly is deployed to SQL Server and stored within the database, this attribute allows SQL to create a CLR routine for the method.

By default, SQL Server 2005 doesn't allow you to execute CLR code, so you'll have to enable it by executing the following command inside a SQL query window (make sure you're connected with sufficient privileges to perform this command):

```
sp_configure 'clr enable', 1
```

After executing this, SQL Server will inform you that the option has changed, but it will not take effect until you issue the following command:

```
reconfigure
```

Now you're ready to start coding. Ordinarily, you would have to create an assembly and then go over to SQL Server and issue several commands within the query window to deploy the assembly and then create a managed stored procedure. However, with Visual Studio 2005, you can create a special type of project called a *SQL Server project.*

Before you create a SQL Server project, you will need to have an instance of SQL Server handy, as well as a database against which you are planning on developing.

When you first create a SQL Server Project, you will be asked for a database reference if you haven't already created one, as shown in Figure 21.1.

With a new SQL Server project in your solution, you are ready to go. Simply right-click the project and highlight the Add submenu. You will see the following list of SQL Server objects appear:

- User-Defined Function
- Stored Procedure
- Aggregate
- Trigger
- User-Defined Type

FIGURE 21.1   Database reference prompt dialog.

Select Stored Procedure and call it TestProcedure. Visual Studio will create a stored procedure stub that looks as follows:

```
using System;
using System.Data;
using System.Data.SqlClient;
using System.Data.SqlTypes;
using Microsoft.SqlServer.Server;


public partial class StoredProcedures
{
[Microsoft.SqlServer.Server.SqlProcedure]
public static void TestProcedure()
{
    // Put your code here
}
};
```

Note that the class is a partial class called StoredProcedures. Whenever you add a new stored procedure to your SQL Server project, it will be part of the partial class StoredProcedures and the static method representing the procedure will be in its own file.

When building C# static methods that will be used as stored procedures, you need to remember the following rules:

- The return type of the method is used as the return value of the stored procedure or function.

- The parameter list of the method is the parameter list of the stored procedure. As such, you should only use data types from the System.Data.SqlTypes namespace.

- Keep in mind that your method has no user interface, so any debugging or tracing you do can't go to a console window. You can still print debug messages the same way you could with stored procedures, however.

Now we make a small modification to the "stub" method provided for us, and we're left with this:

```
using System;
using System.Data;
using System.Data.SqlClient;
using System.Data.SqlTypes;
using Microsoft.SqlServer.Server;


public partial class StoredProcedures
{
[Microsoft.SqlServer.Server.SqlProcedure]
public static void TestProcedure(out SqlString outVal)
{
    // Put your code here
    outVal = "Hello World";
}
};
```

When you build this project, the assembly is compiled into a DLL, but that's it. In order to get your stored procedure onto the server, you need to debug your application. This will deploy your assembly to SQL Server, register your stored procedure, and then execute a test script found in the Test Scripts folder of your solution called Test.sql. To execute just this stored procedure without running a test script, open your Server Explorer pane, browse to the stored procedure you just created, right-click the procedure, and choose Execute. Finally, select <NULL> for the input to the @outVal parameter. When you execute the stored procedure, the following text will appear in your output window:

```
Running [dbo].[TestProcedure] ( @outVal = <NULL> ).

No rows affected.
(0 row(s) returned)
```

```
@outVal = Hello World
@RETURN_VALUE =
Finished running [dbo].[TestProcedure].
```

This is just the beginning. As you will see in the section on utilizing the new server-side SQL library, accessing data and returning data to the caller are both extremely easy tasks managed by powerful tools.

Building C# User-Defined Functions

A function in SQL Server is just that: a function that can be invoked from within any T-SQL statement that will return a value. SQL Server has many built-in functions for string concatenation, mathematics, data type conversion, and much more. With the integration of the CLR into SQL Server 2005, you can now write your own user-defined functions in C#.

In many circumstances, you need to perform some bit of logic on a column or a couple of columns in order to provide a calculated column. What often happens in that situation is that either the logic is too difficult to represent in T-SQL or the calculation is just too slow, so developers leave the columns unaltered, and then perform the calculated column on the client side in C#. Now you can place that complex logic on the server, and gain a performance boost from not having to perform the calculations on the client.

To illustrate this, without getting bogged down in a complex calculation, the next example will create a C# user-defined function that takes a customer's first name, last name, and middle initial as parameters, and returns a string containing the appropriate full-name display.

Add a new user-defined function to your project by right-clicking the project, highlighting Add, and then clicking User-Defined Function. You'll be presented with an empty stub that looks similar to the empty stored procedure stub from the preceding section. However, this method starts off with a return type (functions *cannot* be void) and is decorated with the `Microsoft.SqlServer.Server.SqlFunction` attribute. The code in Listing 21.1 shows this name-formatting function.

LISTING 21.1   C# User-Defined Function

```
using System;
using System.Text;
using System.Data;
using System.Data.SqlClient;
using System.Data.SqlTypes;
using Microsoft.SqlServer.Server;

public partial class UserDefinedFunctions
{
[Microsoft.SqlServer.Server.SqlFunction]
public static SqlString NameDisplay(
```

LISTING 21.1   Continued

```
    SqlString firstName,
    SqlString lastName,
    SqlString middleInitial)
{
    // we have access to the StringBuilder, a much better
    // concatenator than string addition
    StringBuilder sb = new StringBuilder();
    sb.AppendFormat("{0}, {1} {2}",
        lastName, firstName, middleInitial);
    return new SqlString(sb.ToString());
}
};
```

The important thing to note here isn't how easy it is to format names. The important thing to note is that you can pass any SQL data type (even the new XML data type) to your own C# function, perform some processing on it, and then return a value that can then be used in a SELECT statement by any code, whether it's someone running a query directly on the server or whether it is within your own C# client application.

If you modify the Test.sql script to contain the following UDF test code

```
select dbo.NameDisplay(c.FirstName, c.LastName, c.MiddleInitial)
as FullName FROM Customers c
```

You will see the following output (assuming you have a Customers table defined):

```
FullName
----------------------
Doe, John Q
Doe, Jane R
Smith, Bob E   Smith, Rob V   Smith, Lob L
Customer, Jethro M
Customer, Ringo R
No rows affected.
(7 row(s) returned)
```

If you have been developing applications based on SQL Server for a long time, you can probably think of several uses for C# user-defined functions that can save you the time and headache of writing them in T-SQL, and also create potential performance improvements.

Creating a C# User-Defined Type

Before we get into the code involved in creating your own user-defined type in SQL Server 2005, it should be pointed out that CLR UDTs are extremely different from any type of custom data structure you may have created for previous versions of SQL Server. A CLR UDT not only has fields for storing data, but it also has behaviors that are defined by C# methods on the UDT class. The larger and more complex a UDT, the more overhead it consumes. As a result, the most efficient use for UDTs is storing simple data over which you want tight control. For example, you could create a UDT in C# that provides a highly customized type of date/time storage, or you could even create one that stores encrypted data. You can provide behaviors (methods) on that type to gain access to the decrypted values.

The *SQL Books Online* reference that you can install with SQL Server 2005 illustrates the use of CLR UDTs with a type called `Point`. What we want to do is to create a table in SQL Server that is storing the positions of all the objects in a fictitious strategy game. This fictitious game uses three-dimensional space, so the UDT that we will create will support three-dimensional points, and will contain a method for determining the distance between two 3D points.

To get started, add a user-defined type called `Point3D` to your project using the same method used to create a user-defined procedure and a user-defined function.

Next, change the default class definition so that it looks like the one shown in Listing 21.2.

LISTING 21.2   Point3D, a User-Defined Type

```
using System;
using System.Data;
using System.Data.SqlClient;
using System.Data.SqlTypes;
using Microsoft.SqlServer.Server;
using System.Text;

[Serializable]
[Microsoft.SqlServer.Server.SqlUserDefinedType(Format.Native)]
public struct Point3D : INullable
{
private bool isNull;
private int x, y, z;

public override string ToString()
{
if (isNull)
    return "NULL";
else
{
    StringBuilder sb = new StringBuilder();
    sb.AppendFormat("{0},{1},{2}", x, y, z);
```

LISTING 21.2 Continued

```
    return sb.ToString();
}
}

public bool IsNull
{
get
{
    // Put your code here
    return isNull;
}
}

public static Point3D Null
{
get
{
    Point3D h = new Point3D();
    h.isNull = true;
    return h;
}
}

// do not invoke this method when the value is null
[SqlMethod(OnNullCall=false)]
public static Point3D Parse(SqlString s)
{
Point3D u = new Point3D();

string rawValue = s.Value;
try
{
    string[] vals = rawValue.Split(',');
    u.x = Int32.Parse(vals[0]);
    u.y = Int32.Parse(vals[1]);
    u.z = Int32.Parse(vals[2]);
}
catch (Exception e)
{
    throw new ArgumentException(
"String format is not a valid 3-D point structure", e);
}
```

LISTING 21.2   Continued

```
return u;
}

[SqlMethod(OnNullCall=false)]
public Double DistanceFromPoint(Point3D origin)
{
return Math.Sqrt(
    (Math.Pow(x - origin.x, 2.0) +
     Math.Pow(y - origin.y, 2.0) +
     Math.Pow(z - origin.z, 2.0)));
}

public int X
{
get { return x; }
set { x = value; }
}

public int Y
{
get { return y; }
set { y = value; }
}

public int Z
{
get { return z; }
set { z = value; }
}
}
```

It looks pretty much like any other C# struct, with a few minor differences. The SqlMethod attribute controls the behavior of the method when invoked within a SQL statement.

To use this new data type, first run your project to complete the deployment and registration of your new type. Then, you can use SQL Server 2005's management console or Visual Studio 2005's server browser for creating a new table. Figure 21.2 shows the table editor from within Visual Studio 2005. Note that the Point3D data type appears just like any other type in SQL.

Two of the key methods that make this type work are the Parse method and the ToString method. The Parse method is what allows you to enter textual data in a grid or send textual data in a SQL statement and have SQL properly create an instance of the

Point3D type. By default, SQL Server 2005 doesn't invoke the ToString method on your type to display it; it displays the raw serialization data.

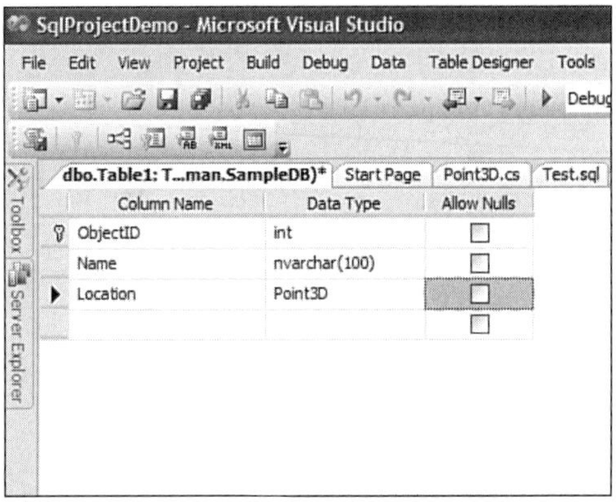

FIGURE 21.2   Creating a table based on the Point3D data type.

Create a new table, GameObjects, with a column for the object's ID, the object name, and the object's location. Then, add in some rows of data, making sure to enter the location points in the format x, y, z.

With the data in place, you can start issuing SQL statements to examine the contents of the data, as shown in the following code:

```
DECLARE @refPoint Point3D
SELECT @refPoint = Location FROM GameObjects WHERE ObjectId=2

select ObjectID, Name, Location.ToString() as CurrentLocation,
 Location.DistanceFromPoint(@refPoint)
FROM GameObjects
```

This SQL statement will give you a list of all the objects in the game, as well as each object's distance from the object with ID 2. The following are the results from the author's sample data:

```
1    Battleship Intrepid       0,0,0     21.6101827849743
2    Starship SAMS             1,5,21    0
3    Battlecruiser DotNettica  9,7,3     19.7989898732233
```

As expected, the distance from object 2 to object 2 is 0. The other objects are displaying the results of the DistanceFromPoint method on the Point3D struct itself.

With this kind of power in hand, you can do a lot of really interesting things. For example, let's say that the Starship SAMS has a radar radius of 20 units. We can easily issue a query that will return all game objects within radar range, as shown in the following lines:

```
select ObjectID, Name, Location.ToString() as CurrentLocation FROM
GameObjects WHERE Location.DistanceFromPoint(@refPoint) < 20 AND ObjectID != 2
```

You can also access the user-defined type from within your regular .NET code using
ADO.NET. All you need to do is add a reference in your client code to the assembly that
contains the UDT. Create a console application and then add a reference to
SqlProjectDemo.dll by browsing for it. Then you can write the code shown in Listing
21.3.

LISTING 21.3   ADO.NET Client Consuming a SQL Server 2005 UDT

```csharp
using System;
using System.Data;
using System.Data.SqlClient;
using System.Collections.Generic;
using System.Text;

namespace ClientHarness
{
class Program
{
static void Main(string[] args)
{
    SqlConnection conn = new SqlConnection(
"data source=localhost; user id=sa; password=...; Initial Catalog=SampleDB");
    conn.Open();

    Point3D origin = new Point3D();
    origin.X = 0;
    origin.Y = 0;
    origin.Z = 0;

    SqlCommand cmd = conn.CreateCommand();
    cmd.CommandText = "SELECT ObjectID, Name, Location FROM GameObjects";

    SqlDataReader rdr = cmd.ExecuteReader();
    while (rdr.Read())
    {
        Console.WriteLine("{0} ({1}) is at {2}. Distance from Origin {3}",
            rdr["ObjectID"], rdr["Name"], ((Point3D)rdr["Location"]).ToString(),
            ((Point3D)rdr["Location"]).DistanceFromPoint(origin));
    }

    rdr.Close();
    cmd.Dispose();
```

LISTING 21.3   Continued

```
    conn.Close();

    Console.ReadLine();
}
}
}
```

When you run this application, you receive the following output:

```
1 (Battleship Intrepid) is at 0,0,0. Distance from Origin 0
2 (Starship SAMS) is at 1,5,21. Distance from Origin 21.6101827849743
3 (Battlecruiser DotNettica) is at 9,7,3. Distance from Origin 11.7898261225516
```

Remember that CLR UDTs are designed specifically for small, simple types that might expose a few behaviors. If you attempt to store complex or hierarchical data in a UDT, you might actually be slowing your application down.

Working with the New Server-Side SQL Library

When writing stored procedures, types, functions, and more, you will need access to data and functionality provided by SQL Server. For example, when writing a C# stored procedure you need to be able to send results out on the "pipe." Also, you will want to be able to run your queries using the existing server-side connection and not have to resort to a client-side ADO.NET connection. All of this is available for you in a few classes, such as SqlContext and SqlPipe.

Table 21.1 shows some of the methods and properties available on the SqlPipe class.

TABLE 21.1   SqlPipe Properties and Methods

Property/Method	Description
IsSendingResults	Indicates whether the SqlPipe is currently sending results to the client. Read-only.
ExecuteAndSend()	Executes the specified command and sends the results on the pipe to the client.
Send()	Sends results to the client on the pipe.
SendResultsStart()	Indicates the beginning of results sent to the client, allowing you to send individual rows. When in this mode, the pipe will only accept calls from SendResultsRow and SendResultsEnd.
SendResultsRow()	Sends a row of data to the client.
SendResultsEnd()	Marks the end of a result set sent to the client.

The code in Listing 21.4 illustrates how to use some of the methods of the SqlPipe class to send results to the client as well as how to create a command parameter that is one of your own UDTs.

LISTING 21.4 Using the `SqlPipe` Class and Creating a UDT Command Parameter

```csharp
using System;
using System.Data;
using System.Data.SqlClient;
using System.Data.SqlTypes;
using Microsoft.SqlServer.Server;


public partial class StoredProcedures
{
[Microsoft.SqlServer.Server.SqlProcedure]
public static void RadarScan(int objectID, int scanRadius)
{
using (SqlConnection conn = new SqlConnection("context connection=true"))
{
    conn.Open();
    SqlCommand cmd = conn.CreateCommand();
    cmd.CommandText =
"SELECT Location FROM GameObjects WHERE ObjectID = " + objectID.ToString();
    Point3D sourceLocation = Point3D.Null;
    SqlDataReader rdr = cmd.ExecuteReader();
    if (rdr.Read())
    {
        sourceLocation = (Point3D)rdr["Location"];
    }
    rdr.Close();

    // now select all objects within radar range
    SqlCommand scanCmd = conn.CreateCommand();
    scanCmd.CommandText =
"SELECT ObjectID, Name, Location.ToString() as CurrentLocation, " +
        "Location.DistanceFromPoint(@pointRef) as DistanceToTarget FROM " +
        "GameObjects WHERE Location.DistanceFromPoint(@pointRef) < " +
scanRadius.ToString() +
        " AND ObjectID != " + objectID.ToString();
    scanCmd.Parameters.Add(new SqlParameter("@pointRef", SqlDbType.Udt));
    scanCmd.Parameters[0].UdtTypeName = "Point3D";
    scanCmd.Parameters[0].Value = sourceLocation;

    // execute the command and send results to the calling client
    SqlContext.Pipe.ExecuteAndSend(scanCmd);
```

LISTING 21.4   Continued

```
   rdr.Close();
} // no need to explicitly shut down connection because of 'using' statement
}
};
```

When this stored procedure is executed in a query environment, it gives the following results (for Object ID of 2, radar range of 20):

```
3    Battlecruiser DotNettica        9,7,3        19.7989898732233
```

These results indicate that, according to the GameObjects table, there is a ship called the "Battlecruiser DotNettica" almost 20 units away, at location (9,7,3). Obviously this procedure could have been written in T-SQL, but if you needed to take into account other factors such as whether that vessel is cloaked, moving, and so on, the C# procedure might prove computationally faster than its T-SQL equivalent.

When you are working with a SQL Server project, you can't just add references as you see fit. When you go to add a reference, you are limited to other projects, and to assemblies already stored in SQL Server, as shown in Figure 21.3.

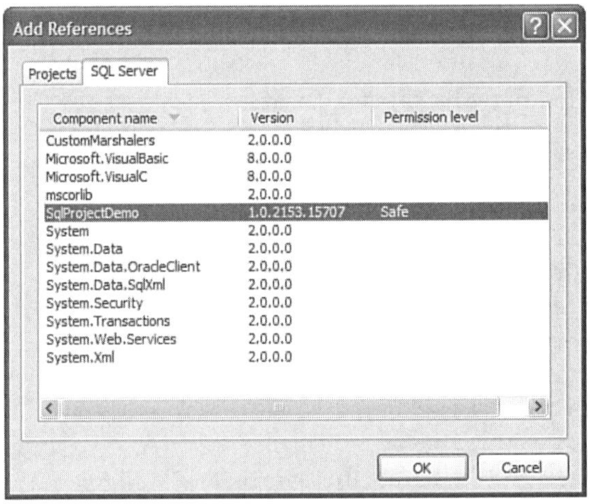

FIGURE 21.3   Adding a reference to a SQL Server project.

Another common task when working with the server-side SQL library is the creation and use of temporary tables. Often developers will need to create a temporary table to store dynamically generated results, and those results are then sent to the client. This same functionality is available to you in C# by giving you the ability to create your own metadata and send records that match that metadata.

The code in Listing 21.5 shows a C# stored procedure that utilizes the SqlPipe class to send its own arbitrary data as well as the accompanying metadata.

LISTING 21.5   Sending Arbitrary Tabular Results

```
using System;
using System.Data;
using System.Data.SqlClient;
using System.Data.SqlTypes;
using Microsoft.SqlServer.Server;

public partial class StoredProcedures
{
[Microsoft.SqlServer.Server.SqlProcedure]
public static void ArbitraryData()
{
    SqlDataRecord record = new SqlDataRecord(
        new SqlMetaData("City", SqlDbType.NVarChar, 100),
        new SqlMetaData("Temperature", SqlDbType.Int));

    // this sends the meta-data information, not the record itself
    SqlContext.Pipe.SendResultsStart(record);

    record.SetString(0, "Denver, CO");
    record.SetInt32(1, 65);

    SqlContext.Pipe.SendResultsRow(record);

    record.SetString(0, "Durango, CO");
    record.SetInt32(1, 43);

    SqlContext.Pipe.SendResultsRow(record);

    SqlContext.Pipe.SendResultsEnd();

}
};
```

Using MARS (Multiple Active RecordSets)

Multiple Active RecordSets is a fairly complex topic, and there are a lot of unseen factors that can determine whether or not you should use this technology. This chapter has a small preview of this technology. For more information on MARS and the impact of using MARS on performance and the database itself, you should consult your favorite SQL Server 2005 reference or the *SQL Server 2005 Books Online* reference that installs with the server itself.

In previous versions of SQL Server, many developers remember getting a common error message that indicates that there is already an open DataReader on the connection, and that in order to open the current `DataReader`, the previous reader needs to be closed. This message arose from the limitation that you could only have one open forward-only result set on any given connection at any given time. The workaround developers used for this was just to make sure that they used new connections all the time, or they opted for low-performance options like reading all the data into a `DataSet` before opening the next `DataReader`.

With the introduction of SQL Server 2005, developers now have the ability to create multiple active result sets on a single connection. This essentially removes the block created by previous versions of SQL Server. The code in Listing 21.6 contains code that would otherwise fail miserably on previous versions of SQL Server 2005 and the .NET Framework.

LISTING 21.6   Using MARS

```
using System;
using System.Threading;
using System.Data;
using System.Data.SqlClient;
using System.Collections.Generic;
using System.Text;

namespace MarsDemo
{
class Program
{
static void Main(string[] args)
{
    // comment this out and use the other conn string
    // to break the app
    SqlConnection conn = new SqlConnection(
      "data source=localhost; initial catalog=SampleDB; integrated security=sspi;
      ➥multipleactiveresultsets=yes");

    // uncomment below to break the sample
    //SqlConnection conn = new SqlConnection(
    //    "data source=localhost; initial catalog=SampleDB;
    ➥integrated security=sspi;");
    conn.Open();

    SqlCommand cmd1 = conn.CreateCommand();
    cmd1.CommandText = "SELECT * FROM Customers";

    SqlCommand cmd2 = conn.CreateCommand();
    cmd2.CommandText = "SELECT * FROM GameObjects";
```

21

LISTING 21.6 Continued

```
SqlDataReader dr1 = cmd1.ExecuteReader();
SqlDataReader dr2 = cmd2.ExecuteReader();

while (dr1.Read())
{
    Console.WriteLine("{0}, {1}", (String)dr1["LastName"], dr1["FirstName"]);
}
while (dr2.Read())
{
    Point3D currentLoc = (Point3D)dr2.GetValue(dr2.GetOrdinal("Location"));
    Console.WriteLine("{0} is at {1}", dr2["Name"], currentLoc.ToString());
}

dr2.Close();
dr1.Close();

Console.ReadLine();
}


}
}
```

The preceding code creates one connection and two commands. Each of these commands is then used to create a new SqlDataReader.

```
MultipleActiveResultSets=true
```

If you remove this option from the connection string, the behavior resembles the previous versions of SQL Server and the .NET Framework, and you get the following error message:

```
There is already an open DataReader associated with this
Command which must be closed first.
```

The downside to MARS is that the execution of the commands on the server is interleaved. This means that a portion of the first command will be executed, and then a portion of the second command will be executed, and so on. You can't rely on which portion will be executed first. If two commands are executed requesting the same rows on the same connection, you could potentially create a deadlock situation where neither command can complete.

You can learn more about these issues in more detail in other SQL Server 2005 references. The important point here is that with MARS, it is possible to have multiple result sets executed on the same connection at the same time. However, this might not always be such a good idea. If the multiple result sets might be competing for the same information or the same table, you might want to consider using separate connections. Just because it is possible doesn't mean it should be overused.

Summary

In this chapter, you've been taken on a whirlwind tour of the new CLR integration features of SQL Server 2005. You've seen how to create stored procedures, user-defined types, and user-defined functions within SQL Server 2005 using the new Visual Studio 2005 "SQL Server Project" template. You also learned that T-SQL is still the fastest way to retrieve data from the database, and now CLR languages are the fastest way to perform complex logic and otherwise computationally expensive operations.

Also, you saw how to use the new SQL Server library for data access on the server side, including the `SqlContext` and `SqlPipe` classes. Finally, you were introduced to yet another new feature of SQL Server 2005 that is of interest to C# developers: MARS. MARS allows you to create and iterate through multiple active result sets at any given time on the same connection. This new feature is not without penalty, however, because the server execution of these commands is interleaved and you need to be wary of this before overutilizing MARS.

PART IV

Developing ASP.NET 2.0 Web Applications

IN THIS PART

Introduction to ASP.NET 2.0 and Web Forms

ASP.NET is a web development framework that provides developers with an advanced, object-oriented interface to the creation and manipulation of HTML that will be rendered to the client. More than that, ASP.NET provides a rich event-driven model that resembles the event-driven model that Windows Forms developers are familiar with. This chapter provides you with an introduction to ASP.NET and a list of the controls and tools that will be available to you for creating compelling web applications using ASP.NET. In addition, this chapter contains a guide to creating and debugging your web applications, handling server-side events in your code, and even a look at how to use one of the powerful new ASP.NET 2.0 features: client callbacks.

Introduction to ASP.NET 2.0

Prior to the first release of ASP.NET, the tools available to developers for creating powerful and compelling web applications were limited and immature.

One of the first widespread tools for creating web applications was the CGI (Common Gateway Interface) standard, which essentially allowed a customized console application to run when invoked from the web and return a stream of text to the end user that served as an HTML page.

A tool that helped make web development commonplace was Active Server Pages (ASP). ASP is a framework that allows developers to embed scripting language (VBScript or JavaScript) code directly in their web pages, drastically increasing the time to market for many applications, especially data-driven web applications.

When the first version of the .NET Framework was released, it was released with ASP.NET. ASP.NET is a framework that takes the concept introduced by classic ASP to a new level. It allows you to write managed, compiled, secure, and reliable code to drive your web application, as well as providing a hefty library of code that automates standard web application tasks such as security, authentication, authorization, membership, and much more.

ASP.NET works by compiling the content in your web application into an assembly that is then used by Internet Information Server (IIS) to service requests for pages and web services. The ASP.NET Framework is made up of several components, including a page and control hierarchy, the page and control compiler, security management, state management, and application configuration. Each of those components is discussed in this section.

Don't worry if some of the information presented in the sections seems a little vague. As you progress through the ASP.NET chapters of this book, each of the items discussed here will be discussed in more detail with plenty of code samples and practical applications.

Page and Control Hierarchy

Tools such as Active Server Pages (ASP) worked by allowing the developer to write script that output text to a web page. This could become extremely tedious, and reading and maintaining code like that could become burdensome.

ASP.NET provides an entirely object-oriented approach to creating web pages and applications. There are classes that represent pages, applications, user controls, server controls, and much more. By allowing controls to become first-class objects, it becomes much easier to create powerful, reusable visual elements that can be reused among multiple pages or applications. Object inheritance can be used to create entire hierarchies of controls with expanding functionality.

ASP.NET 2.0 provides additional features that allow your applications to support skins and themes for enhancing an application's look and feel. Another feature new to ASP.NET 2.0 is the concept of master pages, which allow for a kind of visual inheritance among pages, further enhancing the code reuse that is already available in ASP.NET.

Introduction to the ASP.NET 2.0 Compiler

Unlike the original versions of ASP, which were driven by scripting languages such as VBScript and JavaScript, ASP.NET is a completely compiled environment. This means that you can create web applications that not only have strong typing, but can catch a myriad of potential problems at compile time and design time. Loosely typed, scripted environments lend themselves to an aggravating scenario in which problems are difficult to find until the program is being tested at runtime under adverse conditions.

The ASP.NET 2.0 compiler makes use of `partial` classes to merge the ASP.NET markup found in `.aspx` and `.ascx` files with the code contained in associated C# files to produce a compiled assembly.

Each ASP.NET page has basically two halves: the half contained in a `.aspx` file that contains HTML markup and ASP.NET server controls, and the other half, which contains the remainder of the code. With `partial` classes, each ASP.NET page produces a single class, even though it is made up of at least two files.

Finally, another major benefit of having fully managed and compiled ASP.NET pages is that each ASP.NET page or control that you create has access to all the same functionality that any other managed application has, and it has that access in a tightly bound fashion. Classic ASP generally required late binding to make use of external components, and those components had to be COM-based.

Security

Above and beyond Code Access Security features that are an inherent part of any managed code application, ASP.NET 2.0 provides a powerful suite of tools and features that help developers create secure applications. ASP.NET has built-in features that manage user authentication using cookies, specially written URLs, Windows authentication, and even support for Microsoft Passport.

Additional providers, tools, and controls are also available that assist in managing user membership on your site, user security roles, and much more.

State Management

HTTP is what is known as a *stateless* protocol. This means that the protocol itself has no support for maintaining state between multiple requests for a page. HTTP on its own can't provide the facilities required to maintain state information on a web application such as shopping carts, control state persisting between subsequent requests for the same page, or even simple things such as the current user's name.

ASP.NET provides facilities for maintaining state that HTTP itself can't provide. There are facilities for managing session state, which is a temporary store of information that persists for a specific user as long as that user is actively using the application. ASP.NET can manage session state directly within the application process, or it can maintain distributed session state to allow your application to share session state among the multiple servers within a Web Farm. In addition to session state, each ASP.NET control can persist its own state between subsequent requests for the same page through a mechanism called `ViewState`. `ViewState` essentially replaces the old technique of using hidden form variables to persist control state information between page requests. It stores information such as a control's items, width, height, state, and more in a specialized string that stores name/value pairs.

The Web Configuration System

The .NET Framework contains built-in functionality that supports the use of application configuration files. These files are XML files that contain information about .NET configuration as well as application-specific configuration.

ASP.NET extends the default .NET Framework configuration files to include several new sections that control web application configuration. By modifying the XML in these configuration files, you can control the authentication and authorization settings for your application, as well as error handling, tracing, debugging, and much more. The use of these configuration files makes deployment a much easier task. You can store connection strings in a configuration file, and then have a different configuration file for each of your build, stage, and production environments. Without such configuration files, managing multiple instances of the same application without writing a lot of unnecessary code would be extremely difficult.

Understanding the ASP.NET Page Life Cycle

The process by which an ASP.NET page is rendered to the browser consists of multiple stages. These stages all have a very distinct purpose in the creation and rendering of your page. A common problem among new ASP.NET developers is injecting code into the wrong stage in the page's life cycle. If you put code in the wrong place, controls that you expect to exist might not exist, or the controls might exist but their state might be nonexistent or unpredictable. This section gives you an introduction to the process that ASP.NET uses to render pages. Understanding this process is absolutely crucial to continuing with more advanced aspects of ASP.NET, such as creating and using your own custom controls.

Stages of ASP.NET Page Rendering

To support the object-oriented framework, the event-driven model, and the capability to persist control state between page requests, ASP.NET has several distinct stages in the life cycle of a page. One key concept to remember is that no matter what, a page will be instantiated and destroyed during the same request. The sequence of stages and events in the life cycle is what allows a page to create a control hierarchy, reconstitute itself from persisted ViewState, render its output, and clean up temporary resources used by the page.

Table 22.1 provides you with the list of stages that occur in the lifetime of an ASP.NET page. It is extremely important to understand these stages before you start creating your own ASP.NET applications.

TABLE 22.1   ASP.NET Page Life Cycle Stages

Stage	Description
Request for Page	The page request starts before a page has been instantiated. When a user requests a page from the web server, ASP.NET checks to see if there is a cached version of the rendered output that can be displayed. If so, the cached version is returned without rerunning the entire Page life cycle. If there is no cached version available, the process continues to the Page Start stage.

TABLE 22.1   Continued

Stage	Description
Page Start	During this stage, the `Page` is instantiated and the input/output properties `Request` and `Response` are set. In addition, the `IsPostback` property is set, indicating whether the request is a new request, or a request originating from a previously rendered ASP.NET page. The `UICulture` property is also set during this stage.
Initialization	During this stage, controls are instantiated and the page's control hierarchy is constructed. Theme and skin information is applied to the page during this stage. Note that the controls are essentially empty at this stage and none of their properties have been restored from view state if the page is a postback.
Load	During this stage, control properties are restored from state if the request is a postback.
Validation	The validation stage is used to validate the state of all controls on the page. The `Validate()` method of all validator controls on the page is invoked, which then determines the state of the page's `IsValid` property. Validation is used to enforce rules on user input.
Postback Event Handling	If the request is a postback, then postback events in response to such things as button clicks, selected index changes, and more are invoked. When creating event handlers, it is important to remember that your event handlers are called *after* the page's `Load` stage.
Render	The `Render` stage is where each control in the `Page`'s control hierarchy is asked to contribute its own rendered output to the rendered output of the entire page. The `Page`'s view state is also included in the output of the page as a hidden form variable at this point.
Unload	When the final rendered output has been produced, and there is no more work to be done by any of the child controls to produce output, the `Unload` stage is entered. In this stage, child controls and the page itself can dispose of resources that were used during any previous stage of the `Page` life cycle.

ASP.NET Page Life Cycle Events

Most of the stages described in Table 22.1 correspond to events that can be handled by your own code. Handling these events allows you to control when your code is executed by placing the code in specific stages of the page's life cycle. Controls that were supplied with ASP.NET, written by you, or provided by a third party are engaged in the life-cycle stages by having their own miniature versions of the `Page` life cycle. The `Page` involves the control in the appropriate stage of the life cycle by triggering control events.

Table 22.2 contains a list of `Page` events, their descriptions, and typical uses.

TABLE 22.2 Page Life Cycle Events

Event	Description
Page_PreInit	Called at the beginning of the Initialize stage. Used to create dynamic controls, set master pages and themes dynamically, and to read/write user profile data. Note that control properties have not yet been restored from view state when this event is called.
Page_Init	Called during the Initialize stage to initialize control properties.
Page_Load	Called during the Load stage to read control properties or update existing control properties. At this stage, control properties have been reconstituted from view state.
(Control Events)	Controls have their events invoked at this stage, such as responding to a button click, the selected index changing on a ListBox, and so on. If your page has validation controls, check the IsValid status of the controls and the page before continuing with your event handler.
Page_PreRender	This event is triggered just before the final version of the page is rendered. If you need to make final tweaks to properties of controls based on information that is only available immediately before rendering, this is the event you should use.
Page_Unload	This event is called immediately before the page is discarded by ASP.NET to dispose of costly resources such as database connections. Also commonly used to write final logging and tracing information.

To further illustrate the page life-cycle events, the code in Listing 22.1 shows you how to create a page that prints some text to the rendered output during each of the crucial life-cycle events. There is a button on the page so that you can click it and see where its event handler appears in the life cycle, as well as see the use of the IsPostback property.

To create this code, open up Visual Studio 2005 and choose File, New, Web Site. Make sure it's a standard C# website and not a starter kit or web service. Drag a single button from the Toolbox onto the form. Double-click it to create an event handler. Switch to the code view and override the many OnXxxx() methods that are already configured as event handlers for the events described in Table 22.2. Your default.aspx.cs file should look very similar to the one in Listing 22.1.

LISTING 22.1 Default.aspx.cs

```
using System;
using System.Data;
using System.Configuration;
using System.Web;
using System.Web.Security;
using System.Web.UI;
using System.Web.UI.WebControls;
using System.Web.UI.WebControls.WebParts;
using System.Web.UI.HtmlControls;
```

LISTING 22.1   Continued

```
public partial class _Default : System.Web.UI.Page
{
    protected void Page_Load(object sender, EventArgs e)
    {
        if (Page.IsPostBack)
            Response.Write("This is a postback request.");
        else
        {
            Response.Write("This is a new request.");
        }
        Response.Write("<br/>Page_Load called.<br/>");
    }

    protected override void OnPreInit(EventArgs e)
    {
        Response.Write("Pre-Init called.<br/>");
        base.OnPreInit(e);
    }

    protected override void OnInit(EventArgs e)
    {
        Response.Write("Init called.<br/>");
        base.OnInit(e);
    }

    protected override void OnInitComplete(EventArgs e)
    {
        Response.Write("Init completed.<br/>");
        base.OnInitComplete(e);
    }

    protected override void OnLoad(EventArgs e)
    {
        Response.Write("Load called.<br/>");
        base.OnLoad(e);
    }

    protected override void OnLoadComplete(EventArgs e)
    {
        Response.Write("Load completed.<br/>");
        base.OnLoadComplete(e);
    }
```

LISTING 22.1   Continued

```
    protected override void OnUnload(EventArgs e)
    {
        // cannot display output here because Response/Request
        // are not available during this stage.
        base.OnUnload(e);
    }
    protected void btnSubmit_Click(object sender, EventArgs e)
    {
        Response.Write("You clicked the submit button.<br/>");
    }
}
```

When you run this application for the first time, you see the output shown in Figure 22.1.

FIGURE 22.1   Page life-cycle event demonstration.

After you click the test button, the output now includes information from the event handler created for the submit button, as shown in Figure 22.2.

As you learn more about control building and you work more with ASP.NET pages, the purpose of the events discussed in this section will become clearer to you.

A fairly new concept, the *postback*, was introduced in Listing 22.1. ASP.NET outputs a JavaScript library that contains many helper functions. One of those functions causes the page to "'post back'" on itself. This function places information in the page's view state that indicates which button was clicked (or which control caused the postback). When the Page life cycle gets to the control event stage, it compares the event that triggered the postback with the event handlers contained in the page, and invokes the appropriate event. In the case of the code in Listing 22.1, the btnSubmit_Click handler was called. The combination of the Page life cycle, postbacks, and some relatively hidden plumbing allows ASP.NET to present the developer with an event-driven model that closely resembles the event-driven model with which Windows developers are very familiar.

FIGURE 22.2   Page life-cycle event demonstration, after clicking the button.

Overview of Controls Provided by ASP.NET

Before creating something new with wood and nails, a carpenter needs to be familiar with the tools at hand. The same is true for working with ASP.NET. Before looking at any more code samples, you should be familiar with the tools that are available to help you create extremely powerful web applications. These tools come in the form of ASP.NET controls that ship with version 2.0 of the .NET Framework. These controls are all briefly described in Table 22.3 according to the category in which they appear on the ASP.NET 2005 Toolbox pane. The Web Part controls are not included in this table, as they will be covered in much more detail in Chapter 26, "Introduction to Web Parts."

TABLE 22.3   Stock ASP.NET Controls

Control	Description
Standard Controls	
Label	The label is just that: simple text used to label other interface elements.
TextBox	An input box.
Button	A standard button.
LinkButton	A button that renders as a hyperlink.
ImageButton	An image that responds to clicks.
CheckBox	A standard check box.
CheckBoxList	A list of check boxes.
RadioButton	A single radio button.
RadioButtonList	A list of radio buttons, allowing only one item in the list to be selected at any time.
Image	An image.

TABLE 22.3   Continued

Control	Description
Standard Controls	
ImageMap	A clickable image map with defined regions.
Table	A standard table, rendering as the HTML `<table>` tag.
BulletedList	Renders as a `<bl>` and its associated list items.
HiddenField	Creates a hidden form field, the value of which you can control with server-side properties.
Literal	Renders whatever raw markup you place in its `Text` Property.
Calendar	Renders an interactive calendar that defaults to displaying today's date.
AdRotator	A component used for displaying a rotating list of advertising banners or images on a page.
FileUpload	A component used for uploading files to the web server. Exposes the uploaded file as a property containing a `Stream` object.
Wizard	Controls the display of a sequence of multiple panels of information rendered in traditional "'Wizard"' format.
Xml	Control responsible for rendering either raw XML or XSLT-transformed XML to a `Page`.
MultiView	Container control for multiple `View` controls, each of which contains a discrete interface containing labels, buttons, and so on. Used to dynamically choose which view to display based on criteria such as state, user identity, or permissions.
Panel	A container for child controls that can be toggled visible or hidden dynamically.
PlaceHolder	A placeholder control. You can use it to "'take up space"' at design time and then fill it dynamically at runtime with child controls or raw HTML.
View	A control that contains child controls to render a subportion of user interface. Used in combination with the `MultiView` control to dynamically render different views based on criteria such as state or user identity.
Substitution	A powerful control that allows you to dynamically integrate dynamic content into cached page output.
Localize	A control very similar to `Literal`, but designed to render localized content.
Data Controls	
GridView	A full-featured control for displaying a grid of data.
DataList	A control that renders a list of data, the look and feel of which is controlled via templates.
DetailsView	A control designed to render a details form.
FormView	Control designed to a render a form.
Repeater	A low-level control for rendering a list of data.
SqlDataSource	A component used to connect to SQL Server.

TABLE 22.3   Continued

Control	Description
Data Controls	
AccessDataSource	Component used to connect to MS Access.
ObjectDataSource	Component used to bind controls to an object.
XmlDataSource	Component used to bind controls to an XML source.
SiteMapDataSource	Component allowing binding to a site map.
ReportViewer	Component designed for displaying data in a report format.
Navigation Controls	
SiteMapPath	Essentially a "'bread crumb"' control for displaying a user's location within a site map.
Menu	Control for rendering an interactive menu.
TreeView	Control for rendering an interactive tree.
Validation Controls	
RequiredFieldValidator	Use this to force a field to have data.
RangeValidator	Use this to require a field to have data within a specified range.
RegularExpressionValidator	Forces an input control's data to match a given regular expression for validating things like phone numbers, e-mail addresses, and so on.
CompareValidator	Forces an input control's data to compare in a specific way to another control's data.
CustomValidator	Allows you to write your own validation routine for a given control's data.
ValidationSummary	Control that displays a summary of all validation failures or indication of success on a given page.
Authentication Controls	
Login	Control that facilitates user authentication.
LoginView	Renders different views based on user authentication status.
PasswordRecovery	Control used to facilitate password recovery.
LoginStatus	Displays user's logged-in status.
LoginName	Displays user's logged-in name.
CreateUserWizard	Wizard control for creating a new user.
ChangePassword	Control allowing user to change password.
HTML Controls (for use only when ASP control is insufficient)	
Input (Button)	A traditional HTML input button.
Input (Reset)	A traditional HTML form reset button.
Input (Submit)	A form submit button.
Input (Text)	A text input control.
Input (File)	An HTML file upload control.
Input (Password)	A password text entry box.
Input (Checkbox)	A checkbox input control.
Input (Radio)	A radio button input control.
Input (Hidden)	A hidden form value control.
Textarea	A multirow text input box.

22

TABLE 22.3   Continued

Control	Description
Standard Controls	
Table	A traditional HTML table control.
Image	A traditional HTML image control.
Select	A select box.
Horizontal Rule	An <hr> tag.
Div	A <div> tag.

Creating and Debugging ASP.NET Applications

The process of creating, debugging, and deploying ASP.NET applications is slightly different than the process for building and deploying Windows Forms applications. This section familiarizes you with the tools and techniques involved in building, deploying, and debugging ASP.NET applications.

Building and Deploying ASP.NET Applications

The first step toward creating an ASP.NET application is the creation of a new website from within Visual Studio 2005. When you create a new website, Visual Studio prompts you for the location of the site. You can store the website on the file system, on a remote server via HTTP, or on a remote server via FTP. This is a new feature that previous versions of Visual Studio did not support. Prior to ASP.NET 2.0, you couldn't create web applications without having a copy of IIS on your development server. This new model allows you to create web applications that can be hosted by Visual Studio 2005's own custom local web server without the need for an IIS installation.

Deploying your web applications after they've been created has also become a lot easier in Visual Studio 2005. If you click the Website top-level menu item and then click Copy Web Site, you will see the website copy screen shown in Figure 22.3.

What you can see from the figure is that you can deploy your website to any location, whether it's accessible via HTTP, FTP, or the file system (so long as you have the appropriate credentials for the destination location). This gives you incredible flexibility in allowing you to deploy your website to development, staging, and production servers all directly from your own workstation within Visual Studio 2005.

ASP.NET applications compile within Visual Studio in the same manner as other applications. The main difference is that the partial class technology creates classes that are combined from the contents of the .aspx files, .ascx files, and so on, and compiles all of those into an assembly used by ASP.NET to service page requests. You will be able to see compile-time errors such as type mismatches, syntax errors, and many more that you would never be able to see in interpreted scripting environments, such as legacy ASP using VBScript or JavaScript.

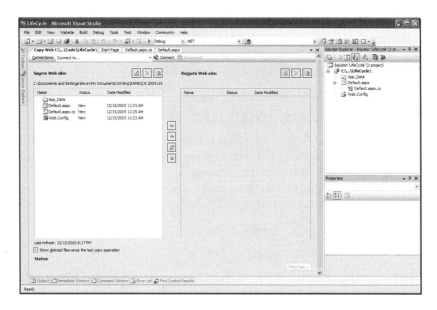

FIGURE 22.3   Website copy screen.

Debugging ASP.NET Applications

You can debug your ASP.NET applications from within Visual Studio 2005, including the ability to stop on breakpoints, step through individual lines of code, and make use of the Immediate window. The only real concern is that if you are debugging code on a remote server via HTTP, that server needs to be configured to allow remote debugging.

To experiment with debugging an ASP.NET application, start up the application created in Listing 22.1 and insert a few breakpoints wherever you like. Then, run the application in debug mode (F5), and you will see that even though you're working with a web application, the code will still stop on the breakpoints, and you still have access to all of the features of the runtime debugger from within Visual Studio

Two classes facilitate logging trace and debug messages from within an ASP.NET application. The first is the `System.Diagnostics.Debug` class, which allows you to write simple information to the debug window. The second, which is specific to ASP.NET, is the `System.Web.TraceContext` class. This class is provided in the `Trace` property of every page and allows you to output debug information to the ASP.NET trace. Using an ASP.NET configuration file, you can have that trace information automatically displayed at the bottom of a page's rendered output or in the output of a special page called `trace.vxd`.

The following are a few lines of code that show how to use these two classes from within an ASP.NET page:

```
Trace.Write("Debug information");
Trace.Write("Diagnostics", "Event X took 10 seconds.");
Trace.Warn("Something bad happened.");
System.Diagnostics.Debug.WriteLine("Debug information");
```

Handling Events and Postbacks

Listing 22.1 gave you a brief look at handling server-side events through ASP.NET pages with a submit button. To illustrate how code typically utilizes both the IsPostback property of the page as well as multiple event handlers per form, Listing 22.2 shows you the ASPX code for a page that presents the user with a simple survey, accepts two different button clicks, and presents the user with results. Listing 22.3 contains the C# code for the event handlers in the partial class.

LISTING 22.2   Handling Multiple Events, ASPX Code

```
<%@ Page Language="C#" AutoEventWireup="true"
    CodeFile="Default.aspx.cs" Inherits="_Default" %>

<!DOCTYPE html PUBLIC "-//W3C//DTD XHTML 1.0 Transitional//EN"
"http://www.w3.org/TR/xhtml1/DTD/xhtml1-transitional.dtd">

<html xmlns="http://www.w3.org/1999/xhtml" >
<head runat="server">
    <title>Untitled Page</title>
</head>
<body>
    <form id="form1" runat="server">
    <div>
        <asp:Label ID="lblWelcome" runat="server"
Text="Label"></asp:Label><br />
        <asp:Panel ID="pnlInput" runat="server">
            Name: <asp:TextBox ID="txtName"
runat="server"></asp:TextBox><br />
            Favorite Color: 
            <asp:ListBox ID="lbColors" runat="server">
                <asp:ListItem Text="White" Value=1 />
                <asp:ListItem Text="Green" Value=2 />
                <asp:ListItem Text="Yellow" Value=3 />
            </asp:ListBox><br />
            <asp:Button ID="btnSubmit" runat="server"
             Text="Submit Survey" OnClick="btnSubmit_Click" /> 
            <asp:Button ID="btnCancel" runat="server"
             Text="Cancel" OnClick="btnCancel_Click" />
        </asp:Panel>
        <asp:Panel ID="pnlResults" runat="server">
```

LISTING 22.2   Continued

```
              <asp:PlaceHolder ID="plhResults" runat="server" />
          </asp:Panel>
      </div>
      </form>
</body>
</html>
```

The page in Listing 22.2 has two panels: one panel for input, and one panel for displaying the results. The idea is to hide the input panel during the postback while revealing the results panel. When the page is first displayed, just the input panel is displayed because the results panel has no controls in the placeholder.

LISTING 22.3   Handling Multiple Events, C# Code

```csharp
using System;
using System.Data;
using System.Configuration;
using System.Web;
using System.Web.Security;
using System.Web.UI;
using System.Web.UI.WebControls;
using System.Web.UI.WebControls.WebParts;
using System.Web.UI.HtmlControls;

public partial class _Default : System.Web.UI.Page
{
protected void Page_Load(object sender, EventArgs e)
{
    if (!Page.IsPostBack)
    {
        lblWelcome.Text =
"Greetings. Please take a few seconds to fill out this
➥survey.<br/>";
        pnlResults.Visible = false;
        pnlInput.Visible = true;
    }
    else
    {
        pnlResults.Visible = true;
        pnlInput.Visible = false;
    }
}

}
```

LISTING 22.3   Continued

```
protected void btnSubmit_Click(object sender, EventArgs e)
{
    // store survey data in database, etc.

    lblWelcome.Text = "Thanks for submitting your survey.";
    plhResults.Controls.Add(new LiteralControl(
        string.Format("You said your name was <b>{0}</b>, and your favorite
        ➥color is <b>{1}</b> ({2})",
        txtName.Text, lbColors.SelectedItem.Text,
        lbColors.SelectedItem.Value)));
}
protected void btnCancel_Click(object sender, EventArgs e)
{
    lblWelcome.Text = "You cancelled your survey submission. Nothing was saved.";
}
}
```

When you run the code in the preceding listings, you will be presented with an input form. You can either fill it out and click Submit, which will show you the information you entered (remember that information is reconstructed from view state during the Initialize stage of the page life cycle), or you can click Cancel and be informed that the results of the survey weren't saved. This provides a good example of where it is appropriate to check for IsPostback and when to perform tasks specific to an individual event.

Building Interactive Dynamic Pages Using Client Callbacks

If you have experience creating full-featured web applications using previous versions of ASP.NET, you have probably run across performance problems involving postbacks. The downside to using server-side events is that in order to trigger such an event, the page must completely reload itself, restore control and page state, and then render according to the new state.

Imagine that you were to create a page where you had three list boxes, and each time you click a list box, the subsequent list box populates with a list of child rows. This is a pretty common pattern, seen in applications where you select a country, then a state, then a city. It is also seen where you select increasing levels of detail from most to least general, such as selecting a company, then a location, then an office. Using purely server-side events, the entire page has to post back and potentially reload all of its data every time the user clicks a list box. This means that to get to the point where the user can proceed, he has clicked three times and caused two potentially slow postbacks.

One solution a lot of developers used in the past was to query all of the data on the first load and then render that data in the form of JavaScript client-side data structures. Then, each time the user clicked a list box, JavaScript would be used to populate the detail lists. This approach yields a pretty fast and reactive web page, but the initial load time becomes horrendous because the browser has to load and parse through mountains of JavaScript data initialization statements. The page size grows exponentially with the amount of data driving the page. This approach creates unwieldy server code and can often be slower than the purely server-side pattern.

The solution to this problem is an incredibly powerful mechanism that essentially allows JavaScript to invoke server-side methods on your page and then receive a response through a callback method that is also written in JavaScript. Callbacks and delegates were covered earlier in the book in Chapter 9, "Events and Delegates." This tool is referred to as a *client callback*, and ASP.NET 2.0 supports this functionality by default. Other tools created by third parties are also available that create similar functionality, such as Ajax .NET.

To allow a control to expose a method to client-side JavaScript, that control needs to implement the `ICallbackEventHandler` interface. This interface requires two methods:

- `void RaiseCallbackEvent(string eventArgument)`—This method is, through code you'll see shortly, invoked by JavaScript. The `string` argument is used to pass information to the method from JavaScript, such as the ID of the parent row for which to retrieve child rows.

- `string GetCallbackResult()`—This method is used to retrieve the results of the previous call to `RaiseCallbackEvent`. The results retrieval method is separate from the `Callback Event` method in order to allow JavaScript to make asynchronous calls in the background.

You can choose to implement this interface at the `Page` level, or at the `Control` level. If you choose to implement the interface at the `Page` level, you will find that you can only support one client callback for the entire page. If this is sufficient, then `Page`-level implementation is definitely the easiest way to go.

However, if you need to invoke multiple client callback methods (for example, you have more than one control that you want to dynamically populate without using an expensive server postback), you will need to create special controls to implement the `ICallbackEventHandler` interface.

Listing 22.4 contains the ASPx code that sets up a sample that will have three list boxes. The first list box is populated on the initial page load by the server. The second and third list boxes will be populated dynamically using client callbacks without incurring the overhead of a full server postback.

LISTING 22.4   ASPx Containing Three List Boxes

```
<%@ Page Language="C#" AutoEventWireup="true"
CodeFile="Default.aspx.cs" Inherits="_Default" %>

<!DOCTYPE html PUBLIC
  "-//W3C//DTD XHTML 1.0 Transitional//EN"
  "http://www.w3.org/TR/xhtml1/DTD/xhtml1-transitional.dtd">

<html xmlns="http://www.w3.org/1999/xhtml" >
<head runat="server">
<title>Client Callback Demo</title>

<script language="javascript">
function CallBackReturnFunction(sReturnValue, oContext)
{
    alert(sReturnValue);

    var oLocations = document.forms[0].lbLocation;
    var oOffices = document.forms[0].lbOffice;

    oLocations.length = 0;
    oOffices.length = 0;

    if (sReturnValue == '') return;

    var aLocations = sReturnValue.split('¦¦');

    for (var i=0;  i < aLocations.length; i++)
    {
        var aOptions = aLocations[i].split('¦');
        oLocations.options[oLocations.length] =
new Option( aOptions[1], aOptions[0]);
    }
}

function CallBackReturnFunction2(sReturnValue, oContext)
{
    var oOffices = document.forms[0].lbOffice;
    oOffices.length = 0;
    if (sReturnValue == '') return;
    var aOffices = sReturnValue.split('¦¦');

    for (var i=0; i < aOffices.length; i++)
    {
```

LISTING 22.4   Continued

```
        var aOptions = aOffices[i].split('¦');
        oOffices.options[oOffices.length] = new Option( aOptions[1], aOptions[0] );
    }

}

function OnError(exception, context)
{
    alert(exception);
}
</script>
</head>
<body>
<form id="form1" runat="server">
<div>
<table width="500" border="0" cellspacing="2" cellpadding="2">
    <tr>
        <th>Company</th>
        <th>Location</th>
        <th>Office</th>
    </tr>
    <tr>
        <td width=33% valign=top>
            <asp:ListBox ID="lbCompany" runat="server"
                OnClick="OnCompanyClick(this.options[this.selectedIndex].value);"
 />         </td>
        <td width=33% valign=top>
            <asp:ListBox ID="lbLocation" runat=server
                OnClick="OnLocationClick(this.options[this.selectedIndex].value);"
 />         </td>
        <td width=33% valign=top>
            <asp:ListBox ID="lbOffice" runat=server></asp:ListBox>
        </td>
    </tr>
    <tr>
        <td colspan=3 align=right>
            <asp:Button ID="btnSubmit" runat=server Text="View Office Details"/>
        </td>
    </tr>
</table>
</div>
</form>
</body>
</html>
```

The preceding ASP code should look pretty straightforward. There are three list boxes and a button. There are also two JavaScript functions: `CallBackReturnFunction` and `CallBackReturnFunction2`. These are both functions that will be called by the client callback framework when results have been made available by the server in response to their initial requests. These requests are made by additional JavaScript functions: `OnCompanyClick` and `OnLocationClick`. As you will see in Listing 22.5, these functions are generated dynamically using the `RegisterClientScriptBlock` method.

LISTING 22.5 Page Code Corresponding to ASPx Code in Listing 22.4

```
using System;
using System.Text;
using System.Data.SqlClient;
using System.Data;
using System.Configuration;
using System.Web;
using System.Web.Security;
using System.Web.UI;
using System.Web.UI.WebControls;
using System.Web.UI.WebControls.WebParts;
using System.Web.UI.HtmlControls;

public partial class _Default : System.Web.UI.Page
{
public CompanyEventControl companyControl = new CompanyEventControl();
public LocationEventControl locationControl = new LocationEventControl();

protected void Page_Load(object sender, EventArgs e)
{
    ClientScriptManager cm = Page.ClientScript;
    this.AddParsedSubObject(companyControl);
    string cbRef = cm.GetCallbackEventReference(companyControl,
        "companyId", "CallBackReturnFunction", "oContext", "OnError", false);
    StringBuilder sb = new StringBuilder();
    sb.Append(
  "<script language=\"javascript\">function OnCompanyClick(companyId)\n");
    sb.Append(
"{ var oContext = new Object(); oContext.CommandName =
➥\"GetLocationsByCompanyID\";\n");
    sb.Append("oContext.CompanyID = companyId;\n");
    sb.AppendFormat("{0};\n", cbRef);
    sb.Append("}\n</script>");
    cm.RegisterClientScriptBlock(this.GetType(), "OnCompanyClick", sb.ToString());

    this.AddParsedSubObject(locationControl);
    string cbRef2 = cm.GetCallbackEventReference(locationControl,
```

LISTING 22.5   Continued

```
        "locationId", "CallBackReturnFunction2", "oContext", "OnError", false);
    sb = new StringBuilder();
    sb.Append(
"<script language=\"javascript\">function OnLocationClick(locationId)\n");
    sb.Append(
"{ var oContext = new Object(); oContext.CommandName =
➥\"GetOfficesByLocation\";\n");
    sb.Append("oContext.LocationID = locationId;\n");
    sb.AppendFormat("{0}\n", cbRef2);
    sb.Append("}\n</script>");
    cm.RegisterClientScriptBlock(this.GetType(), "OnLocationClick", sb.ToString());

    if (!Page.IsPostBack)
        PopulateCompanies();


}

void PopulateCompanies()
{
    SqlConnection conn =
new SqlConnection("Data Source=localhost; Initial Catalog=SampleDB;
➥Integrated Security=SSPI;");
    conn.Open();
    SqlCommand cmd = conn.CreateCommand();
    cmd.CommandText = "SELECT CompanyID, Description FROM Companies";
    DataTable companies = new DataTable("Companies");
    SqlDataAdapter da = new SqlDataAdapter(cmd);
    da.Fill(companies);
    lbCompany.DataTextField = "Description";
    lbCompany.DataValueField = "CompanyID";
    lbCompany.DataSource = companies;
    lbCompany.DataBind();
}
}
```

Don't worry if this looks a little complex. As you progress through the book, the techniques used here will become second nature to you. Keep this sample handy as you go through the rest of the examples in the ASP.NET section and try to apply the technique of client callbacks to the other techniques you're learning.

The code in Listing 22.5 essentially indicates that two controls, CompanyEventControl and LocationEventControl, are going to be event handlers for client callbacks. Listing 22.6

22

contains the source code for both of these classes. Their sole purpose is to take a request indicating a parent row and return a specially serialized string (one that can be easily decomposed by JavaScript) containing the appropriate rows.

LISTING 22.6   `ICallbackEventHandler` Implementations

```
using System;
using System.Text;
using System.Data;
using System.Data.SqlClient;
using System.Configuration;
using System.Web;
using System.Web.Security;
using System.Web.UI;
using System.Web.UI.WebControls;
using System.Web.UI.WebControls.WebParts;
using System.Web.UI.HtmlControls;


/// <summary>
/// Summary description for CompanyEventControl
/// </summary>
public class CompanyEventControl : Control, ICallbackEventHandler
{
private DataTable locations;
public CompanyEventControl()
{
//
// TODO: Add constructor logic here
//
}


#region ICallbackEventHandler Members

public string GetCallbackResult()
{
StringBuilder sb = new StringBuilder();
foreach (DataRow row in locations.Rows)
{
    sb.AppendFormat("{0}|{1}||", row["LocationID"], row["Description"]);
}
return sb.ToString();
}


public void RaiseCallbackEvent(string eventArgument)
{
```

LISTING 22.6   Continued

```
using (SqlConnection conn = new SqlConnection(
    "data source=localhost; initial catalog=SampleDB; Integrated Security=SSPI;"))
{
    conn.Open();
    SqlCommand cmd = conn.CreateCommand();
    cmd.CommandText =
"SELECT LocationID, Description FROM Locations WHERE CompanyID = " +
  eventArgument;
    SqlDataAdapter da = new SqlDataAdapter(cmd);
    locations = new DataTable();
    da.Fill(locations);
}
}


#endregion
}
public class LocationEventControl : Control, ICallbackEventHandler
{
private DataTable offices;

public LocationEventControl()
{
//
// TODO: Add constructor logic here
//
}

#region ICallbackEventHandler Members

public string GetCallbackResult()
{
StringBuilder sb = new StringBuilder();
foreach (DataRow row in offices.Rows)
{
    sb.AppendFormat("{0}¦{1}¦¦", row["OfficeID"], row["Description"]);
}
return sb.ToString();
}

public void RaiseCallbackEvent(string eventArgument)
{
```

LISTING 22.6   Continued

```
using (SqlConnection conn = new SqlConnection(
    "data source=localhost; initial catalog=SampleDB; integrated security=SSPI;"))
{
    offices = new DataTable("Offices");
    conn.Open();
    SqlCommand cmd = conn.CreateCommand();
    cmd.CommandText =
"SELECT OfficeID, Description FROM Offices WHERE LocationID = " +
  eventArgument;
    SqlDataAdapter da = new SqlDataAdapter(cmd);
    da.Fill(offices);
}
}

#endregion
}
```

The code in Listing 22.6 responds to a client callback event triggered by client-side JavaScript and retrieves the appropriate child rows given the parent's ID (passed as the eventArgument parameter). Because JavaScript isn't going to be able to work with native .NET structures, the response to client callbacks is always going to be a string. In this case, the code used the pipe (|) and double-pipe (||) characters as column and row delimiters respectively.

Figure 22.4 shows a sample of what a page looks like that was populated using client callbacks. Keep in mind that the first list box is populated on the initial page load, and the second two list boxes are populated dynamically using client-side JavaScript and server-side client callback events.

Using Client Callbacks

Even if you don't completely follow the code used to implement client callbacks, I strongly urge you to run the sample provided with the book. As you progress throughout the book, go back to this sample and, as a useful exercise, try to change the book's samples from purely server-side postbacks into samples that implement client callbacks for increased performance. The task of converting purely postback code to client callback code will rapidly increase your ASP.NET proficiency. Client callbacks are the steppingstone to Microsoft's Atlas implementation of AJAX technology, and understanding how they work will help ease the transition into AJAX-style application development.

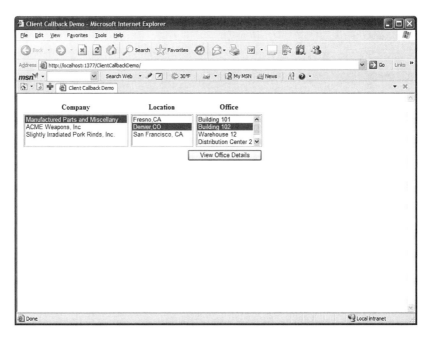

FIGURE 22.4   Using client callbacks.

Summary

This chapter provided you with an in-depth introduction to the world of creating power-ful applications using ASP.NET 2.0. You learned the basics of how ASP.NET takes ASPX files and C# files and merges them into an assembly that is then used to service requests from users. This chapter also provided an overview of all of the stock controls that ship with ASP.NET, including the new controls specific to ASP.NET 2.0 such as the GridView, all of the integrated security controls such as Login and LoginView, and site navigation controls such as the SiteMapPath and the powerful new Menu control. Finally, the chapter concluded by giving you sample code for working with postbacks and event handling, and even a glimpse at the high-performance client/server hybrid *client callback* feature. At this point, you should be well equipped to take your ASP.NET learning to the next level and start diving into some of the amazing features of ASP.NET 2.0 such as personalization, customization, data-driven applications, security, web services, and much more.

CHAPTER **23**

State Management in ASP.NET 2.0

Τhe web is inherently stateless because all web pages are served up using the stateless HTTP (or HTTPS) protocol. That means that there is no protocol-level mechanism that allows a web page to maintain information from one request to the next. Without outside help, web pages cannot maintain information about an application, a user's session, or even about previous requests for the same page.

This chapter shows you how to manage the various types of state that are critical to all web applications: application state, session state, and view state. Code samples are provided with discussion on utilizing all of these state management tools. Creating custom session state providers, as well as other types of providers, is covered in Chapter 29, "Creating Custom ASP.NET Providers."

Working with Application State

When developing web applications, it is often necessary to maintain information that is applicable to the entire site. Site-wide information is often stored in databases, but can also be stored in application state within ASP.NET. If the information you need to store is small, but will be accessed quite often, then using application state will be faster and more memory-efficient than continually reading and writing site-wide data to and from a database.

Application state is accomplished through the storage of name/value pairs in an instance of the HttpApplicationState class. Every page in an ASP.NET application has access to this instance in the page's Application property. The HttpApplicationState class operates just like any other dictionary, where you can set and retrieve values using numeric or string indexes:

```
Application["myValue"] = 21;
Application.Add("anotherValue") = "Hello";
foreach (string key in Application.AllKeys)
{
    Response.Write(Application[key]);
}
```

Because application state is stored in such a wide scope, you can potentially have hundreds or even thousands of page requests attempting to write to the same state variable at the same time. As you saw in Chapter 10, "Multithreaded Programming," data can quickly become corrupted when accessed by multiple threads at the same time without proper protection. You can protect code that writes to an application state variable from simultaneous writes by using the Application.Lock() and Application.UnLock() methods. These methods are essentially wrappers around the C# lock keyword, using the application state object as the lock source, as shown in the following example:

```
Application.Lock();
Application["myVariable"] = 121;
Application.UnLock();
```

With the preceding lines of code, you can guarantee that only one request will write to application state at any given time.

> **TIP**
>
> Be careful when you use the Application.Lock() and Application.UnLock() methods. If you accidentally lock the application without unlocking it, you could wind up causing a large slowdown or even page failure. You might want to consider using a code snippet for application state access that automatically includes a corresponding UnLock() method for the Lock() method, guaranteeing that you will always unlock the application state object when you're done writing the state variable. Make sure that you unlock the application state as soon as possible to avoid keeping other pages waiting for state data.

If you add a "Global Application Class" file to your project, you will add the Global.asax file. This file contains several events that can be used to initialize state. One such event is the Application_Start event, which can be used to initialize application state variables, as shown in the following code:

```
void Application_Start(object sender, EventArgs e)
{
    // Code that runs on application startup
    Application["counter"] = 0;
}
```

Listing 23.1 shows the ASPX and C# code for a page that displays the current value of an application-wide counter variable as well as prompting the user to click a button to increment the counter.

LISTING 23.1   Using Application State

```
<%@ Page Language="C#" AutoEventWireup="true"
CodeFile="Default.aspx.cs" Inherits="_Default" %>

<!DOCTYPE html PUBLIC
"-//W3C//DTD XHTML 1.0 Transitional//EN"
"http://www.w3.org/TR/xhtml1/DTD/xhtml1-transitional.dtd">

<html xmlns="http://www.w3.org/1999/xhtml" >
<head runat="server">
<title>Untitled Page</title>
</head>
<body>
<form id="form1" runat="server">
<div>
<asp:Label ID="lblAppCounter" runat="server" /><br /><br />
Press the "Increment Counter" button to increase the application-wide counter<br />
<asp:Button ID="btnIncrement" runat="server"
OnClick="btnIncrement_Click" Text="Increment Counter" /><br />

</div>
</form>
</body>
</html>

Default.aspx.cs
using System;
using System.Data;
using System.Configuration;
using System.Web;
using System.Web.Security;
using System.Web.UI;
using System.Web.UI.WebControls;
using System.Web.UI.WebControls.WebParts;
using System.Web.UI.HtmlControls;

public partial class _Default : System.Web.UI.Page
{
protected void Page_Load(object sender, EventArgs e)
{
```

23

LISTING 23.1   Continued

```
    UpdateCounterLabel();
}
protected void btnIncrement_Click(object sender, EventArgs e)
{
    Application["counter"] = (int)Application["counter"] + 1;
    UpdateCounterLabel();
}

private void UpdateCounterLabel()
{
    lblAppCounter.Text = string.Format(
      "Current value of application-wide counter is <b>{0}</b>.<br/>",
        Application["counter"]);
}
}
```

As mentioned earlier, you want to use application state to store small amounts of frequently accessed information. The larger the data you store in the application state, the higher the risk of having application state objects slow down your application. Larger amounts of less frequently accessed data would be more efficiently stored in a database or in an application configuration file.

Working with Session State

A user's session is the time period from when he makes his first request in an application until he leaves the site. A user's session ends when the web application has not received a request from that user within a specified timeout period.

Session state allows the web application to store and retrieve information that pertains to the given user and her session. This information often includes things such as the user's list of security privileges, shopping cart, wish list, or temporary data used for specific pages, such as the most recently browsed products or the last set of search criteria used.

Sessions are identified with a unique identifier that is generated for each session. In most cases, the user's session ID is stored in a temporary cookie in the browser's memory. When the browser makes a request for a page, it sends the collection of cookies that apply for the site, including the user's session ID. This allows the server to locate all of the data stored for a given user based on the user's session ID.

If the user has disabled cookies in her browser, you can use a special technique that rewrites website URLs so that each URL contains the user's session ID. This allows the server to access the user's session state without reading it from the collection of cookies transmitted by the browser.

This section covers the various ways in which you can maintain session state within an ASP.NET application, such as the in-process state provider and out-of-process state providers like the ASP.NET State Server and SQL Server. You will also learn how to handle events specific to session state within your ASP.NET application.

Using the Default In-Process State Provider

Because all session state providers expose the same functionality, the use of each provider will appear to be very similar. However, there are some major differences among the providers that can cause potential problems if you aren't aware of them.

The default session state provider can handle pretty much anything you want to store in a session, within reason. The more data you store in the session state, the larger the memory footprint of your application.

Managing Session Variables

When deciding on what you want to store in session state and what you want to store in a relational back end such as SQL Server or Oracle, you should consider a few things. First, consider the size of the data being stored. Is it fairly small? Secondly, consider that you can have as many open sessions as you have simultaneous users. In fact, you can have more than that if you have a long session timeout period. So, for every piece of data you plan on storing in session, multiply the size of that data by the maximum number of users you expect to have visiting your site at any given time, plus 5%. This will give you a worst-case-scenario memory cost for storing that item in the session state. If you absolutely must store that data in the session, and that data is extremely costly memory-wise, consider using SQL Server as your session state provider because it is designed to handle larger data sizes.

All session state is exposed through an instance of the `System.Web.SessionState.HttpSessionState` class in the `Session` property of the `Page` class. Table 23.1 contains the list of properties available for the `HttpSessionState` class, and Table 23.2 contains the list of methods available for that class.

TABLE 23.1   Commonly Used `HttpSessionState` Properties

Property	Description
CookieMode	Indicates whether the session state is currently configured for cookieless (URL rewriting) operation or normal operation. Values are : AutoDetect (detect if browser supports cookies; if not, use URL rewriting), UseCookies (always use cookies), UseDeviceProfile (checks browser capabilities to determine use of cookies), and UseUri (always use URL rewriting).
Count	Returns the number of data items stored in the session. Note that this count, and all other data, is *for the current user session*.
IsCookieless	Indicates if the session ID is stored in the URL.
IsNewSession	Indicates that the session was created on the current request. Very handy for detecting a user's first page hit on a site.
IsReadOnly	Indicates whether the session is read only.
IsSynchronized	Indicates whether access to session variables is thread-safe (synchronized).
Item	Get or set individual session items. C# allows the use of the indexer ([ ]) notation instead of this property.

23

TABLE 23.1   Continued

Property	Description
Keys	The keys of all items stored in session state.
LCID	Gets or sets the locale of the current session.
Mode	Gets the current state mode (provider): Custom, InProc, Off, SqlServer, or StateServer.
SessionID	Returns the unique ID string of the current session.
StaticObjects	Gets a list of all objects declared as static by <object> tags within Global.asax, scoped as session scope.
SyncRoot	Object against which thread-safe locks can be made to synchronize access to data items.
Timeout	Indicates the amount of time (in minutes) that can elapse between requests for pages without expiring the user's session. If the timeout period elapses without a page request by the same user, the user's session expires.

TABLE 23.2   HttpSessionState Methods

Method	Description
Abandon	Abandons the current session, removing all data items from the user's session. The next page request made by this user will create a new session.
Add	Adds a new data item to session state.
Clear	Removes all data items from session state.
Remove	Removes a data item from session state.
RemoveAll	Removes all items from session state.
RemoveAt	Removes the data item from the indicated index.

To get started working with session state, create a new website using the menu option File, New, Web Site. This will create an empty website with a single page: default.aspx. By default, in-process session state is enabled. Drop two labels onto the default.aspx page called lblStatus and lblCounter, separated by <br> tags. Finally, drop a button onto the page called btnSubmit with the text "Click Here". Double-click the button to rig up an empty event handler, and then set the C# code portion of the page to match the code contained in Listing 23.2.

LISTING 23.2   Session State Demo

```
using System;
using System.Data;
using System.Configuration;
using System.Web;
using System.Web.Security;
using System.Web.UI;
using System.Web.UI.WebControls;
using System.Web.UI.WebControls.WebParts;
using System.Web.UI.HtmlControls;
```

LISTING 23.2   Continued

```
public partial class _Default : System.Web.UI.Page
{
protected void Page_Load(object sender, EventArgs e)
{
    lblStatus.Text = string.Format("This is a(n) {0} session!",
        Session.IsNewSession ? "New" : "Old");
    if (Session.IsNewSession)
        Session["counter"] = 0;

    UpdateCounterDisplay();
}


protected void UpdateCounterDisplay()
{
    lblCounter.Text = string.Format("Counter value is <b>{0}</b>",
Session["counter"]);
}
protected void btnSubmit_Click(object sender, EventArgs e)
{
    Session["counter"] = (int)Session["counter"] + 1;
    UpdateCounterDisplay();


}
}
```

This page basically displays the value of a session counter, along with some text that indicates whether the session was created during that request or not (using the IsNewSession property). The first time you run this application (just press F5 in Visual Studio and choose Yes to have a debug-enabled Web.config file created for you), you will see the page shown in Figure 23.1.

After clicking the Click Here button a few times to increment the session counter, not only can you see the session counter being incremented, but Figure 23.2 also shows that the session is no longer a new session.

You can add the following lines of code to the preceding sample to display the name and value of every piece of data stored in the session:

```
Response.Write("<hr/>");
foreach (string key in Session.Keys)
{
    Response.Write(string.Format("<B>{0}</B>: {1}<br/>", key, Session[key]));
}
Response.Write("<hr/>");
```

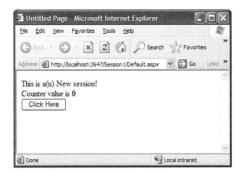

FIGURE 23.1   First run of a session state demo.

FIGURE 23.2   Subsequent run of a session state demo.

Working with the default, in-process session state provider is fairly easy. No initial setup is required, you don't have to change the `Web.config` file to support it, and you don't have any firm restrictions on the kinds of objects that can be placed in session state. The next two providers discussed both require manipulation of the `Web.config` file and have requirements on the types of objects that can be stored and retrieved.

> **TIP**
>
> Keep in mind that the `Session` object's keys are all strings. This also means that the keys are case sensitive. In an application that has dozens of session keys and data items, it can quickly become a maintenance nightmare for large teams to remember which keys are being used for which variables. In such a situation, it is often helpful to create a wrapper around the `Session` object that takes an enumeration as parameters. Instead of accessing the `Session` via code like `Session["myVariable"]`, you could access it via `SessionWrapper[SessionKeys.MyVariable]`. This way, anyone on the team who needs a new session key must either reuse an existing key or add one to the SessionKeys enumeration.

Using the ASP.NET State Server Provider

The State Server is a Windows service provided by ASP.NET 2.0 that is installed whenever ASP.NET is installed on a machine. By default, this service is off. As mentioned earlier, your code will work directly with the HttpSessionState class instance stored in the Session property of the Page class regardless of which state provider you select.

The reason for using an out-of-process state server is simple: web farms. In a web farm, more than one server is used to host multiple copies of the same web application that act as one. These web applications need to be able to share the same session state, because a user could make requests of multiple servers throughout their session, and the session state needs to remain consistent between those requests. The ASP.NET State Server is a lightweight out-of-process server. SQL Server can be used as a "heavyweight" out-of-process state server.

The ASP.NET State Server must be turned on and configured before you can use it. To turn it on, open the Services control panel, right-click it, and choose Start. If you are going to want it on all the time for your application, you will need to make sure that the service is always on (by default it is set to Manual). Figure 23.3 shows the Services control panel with the State Server service highlighted.

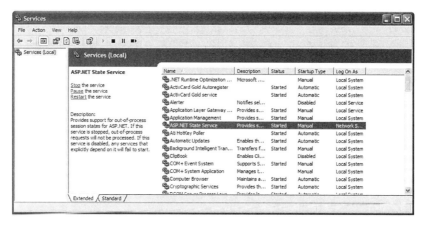

FIGURE 23.3 The State Server service.

To use the State Server service, you'll need to modify the Web.config of your website to indicate the use of the State Server in the <sessionState> element, as shown in Listing 23.3.

LISTING 23.3 A Web.config File Modified to Work with the State Server Service

```
<?xml version="1.0"?>
<configuration>
  <appSettings/>
  <connectionStrings/>
  <system.web>
```

LISTING 23.3   Continued

```
    <compilation debug="true"/>
    <sessionState mode="StateServer"
        stateConnectionString="tcpip=localhost:42424" />
    <authentication mode="Windows"/>
  </system.web>
</configuration>
```

The `stateConnectionString` attribute is the most crucial part of the configuration. This string takes the format `tcpip=address:port`. You can use `localhost` or `127.0.0.1` if the state server is local to the web application, or you can specify a host name or IP address for a remote server. The state server always listens on the same port, but you can put the state server on any machine you like.

After you have modified the `Web.config` file and you have turned on the State Server service, you're ready to go. There is one caveat, however: *You cannot store and retrieve nonserializable objects or* `MarshalByRefObjects`. Any attempt to store an object that inherits from `MarshalByRefObject` or that is not marked as serializable will result in the following error message:

```
Unable to serialize the session state. In 'StateServer' and 'SQLServer' mode,
ASP.NET will serialize the session state objects, and as a result non-serializable
objects or MarshalByRef objects are not permitted. The same restriction applies if
similar serialization is done by the custom session state store in 'Custom' mode.
```

The reason that ASP.NET serializes session state objects for out-of-process servers is their out-of-process nature. If ASP.NET attempted to store an actual object reference, that reference would be tied directly to the one server that tried to store the reference. Put simply: the complexity of the `Remoting` code that would be required to get object references to be stored in an out-of-process state server make it nearly impossible to accomplish. As such, ASP.NET serializes all objects being stored in out-of-process state servers.

TIP

Not only do you need to make sure that you aren't using a `MarshalByRefObject` class, but you need to make sure that your class is marked as `Serializable`. One common problem that developers run into, even though their class is marked `Serializable`, is in state consistency. If "side-effect" code takes place in a `set` or a `get` accessor, there is a chance that the serialization code in ASP.NET might not give you back the same object you stored. To avoid these pitfalls, developers often make a rule such that only `structs` can be stored in session state, with only public fields. Excessive use of private fields, side-effect code (code inside accessors), or even parameterized constructors can lead to serialization inconsistency.

To try out the State Server session provider, you can basically follow the same steps you followed in the preceding sample: create a website, drop two labels onto the form (lblStatus and lblCounter), and drop a button on the form named btnSubmit. Double-click the button to wire up the event handler.

Before you do anything else, add a struct to your project (you might be prompted to create the App_Code folder) called Customer:

```csharp
using System;
using System.Data;
using System.Configuration;
using System.Web;
using System.Web.Security;
using System.Web.UI;
using System.Web.UI.WebControls;
using System.Web.UI.WebControls.WebParts;
using System.Web.UI.HtmlControls;


/// <summary>
/// Really good guideline for out-of-proc state:
/// 1. structs only
/// 2. lightweight
/// 3. must be serializable
/// 4. use only public fields, no accessors
/// 5. no private members
/// 6. constructors cannot create a state that is unachievable
///     through simple property/field setting (serialization/deserialization)
/// </summary>
[Serializable()]
public struct Customer
{
    public string FirstName;
    public string LastName;

    public Customer(string last, string first)
    {
        FirstName = first;
        LastName = last;
    }
}
```

Now you can set the C# (default.aspx.cs) to the code shown in Listing 23.4.

LISTING 23.4   Using a Serializable Struct In an Out-of-Process Session State Server

```csharp
using System;
using System.Data;
using System.Configuration;
using System.Web;
```

LISTING 23.4   Continued

```
using System.Web.Security;
using System.Web.UI;
using System.Web.UI.WebControls;
using System.Web.UI.WebControls.WebParts;
using System.Web.UI.HtmlControls;

public partial class _Default : System.Web.UI.Page
{
protected void Page_Load(object sender, EventArgs e)
{
    if (Session.IsNewSession)
    {
        lblStatus.Text = "This session is <b>New</b>.";
        Session["counter"] = 0;
        Session["customer"] = new Customer("Hoffman", "Kevin");
    }
    else
    {
        lblStatus.Text = string.Format(
            "This session is <b>Old</b>. Stored Customer is {0}",
            ((Customer)Session["customer"]).LastName + ", " +
            ((Customer)Session["customer"]).FirstName);
    }

    UpdateCounterLabel();
}

private void UpdateCounterLabel()
{
    lblCounter.Text = string.Format(
        "Counter value is <b>{0}</b>.",
        Session["counter"]);
}
protected void btnSubmit_Click(object sender, EventArgs e)
{
    Session["counter"] = (int)Session["counter"] + 1;
    UpdateCounterLabel();
}
}
```

As long as you remember the fact that the ASP.NET State Server service is designed for lightweight (small amounts of data), out-of-process (consistently serializable) session state management, you will be able to take full advantage of this provider.

Using the SQL Server Session State Provider

The SQL Server session state provider is designed for more robust out-of-process session state management. This means that SQL Server can handle a larger number of concurrent user sessions than the ASP.NET State Server. It can also handle larger amounts of data per session than the ASP.NET State Server (though that too is not without limit).

There are two steps to getting the SQL Server session state provider to work. First, you need to create the state management database within your SQL Server instance. Second, you need to modify `Web.config` to point to that SQL Server instance.

To install the appropriate schema in SQL Server, you can run the `InstallSqlState.sql` script *on the server on which the SQL Server instance resides*. Do not attempt to run this script on your web server (unless that is also your SQL Server). You can find this script in `%SystemRoot%\Microsoft.NET\Framework\version`. For example, on the author's machine, the file was in

`C:\Windows\Microsoft.NET\Framework\v2.0.50727`

To run this script, you should *not* execute it from within SQL Server 2005 Management Studio. Instead, you should run the script using the `aspnet_regsql` command-line tool. To use this tool, open a Visual Studio 2005 Command Prompt window. To get the full help text, type **aspnet_regsql -?**. You can also use this tool to add support for other providers in SQL Server such as roles, membership, profiles, personalization, and so on.

You use the `sstype` option to indicate the type of session state support to add to the SQL Server database:

- Temporary—The session state will be temporary and stored in the `tempdb` database. This is an ideal option for most situations because `tempdb` cleans itself up and you don't have to worry about maintenance. If you don't need to be able to restore session state if your SQL Server crashes, this is the option you should use.
- Persistent—The session state will be stored in a SQL database called `ASPState`. The stored procedures for maintaining session state will also be stored in this database.
- Custom—The session state data and corresponding stored procedures will both be placed in a database named on the command line using the `-d` option.

When you create the session state database at the command line, you also need to specify the SQL connection information, as shown in the following line of code:

`aspnet_regsql -S localhost -ssadd -sstype p -E`

The `-E` option uses a trusted connection to SQL Server using the current Windows credentials. To specify an alternate username and password, you can use the `-U` and `-P` options. Figure 23.4 shows the SQL Server 2005 Management Studio application examining the contents of the newly created `ASPState` database.

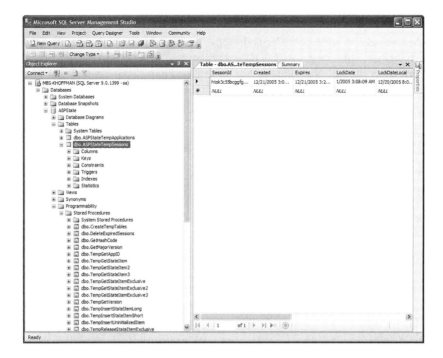

FIGURE 23.4   The `ASPState` database.

With the session state management database properly configured in your SQL Server (you can do this in SQL Express as well, provided you give `.\SQLExpress` for the server name for the local SQL Express instance), you can then start using SQL Server for your session state store.

Because the code in Listing 23.4 is designed to work using serializable structures with an out-of-process session state store, it is ideal to use as a sample to test SQL Server session state management.

Take the code from that sample and modify the `Web.config` file to contain a new `<sessionState>` element as shown in the following example:

```
<?xml version="1.0"?>
<configuration>
    <appSettings/>
    <connectionStrings/>
    <system.web>
    <sessionState mode="SQLServer"
      sqlConnectionString="data source=localhost; Integrated Security=SSPI;" />
        <compilation debug="true"/>
        <authentication mode="Windows"/>
    </system.web>
</configuration>
```

Note that the connection string for the SQL Server session state store doesn't contain the database name. You never supply the database name unless you have used the Custom Database option from the `aspnet_regsql` command-line tool. This allows your application to use temporary and persistent session state management interchangeably without having to modify your `Web.config` file.

Handling Session State Events

If your application has a `global.asax` file (you can add this by choosing to add a new item, and selecting Global Application Class from the template list), you can write code that responds to several events specific to session state.

Your code can respond to events triggered when a user's session is first created and when a user's session is terminated. A session is created when a user makes a request for a page in your application and has no current session ID. A session is terminated when a specified time period has elapsed since the user's last request for any page within the application.

In the `global.asax` file there are two methods specific to session state events: `Session_Start` and `Session_End`. The start event is extremely useful for initializing data to make it available to the rest of the application, such as counters and other data. The end event is used to clean up data related to the user's session. You don't need to use the end event to manually remove items from the user's session because those will be automatically disposed, but you can use this event to perform other operations such as database queries that need to be done when a user is no longer connected to a website.

To illustrate these two events, you can create a sample application that maintains a list of all connected users at the application level and a counter at the session level.

> **Session_End**
>
> Keep in mind that the `Session_End` event is only raised when the session state mode is set to `InProc`. This event is meaningless and will never be fired in any out-of-process mode such as SQL Server, State Server, or your own custom state provider implementation.

The code for such a `global.asax` file is contained in Listing 23.5.

LISTING 23.5   Event Handling in `global.asax`

```
<%@ Application Language="C#" %>

<script runat="server">

void Application_Start(object sender, EventArgs e)
{
// Code that runs on application startup

}
```

LISTING 23.5   Continued

```
void Application_End(object sender, EventArgs e)
{
//  Code that runs on application shutdown

}

void Application_Error(object sender, EventArgs e)
{
// Code that runs when an unhandled error occurs

}

void Session_Start(object sender, EventArgs e)
{
  System.Collections.Generic.List<string> users = null;
  if (Application["users"] == null)
  {
    users = new System.Collections.Generic.List<string>();
    Application["users"] = users;
  }
  else
    users =
      (System.Collections.Generic.List<string>)Application["users"];

 users.Add(Context.User.Identity.Name.Substring(
 Context.User.Identity.Name.IndexOf('\\')+1,
 Context.User.Identity.Name.Length -
 Context.User.Identity.Name.IndexOf('\\')-1));
 Session["counter"] = 0;
}

void Session_End(object sender, EventArgs e)
{
 System.Collections.Generic.List<string> users =
   (System.Collections.Generic.List<string>)Application["users"];
 users.Remove(User.Identity.Name);
}
</script>
```

The code in the preceding listing adds the user's name (with the domain name stripped off) to an application-wide List<string> class when a session starts and removes that same name from the list when the user's session ends. This effectively creates a "who's online" list that can then be rendered by any page. A sample of this is included with the chapter's code, but you could try to create a "who's online" page on your own as an exercise.

Working with View State

View state is the means by which controls on a page can maintain state information between requests. HTTP is inherently stateless, so additional coding needed to be done to allow a control's state to persist between multiple requests for the same page. For example, if a user selects the third item in a drop-down list, checks a box, and enters some text in a text box, you will want that information to be made available to you in your server code so that you can process it, validate it, or persist the information in a database.

This is all made possible using the mechanism called view state. When a page is almost finished its rendering phase, it creates a hidden form field called __VIEWSTATE. This hidden input tag contains the state for all controls on the entire page in a serialized fashion. When you view the source for an ASP.NET page, you will see the view state tag as shown in the following code:

```
<input type="hidden" name="__VIEWSTATE" id="__VIEWSTATE" value="..." />
```

View state is restored from this hidden input tag during the initialization phase of the page life cycle and made available to the developer in the ViewState property of the Page class. The ViewState property is an instance of the StateBag class.

To place a value into view state to be restored on a subsequent postback, you can use indexer notation as shown in the following code:

```
ViewState["customValue"] = 21;
```

And then on a subsequent postback, you can check the value you stored with the following code:

```
if (Page.IsPostback)
    if (ViewState["customValue"] != null)
        Response.Write(ViewState["customValue"]);
```

> **TIP**
>
> As long as you know when view state is restored and saved, you will find it easy to work with. If you attempt to access view state before the initialization stage of the page life cycle or attempt to change view state after the rendering stage, the results will be unpredictable. View state is not dynamic like session state. It is restored once at page initialization, and output in the form of a hidden input tag once at page render completion.

As you will see in Chapter 30, "Developing ASP.NET Controls," controls maintain their own state using the ViewState collection. For example, the ListBox control stores the list of items in the list box in view state, and it stores the currently selected item. This allows a page to access the database once to retrieve the data, and then pass the data to subsequent requests using view state, creating a faster and more scalable solution. This pattern is used in virtually all ASP.NET controls.

Despite the power and flexibility that view state provides, it can be overused. Using view state to store large amounts of data can cause problems for users with slower connections.

In a hypothetical scenario, a page retrieves 3,000 rows of data and then instructs a GridView control to render page 3, displaying 20 rows. If this GridView is maintaining the entire set of data between requests, the GridView will actually be placing 3,000 rows of data into view state. As a rule of thumb, storing data in view state actually consumes more space than the raw value. Therefore, storing a 32-bit integer in view state is going to consume far more data than just 4 bytes because the *name* of the view state item is also stored in view state.

In a production application, you will probably find that you need to reach a balance. Using view state for every control on your page regardless of whether its value needs to be persisted between requests can lead to a severe bloating of the view state hidden form field (which increases page size as a result). Querying the database on every request is also going to cause problems for your database.

What most developers do is find middle ground. They will disable view state for all controls that have static values or values that are irrelevant on postback. Developers can also do things like only query a single page of data from the database so that only a small number of rows are stored in view state. It will be up to you to find the middle ground that satisfies your performance, scalability, and time-to-market requirements.

TIP

One approach that seems to work well is to get the initial version of a page done relying heavily on view state and default data-binding code. When the initial version is completed, you can analyze the size of the view state (figure out how long it takes to download view state on the slowest end-user connection) and determine how much view state (if any) you need to trim from the page to decrease download time. One thing you never want to do is waste weeks of development time to create a performance improvement that most users won't be able to see. Always weigh the cost of improvement against visible benefits to the end user.

State Management in Web Farms

So far you've been reading how to manage state for a web application using various techniques. You've seen how to manage application state using the Application object, and you've seen how to manage both in- and out-of-process session state using the Session object and the available session state providers. What hasn't been discussed is how all of this is impacted when your application is running in a web farm.

Web farms are a topic that don't seem to get enough coverage in printed material, and people are unfortunately forced to learn how to code in a farm environment the hard way: write code, watch it break, rewrite the code.

A *web farm* is an environment in which multiple servers are all running copies of the same application. Windows software or special routers are used to distribute requests for a page between the different servers either for load balancing or to provide failover support in case a server goes down.

Three types of state need to be addressed within a web farm: application state, session state, and view state.

Using Application State in Web Farms

When you access the `Application` object, you are doing so at the `AppDomain` scope. Applications running on other servers will be running within different `AppDomains`. This means that when one server accesses the `Application` object, it is not accessing the same data as the other servers.

You can get around this in several ways. The first and easiest method is to simply avoid using the `Application` object's dictionary for storing data. If your design doesn't allow for storing application-wide data in this object, no additional coding is required to make your application "state safe" in a web farm.

> **TIP**
>
> A rule I live by is: "Statelessness is next to godliness." In large-scale enterprise applications, the maintenance of state decreases the rate at which the application can scale, and often introduces huge problems with performance and design. If you find yourself having to graph out state changes just to keep up, you may need to take another look at your design. As a rule, if you can avoid requiring state at all, your large-scale enterprise design will thank you for it.

If you absolutely have to have application-wide state storage, and you can't accomplish that using the database, you can create a web service hosted by a designated server in your farm that exposes central state management at the application level. You can also do this using a business object and a Singleton Remoting server. Web services are covered in Chapter 32, "Exposing Functionality with Web Services," and Remoting is covered in Chapter 41, "Remoting." The Web Services and Remoting options should be considered a last resort if you need application state in your web farm and can't accomplish it using a database.

Using Session State in Web Farms

Session state is far easier to scale from the single-server environment to a web farm environment. As you saw earlier in this chapter, you can use the ASP.NET State Server service or SQL Server as an out-of-process session state manager. Because session state is being managed outside the `AppDomain` scope of a single application, session state can be easily shared among all the applications participating in a single farm.

All the usual session state caveats apply here: Keep the data stored in the session small, *consistently* serializable, and pertinent. In this context, "pertinent" means that you should make sure that you *need* to store that information in session state, and that the information stored in the session is not duplicated anywhere else. For example, don't bother storing the user's authenticated name in session because it is already available in the `User.Identity.Name` property.

Using View State in Web Farms

Part of the overhead involved in view state that makes this author strongly recommend against its overuse is that view state is tamper-proof. This means that, by default, someone cannot send artificial view state to a page, nor can they take view state that originated on one server and send it to another.

This presents a problem in a web farm because view state is validated based on the server from which it originated. If a user requests a page from `ServerA` and then clicks a button on that page, it is highly likely that the resulting postback request could be sent to the same page on `ServerB`. To fix this problem, you can use the `Web.config` file to specify the validation settings for view state as well as keys used in the encryption of view state. If all servers are using the same keys to work with view state, all servers in the farm can read view state generated by any other server in the farm.

In addition to the hash validation of view state that prevents tamper proofing, view state can be encrypted if you will be posting back sensitive information. There are a variety of publicly available tools that will decode unencrypted view state and show you all the data contained within. If you have sensitive information stored in view state that needs to be posted back over a non-SSL request, you can encrypt view state.

This problem is corrected for web farms by using the `<machineKey>` element in `Web.config`. By default, this element is configured to allow the server to automatically generate its own key pair and to use SHA1 for the hashing algorithm used to verify view state. It can also be used to encrypt other things that you will see later in the book, such as the forms authentication ticket and the `Role` authorization cookie.

You will want to supply manually generated values for the `validationKey` and `decryptionKey` attributes of the `<machineKey>` element, and share those values among all servers in your web farm for proper operation. You can either create these keys on your own, or you can use the `RNGCryptoServiceProvider` (cryptographically sound random number generation) to build the keys. Three different types of hash validation can be performed on view state: SHA1, AES, and 3DES (Triple DES). For more information on how to use these and other cryptographic techniques, refer to Chapter 15, "Cryptography and Data Protection." To build cryptographically random keys, you should use the following Microsoft-recommended key sizes:

- SHA1—`validationKey` set to a value containing 64 bytes (128 hex characters)

- AES—`decryptionKey` set to a value containing 32 bytes (64 hex characters)

- 3DES—`decryptionKey` set to a value containing 24 bytes (48 hex characters)

A sample `Web.config` file configured properly for a web farm might contain the following elements inside the `<system.web>` element:

```
<pages enableViewStateMac="true" viewStateEncryptionMode="Always" />
<machineKey validation="SHA1" validationKey="..." decryptionKey="..." />
```

With these elements in place, all servers in a web farm will both validate and encrypt view state data using the same validation algorithm and the same keys. This allows view state from the same page on different servers to function properly in a web farm environment.

Summary

State management has always been a crucial aspect of creating web applications. Although ASP.NET 2.0 makes state management relatively easy, it doesn't absolve you from the responsibility of deciding how to use stored state. This chapter has illustrated the various aspects of working with application state, session state, and view state, as well as how state management techniques vary when working within a web farm environment. The information contained in this chapter is designed as much to show you *how* to use the state management techniques as it is to show you *when* to use them. If you keep the information and guidelines contained in this chapter in mind when designing your next ASP.NET web application, you will find the task of state management much easier and the solution much clearer.

CHAPTER 24

Using Master Pages

Master Pages are just one of the many new productivity features included with ASP.NET 2.0. The use of Master Pages allows your web application to easily maintain a consistent look and feel.

Before ASP.NET 2.0, the task of creating a consistent look and feel was often tedious and time consuming. This chapter first takes you through a quick tour of what it looks like to create a consistent look and feel in ASP.NET 1.1. After that, you will see an introduction to the basic concepts behind Master Pages.

By the end of the chapter you will be able to perform everything from simple Master Page tasks to some of the more advanced techniques that you can use in your own high-quality web applications.

The World Before Master Pages

Before you can really understand how much time and effort Master Pages can save developers, you should know what it was like performing a similar task in ASP.NET 1.1. This section gives you information on the practical need for a consistent (and easily modifiable) GUI for your web applications and shows you how much effort was involved in creating such a GUI for an ASP.NET 1.1 application.

If you have a lot of experience with the frustration of creating common and consistent layouts for ASP.NET, you thoroughly understand the problems that Master Pages solve and you can probably skim some of this section and skip to the Master Pages introduction.

The Need for a Consistent GUI

Anyone who has had to do web design for more than five minutes will tell you that one of the most important aspects of good design is consistency. If your home page is extremely artistic and covered with all kinds of flashy artwork and the rest of your site is functional but bland, your users will be discouraged and put off by the lack of consistent look and feel. If your entire website has extremely professional graphics, but no two web pages have the same color scheme, your users will be just as disappointed with your application.

In most cases, designers prefer to have the entire site follow a consistent look and feel. This doesn't mean that the whole site needs to be one color, but each functional area of the site should contain pages that are visually similar. Users should be able to tell where they are and what they are doing as much from the "feel" of the page as from the text on it.

The problem is that professional-looking pages and consistent GUIs often involve a lot of redundant HTML, even with the use of style sheets. Almost every time you sit down to start work on a website, the first thing you need to do is come up with a way to standardize the pages for that site. Not only do developers need to be able to create a consistent look and feel, but they need to be able to make changes to the GUI that affect the entire site without having to manually edit every single page in the site.

Creating a Consistent GUI in ASP.NET 1.1

Although ASP.NET introduced the concept of reusable server-side controls and those controls drastically improved the development process, there is still nothing built directly into ASP.NET 1.1 that supports the notion of creating a standardized look and feel throughout an entire website or functional areas within that site.

The solution in ASP.NET 1.1 was to create a set of reusable controls (often User Controls for ease of use) that could be included on every page within a functional area to provide a common look and feel as well as some common functionality. This was done to add things like navigation strips on the left side of a page, headers on top, footers on the bottom, and often navigation or toolstrips on the right side of a page.

After you created the user controls, you then had to lay out each and every page within your site to include those controls in the right place. This was an extremely error-prone process because a typo or failed paste operation on a page could create an unintended gap in the consistent look and feel or even bugs. Figure 24.1 illustrates what a sample of the HTML required to lay out a consistent look and feel looks like. With graphics and styles added into the HTML, that layout code would have to be pasted into each new page.

As you can see, this process is cumbersome, repetitive, and extremely prone to errors. The rest of this chapter will show you how the use of Master Pages in ASP.NET 2.0 makes the process of creating a consistent look and feel for your web site smooth, elegant, reliable, and easy to maintain.

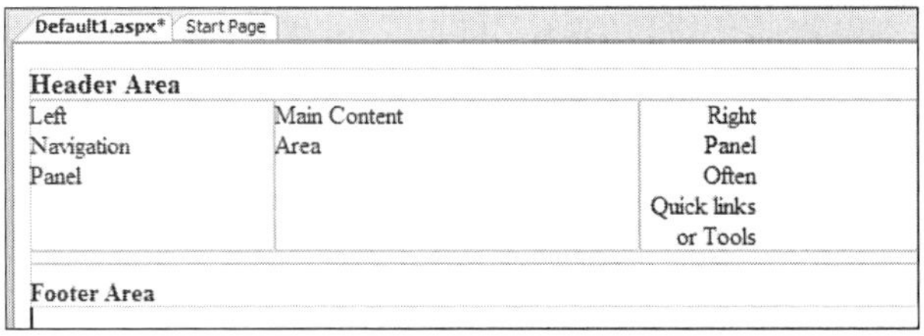

FIGURE 24.1   A minimal layout design required for each page to have a consistent look and feel in ASP.NET 1.1.

Introduction to Master Pages

Master Pages are a framework that is built into ASP.NET that provide for the creation and maintenance of reusable page templates that can be used to give a website a consistent look and feel.

Some of the more adventurous programmers may have even created their own frameworks for ASP.NET 1.1 that provided similar functionality. The good news is that the capability provided by Master Pages is provided as an integrated feature of ASP.NET 2.0.

Master Pages and Content Pages

Master Pages is actually a broad term that really encompasses two distinct concepts:

- The Master Page
- The Content Page

The Master Page

The Master Page functions just like any other ASP.NET page, with a few exceptions. The role of the Master Page is to provide a master layout to which all content pages (defined shortly) using the master must adhere. It can (and should) contain standard HTML, styled elements, server-side controls, and even C# code if necessary. It also contains placeholder controls that indicate where content can appear in associated content pages.

The Content Page

The content page is subservient to a single master page. It defines the content that appears in the placeholders defined within the master page. Interestingly enough, a content page can be a master page for one or more additional content pages. That topic will be explained later in this chapter in the section on advanced topics.

Creating Your First Master Page

Now that you're familiar with the basic concepts behind Master Pages and the need that created them, you can create your own Master Page.

To create a new master page using Visual Studio, simply create a new web project. When you have a new web application, right-click the project, choose Add New Item and then select the Master Page template from the list.

The empty master page contains the code in Listing 24.1.

LISTING 24.1   An Empty Master Page

```
<%@ Master Language="C#" AutoEventWireup="true"
   CodeFile="MasterPage.master.cs" Inherits="MasterPage" %>
<!DOCTYPE html PUBLIC "-//W3C//DTD XHTML 1.1//EN"
   "http://www.w3.org/TR/xhtml11/DTD/xhtml11.dtd">

<html xmlns="http://www.w3.org/1999/xhtml" >
<head runat="server">
    <title>Untitled Page</title>
</head>
<body>
    <form id="form1" runat="server">
    <div>
        <asp:contentplaceholder id="ContentPlaceHolder1" runat="server">
        </asp:contentplaceholder>
    </div>
    </form>
</body>
</html>
```

As you can see, there is a single `ContentPlaceHolder` control defined by default. You can change the layout to include as many content placeholders as you like.

To create content placeholders to represent the layout shown in Figure 24.1, you can create a master page like the one described in Listing 24.2. If you are following along, call this Master Page `SiteMaster.master` so that it can be used in later samples in this chapter.

LISTING 24.2   A Master Page with Multiple Content Placeholders (`SiteMaster.master`)

```
<%@ Master Language="C#" AutoEventWireup="true"
 CodeFile="SiteMaster.master.cs" Inherits="SiteMaster" %>
<!DOCTYPE html PUBLIC "-//W3C//DTD XHTML 1.1//EN"
"http://www.w3.org/TR/xhtml11/DTD/xhtml11.dtd">
<html xmlns="http://www.w3.org/1999/xhtml" >
<head runat="server">
    <title>Untitled Page</title>
</head>
<body>
    <form id="form1" runat="server">
```

LISTING 24.2   Continued

```
<table width=100% border=0 cellspacing=1 cellpadding=1>
    <tr>
        <td width=150 valign=top>
            This is a fixed content left side
        </td>
        <td valign=top>
            <asp:ContentPlaceHolder ID="plhMain" runat=server>
                Content in the middle goes here</asp:ContentPlaceHolder>
        </td>
        <td width=150 valign=top align=right>
            This is a fixed content right side
        </td>
    </tr>
    <tr>
        <td colspan=3>
            <asp:ContentPlaceHolder ID="plhFooter" runat=server>
                The footer goes in this content area
            </asp:ContentPlaceHolder>
        </td>
    </tr>
</table>
</form>
</body>
</html>
```

Take some time to flip back and forth between the HTML view and the design view after you create your first master page so that you can get used to the difference between fixed areas of content and areas of content that will be defined by Content Pages themselves.

Creating Your First Content Page

To create a content page based on an existing master, you just follow the same steps you would follow if you were creating a new Web Form, with one small exception.

Right-click the existing web project and choose Add New Item. When the dialog appears, click to select the Web Form template, and down at the bottom of the dialog box, make sure that the Select Master Page option is clicked. When you click the Add button, you will then be prompted to choose the master page to which the Content Page will be associated. If you were following along with the preceding sample, create a new Web Form called ContentSample3.aspx and choose the SiteMaster.master file as the master page. The first thing you should notice is that when you create the content page, Visual Studio has automatically created some empty Content elements. Switch to design view and you will see where those elements fit within the context of the Master Page.

Enter the code for ContentSample as shown in Listing 24.3.

LISTING 24.4   HTML Source for `ContentSample3.aspx`, a Web Form Using a Master Page

```
<%@ Page Language="C#"
  MasterPageFile="~/SiteMaster.master"
  AutoEventWireup="true" CodeFile="ContentSample.aspx.cs"
  Inherits="ContentSample" Title="Untitled Page" %>
<asp:Content ID="Content1" ContentPlaceHolderID="plhMain" Runat="Server">
    This will appear in the main content area
</asp:Content>
<asp:Content ID="Content2" ContentPlaceHolderID="plhFooter" Runat="Server">
    &copy;2005 SAMS Press, Inc. All rights reserved. Ad Nauseum.
</asp:Content>
```

Now highlight the `ContentSample` page in the project and start it up in the debugger. You will see a page that looks much like the one shown in Figure 24.2.

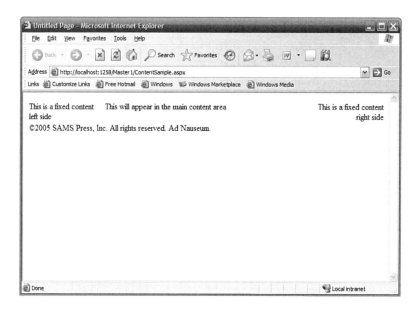

FIGURE 24.2   The `ContentSample` page, demonstrating the use of a Master Page and multiple content areas.

Using a Default Master Page

When you create a content page, there is a special metacommand statement that indicates the associated master page that is part of the `@Page` statement: `MasterPageFile`. If you want to enforce more control over the look and feel of your site, but you don't want to have to manually change every single page in your site, you can define a default master page.

Another use for default master pages allows you to change the master page for a group of content pages without modifying the individual pages. For example, you might want to change the master page for a short period of time to put up a seasonal look and feel such as a page styled for Christmas or Halloween.

To specify a default master page, you can make use of the `<pages>` element in a website's `web.config` file, as shown in the following example:

```
<pages masterPageFile="~/SiteMaster.master" />
```

The only issue I have with the default master page approach is that if you remove the master indication from the content page, the visual designer won't properly display the master layout. Losing some interactivity in the designer is a small price to pay for being able to use the `<pages>` directive to define a default master page. Keep in mind that each subdirectory can contain its own `web.config` file and thus could also contain its own `<pages>` directive to define a default master page for the directory. This lack of functionality in the designer may change in the final release of Visual Studio 2005.

Master Pages "Under the Hood"

When you create a master page, you are actually creating a class of type `System.Web.UI.MasterPage`. This class inherits from `UserControl`, which in turn inherits from `TemplateControl`. This should give you some idea that at the core of the Master Pages system, you are really just dealing with a specialized user control that is designed to render content within special placeholders.

At runtime, the master page is compiled and the content contained within the content areas is compiled as well. One really important thing to keep in mind that will become more important in the advanced section is the notion that when a content page is rendered, the rendering is relative to the content page's location, not the master page's location. The master page itself can also be accessed programmatically at runtime via the `Master` property on the `Page` object, and you will see more about this property in the next section.

Advanced Master Pages Techniques

This section covers some of the more advanced techniques that are useful when dealing with Master Pages, such as nesting, the use of the `Master` property, strongly typed Master Pages, and the intricacies of handling relative paths when dealing with rendered content pages.

The real power of Master Pages shines when you begin adding reusable code to them as well as reusable user interface elements and styles.

Nested Master Pages

You can actually indicate that one master page is the master of another. There are a few restrictions to doing this and it can be a bit tricky to get working properly the first time you try it.

The main restriction is that when a master page is a child master page, the top-level element in the ASPX for that page *must* be a Content control and nothing else. Often when people think of nesting they think of classic ASP or even ASP.NET, where two different user controls were included back-to-back in a page, as shown in the following snippet:

```
<custom:TopHeader id="topHeader" runat=server /><br/>
<custom:MidHeader id="midHeader" runat=server/><br/>
```

The trouble here is that the preceding code is actually a linear sequence of controls, and not a nesting of controls. When you define the topmost master page, you define content areas in which other master pages will render themselves. The child master pages then define content placeholders that content pages will fill, completing the rendered pages. Take a look at Figure 24.3 to see an illustration of how master page nesting works to create a complete rendered page.

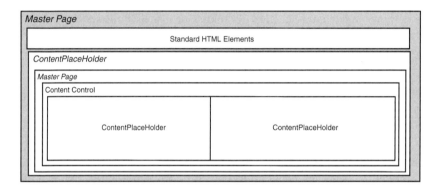

FIGURE 24.3   Illustration of Master Page nesting with Content Pages.

One thing to keep in mind when working with nested Master Pages is that the Visual Studio designer will not render any portion of a nested Master Page hierarchy except the topmost parent. All nested master pages and all content pages that utilize those master pages will not display in design mode, so you will have to do it the "old-fashioned" way and actually run the page to see what the final rendering looks like.

The "Master" Property

There's more to Master Pages than just creating reusable layout and style to maintain a consistent look and feel. Master Pages are also accessible programmatically at runtime. Each ASP.NET 2.0 page has a property called Master that is of type MasterPage.

You can use this property to access a host of properties and methods to provide common functionality across all pages that are associated with a given Master Page. Because MasterPage inherits from System.Web.UI.Page you can access all page-related properties of the master page.

More commonly, however, developers will expose methods and properties on the master page that provide functionality that can be shared among all pages that utilize the master.

For example, in the preceding nesting example you saw a Master Page used for an R&D department in a fictitious company. Assume that you need to provide a function called `IsDevelopmentSupervisor` that you want to be available to all pages within R&D that will indicate whether the current user is an R&D supervisor. You could add the following method to the `RDMaster.master` code-behind:

```
public bool IsDevelopmentSupervisor()
{
  return (Context.User.Identity.Name.ToUpper() == "KEVIN");
}
```

Obviously in a production application you would replace this logic with something that queried the current user's Role membership, but the code is fine for this sample.

If you type "Master." into the `Page_Load` event handler in the code-behind for the `RDdefault.aspx` page, you'll notice that the method you just entered isn't there. Even after you rebuild the entire solution it won't appear. This is because the `Master` property is of type `MasterPage`. If you want access to a member of a *specific* Master Page, you will need to typecast it, as shown in the following code found in the `RDdefault.aspx.cs` file:

```
protected void Page_Load(object sender, EventArgs e)
{
    if (((RDmaster)Master).IsDevelopmentSupervisor())
    {
      Response.Write("Greetings, Boss.");
    }
    else
      Response.Write("Greetings.");
}
```

The preceding code typecasts the `Master` property to the `RDmaster` class where the `IsDevelopmentSupervisor` method has been defined.

Strongly Typed Master Pages

Sometimes you will be writing code for pages and not know at design time which master the page will be associated with, but that isn't the most common scenario. More often than not, you will probably know at design time the type and file of the Master Page. If you know that information, you can give ASP.NET the information and it will provide you with a strongly typed `Master` property.

To create a strongly typed `Master` property, you just use the `MasterType` command in the ASPX file as follows:

```
<%@ MasterType VirtualPath="~/RDmaster.master"  %>
```

If you do this, you'll be reminded of another incredibly handy feature in VS 2005: IntelliSense works inside the <%@ %> tags. After you recompile the page, you can change the previous typecasting code into the following, and it will even support IntelliSense:

```
protected void Page_Load(object sender, EventArgs e)
{
  if (Master.IsDevelopmentSupervisor())
    Response.Write("Greetings, Boss.");
  else
    Response.Write("Greetings.");
}
```

Handling Relative Paths

A common problem among developers working on ASP.NET 1.1 sites is that the use of User Controls could create issues with relative paths. For example, if a user control refers to a relative path, that path will be treated as relative to the *container* of the control at runtime. This makes locating images, files, and other URLs somewhat of a mess when dealing with a lot of User Controls in different locations.

The same problem can arise when dealing with Master Pages. Take a look at the following simple HTML tag:

```
<img src="images/navBorder.jpg" alt="Navigation Border" />
```

The hard thing to remember about Master Pages is that they aren't really pages on their own; they simply provide the ability to lay out content in containers. As a result, the HTML rendered by the code in the Master Page will actually render *relative to the content page*.

The way to get around this is to make appropriate use of server-side controls. As you probably know, there is a server-side control for virtually every HTML tag, including the img tag.

If you are putting HTML into a Master Page, and you know that the relative path of the code in the Master Page is not going to be the same as the relative path in the Content Page, then you can just put a runat="server" tag inside the control, and ASP.NET will take care of determining the appropriate location of the image. So, to make the image tag render appropriately regardless of where the Content Page exists in the directory structure, just change the code to look as follows:

```
<img src="images/navBorder.jpg" alt="Navigation Border" runat="Server"/>
```

Because server-side controls consume memory and add to the processing time of your page, you should use them sparingly. A good way to deal with it is to create the Master Page without a single server-side image or URL control and then to selectively convert client-side controls into server-side controls until the Content Page renders properly.

Summary

This chapter provided you with an introduction to Master Pages. The key to understanding why Master Pages are so incredibly useful is understanding the programming and layout headaches created by previous versions of ASP.NET and legacy web development environments such as ASP.

Master Pages are a key part of the essential idea behind ASP.NET: making the development process easier, faster, more scalable, and far more reusable than in previous versions. By using Master Pages, you can create reusable layouts to provide a consistent look and feel, as well as create standardized code that can be made available to all pages that use a particular master page. By making the use of Master Pages a standard practice when creating your ASP.NET applications, you can significantly decrease the User Interface development time while also decreasing the UI maintenance time, as well as providing standard functionality to groups of related pages.

24

ASP.NET Personalization and Customization

As websites become more full-featured, their peers too need to become more full-featured and robust. One of the features of modern websites that most users have come to expect (often at the pain and expense of the developer) is the ability to personalize and customize their own experience on that website. This feature is often used in portals such as Yahoo, Google, MSN, and so on. Users want to be able to change the look and feel of the website as well as supply information that tailors content to themselves, such as their zip code, interests, hobbies, and so on. This chapter shows you how new features of ASP.NET 2.0 allow you to give users this functionality by using themes, skins, and user profiles.

User Interface Tailoring with Themes and Skins

Before ASP.NET 2.0, a developer had to hand-code the "engine" that provided support for user customization of look and feel. This engine typically resulted in the user selecting a theme from a list. Under the hood, the user's selection would be used to dynamically choose which Cascading Style Sheet (CSS) would be used to support the HTML output of a given page. If a user selected the 'Green' theme, the engine would dynamically decide to use Green.css as a page's style sheet, using various shades of green and complementary colors. Likewise, if the user chose the 'Red' theme, the page would be rendered using the Red.css style sheet.

The good news for developers is that this dynamic theme engine is built into ASP.NET 2.0. All of the work required to dynamically change the look and feel of a page has been done for us, and much more.

The creation of themes is the easy part. The hard part is populating the themes with the right styles and UI elements to make them compelling to your users. Themes are so modular that they can easily be created by a designer and then handed to the developer upon completion.

ASP.NET has several custom folder names that it recognizes within an ASP.NET application. Each of these folders has a unique purpose. For example, the App_Code folder contains classes that will be compiled and visible to the entire application. For themes, the App_Themes folder contains all of the themes installed for a given application.

To create a themes folder, first create an empty ASP.NET website called ThemesSkins. Then, right-click the project in Visual Studio, choose Add ASP.NET Folder, and then select Theme. This will create a new folder called App_Themes.

To create a new theme, right-click the App_Themes folder and add a new folder. The name of the folder will be the name of the theme, so choose the folder name carefully.

To this folder, you can add style sheets (.css files) and skin files. The purpose of the style sheet is fairly obvious: The ASP.NET theme engine reads *all* style sheets in the folder (determined by the page's current theme setting) and includes them as standard stylesheet links in the rendered output.

Skin files contain control definitions. Within a theme, you can have multiple skins (represented by a unique ID). By using skin files, you can define the default behavior of a grid view based on a theme, and you can even define alternate UI settings for that grid view based on the skin ID. For example, the default behavior for a grid in the 'Blue' theme could be to display regular rows with a white background and alternating rows with a blue background. You could define an 'Inverse' skin that indicates that the grid view should be displayed with blue regular rows and white alternating rows. The possibilities are endless, and the power put in the hands of graphic designers and web designers is enormous.

To get started and see how themes work, create three folders in your App_Themes directory: Blue, Red, and Green. In each of those folders, add a new style sheet of the same name, for example, Blue.css or Red.css. Finally, add a new skin file called Controls.skin to each of the folders. Then create a master page called Site.master, delete the standard default.aspx, and then create a new one that utilizes Site.master as its master page. After all this, you should have a directory structure that looks like the one shown in Figure 25.1.

There are two ways to control what theme a page uses for rendering. The first is to use the <pages> element in the Web.config file, as shown in the following line:

```
<pages theme="Green"/>
```

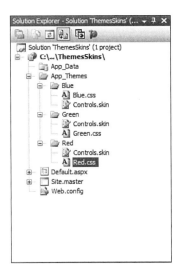

FIGURE 25.1   Creating a themed application.

This line of XML in the configuration file indicates that all pages within the application will default to the Green theme. Each page can individually override the theme choice in one of two ways.

The second way involves using the @Page directive at the top of the page, as shown in the following example:

```
<%@ Page Language="C#" MasterPageFile="~/Site.master"
AutoEventWireup="true" CodeFile="Default.aspx.cs"
Inherits="_Default" Title="Home Page"
 Theme="Red" %>
```

This code is used by a page to override the Web.config setting and force the page to use the "Red" theme. You can also programmatically set the page's current theme. Because the page's theme selection has such a drastic impact on how the page is rendered, that selection needs to be done early in the page's life cycle. The following code shows a page's OnPreInit method overridden to programmatically set the page theme:

```
protected override void OnPreInit(EventArgs e)
{
    base.OnPreInit(e);
    Theme = "Green";
}
```

If you attempt to set the page's theme at any other stage in the page life cycle, you will get a runtime error.

To see the theme system in action, add some content to the master page and the `default.aspx` page and set the background color in each of the themes' `css` file to the appropriate color (for example, set the `background-color` style attribute in `Blue.css` to blue).

When you run the application the first time, you should see the default behavior (no theme). Experiment with changing the `Web.config` theme setting and the page's setting and programmatic setting to see how that affects the display. The programmatic change of the theme setting overrides all previous theme selections for that page.

Next, let's add some skins to dynamically control the appearance and behavior of specific controls. To do this, open up the `Controls.skin` file in the `Green` theme and add the following code:

```
<%-- default button --%>
<asp:Button runat="server" ForeColor="Green" BackColor="White" />

<%-- button appears when flat skinid is selected --%>
<asp:Button runat="server" ForeColor="Green"
  BackColor="White" BorderStyle="None" SkinID="Flat" />

<%-- button appears when 'inverse' skin is selected --%>
<asp:Button runat="server" ForeColor="White"
  BackColor="Green" SkinID="Inverse" />
```

The code in a `skin` file contains partial control definitions. You must include the `runat="server"` portion, but you cannot set the `ID` property of the control. In addition, you can only set UI and display properties. This means that you can set the regular and alternating styles on a grid, but you cannot set its data source within the skin file.

> **TIP**
>
> You can choose to include all of your control definitions for the theme in a single skin file (for example, `Controls.skin`), but that can get extremely difficult to maintain on a large project. If you have several skins, and each skin has unique control definitions, it can be more efficient to create a different skin file for each skin ID. For example, you might create a `Normal.skin` file for the default control definitions for the theme, and an `Inverse.skin` for inverted controls, and so on. Using this method can make skins easier to create for designers and easier for developers to maintain.

Now, create a new page called `skindemo.aspx` and choose your `Site.master` master page. If you created a content placeholder in the master page, you can set the following code in the `skindemo.aspx` file:

```
<%@ Page Language="C#" MasterPageFile="~/Site.master" AutoEventWireup="true"
 CodeFile="skindemo.aspx.cs" Inherits="skindemo"
 Title="Untitled Page"
 Theme="Green"%>
```

```
<asp:Content ID="Content1" ContentPlaceHolderID="cplhMain" Runat="Server">
    <asp:Button ID="defaultButton" runat="server"
        Text="This is the default button" />
    <asp:Button ID="flatButton" runat="server"
        Text="This is a flat button" SkinID="Flat" />
    <asp:Button ID="inverseButton" runat="server"
        Text="This is inverse" SkinID="Inverse" />
</asp:Content>
```

When you run this page in the debugger, you will see your master page content and the child content merged onto a green background. The first button will display with a standard border, the second button has no border, and the third button has a regular border but the colors are inverted.

The power of the new IntelliSense in Visual Studio 2005 never ceases to impress. If you were typing the code in by hand and following along, you probably noticed that as you typed SkinID= IntelliSense actually popped up and displayed a list of skins defined. The new IntelliSense is shown in Figure 25.2.

FIGURE 25.2   IntelliSense displaying a list of defined skins.

You can also create a *global* theme. A global theme is one that is available to all applications on a given server. This can be particularly useful if you have multiple applications running on the same server that you want to share a set of common themes as well as have their own private themes. To create a global theme, you follow the same rules as for creating a page theme, except that the global theme is stored in the following directory:

```
[IIS root]\aspnet_client\system_web\[version\Themes\[Theme]
```

So on my system, a global theme called Christmas might be in the following directory:

```
C:\inetpub\wwwroot\aspnet_client\system_web\2_0_50727\Themes\Christmas
```

By default, the global Themes directory hasn't been created, so you will have to create it when you create your first global theme.

As you can see, the mechanics of creating and using skins has been made extremely simple by the new ASP.NET theme support. The hard part is, as it should be, in the design of the style sheets and skin files. Because skins are file-based and extremely modular, the web and graphic designers can create these files on their own and insert them into the website as they become available without hindering the rest of the development process.

25

TIP

When building themes, you can have images that are specific to an individual theme. When you refer to that image from a control in a skin file, the URL is *relative to the theme directory*. This means that an image stored in `App_Themes\Blue\images\logo.jpg` would be referred to as `<asp:Image ImageUrl=""images\logo.jpg""/>`.

Working with ASP.NET User Profiles

It is becoming harder and harder to find web applications that don't store information in user profiles. Information such as a user's name, e-mail address, phone number, and even credit card information is stored by so many websites that most users are pretty used to filling out profiles and new-user forms on websites.

In the past, every time you needed an application that maintained user profile information, you had to create a database (or at least a few tables in an existing database) to store that information and probably a library of classes that encapsulated the interaction with the back-end profile store. That task has been made obsolete in ASP.NET 2.0. This section of the chapter shows you how to configure application services (used to store profiles and much more, such as membership data), how to use an ASP.NET profile provider, and finally how to write code that allows the storage and retrieval of user profile data.

Configure Application Services

To store profile information in an underlying database, you need to have the database created and the appropriate tables and stored procedures created. Fortunately, ASP.NET provides a wizard that walks you through the process of creating the application services database. Application services consist of membership data, profile data, personalization data (discussed in Chapter 26, "Introduction to Web Parts"), role data, and event data. This allows you to create one application services database, and it will take care of many of the tasks that used to require manual development effort in previous versions of ASP.NET.

To create a new database or configure an existing one for application services, you need to use the ASP.NET SQL Server Setup Wizard that ships with ASP.NET. It is a command-line tool called `aspnet_regsql`. This tool will automatically be in your path if you open up a Visual Studio 2005 Command Prompt (in the `Visual Studio Tools` subfolder under `Visual Studio 2005` in your Start menu).

When you execute `aspnet_regsql` with no parameters, you will first be prompted with a screen indicating the application's purpose. When you click Next, you will see the screen displayed in Figure 25.3.

You will be prompted for the name of the SQL Server in which the application services database will be created, as well as for credentials (or you can use default Windows credentials). Keep in mind that all you're doing at this stage is creating the database; none of the information you enter here will be recorded in any ASP.NET application.

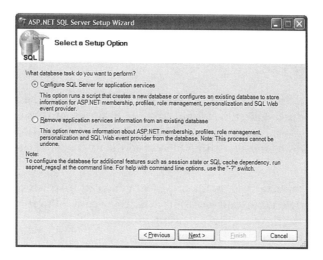

FIGURE 25.3   ASP.NET SQL Server Configuration Wizard.

After you follow all the directions in the ASP.NET SQL Server Configuration Wizard, you can go into your SQL Server Management Studio and look at the contents of the database you just created. It doesn't have to make much sense because the ASP.NET providers expose a very robust API for interacting with that data.

Configuring the Profile Provider

When the application services database has been created and is ready for use, you will need to create an application that utilizes that database for its profile provider.

> **Using Application Services**
>
> It might get confusing when you use application services because of the Provider model. There are multiple ASP.NET providers and a SQL provider for membership, roles, profiles, and more. When you create an application services database, it creates tables and stored procedures that can support *all* of the ASP.NET SQL providers. In this fashion, you can create a single connection string to your application services database and reuse that connection string for all of your providers.

To configure your application to use a specific profile provider, you need to use the `<profile>` element and the `<connectionStrings>` element of the `Web.config` file.

Create a new ASP.NET application called `UserProfiles` and leave all of the default content in place. Add a `Web.config` file to the project.

The first step to configuring an application to use a profile provider is to create a connection string that points at the application services database, as shown in the following code:

```
<connectionStrings>
    <add connectionString="server=localhost; database=ASPNET_AppServices;
    ➥Trusted_Connection=true;" name="appSvcs"/>
</connectionStrings>
```

This creates a connection string that will establish a connection to the application services database created during the wizard (the one in the example is called `ASPNET_AppServices`—you will have to replace the database name with the name of the one you created). This connection string follows all the rules of standard ADO.NET SQL connection strings.

The next step is to configure the profile provider by indicating which connection string the profile provider will use to connect to its data. You also need to specify the type of the profile provider. In this case, we'll be using the `System.Web.Profile.SqlProfileProvider`.

The `<profile>` section (contained within `<system.web>`) looks like the one shown in the following code:

```
<profile defaultProvider="AppServicesProvider">
  <providers>
    <add name="AppServicesProvider"
         type="System.Web.Profile.SqlProfileProvider"
         connectionStringName="appSvcs"/>
  </providers>
  <properties>
     <add name="FirstName" type="string" allowAnonymous="true"/>
  </properties>
</profile>
```

The `<profile>` element indicates which provider defined within the subelement `<providers>` will be used as the default provider. The `<properties>` element will be discussed in the "Using ASP.NET Profiles" section.

If you run your application as it is now with just the default content and the modified `Web.config`, you will get a runtime error if the connection to the profile data source failed, and your application will run just fine if the profile data source connection worked properly.

Using ASP.NET Profiles

At its very core, a user profile is really nothing more than a collection of name-value pairs. For example, a sample user profile might contain the following name-value pairs:

- `FirstName : Kevin`

- `LastName : Hoffman`

- Profession : Author

- FavoriteColor : Blue

If you create a database table that contains user profile data and just the columns from the preceding list, you could write code that reads and writes user profiles from that table. The problem is that user profiles tend to grow over time, and you may need to add or remove columns at some point in your application's life. If you have a fixed set of columns in that table, this kind of maintenance can become a nightmare.

The ASP.NET profile providers fix this problem by allowing the properties that belong to a user's profile to be *arbitrary*. You can define the list of properties that you want to manage for your users directly within your Web.config file. The profile provider takes care of the details of persisting and retrieving the data, leaving you with a very simple API for managing user profile data: the Profile object.

The Profile object is available to all web pages, and inherits from System.Web.Profile.ProfileBase. Table 25.1 lists the properties that come with the base profile class.

TABLE 25.1   ProfileBase Properties

Property	Description
Context	Returns the settings context for the profile.
IsAnonymous	Indicates whether the profile is anonymous.
IsDirty	Indicates whether changes have been made to the profile since it was last stored in the backing store.
IsSynchronized	Indicates whether access to the profile object is thread-safe.
Item	Gets a profile property by index or by property name. Uses the [ ] indexer notation in C#.
LastActivityDate	Gets the last date and time when the profile was modified or read.
LastUpdatedDate	Gets the last date and time when the profile was last modified.
Properties	Static property that returns a list of configured properties for the profile.
PropertyValues	Returns the list of property values for the given profile.
Providers	Gets a collection of profile providers configured.
UserName	Gets the user name of the profile. Name of the profile depends on the Web.config authentication mode used. Authentication is covered in Chapter 28, "Securing Your ASP.NET Applications."

In addition to the stock properties defined by the ProfileBase class, ASP.NET actually adds a property to the Profile object for every property you have defined in Web.config. For example, if you have defined the FirstName property in Web.config (see the <profile> element from the preceding section), you can write code that looks like this:

```
lblFirstName.Text = Profile.FirstName;
Profile.FirstName = txtFirstName.Text;
```

This is extremely powerful because even at design time, you have a strongly typed, IntelliSense-aware set of properties that are read from `Web.config`. Defining a property in the `<properties>` subelement of the `<profile>` element is fairly easy. You use the following format:

```
<add name="FirstName" type="string" allowAnonymous="true"/>
```

The name of the property is self-explanatory. This name will also be used as a property name on the dynamically constructed `Profile` object. The `type` attribute indicates the data type. You can actually use any .NET data type, even one you have created:

```
<add name=""ShoppingCart"" type=""MyApp.Utilities.ShoppingCart"" />
```

The only requirement on the data type of the profile property is that it must be a type that can be resolved from the ASP.NET project, so the type needs to be either in the `App_Code` directory of the application or in an assembly that is referenced by the project.

> **NOTE**
>
> If you are planning on using a custom-created type as a profile property, that type must be serializable. You should follow the same rules for out-of-process session-state data when determining what to store in a user's profile: It must be consistently serializable. When you serialize and then deserialize the object, it should represent exactly the same data. There should be no "side-effect" code in any property accessors, and it should have an empty default constructor.

The `allowAnonymous` attribute indicates whether an anonymous profile (a profile owned by an unauthenticated user) should have that property. In such situations, you might choose to allow an anonymous user to have a shopping cart and then migrate their anonymous profile to a named profile as they create an account during the checkout process. When they have a named profile, they can have additional properties such as a name, address, billing and shipping information, and so on.

To illustrate how to use profiles and profile properties, let's get started with a full `Web.config` that stores the user's first and last names as well as the number of times that the user has hit the home page. Listing 25.1 contains a complete `Web.config` using the previously configured application services database and three profile properties, all of which are allowed by anonymous users.

LISTING 25.1   A `Web.config` Supporting Profile Properties

```
<?xml version="1.0"?>

<configuration>
<appSettings/>
<connectionStrings>
  <add connectionString="server=localhost; database=ASPNET_AppServices;
  ➥Trusted_Connection=true;" name="appSvcs"/>
```

LISTING 25.1   Continued

```
</connectionStrings>
<system.web>

<compilation debug="true"/>

  <anonymousIdentification enabled="true"/>
  <profile defaultProvider="AppServicesProvider">
    <providers>
      <add name="AppServicesProvider"
        type="System.Web.Profile.SqlProfileProvider"
        connectionStringName="appSvcs"/>
    </providers>
    <properties>
      <add name="FirstName" type="string" allowAnonymous="true"/>
      <add name="LastName" type="string" allowAnonymous="true"/>
      <add name="HomeHits" type="int" allowAnonymous="true"/>
    </properties>
</profile>
</system.web>
</configuration>
```

Now add a page to your application called `MyProfile.aspx`. This page will be responsible for allowing the users to edit their first and last names, as well as displaying the number of times they have accessed the home page of the application. The source code for `MyProfile.aspx.cs` is shown in Listing 25.2.

LISTING 25.2   MyProfile.aspx.cs

```
using System;
using System.Data;
using System.Configuration;
using System.Collections;
using System.Web;
using System.Web.Security;
using System.Web.UI;
using System.Web.UI.WebControls;
using System.Web.UI.WebControls.WebParts;
using System.Web.UI.HtmlControls;

public partial class MyProfile : System.Web.UI.Page
{
    protected void Page_Load(object sender, EventArgs e)
    {
```

LISTING 25.2   Continued

```
        if (!Page.IsPostBack)
        {
            txtFirstName.Text = Profile.FirstName;
            txtLastName.Text = Profile.LastName;
            lblHomeHits.Text = Profile.HomeHits.ToString();
        }
    }
    protected void btnSave_Click(object sender, EventArgs e)
    {
        Profile.FirstName = txtFirstName.Text;
        Profile.LastName = txtLastName.Text;
        Profile.Save();
    }
}
```

The code is pretty straightforward. If the page is not a postback, the user's profile information is loaded into the appropriate text box and label controls. After the user clicks Save, the user's profile information is modified according to the data contained in the two text boxes, and the Profile.Save() method is called to ensure the data is stored in the database. Any developers who have had to code their own profile storage system can appreciate how incredibly powerful it is to now have design-time, strongly typed profile properties and to have the complexity of storing and retrieving those profiles handled automatically by ASP.NET's SQL Profile Provider.

The only remaining piece of work that needs to be done to create a full-featured application using profiles is to migrate the anonymous profile to a real profile when the anonymous user becomes authenticated. To handle this situation, just add the following method to the Global.asax.cs file:

```
public void Profile_OnMigrateAnonymous(object sender,
➥ProfileMigrateEventArgs args)
{
   // locate the anonymous profile being migrated
   ProfileCommon anonProfile = Profile.GetProfile(args.AnonymousID);

   // set new profile data to data from the ''old'' anon profile
   Profile.FirstName = anonProfile.FirstName;
   Profile.LastName = anonProfile.LastName;
   Profile.HomeHits = anonProfile.HomeHits;
   Profile.Save();

   // remove the anon profile and the associated cookie
   ProfileManager.DeleteProfile(args.AnonymousID);
   AnonymousIdentificationModule.ClearAnonymousIdentifier();
}
```

Because an anonymous profile can only be migrated to a named profile when the user goes from being anonymous to being authenticated, you will probably not run into this situation until you start using the Membership provider that is discussed in Chapter 28, "Securing Your ASP.NET Applications." Keep this code in mind, and when you're done with both this chapter and Chapter 28, you can try to create an application that uses both Membership and Profile providers not only to authenticate users, but also to store their profile information.

User Customization with Themes and Profiles

Perhaps one of the most powerful uses of both profile and theme technology is to combine the two by allowing the users to choose their own theme and store that choice as a profile property. The Theme property of the Page object is a string type, so you can add a user profile property to store the currently selected theme with the following <add> element in the <properties> element of the <profile> element:

```
<add name="Theme" type="string" allowAnonymous="true"/>
```

To see this all work together, go back to the ThemesSkins solution you created earlier if you were following along. That web application has three themes defined: Blue, Red, and Green. It also has a Site.master page with some random content in it just to illustrate that themes are applied to the final rendering and don't interfere with Master Page composition. The Controls.skin file in all of the themes has been modified to make sure that they all had Flat and Inverse button definitions to make the sample show up more clearly.

The first thing to do is to modify the Site.master so that it is displaying the name of the user's currently selected theme. To do this, just add a label anywhere you want in the Site.master and set the page's code as follows:

```
using System;
using System.Data;
using System.Configuration;
using System.Collections;
using System.Web;
using System.Web.Security;
using System.Web.UI;
using System.Web.UI.WebControls;
using System.Web.UI.WebControls.WebParts;
using System.Web.UI.HtmlControls;

public partial class Site : System.Web.UI.MasterPage
{
    protected void Page_Load(object sender, EventArgs e)
    {
```

25

```
            lblTheme.Text = Profile.Theme;
        }
}
```

Next, you'll want to create a `MyProfile.aspx` page used to allow the users to view and save their own profiles just as you did in the preceding section. Set the ASPX code as follows:

```
<%@ Page Language="C#"
   MasterPageFile="~/Site.master"
   AutoEventWireup="true"
   CodeFile="MyProfile.aspx.cs"
   Inherits="MyProfile"
   Title="My Profile" %>

<asp:Content ID="Content1" ContentPlaceHolderID="cplhMain" Runat="Server">
First Name: <asp:TextBox ID="txtFirstName" runat="server" /><br />
Last Name: <asp:TextBox ID="txtLastName" runat="server" /><br />
Theme: <asp:DropDownList ID="dlTheme" runat="server">
        <asp:ListItem Text="Blue Theme" Value="Blue" />
        <asp:ListItem Text="Green Theme" Value="Green" />
        <asp:ListItem Text="Red Theme" Value="Red" />
</asp:DropDownList><br />
<asp:Button ID="btnSave" runat="server"
  Text="Save Profile" OnClick="btnSave_Click" />
</asp:Content>
```

Then enter the following code for `MyProfile.aspx.cs`:

```
using System;
using System.Data;
using System.Configuration;
using System.Collections;
using System.Web;
using System.Web.Security;
using System.Web.UI;
using System.Web.UI.WebControls;
using System.Web.UI.WebControls.WebParts;
using System.Web.UI.HtmlControls;

public partial class MyProfile : System.Web.UI.Page
{
    protected void Page_Load(object sender, EventArgs e)
    {
        if (!Page.IsPostBack)
        {
            txtFirstName.Text = Profile.FirstName;
```

```
            txtLastName.Text = Profile.LastName;
        }

    }
    protected void btnSave_Click(object sender, EventArgs e)
    {
        Profile.FirstName = txtFirstName.Text;
        Profile.LastName = txtLastName.Text;
        Profile.Theme = dlTheme.SelectedValue;
        Profile.Save();
    }
}
```

The last step is to modify any existing pages so that they dynamically set the theme based on the user's profile. Add the following lines of code to any existing page to do just that:

```
protected override void OnPreInit(EventArgs e)
{
    base.OnPreInit(e);
    Page.Theme = Profile.Theme;
}
```

This framework allows your users to select the look and feel that they prefer most, with very little work done by the developer. When the themes have been created either by the developer or by designers, the hard work is done. Setting up a profile property to store the user's theme is just a matter of adding one line to the Web.config file, and modifying a page to dynamically change its theme based on the user's profile only takes a few more lines of code. If all your pages inherit from the same base page, you could make that change in the base page and your entire site could automatically have the dynamic theme selection ability. Figure 25.4 shows a page where the theme name is displayed by Site.master and the rest of the content has been skinned and themed dynamically based on the user's profile (though the color might not be obvious).

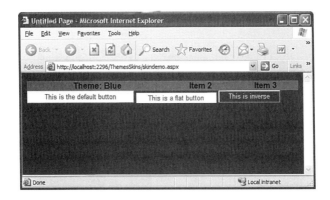

FIGURE 25.4   Themes, skins, and user profiles in action.

Summary

In previous versions of ASP.NET, giving the users the ability to modify their own profiles and storing those profiles in a back-end database was a commonly required activity. It was also tedious and increased the time to market for virtually any product that required it. Developers often created their own reusable user profile APIs and databases to ease the pain of this task. With ASP.NET 2.0, the task of storing and retrieving user profile data is handled automatically, and adding profile properties is as simple as modifying the `Web.config` file.

The notion of creating themes and skins was often left for the most advanced sites because it required a lot of extra code and often made pages more difficult to read and maintain. With ASP.NET 2.0, theme and skin support is built into every application with very little overhead in a modular, easy-to-use fashion.

Combining the power of user profiles with themes and skins allows the users to choose the way the site looks and feels, giving them control and flexibility over the site and allowing them to feel that they have the ability to customize their own experience.

The next chapter, "Introduction to Web Parts," will take the user's ability to customize his own experience to the next level and uses the application services database discussed in this chapter.

Introduction to Web Parts

In Chapter 25, "ASP.NET Personalization and Customization," you learned how to use themes, skins, and user profiles to store meaningful information about users and to enable those users to make decisions about the look and feel of individual pages or an entire website.

This chapter introduces you to the concept of Web Parts, which give users control over both the layout and the content of pages, providing an extremely powerful user experience. You will learn the basics of what Web Parts are and how they work, as well as how to place Web Parts on a page, create Web Parts, and even build connected Web Parts.

Web Part Basics

Web Parts are special controls that are designed to provide the user with discrete units of functionality that can be placed on a page in virtually any location. A discrete unit of functionality essentially means that the Web Parts are designed to perform specific tasks such as displaying an inbox, providing a task list, displaying the current weather, and so on. Web Parts are not entire applications encapsulated in a control. The suite of Web Part tools allows the developer to quickly and easily create pages (called Web Part Pages) that host Web Parts. Such pages can allow users to control the layout by dragging and dropping Web Parts to move them into the location that the user chooses. Users can also control Web Part properties; they can minimize or even close Web Parts just as they would manipulate Windows on their desktop. All of this functionality is virtually free for the developer utilizing the Web Parts suite of controls and ASP.NET 2.0.

There are many reasons to use Web Parts. If you want to provide your users with functionality, but you want your users to be able to choose what data is presented to them, and *how* that data is presented to them, Web Parts will definitely provide you with a huge boost in productivity, time to market, and application functionality.

Web Parts make use of the personalization provider to store personalization data. When a Web Part is added to a page, it contains both shared data and personalization data. This means that a control can have a set of properties that are shared among all users. When a user chooses to customize that Web Part, his personalization data overrides the shared data, creating user-specific settings. For example, you could create a Weather Web Part that has a shared setting of `ZipCode` that defaults to the ZIP code of the website's headquarters. When users choose to customize that Web Part with their own ZIP code, they create a user-specific setting that overrides the shared default.

Figure 26.1 shows a conceptual mock-up of what a sample Web Part Page might look like. The page has been divided into zones in which Web Parts can reside. The page in Figure 26.1 has Web Parts for displaying news, weather, a to-do list, the user's inbox, and a site navigation control. A fully functioning Web Part Page containing these Web Parts would allow the user to choose which parts were visible, where those parts sat on the page, and even things like whether the part should display a header or a border. If the Web Part had custom properties (such as the ZIP code for local weather), the user could also choose to supply that information.

FIGURE 26.1   A Web Part Page conceptual diagram.

Several controls and classes provide the core framework for Web Parts. Table 26.1 contains a list of the key component controls required to make the Web Parts functionality possible.

TABLE 26.1   Web Part Controls

Control	Description
WebPartManager	The WebPartManager is a UI-less component that resides on a Web Form and manages all Web Parts on that page. Every Web Part Page has one and only one WebPartManager.
WebPartZone	A special type of container control that contains Web Parts within a ZoneTemplate. Pages are typically divided into zones such as a header, footer, center, left, and right.
EditorZone	A container control that contains Web Parts that enable users to edit and personalize Web Parts on a page.
CatalogZone	A container control that contains CatalogPart controls. Use this zone to provide users with a list of Web Parts that they can add to a page that might not be on the page by default.

Additional controls are used in conjunction with the ones listed in Table 26.1, but the ones in Table 26.1 are the controls you should be concerned with at the top level.

The key to working with Web Parts is in knowing what they can and cannot do. Every time you add a server or user control into a ZoneTemplate within a WebPartZone, that control is encapsulated within a GenericWebPart control. Before you start coding your own Web Parts and working with them, you should know how this class works, because it and the WebPart class form part of the foundation of the Web Parts framework. The GenericWebPart class is generated at runtime to allow user controls and other non-Web Part controls to have access to Web Part functionality.

Tables 26.2 and 26.3 show some of the common properties and methods of the WebPart class, the class from which all Web Parts (including GenericWebPart) inherit.

TABLE 26.2   Common WebPart Properties

Property	Method
AllowClose	Indicates whether the user can close the Web Part. When a Web Part is closed, its associated control bar is also hidden from the page in the default display mode.
AllowConnect	Indicates whether the part can be connected to other parts (connected Web Parts are covered later in this chapter).
AllowEdit	Indicates whether the user can edit the properties of the Web Part.
AllowHide	Indicates whether the user can hide the part.
AllowMinimize	Indicates whether the user can minimize the Web Part.
AllowZoneChange	Indicates whether the user can move the part between zones. Some parts require a minimum amount of room to display and shouldn't be allowed to be moved into a smaller zone.
CatalogIconImageUrl	Gets or sets the icon used to represent the Web Part within a catalog of Web Parts.
ChromeState	Gets or sets whether a Web Part is minimized or normal.
ChromeType	Gets or sets the type of border that surrounds the Web Part.

26

TABLE 26.2 Continued

Property	Method
ConnectErrorMessage	Message displayed to users if a failure occurs when attempting to connect the Web Part to another part.
Description	Gets a description of the Web Part that will be displayed in catalogs and tooltips.
DisplayTitle	The title text displayed in the title bar of the Web Part.
ExportMode	Indicates the portion of the Web Part's properties that can be exported.
HasSharedData	Indicates whether the Web Part has shared personalization data.
HasUserData	Indicates whether the Web Part has user-specific personalization data associated with it.
HelpMode	Indicates the type of help UI displayed for the Web Part.
HelpUrl	The page to open when a user requests help for the part.
Hidden	Indicates whether the part is hidden.
IsClosed	Indicates whether the Web Part is closed.
IsShared	Indicates whether the Web Part is shared.
Subtitle	(Read Only) A string added with the Title property that indicates the full title of the Web Part.
Title	The title of the Web Part.
TitleIconImageUrl	The URL indicating the Web Part's icon in the title bar.
Verbs	The collection of custom verbs associated with the part.
Zone	Gets the zone in which the Web Part currently resides.
ZoneIndex	Gets the relative position within the zone of the Web Part within its current zone.

TABLE 26.3 Part-Specific Control Methods

Method	Description
CreateEditorParts	Creates instances of custom editor parts that can be used to edit the Web Part in edit mode.
SetPersonalizationDirty	Sets a flag that indicates that the data has changed for the Web Part and needs to be updated in the underlying personalization store.

Using a Personalization Provider

Using the personalization provider is actually pretty easy. All of the code that communicates directly with the provider is contained within the Web Parts set of controls and classes. This means that the only work you need to do is to configure the personalization database and modify the Web.config file to indicate the appropriate provider connection string.

Creating the personalization database is actually done by creating the Application Services database using the instructions in Chapter 25.

Open a Visual Studio 2005 Command Prompt window and type **aspnet_regsql** on the command line. You will be presented with the ASP.NET SQL Server Configuration Wizard. This wizard will prompt you for the location of a SQL Server instance as well as the credentials needed. You can also choose whether you want to create the Application Services information in a new database or configure an existing one. When you have completed this wizard, you will have created an Application Services database that hosts the data, metadata, and stored procedures required to support the membership, roles, profile, and personalization providers.

After you have created your Application Services database and you've verified that it is available and ready to be accessed, you need to modify your web application's Web.config file to point the personalization provider at this location. A sample Web.config configured for personalization is shown in Listing 26.1.

LISTING 26.1   A Personalization-Enabled Web.config File

```
<?xml version="1.0"?>
<configuration>
<appSettings/>
<connectionStrings>
    <add name="AppSvcsConnection"
     connectionString="database=ASPNET_AppServices;
     ➥server=localhost; Trusted_Connection=true;"/>
  </connectionStrings>
  <system.web>
    <webParts>
            <personalization defaultProvider="appSvcs">
        <providers>
        <add name="appSvcs"
            connectionStringName="AppSvcsConnection"
            type="System.Web.UI.WebControls.WebParts.SqlPersonalizationProvider"/>
        </providers>
      </personalization>
    </webParts>
    <compilation debug="true"/>
  <authentication mode="Windows"/>
</system.web>
</configuration>
```

This Web.config file indicates that the System.Web.UI.WebControls.WebParts.SqlPersonalizationProvider will be used as the personalization provider, and it will use the database indicated by the connection string named AppSvcsConnection.

Run an empty default.aspx in an application with the Web.config file from Listing 26.1 and see if it works. If no runtime errors occur while trying to load the default page, you can assume that a personalization connection was made to the database and you can continue on to the next section to create your first Web Part Page. If you do have errors, there is usually enough information in the error message to indicate what went wrong. Make sure to change the `database` and `server` options in your connection string to match the information you provided when you created the Application Services database using the `aspnet_regsql` wizard.

Building Your First Web Part Page

The steps in this section walk you through the process of creating your first Web Part Page. At first it can seem very overwhelming as there are a lot of new controls to use and a lot of new terminology. After you have completed the Web Part Page, you are strongly encouraged to play with it, modify it, and experiment with it before continuing on to the next section so that you can familiarize yourself with the behavior and functionality of Web Parts within ASP.NET 2.0. Rather than have you examine the completed solution, this section is designed to walk you through all of the individual steps required in creating a Web Part Page so that you can gain a thorough understanding of the process and can reuse that process in your own applications. Use the following walk-through to create your first web part page:

1. Create a new ASP.NET web application called `FirstWebPartPage`. When you have the application created, modify the `Web.config` so that it points to the personalization provider created in the preceding section. Your new `Web.config` should look a lot like the one shown in Listing 26.1.

2. You will want to divide your page up into zones. A zone is a container for Web Parts and is often used to divide content areas of differing sizes and purposes. Common scenarios involve top zones, side bars, central content zones, footers, and occasionally right-justified side bars. In this case, open `default.aspx` and create a three-column table in between the default `<div>` tags. Make sure that your View menu (when looking at the designer view) has both Non-Visual Controls and Details checked so that you can see everything that's going on in both source view and design view.

3. Open your Toolbox and expand the Web Parts group. Drag the `WebPartManager` component from the Toolbox onto your web page (this works in either design or HTML view) directly above the three-column table created in step 2. Rename the component to `wpManager`. The `WebPartManager` provides the plumbing necessary to convert a standard page of static controls into a dynamic Web Part Page.

4. Drag a `WebPartZone` from the Toolbox into the leftmost table cell in the first row of the table you created earlier. Call this control `zoneSideBar`. Set the `HeaderText` property to `"Side Bar"`.

5. Drag another `WebPartZone` control from the Toolbox into the middle column of the table. Call that control `zoneMain`. Set the `HeaderText` property to `"Main Zone"`.

6. At this point you should have a `WebPartManager` followed by a three-column table. The left column should contain the `zoneSideBar` control and the middle column should contain the `zoneMain` control. From the design view, drag a `TreeView` control

and drop it in the box framed by the side bar zone. Feel free to add random nodes and format it as you see fit. The important thing to note is that when you switch to source view, you will see that the `TreeView` is now contained within a `ZoneTemplate` element inside the `zoneSideBar` control. At runtime, the `TreeView` control will automatically become the child control of a `GenericWebPart`, giving it access to all of the functionality provided by the Web Parts engine.

7. You might notice that in the design view, the `TreeView` control is inside another frame labeled "Untitled" with the Web Part menu down-arrow icon. This is because the `TreeView` is actually inside an unlabeled `GenericWebPart`. To fix this, you can add `title="Tree"` to the `TreeView`'s declaration. You'll get a warning message about it in the source view, but you can ignore it because when you switch back to the design view, `"Untitled"` will have been replaced with `"Tree"`.

8. Now drag three different labels into the `zoneMain` zone control. Don't worry about separating them with `<br/>` tags—the fact that they are contained within a `WebPartZone` will automatically make them appear within their own frames. Call them `lblOne`, `lblTwo`, and `lblThree` respectively. You can add whatever text you like to them. Set the `Title` property on them using the source view. If you feel like it, you can right-click `zoneSideBar` and `zoneMain`, choose Auto Format, and select something more colorful than the default zone colors. Figure 26.2 shows a screenshot of the author's designer at this stage of the walkthrough.

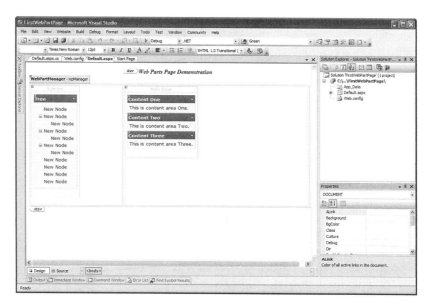

FIGURE 26.2   Visual Studio 2005 Designer, building a Web Part Page.

9. When you run your application now, you should see four different Web Parts on the page. Each of them has a drop-down menu that appears when you click the down-arrow icon that contains a "Minimize" link and a "Close" link. If this isn't

the case, go back over the preceding steps to make sure you didn't miss anything before continuing.

Web Part Page Caveats

As you play with the Web Part Page, you might end up clicking the Close link. If you do this, and you don't have some facility on the page to switch the Web Part Zones into Edit mode, you will never see that Web Part again. The personalization provider will have recorded the closed state of that Web Part, and the only way to get it back is to switch the zones into Edit mode so that you can edit the properties of the closed Web Part to make it visible again. A lot of developers familiar with SharePoint often take it for granted that such an ability to switch to edit mode exists by default. As you'll see in this walkthrough, you will need a user control that allows your page to switch into and out of edit mode. The good news is that this control can be used on as many pages in as many applications as you like.

---

10. At this point, you now have a functioning Web Part Page that is displaying multiple Web Parts in multiple Web Part Zones. The problem now is that you don't have any way of switching the page into edit mode to allow the user to change the layout of the parts and their properties. To enable the user to switch between edit and browse modes, you'll need to create a user control to facilitate that change. To get started, right-click the web application and choose Add New Item and choose Web User Control. Call the control `PageStateSwitcher.ascx`.

11. MSDN's walkthrough of creating a Web Part Page contains the complete source code for a user control that enables page state switching. However, at the time of this writing, that walkthrough appears to be for Beta 2 and won't work properly. Because this task is virtually essential for every single Web Part Page you create, the author is providing the source code for his version of that control, which works with the retail version of Visual Studio 2005. First, set the `PageStateSwitcher.ascx` code to the following:

```
<%@ Control Language="C#" AutoEventWireup="true"
➥CodeFile="PageStateSwitcher.ascx.cs" Inherits="PageStateSwitcher" %>
<asp:Panel ID="pnlPageMode" runat="server" BackColor="PaleGoldenrod"
➥BorderWidth="1" BorderColor="black" Width="250">
    <asp:Label ID="lblPageMode" runat="server" Text="Display Mode"
    ➥Font-Bold="true" Width="100"/> 
    <asp:DropDownList ID="dlDisplayModes" runat="server" AutoPostBack="true"
     OnSelectedIndexChanged="dlDisplayModes_SelectedIndexChanged"/><br />
    <asp:LinkButton ID="lnkbReset" runat="server"
      Text="Reset User Data to Default" OnClick="lnkbReset_Click" /><br />
    <asp:Panel ID="pnlScopeChange" runat="server"
      Font-Size="9pt" BackColor="lightgray" Width="250"
      GroupingText=" Scope Change "
        Visible="false">
        <asp:RadioButton ID="rdoUser" runat="server"
```

```
                Text="User" AutoPostBack="True" GroupName="ScopeChange"
                ↪OnCheckedChanged="rdoUser_CheckedChanged" />
            <asp:RadioButton ID="rdoShared" runat="server"
                Text="Shared" AutoPostBack="True" GroupName="ScopeChange"
                ↪OnCheckedChanged="rdoShared_CheckedChanged" />
        </asp:Panel>
    </asp:Panel>
```

12. Now open the `PageStateSwitcher.ascx.cs` file and enter the following source code:

```
using System;
using System.Data;
using System.Configuration;
using System.Collections;
using System.Web;
using System.Web.Security;
using System.Web.UI;
using System.Web.UI.WebControls;
using System.Web.UI.WebControls.WebParts;
using System.Web.UI.HtmlControls;

public partial class PageStateSwitcher : System.Web.UI.UserControl
{
private WebPartManager mgr;

protected void Page_Load(object sender, EventArgs e)
{
}

protected override void OnInit(EventArgs e)
{
    base.OnInit(e);
    mgr = WebPartManager.GetCurrentWebPartManager(Page);

    foreach (WebPartDisplayMode mode in mgr.SupportedDisplayModes)
    {
        // if the mode is available, add it to the dropdown
        if (mode.IsEnabled(mgr))
        {
            string modeName = mode.Name;
            dlDisplayModes.Items.Add(new ListItem(
                modeName, modeName));
        }
    }
```

```csharp
        if (mgr.Personalization.CanEnterSharedScope)
        {
            pnlScopeChange.Visible = true;
            if (mgr.Personalization.Scope == PersonalizationScope.User)
                rdoUser.Checked = true;
            else
                rdoShared.Checked = true;
        }
    }

    protected void dlDisplayModes_SelectedIndexChanged(object sender, EventArgs e)
    {
        string selectedMode = dlDisplayModes.SelectedValue;
        WebPartDisplayMode newMode = mgr.SupportedDisplayModes[selectedMode];
        if (newMode != null)
            mgr.DisplayMode = newMode;
    }

    protected override void OnPreRender(EventArgs e)
    {
        ListItemCollection lic = dlDisplayModes.Items;
        int curMode = lic.IndexOf(lic.FindByText(mgr.DisplayMode.Name));
        dlDisplayModes.SelectedIndex = curMode;
    }

    protected void rdoUser_CheckedChanged(object sender, EventArgs e)
    {
        if (mgr.Personalization.Scope == PersonalizationScope.Shared)
            mgr.Personalization.ToggleScope();
    }
    protected void rdoShared_CheckedChanged(object sender, EventArgs e)
    {
        if ((mgr.Personalization.Scope == PersonalizationScope.User) &&
            (mgr.Personalization.CanEnterSharedScope))
        {
            mgr.Personalization.ToggleScope();
        }
    }
    protected void lnkbReset_Click(object sender, EventArgs e)
    {
        mgr.Personalization.ResetPersonalizationState();
    }
}
```

13. Now go back to `default.aspx` in whatever view you want and drag `PageStateSwitcher.ascx` from the Solution Explorer onto the design surface below the three-column table, just before the last `</div>` tag.

14. Run `default.aspx` and play around with the page for a while. Notice that when you switch the page into Design mode, borders appear around each zone as well as the zone's name. To watch the real magic happen, left-click and hold on a Web Part's title bar (while in Design mode) and *drag* it into some other location. You can move Web Parts between zones as well as change their display order. To prove that personalization is remembering your changes, make some visible changes to the page, close the page, and then reopen it. It will reappear in the same state in which you left it.

Entering Shared Scope

By default, users cannot enter shared scope. This means that when you run the application at this point in the walkthrough, the scope-changing panel will never appear. To allow your users to enter shared scope, you can add the following lines to the `<personalization>` section of your `<webParts>` element in `Web.config`:

```
<authorization>
  <allow users="*" verbs="enterSharedScope"/>
</authorization>
```

If you want finer-grained control over who can enter shared scope, you can make use of a role provider and only allow users who belong to specific roles to enter shared scope. This is definitely recommended for production scenarios because you do *not* want every user of your web application to be able to make global changes to the layout of a page.

---

15. Now that you have a Web Part Page that has multiple Web Part Zones and multiple Web Parts and has a control that allows users to switch into Design mode, you need some additional tools to allow users to make changes to Web Part properties. These tools fit nicely into an `EditorZone`. To create an `EditorZone`, drag one from the Toolbox into the third column of the table that hasn't been used yet. Rename this control to `zoneEditor`.

16. Drag an `AppearanceEditorPart` and a `LayoutEditorPart` into the `EditorZone` control. You'll see that both of those parts will also be wrapped in a `ZoneTemplate` control. Note that if you drag these controls while in source view, you will have to create the `ZoneTemplate` element manually.

17. If you haven't already been impressed by the Web Parts engine so far, you will definitely be at this step. Run the application again and you will see that there is a new display mode: Edit. Select that mode and all of the Web Parts on the page again switch into what looks like design mode. However, if you select one of their dropdown menus, you'll see a new Edit option. Click that and all of the editors contained within the `EditorZone` will appear, as shown in Figure 26.3.

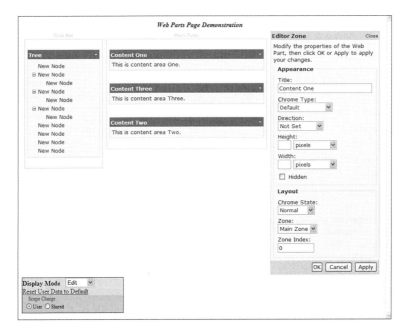

FIGURE 26.3   A Web Part Page with editing enabled.

18. So far you've seen how to declaratively add Web Parts to a Web Part Page by placing them directly in the aspx within a WebPartZone. With a little bit of work, you can also allow users to interactively select which Web Parts they want on their page by picking them from a catalog. To add catalog support to your page, start by dragging a CatalogZone control onto your page directly below the EditorZone you just created.

19. You can add a couple of different kinds of catalog parts, but the one you'll add in this walkthrough is the DeclarativeCatalogPart, which allows you to declare the list of parts contained in the catalog directly within the page. Drag the DeclarativeCatalogPart from the Toolbox in design view into the CatalogZone just created. VS will create the ZoneTemplate for you.

20. You can either drag controls onto the surface of the DeclarativeCatalogPart, or you can go into source view and create a WebPartsTemplate child element and declare the controls within that element. For this walkthrough, place a Calendar, a TextBox, and a Label with some random text into the WebPartsTemplate. Also remember that you can add any control here: a user control, a standard ASP.NET server control, or a control you have created that inherits directly from WebPart.

21. After you've added a couple of controls to the catalog's WebPartsTemplate, add a Title property to each of them so that the catalog has some way of displaying a description of the Web Part to the user. The code for your DeclarativeCatalogPart will look similar to this:

```
<asp:DeclarativeCatalogPart ID="DeclarativeCatalogPart1" runat="server">
    <WebPartsTemplate>
        <asp:Calendar ID="calendar1" runat="server" Title="Misc Calendar" />
        <asp:TextBox ID="txtTest" runat="Server" Title="Test Text Box" />
        <asp:Label ID="lblTest" runat="server" Title="Sample Label" />
    </WebPartsTemplate>
</asp:DeclarativeCatalogPart>
```

22. When you run the application now, you will find that yet another display mode has
    been added to the drop-down list: Catalog. Select this display mode and the
    CatalogZone will appear. It will then display a list of checkboxes next to the titles of
    the controls you added in step 20. You can see how the catalog will allow you to
    add Web Parts by selecting them and choosing the zone in which you want them to
    appear. Figure 26.4 shows a sample page after the user has added the Calendar
    control to the Side Bar zone.

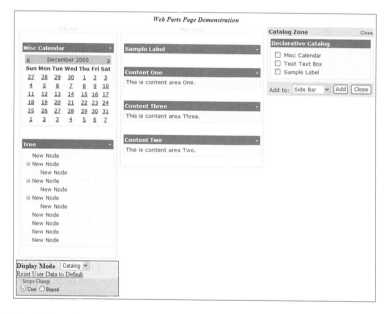

FIGURE 26.4   Using the catalog zone to add Web Parts at runtime.

23. Again, to be sure that personalization storage is working properly, if you close the
    page after making changes by using the Catalog and then reopen the page, it will
    remember all of those changes so long as you are still authenticated as the same
    user (this walkthrough is using Windows authentication).

26

Creating Web Parts

There are several different ways to create a Web Part. The first and easiest way is to simply take an existing ASP.NET control and place it inside a `ZoneTemplate`. At runtime, that control will automatically be wrapped inside a `GenericWebPart` control. This automatic promotion of regular controls to Web Parts makes using existing controls in Web Part Pages extremely easy.

A second way to create Web Parts is to create a control that derives from the `WebPart` class. Although this approach provides the developer with the most direct control over the behavior of the Web Part, it also doesn't allow you to use a designer and requires you to have some knowledge of custom control creation, which is covered in Chapter 30, "Developing ASP.NET Controls."

The third way is to create a user control that performs the function you want. After the user control has been created, you can place it within a `WebPartZone` and it will not only function like a standard Web Part, but it will also have access to all of the Web Part functionality available in the ASP.NET Web Part engine.

Creating user controls isn't the focus of this chapter, but there are some additional things that you can do within a user control or within any other class to make the control compatible with the personalization provider. If you create a Web Part and you want to be able to expose a property of that Web Part so that the data can be stored in the personalization store, you can use the `PersonalizableAttribute` class. You use this attribute to decorate a property just as you would with any other attribute, as shown in the following code:

```
[Personalizable(PersonalizationScope.User)]
public string ZipCode
{
    get { return zip; }
    set { zip = value; }
}
```

You can also use the `WebDescriptionAttribute` and `WebDisplayNameAttribute` attribute classes to further decorate a property so that it will show up properly in an `EditorZone`. `WebDescriptionAttribute` indicates the tooltip that will be used for a Web Part property, whereas `WebDisplayName` indicates the friendly name that will be displayed for a Web Part property:

```
[Personalizable(PersonalizationScope.User)]
[WebDisplayName("Zip Code")]
[WebDescription("Zip Code Used for Local Weather Forecast")]
public string ZipCode { ... }
```

The next section on building connected Web Parts will give you a thorough walkthrough of creating user control-based Web Parts.

Building Connected Web Parts

One of the most powerful things that can be done by Web Parts is to share data among parts within the same zone or even between different zones. A really common scenario among portal-style pages is to provide information based on the user's ZIP code. For example, when you log on to a portal for the first time, you typically add content to your page like local movie listings, weather reports, and local news. All of these could easily be written as ASP.NET 2.0 Web Parts. The issue is how to feed all of the Web Parts the same information: your ZIP code.

Data is shared among Web Parts in ASP.NET 2.0 using a publish/consume model. A Web Part can publish a piece of information that can then be consumed by any other Web Part that knows how to consume that information. This means that you could create a Web Part that prompts the user for her ZIP code and then publishes that information to all interested Web Parts. Without prior knowledge of other existing Web Parts, a developer could create a Web Part that consumes ZIP codes and an end user or administrator could utilize a ConnectionsZone to hook up publishers and consumers on the same page.

This is all made possible through a contract by which publishers and consumers both must abide. As you know, in programming terms, a contract is an interface. When a Web Part publishes data, it publishes that data in the form of an instance of an object that implements a specific interface. All a consumer has to do is implement a method that receives an instance of that same interface. The Web Part plumbing in the underlying connection takes care of calling the publishing method on the publisher and the consuming method on the consumer.

To illustrate connected Web Parts, this section walks you through adding a shared interface and two new user controls to the solution developed in the previous section, FirstWebPartPage.

Before creating any controls, add an App_Code folder to your web application and place the IZipCode interface in it. The code for the IZipCode interface is quite simple:

```csharp
using System;
using System.Data;
using System.Configuration;
using System.Web;
using System.Web.Security;
using System.Web.UI;
using System.Web.UI.WebControls;
using System.Web.UI.WebControls.WebParts;
using System.Web.UI.HtmlControls;

public interface IZipCode
{
    string ZipCode { get; set; }
}
```

This simple interface indicates to any consumers that the data being published is a string representing a ZIP code.

The first control is a simple control that prompts the user for his ZIP code. The beautiful thing about it is that the user's ZIP code can then be automatically stored in the personalization provider and remembered every time that same user loads the page. Create a new application subfolder called `Controls` and add a new web user control to it called `ZipCodeSelector`. The ascx code for this control is extremely simple:

```
<%@ Control Language="C#" AutoEventWireup="true"
  CodeFile="ZipCodeSelector.ascx.cs" Inherits="Controls_ZipCodeSelector" %>
Zip Code: <asp:TextBox ID="txtZip" runat="server" /> 
<asp:Button ID="btnSetZip" runat="server" Text="Set" OnClick="btnSetZip_Click" />
```

The C# code that drives the control looks like this:

```
using System;
using System.Data;
using System.Configuration;
using System.Collections;
using System.Web;
using System.Web.Security;
using System.Web.UI;
using System.Web.UI.WebControls;
using System.Web.UI.WebControls.WebParts;
using System.Web.UI.HtmlControls;

public partial class Controls_ZipCodeSelector :
System.Web.UI.UserControl, IZipCode
{
private string zip = string.Empty;

[Personalizable(PersonalizationScope.User)]
[WebDisplayName("Zip Code")]
[WebDescription("Zip Code Made Available to Connected Controls for localized
data")]
public string ZipCode
{
    get { return zip; }
    set { zip = value; }
}

protected void Page_Load(object sender, EventArgs e)
{

}
```

```
protected override void OnPreRender(EventArgs e)
{
    base.OnPreRender(e);
    if (zip != null)
        txtZip.Text = zip;
}

[ConnectionProvider("Zip Code Data Provider", "ZipCodeProvider")]
public IZipCode ProvideIZipCode()
{
    return this;
}

protected void btnSetZip_Click(object sender, EventArgs e)
{
    zip = txtZip.Text;
    txtZip.Text = string.Empty;
}
}
```

The PersonalizableAttribute attribute class marks the ZipCode property as one that is not only managed by the personalization provider, but in this case it also indicates that the ZipCode property is managed at the User scope.

Under the hood, when you place a Web Part on a page that has a ConnectionProvider attribute on it, that tells the Web Part framework that the Web Part is publishing data.

To create a Web Part that consumes the data published by the ZipCodeSelector control, add a new Web User Control to the Controls folder and call it WeatherPart. We're not actually going to create a real weather control, so all you need to do is add the following code to your ascx file:

```
Currently Displaying the Weather for <asp:Label ID="lblZip" runat="server" />
```

Then you can modify WeatherPart.ascx.cs so that it contains the following code to consume a ZIP code:

```
using System;
using System.Data;
using System.Configuration;
using System.Collections;
using System.Web;
using System.Web.Security;
using System.Web.UI;
using System.Web.UI.WebControls;
using System.Web.UI.WebControls.WebParts;
using System.Web.UI.HtmlControls;
```

26

```
public partial class Controls_WeatherPart : System.Web.UI.UserControl
{
private IZipCode zipProvider = null;

[ConnectionConsumer("Zip Code Consumer", "ZipCodeConsumer")]
public void GetIZipCode(IZipCode Provider)
{
    zipProvider = Provider;
}


protected override void OnPreRender(EventArgs e)
{
    base.OnPreRender(e);
    // take advantage of short-circuiting here
    if ((zipProvider != null) && (zipProvider.ZipCode != string.Empty))
        lblZip.Text = zipProvider.ZipCode;
    else
        lblZip.Text = "(No Data)";
}
protected void Page_Load(object sender, EventArgs e)
{

}
}
```

The reason the preceding code uses the `PreRender` event is because, as the developer, you can't be absolutely sure when during the control's life cycle the connection data will be transferred. So the safest bet is to use the last event in the control life cycle before rendering to process the data being shared over the connection to guarantee that the data has been delivered. You will find that if you use the standard `Page_Load` method, the `zipProvider` instance will be `null`.

Build the solution to make sure everything compiles properly. Next, open up `default.aspx` again and select the `CatalogZone` control you placed in the designer earlier. Select the control's context menu and then click Edit Templates. This will open up the inside of the `DeclarativeCatalogPart` and allow you to drop additional controls into the catalog. Drag both of the controls created in this section into the area and then switch to design view to set the `Title` property. The new `DeclarativeCatalogPart` region should look something like this:

```
<asp:DeclarativeCatalogPart ID="DeclarativeCatalogPart1" runat="server">
<WebPartsTemplate>
    <asp:Calendar ID="calendar1" runat="server" Title="Misc Calendar" />
    <asp:TextBox ID="txtTest" runat="Server" Title="Test Text Box" />
    <asp:Label ID="lblTest" runat="server" Title="Sample Label" />
    <uc2:WeatherPart ID="WeatherPart1" runat="server" Title="Weather Consumer" />
```

```
    <uc3:ZipCodeSelector ID="ZipCodeSelector1" runat="server" Title="Zip Provider"
/>
</WebPartsTemplate>
</asp:DeclarativeCatalogPart>
```

To allow users to modify the connection properties of connected Web Parts, you need a
`ConnectionsZone`, so drag one of those from the Toolbox into the third column of the
table right below the `EditorZone` and `CatalogZone`.

Now you're ready to run the application. When you run it, you will see that a new
display mode, Connect, has been added to the display mode selector created earlier.
Before using that mode, open the Catalog mode and add the two new Web Parts to the
main zone. The ZIP code selector should contain an empty text box and the weather Web
Part should display the "(no data)" phrase because it hasn't been connected and isn't
receiving data.

Switch the page into Connect mode and click the drop-down menu for the ZIP code
provider Web Part. Click the new Connect menu option. You will then be able to choose
the destination control from a drop-down list of compatible controls. If there were 10
controls on the page that consumed ZIP codes using the `IZipCode` interface, all 10 of
them would appear in the drop-down list. A portion of the page containing the connection editor for the ZIP code provider Web Part is shown in Figure 26.5.

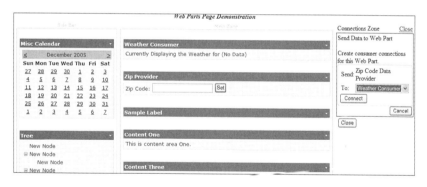

FIGURE 26.5   Connecting a provider to a consumer using a connections zone.

When you connect the Web Parts and switch back to the Browse mode of the page, you
won't notice any immediate difference because you still haven't given the ZIP code
provider part a ZIP code. Enter a ZIP code and click the Set button. As soon as you click
that button, you should not only see that the ZIP code remained in the text box, but that
the weather consumer part has received the ZIP code, as shown in Figure 26.6.

Finally, close the page and then reopen it. You will see that the ZIP code provider has
remembered your ZIP code because of the attributes used on the `ZipCode` property. As a
result, that Web Part has also provided the ZIP code to the weather consumer part—all
without you having to do any additional work.

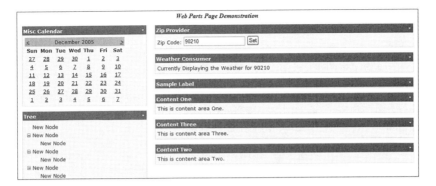

FIGURE 26.6   Web part data provider and consumer in action.

Summary

This is a fairly dense chapter, packed full with information about Web Parts and the ASP.NET 2.0 Web Part framework. Throughout this chapter you learned what Web Parts are, how they work, and how you can deploy them on Web Part Pages. In addition, this chapter presented quite a bit of information about the extensive use of the personalization provider by the Web Parts framework and how you can make that work for you. This chapter is by no means the definitive reference for all things related to Web Parts, but it has provided you with enough information so that you can get started with Web Parts and you can make informed design decisions when presented with the opportunity to create a solution involving Web Parts.

CHAPTER **27**

Building Rich, Data-Driven Web Applications

Unless you're creating the most basic of applications on the web, your application will need to interact with data. It will need to retrieve data from some location for display to the user or perhaps for being processed by business logic. You will also surely need to be able to send data to a data source. Sending data to a data source takes place when you need to change existing data, create new data, or delete existing data. All of these operations are standard for pretty much any web application that does anything more than simply display static text.

This chapter shows you the basics of how data binding works in ASP 2005 and how you can use the new controls, classes, and functionality to dramatically speed up the development time for data-bound Web Forms, increasing scalability, performance and ease of maintenance in the process.

Introduction to Data Binding in ASP.NET

Data binding refers to the act of "binding" user interface elements to underlying data through some means. This chapter does not focus much on how previous versions of ASP.NET accomplished data binding except to briefly compare and contrast. Although the new ASP.NET controls can be bound the "old way" as well as the new ASP 2005 way, you will see a huge improvement in productivity by writing your code to take advantage of some of the new features. This section introduces you to the data source pattern that exists in both ASP 2005 and Windows Forms and how to create data sources. Finally, this section will finish up with an overview of the wide variety of controls available to you for using as-is or for extending through inheritance.

The Data Source Model

Data sources are just that: sources of data. The new data source model is designed in such a way that you can create a data source for any type of underlying data, and the UI control can then bind to the data source and not directly to the data. This allows the UI control to focus simply on rendering data and not on the underlying format of the data. For example, using various data sources you can now bind a single control to an XML document, to a `DataSet`, to a strongly typed collection of objects, to the results of a stored procedure execution in SQL, or to the results of an OLEDB query, and much more.

The steps required to connect your controls to a data source are extremely simple. First, you create your data source (discussed shortly), and then you drag a bindable control onto the form, select the data source from the drop-down box, and you're well on your way to creating a rich, interactive, and data-driven web page.

Creating Data Sources

Creating a data source is a simple task. After you've created an empty website through Visual Studio 2005, create a new Web Form. To create a data source, you drag one of the five built-in data source components onto your form. The following is a brief description of the data source components that come with ASP.NET:

- `SqlDataSource`—A data source used to access data contained in a SQL Server 2000 (or higher, including SQL 2005) database.

- `AccessDataSource`—A data source used to connect to data contained in a Microsoft Access (.mdb) file.

- `ObjectDataSource`—An extremely powerful data source component that allows you to connect a UI control to an arbitrary object.

- `XmlDataSource`—A data source used to connect to data contained within an XML document.

- `SiteMapDataSource`—A data source designed to connect to the data representing a site map.

After you drag the data source onto the form, the Data Source Configuration Wizard dialog will appear. This wizard will walk you through the process of configuring all the aspects of your data source. This includes specifying the query that obtains the data as well as additional queries (or stored procedures, if applicable) used for Create, Update, and Delete operations. With those operations defined, you can then use the stock ASP.NET controls to create, retrieve, update, and delete data from your data source whether the data is in an XML file, a SQL database, an Access database, or an instance of an object within your application.

To see this in action, open the Toolbox panel in Visual Studio and drag an AccessDataSource component onto your form. This should automatically bring up the smart tag menu. From here, click the Configure Data Source option. This will bring up a screen asking you for the filename of the Access database to which the data source will attach. Browse to the location of your Northwind.mdb file (this file is included with Visual Studio 2005 in one of the sample directories) and click Next, bringing up the screen shown in Figure 27.1.

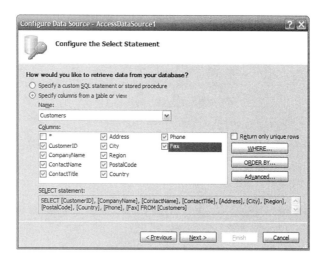

FIGURE 27.1   SELECT statement configuration for an Access data source.

Select each column specifically (instead of clicking the asterisk) and then click Next to move to the next step in the wizard. The next step allows you to click Test Query to see a preview of the data that will be appearing in the control. After you've tested the query, click Finish and the Data Source Configuration Wizard will finish.

Drag a GridView control onto the form, autoformat it however you like, and set the data source to the Access data source you just created (named AccessDataSource1 by default). When you run this page in debug, you will see output that looks like Figure 27.2.

This is great, but it only allows you to view the data. The GridView also allows you to update and delete existing rows. The great thing about data sources is that the Create, Retrieve, Update, and Delete commands are all stored in the data source, and the control need not have any knowledge of those commands. To configure your data source for insert, update, and delete operations, go back to the Configure Data Source Wizard and click "Next" to get to the screen where you choose the columns for your SELECT statement. Click the Advanced button and you will see the dialog shown in Figure 27.3, which asks if you want to autogenerate UPDATE, DELETE, and INSERT statements.

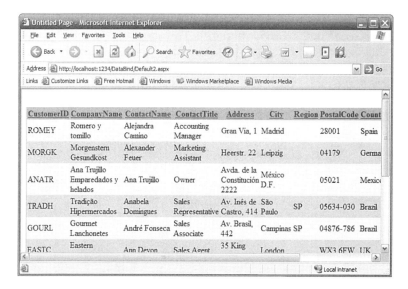

FIGURE 27.2   A GridView connected to an Access data source.

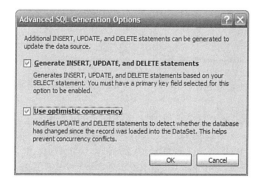

FIGURE 27.3   Dialog prompting to autogenerate UPDATE, DELETE, and INSERT statements.

Before you think this is actually going to work, go into the properties for the data source and take a look at the InsertQuery, UpdateQuery, and DeleteQuery properties. There is an extremely useful miniature query builder that will pop up when you open these properties. More often than not, autogenerated queries are either not efficient enough or simply don't work at all. However, they are a good starting point for you to go in and optimize them to work properly. After a small tweak to make it work properly, the screenshot shown in Figure 27.4 shows a functioning update query.

The only thing that a GridView can't do is utilize the InsertQuery property of the data source. This section won't get into details on how to do that because the section "Using Data-Bound Controls" later in this chapter covers utilizing the various controls that can be data-bound.

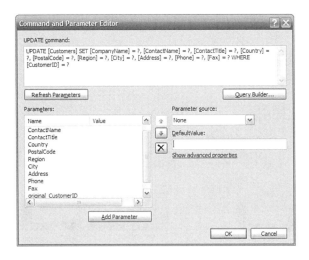

FIGURE 27.4   A functioning update query for an Access Data source.

Data-Bound Control Hierarchy

Almost every single control that comes with ASP.NET 2.0 can be involved in the data-binding process in some way. However, there is a smaller list of controls that are designed specifically for working in a data-bound fashion, whether it is to display and edit the details of a single row of data or to display and edit multiple rows in a sorted, paged, or even filtered way. This list is shown in Figure 27.5.

The following is a brief overview of the controls shown in the hierarchy in Figure 27.5. The next section of this chapter will show you how to use each of these controls.

- AdRotator—A standard control for rotating advertisement information from a data-bound source

- ListBox—A standard list box control that displays multiple elements at a time, and can allow single or multiple selection of items

- CheckBoxList—A list of checkboxes that can be rendered in several modes from a data source

- DropDownList—A traditional "combo box"-style control whose elements and currently selected item can be pulled from a data source

- RadioButtonList—A list of radio buttons that can be rendered in several modes from a data source

- DetailsView—A composite control that can render a detail view showing the columns and values for a specific data row

27

- `FormView`—A composite control that renders an interactive form populated by a data source

- `GridView`—A grid-style view of data from a data source that is extremely powerful and can support in-line edit and deletion of data

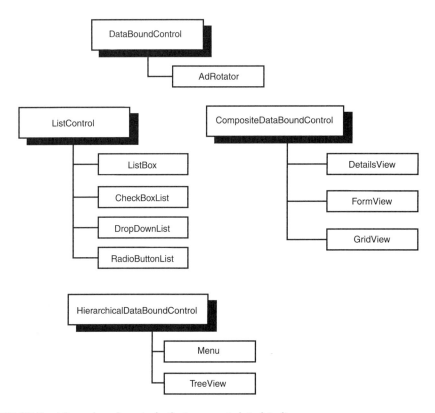

FIGURE 27.5 Hierarchy of controls that support data binding.

Using Data-Bound Controls

Many controls support binding, but thanks to the use of the data source model, many of the simpler controls are self-explanatory and easy to work with, such as the `CheckBoxList` and the `ListBox`. This section covers some of the more powerful controls and gives you an introduction to their use. For a more thorough examination of all ASP.NET 2.0 controls, you should consider reading one of the books that are specific to ASP.NET 2.0, such as *ASP 2005 Unleashed*, from Sams Publishing (ISBN: 0672328232).

Using the `GridView` Control

Earlier in this chapter you saw a brief introduction to the `GridView` control. This control is responsible for rendering a list of items in a grid format, and can be configured to allow for inline editing and deleting of existing rows if the data source to which the control is connected has a `DeleteCommand` and an `UpdateCommand` defined. If you set the `AutoGenerateDeleteButton`, `AutoGenerateEditButton`, and `AutoGenerateSelectButton` properties, the manual tasks previously required of the `DataGrid` in ASP.NET 1.1 will be taken care of. In fact, you won't have to write any of your own update code because the data source will perform the update (or delete) at the request of the `GridView`.

Using the `DetailsView` Control

The `DetailsView` control is used for displaying the details for a single row of data. Most often when a user interface calls for the display of multiple rows of data in a grid format, the same interface requires that a row's details eventually be displayed, either on the same page or on a different page.

If you've been following along, drag a `DetailsView` control onto the form and set its data source to the same as the `GridView`, `AccessDatasource1`. Make sure to set the `EnablePaging` property to true. The one thing to keep in mind that is to the `DetailsView` control, one row is equivalent to one page. Therefore, to set the row being viewed or edited, you simply set the `PageIndex` property.

With both a `GridView` and a `DetailsView` on the same page, you might assume that if you click the Select button on the `GridView` (this button appears when your `GridView` allows row selection), the `DetailsView` will automatically move to the selected row. This would be true if the data source supported the notion of currency (maintaining current row in state), but ASP.NET 2.0 data sources do not support currency, with good reason. To make a `GridView` and a `DetailsView` sync up when the user selects a row in the `GridView`, all you have to do is add the following line of code to the `GridView`'s `SelectedIndexChanged` event handler:

```
DetailsView1.PageIndex = GridView1.SelectedIndex;
```

If you're familiar with ASP.NET 1.1 programming, you are probably wondering where the call to `DataBind()` is for the `DetailsView`. There is no need because all new ASP.NET 2.0 controls that support data binding indicate to the ASP.NET framework whether or not something has changed with the control that requires it to rebind. This facet of ASP.NET saves a lot of time and effort on behalf of the programmer, who no longer has to write complicated code to determine whether binding needs to take place or create convoluted workarounds to avoid double-binding the same data.

Using the `FormView` Control

The `FormView` control is similar to the `DetailsView` control. The main difference between the two is that the `DetailsView` is preconfigured to work in tabular data fashion, whereas the `FormView` requires the developer to define the templates for items in read-only and edit mode.

To see the `FormView` in action, create a new Web Form and copy the `AccessDataSource1` data source from the previous page onto the new page. Then, drag a `FormView` onto the page and make sure to enable paging (remember that one page on a detail/form control is the same as one row in a grid control).

Set the control up so that the form view control looks as follows:

```
<asp:FormView ID="FormView1" runat="server"
BackColor="LightGoldenrodYellow"    BorderColor="Tan"
  BorderWidth="1px" CellPadding="2"
DataSourceID="AccessDataSource1" ForeColor="Black"    AllowPaging="True">
  <FooterStyle BackColor="Tan" />
  <PagerStyle BackColor="PaleGoldenrod"
ForeColor="DarkSlateBlue"    HorizontalAlign="Center" />
  <HeaderStyle BackColor="Tan" Font-Bold="True" />
  <EditRowStyle BackColor="DarkSlateBlue" ForeColor="GhostWhite" />
  <ItemTemplate>
    <table width="100%" border=1 cellspacing=0 cellpadding=0 bordercolor=black>
      <tr>
        <td width="100">
          Company Name
        </td>
        <td>
          <%# Eval("CompanyName") %>
        </td>
      </tr>
      <tr>
        <td>
          Contact Name
        </td>
        <td>
          <%# Eval("ContactName") %>
        </td>
      </tr>
    </table>
  </ItemTemplate>
  <PagerSettings Mode="NextPreviousFirstLast" />
</asp:FormView>
```

The really important piece to remember in the preceding code is the `Eval` method. This method is a part of the `Page` class itself and, as such, is available through partial class technology to the code on the `.aspx` page. It is far easier syntax to use than the `DataBinder.Eval()` method that was required by ASP.NET 1.1 and earlier. In short, it will evaluate the property indicated on whatever data context is applicable for the template. In the case of the preceding code, it is evaluating the properties on a single row of the `Customers` table in the Northwind sample Access database. You can also pass a format string to this method to further control the output.

Using the TreeView

The TreeView control (found in the "Navigation" section of the Toolbox) is a data-bound control that is responsible for rendering data in a hierarchical fashion. Tree-style controls are extremely useful for displaying hierarchies such as the relationship between parent rows and child rows, site navigation trees, and much more.

Although you can manually populate the nodes of a TreeView control programmatically, this section will show you how to bind a TreeView to a data source. This control is a hierarchical control and as such must be bound to a hierarchical data source, such as a site map or an XML data source.

One of the best features of the TreeView control is that you can use a design-time editor to graphically pick out which attributes will supply the node labels and which attributes will supply node values given a certain hierarchy.

To see how this all works, create a new page called TreeView.aspx and drag a TreeView control onto the page. Now add a new XML file to the App_Data folder in the solution and call it BuddyList.xml. Enter the following XML for the file:

```xml
<?xml version="1.0" encoding="utf-8" ?>
<Buddylist name="My Contacts">
<Group name="Co-Workers">
    <Buddy name="Joe"/>
    <Buddy name="John"/>
</Group>
<Group name="Everybody Else">
    <Buddy name="Steve"/>
    <Buddy name="Bob"/>
</Group>
</Buddylist>
```

With the XML file in place, you can create an XML Data source using the BuddyList.xml file as a source.

Open up the smart tag menu on the TreeView control and select the XML data source as the data source. Then select the option to configure the TreeNode data bindings. A dialog like the one shown in Figure 27.6 will appear, allowing you to select the attributes that populate various nodes of the tree. You can also autoformat the tree view for a specific application, such as a Contact list in this scenario.

When you run the page you can see how the XML file you created has been mapped onto the hierarchical structure of the TreeView control, as shown in Figure 27.7.

27

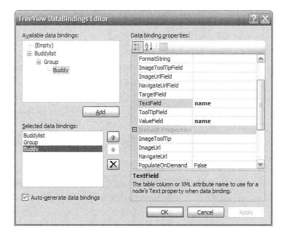

FIGURE 27.6   TreeNode data bindings editor.

FIGURE 27.7   A TreeView autoformatted for Contacts bound to an XML file.

Advanced Data-Binding Techniques

You can do a lot of things with data-bound controls. When you get out of the realm of small sample applications, you often start creating your own controls and creating multi-tier applications. The discussion of creating your own controls is better left to a book specializing on ASP.NET, such as *ASP 2005 Unleashed*, from Sams Publishing (0672328232).

When you begin adding tiers to your application, binding directly to a connected data source such as SQL Server or Oracle becomes impractical. In addition, you might be pulling data from a web service or from some other service provided by code written for the Windows Communication Framework. In these cases you don't want to bind directly to the data source for a number of reasons, not the least of which include potentially poor performance and scalability. To deal with multiple tiers or other situations where you want to bind to custom data, you can use an `ObjectDataSource`.

Creating and Utilizing an Object Data Source

Object data sources are data sources that read and write information to a class instance rather than to a connected source such as SQL Server or Oracle. To create an object data source, all you have to do is drag an Object Data Source onto your form and choose the class to which it will be bound.

This means that you'll have to create the class before you drag the object data source control. In an n-tier application scenario, this probably won't be difficult because many n-tier applications have business objects that supply strongly typed properties as well as methods to support the standard CRUD (Create, Retrieve, Update, Delete) functionality.

This sample will show you how to create an Object Data Source from a typed `DataSet`. This is the quickest way to get an object data source running from scratch because an object data source requires you to create your own implementation of the create, retrieve, update, and delete methods. After you have tried object binding with a typed `DataSet`, you can move on to implementing it with your own business objects.

The first step is to add a typed `DataSet` to your project. I created a typed `DataSet` called `UsersDataSet`, which has basic schema support for a string-based user ID, a first name, and last name. These users are stored in a SQL Express database on my machine. When you create a new `DataSet` in your solution, it will prompt you to choose a connection string and will allow you to automatically connect the `DataSet` to a database such as SQL Express. Although you don't have to connect your `DataSet` to a live source of data, it does make this sample easier.

With the `DataSet` created, you can then drag an `ObjectDataSource` component onto your Web Form. Use the wizard to select the data source. When you select the typed `DataSet`, the wizard will recognize the data object immediately and automatically select the appropriate methods for Select, Create, Update, and Delete operations.

Finally, with the `ObjectDataSource` created, you can drag a `GridView` component onto your form and select the object data source you just created as the data source.

Figure 27.8 shows the combination of the `GridView` control running against an `ObjectDataSource`. When you run this page, the `GridView` and the `ObjectDataSource` will enable a user to edit the contents of the data set, while persisting those same contents to a connected database, all without requiring you to write a single line of code.

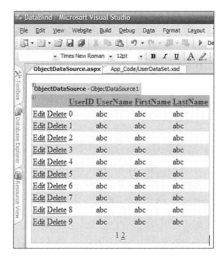

FIGURE 27.8   A `GridView` and an `ObjectDataSource` working against a typed *DataSet*.

Summary

This chapter introduced you to the new method of binding user interface controls to various sources of data in the new version of ASP.NET. Although the old `DataBind()` syntax is still available, the new method of using data sources such as a SQL data source, XML data source, or object data sources is quicker, easier, and can produce some extremely powerful results with very little effort on the part of the programmer.

If you want more detail on how data binding works, and how to create your own custom data-bound controls, you can look at *ASP 2005 Unleashed* by SAMS Publishing (0672328232). This chapter provides enough of an overview of data-bound controls to get you into Visual Studio and coding.

CHAPTER 28

Securing Your ASP.NET Applications

"Security" is a term that is often overused and encompasses so many different topics that it can be confusing. When someone is talking about securing an application, often they are talking about things completely irrelevant to our needs. To distill the concept of security down a bit, the topic of security in this chapter is limited to just the notion of securing an ASP.NET application.

In this chapter, you will learn the important distinction between *authentication* and *authorization.* You will learn how to identify the users connecting to your websites as well as how to discern what they can and cannot do. You will also get an introduction to some of the new ASP.NET controls relating to users and security. Finally, you will see how to use and extend the new Membership provider that comes with ASP.NET 2.0.

Security Through Authentication

Regardless of what type of application you are creating in ASP.NET, the chances are very high that you will want to be able to identify the users who are connecting to your website. If you want to do something as simple as provide a personalized greeting or something as complex as identifying the user through some corporate single sign-on system, you will need to make use of some form of authentication. *Authentication* is the process of identifying *who* a particular user of your web application is by obtaining some set of credentials from the user and verifying those credentials against some authority. The authority can be a custom database, an Active Directory, or a single sign-on authority such as Microsoft Passport.

Authentication in ASP.NET works on the premise of providers. You choose which provider is providing authentication services for your application through a setting in the `Web.config` file.

You indicate the authentication provider within `Web.config` by setting the `<authentication>` element as follows:

```
<authentication mode="[Windows|Forms|Passport|None]"/>
```

Three authentication providers come with ASP.NET: Windows, Forms, and Passport. If you choose "None" for your authentication provider, ASP.NET will not do anything whatsoever to identify the person requesting each page. In the next few sections of this chapter you will see how to use the three authentication providers.

Two main interfaces are used by all of the authentication providers: `IPrincipal` and `IIdentity`. These two interfaces allow for a standard method of identifying authenticated users.

When a user has been authenticated (even if that authentication failed), an ASP.NET page has access to the user credentials and other authentication through the web context. All pages have access to the web context through an instance of the `HttpContext` class, which you can access via the `HttpContext.Current` property. To obtain an `IPrincipal` representing the current user, you can make use of the `HttpContext.Current.User` property.

Windows Authentication

Windows authentication for ASP.NET is provided by the `WindowsAuthenticationModule` class (found in the `System.Web.Security` namespace). When a user is authenticated using Windows authentication, the provider will create an instance of the `WindowsPrincipal` class and make it available through the web context.

Windows authentication works by taking whatever Windows-based credentials (clear text, integrated, and so on) were supplied by Internet Information Server (IIS) and providing them to the ASP.NET application through the `WindowsPrincipal` and `WindowsIdentity` classes.

Because Windows authentication is the default authentication provider for ASP.NET, it is extremely easy to create a sample application to test it out. To do so, create a new C# website called `Authentication`. After you've done this, add the following lines of code to the `Page_Load` event handler of the default Web Form that comes with the application:

```
Response.Write(User.Identity.Name + "<BR>");
Response.Write("User is authenticated? " +
    User.Identity.IsAuthenticated.ToString() + "<BR>");
Response.Write("Authentication Method: " +
    User.Identity.AuthenticationType.ToString() + "<BR>");
```

The `User` object is made available to all ASP.NET web pages. If you are writing a server control or a user control, you can access the `User` object by using `Page.User` or

`HttpContext.Current.User`. Figure 28.1 shows the output of this page when run under Windows authentication. Obviously the name of the user will change, but everything else should look very similar in your own development environment.

FIGURE 28.1   The output of a page displaying Windows authentication information.

Passport Authentication

Passport authentication is handled by the Passport authentication provider. Passport is a centralized authentication service provided by Microsoft. Your application benefits in that users can reuse the same Passport on any number of sites while still maintaining their own privacy. Your application, by making use of Passport, can skip a lot of the process usually involved in creating an authentication scheme. If you are developing on Windows Server 2003, you already have all the tools you need in order to work with Passport authentication. If you are not using Windows Server 2003, you will need to download the Passport SDK. For information on the Passport SDK and how to support Passport authentication on your website, go to http://www.passport.com/business. In order to see the documentation you will have to have a Passport of your own.

Much like Forms authentication (covered in the next section), Passport authentication works with cookies. When a user opens a browser to a Passport-secured website, the client's cookies are examined for a valid Passport authentication ticket. If it is found, the user is seamlessly delivered to the secured resource. If no such ticket is found, the user is redirected to the Passport authentication page hosted by Microsoft. After authentication takes place, the user is then redirected to the original secured resource. Because the user now has a valid Passport authentication ticket, the client is then given access to the protected resource.

The `PassportAuthenticationModule` detects the presence of a valid Passport and then creates a `PassportIdentity` instance, which then becomes available from within the `User` object as shown in the preceding samples.

The `PassportIdentity` class offers several additional methods and properties that are useful when creating a Passport-secured website. For a full reference on the `PassportIdentity` class, consult the MSDN documentation at http://msdn.microsoft.com

28

and the Passport SDK, which can be found at http://www.passport.com/business and is included with Windows Server 2003.

Forms Authentication

Forms authentication is the most commonly used means of authentication for public-facing websites. The reason for this is that there are often concerns with securing a website with Windows authentication that must be accessible to users who don't belong to a domain and to users accessing the site across any number of router configurations, as well as a need for protection of credentials.

As mentioned in the Passport section, Forms authentication is cookie-based. This means that when a user has authenticated to a website, that fact is stored in a cookie on the user's machine. If the website fails to find an authentication cookie, the user is redirected to a login page where they can supply their credentials (or in some cases they can register a new account).

Forms authentication has several options that can be configured through the `Web.config` file. The options for the `<forms>` element in the `Web.config` file are shown in the following code:

```
<authentication mode="Forms">
   <forms name="name"
        cookieless=UseCookie¦UseUri¦AutoDetect¦UseDeviceProfile
        defaultUrl=[URL]
    domain=domain name
        loginUrl="url"
    protection="All¦None¦Encryption¦Validation"
    timeout="30"
    path="/"
        requireSSL="true¦false"
        slidingExpiration="true¦false">
    <credentials passwordFormat="Clear¦SHA1¦MD5">
      <user name="username" password="password"/>
    </credentials>
  </forms>
</authentication>
```

The following is a quick summary of some of the options shown in the preceding example:

- `protection`—Indicates the protection used to secure the Forms authentication cookie

- `timeout`—Indicates the amount of time (in minutes) that will elapse before a Forms authentication cookie will expire

- `credentials`—Allows you to manually specify a list of users who can use your application directly in the `web.config` file

Also keep in mind that Visual Studio 2005 has a far more active and alert IntelliSense system than previous versions—you will be able to see all of the options available to you while typing directly into the `web.config` file.

The `<forms>` element only indicates how you are going to protect the pages on your website, not which locations you plan on protecting. To protect every page in your application except the login page, you can use a `web.config` file that looks like this:

```
<?xml version="1.0"?>
<configuration xmlns="http://schemas.microsoft.com/.NetConfiguration/v2.0">
    <appSettings/>
    <connectionStrings/>
    <location path="login.aspx">
        <system.web>
            <authorization>
                <allow users="*"/>
            </authorization>
        </system.web>
    </location>
    <system.web>
        <compilation debug="true"/>
        <authentication mode="Forms">
            <forms loginUrl="login.aspx" name="MyApp" protection="All"/>
        </authentication>
        <authorization>
            <deny users="?"/>
        </authorization>
    </system.web>
</configuration>
```

The `authorization` section indicates who has been granted access and who has been denied access. The wildcards ? and * indicate anonymous (unauthenticated) users and all users, respectively. You will see more about the `authorization` element later in the chapter in the section "Security Through Authorization."

When you use the `FormsAuthentication` class, several static methods are available to you for dealing with Forms authentication, including the following:

- `RedirectFromLoginPage`—This method authenticates the user (saves their cookie) and redirects from the login page back to the original protected resource.

- `RedirectToLoginPage`—This method sends the user to the login page, the URL of which is defined in `Web.config`.

- `HashPasswordForStoringInConfigFile`—This method is a handy, quick way of storing a user's password in an encrypted hash.

- `SetAuthCookie`—This method authenticates the user but performs no additional processing (such as redirection to a protected resource).

28

- SignOut—This method will expire the current user's Forms authentication cookie.

- Authenticate—If you are storing the user credentials in the Web.config, you can use this method to validate a username/password combination against those stored in the config file.

With a quick change to the preceding application and a call to FormsAuthentication.RedirectFromLoginPage, you can create a quick sample of Forms authentication. The three lines of code you used to display the WindowsIdentity details can also be used to show the same information from Forms authentication, as shown in Figure 28.2.

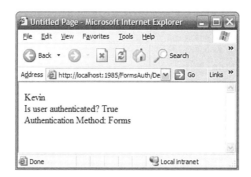

FIGURE 28.2   Forms authentication in action.

If you have experience with Forms authentication in previous versions of ASP.NET, you may think that this section is a little small. I am deliberately leaving out some of the more tedious programming tasks associated with authentication such as creating login pages, status controls, and so that on. Later in this chapter there is a section ("The ASP.NET Security Controls") covering a host of new UI controls that automate a great deal of the common tasks associated with authentication that work with any authentication provider, not just Forms.

User Management with Membership

Authentication requires that a set of credentials supplied by the user be validated against some previously stored set of credentials. The means by which you store the user credentials is completely up to you. You can store them in a SQL Server instance, you can store them in an XML file, or an Access database, or even the Web.config file.

Every web application that requires a user to log in must deal with the issue of storing the information about the website's members and their credentials. ASP.NET 2.0 provides a new API, the Membership API. This API abstracts the management of user storage and credentials in a standard way. As you will find out later in this chapter, there is also a set of standard controls that are fully compatible with the membership API.

The Membership API consists of the set of classes provided by ASP.NET for dealing with Membership that reside in the `System.Web.Security.Membership`. This API provides the following functionality:

- User management—Create, edit, and delete users.

- Membership data management—Maintain membership data, such as email addresses.

- Authentication—The membership API is capable of validating supplied user credentials against the credentials contained in the membership store.

- Advanced password management—Not only does the Membership API give you easy access to methods for changing user passwords, but through Membership, users can also retrieve and reset their own passwords.

The bottom line is that now the majority of the tasks you had to code manually each time you created an ASP.NET v1.x website are now bundled for you in a secure, easy-to-use library that is available to every ASP.NET 2.0 web application.

The first step to using Membership on any application is to make sure that the ASP.NET Membership schemas are installed properly. These schemas are installed in an instance of SQL Server, or your default SQL Express instance. If this was not already done for you at the time ASP.NET was installed, you can use the command-line utility `aspnet_regsql.exe` to do the job for you. You can find this tool in `[drive:]\windows\Microsoft.NET\Framework\v[version]`.

The next thing you need to do is create a connection string for the Membership provider to use. This connection string will be stored in the new `<connectionStrings>` element in `Web.config`. If you installed the full version of SQL Server 2005, you will have a standard connection string. If you are using the Express version of SQL 2005, you will have a slightly different connection string. The following is the line of XML I used for my Membership connection string after installing the schemas into my copy of SQL Express:

```
<connectionStrings>
<romove name-"LocalSqlServer"/>
<add name="LocalSqlServer"
    connectionString="Data Source=.\SQLExpress;Integrated Security=True;User
    ➥Instance=True;AttachDBFilename=¦DataDirectory¦aspnetdb.mdf" />
</connectionStrings>
```

Note that if you're using a full version of SQL Server, you should replace the `.\SQLExpress` instance name with the server name (and possible instance name) of your full installation of SQL Server. Next, you need to configure the Membership API from within the `Web.config` file. The following is a sample Membership provider configuration:

```
<membership defaultProvider="SqlProvider"
  userIsOnlineTimeWindow="5">
  <providers>
```

```
  <clear/>
    <add name="SqlProvider"
         type="System.Web.Security.SqlMembershipProvider"
         connectionStringName="LocalSqlServer"
         applicationName="MembershipSample"
         enablePasswordRetrieval="false"
         enablePasswordReset="true"
         requiresQuestionAndAnswer="true"
         requiresUniqueEmail="true"
         passwordFormat="Hashed" />
  </providers>
</membership>
```

When you look at this configuration, the individual attributes of the <add> element correspond directly to some of the static properties of the Membership class.

Before we get into any serious Membership coding, let's take a look at some of the properties and methods of the Membership class, which are shown in Tables 28.1 and 28.2.

TABLE 28.1   System.Web.Security.Membership Properties

Property	Description
ApplicationName	The name of the application.
EnablePasswordReset	Indicates whether the user can request that their password be reset.
EnablePasswordRetrieval	Indicates whether the user can request to have their password given to them. Optionally requires the user to answer a security question.
MaxInvalidPasswordAttempts	The number of times a user can enter an incorrect password.
MinRequiredNonAlphaNumericCharacters	Password strength property indicating the minimum number of non-alphanumeric characters required for a "strong" password.
MinRequiredPasswordLength	Indicates the minimum size (in characters) of a strong password.
PasswordAttemptWindow	The number of minutes between the maximum password failures before the user is locked out.
PasswordStrengthRegular-Expression	A regular expression used to validate passwords. If the expression fails, the supplied password is too weak and will not be accepted.
Provider	Gets a reference to the default Membership provider.
Providers	The collection of available membership providers.
RequiresQuestionAndAnswer	Indicates whether the security question is required in order to retrieve or reset a password.
UserIsOnlineTimeWindow	The number of minutes since user's last activity that will elapse before the user is considered offline.

TABLE 28.2 `System.Web.Security.Membership` Methods

Method	Description
`CreateUser`	Creates a new user in the database specified in the provider configuration
`DeleteUser`	Removes a user from the Membership system
`FindUsersByEmail`	Searches through the user data, returning users with the given email address
`FindUsersByName`	Searches through the user data, returning users whose name matches the input
`GeneratePassword`	Creates a random password that is sufficiently strong to pass the strength validation test
`GetAllUsers`	Retrieve all of the users in the database
`GetNumberOfUsersOnline`	Gets the number of users currently using the application (within the configured inactivity period)
`GetUser`	Retrieves the membership information for a specific user
`GetUserNameByEmail`	Gets the user name for the user whose email address matches the input
`UpdateUser`	Commits changes made to the user to the Membership database
`ValidateUser`	Validates the supplied username and password against the Membership database

The impact of a standardized membership API is extremely significant. This allows for developers of membership-enabled ASP.NET applications to learn one simple API for managing users, and the only difference between one application and the other is the `Web.config` setting for the provider and connection string. I can't stress enough how incredibly useful the new provider model is for ASP.NET developers. Later in this chapter you will see how to create your own Membership provider.

To recap, the following are the steps to take in order to enable Membership in your ASP.NET application:

1. Verify that the Membership schemas are installed in your database. You can do this with the `aspnet_regsql.exe` tool.

2. Add your connection string to the `Web.config` file.

3. Set up the `<membership>` element in `Web.config`.

4. Begin using the Membership API and UI Controls.

Security Through Authorization

In the preceding section you saw that regardless of what means of authentication is used, all users will appear to ASP.NET pages as an instance of `IPrincipal`, which in turn has an `Identity` property of type `IIdentity`. Using these standard interfaces, your code can function properly under any authentication scheme. The next section of this chapter deals with the concept of *authorization*, which is the process by which an authenticated user is permitted or denied access to specific resources. In other words, authentication deals with *who* a user is, and authorization deals with *what* the user can *do*.

Authorization with Roles

As you saw in the preceding section of this chapter, authentication is supported largely by the Membership API and Membership providers like the SQL Membership provider. The Provider model is used throughout ASP.NET to create standard interfaces in commonly used design patterns. Membership is something that virtually every ASP.NET website has to deal with in some form, so the Membership provider was used to standardize how that is done, creating a huge benefit for developers.

Authorization in ASP.NET applications is largely supported by the Role provider. A Role provider is a pluggable provider that gives programmers a standard API for determining users' role membership as well as manipulating the roles to which users belong. If you use the provider model, the code for your role-based application will be identical whether the user role membership is stored in SQL Server, Access, Active Directory, or some other proprietary data store.

Just as with the Membership provider, you need to tell your application which Role provider you're using. The first step is to define a connection string. If you followed along with the preceding example, you already have a connection string in your `Web.config` file. The next step is to define the `<roleManager>` element. An example of a `<roleManager>` element is shown in the following code:

```
<roleManager
  defaultProvider="SqlProvider"
  enabled="true" cacheRolesInCookie="true"
  cookieName=".ASPROLES" cookieTimeout="30"
  cookiePath="/" cookieRequireSSL="false"
  cookieSlidingExpiration="true" cookieProtection="All">
  <providers>
    <add name="SqlProvider"
        type="System.Web.Security.SqlRoleProvider"
        connectionStringName="LocalSqlServer"
        applicationName="RolesDemo"/>
  </providers>
</roleManager>
```

Access to the majority of the functionality available through the Role management provider is available through the `Roles` class. Table 28.3 lists some of the properties of the `Roles` class and Table 28.4 lists some of its methods that you will be using in your own role-based security implementation.

TABLE 28.3 Roles Properties

Property	Description
ApplicationName	The name of the application for which role data is stored.
CacheRolesInCookie	Indicates whether the role information is cached in a cookie. If there is more information than a cookie can hold, only recent Roles are stored in the cookie and the rest are fetched as needed.
CookieName	Gets or sets the name of the cookie used for role caching.
CookiePath	The path of the cookie that was set by CookieName.
CookieProtectionValue	Indicates how the role names are protected within the cookie.
CookieRequireSSL	Indicates whether the role name cache cookie requires SSL in order to be given to the server.
CookieSlidingExpiration	The sliding expiration period for the role name cache cookie.
CookieTimeout	The timeout period for the role name cache cookie.
CreatePersistentCookie	Indicates whether the cookie for storing role name caches is persistent or session-based.
Domain	The domain of the role name cache cookie.
Enabled	Indicates whether role management is enabled for the current application. The default is true.
MaxCachedResults	Indicates the maximum number of roles that can be cached for a user.
Provider	Gets the Role provider for the current application.
Providers	Gets the collection of all Role providers for the current application.

TABLE 28.4 Roles Methods

Method	Description
AddUsersToRole	Adds a list of users to a given role.
AddUsersToRoles	Adds a list of users to a list of roles.
AddUserToRole	Adds a user to a role.
AddUserToRoles	Adds the user to a list of roles.
CreateRole	Creates a new role in the underlying role store.
DeleteCookie	Deletes the role name cache cookie.
DeleteRole	Deletes a role from the data source. Existing users will no longer be a part of the deleted role.
FindUsersInRole	Returns the list of users in a given role that match the supplied username wildcard.
GetAllRoles	Returns the list of all roles configured in the system.
GetRolesForUser	Returns the list of all roles to which the user belongs.
GetUsersInRole	Returns the list of all users belonging to the supplied role.
IsUserInRole	Indicates whether the user (current or supplied) is in the supplied role.
RemoveUserFromRole	Removes the user from the indicated role.
RemoveUserFromRoles	Removes the user from the indicated roles.
RemoveUsersFromRole	Removes the specified list of users from the specified role.
RemoveUsersFromRoles	Removes the list of users from the specified roles.
RoleExists	Indicates whether a role with the supplied name exists in the data store.

28

As you will see in the next section, working with Users and Roles when using the Membership and Role providers has already been wrapped into a few extremely handy server controls that ship with ASP.NET 2.0. To see how the Role system works programmatically, try walking through a quick sample.

The first thing you need to do is create a user. To create a new user, you can use the `Membership.CreateUser` method as shown in the following code:

```
string newPassword = Membership.GeneratePassword(8, 2);
MembershipCreateStatus status;
Membership.CreateUser("kevin", newPassword,
  "kevin@kevin.com", "What is the answer?", "42", true,
  out status);
Response.Write("Attempt to create user 'kevin' with password '" +
  newPassword + "' was " + status.ToString() + "<BR>");
```

When you have a user, you can start playing around with the Role membership system. For example, the following code creates several new Roles and adds the current user to a few of them:

```
Roles.CreateRole("Administrators");
Roles.CreateRole("Validated Users");
Roles.CreateRole("Applicants");

Roles.AddUserToRole("kevin", "Administrators");
Roles.AddUserToRole("kevin", "Validated Users");
Response.Write("User 'kevin' belongs to the following Roles:<BR>");
foreach (string roleName in Roles.GetRolesForUser("kevin"))
{
  Response.Write(
    string.Format("<b><i>{0}</b></i><br>", roleName));
}
```

I can't stress enough how important the impact of the provider model is. The common tasks of building a Membership and Role system —which most of us have built over and over again for many different ASP.NET applications—have been completely abstracted into a provider model. This allows you to create standardized code that works against a standard Membership and Role system, and you will know that your code will work on any other application that is using the Membership and Role providers.

The ASP.NET Security Controls

One of the things that is possible now through the use of the Membership and Role providers is the creation of a standardized set of controls that provide a customizable user interface for many of the common tasks related to securing an ASP.NET application.

With previous versions of ASP.NET, you not only had to create your own Membership and Role system, but you also had to create your own controls for facilitating login, user validation, password entry, display of the currently logged-in user, and much more. This section shows you the new controls that ship with ASP.NET 2.0 that sit on top of the provider model and will *drastically* reduce the amount of code you have to write and the amount of time you have to spend writing redundant security code.

Login

The Login control is a control that facilitates the prompting for a user's name and password. In addition, it can display a checkbox that controls whether or not the validation cookie is persistent. To use it, simply create a login page (usually called login.aspx) for your web application and open up the Toolbox. From the Toolbox, in the Login group, drag the Login control onto your form. This control has a host of configurable options. You can customize the appearance of every aspect, you can specify the URLs for icons for each option, you can choose whether to include a link to create a new user, and you have many more choices. Figure 28.3 shows a login control on a form that is fully functional, attached to the default Membership provider, and took just minutes to create.

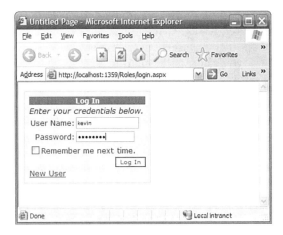

FIGURE 28.3   The Login control in action.

LoginName

The LoginName control is a simple control that displays the name of the currently logged-in user, regardless of the means by which they logged in. To use it, just drag it onto the form in the location where you want the user's name to appear and then change the properties to customize the look and feel as needed. For example:

```
<asp:LoginName ID="LoginName1" runat="server"
FormatString="Welcome to the site, {0}" />
```

This will display the text "Welcome to the site, Kevin" if the user name is "Kevin." If the user is not authenticated, the `LoginName` control will be empty and not render any text.

LoginStatus

The `LoginStatus` control indicates the user's logged-in status by presenting them with a link. If they are logged in, there is a link that will let them log out. If they are logged out, there is a link to let them log in. You can configure the URLs the user will be sent to for each action or use the defaults. As with many of the other controls, all you have to do is just drag this control into the appropriate location from the Toolbox and you're ready to go. Note that if your application doesn't allow anonymous access to the page on which the `LoginStatus` control exists, the user will be redirected to the login page upon clicking the Logout link.

LoginView

Of all of the new controls that ship with ASP.NET 2.0, the `LoginView` control provides what is probably one of the biggest savings in terms of effort and lines coded.

In past versions of ASP.NET, there was no easy way to design a page where certain users saw one piece of content while other users saw a different piece of content based on their Role membership. In addition, it was also cumbersome to render a page where logged-in users saw one view and anonymous users saw a different view. The `LoginView` control makes all of that easy and you can use the smart tags inside the Visual Studio 2005 editor to switch between views or use the HTML source and edit the views manually.

The `LoginView` control allows you to encapsulate several different views using templates and show them to the user depending on their security access and logged-in status:

- `LoggedInTemplate`—This view is displayed to the user when they are logged in.

- `AnonymousTemplate`—This view is shown to an anonymous user.

- `Role Groups`—You can optionally render a different piece of content for the user based on their role membership. If the user is a member of one of the role groups listed, the role group template will be displayed *instead of* the `LoggedInTemplate`.

Take a look at the following code snippet, which uses some of the Roles defined earlier to render different content to different security levels:

```
<asp:LoginStatus ID="LoginStatus1" runat="server" /><Br />

<asp:LoginView ID="LoginView1" runat="server">
  <AnonymousTemplate>
    Greetings Guest User!<br />
  </AnonymousTemplate>
  <RoleGroups>
```

```
    <asp:RoleGroup Roles="Administrators,Validated Users">
      <ContentTemplate>
        <asp:LoginName ID="LoginName1" runat="server"
          FormatString="Welcome to the site, {0}" /><br />
        You have full access to this page!
      </ContentTemplate>
    </asp:RoleGroup>
    <asp:RoleGroup Roles="Applicants">
      <ContentTemplate>
        You are an applicant and, as such,
        do not have full access to this page.
      </ContentTemplate>
    </asp:RoleGroup>
  </RoleGroups>
</asp:LoginView>
```

As you can see, it is extremely easy to take entire sections of your page and render different views conditionally based on security clearance, role membership, and authentication
status. In the preceding sample, members of the Administrators and Validated Users roles
will be given access to secure information, whereas members of the Applicants role will
only receive a limited view of the page. You no longer have to create multiple panels and
write code that conditionally makes some panels visible or invisible in your code-behind.
It is now easy to separate the views of the page, the code is efficient and reusable, and
anyone else reading your code should have no trouble figuring out what information is
bound for which users.

PasswordRecovery

As we all know, users forget their passwords. One of the most annoying tasks of creating a
secure ASP.NET application in version 1.1 was figuring out just how to support users who
had forgotten their passwords. Often a complex series of pages needed to be created to
deal with this situation, taking time and productivity away from coding the actual application and business logic.

With ASP.NET 2.0, you can simply drag the PasswordRecovery control onto a form, and
that form then automatically supports password recovery. If your membership provider
has been configured to require the user to answer a security question, the
PasswordRecovery control will not only prompt the user for that answer, but will validate
the answer. You will need to tell the PasswordRecovery control the information it needs
to construct and send e-mail messages, but other than that it takes very little effort to use.

Figure 28.4 shows this control prompting the user for their security question. If the user
enters the correct answer, their password will be emailed to them based on the email
address stored for that user in the data source.

FIGURE 28.4   The `PasswordRecovery` control in action.

ChangePassword

The `ChangePassword` control allows the end user to change their password. The control handles all of the work of verifying the old password, ensuring that the new password meets the password strength requirements, and storing the new password in the underlying Membership data store. Just like all the other controls in this section, the display is incredibly customizable, allowing you to specify text and icons for every major part of the control. In addition, you can choose to redirect the user to a different page if the password change was successful. To use this control, just drag it onto a form and you're ready to go.

CreateUserWizard

The task of creating a new user is now also made extremely easy. To create a page that will create a new user, simply create an empty form and then drag a `CreateUserWizard` control onto it. By default, this control will prompt the user for their user name, email address, password (including confirmation), and a security question if the Membership provider is configured accordingly.

You can choose to add your own custom steps to the middle of the process, prompting the user for additional information or injecting your own code into the process. One possible use for the additional steps for this wizard is to prompt for additional information or to do things like prompt for confirmation of a EULA or privacy policy. Figures 28.5 and 28.6 show the `CreateUserWizard` control in action.

FIGURE 28.5   The `CreateUserWizard` first page.

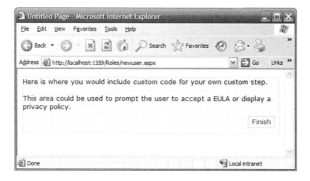

FIGURE 28.6   The `CreateUserWizard` displaying a custom wizard page.

Advanced ASP.NET Security

This section of the chapter is about one of the more advanced topics concerning ASP.NET security: securing sensitive configuration settings. If you are looking for information on general security or general encryption, other chapters in this book are more appropriate, such as Chapter 15, "Cryptography and Data Protection." This section deals only with advanced ASP.NET security topics.

Using Protected Configuration Settings

When you create your ASP.NET application, more often than not, the connection strings used by your data tier end up in the `Web.config` file. This is even more common in

ASP.NET 2.0, where there is a special `connectionStrings` element that is part of every application configuration file, whether it is for ASP.NET or Windows Forms.

The problem with this pattern is that it leaves your valuable connection string information completely exposed. If you are using password-based authentication against the database server, the username and password of a database user are sitting in plain text in the file, along with the name and/or IP address of the database server itself. In some situations you cannot afford to have this information available for viewing, but you still want the ease of use of the .NET configuration API.

With .NET 2.0, there is now a way to encrypt sections of a configuration file using the same technique that is used to encrypt pieces of SOAP envelopes when using secure Web Services. This encryption (and associated decryption) is done with the `aspnet_regiis.exe` tool, which is found in the following directory:

```
[drive]:\[windows directory]\Microsoft.NET\Framework\v[version]
```

Using the `-pe` option, you can encrypt a section of a `Web.config` file hosted as a virtual directory in IIS. Using the `-pef` option, you can encrypt a section of a `Web.config` file in a physical directory if you are not using IIS and you're just using Visual Studio 2005's built-in web server to test your applications.

To start this sample, create a new Web Site called `ProtectedSettings`. Add a `Web.config` file to it and add the following `<connectionStrings>` element:

```
<connectionStrings>
   <add name="SqlServices"
connectionString="Data Source=".\SQLExpress; Integrated Security=SSPI;
➥Initial Catalog=Northwind;" />
</connectionStrings>
```

This is a simple connection string. The problem is that if this connection string contained sensitive machine names and passwords, we would need to be able to encrypt that to prevent prying eyes from seeing it while still allowing the application to access the information.

To encrypt this section, in a file-based web application, you can enter a command similar to the one in the following code:

```
aspnet_regiis -pef "connectionStrings"
"d:\sams\c# unleashed 2005\chapters\28\code\protectedsettings"
-prov "RSAProtectedConfigurationProvider"
```

Obviously you won't want to have the carriage returns in your command-line statement. After running this command, your new `Web.config` file looks like the text shown in Listing 28.1.

LISTING 28.1   A Web.config File Containing an Encrypted Connectionstrings Element

```
<?xml version="1.0"?>
<configuration xmlns="http://schemas.microsoft.com/.NetConfiguration/v2.0">
    <protectedData>
        <protectedDataSections>
            <add name="connectionStrings"
provider="RsaProtectedConfigurationProvider" inheritedByChildren="false"/>
        </protectedDataSections>
    </protectedData>
    <appSettings/>
    <connectionStrings>
        <EncryptedData
Type="http://www.w3.org/2001/04/xmlenc#Element"
➥xmlns="http://www.w3.org/2001/04/xmlenc#">
            <EncryptionMethod
Algorithm="http://www.w3.org/2001/04/xmlenc#tripledes-cbc"/>
            <KeyInfo xmlns="http://www.w3.org/2000/09/xmldsig#">
                <EncryptedKey Recipient=""
xmlns="http://www.w3.org/2001/04/xmlenc#">
                    <EncryptionMethod
Algorithm="http://www.w3.org/2001/04/xmlenc#rsa-1_5"/>
                    <KeyInfo xmlns="http://www.w3.org/2000/09/xmldsig#">
                        <KeyName>Rsa Key</KeyName>
                    </KeyInfo>
                    <CipherData>
                        <CipherValue>...</CipherValue>
                    </CipherData>
                </EncryptedKey>
            </KeyInfo>
            <CipherData>
                <CipherValue>...</CipherValue>
            </CipherData>
        </EncryptedData>
    </connectionStrings>
    <system.web>
        <compilation debug="true"/>
        <authentication mode="Windows"/>
    </system.web>
</configuration>
```

I cut out the actual hexadecimal characters of the encrypted data and replaced them with ellipses (…) in Listing 28.1 to make it easier to read. To prove that even after the encryption process you can still read the configuration file just as before from within the

28

ASP.NET application, create a Web Form with the following lines of code in the code-behind:

```
foreach (ConnectionStringSettings css in ConfigurationManager.ConnectionStrings)
{
  Response.Write(css.Name + ": " + css.ConnectionString + "<BR/>");
}
```

When you debug this page in Visual Studio 2005, you should see that the connection string has been completely decrypted for you and is ready to pass to your ADO.NET data provider of choice.

Keep in mind that the private key used to encrypt the data contained in the web.config file isn't actually written inside that file. This means that if you copy the encrypted web.config from one server to another, the second server will be unable to decrypt the information. For more information on using private key encryption and how to deal with the issues that arise from sharing information among multiple servers, check out Chapter 15.

Summary

This chapter introduced you to some of the incredibly useful new features of ASP.NET that dealt with security. Security consists of basically two things: authentication and authorization. You saw how to authenticate users using the different authentication providers that ship with ASP.NET and how to work with the Membership provider. In addition, you saw how to authorize users by determining and manipulating their role membership with the Role provider. Finally, you saw how to protect sensitive information contained within the Web.config file by selectively encrypting certain sections.

You should now have a firm grasp of how to protect the information in your configuration file and how to identify and authorize users of your web application, regardless of where you are storing your user information. The next chapter will provide you with even more advanced ASP.NET techniques, including how to create your own custom providers.

CHAPTER **29**

Creating Custom ASP.NET Providers

ASP.NET 2.0 is built around the concept of providers. In previous versions of ASP.NET, you could customize various aspects of ASP.NET's behavior, but the methods for doing so and the difficulty of doing so varied greatly from one task to another.

With providers, there is a standard way to customize and replace different aspects of ASP.NET with your own code. With this version of ASP.NET, you can customize how ASP.NET does everything from authentication to authorization and even storing user profiles, session state, and site maps.

This chapter introduces you to the many providers available for your customization. It includes three fully functioning custom providers based on XML files, as well as information on the other providers. This chapter is very code-heavy, so I don't recommend trying to read this chapter in a few quick minutes. The code listings in this chapter tend to be longer than most of the code listings in the rest of the book. As such, to follow along you may want to use the actual code accompanying the book rather than trying to type the samples line-by-line.

The Membership Provider

The Membership provider is what ASP.NET uses to store and validate user credentials. Through a consistent API and object model, developers can create code that works with Membership providers that will continue to function properly, regardless of the underlying credentials database (SQL, XML, Oracle, Access, and so on). In fact, ASP.NET ships with several visual controls that work with the Membership provider, such as the `Login`, `LoginStatus`, and `LoginView` controls. This section shows you the functionality provided by the `MembershipProvider` abstract base class, discusses the creation of a Membership schema, and then shows you the code and installation instructions for a sample custom Membership Provider.

Introduction to the `MembershipProvider` **Base Class**

To create your own custom Membership Provider, you need to create a class that inherits from `MembershipProvider`. Before doing that, you should know what methods and properties are exposed by this class, their purpose, and what functionality you should include in your derivative class. Tables 29.1 and 29.2 illustrate the properties and methods you will be overriding in your custom implementation.

TABLE 29.1   `MembershipProvider` Properties

Property	Description
ApplicationName	The name of the application. Used to differentiate between users with the same name but in two different applications.
EnablePasswordReset	Indicates whether users can request to have their passwords reset.
EnablePasswordRetrieval	Indicates whether users can have their passwords sent to them upon request.
MaxInvalidPassword-Attempts	The number of times a user can fail a validation attempt before being locked out.
MinRequiredNonAlpha-NumericCharacters	The minimum number of non-alphanumeric characters required for a strong password.
MinRequiredPasswordLength	The minimum number of characters required for a strong password.
PasswordAttemptWindow	The time period, in minutes, that can elapse between times when a user exceeds the `MaxInvalidPasswordAttempts` value.
PasswordFormat	The format of passwords: Clear, Hashed, or Encrypted.
PasswordStrengthRegularExpression	The regular expression used for validating new passwords.
RequiresQuestionAndAnswer	Indicates whether or not the user must supply the answer to their secret question to change, reset, or request their password.
RequiresUniqueEmail	Indicates whether the user data store can contain multiple users with the same email address.

TABLE 29.2 `MembershipProvider` Methods

Method	Description
ChangePassword	Changes the user's password.
ChangePasswordQuestion-AndAnswer	Changes the user's password as well as the question/answer pair.
CreateUser	Creates a new user.
DeleteUser	Deletes an existing user.
FindUsersByEmail	Returns a list of users whose email address matches the one supplied.
FindUsersByName	Returns a list of users whose user name matches the supplied name.
GetAllUsers	Returns all of the users in the underlying data store.
GetNumberOfUsersOnline	Returns the number of users in the data store who have been active within the configured timeout period.
GetPassword	Returns a given user's password. This is the data store format, so it may be hashed or encrypted.
GetUser	Returns a `MembershipUser` object based on a supplied unique identifier.
GetUserNameByEmail	Returns the name of the user whose email address matches the one supplied.
ResetPassword	Resets the user's password.
UnlockUser	If a user has been locked out, this method will clear that status.
UpdateUser	Updates changes made to a given user to the underlying data store.
ValidateUser	Validates the supplied credentials.

Implementing a Membership Schema

When working with your own custom Membership Provider, the main thing to keep in mind is that the Membership provider works almost exclusively with the following classes: `MembershipUser` and `MembershipUserCollection`. The `MembershipUserCollection` class is just a simple collection class containing `MembershipUser` instances. The `MembershipUser` class will provide you with your biggest clue as to what information your MemberShip schema needs to define. This class is a fairly straightforward placeholder with a few methods and the following properties:

- `Comment`—Application-specific (string) data related to the user.

- `CreationDate`—The date the user was created.

- `Email`—The user's email address.

- `IsApproved`—Whether the user has been approved or not.

- `IsLockedOut`—The user's locked-out status.

- `IsOnline`—Indicates whether the user is online.

- `LastActivityDate`—The last time the user performed an action related to membership.

- `LastLockoutDate`—The last time the user was locked out.

- `LastLoginDate`—The last time the user logged in.

- `LastPasswordChangedDate`—The last time the user's password was changed.

- `PasswordQuestion`—The user's secret question used for password operations.

- `ProviderName`—The name of the Membership Provider. This always corresponds to the name as defined in `Web.config`.

- `ProviderUserKey`—The provider-specific unique identifier for the given user. The actual key depends on which provider you're using.

- `UserName`—The user's name.

As with all of the schemas for all custom providers in this chapter, I am designing an XML-based custom provider. The quickest and easiest way to get some code up and running that will read and write to and from an XML file while still maintaining a relational view for easy access is to use a typed dataset. The typed dataset, like a regular dataset, can easily persist itself in an XML file. Figure 29.1 shows this typed dataset in the Visual Studio Designer.

FIGURE 29.1   The `MembershipDataSet` typed dataset.

Creating a Custom Membership Provider

Now that you've seen the typed dataset that is going to be the XML file in which the custom Membership information will be stored and you've also seen the list of properties and methods that you need to override in order to create your own Membership provider—you can finally get started on the coding.

To get started, create a C# Class Library called XMLProviders. You can delete the Class1.cs file that comes in the library because you have to rename it anyway. Next, make sure that this Class Library has a reference to System.Configuration. If it doesn't have a reference to System.Web, make sure it has that as well.

The basic premise behind this custom Membership provider is that every call to the provider that normally would have connected to a SQL Server database, an Oracle database, or an Access database is going to instead connect to a single XML file on the hard disk of the server. The code in Listing 29.1 contains the first class in this Class Library: MembershipProvider.cs.

Through the magic of partial classes, some of the private utility methods that make the code in Listing 29.1 possible are contained in a separate file called MembershipProvider_Utils.cs, but are still part of the class. These have been omitted from the listing to save room in the chapter, but the methods are available in the code accompanying the book. The methods in that file include InitializeData, SaveData, LoadKey, HexStringToByteArray, ComparePassword, GetClearPassword, ConvertPasswordForStorage, GetUserByName, CopyUserRowToMembershipUser, CopyMembershipUserToRow, QueryUsers (the workhorse of the entire class), and GetUserByNameAndPassword. Most of the encryption code in the utility file is inspired by some of the sample code for a custom Membership provider in the WinFX SDK published by MSDN. You are free to choose your own encryption methods if you like, but the code in this file and in the WinFX SDK samples is quite secure.

LISTING 29.1   The XML Membership Provider Class

```
using System;
using System.Configuration;
using System.Collections.Generic;
using System.Text;
using System.Web;
using System.Web.Security;
using System.Web.Configuration;
using System.IO;
using System.Data;

namespace SAMS.CustomProviders.XML
{
  public partial class MembershipProvider :
  System.Web.Security.MembershipProvider
{
  private MembershipDataSet memberData;
  private string name;
  private string memberFile;
  private bool enablePasswordReset = false;
  private bool enablePasswordRetrieval = false;
  private string applicationName;
```

LISTING 29.1   Continued

```
  private byte[] decryptionKey;
  private byte[] validationKey;
  private bool requiresQuestionAndAnswer = false;
  private bool requiresUniqueEmail = false;
  private MembershipPasswordFormat passFormat =
    MembershipPasswordFormat.Hashed;
  private int maxInvalidPasswordAttempts;
  private int minRequiredNonAlphanumericCharacters;
  private int minRequiredPasswordLength;
  private int passwordAttemptWindow;
  private string passwordStrengthRegularExpression;

  public override void Initialize(string name,
    System.Collections.Specialized.NameValueCollection config)
  {
    this.name = name;
    if (config["applicationName"] != null)
      applicationName = config["applicationName"];
    if (config["enablePasswordRetrieval"] != null)
      enablePasswordRetrieval = Convert.ToBoolean(
config["enablePasswordRetrieval"]);
    if (config["enablePasswordReset"] != null)
      enablePasswordReset = Convert.ToBoolean(config["enablePasswordReset"]);
    if (config["requiresQuestionAndAnswer"] != null)
      requiresQuestionAndAnswer =
        Convert.ToBoolean(config["requiresQuestionAndAnswer"]);
    if (config["requiresUniqueEmail"] != null)
      requiresUniqueEmail =
        Convert.ToBoolean(config["requiresUniqueEmail"]);
    if (config["maxInvalidPasswordAttempts"] != null)
      maxInvalidPasswordAttempts =
        Convert.ToInt32(config["maxInvalidPasswordAttempts"]);
    if (config["minRequiredNonAlphanumericCharacters"] != null)
      minRequiredNonAlphanumericCharacters =
        Convert.ToInt32(config["minRequiredNonAlphanumericCharacters"]);
    if (config["minRequiredPasswordLength"] != null)
      minRequiredPasswordLength = Convert.ToInt32(
config["minRequiredPasswordLength"]);
    if (config["passwordAttemptWindow"] != null)
      passwordAttemptWindow = Convert.ToInt32(
config["passwordAttemptWindow"]);
    if (config["passwordStrengthRegularExpression"] != null)
```

LISTING 29.1   Continued

```
     passwordStrengthRegularExpression =
config["passwordStrengthRegularExpression"];

  if (config["passwordFormat"] != null)
  {
    switch (config["passwordFormat"].ToLower())
    {
       case "clear":
         passFormat = MembershipPasswordFormat.Clear;
         break;
       case "hashed":
         passFormat = MembershipPasswordFormat.Hashed;
         break;
       case "encrypted":
         passFormat = MembershipPasswordFormat.Encrypted;
         break;
       default:
         throw new ConfigurationErrorsException(
           string.Format("Unknown password format {0}.",
           config["passwordFormat"]));
    }
  }

memberFile =
   ConfigurationManager.ConnectionStrings[
      config["connectionStringName"]].ConnectionString;
InitializeData();
LoadKey(config);
}

/*
 * Various simple get/set properties excluded from code listing
 * for clarity
 */

public override bool ChangePassword(string username, string oldPassword,
string newPassword)
{
  MembershipDataSet.UsersRow user = GetUserByName(username);
  if (user == null)
    throw new InvalidDataException("No such user exists.");
```

29

LISTING 29.1   Continued

```
  if (!ComparePassword(oldPassword, user.Password))
    throw new ApplicationException("Existing password does not match.");

  user.Password = ConvertPasswordForStorage(newPassword);
  user.LastPasswordChangedTimeStamp = DateTime.Now;
  SaveData();
  return true;
}

public override bool ChangePasswordQuestionAndAnswer(string username,
string password,
  string newPasswordQuestion, string newPasswordAnswer)
{
   MembershipDataSet.UsersRow user =
     GetUserByNameAndPassword(username, password);

   user.PasswordQuestion = newPasswordQuestion;
   user.PasswordAnswer = newPasswordAnswer;
   SaveData();
   return true;
}

public override MembershipUser CreateUser(string username, string password,
string email,
    string passwordQuestion, string passwordAnswer, bool isApproved,
    object providerUserKey, out MembershipCreateStatus status)
{
  status = MembershipCreateStatus.UserRejected;

  MembershipDataSet.UsersRow user = GetUserByName(username);
  if (user != null)
  {
    status = MembershipCreateStatus.DuplicateUserName;
    return null;
  }
if (requiresUniqueEmail)
{
  MembershipDataSet.UsersRow[] users =
    (MembershipDataSet.UsersRow[])memberData.Users.Select(
       "Email='" + email + "' AND ApplicationName='" + applicationName + "'");
  if ((users != null) && (users.Length > 0))
  {
    status = MembershipCreateStatus.DuplicateEmail;
```

LISTING 29.1   Continued

```
    return null;
  }
}
Guid newUserId = Guid.NewGuid();
MembershipDataSet.UsersRow newUser = memberData.Users.NewUsersRow();
newUser.UserId = newUserId;
newUser.UserName = username;
newUser.Password = ConvertPasswordForStorage(password);
newUser.Email = email;
newUser.ApplicationName = applicationName;
newUser.PasswordQuestion = passwordQuestion;
newUser.PasswordAnswer = passwordAnswer;
newUser.IsApproved = isApproved;
newUser.LastActivityTimeStamp = DateTime.Now;
newUser.LastLoginTimeStamp = DateTime.Now;
newUser.Comment = string.Empty;
newUser.UserCreationTimeStamp = DateTime.Now;
newUser.LastPasswordChangedTimeStamp = DateTime.Now;
memberData.Users.AddUsersRow(newUser);
SaveData();
MembershipUser newMembershipUser = new MembershipUser(name,
    username, providerUserKey, email, passwordQuestion, string.Empty,
    isApproved, false, DateTime.Now, DateTime.Now, DateTime.Now, DateTime.Now,
    DateTime.MinValue);
status = MembershipCreateStatus.Success;
return newMembershipUser;
}


public override bool DeleteUser(string username, bool deleteAllRelatedData)
{
  MembershipDataSet.UsersRow user = GetUserByName(username);
  if (user == null)
    throw new ApplicationException("No such user exists.");
  user.Delete();
  SaveData();
  return true;
}


public override MembershipUserCollection FindUsersByEmail(string emailToMatch,
    int pageIndex, int pageSize, out int totalRecords)
{
    MembershipUserCollection uc = QueryUsers(
      "Email='" + emailToMatch + "' AND ApplicationName='" + applicationName + "'",
```

29

LISTING 29.1   Continued

```
      pageIndex, pageSize, out totalRecords);
    return uc;
}

public override MembershipUserCollection FindUsersByName(string usernameToMatch,
    int pageIndex, int pageSize, out int totalRecords)
{

    MembershipUserCollection uc = QueryUsers(
      "UserName='" + usernameToMatch + "' AND ApplicationName='" +
applicationName + "'",
    pageIndex, pageSize, out totalRecords);
    return uc;
}

public override MembershipUserCollection GetAllUsers(int pageIndex,
int pageSize, out int
    totalRecords)
{
    MembershipUserCollection uc = QueryUsers(
      "ApplicationName='" + applicationName + "'", pageIndex,
pageSize, out totalRecords);
    return uc;
}

public override int GetNumberOfUsersOnline()
{
    int totalRecords;
    MembershipUserCollection uc = QueryUsers(
      "LastActivityTimeStamp >= " + DateTime.Now.AddMinutes(-1 *
      Membership.UserIsOnlineTimeWindow).ToString(),
      0, 1, out totalRecords);
    return totalRecords;
}

public override string GetPassword(string username,
string answer)
{
    if ((!enablePasswordRetrieval) ||
    (passFormat == MembershipPasswordFormat.Hashed))
      throw new
      ApplicationException(
        "Current configuration settings prevent password retrieval.");
```

LISTING 29.1 Continued

```
  MembershipDataSet.UsersRow user = GetUserByName(username);
  if (user == null)
    throw new ApplicationException("No such user exists.");
  if (requiresQuestionAndAnswer)
  {
    if (user.PasswordAnswer.ToUpper() != answer.ToUpper())
    {
      throw new ApplicationException(
        "Security question answer supplied is incorrect.");
    }
  }
  return GetClearPassword(user.Password);
}

public override MembershipUser GetUser(string username, bool userIsOnline)
{
  MembershipDataSet.UsersRow user = GetUserByName(username);
  MembershipUser mu;
  if (userIsOnline)
  {
    user.LastActivityTimeStamp = DateTime.Now;
    SaveData();
  }
  mu = new MembershipUser(
    name, user.UserName, user.UserId,
    user.Email, user.PasswordQuestion, user.Comment,
    user.IsApproved, false, user.UserCreationTimeStamp, user.LastLoginTimeStamp,
    user.LastActivityTimeStamp, user.LastPasswordChangedTimeStamp,
DateTime.MinValue);
  return mu;
}

public override MembershipUser GetUser(object providerUserKey, bool userIsOnline)
{
  DataRow[] rows =
    memberData.Users.Select(
      "UserId='" + ((Guid)providerUserKey).ToString() + "'");
  if ((rows != null) && (rows.Length > 0))
  {
    MembershipDataSet.UsersRow user = (MembershipDataSet.UsersRow)rows[0];
  MembershipUser mu;
  if (userIsOnline)
  {
```

29

LISTING 29.1   Continued

```
      user.LastActivityTimeStamp = DateTime.Now;
      SaveData();
    }
    mu = new MembershipUser(
          name, user.UserName, user.UserId,
          user.Email, user.PasswordQuestion, user.Comment,
          user.IsApproved, false, user.UserCreationTimeStamp,
user.LastLoginTimeStamp,
          user.LastActivityTimeStamp, user.LastPasswordChangedTimeStamp,
          DateTime.MinValue);
    return mu;
  }
  else
  {
    throw new ApplicationException("Specified user does not exist.");
  }
}

public override string GetUserNameByEmail(string email)
{
  MembershipDataSet.UsersRow user;
  DataRow[] rows =
    memberData.Users.Select(
    "Email='" + email + "'" +
    " AND ApplicationName='" + applicationName + "'");
  if ((rows != null) && (rows.Length > 0))
  {
    user = (MembershipDataSet.UsersRow)rows[0];
    return user.UserName;
  }
  else
    throw new ApplicationException(
"No such user exists with given e-mail address.");
}


public override string ResetPassword(string username, string answer)
{
  if (!enablePasswordReset)
    throw new ApplicationException(
      "Cannot reset password under current provider configuration settings.");
```

LISTING 29.1   Continued

```
  MembershipDataSet.UsersRow user = GetUserByName(username);
  if (user == null)
   throw new ApplicationException("No such user found.");

  string newPw =
    Membership.GeneratePassword(minRequiredPasswordLength,
      minRequiredNonAlphanumericCharacters);
  user.Password = ConvertPasswordForStorage(newPw);
  user.LastPasswordChangedTimeStamp = DateTime.Now;
  SaveData();
  return newPw;
}

public override bool UnlockUser(string userName)
{
  // this provider doesn't lock users out, so just do nothing.
  return true;
}

public override void UpdateUser(MembershipUser user)
{
  DataRow[] rows =
    memberData.Users.Select(
      string.Format("UserId={0}", ((Guid)user.ProviderUserKey).ToString()));
  if ((rows !=null) && (rows.Length > 0))
  {
    MembershipDataSet.UsersRow userRow =
      (MembershipDataSet.UsersRow)rows[0];
    CopyMembershipUserToRow(user, userRow);
    SaveData();
  }
else
    throw new ApplicationException("No such user found to update.");
}

public override bool ValidateUser(string username, string password)
{
  MembershipDataSet.UsersRow user = GetUserByName(username);
  if (user == null)
    return false;

  if (!ComparePassword(password, user.Password))
    return false;
```

LISTING 29.1   Continued

```
  user.LastLoginTimeStamp = DateTime.Now;
  user.LastActivityTimeStamp = DateTime.Now;
  SaveData();

  return true;
}


}
}
```

Configuring and Installing the Membership Provider

After you have created the Membership Provider class and your XMLProviders Class
Library compiles without a hitch, you need to configure your provider for use with an
ASP.NET application. This is done through a Web.config setting called <membership>. You
saw a little bit about this element in Chapter 28 where you learned how to use the
Membership provider. The following is a sample <membership> element element
(Web.config files);Membership provider, configuring> that is configured to use the custom
XML membership provider created in Listing 29.1:

```
<membership defaultProvider="xmlMembership" userIsOnlineTimeWindow="15">
<providers>
<add name="xmlMembership"
    type="SAMS.CustomProviders.XML.MembershipProvider"
    connectionStringName="membershipProvider"
    enablePasswordRetrieval="false"
    enablePasswordReset="true"
    requireQuestionAndAnswer="true"
    applicationName="CustomProviderDemo"
    requiresUniqueEmail="false"
    passwordFormat="Hashed"
    minRequiredNonAlphanumericCharacters="2"
    minRequiredPasswordLength="2"
    maxInvalidPasswordAttempts="3"
    passwordAttemptWindow="30"
    passwordStrengthRegularExpression=""
    description="Stores and Retrieves membership data from an XML file"
    decryptionKey="34a266624e967adf6e92937c5341e931e73f25fef798ba75"
    validationKey="34a31f547c659b6e35edc029dd3abbe42f8936
    ➥cb2b24fff3e1bef13be429505b3f5becb5702e15bc7b98cd6fd2b7702
    ➥e46ff63fdc9ea8979f6508c82638b129a" />
</providers>
</membership>
```

The first important attribute is the `type` attribute. This tells ASP.NET where to find the class that derives from `MembershipProvider`, as that class will be instantiated the first time any Membership operations are performed in the application. In the case of my sample provider, the type is `SAMS.CustomProviders.XML.MembershipProvider`. In order for this to work, the web application needs to have a copy of the Assembly in which that type is defined in its `bin` directory. The easy way to do this is just to make sure that the web application references the `XMLProviders` project. If you are deploying your providers without regard to application, you can install them in the Global Assembly Cache (GAC), in which case you would need to supply a fully qualified type name including the type name, Assembly name, version number, and culture identifier for the `type` attribute.

The Role Provider

The Role provider is used for determining user authorization. It performs a fairly simple function: maintain which users belong to which Roles. One really key thing to remember is that the Role provider can function independently of (and even without) the Membership provider. This means that the user names used in conjunction with the Role provider *don't have to match* the user names used for Membership. Obviously it is in your best interest to allow them to match, but it is helpful for the custom `RoleProvider` programmer to know that you don't need access to the Membership database to create a Role provider. This section of the chapter introduces you to the `RoleProvider` abstract base class, shows you how to create your own Role schema, and then shows you how to create your own custom `RoleProvider`.

Introduction to the `RoleProvider` Base Class

The `RoleProvider` base class is a fairly straightforward class. By inheriting from that class and overriding its implementation with your own, you can allow the user role membership data to be stored anywhere you like. In the example discussed in this section, I'm using an XML file on the web server. Tables 29.3 and 29.4 give you a list of the properties and methods of the `RoleProvider` class that you will be overriding to create your own implementation.

TABLE 29.3   RoleProvider Properties

Property	Description
ApplicationName	The only required property for a RoleProvider—used to distinguish between multiple applications managed by the same provider

TABLE 29.4   RoleProvider Methods

Method	Description
AddUsersToRoles	Adds a list of users to a list of Roles
CreateRole	Creates a new Role in the data store
DeleteRole	Deletes a Role in the data store

29

TABLE 29.4   Continued

Method	Description
FindUsersInRole	Returns an array of user names (Strings) where the user name matches the one supplied within the supplied Role name
GetAllRoles	Gets a list of all Roles in the data store
GetRolesForUser	Gets a list of all the Roles to which a given user belongs
IsUserInRole	Indicates whether the user (either current or supplied by parameter) is in a given role
RemoveUsersFromRoles	Removes a list of users from a list of roles
RoleExists	Indicates whether a given role name exists in the underlying data store

Implementing a Role Schema

As with the Membership schema, the data you need to maintain in your custom provider implementation is dictated by the methods exposed by the provider, and the classes utilized by that provider. The Role provider has fewer rules that need to be followed than the Membership provider, so there is more flexibility with how you store the underlying data. For example, the Membership provider made extensive use of the MembershipUser and MembershipUserCollection classes, and as such the properties of those classes dictated the schema of the stored data.

The RoleProvider interface consists mainly of passing strings and arrays of strings, and returning strings, arrays of strings, and Boolean values indicating membership in Roles. This makes the typed dataset fairly straightforward. You'll need a table to store the list of Roles, and then you'll need a table to store the list of users that belong to each role. Because all Role membership checking is done on the user's name or ID (the string UserName property in the Membership provider, also the UserName property used by the IPrincipal interface), you only need to store the user name in the detail table, as illustrated in Figure 29.2.

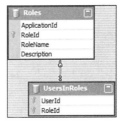

FIGURE 29.2   The RoleDataSet typed dataset.

Creating a Custom Role Provider

The code for the RoleProvider is fairly straightforward. After you add the RoleDataSet to the XMLProviders project, you can then add the RoleProvider class shown in Listing 29.2. The main thing to keep in mind when looking at this class is that the ultimate reason for the Role provider is to simply determine the roles to which each user belongs, and nothing more. Often the hardest part about creating custom providers is avoiding the pitfall of trying to make them do more work than they are responsible for.

LISTING 29.2   The XML RoleProvider Class

```
using System;
using System.Data;
using System.IO;
using System.Configuration;
using System.Web;
using System.Collections.Generic;
using System.Text;
using System.Web.Security;

namespace SAMS.CustomProviders.XML
{
class RoleProvider : System.Web.Security.RoleProvider
{
  private string name;
  private string roleFile;
  private string applicationName;
  private RoleDataSet roleData;

  public override string Description
  {
    get { return "XML File-Based ASP.NET 2.0 Role Provider"; }
  }

  private void InitializeData()
  {
    roleData = new RoleDataSet();
    if (File.Exists(roleFile))
      roleData.ReadXml(roleFile);
  }

  private void SaveData()
  {
    roleData.AcceptChanges();
    roleData.WriteXml(roleFile);
  }

public override void Initialize(string name,
  System.Collections.Specialized.NameValueCollection config)
{
```

LISTING 29.2   Continued

```
  try
  {
    this.name = name;
    ApplicationName = config["applicationName"];
    roleFile =
     ConfigurationManager.ConnectionStrings[
        config["connectionStringName"]].ConnectionString;
    InitializeData();
  }
  catch (Exception e)
  {
    System.Diagnostics.Debug.WriteLine(e.ToString());
  }
}

public override string Name
{
get { return name; }
}

public override void AddUsersToRoles(string[] usernames, string[] roleNames)
{
  foreach (string userName in usernames)
  {
    foreach (string roleName in roleNames) {
        int roleId = ((RoleDataSet.RolesRow)
          roleData.Roles.Select("RoleName='" + roleName + "'")[0]).RoleId;
        RoleDataSet.UsersInRolesRow newRow =
          roleData.UsersInRoles.NewUsersInRolesRow();
        newRow.UserId = userName;
        newRow.RoleId = roleId;
        roleData.UsersInRoles.AddUsersInRolesRow(newRow);
        SaveData();
  }
 }
 }

public override string ApplicationName
{
 get { return applicationName; }
 set
 {
```

LISTING 29.2   Continued

```
    applicationName = value;
  }
}

public override void CreateRole(string roleName)
{
  RoleDataSet.RolesRow newRole = roleData.Roles.NewRolesRow();
  newRole.RoleName = roleName;
  newRole.ApplicationId = applicationName;
  newRole.Description = roleName;
  roleData.Roles.AddRolesRow(newRole);
  roleData.AcceptChanges();
  SaveData();
}

public override bool DeleteRole(string roleName, bool throwOnPopulatedRole)
{
  RoleDataSet.RolesRow delRole = (RoleDataSet.RolesRow)
    roleData.Roles.Select("RoleName='" + roleName + "'")[0];
  DataRow[] users = roleData.UsersInRoles.Select("RoleId=" + delRole.RoleId);
  if ((users.Length > 0) && (throwOnPopulatedRole))
    throw new
    InvalidOperationException("Cannot delete a role to which users are assigned.");
  else
  {
    foreach (DataRow userInRole in users)
    {
        userInRole.Delete();
    }
    delRole.Delete();
    roleData.AcceptChanges();
    SaveData();
    return true;
  }
}

public override string[] FindUsersInRole(string roleName, string usernameToMatch)
{
  List<string> al = new List<string>();
  RoleDataSet.UsersInRolesRow[] users =
  (RoleDataSet.UsersInRolesRow[])roleData.Roles.Select(
"RoleName = '" + roleName + "'");
  foreach (RoleDataSet.UsersInRolesRow user in users)
  {
```

29

LISTING 29.2   Continued

```
    if (user.UserId.ToUpper() == usernameToMatch.ToUpper())
      al.Add(user.UserId);
  }
  return al.ToArray();
}

public override string[] GetAllRoles()
{
  List<string> al = new List<string>();
  foreach (RoleDataSet.RolesRow role in
    (RoleDataSet.RolesRow[])
      roleData.Roles.Select("ApplicationId='" + applicationName + "'"))
  {
    al.Add(role.RoleName);
  }
  return al.ToArray();
}

public override string[] GetRolesForUser(string username)
{
  List<int> roleIds = new List<int>();
  RoleDataSet.UsersInRolesRow[] users =
    (RoleDataSet.UsersInRolesRow[])
      roleData.UsersInRoles.Select("UserId = '" + username + "'");
  foreach (RoleDataSet.UsersInRolesRow user in users)
  roleIds.Add(user.RoleId);
  List<string> roleNames = new List<string>();
  foreach (int roleId in roleIds)
  {
    RoleDataSet.RolesRow theRow =
     (RoleDataSet.RolesRow)roleData.Roles.Select("RoleId=" + roleId)[0];
    if (theRow.ApplicationId.ToUpper() == applicationName.ToUpper())
      roleNames.Add(theRow.RoleName);
  }
  return roleNames.ToArray();
}

public override string[] GetUsersInRole(string roleName)
{
  List<string> users = new List<string>();
  int roleId = GetRoleId(roleName);
  foreach (RoleDataSet.UsersInRolesRow user in
    (RoleDataSet.UsersInRolesRow[])
```

LISTING 29.2   Continued

```
      roleData.UsersInRoles.Select("RoleId=" + roleId.ToString()))
  {
    users.Add(user.UserId);
  }
  return users.ToArray();
}


private int GetRoleId(string roleName)
{
  DataRow[] rows =
    roleData.Roles.Select(
      "RoleName='" + roleName + "' AND ApplicationId='" + applicationName + "'");
  if (rows == null)
    return -1;
  if (rows.Length == 0)
    return -1;
  return ((RoleDataSet.RolesRow)rows[0]).RoleId;
}


public override bool IsUserInRole(string username, string roleName)
{
  int roleId = GetRoleId(roleName);
  RoleDataSet.UsersInRolesRow[] users =
    (RoleDataSet.UsersInRolesRow[])
      roleData.UsersInRoles.Select("RoleId=" + roleId.ToString());
  return (users.Length > 0);
}


public override void RemoveUsersFromRoles(string[] usernames, string[] roleNames)
{
  foreach (string userId in usernames)
  {
    foreach (string roleName in roleNames)
    {
     int roleId = GetRoleId(roleName);
     RoleDataSet.UsersInRolesRow userRoleRow =
       ((RoleDataSet.UsersInRolesRow[])
           roleData.UsersInRoles.Select("UserId='" + userId +
           "' AND RoleId=" + roleId.ToString()))[0];
     userRoleRow.Delete();
    }
  }
```

29

LISTING 29.2   Continued

```
  SaveData();
}

public override bool RoleExists(string roleName)
{
  return (GetRoleId(roleName) != -1);
}
}
}
```

Configuring and Installing the Role Provider

The configuration and installation of the Role provider follows the same rules as the Membership provider. If you want your provider to be shared among more than one application on a server, you should probably install the provider into the GAC so that you don't have to have multiple copies of your provider scattered throughout a server.

To configure the Role provider, you use the `<roleManager>` `Web.config` element that you were introduced to in Chapter 28. A sample `<roleManager>` element designed to work with the code in this chapter is shown in the following code:

```
<roleManager defaultProvider="xmlRoles" enabled="true" cacheRolesInCookie="true"
    cookieName=".ASPROLES"
cookieTimeout="30" cookiePath="/" cookieRequireSSL="false"
    cookieSlidingExpiration="true" cookieProtection="All">
    <providers>
      <add name="xmlRoles"
        type="SAMS.CustomProviders.XML.RoleProvider"
        connectionStringName="roleProvider"
        applicationName="CustomProviderDemo" />
</providers>
</roleManager>
```

The `connectionStringName` attribute points to the following connection string stored in the `<connectionStrings>` element, which is just the physical location of the XML file:

```
<add name="roleProvider"
    connectionString="D:\SAMS\C# Unleashed 2005\Chapters\29\Code\Data\Roles.XML"/>
```

The ProfileProvider

The ProfileProvider is probably one of the most versatile providers in ASP.NET. It doesn't store user credentials or user role membership. Instead, this provider is responsible for storing arbitrary properties about the users themselves. As you have seen in previous chapters, when you define user profile properties in the Web.config file, you can use them in a strongly typed fashion at compile time in the Visual Studio environment using the Profile static class within a Web Form.

Introduction to the ProfileProvider Base Class

The ProfileProvider abstract base class provides methods that deal with locating user profiles, reading and writing properties on those profiles, and modifying, creating, and deleting those profiles. Table 29.5 contains the methods that you will be overriding in your custom implementation of the ProfileProvider class.

TABLE 29.5   ProfileProvider Methods

Method	Description
DeleteInactiveProfiles	Deletes all user profile data for profiles where the last activity date was older than the indicated date
DeleteProfiles	Deletes a list of user profiles as indicated by the user profiles in the supplied ProfileInfoCollection object
FindInactiveProfilesByUserName	Finds a list of inactive users where the supplied user name matches
FindProfilesByUserName	Finds a list of users where the supplied user name matches (regardless of whether the profile is inactive)
GetAllInactiveProfiles	Gets all profiles where the last activity date was older than the indicated date
GetAllProfiles	Gets all profiles in the data store
GetNumberOfInactiveProfiles	Gets the number of inactive profiles contained in the store

Implementing a Profile Schema

A quick examination of the ProfileProvider abstract base class reveals that a lot of the interface takes place with the ProfileInfo and ProfileInfoCollection classes. The ProfileInfo class has very few properties and only tracks basic information such as UserName, IsAnonymous, LastActivityDate, LastUpdatedDate, and Size. More important than storing the user name is the storage of profile properties. In most Profile providers, developers can create arbitrary properties.

If you are going to create a custom provider, you will need to be able to store arbitrary data associated with a given user. To do this, I used a parent-child table where the child table contained rows of name-value pairs associated with a specific user. Figure 29.3 shows the typed dataset ProfileDataSet. The only really important thing of note in the schema shown in Figure 29.3 is that the UniqueId column is a System.Guid and it is generated programmatically each time a new row is created.

29

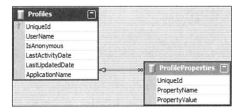

FIGURE 29.3   The `ProfileDataSet` typed dataset.

Creating a Custom Profile Provider

As with the previous providers, I have split the Provider implementation and the private utility methods into two files so that the code is easy to read and follow. The utility methods that are not included in Listing 29.3 are: `InitializeData`, `SaveData`, `AppendAuthOptionToQuery`, `GetProfileByUserName`, `CreateUserProfile`, `QueryProfiles`, `ProfileRowsToProfileInfoCollection`, `ProfilesRowToProfileInfo`, `GetProfileProperty`, and `TouchActivityDates`.

LISTING 29.3   The XML Profile Provider

```
using System;
using System.Xml;
using System.Configuration;
using System.Web;
using System.Web.Profile;
using System.Web.Security;
using System.Collections.Generic;
using System.Text;
using System.Collections;

namespace SAMS.CustomProviders.XML
{
public partial class ProfileProvider : System.Web.Profile.ProfileProvider
{
  private string profileFile = string.Empty;
  private string name = string.Empty;
  private ProfileDataSet profileData = null;
  private string applicationName = string.Empty;

public override void Initialize(string name,
    System.Collections.Specialized.NameValueCollection config)
{
  this.name = name;
  if (config["connectionStringName"] != null)
    profileFile =
```

LISTING 29.3   Continued

```
    ConfigurationManager.ConnectionStrings[
      config["connectionStringName"]].ConnectionString;
  else
    profileFile = @"D:\SAMS\C# Unleashed 2005\Chapters\29\Code\Data\Profiles.XML";
  if (config["applicationName"] != null)
    applicationName = config["applicationName"];
  else
    applicationName = HttpContext.Current.Request.ApplicationPath;
  InitializeData();
}

public override string Description
{
  get { return "XML Profile Provider"; }
}

public override string Name
{
  get { return name; }
}

public override int DeleteInactiveProfiles(ProfileAuthenticationOption
    authenticationOption, DateTime userInactiveSinceDate)
{
  string query = string.Format(
    "ApplicationName='{0}' AND LastActivityDate <= '{1}'",
    applicationName, userInactiveSinceDate);

  int totalRecords;
  ProfileDataSet.ProfilesRow[] profiles = QueryProfiles(query,
    authenticationOption, 0, Int32.MaxValue, out totalRecords);
  foreach (ProfileDataSet.ProfilesRow profile in profiles)
  {
    profile.Delete();
  }
  SaveData();
  return totalRecords;
}

public override int DeleteProfiles(string[] usernames)
{
  int x = 0;
  foreach (string user in usernames)
  {
```

LISTING 29.3   Continued

```
    ProfileDataSet.ProfilesRow profile = GetProfileByUserName(user);
    profile.Delete();
    x++;
  }
  SaveData();
  return x;
}

public override int DeleteProfiles(ProfileInfoCollection profiles)
{
  int x = 0;
  foreach (ProfileInfo pi in profiles)
  {
    ProfileDataSet.ProfilesRow profile = GetProfileByUserName(pi.UserName);
    profile.Delete();
    x++;
  }
  SaveData();
  return x;
}

public override ProfileInfoCollection
FindInactiveProfilesByUserName(ProfileAuthenticationOption authenticationOption,
  string usernameToMatch,
DateTime userInactiveSinceDate, int pageIndex, int pageSize,
  out int totalRecords)
{
  string query = string.Format(
    "UserName='{0}' AND ApplicationName='{1}' AND LastActivityDate <= '{1}'",
    usernameToMatch, applicationName, userInactiveSinceDate);

  ProfileDataSet.ProfilesRow[] profiles = QueryProfiles(
    query, authenticationOption, pageIndex, pageSize, out totalRecords);

  return ProfileRowsToProfileInfoCollection(profiles);
}

public override ProfileInfoCollection FindProfilesByUserName(
ProfileAuthenticationOption
  authenticationOption, string usernameToMatch, int pageIndex,
  int pageSize, out int totalRecords)
{
  string query = string.Format(
    "UserName='{0}' AND ApplicationName='{1}'",
```

LISTING 29.3   Continued

```
    usernameToMatch, applicationName);
  ProfileDataSet.ProfilesRow[] profiles = QueryProfiles(
    query, authenticationOption, pageIndex, pageSize, out totalRecords);
  return ProfileRowsToProfileInfoCollection(profiles);
}

public override ProfileInfoCollection
GetAllInactiveProfiles(ProfileAuthenticationOption
  authenticationOption, DateTime userInactiveSinceDate,
  int pageIndex, int pageSize, out int totalRecords)
{
  string query = string.Format(
    "LastActivityDate <= '{0}' AND ApplicationName='{1}'", userInactiveSinceDate,
    applicationName);
  ProfileDataSet.ProfilesRow[] profiles = QueryProfiles(
    query, authenticationOption, pageIndex, pageSize, out totalRecords);
  return ProfileRowsToProfileInfoCollection(profiles);
}

public override ProfileInfoCollection GetAllProfiles(ProfileAuthenticationOption
    authenticationOption, int pageIndex, int pageSize, out int totalRecords)
{
  string query = string.Format(
    "ApplicationName='{0}'", applicationName);
  ProfileDataSet.ProfilesRow[] profiles = QueryProfiles(
    query, authenticationOption, pageIndex, pageSize, out totalRecords);
  return ProfileRowsToProfileInfoCollection(profiles);
}

public override int GetNumberOfInactiveProfiles(ProfileAuthenticationOption
  authenticationOption, DateTime userInactiveSinceDate)
{
  int totalRecords;
  ProfileInfoCollection pic = GetAllInactiveProfiles(authenticationOption,
    userInactiveSinceDate, 0, Int32.MaxValue, out totalRecords);
  return totalRecords;
}

public override string ApplicationName
{
get
{
  return applicationName;
}
```

29

LISTING 29.3   Continued

```
set
{
  applicationName = value;
}
}

public override System.Configuration.SettingsPropertyValueCollection
GetPropertyValues(
    System.Configuration.SettingsContext context,
    System.Configuration.SettingsPropertyCollection collection)
{
  string userName = (string)context["UserName"];
  bool isAuthenticated = (bool)context["IsAuthenticated"];

  ProfileDataSet.ProfilesRow user = GetProfileByUserName(userName);
  if (user == null)
    user = CreateUserProfile(userName, isAuthenticated);

  SettingsPropertyValueCollection svc = new SettingsPropertyValueCollection();
  foreach (SettingsProperty prop in collection)
  {
    SettingsPropertyValue propValue = new SettingsPropertyValue(prop);
    ProfileDataSet.ProfilePropertiesRow propRow = GetProfileProperty(
      user, prop.Name);
    if (propRow != null)
    {
      propValue.PropertyValue = propRow["PropertyValue"];
    }
    svc.Add(propValue);
  }
  TouchActivityDates(user, true);
  return svc;
}

public override void SetPropertyValues(
System.Configuration.SettingsContext context,
    System.Configuration.SettingsPropertyValueCollection collection)
{
  string userName = (string)context["UserName"];
  bool isAuthenticated = (bool)context["IsAuthenticated"];
```

LISTING 29.3   Continued

```
ProfileDataSet.ProfilesRow user = GetProfileByUserName(userName);
if (user == null)
  user = CreateUserProfile(userName, isAuthenticated);

foreach (SettingsPropertyValue propValue in collection)
{
  ProfileDataSet.ProfilePropertiesRow propRow =
    GetProfileProperty(user, propValue.Name);
  if (propRow != null)
    propRow["PropertyValue"] = propValue.PropertyValue;
  else
  {
    propRow = profileData.ProfileProperties.NewProfilePropertiesRow();
    propRow["UniqueId"] = user.UniqueId;
    propRow["PropertyValue"] = propValue.PropertyValue;
    propRow["PropertyName"] = propValue.Name;
    profileData.ProfileProperties.AddProfilePropertiesRow(propRow);
  }
  }
  SaveData();
  TouchActivityDates(user, false);
}
}
}
```

Configuring and Installing the Profile Provider

The Profile provider also has its own Web.config entry. As with the other providers, if you plan on sharing the provider among multiple applications on the same server, you should install the provider into the Global Assembly Cache. Otherwise, you are fine just ensuring that the provider's Assembly is in your web application's bin directory.

The first thing you need is a connection string in the <connectionStrings> Web.config element:

```
<add name="profileProvider"
    connectionString=

"D:\SAMS\C# Unleashed 2005\Chapters\29\Code\Data\Profiles.XML"/>
```

Next you can add the <profile> element to the Web.config file:

```
<profile defaultProvider="xmlProfile" enabled="true">
<providers>
<add name="xmlProfile"
```

```
type="SAMS.CustomProviders.XML.ProfileProvider"
applicationName="CustomProviderDemo"
connectionStringName="profileProvider" />
</providers>
<properties><add name="ShoeSize"
type="System.Int32" allowAnonymous="false" />
<add name="FavoriteColor"
type="System.String" allowAnonymous="false" />
</properties>
</profile>
```

Additional Providers

This section provides you with a brief introduction to some of the other providers that you can customize. Given what you have learned already about customizing the `ProfileProvider`, the `MembershipProvider`, and the `RoleProvider`, you should have no trouble using that knowledge to create your own custom providers for each of the items discussed in the rest of this section.

Introduction to the `SessionState` Provider

The session state provider is used to maintain session state for a web application. The session state is essentially a collection of name-value pairs that are associated with a session identifier. This session identifier is stored as a cookie (or embedded in the URL depending on session state configuration) on the client's machine. Each time a user requests a page, the session state for that user is accessible by means of the user's session identifier.

To create your own session state provider, you must override the `SessionStateProviderBase` class in the `System.Web.SessionState` namespace. The list of methods for that class is shown in Table 29.6.

TABLE 29.6   `SessionStateStoreProviderBase` Methods

Method	Description
CreateNewStoreData	Creates a new `SessionStateStoreData` instance for use with a web request
CreateUninitializedItem	Creates a new session state item to the data store
EndRequest	Invoked at the end of a request
GetItem	Obtains a session state item based on an ID and an `HttpContext` instance
GetItemExclusive	Gets an item and locks access to that item exclusively to the caller
InitializeRequest	Initializes a web request
ReleaseItemExclusive	Releases the exclusivity lock on a session state item obtained through `GetItemExclusive`
RemoveItem	Removes a state item name-value pair

TABLE 29.6   Continued

Method	Description
`ResetItemTimeout`	Updates the expiration date of a session item
`SetAndReleaseItemExclusive`	Updates the session state item and clears the exclusive lock on the item
`SetItemExpireCallback`	Sets the delegate to be invoked when an item expires

Introduction to the `SiteMap` Provider

The `SiteMap` Provider is responsible for maintaining a site hierarchy. Essentially it is responsible for storing a tree structure, where each node in the tree has a description of a page as well as a link to that page. Site Map Providers make it possible to create "breadcrumb"-style controls that illustrate where a user is within a site hierarchy.

To create your own Site Map Provider, you need to create a class that inherits from `System.Web.SiteMapProvider`. The good thing about this particular provider is that not only does ASP.NET ship with an XML version, but the XML version is the default. Microsoft has provided an `XmlSiteMapProvider` that allows you to define your site map within an XML file.

However, if you are already storing your site map in a database such as SQL Server or Oracle in your own schema, you might want to create your own provider. Table 29.7 illustrates the methods of the `SiteMapProvider` class that you must override in order to implement your own custom Site Map Provider.

TABLE 29.7   `SiteMapProvider` Methods

Method	Description
`FindSiteMapNode`	Retrieves a `SiteMapNode` object based on a URL
`FindSiteMapNodeFromKey`	Finds a site map node based on the supplied key
`GetChildNodes`	Gets the child site map nodes of a given site map node
`GetCurrentNodeAndHint-AncestorNodes`	Retrieves the current site map node as well as a set number of ancestors (-1 for all)
`GetCurrentNodeAndHint-NeighborhoodNodes`	Retrieves the current site map node as well as neighborhood (under same parent) nodes
`GetParentNode`	Retrieves the parent node
`GetParentNodeRelativeToCurrent-NodeAndHintDownFromParent`	Optimized fetch for an ancestor node and the ancestor's descended nodes
`GetParentNodeRelativeToNodeAnd-HintDownFromParent`	Same as the preceding, but relative node is supplied rather than implied as "current"
`HintAncestorNodes`	Retrieves ancestor nodes of a given node
`HintNeighborhoodNodes`	Retrieves peer (same parent) nodes of a given node
`Initialize`	Initializes the `SiteMapProvider`
`IsAccessibleToUser`	Indicates whether the indicated site map node can be displayed to the user in the current context

29

The basic idea behind the site map provider is that the code is maintaining a tree structure with page-related information. You can come up with a fairly simple schema to manage this. The caveat here is that often many tree structures in relational databases perform slowly, so when implementing your own Site Map provider make sure to take advantage of the Hint*xxxx* methods and provide very fast (and cacheable) results.

Summary

As I explained at the beginning of this chapter, this was an extremely code-heavy chapter. Even though one of the most significant additions to ASP.NET 2.0 is the fact that virtually everything is faster, easier, and achievable with less code—you can still roll up your sleeves and get down in it.

This chapter showed you that, with a little bit of effort in the creation of your own custom providers, you can do some up-front work that will allow you to create sites that will seamlessly plug into your own authentication, membership, roles and profile stores, regardless of where they're stored or how they're stored. ASP.NET's core utilizes the provider model for everything, so as long as your code inherits from one of the base provider classes, your code will cooperate fully with ASP.NET. You saw custom XML-based implementations of the `ProfileProvider` class, the `RoleProvider` class, and the `MembershipProvider` class as well as introductions to the `SiteMapProvider` class and the `SessionStateStoreProviderBase` class.

When creating custom providers, you can find the list of requirements for a given provider in its associated interface. For example, `IMembershipProvider` tells you everything you need to know in order to create your own membership provider.

You also saw a good example of using partial classes. The implementations of the providers were split into multiple files: one file containing the strict interface implementation and the other file containing private utility methods. This is done to make the code easier to read and maintain.

After completing this chapter, you should have a thorough knowledge of how all of the various ASP.NET 2.0 providers work as well as how to implement your own. You should also be able to determine when you need to create your own and when you can rely on the existing providers that come with ASP.NET 2.0.

CHAPTER **30**

Developing ASP.NET Controls

ASP.NET radically increases the productivity of web developers by running atop the .NET Framework and providing a large suite of powerful controls that do everything from accept simple input to display complex, interactive, data-bound grids.

Occasionally you may run into a situation where you have a need for a reusable control that isn't already implemented by the base set of controls that ship with ASP.NET. In that case, you can use C#, object-oriented programming, and existing ASP.NET classes to create your own custom controls to extend ASP.NET's already powerful feature set. This chapter shows you how to create everything from simple user controls to complex, nested server controls that maintain their own view state.

Building User Controls

User controls are essentially miniature versions of a standard ASP.NET Web Form. They have markup source that is converted into a partial class as well as underlying code that combines with the markup code to produce an executable unit of user interface very similar to a Web Form.

If you want to create a control that you can reuse multiple times throughout your application and you want to do it quickly, creating a user control is probably your best option. The only real downside to user controls is that they don't lend themselves to being reused among multiple projects. If you are creating a library of reusable controls that will be used by multiple applications or even by your own customers, you would be better served by using server controls (discussed in the next section).

To start with, create the most basic control: a control that displays "Hello World". Create a new ASP.NET application called ControlsDemo. Right-click the project and select Add New Item. Select Web User Control and call that control HelloWorld.ascx.

Set the source view of the page to the following code:

```
<%@ Control Language="C#" AutoEventWireup="true"
CodeFile="HelloWorld.ascx.cs" Inherits="HelloWorld" %>
Hello World
```

It's a pretty simple control. The Control tag looks very similar to the Page tag that you find on standard pages. You can configure various options such as content caching using this tag.

To use this control on a page, go to the design view of any page in your web application and simply drag HelloWorld.ascx from the Solution Explorer onto the design surface. Unlike previous versions of ASP.NET, version 2.0 does not require you to manually register the control, as dragging the file into the designer autogenerates the following control registration at the top of the file:

```
<%@ Register Src="HelloWorld.ascx" TagName="HelloWorld" TagPrefix="uc1" %>
```

> **NOTE**
>
> This only works when dragging onto the design surface. If you drag a control from the Solution Explorer into an HTML view, you will end up with a URL pointing to that file, and not the registered control reference.

You can change the tag's prefix if you like, but the control will appear on the .aspx page using the uc# prefix by default, as shown in the following line:

```
<uc1:HelloWorld ID="HelloWorld1" runat="server" />
```

When ASP.NET encounters a user control tag like the preceding one when rendering a page, it stops what it's doing and renders the user control in place. This operation is a nested operation, so if that user control contains further user controls, those will be rendered in their appropriate relative positions. When you run the page with your "Hello World" control on it, you get a fairly predictable output that is shown in Figure 30.1.

Obviously you're going to want to create more than just a control that displays simple text. In this next sample, you'll create a user control that combines several child controls to create a reusable piece of UI functionality.

Start by adding a new web user control to the project called LabelledTextBox.ascx. Drag a Label and a TextBox into this control. The .ascx source should look something like this:

```
<%@ Control Language="C#" AutoEventWireup="true"
CodeFile="LabelledTextBox.ascx.cs" Inherits="LabelledTextBox" %>
<asp:Label ID="lblText" runat="server" /> 
<asp:TextBox ID="txtText" runat="server" />
```

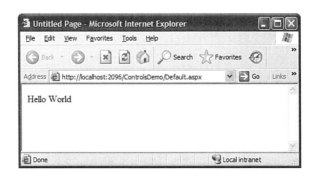

FIGURE 30.1 A simple user control.

Because the user control is just another class, you can expose properties on that class to control its behavior. For example, you can create properties on the user control that can be used to set properties on the Label and TextBox, as shown in the source for LabelledTextBox.ascx.cs:

```
using System;
using System.Data;
using System.Configuration;
using System.Collections;
using System.Web;
using System.Web.Security;
using System.Web.UI;
using System.Web.UI.WebControls;
using System.Web.UI.WebControls.WebParts;
using System.Web.UI.HtmlControls;

public partial class LabelledTextBox : System.Web.UI.UserControl
{
protected void Page_Load(object sender, EventArgs e)
{

}

public string LabelText
{
```

30

```
    get { return lblText.Text; }
    set { lblText.Text = value; }
}

public string Text
{
    get { return txtText.Text; }
    set { txtText.Text = value; }
}

}
```

Properties on a custom ASP.NET control can be set programmatically or they can be set declaratively in the markup. The ASP.NET engine will take all declarative property assignments and try to match them to properties on the underlying class. Take a look at the following code that sets the Text and LabelText properties of the user control:

```
<%@ Page Language="C#" AutoEventWireup="true"
CodeFile="Default.aspx.cs" Inherits="_Default" %>

<%@ Register Src="LabelledTextBox.ascx"
TagName="LabelledTextBox" TagPrefix="uc2" %>

<%@ Register Src="HelloWorld.ascx" TagName="HelloWorld" TagPrefix="uc1" %>

<!DOCTYPE html PUBLIC "-//W3C//DTD XHTML 1.0 Transitional//EN"
"http://www.w3.org/TR/xhtml1/DTD/xhtml1-transitional.dtd">

<html xmlns="http://www.w3.org/1999/xhtml" >
<head runat="server">
<title>Untitled Page</title>
</head>
<body>
<form id="form1" runat="server">
<div>
    <uc1:HelloWorld ID="HelloWorld1" runat="server" />
    <uc2:LabelledTextBox ID="LabelledTextBox1"
      LabelText="Favorite Color" Text="Blue" runat="server" />
</div>
</form>
</body>
</html>
```

You can also programmatically change property values on a web user control from within the code-behind (.cs file) for a page or parent control:

```
LabelledTextBox1.LabelText = "Enter your Favorite Color";
```

As mentioned earlier, an ASP.NET web user control functions exactly like a "mini" ASP.NET page, so you can leverage all of the skills you have developed for building ASP.NET pages and apply them to building ASP.NET web user controls.

Creating Server Controls

A *server control* trades off the ease of use of having separate UI and code elements by giving the developer tighter control of the rendering process. This control comes at a price, however: It is often more time-consuming to produce server controls than user controls. Despite the relative difficulty, many developers prefer using server controls because they are easy to share among multiple projects and the developer has precise control over the control's output and its behavior. Server controls also have the advantage of being easily bundled and can be sold to other developers by component and control vendors.

Within the narrow scope of this single chapter, you will not get a thorough and comprehensive coverage of all aspects of creating server controls within ASP.NET. However, this next section will get you started creating those controls and possibly whet your appetite for a book like Stephen Walther's *ASP.NET 2.0 Unleashed* (ISBN: 0672328232).

Before getting into the specifics of creating a custom server control, you should familiarize yourself with the capabilities of the `WebControl` class. You create custom server controls by creating classes that inherit from `WebControl`. Tables 30.1 and 30.2 contain a list of commonly used properties and methods of the `WebControl` class.

TABLE 30.1   `WebControl` Properties

Property	Description
AccessKey	The key that allows quick access to the control.
BackColor	The background color used for the control.
BorderColor	The control's border color.
BorderStyle	The control's border style.
BorderWidth	The control's border width.
Controls	A collection of the child controls contained within the control.
CssClass	The Cascading Style Sheet (CSS) used by the control.
Enabled	Boolean indicating whether the control is enabled.
EnableTheming	Enables support for ASP.NET 2.0 themes.
EnableViewState	Indicates whether view state is active for this control.
Font	The control's font.
ForeColor	The control's foreground color.
ID	The control's ID.
SkinID	The currently selected skin for the control.
ToolTip	The ToolTip for the control displayed when the mouse hovers over the control.
Visible	Indicates whether the control is rendered visibly on the page.
Width	The control's width.

30

TABLE 30.2 WebControl Methods

Method	Description
DataBind	Binds a data source to the control.
Focus	Sets the current input focus to the control.
HasControls	Indicates whether the control contains child controls.
RenderBeginTag	Renders the HTML tag used to begin the rendering of the control. Default tag is .
RenderControl	Outputs the control contents.
RenderEndTag	Renders the HTML completion tag that wraps the control. Default is .

As you saw in the preceding example, you can define properties on a control class that can be set declaratively at design time or programmatically at runtime. With a custom server control, it is more difficult to determine the context of those properties because you don't have editable access to the control tree at design time as you do with a web user control. To help the user figure out what each property means and how it should be used, there are several attributes that you can use to decorate a server control property. Some of the more common ones are

- Bindable—This attribute indicates whether the associated property can be bound to a data source.

- Category—This attribute indicates the category within the property editor in which the property should appear. For example, properties such as Font, ForeColor, and BackColor all show up in the Appearance category.

- DefaultValue—This attribute indicates the default value of the property when no value has been supplied at design time or runtime.

- Description—This attribute provides a long description of the property.

- Localizable—This attribute indicates whether the property will have different values based on different cultural locations and language settings.

To follow along, add a new Class Library project to the solution in which the control website was created. Add a reference to System.Web from within this class library and you're ready to start creating server controls in this library.

Add a new class to the class library called TextBoxButton. This class is going to be a server control that will contain a text box and a button to illustrate the principle of a custom server control with child controls. In addition, you will also see how to "bubble" events from within a server control up to the page in which the control resides.

Make sure the code for the TextBoxButton class looks like the code in Listing 30.1.

LISTING 30.1 The TextBoxButton Class

```
using System;
using System.ComponentModel;
using System.Data;
```

LISTING 30.1 Continued

```csharp
using System.Configuration;
using System.Web;
using System.Web.Security;
using System.Web.UI;
using System.Web.UI.WebControls;
using System.Web.UI.WebControls.WebParts;
using System.Web.UI.HtmlControls;

/// <summary>
/// Summary description for TextBoxButton
/// </summary>
namespace CustomControls
{
public class TextBoxButton : WebControl
{
public event EventHandler buttonClick;
private Button btn;
private TextBox txBox;

public TextBoxButton()
{
    //
    // TODO: Add constructor logic here
    //
}

[Bindable(true),
   Category("Appearance"),
   DefaultValue("Button"),
   Description("The Text on the Button"),
   Localizable(true)]
public string ButtonText
{
    get { EnsureChildControls(); return btn.Text; }
    set { EnsureChildControls(); btn.Text = value; }
}

[Bindable(true),
   Category("Appearance"),
   DefaultValue(""),
   Description("The Text within the Text Box"),
   Localizable(true)]
public string Value
{
```

LISTING 30.1   Continued

```
    get { EnsureChildControls(); return txBox.Text; }
    set { EnsureChildControls(); txBox.Text = value; }
}

protected override void CreateChildControls()
{
    txBox = new TextBox();
    Controls.Add(txBox);
    btn = new Button();
    btn.Click += new EventHandler(btn_Click);
    Controls.Add(btn);
}

protected override void RenderContents(HtmlTextWriter writer)
{
    base.RenderContents(writer);
}

void btn_Click(object sender, EventArgs e)
{
    if (buttonClick != null)
        buttonClick(sender, e);
}
}
}
```

However tempting it may be, you should never instantiate new child controls from within a control's constructor. It is often difficult to remember that the instantiation and configuration of controls is done in an entirely separate stage of the control life cycle than the rendering. Because of this, use the CreateChildControls method to establish the control tree and use the RenderContents method to make any specific changes to the child controls.

In Listing 30.1 the property definitions should be fairly self-explanatory. The property values are derived from property values on child controls, and thus require the use of the EnsureChildControls() method to make sure that the child controls exist before retrieving or setting their properties.

To let the page hosting the control respond to the event when a user clicks the nested button within TextBoxButton, you need to support a process called "bubbling." When an event is fired and handled within one class and that class then publishes an event representing the same occurrence to another class, the event is considered to be "bubbled." The phrase comes from an analogy related to bubbles rising to the surface of a liquid.

For this control to support event bubbling, it needs to publish an event using the following line of code:

```
public event EventHandler buttonClick;
```

When this control handles the `Click` event from the child `Button` control, it allows any container control to respond to the same event by bubbling it up one level:

```
void btn_Click(object sender, EventArgs e)
{
    if (buttonClick != null)
        buttonClick(sender, e);
}
```

Build the class library and then add a reference to the `CustomControls` project from the web application project. After building the solution this way, create a new Web Form. An extremely useful feature is that the Toolbox has detected the presence of a web control within an assembly in the solution and has added it in a category called "ControlsDemo Components" (assuming your web project is called `ControlsDemo`).

When you drag the control from the special category on the control Toolbox, you will see a preview of the control's rendered output using default values. The Properties Editor panel will contain all of the custom properties that you defined on your control and will reflect the settings of the custom attributes applied to those properties, as shown in Figure 30.2.

FIGURE 30.2   Properties Editor panel for a custom server control.

30

Using your knowledge of C#, object-oriented programming, the ASP.NET page life cycle, and the functionality and features of the `WebControl` class, you can create some very powerful controls.

Managing State Within Server Controls

With the introduction of ASP.NET 2.0, there are now two kinds of state management at the disposal of control developers: view state and control state. ASP.NET 2.0 makes a distinction between page-wide view state and control state to allow developers to turn off view state for an entire page to speed up performance, and selectively allow individual controls to maintain their state.

View state is a feature of ASP.NET that allows controls and the page itself to maintain state between requests by storing that state information in a hidden form variable. The contents of that hidden form variable are exposed through an instance of the `StateBag` class as the `ViewState` object. You can read and write name-value pairs using the following syntax:

```
int selectedIndex = ViewState["selectedIndex"];
ViewState["selectedIndex"] = comboBox1.SelectedIndex;
```

Although view state is an incredibly powerful tool and facilitates many things in ASP.NET that required a lot of tedious programming before ASP.NET was released, it can become a performance problem. For example, in ASP.NET 1.1, if a `DataGrid` was bound to several hundred rows of data, all of that data could end up in view state in order to avoid requerying the server. The nature of the view state hidden form variable led to incredibly large page sizes in this situation. Before ASP.NET 2.0, control builders either had to rely on view state or they had to use some other mechanism to maintain state between page requests.

The size of view state became a burden for controls that only needed to maintain small amounts of data between requests. With ASP.NET 2.0, *control state* can be used to maintain small pieces of information between requests, whereas view state is still useful for storing large amounts of data.

Control state management follows a different model than view state. Rather than accessing the name/value pairs stored in the `ViewState` object, any control that you build should override the `LoadControlState(object)` and `SaveControlState()` methods that are now part of the `WebControl` class.

The `LoadControlState` method is used to restore the control's state from the object supplied as a method parameter. `SaveControlState` is used to return the object that constitutes the control's state. These two methods combined allow the control to manage its own state without resorting to the `ViewState` object. Keep in mind that control state should only be used for small values and control state *cannot be disabled*. Even if the page or the control has had `EnableViewState` set to `false`, control state code will still work properly.

Listing 30.2 contains the source code for a custom server control named `StateControl`. It is a control that uses `ViewState` for storing a list of strings to which the control is bound and it uses `ControlState` for storing the currently selected index to highlight an individual string.

LISTING 30.2   Custom Control Using View State and Control State

```csharp
using System;
using System.Drawing;
using System.Security.Permissions;
using System.Collections;
using System.Collections.Generic;
using System.ComponentModel;
using System.Data;
using System.Configuration;
using System.Web;
using System.Web.Security;
using System.Web.UI;
using System.Web.Util;
using System.Web.UI.WebControls;
using System.Web.UI.WebControls.WebParts;
using System.Web.UI.HtmlControls;

namespace CustomControls
{
public class StateControl : CompositeControl
{
private List<string> stringList = null;
private int selectedIndex = -1;
private Table mainTable = null;

public List<string> DataSource
{
    get
    {
        if (stringList == null)
            stringList = (List<string>)ViewState["stringList"];
        return stringList;
    }
    set
    {
        stringList = value;
        ViewState["stringList"] = value;
    }
}

public int SelectedIndex
{
```

30

LISTING 30.2   Continued

```
    get { return selectedIndex; }
    set { selectedIndex = value; }
}

public override void DataBind()
{
    base.DataBind();
    EnsureChildControls();
    for (int x = 0; x < DataSource.Count; x++)
    {
        TableRow tr = new TableRow();
        if (selectedIndex == x)
            tr.BackColor = Color.LightBlue;
        else
            tr.BackColor = Color.White;

        TableCell td = new TableCell();
        td.Text = DataSource[x];
        tr.Cells.Add(td);
        mainTable.Rows.Add(tr);
    }
}

protected override void LoadControlState(object savedState)
{
    Page.Response.Write("LoadConstrolState: " + savedState.ToString()+"<br/>");
    selectedIndex = (int)savedState;
}

protected override object SaveControlState()
{
    Page.Response.Write("SaveControlState: " + selectedIndex.ToString()+"<br/>");
    return selectedIndex;
}

protected override void RenderContents(HtmlTextWriter writer)
{
    base.RenderContents(writer);
}

protected override void CreateChildControls()
{
    Page.RegisterRequiresControlState(this);
    mainTable = new Table();
```

LISTING 30.2   Continued

```
    mainTable.Width = new Unit(100, UnitType.Percentage);
    Controls.Add(mainTable);
}
}
}
```

The DataSource property makes use of the ViewState object to retrieve the data from view state if it wasn't set during the page load. This allows the control to maintain the list of strings between page requests without requiring the host page to set them every time. The LoadControlState and SaveControlState overridden methods load and store the value of selectedIndex, and the DataBind() method uses that value to selectively determine which row to highlight in light blue. Finally, the following line tells the page framework that this control takes part in control state persistence:

```
Page.RegisterRequiresControlState(this);
```

Without this line of code, ASP.NET will not restore the control's state. Listing 30.3 contains the code for the page that hosts this control.

LISTING 30.3   A Page Hosting a State-Persisting Control

```
using System;
using System.Data;
using System.Configuration;
using System.Collections;
using System.Collections.Generic;
using System.Web;
using System.Web.Security;
using System.Web.UI;
using System.Web.UI.WebControls;
using System.Web.UI.WebControls.WebParts;
using System.Web.UI.HtmlControls;

public partial class StateDemo : System.Web.UI.Page
{
protected void Page_Load(object sender, EventArgs e)
{
if (!Page.IsPostBack)
{
    List<string> stringList = new List<string>();
    stringList.Add("String One");
    stringList.Add("String Two");
    stringList.Add("String Three");
    StateControl1.DataSource = stringList;
```

LISTING 30.3 Continued

```
    StateControl1.SelectedIndex = 2;
}
StateControl1.DataBind();
}


protected override void OnPreRender(EventArgs e)
{
base.OnPreRender(e);
Response.Write("Requires control state: " +
  RequiresControlState(StateControl1) + "<br/>");
}


protected void button1_Click(object sender, EventArgs e)
{
Response.Write("Button was pressed, this is a post back.<br/>");
Response.Write("StateControl Selected Index: " +
    StateControl1.SelectedIndex.ToString() +"<br/>");
}
}
```

This code illustrates how you can create custom server controls that take part in view state and control state.

Summary

Despite the vast array of functionality provided by the controls that come with ASP.NET 2.0, there will undoubtedly be occasions when developers need to create their own controls. These controls can be simple user controls or custom server controls. This chapter showed you how easy it can be to create both types of controls, as well as how to manage state from within controls. After reading this chapter, you should be familiar with the concepts involved in creating user controls and know enough to continue your learning with a more detailed reference if you plan on creating more powerful and complex controls.

CHAPTER 31

ASP.NET Management and Monitoring

Administering and monitoring an ASP.NET application can be a tedious and difficult task. Often, due to the complexity of attempting to monitor the internal behavior and health of an ASP.NET application, developers are the ones tasked with performing the ongoing maintenance and monitoring of these applications. This chapter illustrates various technologies and techniques that can make applications easier to administer, configure, and monitor by IT staff as well as developers.

Introducing the New Health Monitoring System

ASP.NET 2.0 comes equipped with a new system that allows for the raising of health monitoring events (also referred to as web events). The main benefit of this system is that because it is completely manageable through configuration files. Operations and other IT staff can monitor the health of deployed web applications without the direct intervention of developers. The health monitoring system is composed of two primary components:

- Web event—A *web event* is a derivative of the `WebBaseEvent` class and is used to contain information pertinent to the event raised and can often contain additional information. For example, several of the event classes that come with the system store information about the application such as its directory, the time of the event, the page in which the event occurred, and so on.

- Web Event provider—A *Web Event provider* is a special class that can subscribe to web events. When the provider receives an event, it can then store the event in a persistence medium like SQL Server or a file on disk, or it can forward the event by sending an e-mail or a text message to a cellular phone.

Events and providers are linked together in your application's `Web.config` file. Event types are assigned to named groups in the `Web.config`'s `<eventMappings>` element. By default, ASP.NET already has several event providers defined as well as event groups.

Table 31.1 shows the web events that come with ASP.NET 2.0.

TABLE 31.1 ASP.NET 2.0 Web Events

Event Class	Description
WebApplicationLifetimeEvent	Indicates important lifetime events in an application such as startup and shutdown.
WebAuditEvent	Base class for all audit-type web events.
WebAuthenticationFailureAuditEvent	Indicates an authentication failure.
WebAuthenticationSuccessAuditEvent	Indicates successful authentication.
WebBaseErrorEvent	Base class for all error-type web events.
WebHeartbeatEvent	Used as a health monitoring timer. Event is raised once per `heartbeatInterval` as defined in the `healthMonitoring` Web.config section.
WebManagementEvent	Base class for web events that contain process details.
WebRequestErrorEvent	Indicates a web request error.
WebRequestEvent	Base class for all web events related to requests.
WebSuccessAuditEvent	Indicates a successful security event.
WebViewStateFailureAuditEvent	Indicates a view state failure.

ASP.NET 2.0 also contains several default web event providers. Those providers are described in Table 31.2.

TABLE 31.2 ASP.NET 2.0 Web Event Providers

Event Provider Class	Description
EventLogWebEventProvider	Stores web event data in the system event log.
SqlWebEventProvider	Stores web event data in SQL Server. Defaults to the `App_Data` folder and a SQL Express database but can be configured for other locations.
WmiWebEventProvider	Sends web events to WMI, converting them into WMI events.
SimpleMailWebEventProvider	These providers send e-mail in response to web events.
TemplatedMailWebEventProvider	
TraceWebEventProvider	Web event data is passed to the ASP.NET page tracing subsystem.

By default, very little of this system is configured. If you don't specify any other web event information in your application's Web.config file, your application will send the All Errors and Failure Audits events to the EventLogWebEventProvider class.

Using the Health Monitoring System

Using the health monitoring system really boils down to manipulating the Web.config file to determine which events are handled by which event providers. As mentioned earlier, errors and failure audits are sent to the system event log by default. Using the Web.config file, you can use additional ASP.NET Web Event providers to handle additional event types.

This section shows you how to use a SQL Server 2005 database table as the destination for error events such as unhandled exceptions. Although the system event log might be handy in a few circumstances, storing all application errors in a central location that can be queried from remote locations is extremely useful. For example, if your application is running in a web farm scenario (multiple web servers hosting the same application), you will want all of the errors to be accessible in the same place and tagged with the name of the machine that originated the error. Logging errors using the SqlWebEventProvider does exactly that.

To start, create a new ASP.NET web application and add a Web.config file to the project. The SQL Web Event provider uses a table called aspnet_WebEvent_Events that is created when you create an application services database using the aspnet_regsql.exe tool.

Listing 31.1 contains the modified Web.config that will utilize the SQL Web Event provider.

LISTING 31.1 A Web.config File Supporting Web Event Persistence in SQL Server

```
<?xml version="1.0"?>
<configuration>
<appSettings/>
<connectionStrings>
<add name="ASPNET_AppServices"
   connectionString="server=localhost; initial catalog=ASPNET_AppServices;
   ➥Integrated Security=SSPI;"/>
</connectionStrings>
<system.web>
<healthMonitoring enabled="true" heartbeatInterval="0">
  <bufferModes>
    <add name="SqlDefault" maxBufferSize="1000"
        maxFlushSize="10" urgentFlushThreshold="10"
        regularFlushInterval="00:05:00" urgentFlushInterval="00:01:00"/>
  </bufferModes>
  <providers>
    <add name="SqlEvents"
```

LISTING 31.1   Continued

```
    type="System.Web.Management.SqlWebEventProvider, System.Web,
    ➥Version=2.0.0.0, Culture=neutral, PublicKeyToken=b03f5f7f11d50a3a"
    connectionStringName="ASPNET_AppServices"
buffer="true" bufferMode="Analysis"/>
  </providers>
  <rules>
  <add name="All Errors Rule"
    eventName="All Errors" provider="SqlEvents"
    profile="Default" minInterval="00:00:30"/>
 </rules>
</healthMonitoring>
<compilation debug="true"/>
<authentication mode="Windows"/>
</system.web>
</configuration>
```

Next, add the following line of code to your `default.aspx.cs` file:

```
throw new ApplicationException("test error");
```

When you run the application, you will get the application exception and VS 2005 will break. Continue execution and then wait a minute or two. Because the `SqlWebEventProvider` class uses a buffered system, the error won't appear within the database immediately. Figure 31.1 shows the contents of the `aspnet_WebEvent_Events` table after an error occurs.

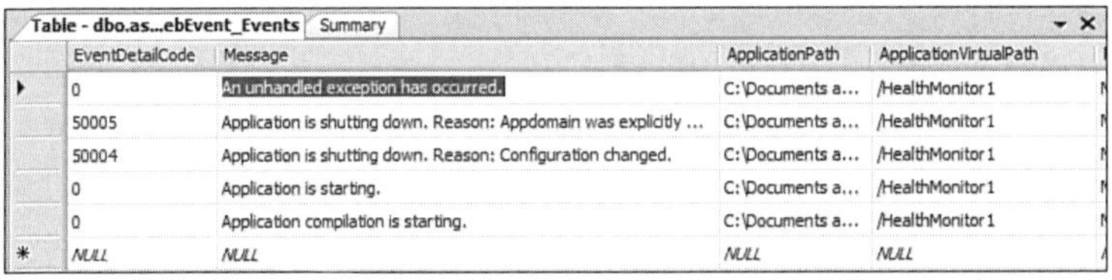

FIGURE 31.1   Storing web errors in SQL Server.

Also shown in this figure are lifetime events. *Lifetime events* indicate significant changes that occur in an application's lifetime such as application startup and shutdown. This information can be important when diagnosing problems with a production server. To support lifetime events in your application, change the preceding `Web.config` to the one shown in Listing 31.2.

LISTING 31.2   A `Web.config` File Supporting Both Errors and Lifetime Events

```xml
<?xml version="1.0"?>
<configuration>
<appSettings/>
<connectionStrings>
<add name="ASPNET_AppServices"
 connectionString="server=localhost; initial catalog=ASPNET_AppServices;
 ➥Integrated Security=SSPI;"/>
</connectionStrings>
<system.web>
<healthMonitoring enabled="true" heartbeatInterval="0">
<eventMappings>
  <add name="Lifetime"
      type="System.Web.Management.WebApplicationLifetimeEvent,
      ➥System.Web,Version=2.0.0.0, Culture=neutral,
      ➥PublicKeyToken=b03f5f7f11d50a3a"/>
</eventMappings>
<bufferModes>
    <add name="SqlDefault" maxBufferSize="1000" maxFlushSize="10"
      urgentFlushThreshold="10" regularFlushInterval="00:05:00"
      urgentFlushInterval="00:01:00"/>
</bufferModes>
<providers>
<add name="SqlEvents"
   type="System.Web.Management.SqlWebEventProvider, System.Web,
   ➥Version=2.0.0.0, Culture=neutral, PublicKeyToken=b03f5f7f11d50a3a"
    connectionStringName="ASPNET_AppServices" buffer="true" bufferMode="Analysis"/>
</providers>
<rules>
  <add name="All Errors Rule"
    eventName="All Errors" provider="SqlEvents"
    profile="Default" minInterval="00:00:30"/>
  <add name="Lifetime Rule" eventName="Lifetime"
    provider="SqlEvents" profile="Default" minInterval="00:00:30"/>
</rules>
</healthMonitoring>
<compilation debug="true"/>
<authentication mode="Windows"/>
</system.web>
</configuration>
```

This configuration file adds a new entry to the `<eventMappings>` section indicating that events in the group "Lifetime" are of the type `WebApplicationLifetimeEvent`. The `<rules>` section indicates that all events in the group "Lifetime" are to be handled by the

`SqlWebEventHandler` class. This provides the necessary hooks to get information like application startup and shutdown stored in the SQL Server database.

> **NOTE**
>
> If you are a tinkerer or just curious, you might try to raise these events manually instead of letting ASP.NET handle them on your behalf. This can't be done, however. All of the default web event classes have an internal protection level so that they cannot be instantiated by code outside the System.Web assembly. This is done deliberately to ensure that only the ASP.NET engine can manually raise the default events. If you want to raise custom events, the next section, "Creating Custom Events," should prove helpful.

Creating Custom Events

Before getting into the details of how to create a custom event, it is important to know when custom events should and should not be created. One important factor to keep in mind is that the developer does not have explicit control over when ASP.NET raises its own default custom events outside of defining event mappings and rules in the `Web.config` file. In other words, a programmer cannot explicitly raise an "Application Startup" event through code. The following guidelines should help you make the decision as to when to create a custom event:

- If your event requires the storage of data that is not already being stored by any of the existing event classes, you should create your own event.

- If you need programmatic control over when to signal the event, you can create your own and inherit from the event you want to manually signal. Keep in mind, however, that ASP.NET already does an excellent job of signaling events at the appropriate time, and you should use the existing events whenever possible.

> **TIP**
>
> A common pitfall that a lot of people run into is that they create a web event that inherits from an existing base event, and then manually fire that event in the same place where ASP.NET would have automatically fired it. For example, if a developer overrides the `WebErrorEvent` and calls the `Raise()` method within the `catch` portion of a `try`/`catch` block, she is essentially reinventing the wheel. In this situation, the *only* reason a developer should take manual control over raising such error events is if the developer needs to store more information in the event than the default ASP.NET `WebErrorEvent` class provides.

The next sample will illustrate the use of a custom web event that will get signaled when a user of a research department's website requests a search. As you'll see in the next section on creating a custom provider, this request can then either be handled automatically via web services or dispatched to a research department employee.

Add a new Class Library project to the solution that contains the website from the previous samples. Add a reference to the System.Web Assembly and add a class to the project called AsyncSearchRequest. Listing 31.3 shows the class that inherits from WebBaseEvent.

LISTING 31.3   The AsyncSearchRequest Class

```
using System;
using System.Web;
using System.Web.Management;
using System.Web.UI;
using System.Web.UI.WebControls;
using System.Collections.Generic;
using System.Text;

namespace SampleEvents
{
public class AsyncSearchWebEvent : WebBaseEvent
{
private DateTime timeRaised;
private string searchCriteria = string.Empty;

public AsyncSearchWebEvent(string message,
    object eventSource,
    int eventCode)
    : base(message, eventSource, eventCode)
{
}

public AsyncSearchWebEvent(string message,
    object eventSource,
    int eventCode,
    int eventDetailCode)
    : base(message, eventSource, eventCode,
    eventDetailCode)
{
}

public override void Raise()
{
    timeRaised = DateTime.Now;
    base.Raise();
}

public override void FormatCustomEventDetails(WebEventFormatter formatter)
{
    formatter.AppendLine("");
```

LISTING 31.3   Continued

```
    formatter.IndentationLevel += 1;
    formatter.AppendLine("-- Custom Event Data --");
    formatter.AppendLine(string.Format("Search Critera: {0}", searchCriteria));
    formatter.AppendLine(string.Format("Event Raised On: {0}",
timeRaised.ToString()));
    formatter.IndentationLevel -= 1;
}

public DateTime TimeRaised
{
    get { return timeRaised; }
    set { timeRaised = value; }
}

public string SearchCriteria
{
    get { return searchCriteria; }
    set { searchCriteria = value; }
}
}
}
```

The constructors were created so that you can see where you can inject your own code into the instantiation process. The FormatCustomEventDetails method is used to provide additional text data that will be logged with the event when sent to a provider.

One of the most powerful features of the new ASP.NET Web Management system is that you can plug any of your custom events into any of the existing event providers or any custom providers that you or a third party create.

Listing 31.4 contains a new Web.config for the web application that associates the newly created custom event with the SQL Server Web Event provider.

LISTING 31.4   A Modified Web.config File Supporting Custom Web Events

```
<?xml version="1.0"?>
<configuration>
<appSettings/>
<connectionStrings>
<add name="ASPNET_AppServices"
    connectionString="server=localhost; initial catalog=ASPNET_AppServices;
    ➥Integrated Security=SSPI;"/>
</connectionStrings>
<system.web>
<healthMonitoring enabled="true" heartbeatInterval="0">
```

LISTING 31.4   Continued

```
  <eventMappings>
    <add name="Lifetime"
        type="System.Web.Management.WebApplicationLifetimeEvent, System.Web,
➡Version=2.0.0.0, Culture=neutral, PublicKeyToken=b03f5f7f11d50a3a"/>
    <add name="SearchEvent"
        type="SampleEvents.AsyncSearchWebEvent, SampleEvents"
        />
  </eventMappings>
    <bufferModes>
        <add name="SqlDefault" maxBufferSize="1000"
maxFlushSize="10" urgentFlushThreshold="10"
regularFlushInterval="00:05:00"
      urgentFlushInterval="00:01:00"/>
    </bufferModes>
    <providers>
        <add name="SqlEvents"
     type="System.Web.Management.SqlWebEventProvider, System.Web,
      ➡Version=2.0.0.0, Culture=neutral, PublicKeyToken=b03f5f7f11d50a3a"
      connectionStringName="ASPNET_AppServices"
buffer="true" bufferMode="Analysis"/>
    </providers>
    <rules>
        <add name="All Errors Rule" eventName="All Errors"
provider="SqlEvents" profile="Default" minInterval="00:00:30"/>
    <add name="Lifetime Rule" eventName="Lifetime"
provider="SqlEvents" profile="Default" minInterval="00:00:30"/>
    <add name="SearchEvents Rule" eventName="SearchEvent"
provider="SqlEvents" profile="Default" minInterval="00:00:30"/>
    </rules>
</healthMonitoring>
<compilation debug="true"/>
<authentication mode="Windows"/>
</system.web>
</configuration>
```

To raise this event, you need to do it manually using the Raise() method on the custom
event class. Because this class isn't part of the default ASP.NET framework, it won't raise
events unless your code forces it to happen, as shown in the following example:

```
SampleEvents.AsyncSearchWebEvent searchEvent =
new SampleEvents.AsyncSearchWebEvent(
    "Search Requested", this, WebEventCodes.WebExtendedBase + 1);
searchEvent.SearchCriteria = "C#";
searchEvent.Raise();
```

Every event requires an event code in order to be raised. Event codes less than 100,000 are the sole property of ASP.NET and cannot be used by custom events. Therefore, your event codes should start at WebExtendedBase and increment from there. Event codes above 100,000 can be reused by any event. After running the preceding code and waiting a few minutes for the event buffer to flush, you will see a new event appear in the aspnet_WebEvent_Events table. The Details column contains the following text:

```
Event code: 100001 Event message: Search Requested Event time: 1/22/2006
1:45:07 PM Event time (UTC): 1/22/2006 8:45:07 PM Event ID:
a0569b9574994157826690f25b38c13f Event sequence: 7 Event occurrence: 1
Event detail code: 0  Application information:     Application domain:
c1085da7-1-127824362038281250     Trust level: Full     Application Virtual Path:
/HealthMonitor1     Application Path: C:\Documents and Settings\Kevin\My Documents
\Writing\SAMS\C# 2005 Unleashed\31\Code\HealthMonitor1\     Machine name: LAB01
Custom event details:                    -- Custom Event Data --     Search Critera:
C#          Event Raised On: 1/22/2006 1:45:07 PM
```

Creating Custom Event Providers

To illustrate how to create a custom Web Event provider, this section will show you how to create a Research Dispatch provider that handles AsyncSearchWebEvent events and dispatches them accordingly. To create a basic Web Event provider, create a class that inherits from the base class BufferedWebEventProvider (you can create an unbuffered one, but this sample uses a buffered provider to provide a comparison with the buffered SqlWebEventProvider class). To see this in action, add a new class called SearchWebEventProvider to the class library that contains the AsyncSearchWebEvent class. This class is shown in Listing 31.5.

LISTING 31.5   A Simple Custom Web Event Provider

```
using System;
using System.Web;
using System.Web.Management;
using System.Web.UI;
using System.Web.UI.WebControls;
using System.Collections.Generic;
using System.Text;

namespace SampleEvents
{
public class SearchWebEventProvider : BufferedWebEventProvider
{
public override void ProcessEvent(WebBaseEvent eventRaised)
{
    if (UseBuffering)
        base.ProcessEvent(eventRaised);
```

LISTING 31.5   Continued

```
    else
        DispatchEvent((AsyncSearchWebEvent)eventRaised);
}

public override void ProcessEventFlush(WebEventBufferFlushInfo flushInfo)
{
    foreach (WebBaseEvent evt in flushInfo.Events)
        DispatchEvent((AsyncSearchWebEvent)evt);
}

public void DispatchEvent(AsyncSearchWebEvent webEvent)
{
    // use this method to decide whether the event
    // should dispatch to a code-resolved search or
    // a human-resolved search (dispatch to a work queue)
}
}
}
```

The code for the provider itself isn't very complex. The complexity can come from choosing the storage medium or notification medium used when handling the event. The preceding sample shows how you can create a simple provider shell to be used with the search event.

Using ASP.NET Performance Counters

Another powerful tool at the disposal of developers and system administrators alike is the use of performance counters. The Performance Monitor tool (found under Administrative Tools, Performance) displays a value-over-time graph of any number of system counters that provide valuable analysis information. Consult your Windows administration guide for more information on system-level performance counters.

ASP.NET 2.0 provides the following performance counters that can be monitored from the Performance Monitor tool. These counters are described in Table 31.3.

TABLE 31.3   ASP.NET 2.0 Performance Counters

Counter	Description
Application Restarts	Number of application restarts since server startup.
Application Running	Number of running ASP.NET applications.
Requests Disconnected	Number of disconnected requests due to a connection failure.
Requests Queued	Number of requests queued and waiting for processing.
Requests Rejected	Number of requests denied due to insufficient resources on the server.
Request Wait Time	Wait time (in milliseconds) of most recent request.

TABLE 31.3   Continued

Counter	Description
Session State Server Connections Total	Total number of connections to the session state server on this machine.
Session SQL Server Connections Total	Total number of connections made to an out-of-process SQL Server for state management.
State Server Sessions Abandoned	Number of abandoned state server sessions.
State Server Sessions Active	Number of currently active state server sessions.
State Server Sessions Timed Out	Total number of timed-out sessions since server startup.
State Server Sessions Total	Total number of state server sessions: sum of active, abandoned, and timed out.
Worker Process Restarts	Total number of times ASP.NET worker processes have restarted.
Worker Process Running	Number of active worker processes.
Application-Specific Counters	
Anonymous Requests	Number of unauthenticated requests.
Anonymous Requests/Second	Average number of anonymous requests/second.
Cache Total Entries	Total number of entries within the cache including ASP.NET entries and programmatically (API) created entries.
Cache Total Hits	Total number of cache hits.
Cache Total Misses	Total number of cache misses.
Cache Total Hit Ratio	Cache hit ratio (ratio of hit to miss).
Cache Total Turnover Rate	Total turnover rate for cache. Turnover rate is number of additions and removals per second. High turnover rate indicates poor cache usage.
Cache API Entries	Number of API-created (non-ASP.NET framework) cache entries.
Cache API Hit Ratio	Hit ratio for API-created cache entries.
Cache API Turnover Rate	Turnover rate for API-created cache entries.
Compilations Total	Total number of compilations performed since process start.
Debugging Requests	Count of total requests during Debugging mode.
Errors During Preprocessing	Total number of preprocessing errors.
Errors During Compilation	Total number of compilation errors.
Errors Unhandled During Execution	Total number of unhandled exceptions. Nothing is counted when a default error page is defined.
Errors Unhandled During Execution/second	Average number of unhandled exceptions/second. Obviously, this number should remain low.
Errors Total	Total number of all types of errors.
Errors Total/Second	Total number of all error types per second.
Output Cache Entries	Number of entries in the output cache.
Output Cache Hits	Total number of output cache hits.
Output Cache Misses	Total number of output cache misses.
Output Cache Hit Ratio	Ratio of output cache hits to misses.
Output Cache Turnover Rate	Turnover rate (sum of additions and deletions).

TABLE 31.3   Continued

Counter	Description
Pipeline Instance Count	Number of active request pipelines.
Request Bytes In Total	Total size in bytes of all requests.
Request Bytes Out Total	Total size in bytes of all responses to requests.
Requests Executing	Total number of requests currently executing.
Requests Failed	Total number of failed requests.
Requests Not Found	Total number of 404 or 414 errors.
Requests Not Authorized	Total number of authorization (401) errors.
Requests Succeeded	Total number of successful requests (HTTP code 200).
Requests Timed Out	Total number of requests timed out (HTTP code 500).
Requests Total	Total number of all requests of all types.
Requests/sec	Average number of requests per second.
Sessions Active	Total number of active sessions. Only includes in-process session states.
Sessions Abandoned	Total number of abandoned sessions (in-process only).
Sessions Timed Out	Total number of timed-out sessions (in-process only).
Sessions Total	Total number of sessions of all types (in-process only).
Transactions Aborted	Total number of all aborted transactions within all ASP.NET applications in this process.
Transactions Committed	Total number of committed transactions.
Transactions Pending	Total number of open transactions waiting to commit or roll back.
Transactions Total	Total number of transactions of all types.
Transactions/sec	Average number of transactions per second.

Summary

The task of monitoring the health of ASP.NET applications has often been difficult and time-consuming in the past. It was also a task that often fell on the shoulders of developers because of the specific constraints and requirements of custom-built monitoring systems. With the use of performance counters and the System.Web.Management namespace for web events, you can create web applications that can be monitored for system impact and performance by non-development staff and you can even monitor important events within your application without having to write complex monitoring systems. Every developer responsible for producing a commercial application should take a look at the ASP.NET performance counters and at web events to see how they can increase the stability and health awareness of their application.

PART V

Web Services

IN THIS PART

Exposing Functionality with Web Services

XML Web Services is a technology that has rapidly grown from a powerful concept to a tried-and true standard, to the point where web services are now an almost ubiquitous standard for developing distributed applications. This chapter provides you with an introduction to web services development and gives you the basics you need to get started integrating web services into your web applications, thin clients, or distributed applications.

Introduction to Web Services

Ever since the early days of client/server applications, applications have benefited from separation of tiers, whether that separation was physical or logical. Applications could communicate with databases that were in remote locations, or using technologies like DCOM, they could communicate with remotely located business logic.

Ever since its creation, the web has been an incredibly powerful tool for disseminating information and content. However, due to the nature of HTML, it has been difficult to use the web to disseminate data in formats that can be easily consumed by client applications.

When powerful new server-side programming technologies became available, such as Active Server Pages, Java, Perl, CGI, and more, developers began creating their own custom solutions to use the web to expose data in a consumable format.

This eventually led to the development of web pages that rendered raw XML that could then be consumed by clients. That led to the development of a standard dialect of XML that defined the contract by which a web service and its client would agree: WSDL (Web Services Description Language).

Using WSDL, modern programming languages could obtain information about functionality exposed over HTTP using web services and then consume that functionality. This provided developers with a whole new model of development that allowed them to expose discrete units of functionality on the Internet and consume it in any language on any platform so long as both the client and server could read and generate XML.

ASP.NET has provided built-in support for web services since its original release. That support has only gotten better in recent versions and will undoubtedly see even more advancements in upcoming releases.

How Web Services Work

Web services describe the methods they expose, including their parameters and return types, in an XML dialect called the Web Services Description Language (WSDL). This language provides a platform-independent description of functionality that can be consumed by any language on any platform that can interpret XML.

Using the information contained in the WSDL document, the functionality can be consumed. In the .NET world, this means that a wrapper class is created around the WSDL exposed by a web service to provide object-oriented access to the underlying web service.

When a method is invoked, it can either be invoked using an HTTP POST statement with simple parameters or it can be invoked by submitting a SOAP (Simple Object Access Protocol) envelope to the ASP.NET web service (represented by a .asmx file on the server). SOAP provides a wire format that can be used to encode method execution requests as well as return values from executed methods. The contents of the POST request or the SOAP envelope are then processed and the requested method is then executed on the server. The return value and any output parameters of that method are then encoded into output that is then sent to the client. A high-level diagram of this process is shown in Figure 32.1.

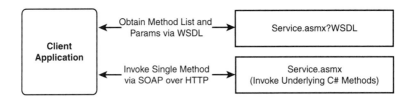

FIGURE 32.1   Two-step process to consume a web service.

Creating a Simple "Hello World" Service

To see how web services work in action, this section walks you through creating the simplest web service you can create: the "Hello World" service.

Start Visual Studio and select File, then New, and then Website. Choose the ASP.NET Web Service template from the menu and call it `HelloWorldService`.

The newly created project contains a C# class file called `Service.cs` in the `App_Code` directory and a `Service.asmx` file in the web application's root directory.

The `Service.asmx` file is the main point of interface for a web service. It can be used to obtain the WSDL contract for the web service as well as to test the service. Highlight the `Service.asmx` file and run the application.

When you run the application in debug mode for the first time, you might be prompted to add a `Web.config` file to the project and enable debugging mode. You will see a new web browser containing a list of the services available within the application. Click the `HelloWorld` link to bring up a web page that looks similar to the one shown in Figure 32.2.

FIGURE 32.2   The `HelloWorld` web service page.

Click the Invoke button to test-run the web service. This web service simply returns the phrase "Hello World" to any application invoking the `HelloWorld()` method. The results of testing this web service are shown in the following lines:

```
<?xml version="1.0" encoding="utf-8" ?>
<string xmlns="http://tempuri.org/">Hello World</string>
```

The output from the web service is in an XML format that can be interpreted by any client aware of the Web Services XML format. To see how .NET, and specifically Visual Studio 2005, handles web services, you need to create a web service client.

To do this, add a new console application project to the existing solution called WSClient. Right-click the new console application project and select Add Web Reference. You will be prompted with a dialog asking for the location of the web service. In this case, the web service is part of the current solution, so you can click the "Web Services in This Solution" link. Then click the displayed link to add a web reference to the "Hello World" web service. Accept localhost as the web service name and click Add Reference.

With the web reference in place, you can modify the code in Program.cs to create an instance of the web service and invoke it, as shown in the following example:

```
using System;
using System.Collections.Generic;
using System.Text;

namespace WSClient
{
class Program
{
static void Main(string[] args)
{
    localhost.Service svc = new localhost.Service();
    Console.WriteLine(svc.HelloWorld());
}
}
}
```

When you run this application, you will see the phrase "Hello World." This phrase comes from the web service in the solution. When the client represented by the localhost.Service wrapper class invokes the HelloWorld() method, the code contained in the Service.cs file on the server (shown in Listing 32.1) is executed.

LISTING 32.1   Service.cs

```
using System;
using System.Web;
using System.Web.Services;
using System.Web.Services.Protocols;

[WebService(Namespace = "http://tempuri.org/")]
[WebServiceBinding(ConformsTo = WsiProfiles.BasicProfile1_1)]
public class Service : System.Web.Services.WebService
{
public Service () {
```

LISTING 32.1   Continued

```
    //Uncomment the following line if using designed components
    //InitializeComponent();
}


[WebMethod]
public string HelloWorld() {
    return "Hello World";
}
}
```

The WebMethodAttribute code attribute class is what marks a method as being exposed to clients via the web service. The WebServiceAttribute class allows you to define additional properties of the web service directly within the code.

Despite how often the "Hello World" sample is used to illustrate the use of new technology, it isn't very practical. The next sample shows you how to create a web service that takes input parameters and returns values both as a method return value and through output parameters.

First, add a new web method to the Service.cs file as shown in Listing 32.2.

LISTING 32.2   Service.cs Containing an Additional Web Method

```
using System;
using System.Text;
using System.Web;
using System.Web.Services;
using System.Web.Services.Protocols;

[WebService(Namespace = "http://tempuri.org/")]
[WebServiceBinding(ConformsTo = WsiProfiles.BasicProfile1_1)]
public class Service : System.Web.Services.WebService
{
public Service () {

    //Uncomment the following line if using designed components
    //InitializeComponent();
}


[WebMethod]
public string HelloWorld() {
    return "Hello World";
}
```

LISTING 32.2   Continued

```
[WebMethod(Description =
"Concatenates two strings, returning the result and length.")]
public int StringConcat(string string1, string string2,
    out string stringTotal)
{
    StringBuilder sb = new StringBuilder();
    sb.Append(string1);
    sb.Append(string2);
    stringTotal = sb.ToString();
    return stringTotal.Length;
}
}
```

The new method takes two input parameters and supplies the concatenation of those two parameters as the third parameter and then returns the length of the new string as the return value.

If you have worked with web services in previous versions of Visual Studio, you will be pleasantly surprised to see that just a few seconds after you add the new method to the web service, the web reference in the console application you created is automatically updated. If it doesn't automatically update, you can just right-click the localhost item in the Solution Explorer and choose Update Web Reference.

Run the web application again and get to the test page for the StringConcat method. Note that you can't test-fire this method from the web any more because of the output parameter.

To see this new method in action, modify the source code to the Program.cs file in the console application to look like the code in Listing 32.3.

LISTING 32.3   Consuming a Web Service Method with Output Parameters

```
using System;
using System.Collections.Generic;
using System.Text;

namespace WSClient
{
class Program
{
static void Main(string[] args)
{
    localhost.Service svc = new localhost.Service();
    Console.WriteLine(svc.HelloWorld());
```

LISTING 32.3   Continued

```
    string conCatResult = string.Empty;
    int conCatLength = svc.StringConcat("The quick brown ",
        "fox ran over the slow 486 DX2/66", out conCatResult);

    Console.WriteLine(string.Format(
        "Concat Result: {0} length {1}", conCatResult, conCatLength));

    Console.ReadLine();
}
}
}
```

The complexity of converting the request for method execution into a portable XML format, transmitting that XML to the remote host, waiting for a response, retrieving the response XML, and finally decoding the response XML into .NET native types is all handled automatically by the Web Service wrapper class. The output of the preceding code is as follows:

```
Hello World
Concat Result: The quick brown fox ran over the slow 486 DX2/66 length 48
```

This book will not spend much time on the details of WSDL, but it does help to see how everything works, including the WSDL describing the service you just created. To see the WSDL for any .NET service, simply append ?WSDL to the end of the URL. The WSDL for the service created in this section is shown in Listing 32.4.

LISTING 32.4   WSDL for a Two-Method Web Service

```
<?xml version="1.0" encoding="utf-8"?>
<wsdl:definitions xmlns:soap="http://schemas.xmlsoap.org/wsdl/soap/"
xmlns:tm="http://microsoft.com/wsdl/mime/textMatching/"
xmlns:soapenc="http://schemas.xmlsoap.org/soap/encoding/"
xmlns:mime="http://schemas.xmlsoap.org/wsdl/mime/"
xmlns:tns="http://tempuri.org/" xmlns:s="http://www.w3.org/2001/XMLSchema"
xmlns:soap12="http://schemas.xmlsoap.org/wsdl/soap12/"
xmlns:http="http://schemas.xmlsoap.org/wsdl/http/"
targetNamespace="http://tempuri.org/"
xmlns:wsdl="http://schemas.xmlsoap.org/wsdl/">
<wsdl:types>
<s:schema elementFormDefault="qualified" targetNamespace="http://tempuri.org/">
  <s:element name="HelloWorld">
    <s:complexType />
  </s:element>
  <s:element name="HelloWorldResponse">
    <s:complexType>
```

LISTING 32.4   Continued

```
        <s:sequence>
          <s:element minOccurs="0" maxOccurs="1"
name="HelloWorldResult" type="s:string" />
        </s:sequence>
      </s:complexType>
  </s:element>
  <s:element name="StringConcat">
    <s:complexType>
      <s:sequence>
        <s:element minOccurs="0" maxOccurs="1" name="string1" type="s:string" />
        <s:element minOccurs="0" maxOccurs="1" name="string2" type="s:string" />
      </s:sequence>
    </s:complexType>
  </s:element>
  <s:element name="StringConcatResponse">
    <s:complexType>
      <s:sequence>
        <s:element minOccurs="1" maxOccurs="1"
name="StringConcatResult" type="s:int" />
        <s:element minOccurs="0" maxOccurs="1"
name="stringTotal" type="s:string" />
      </s:sequence>
    </s:complexType>
  </s:element>
</s:schema>
</wsdl:types>
<wsdl:message name="HelloWorldSoapIn">
<wsdl:part name="parameters" element="tns:HelloWorld" />
</wsdl:message>
<wsdl:message name="HelloWorldSoapOut">
<wsdl:part name="parameters" element="tns:HelloWorldResponse" />
</wsdl:message>
<wsdl:message name="StringConcatSoapIn">
<wsdl:part name="parameters" element="tns:StringConcat" />
</wsdl:message>
<wsdl:message name="StringConcatSoapOut">
<wsdl:part name="parameters" element="tns:StringConcatResponse" />
</wsdl:message>
<wsdl:portType name="ServiceSoap">
<wsdl:operation name="HelloWorld">
  <wsdl:input message="tns:HelloWorldSoapIn" />
  <wsdl:output message="tns:HelloWorldSoapOut" />
</wsdl:operation>
```

LISTING 32.4   Continued

```
<wsdl:operation name="StringConcat">
  <wsdl:documentation
xmlns:wsdl="http://schemas.xmlsoap.org/wsdl/">
Concatenates two strings, returning the result and length.</wsdl:documentation>
  <wsdl:input message="tns:StringConcatSoapIn" />
  <wsdl:output message="tns:StringConcatSoapOut" />
</wsdl:operation>
</wsdl:portType>
<wsdl:binding name="ServiceSoap" type="tns:ServiceSoap">
<soap:binding transport="http://schemas.xmlsoap.org/soap/http" />
<wsdl:operation name="HelloWorld">
  <soap:operation soapAction="http://tempuri.org/HelloWorld" style="document" />
  <wsdl:input>
    <soap:body use="literal" />
  </wsdl:input>
  <wsdl:output>
    <soap:body use="literal" />
  </wsdl:output>
</wsdl:operation>
<wsdl:operation name="StringConcat">
  <soap:operation soapAction="http://tempuri.org/StringConcat"
style="document" />
  <wsdl:input>
    <soap:body use="literal" />
  </wsdl:input>
  <wsdl:output>
    <soap:body use="literal" />
  </wsdl:output>
</wsdl:operation>
</wsdl:binding>
<wsdl:binding name="ServiceSoap12" type="tns:ServiceSoap">
<soap12:binding transport="http://schemas.xmlsoap.org/soap/http" />
<wsdl:operation name="HelloWorld">
  <soap12:operation soapAction="http://tempuri.org/HelloWorld"
style="document" />
  <wsdl:input>
    <soap12:body use="literal" />
  </wsdl:input>
  <wsdl:output>
    <soap12:body use="literal" />
  </wsdl:output>
</wsdl:operation>
<wsdl:operation name="StringConcat">
  <soap12:operation
```

LISTING 32.4   Continued

```
soapAction="http://tempuri.org/StringConcat" style="document" />
  <wsdl:input>
    <soap12:body use="literal" />
  </wsdl:input>
  <wsdl:output>
    <soap12:body use="literal" />
  </wsdl:output>
</wsdl:operation>
</wsdl:binding>
<wsdl:service name="Service">
<wsdl:port name="ServiceSoap" binding="tns:ServiceSoap">
  <soap:address
location="http://localhost:3179/HelloWorldService/Service.asmx" />
</wsdl:port>
<wsdl:port name="ServiceSoap12" binding="tns:ServiceSoap12">
  <soap12:address
location="http://localhost:3179/HelloWorldService/Service.asmx" />
</wsdl:port>
</wsdl:service>
</wsdl:definitions>
```

There is a lot going on in the preceding WSDL document. The basic idea is that operations (remote method invocations) are defined and associated with specific ports (URLs). For each operation, there are elements defined as input and elements defined as output. By consuming this WSDL document, a web service client is able to format messages sent to the service and interpret response messages from the service.

Creating Transactional Services

Imagine that you are creating a web service for a bank and you have several methods on that web service: Transfer, Inquiry, and Deposit. In order to produce the most reliable web service possible, you need to make it so that if an error occurs during a Transfer or a Deposit method call, the changes will be rolled back in order to avoid placing a customer's bank account in an inconsistent state. The Inquiry method doesn't need to have any transactional support because it is a read-only method, and an exception within that method call won't create inconsistent data.

The way transactional support is added to a web service method is through the TransactionOption parameter to the WebMethod attribute. Listing 32.5 shows the three sample web methods discussed in the preceding paragraph, two of which have been set to use transactions.

LISTING 32.5 Transactional Web Services

```
[WebMethod(Description="Transfers money between accounts.",
    TransactionOption=System.EnterpriseServices.TransactionOption.Required)]
public void Transfer(string sourceAccount, string destAccount,
    decimal amount)
{
    // transfer 'amount' from 'sourceAccount' to 'destAccount'
}

[WebMethod(Description="Inquires about a specific bank account's balance.")]
public decimal Inquiry(string account)
{
    return 0.0m;
}

[WebMethod(Description="Deposits money into an account.",
    TransactionOption=System.EnterpriseServices.TransactionOption.Required)]
public void Deposit(string destAccount, decimal amount)
{
    // deposit 'amount' into 'destAccount'
}
```

The TransactionOption enumeration tells the underlying transaction system how to handle transactions. In the preceding code, Required indicates that if a transaction already exists, it will be reused; otherwise, a new transaction will be created. The transaction system used to support transactional web services is found in the System.EnterpriseServices namespace, which is part of the COM+ system. COM+ and Enterprise Services are discussed in Chapter 40, "Using Enterprise Services."

If any of the transactional methods throw an exception, the current transaction will be rolled back and any changes will be lost. Keep in mind that *only transaction-aware resources will roll back*. This means that if your code makes changes to a disk file during the transactional method and an exception occurs and the transaction is rolled back, the disk file will *still contain any changes made during the method call*. Resources like SQL Server connections, Oracle connections, Microsoft Message Queues, and others are all aware of transactions and capable of rolling back changes.

Managing State in Web Services

A web service is really nothing more than a specialized type of ASP.NET page. As such, a web service is actually part of an ASP.NET web application and can take advantage of application state management techniques such as using the Application object. In addition, session state can be enabled or disabled using properties of the WebMethod attribute.

State should be used sparingly within web services. Maintaining state between multiple calls to the same web service can potentially lead to scalability problems and even

inconsistent data. If you absolutely have to make use of some means of state maintenance, then consider using session state over application state, because application state
can grow rapidly and has the potential of creating memory problems. Refer to Chapter
23, "State Management in ASP.NET 2.0," for more details on the reasons for and against
the various types of state management.

To enable session state and use application state within a web service, you can use code
similar to the code in Listing 32.6.

LISTING 32.6   State-Aware Web Service

```
[WebMethod(Description="Sets a session state variable",
    EnableSession=true)]
public void SetSessionVariable(string variable, string value)
{
    Session[variable] = value;
}


[WebMethod(Description="Queries a session state variable",
    EnableSession=true)]
public string QuerySessionVariable(string variable)
{
    return (string)Session[variable];
}


[WebMethod(Description="Sets an application-wide variable")]
public void SetAppVariable(string variable, string value)
{
    Application[variable] = value;
}


[WebMethod(Description="Obtains an application-wide variable")]
public string GetAppVariable(string variable)
{
    return (string)Application[variable];
}
```

Deciding which state management method you want to use will be a decision very similar
to the decision made for a standard ASP.NET application's state management solution.
The difference is that web services tend to be invoked more frequently than web pages
and typically have different usage patterns. You will generally want to keep state maintenance for web services even lower (if used at all) than what is used for ASP.NET Web
Forms applications. This is because each method should be considered a discrete unit of
functionality, and subsequent method calls should not normally depend on state created
by previous method calls.

Summary

This chapter provided you with a brief introduction to the world of web services programming without bogging you down in too much detail. The chapter covered how to create web service applications and add web methods to services within those applications. You saw how to create regular web services as well as web services that take advantage of state management as well as transactions. Chapter 33, "Advanced Web Services Programming," will provide you with an even more detailed coverage of web services as well as explain some advanced concepts not covered in this chapter.

32

CHAPTER **33**

Advanced Web Services Programming

Learning the appropriate syntax for creating web services is certainly important, but it is definitely not where the majority of work with web services takes place. Creating web services that add value in loosely coupling application components hinges more on effective design and appropriate technology decisions than it does on your knowledge of web service attributes.

This chapter introduces you to some of the techniques and design patterns that are used to create web services that add value to distributed applications, such as designing with Service-Oriented Architecture (SOA) in mind, discovering information about web services dynamically at runtime, maintaining a secure environment with web services, and even how to bind Windows Forms components to data returned from web services.

Designing for Service-Oriented Architectures (SOA)

Service-Oriented Architecture (SOA) as a design pattern has been gaining a lot of momentum lately. As technology advances and provides more and more power, SOA gradually shifts from a theory about how software should be developed to a case study in how software *is* developed.

SOA is considered to be the evolution of object-oriented programming by some people in the industry, whereas others consider it to be completely unrelated to the goals and purposes of object-oriented programming.

Before you can grasp the true definition of SOA, you need to understand the goals that drive this architecture. Achieving loose coupling among application components is a primary goal of SOA.

Loose Coupling and Dependencies

As time goes on and companies produce larger volumes of code, the need to reuse previously created functionality instead of rewriting it from scratch becomes more important. In fact, many times the cost of rewriting functionality instead of reusing it can mean the difference between a project that gets completed and a project that never makes it out of the first design meeting.

This introduces the concept of a dependency. Developers and designers alike often group the two different kinds of dependencies together, and this prevents the creation of the best application possible. There are two different kinds of software dependencies:

- Real dependency—A *real dependency* refers to functionality or services that one system consumes from another system. A system can be a small subsection of code or it can refer to an entire application. Real dependencies always exist and cannot be mitigated with coding techniques or varying architectures.

- Artificial dependency—An *artificial dependency* is the set of constraints imposed by a system on a system that intends to consume functionality. Common artificial dependencies are things such as language or platform dependencies (requiring C, C++, or Linux, for example), infrastructure dependencies, and more. An artificial dependency always exists, but it can be mitigated using various techniques.

What often happens is that an artificial dependency is listed simply as a dependency or a requirement that must be fulfilled without any further discussion. This prevents the mitigation of this dependency and prevents the creation of the best application possible and maximum reuse of functionality.

What all of us strive for is the complete, or as nearly complete as possible, mitigation of the artificial dependencies within a system. This means that when examining dependencies, you need to make a clear distinction about which dependency is based purely on required functionality and which dependency is based on artificial limitations imposed on the feature consumer by the provider.

SOA as a Way of Life

SOA is an architectural pattern in which the main goal is to achieve loose coupling by reducing artificial dependencies within a system. Within SOA, there are services (also called providers) and consumers. A *service* is a discrete unit of work that accomplishes some task requested by a consumer. The loose coupling is achieved when the dependency that a consumer has on a specific provider is *only that the provider accomplish a specific task*, and that there are few or no artificial dependencies in the way. When loose coupling is achieved, the service can be consumed by any consumer that knows the agreed-upon message format to talk to the provider. Likewise, the consumer can use *any* provider of the same type.

In traditional object-oriented programming, the consumer and provider are very tightly coupled, and may even be part of the same class or library of classes. This is where SOA and OOP spread apart in philosophy. OOP traditionally indicates that data and the methods that process that data should be bound together, whereas SOA strives to separate the information from the processing of the information to allow one processor to perform its task on data from multiple consumers and one consumer to send its data to multiple processors without having any impact on the system.

The concept of reusable providers and consumers can become more apparent when applied to a real-world scenario. In the real world, we consume services because those services are either too costly or take too much time for us to do ourselves. In some cases, such as performing specialized tasks for which we have no aptitude, we would be completely unable to do the job ourselves, even if we had the time and money. For example, if I were to attempt to put a new roof on my house without getting the help of a professional, the results would be disastrous. This is called an "area of concern." Some existing services simply do the job better than the consumer could; you might consider some services to be "'experts."

At a hardware level, a device near and dear to the hearts of many developers can be considered a service provider: the Xbox. It provides a service of playing games. You, as the consumer, supply the information (games) to the service provider. As an output, you receive entertainment (and hopefully a high score). The service provider (Xbox) can provide the game-playing service to any input that meets the specified format. The input that you use on one Xbox can be used on any other Xbox because the service provider knows the format of the data being used as input. You can say that the Xbox is loosely coupled from the consumer in that you can play your games on *any* Xbox, and your Xbox can play games owned by any other consumer. The only dependency on the Xbox is a real dependency in that you must use the Xbox functionality in order to play an Xbox game.

Now that you know what SOA is, what its purpose is, and how similar models appear in everyday life, let's take a look at an example of SOA implemented in software.

In this hypothetical scenario, a company has decided to provide a unified storefront. It has purchased several smaller companies that used to sell products individually such as a bookstore, a DVD store, a CD store, and a company that sold consumer electronics online. The new, larger company wants to be able to provide all of the products of each individual child company in a unified storefront. In addition, the larger company wants to have several different sites that all share the same catalog and product fulfillment system so that they can be branded, styled, and customized for different companies.

Without SOA, creating a solution like this would be a daunting task. Even if a solution could be developed without SOA, it would be an extremely rigid and brittle solution that would break at the slightest attempt for expansion or modification because of the tight coupling and the numerous interdependencies.

Using Service-Oriented Architecture, the company decides to create a catalog service that can be used as an interface to the product catalogs of each of the individual child companies and a dispatcher service that is used to funnel requests for catalog information and features from the front-end applications to the appropriate catalog service based on the type of product. In addition, loosely coupled shipping and credit-card–charging services will be used for maximum scalability and growth potential. This allows each of the product catalog hosts to provide their catalog to any front-end store, and the front-end stores can work with any catalog. In addition, additional shipping providers, credit-card management systems, and even product catalogs can be added to the system with very little impact on existing code. Figure 33.1 illustrates this particular SOA case study.

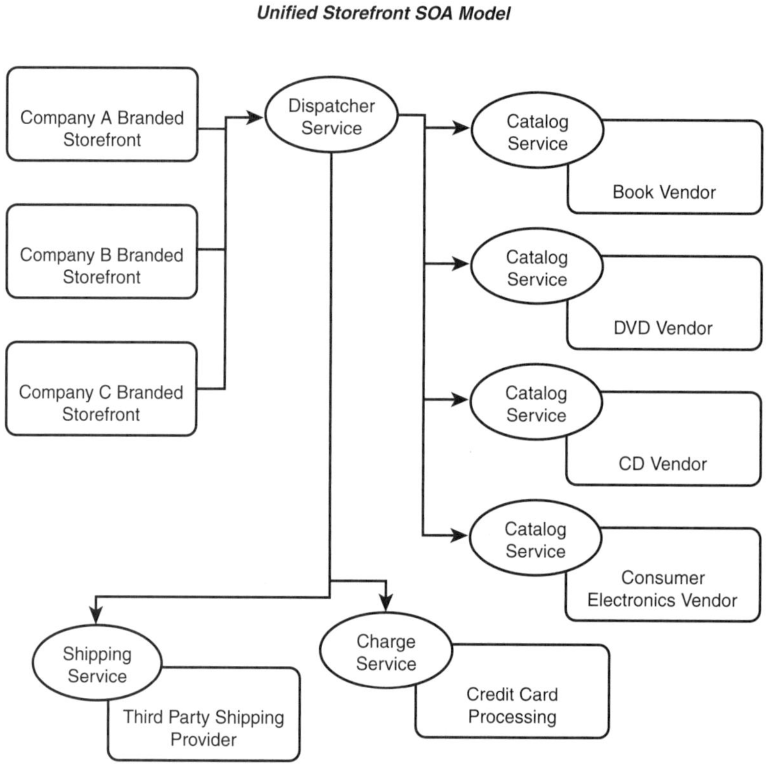

Unified Storefront SOA Model

FIGURE 33.1   Service-oriented architecture model—unified storefront.

This is by no means the only solution to the problem described. However, it does illustrate how the use of SOA and loosely coupled systems can dramatically reduce risk normally associated with a project of this size and can create an environment that is agile and able to cope with change and expansion without requiring a lot of rework and refactoring effort on the part of developers.

Using Web Service Discovery

Loose coupling is a recurring theme whenever developing and designing web services for distributed applications. As mentioned in the preceding section, the more artificial dependencies you can remove, the better. One such dependency is hard-coded information about the web service to which a consumer connects. Using Web Services Discovery, client code can be more versatile and agile in its consumption of web services.

Web Services Discovery works on the basis of discovery documents. A discovery document contains vital information about web services contained on a web server. Discovery documents are created on servers with a `.disco` extension to provide location information about web services hosted by a server. In addition, you can append the `?disco` argument to the end of a request for an ASP.NET web service `.asmx` file to retrieve a discovery document for that service.

Using discovery documents, and other directory facilities such as UDDI to provide dynamic location of web services, you can further remove artificial dependencies from your solution.

The `System.Web.Services.Discovery` namespace is where the .NET Framework provides tools for reading and writing discovery documents and performing other discovery-related tasks.

To see discovery in action, first create a new web service called `ServiceToDiscover` and just leave the default "Hello World" service there in the `Service.asmx` file. Add another web service called `SecondService.asmx` to the project. When you add the `?disco` postfix to the web service URL, for example, `http://localhost/ServiceToDiscover/Service.asmx?disco`, you get an XML document that looks similar to this:

```
<?xml version="1.0" encoding="utf-8" ?>
<discovery
  xmlns:xsi="http://www.w3.org/2001/XMLSchema-instance"
  xmlns:xsd="http://www.w3.org/2001/XMLSchema"
  xmlns="http://schemas.xmlsoap.org/disco/">
  <contractRef ref="http://localhost/ServiceToDiscover/Service.asmx?wsdl"
docRef="http://localhost/ServiceToDiscover/Service.asmx"
xmlns="http://schemas.xmlsoap.org/disco/scl/" />
  <soap address="http://localhost/ServiceToDiscover/Service.asmx"
 xmlns:q1="http://tempuri.org/" binding="q1:ServiceSoap"
xmlns="http://schemas.xmlsoap.org/disco/soap/" />
  <soap address="http://localhost/ServiceToDiscover/Service.asmx"
xmlns:q2="http://tempuri.org/" binding="q2:ServiceSoap12"
xmlns="http://schemas.xmlsoap.org/disco/soap/" />
</discovery>
```

Probably the most important part of the discovery document is the information that points to the location of the WSDL contract data. The WSDL contract is used to construct client proxies capable of communicating with the web service.

The code in Listing 33.1 shows how to use the `System.Web.Services.Discovery` namespace to read and process the information contained in a remote `.disco` file. This Windows Forms application places each contract reference and SOAP binding in separate `ListView` controls.

LISTING 33.1   Using `System.Web.Services.discovery` to Process Discovery Documents

```
using System;
using System.Collections.Generic;
using System.ComponentModel;
using System.Data;
using System.Drawing;
using System.Text;
using System.Windows.Forms;
using System.Web.Services;
using System.Web.Services.Discovery;

namespace DiscoClient
{
public partial class Form1 : Form
{
private DiscoveryDocument doc = null;

public Form1()
{
InitializeComponent();
}

private void button1_Click(object sender, EventArgs e)
{
DiscoveryClientProtocol discoClient = new DiscoveryClientProtocol();
discoClient.Credentials = System.Net.CredentialCache.DefaultCredentials;
doc = discoClient.DiscoverAny(txtDiscoverUrl.Text);
listView1.Items.Clear();
listView2.Items.Clear();

foreach (object discoRef in doc.References)
{
    ListViewItem lvi = new ListViewItem();
    // contract reference
    if (discoRef is ContractReference)
    {
        ContractReference cRef = (ContractReference)discoRef;
        lvi.Text = cRef.DefaultFilename;
        lvi.SubItems.Add(cRef.Url);
```

LISTING 33.1   Continued

```
        listView1.Items.Add(lvi);
    }
    else if (discoRef is SoapBinding)
    {
        SoapBinding sb = (SoapBinding)discoRef;
        lvi.Text = sb.Address.ToString();
        lvi.SubItems.Add( sb.Binding.Name );
        listView2.Items.Add(lvi);
    }
 }


}
}
}
```

Figure 33.2 shows the output of this application after processing a discovery document.

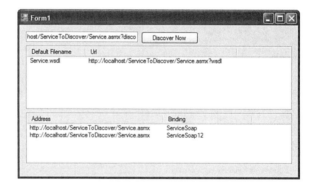

FIGURE 33.2   Reading information from discovery documents.

Using Custom SOAP Headers

SOAP is the wire format used to communicate with web services. In SOA implementations, SOAP is used in Document mode. A less-often-used standard is SOAP-RPC, which is a special form of SOAP used to serialize Remote Procedure Calls. When SOAP documents are used as input parameters to methods, the wire format becomes more flexible and prevents additional artificial dependencies that are typically created when using SOAP-RPC.

Another feature that SOAP allows for is the use of custom headers. Attached to the top of any SOAP envelope, there can be a header that contains additional information. The great thing about using .NET with SOAP headers is that the information contained in a SOAP header can be carried from one method call to the next without explicitly writing additional code. This allows for information that needs to be transmitted to multiple methods to be sent without impacting the parameter list of each method.

The ASP.NET Web Services infrastructure insulates you from the complexities of constructing and decoding the XML that forms SOAP headers and allows you to concern yourself with the data contained within them.

The first code sample illustrates how to add a SOAP header to a web service method. This is a two-step process:

1. Create a class that derives from SoapHeader and declare an instance of that class as a public member within the web service.

2. Use the SoapHeaderAttribute to indicate the name of the SOAP header that will be used by a given method, as well as the header direction and whether that header is required.

To see this in action, take a look at the code in Listing 33.2, which contains the source code for a web service called SoapHeaderTest.asmx.

LISTING 33.2   Using SOAP Headers in a Web Service

```
using System;
using System.Web;
using System.Collections;
using System.Web.Services;
using System.Web.Services.Protocols;

/// <summary>
/// Use this class to represent a soap header
/// It will be serialized and deserialized for
/// communication within a SOAP envelope
/// </summary>
public class TestSoapHeader : SoapHeader
{
public string FirstValue;
public string SecondValue;
}
/// <summary>
/// Summary description for SoapHeaderTest
/// </summary>
[WebService(Namespace = "http://tempuri.org/")]
[WebServiceBinding(ConformsTo = WsiProfiles.BasicProfile1_1)]
public class SoapHeaderTest : System.Web.Services.WebService
{
public TestSoapHeader TestHeader;
```

LISTING 33.2 Continued

```
public SoapHeaderTest()
{

    //Uncomment the following line if using designed components
    //InitializeComponent();
}

[WebMethod]
public string HelloWorld()
{
    return "Hello World";
}

[WebMethod]
[SoapHeader("TestHeader", Direction=SoapHeaderDirection.InOut)]
public string HeaderEnabledMethod(string message)
{
    if (TestHeader != null)
    {
        string output = string.Format(
            "The Message you sent was {0}. The soap header contained {1} and {2}.",
            message, TestHeader.FirstValue, TestHeader.SecondValue);
        TestHeader.FirstValue += " (modified)";
        TestHeader.SecondValue += " (modified)";
        return output;
    }
    else
        return string.Format(
            "The message you sent was {0}.", message);
}
}
```

One thing worth pointing out is that you can have bidirectional SOAP headers. This means that when the web service method is done executing, the current values of the SOAP header are then serialized back into the output of the web service. The client proxy takes care of the underlying work involved in reloading the headers from the SOAP envelope, making it a very seamless and easy-to-use system.

You add references to header-enabled web services in the same manner as standard web services. The only difference is that the SOAP header appears as a member of the service proxy, allowing the client code to manipulate the header before making a method call, as shown in Listing 33.3.

LISTING 33.3   Programming with SOAP Headers: Client Code

```
private void button2_Click(object sender, EventArgs e)
{
    localhost.SoapHeaderTest svc = new DiscoClient.localhost.SoapHeaderTest();
    svc.TestSoapHeaderValue = new DiscoClient.localhost.TestSoapHeader();
    svc.TestSoapHeaderValue.FirstValue = "one";
    svc.TestSoapHeaderValue.SecondValue = "two";
    string output = svc.HeaderEnabledMethod("Hello World");
    output = string.Format("Message from service : {0}\nHeader : {1} / {2}\n",
        output, svc.TestSoapHeaderValue.FirstValue,
        svc.TestSoapHeaderValue.SecondValue);
    MessageBox.Show(output);
}
```

When you run a Windows Forms test harness application and click the button to launch the preceding code, the `MessageBox` output is shown in Figure 33.3.

FIGURE 33.3   Output from SOAP header example.

SOAP headers allow the web service and client to exchange information in a very loose manner without changing the list of parameters on the service methods. As you know, any change to a web service method signature that a client isn't aware of will cause the client to break.

Programming Secure Web Services

Even though a lot of free, public web services are available on the Internet at the moment, the majority of all web service development is still in creating web services that can only be used by a certain set of users. In other words, clients need to be able to prove their eligibility to consume the service.

Using WSE (Web Services Extensions), a downloadable tool library from Microsoft, you can take advantage of the WS-Security standard and have some extremely powerful security features. WSE is beyond the scope of this chapter and often provides more functionality than is desired for simple authentication of clients. This section shows you a very good pattern for authenticating clients in a secure way without impacting the performance of the web service.

Before taking a look at the final pattern, you should know about some of the other alternatives that usually are not chosen. The simplest (for the client) means of authenticating clients is to pass the username and password in the SOAP header to every single method call, and then each web service method would validate those credentials and refuse to perform the work if the credentials fail to verify. There are a number of problems with this pattern. The biggest is that passwords are being transmitted in clear text via XML over the Internet. To fix that problem and protect passwords, you would have to make every single method call to the web service over SSL, or hash the password using an algorithm known to the service. No matter what you do, a lot of unnecessary overhead is still incurred for every web service method. There is already a lot of natural latency that occurs as part of using web services, so adding further overhead to method calls is not a viable option.

Another option would be to use session state. The client would make a call to a web method that validates credentials. If the credentials are valid, the client has access to the rest of the service's functionality for the remainder of the session. On the surface, this might appear to be a fine solution. However, session cookies can be faked by malicious software intercepting communications between the service consumer and service provider and session state incurs an SOA penalty on the server; SOA relies heavily on the idea that services should be as stateless as possible.

The pattern that combines the best of the previous recommendations is one that uses a concept called a *token store*. One service, often called `Login.asmx` or `Security.asmx`, is only accessible via SSL. It has a method for validating user credentials. If the credentials are verified, this service returns an authentication token that is really just an arbitrary string. This token often takes the form of a GUID (Globally Unique Identifier). That GUID is then passed to subsequent non-SSL calls to the real service in the SOAP header. The web method then processes the SOAP header and determines if the token is a valid token. If the token is invalid, the method throws an exception and no work is done. Figure 33.4 shows a conceptual diagram of this model.

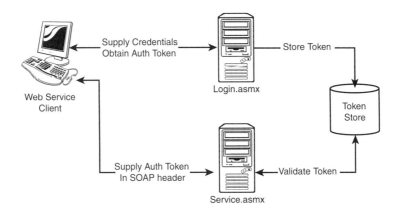

FIGURE 33.4   Using the token store web services authentication model.

The model illustrated in Figure 33.4 should be sufficient for most medium-security requirements. However, a problem still exists because an intruder can intercept a SOAP envelope containing a valid authentication token and reuse that token to send altered messages to the server. In this case, messages can be digitally signed using certificates that verify not only the authenticity of the sender of the message but also that the message was not tampered in transit. If your security situation requires tight constraints such as this, you should consider using WSE for your web service security needs. You can find more information about WSE at `http://msdn.microsoft.com/webservices/webser-vices/building/wse/default.aspx`. If you want to download WSE 3.0, the version of WSE that works in conjunction with ASP.NET 2.0, you can get the library at `http://www.microsoft.com/downloads/details.aspx?familyid=018a09fd-3a74-43c5-8ec1-8d789091255d&displaylang=en`.

Data-Binding Windows Forms to Web Services

One of the powerful new features of Windows Forms is the consolidated Data Sources panel. This panel shows you a list of available data sources that can then be dragged onto any form in the application. For example, if you have created a `DataSet`, that `DataSet` will appear in the Data Sources panel and you can then drag it onto the surface of a form, creating either a grid view or a details view.

One of the types of data sources is a web service. This section of the chapter walks you though building a web service that returns data through a web method. The schema of this data is then interpreted as a data source by the Windows Forms client, allowing that client to bind directly to data returned by a web service.

The following steps will walk you through the process of using a web service as a data source. While reading these steps, it is important to keep in mind a very important distinction: *The web service itself is not the data source—only the data types returned from that service are considered data sources*. In other words, a web service data source will not automatically invoke methods; it only obtains the schema from the web service and uses that schema to prepare the data source.

The following steps will take you through the process of binding to a web service:

1. Create a new ASP.NET web service application by selecting File, then New, then Website from within Visual Studio 2005. You can call the service anything you like.

2. Add a class called `Customer` to the `App_Code` directory within the service. The `Customer` class should have a few basic public string fields, such as `FirstName`, `LastName`, and `CustomerID`.

3. Add a method to the service called `GetAllCustomers()` with the following code:

```
[WebMethod(Description="Retrieve all Customers")]
public List<Customer> GetAllCustomers()
{
```

```
    List<Customer> custList = new List<Customer>();
    custList.Add(new Customer("Kevin", "Hoffman", "customer001"));
    custList.Add(new Customer("John", "Doe", "customer002"));

    return custList;
}
```

4. Add a new Windows Forms project to the solution called WSBindingClient. *Do not add a web reference to the new project at this point.*

5. Open the Data Sources pane and click the Add New Data Source button.

6. Select Web Service as the data source type and browse the current solution for web services.

7. Select the "Service" service from the provided list.

8. Click the Add Reference button. You will see a confirmation dialog that indicates that all of the objects returned by the web service will be added to the Data Sources window. Confirm this by clicking Finish.

9. Figure 33.5 shows what your Data Sources window should look like after completing step 8.

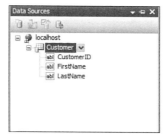

FIGURE 33.5   The Data Sources window after adding a web service data source.

10. Drag the Customer item from the Data Sources window onto the main form.

11. Switch to the code view beneath the form and add the following two lines of code below the call to InitializeComponent(); in the form's constructor:

```
localhost.Service svc = new localhost.Service();
customerBindingSource.DataSource = svc.GetAllCustomers();
```

12. Run the application. You should see a DataGridView that contains the two rows of data provided by the web service, as shown in Figure 33.6.

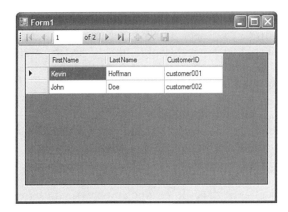

FIGURE 33.6   A DataGridView populated by a web service.

Unlike other kinds of data sources that can be automatically updated by the controls to which they are bound, you will have to write your own code to invoke the appropriate update methods on the web service because there is no way for the data source to know which methods on which web service to invoke in response to data change events. However, even with that minor bit of required coding, the ability to bind controls to data retrieved directly from web services is a powerful tool, especially for smart client applications and SOA infrastructures.

Summary

The art to building great web services has very little to do with writing code. Most of the work in building web services is in design and architecture. This chapter provided you with an overview of the goals and concepts behind Service-Oriented Architecture and how that applies to building web services. This chapter also covered a few techniques that can help to reduce artificial dependencies, such as using SOAP headers for data transmission and implicit authentication, as well as a handy shortcut for binding data in a Windows Forms control to information retrieved from a web service.

PART VI

Developing Windows Forms 2.0 Applications

IN THIS PART

CHAPTER **34**

Introduction to
Windows Forms 2.0

W indows Forms is one of the core components of the
.NET Framework. It allows developers to create extremely
powerful and interactive applications that run on any
Windows platform on which the .NET Framework v2.0 has
been installed. Windows Forms represents a radical increase
in time to market, ease of maintenance, and ease of deployment over other unmanaged development environments
such as Visual Basic 6 and unmanaged Visual C++. This is
the first of several chapters that will help turn you into an
effective Windows Forms developer. This chapter provides
an introduction to Windows Forms, how it works, and how
you can start creating Windows Forms applications using
Visual Studio 2005.

Windows Forms Basics

At its core, Windows Forms is a collection of classes all
created in the .NET Framework. These classes provide a
completely object-oriented encapsulation of creating and
manipulating user interface elements such as forms, dialog
boxes, user input, enhanced graphical output, and much
more.

Although you can create virtually any type of application
using the .NET Framework SDK and Notepad, Visual Studio
includes a plethora of tools and designers that make creating Windows Forms applications a smooth and efficient
process that has become even faster and more powerful
with the current version of Visual Studio.

Figure 34.1 illustrates how Windows Forms fits in with the
rest of the .NET Framework, including ASP.NET applications,
Windows Service applications, and console applications.

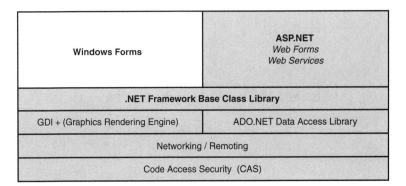

FIGURE 34.1   Windows Forms within the .NET Framework.

Because of the object-oriented nature of the .NET Framework and of Windows Forms, you can accomplish a lot of things with Windows Forms that are virtually impossible without it. For example, you can use inheritance to create forms that inherit from other forms and you can also use inheritance to create your own custom controls that derive from existing controls. For example, with only a few lines of code you could create a text box with your own custom behavior added to it while reusing all of the existing behavior inherent in a text box control.

Windows Forms Versus Web Forms

One of the most common tasks when designing a new application is deciding whether to use Windows Forms or Web Forms. The incredible power, flexibility, and scalability of applications developed using the .NET Framework blurs the line between traditional Windows applications and web applications.

> **Windows Update Is Your Friend**
>
> Ever since Windows Update started pushing the .NET Framework 1.0 to Windows users through its BITS background transfer system, developers of .NET applications have been extremely happy. The reason is that before that time, developers could not count on users already having the .NET Framework on their machines, so deployment of Windows Forms applications was problematic. With .NET 2.0 available through Windows Update, developers can actually make the business assumption that the majority of Windows XP users already have the .NET Framework installed on their PCs. This is a tremendous advantage in the Windows versus web argument in terms of ease of deployment.

There are many arguments for and against Windows Forms applications. Most of the positives for Windows Forms include the fact that a Windows Forms application can have a far more interactive and graphically rich interface, whereas Web Forms applications tend to take less time to build. Table 34.1 takes a look at the various concerns for building applications and indicates whether Web Forms or Windows Forms (or both) support such features.

TABLE 34.1   Decision Support Table: Windows Forms Versus Web Forms

Feature	WinForms	Web Forms
Deployment Deployment of Windows Forms applications is made easier using ClickOnce, whereas web applications are available via a web browser that virtually all Windows users possess. Web applications are still often considered "zero deployment" applications, however.	✓	✓
Time to Market In most cases, web applications of similar complexity take less time to develop than their Windows Forms counterparts.		✓
Interactivity The time and effort required to produce the same highly interactive environment that is the Windows Forms hallmark in an ASP.NET application negates ASP.NET's time-to-market advantage.	✓	
Rich User Interface Both Windows and Web Forms can create extremely rich and visually pleasing user interfaces in their own ways with their own strengths. However, combining the interactivity and reactivity of WinForms here with GDI+ (2D graphics) capability gives Windows Forms the edge.	✓	✓
Scalability Because both ASP.NET and Windows Forms are based on the .NET Framework, they can both scale equally well within their own environments using core .NET technologies.	✓	✓
Enterprise/Distributed Web applications can be expanded using web farms, out-of-process state management, and much more. Both application types can make use of COM+ services, remoting, and web services to build distributed solutions.	✓	✓
Mobile Windows Forms applications can be converted to run on the Compact Framework for PocketPCs, whereas ASP.NET applications can dynamically render "lite" markup depending on the feature set of the mobile browser.	✓	✓

34

The bottom line is that although the two platforms are radically different in their purpose, they have very few technical differences that would sway a developer in one direction over the other. In most cases, the decision of Windows versus web comes down to the type of application being created and the environment in which it must be deployed. Time to market and interactivity are the only two major categories in which ASP.NET and Windows Forms evince a large difference in ability. The rest of this chapter should get you started building Windows Forms applications.

Creating a Windows Forms Application

Creating a Windows Forms application is a fairly simple process. You start off by opening Visual Studio 2005 and choosing to create a new project. After selecting the appropriate language from the left side of the project creation dialog (assuming you have more than one language installed), click the Windows tree node. The following project types will appear:

- Windows Application—Creates an empty Windows application with an empty form.

- Class Library—Creates an assembly that contains a library of classes. You have created many of these throughout the course of this book.

- Windows Control Library—Creates an assembly that is designed to contain a library of custom Windows Forms controls.

- Windows Service—Creates an executable application without any user interface with the appropriate code and hooks to run as a service within the Services Control Panel.

- Console Application—You have created countless console applications if you have been following along throughout this book; creates an executable application that utilizes the Windows Command Prompt console for input and output.

You also might see some additional project types depending on your Visual Studio installation, but the ones listed here are the ones that apply to Windows Forms programming.

To create your first Windows Forms application, click on the "Windows Application" template, provide a name for the application and a location for your code, and click OK to continue. Most of what is presented to you should seem quite familiar. Rather than having the Web Forms Designer window allowing you to build your web application, you have an image of an empty form and a Toolbox full of Windows Forms tools that looks something like the image shown in Figure 34.2.

The next section will teach you the basics of building a powerful user interface using the Windows Forms Designer.

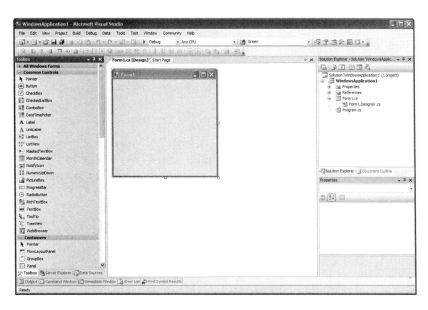

FIGURE 34.2   An empty Windows Forms application.

Using the Windows Forms Designer

The Windows Forms Designer is the interactive tool used to graphically lay out and configure the elements of your user interface. You use this designer to create and manipulate forms as well as to design and lay out the controls on those forms.

To get started using the Windows Forms Designer, drag a control (any simple control should do) onto a form. As you are dragging you'll see a small outline that indicates the point at which the control will be inserted. When you let go of the control, it will appear completely at the designated insertion point.

When a control is on the surface of a form, you can configure all of the control's properties using the Properties window. By default, this window shows up in the bottom right of the Visual Studio screen below the Solution Explorer window. If the window is not visible, you can make it visible by selecting View, Properties Window. You can also use the hotkey Ctrl+W, P. This will open the Properties window if it has been closed and will then set the focus to that window. Inside the Properties window you can configure virtually every aspect of a control. If you click the lightning-bolt icon from within the Properties window, you can also see a list of all the events exposed by a given control (such as an event for when the control is clicked, double-clicked, and so on). If you double-click an empty space next to an event, you can create an event handler for that event on that control.

The list of properties that belong to a given control is specific to that control, and many control properties will be covered in Chapter 35, "The Windows Forms Control Library." The most important things that you will use the forms designer for are navigating control structures, which can be made significantly easier by the Document Outline window; aligning and justifying controls using the new SnapLines feature; and finally, you will be using the designer to make sure that as the host form grows and shrinks, the size and layout of the controls on the form adjust accordingly. You can perform all of these tasks using the designer and without having to write a single line of code.

Using the Document Outline Window

The Document Outline window is an extremely powerful tool that allows a developer to rapidly locate an individual control that might be nested deep within other controls on a form. Despite its power, this window is often overlooked or even forgotten by many developers.

> **TIP**
>
> Even if you don't use it all the time, you should get in the habit of making sure that the Document Outline window has been opened at the beginning of a project. That way it will appear as a tab next to Solution Explorer. With it sitting in a visible location in your workstation, you are more likely to notice it and make use of it. With simple interfaces it may be completely unnecessary, but when you start creating complex interfaces with many levels of nested controls, you may wonder how you managed to survive without it.

This window, shown in Figure 34.3, displays controls in a tree so that you can get a quick list of all controls on the form as well as a reference of where those controls all are in relation to each other. When you have many levels of nesting, it can become extremely difficult or even impossible to properly click on and select child controls using just the visual designer. If you run into that situation, you can use the Document Outline window to quickly find and select the control you need.

FIGURE 34.3   The Document Outline window.

Lining Up Controls with SnapLines

One of the most helpful and powerful new features of the Visual Studio 2005 Forms Designer is the use of SnapLines. *SnapLines* are a new feature that allow you to visually align controls while maneuvering them around the design surface.

With previous versions of Visual Studio, one of the most annoying and tedious tasks involved in Windows Forms development was lining up controls. Previous versions of Visual Studio supported control alignment by littering a containing surface with little grid points. You could move a set of controls so that it looked as if they would all start at the same point, but more often than not there would be discrepancies. Sometimes it would be so difficult to line up the controls that developers would have to go into the control properties and manually modify a control's X and Y coordinates within a container.

This kind of tedium is no longer required when working with Windows Forms 2.0. To see a quick example of SnapLines in action, drag a Label control from the Toolbox onto a blank form. Now click the label and hold to drag and move the label around the outside edge of the form. As you approach an edge of the form, a blue SnapLine appears that visually shows you the recommended distance between the current control and the form's edge. If you move the Label control to the top left corner of the form, you will see that both a vertical and horizontal SnapLine appear to guide the control's placement, as shown in Figure 34.4.

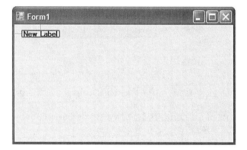

FIGURE 34.4   SnapLines used to recommend margins.

You can also use SnapLines to align controls relative to each other. One of the most common tasks in creating Windows Forms user interfaces is aligning a text label with an input control such as a TextBox. This alignment task used to be time-consuming and frustrating. To see how easy it is with SnapLines, drag a TextBox control onto the form and move it near the right edge of the label. As you do so, a set of SnapLines appears. When the TextBox control is in a position near the right of the label, a pair of SnapLines appears and the TextBox control snaps into a position that puts it at the exact same level as the label. You can experiment with this by dragging more controls onto the form and seeing where the SnapLines appear. When you align a TextBox near a Label, you can see a pink SnapLine that indicates that even though the outside edges of the controls might not be aligned, the text contained within them will appear at the same level.

As you learn more about Windows Forms and you start experimenting more with the designer and creating sample applications in the upcoming chapters, you will grow to love the SnapLines feature; it will quickly become a feature that you can't live without.

Creating Resizable Forms

As you will see in the next section, creating forms that respond properly to different environments and being shrunk or expanded can go a long way toward creating a compelling user interface.

Thankfully, you can accomplish a great deal toward making your form and its contained controls resizable using a few control properties and some features of the designer.

Dock

All controls have a `Dock` property. This property indicates the docking mode of the control. It essentially indicates which borders of the control are bound to the container. A little graphical tool pops up when you select the `Dock` property of a control, which helps you determine what docking mode you want for the control. That pop-up is shown in Figure 34.5.

FIGURE 34.5   Dock selection pop-up.

As you can see from the image, you have the following docking mode options:

- Left—Docks the control so that its left border is "stuck" to the left border of the container.

- Right—Docks the control so that its right border is "stuck" to the right border of the container.

- Fill—Docks the control so that it fills the entire container.

- Top—Docks the control so that its top border is "stuck" to the top border of the container.

- Bottom—Docks the control so that its bottom border is "stuck" to the bottom border of the container.

Experiment with the various docking modes by picking a random control and putting it on a form and then setting the `Dock` property. With a single control and just a form, it might not look like a very powerful property. However, when you start working with nested controls and nested docks, things can get interesting quickly.

Anchor

As you saw when experimenting with the Dock property, the control moves from wherever it was before so that it can attach itself to the designated container border, or it expands to fill the entire container. Sometimes that is the desired behavior, but other times you may want more finely grained control over your interface. This is where the Anchor property comes in.

Rather than defining the border to which the control is attached, the Anchor property defines the *border with which the control will resize*. For example, you can have a control that will automatically grow and shrink horizontally as the form grows and shrinks but remains in its original vertical position. You can also accomplish the opposite and have a control that sizes vertically as the form is sized, but it remains in its original horizontal location. You can even have a control that expands horizontally and vertically but still doesn't consume the entire container as a Dock property would if it was set to Fill.

When you define an anchor, the anchor selection pop-up shown in Figure 34.6 appears. This pop-up is a handy visual indicator as to which control borders will stretch or shrink when the container stretches or shrinks.

FIGURE 34.6   The anchor selection pop-up.

Using the Dock and Anchor properties combined with control nesting (controls that contain other controls), the developer can easily create extremely powerful user interfaces that respond appropriately when a form is resized. Before these properties existed, developers had to manually write code to resize and adjust every control on a form in response to a window resize event. Such tedious coding is no longer required.

Elements of Good User Interface Design

Some people believe that that developers don't need to know anything about what constitutes good design. This author couldn't disagree more. Most developers have a fairly firm grasp of what works and what doesn't as far as user interfaces are concerned: Developers spend more time consuming user interfaces than almost all other computer users. This section provides a quick reference for some simple rules that can help produce friendly and powerful user interfaces.

Design with Colors

Everyone likes a colorful interface. The problem is that too much color, especially colors that don't go well together, can turn a user off quickly. When deciding on colors it is generally a good idea to use a theme of colors: varying shades of the same color and complementary colors. Keep in mind how long a user will be spending looking at your application and keep the flashy colors for things like splash screens and the subtle colors for screens where the users will be spending a lot of their time.

Size Awareness in Design

A lot of really ugly user interfaces are the result of bad proportions. The adage "bigger is better" doesn't always apply to user interface design. When using icons for buttons that will be on the screen a lot and clicked quite often, use smaller icons. For launch panel icons that might only appear once per application use, you can use bigger and more elaborate images. Also make sure that your choice of font family and style are ones that are visually pleasing. Again, keep in mind how long the users will be looking at a screen and how much work and clicking they will be doing: When a user's eye has to frequently switch from large text to small text, large images to small images, or even bright colors to dim colors, that causes eyestrain. If your application is hurting your users' eyes, it might not last very long.

Complexity in Design

Although you might be tempted to cram as much information on a screen as possible in order to reduce the user's click count (see the next subsection), a crowded interface screen is usually a screen no one wants to look at. When building a user interface you always need to balance the amount of information being presented to the user with the tasks the user needs to accomplish. If the user only needs a portion of the information at a time, you can probably reduce the complexity of the screen and make the interface more appealing as a result.

Click Count Awareness in Design

When reducing the complexity of each screen, you can often fall into the trap of creating too many screens or forms. When this happens, it can often take the user an excessive number of clicks or keystrokes to get to the information they want. If the complexity of *reaching* the information is greater than the complexity of the information itself, the user will definitely not enjoy the experience.

Design Intuitiveness

Last but not least, your user interface should be intuitive. If the users cannot figure out how to accomplish their task without reading a lengthy manual or opening some online help, the interface itself might be too complex or structured poorly. Obviously there are some applications where reading the manual is required, but the vast majority of individual user tasks should be fairly obvious. If you find that a lot of users are stopping their workflow to continually refer to documentation, you might want to consider changing the layout of the screen to be more intuitive.

Summary

This chapter has provided you with a brief introduction to the realm of Windows Forms development. It contained an introduction to Windows Forms that included an overview of the technology, how it works, and where it fits within the overall .NET Framework. Next, this chapter walked you through creating a Windows Forms application and gave you a quick tour of some of the highlights of using the Windows Forms Designer to build your user interfaces. Finally, the chapter was rounded out by a brief discussion on some of the concepts involved in building powerful, interactive, and appealing user interfaces. You should now be ready to move on to learning about the Windows Forms control library, data access using Windows Forms, Smart Clients, and much more in the upcoming chapters.

34

The Windows Forms Control Library

W hen full-featured IDEs (Integrated Development Environments) were just becoming the standard for rapid application development for Windows applications, the size of the IDE's control toolbox determined whether the language was the best tool for the job. For example, when comparing Delphi and Visual Basic, Delphi's library of reusable UI controls was not only larger, but many developers considered the VCL (Visual Control Library) to be faster and easier to use. Visual Basic users often had to resort to third-party ActiveX controls to obtain rich user interface programmability.

With the advent of Windows Forms, the library of controls is written for the .NET Framework. As a result, any .NET language has complete access to the base library of Windows Forms controls, whether that language is C#, VB.NET, or even Delphi for .NET.

With Visual Studio 2005, the toolbox of Windows Forms controls has grown significantly. New controls have been added and old controls have been modified and improved. This chapter takes you through a whirlwind tour of every single control available in the Visual Studio 2005 Windows Forms control Toolbox. As you progress through the book to other Windows Forms chapters, many of these controls will be used again with more detailed explanations and code samples.

The Common Controls Toolbox

The Common Controls Toolbox category is essentially a "Miscellaneous" category. It contains the controls that you will typically find in every single Windows Forms application such as buttons, text boxes, check boxes, radio buttons, and so on. This section provides an overview of each of these controls and what they do, as well as how and when they should be used.

The `Button` Control

The button is the de facto standard for user interactivity. If a user wants to confirm changes, open a new window, start or complete a task, or virtually any other major task, that task is often represented by a `Button` of some kind. Buttons can be standard buttons or they can have a flat appearance or even be made up of images. Most of the work done by buttons is accomplished through the `Click` event.

The `CheckBox` Control

A check box is a graphical expression of a Boolean value. If the box is checked, the underlying value is `true`. If the box is not checked, the underlying value is `false`. You can respond to events such as when the checked status of the box changes, and so on. Check boxes can be data-bound directly to any Boolean value.

The `CheckedListBox` Control

The `CheckedListBox` control is an extremely powerful and handy tool. It displays a list of items in much the same way as a `ListBox` control, and when an item is selected, the `CheckBox` control associated with that item becomes checked. You can obtain the list of items currently selected in the control with the `SelectedItems` property. If you need to present the user with several checkboxes and you want those to be formatted in an organized list, this control will help.

The `ComboBox` Control

The `ComboBox` is another control that you will see in just about every Windows Forms application somewhere. Its responsibility is to present the user with a list of options and allow her to select one. You can set the `ComboBox`'s `DropDownStyle` to control its behavior. The `Simple` mode allows the user to manually type in the text portion with the list portion of the `ComboBox` remaining visible. The `DropDown` mode is the same as `Simple`, except that the user must click the down-arrow to reveal the item list. Finally, the `DropDownList` mode is one of the most common modes and doesn't allow the user to manually type anything; she must select an item from the list. If a user needs to select a single value (or provide his own) from a list of values, the `ComboBox` control is the right tool for the job.

The `DateTimePicker` Control

The `DateTimePicker` is a handy control that looks similar to a `ComboBox` on the surface, but when you click the down arrow on this control, a calendar appears. This calendar allows you to navigate month by month or advance or reverse years. When the user clicks on a specific date, that date becomes the `Value` property of the control, which is of type `DateTime`. Today's date shows up highlighted with a box around it. The programmer can also choose the format in which the selected date appears for maximum flexibility. Figure 35.1 shows a DateTimePicker in action.

FIGURE 35.1   A DateTimePicker control.

The Label Control

Labels are pretty simple controls. If you want to include some text on a form that is just there for decoration and doesn't do much beyond that, the Label is the control you need. Just put it where you want, set the margins, padding, justification, foreground color, background color, and the Text property, and you're ready to go.

The LinkLabel Control

The LinkLabel control works very much like the standard Label control, except that it renders like an HTML hyperlink. The default foreground color is the same blue that most browsers use as the default hyperlink color. The LinkLabel has a LinkClicked event that you can use to respond to when a user clicks on the active text of the label. The following few lines of code are used as an event handler for a LinkLabel with the Text property of "Go to SAMS Publishing":

```
private void linkLabel1_LinkClicked(object sender, LinkLabelLinkClickedEventArgs e)
{
    Process p = new Process();
    p.StartInfo =
      new ProcessStartInfo("http://www.samspublishing.com");
    p.Start();
}
```

In three simple lines of code, you can have a user click a link and use the current default browser to open a link to any URL. You don't have to use the LinkLabel for opening web pages, however. It is ideally suited for supplying pop-ups of help information and launching small subforms.

The `ListBox` Control

The `ListBox` is pretty self-explanatory. It is a box that holds a list of items. You can load the list of items programmatically, at design time, or through any of the data-binding features of Windows Forms. You can access the list of items through the `Items` property, and you can get the selected item or items with the `SelectedItem` and `SelectedItems` properties respectively. You can also obtain the numerical indices of selected items using the `SelectedIndices` property. You typically use this control if you need to present the user with a list of options and allow them to select one or more of those items.

The `ListView` Control

The `ListView` takes the concept of a `ListBox` and adds quite a bit of additional functionality. There is so much power in this control that in previous versions of Windows Forms, developers often preferred this control over the `DataGrid` for displaying grids of data. The `ListView` supports multiple display modes that the developer can switch programmatically or the user can select them (if the developer provides that ability). These modes are: `LargeIcon`, `Details`, `SmallIcon`, `List`, and `Tile`. The `LargeIcon` and `SmallIcon` modes are graphical display modes that display an icon as well as the text of the list item. The `Details` mode displays the list in a set of rows and columns in tabular fashion. The first column contains the list item's `Text` property, while each additional column represents one of that item's subitems. `List` mode just displays the list items in a simple list format with no additional information. You can specify the images used for the `ListView` using the `SmallImageList`, `StateImageList`, and `LargeImageList` properties.

One of the new features of the `ListView` that was added for the 2.0 version of Windows Forms is the use of groups. The `ListView` control will now allow you to group list items and display group headers in the list. The `LargeIcon`, `SmallIcon`, `Tile`, and `Details` modes support the display of list item groups.

The `MaskedTextBox` Control

The `MaskedTextBox` control is another new addition with the 2005 set of controls. This `TextBox` allows the programmer to define a *mask* that indicates the allowed input. When a user starts typing in a masked text box, the input will simply be rejected if it doesn't match the mask. This means that developers can use the `MaskedTextBox` to allow only numeric data or only phone numbers that match a specified format.

When you set the `Mask` property of the `MaskedTextBox` control, you will see the Input Mask dialog shown in Figure 35.2. This dialog lets you select from a number of useful pre-created masks (such as phone number, e-mail address, and so on), or you can pick the `<Custom>` mask and define your own pattern using mask rules.

The `MonthCalendar` Control

The `MonthCalendar` control is essentially like a `DateTimePicker` except that there is no text-entry portion. The calendar is always visible and users can use the controls on the calendar to navigate forward and backward in time. Today's date is highlighted just as it is with the `DateTimePicker` control.

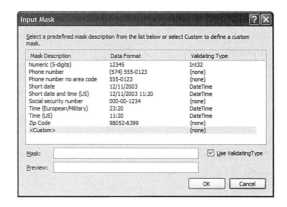

FIGURE 35.2   The Input Mask dialog for a `MaskedTextBox` control.

The `NotifyIcon` **Control**

The `NotifyIcon` control is extremely powerful and has even received a bit of a boost in Windows Forms 2.0. This component, when you drag it onto your form, allows you to display an icon in the Windows system tray where you typically see icons for your virus scanner, instant message system, and any other background applications you might be running.

You can set the `Icon` property of the control at design time or programmatically at runtime to have the icon change depending on the state of your application. You can even create a timer to swap the icon every few milliseconds to create a blinking or flashing icon.

Something new with 2.0 is the ability to work with the Windows XP notification balloons. These balloons should be familiar to anyone who uses Windows XP—Windows Update displays them when updates are ready to download. Using the `ShowBalloonTip` method, you can quickly create a compelling notification from the system tray like the one shown in Figure 35.3.

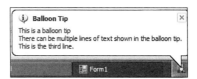

FIGURE 35.3   Using balloon tips with the `NotifyIcon` component.

The `NumericUpDown` **Control**

The `NumericUpDown` is a simple text control that allows users to enter a number or use a combination of up and down arrows to increase and decrease the number. You can set the amount that is incremented by the arrows using the `Increment` property and you can set the current number using the Value property. When users need to enter numeric data into a text box, this control is often more appropriate than a standard TextBox control or even a MaskedTextBox control.

The PictureBox Control

The PictureBox control is responsible for displaying an image. Wherever you place the control you can have an image displayed. This image can be set dynamically at runtime or it can be loaded from any number of file formats such as bitmap, JPG, PNG, and so on. The developer has control over the alignment, scale/stretch, position, and much more. Images can even be loaded at design time from project resources using just the designer— this task used to require additional coding in previous versions of Windows Forms.

The ProgressBar Control

The ProgressBar is a fairly simple control that graphically displays progress. After you set the Maximum, Minimum, and Value properties, the progress bar will graphically display the percentage of completion. Progress bars are used primarily to provide the user with a graphical indication that something is taking place in the background and could potentially be a long-running task. The new 2.0 ProgressBar uses the familiar Windows XP-style progress bar. As each new item appears within the bar, it animates itself into the bar by spreading out vertically. You can see this if you increase the MarqueeAnimationSpeed property and then slowly change the Value property of the ProgressBar.

The RadioButton Control

A RadioButton is a control that works in a way that is similar to a CheckBox. Radio buttons are small circles that have a dot in them if they are selected and are hollow otherwise. Radio buttons are typically used in groups to allow a user to select only one option from a list of options.

The TextBox Control

The TextBox control is a simple input control that allows users to enter free-form text in either single or multiline input modes. As with all stock .NET controls, the TextBox control supports Unicode input, so users typing in languages that have more than 255 characters, such as Chinese or Hindi, will be able to use all of the .NET controls without the developer having to do any additional work.

The RichTextBox Control

The RichTextBox control works in a way that is very similar to the TextBox control, but allows the text to have additional properties such as varying fonts, colors, sizes, and styles such as bold, italic, or underlined. The RichTextBox control is often underestimated. It is actually a small word processor bundled into a single control. In addition to standard formatting, this control also supports bulleted lists and other more advanced word processing features. You can also save and load the contents of a RichTextBox control. The only real work the developer needs to do is provide the interface that changes the properties of the selection. This is the same method Microsoft Word uses to change text attributes. The RichTextBox control has properties such as SelectionFont and SelectionColor to change the current font and color properties. When you examine the Text property of the control, you will get the raw text without the formatting.

The ToolTip Control

The ToolTip control is a powerful new addition to the set of controls available in Windows Forms. The ToolTip control is one of the "provider" types of components. When you place it on a form, you are defining a template for how tooltips should be displayed, not the tooltip itself. When the ToolTip is on the form, all other controls on that form will gain an additional property that looks like ToolTip on ToolTip1. Using the ToolTip control, you can specify the animation speed of the pop-up tip, you can specify the icon that will be displayed, and you can even customize the foreground and background colors used to display the tooltip. These tooltips are much better looking than the ones that were possible using previous versions of Windows Forms. A tooltip with an icon is displayed in Figure 35.4.

FIGURE 35.4   The ToolTip control in action.

You can also set tooltips programmatically using the following syntax:

```
toolTip1.SetToolTip(checkBox1, "This is the tool tip for check box 1");
```

The TreeView Control

The TreeView control is a control that is designed to display a hierarchical list of items. There are top-level (referred to as *root*) nodes and each node can have its own list of child nodes, and so on. TreeViews are exceptionally well suited for allowing browsing and navigating through large amounts of data if that data is hierarchical in nature. The ability to expand and collapse nodes allows the user to see only the information important to them at the time. You can bind the nodes of a TreeView at runtime to a data source, you can edit the nodes at design time, and you can manually modify the nodes at runtime by accessing the TreeView's Nodes property. You also have control over where lines are drawn on the tree, which icons appear next to nodes, and much more. You can even have check boxes appear next to each node, giving you a Boolean value that you can use to allow the user to select multiple nodes within the control.

The `WebBrowser` Control

The `WebBrowser` is a new control that allows your application to open local or remote web pages in a powerful and easy-to-use control. The control supports clicking hyperlinks to open other pages, and will even display Flash animations if you have the Flash player installed. All you need to do is set the `Url` property and the control does the rest of the work for you. It is an extremely powerful control and not only allows your application to view remote websites, but can be used to further blur the line between Windows Forms and Web Forms applications by rendering dynamically generated HTML directly within a Windows Form.

Containers

Containers are used to create extremely powerful and visually appealing user interfaces. A *container*, as its name implies, is a container for other controls. Each container has a unique purpose and it handles its child controls in a very different way. This section provides you with an overview of the containers available in Visual Studio 2005, what they do, and how you can use them in your applications.

The `FlowLayoutPanel` Control

The `FlowLayoutPanel` and the `TableLayoutPanel` are quite possibly two of the most powerful controls to be added to Windows Forms in version 2.0. When working with HTML and ASP.NET, you create markup elements that contain yet more markup elements. These elements are then rendered to the user according to the options specified by the markup. This compositional style of rendering allows HTML designers to create extremely fluid user interfaces that can display a variety of data to the user in ways that you could never really accomplish using Windows… until now.

When you add ASP.NET controls to a form, those controls (assuming the page is in Flow Layout mode) "flow" one after the other to the user. If there are more controls than there is room horizontally in the container, those controls can then automatically wrap.

Using the `FlowLayoutPanel` in Windows Forms, you can simply add controls to the panel and it will deal with adjusting the relative positions of all child controls. You can specify the flow direction using the `FlowDirection` property and can control the automatic wrapping feature using the `WrapContents` property. The control can even be configured to expand itself dynamically as more controls are added to it. Another extremely handy feature is that you can specify a `BackgroundImage` for the control and the layout of that image. If you have ever needed to dynamically add controls to a form and found the task of manually computing the X and Y coordinates of each new control to be tedious and time-consuming, the `FlowLayoutPanel` will probably be your favorite new control. You can experiment with this control at design time by randomly dragging controls into it and modifying the flow direction, wrap, and autosize settings to see how they affect the relative positions of the child controls.

The `GroupBox` Control

The `GroupBox` provides a container for child controls. It has a caption or title. This box can have varying types of borders, background colors, background images, and more to create a very appealing UI element. It is often used to group related controls on a single form, such as a list of radio buttons, related check boxes, and so on.

The `Panel` Control

The `Panel` is the basic container. Although containers provide things like background colors and borders, one of their most important uses is to play host to docking controls. When you dock a control, it "sticks" to the border of its parent container. If the parent container is a fixed-size panel, you have a lot of control over the appearance and functionality of the docked control.

The `SplitContainer` Control

The `SplitContainer` replaces the splitter found in previous versions of Windows Forms. This container control contains two separate panels. The user can drag the middle bar (referred to as the split) to size each of the panels. You can even change the `Orientation` property so that the `SplitContainer` will split a region vertically or horizontally. Probably the most recognizable use of splitters in an application is in Microsoft Outlook. In Outlook, the tree containing things like your Inbox, Outbox, Sent Items, and so on is separated from the panel in which your messages are displayed, using a splitter control.

The `TabControl` Control

The `TabControl` is a control that makes it easy to segment large or complex user interfaces into something more manageable. If you place controls in "tabs," the user can switch between tabs and enter information. Tabs are often used for spitting a user interface into multiple categories. You can access individual tab pages programmatically using the `TabPages` property. The designer allows you to change the active tab and then you can simply drag controls from the Toolbox into each page.

The `TableLayoutPanel` Control

The `TableLayoutPanel` works in a way very similar to the `FlowLayoutPanel`. The difference is in how child controls are handled. Instead of flowing controls either vertically or horizontally, controls in a `TableLayoutPanel` reside in specific table cells. You can define the rows and columns and even use HTML-like column span and row spans to create complex table structures. When you add controls to the `TableLayoutPanel`, you can drag them into specific cells. At runtime, you can set the cell in which a control resides by using the following syntax:

```
tableLayoutPanel1.SetCellPosition(label1,
          new TableLayoutPanelCellPosition(col, row));
```

Using code like this, you can dynamically size a `TableLayoutPanel` at runtime as well as dynamically add and maneuver controls within the layout panel.

Menus and Toolbars

The "Menus and Toolbars" category in the Toolbox contains controls that are responsible for providing pop-up contextual menus, main form-wide menus, strips that contain buttons and other interactive content, and the status bar strip. This section provides you with an overview of the controls in this category.

The ContextMenuStrip Control

The ContextMenuStrip control is a menu strip that appears when the user right-clicks on a control to bring up a list of options that relate to the context at hand. For example, when a user right-clicks the name of a contact in a contact list, a context menu could appear providing options relating specifically to that contact. Figure 35.5 shows a ContextMenuStrip in action. As you can see from this figure, the menus in Windows Forms 2.0 are all upgraded from previous versions, and adding iconic treatment to the menus is now only a few clicks away.

FIGURE 35.5   The ContextMenuStrip control.

The MenuStrip Control

The MenuStrip control is very much like the ContextMenuStrip. Menus created using this control are used to provide a menu that is typically docked on the top of a form.

The StatusStrip Control

The StatusStrip control allows you to display a wide variety of content that is docked to the bottom of a form. This area is usually used to display status messages to keep the user informed about tasks that may be going on in the background or the task most recently performed. You can also use this area to display the current time, currently logged-in user, status icons, and more.

The ToolStrip Control

The ToolStrip is a strip that contains interactive content such as buttons, dividers, text, icons, and so on. These ToolStrips function exactly the same way the toolbars in Microsoft Office function. In fact, the look and feel is almost the same as that of Microsoft Office. The ToolStrip provides more enhanced functionality and a much more professional look than the toolbar controls provided in previous versions of Windows Forms.

The `ToolStripContainer` Control

The `ToolStripContainer` provides a way of storing `ToolStrips` such that they can be moved around and dragged along the top, left, right, and bottom of the container. You can dynamically add and remove `ToolStrips` from a container at runtime, giving you a lot of the functionality that required significant development time in the past at your fingertips for free. Again, the `ToolStripContainer` can add a lot of power to an application and a lot of functionality that resembles Microsoft Office.

The Data-Related Controls

As you will see as you learn more about Windows Forms, working with data is one of the most common tasks for any Windows Forms developer. This section walks you through the controls in the Toolbox that are in the "Data" category including what they do and how you use them. You'll see a lot more of these controls in Chapter 37, "Data Binding with Windows Forms 2.0."

The `DataSet` Control

When you drag a `DataSet` from the Toolbox onto a form, you are prompted for whether you want the `DataSet` to be based on a typed `DataSet` or a standard `DataSet` with no schema. If you select Typed DataSet, you can pick one from the current project or from any referenced assembly. After you select the type of `DataSet` you want, a new component will appear at the bottom of the designer that can then be used in conjunction with other data controls as an instance of a `DataSet` or typed `DataSet`.

The `DataGridView` Control

As you will see in Chapter 37, the `DataGridView` is an extremely powerful replacement for the old `DataGrid` control that came with previous versions of Windows Forms. This new grid is far easier to customize and control and has a lot of powerful new features, including a "virtual" mode that allows for extremely memory-efficient grids that can contain large numbers of records.

The `BindingSource` Control

The `BindingSource` control is a kind of "middle man" for data binding. When you have any type of data that can be bound, you can drag a `BindingSource` onto the form and select that `BindingSource` control's `DataSource` property. The `BindingSource` control can then be used as the target for any other control's `DataSource` property, and all `BindingSource` instances show up in the browse boxes for locating sources of data in the designer.

The BindingNavigator Control

The BindingNavigator control is a customized ToolStrip that contains buttons and actions appropriate to navigating through a list of data-bound items. It comes with buttons for navigating to the first, last, next, and previous records, as well as buttons for creating new records and deleting the current record. You can respond to events from this control for further customization and you can even add your own additional buttons to the navigator's ToolStrip.

The ReportViewer Control

The ReportViewer control should not be underestimated. A lot of people leave it out when discussing the new features in Windows Forms 2.0, but it's one of the controls used most often in the author's Windows Forms applications in commercial applications. This control has a ServerReport property that allows the developer to point to the location of a report hosted on the web such as a SQL 2005 Reporting Services report, and it has a LocalReport property that allows it to run a report using a .rdlc file that was designed within Visual Studio 2005. Directly in Visual Studio 2005, you can create a report, configure data sources within that report, and then bind the data sources in the report to live runtime data sources programmatically or even at design time. The power of this single control is incredible.

The Components Toolbox Group

Components are controls that can be dragged into the designer and manipulated at design time but have no actual user interface. These components are used for things like performing tasks in the background, setting up timed events, providing error and help text to other controls on a form, and even things like monitoring the file system, searching Active Directory, storing images, and much more. This section walks you through the "Components" category of the Toolbox and illustrates what the components are and how they should be used.

The BackgroundWorker Component

The BackgroundWorker component facilitates multithreaded programming by providing methods that notify the foreground (the main UI) thread when progress has occurred and has been completed. All you really need to do is define the method that will perform the background task and periodically call ReportProgress from within your background thread, and the complexities previously required of Windows Forms multithreaded programming are all handled.

The DirectoryEntry Component

The DirectoryEntry component is used to represent a single information entry within an LDAP directory source such as Active Directory or ADAM (Active Directory Application Mode).

The DirectorySearcher Component

The DirectorySearcher component provides the ability to search through an LDAP directory source for information and return results in the form of DirectoryEntry lists.

The ErrorProvider Component

As you saw with the ToolTip control, provider-type controls extend existing controls by adding properties to the designer view and allowing you to set those extended properties programmatically at runtime. The ErrorProvider allows your user interface to bring up icons next to input fields that have invalid data in them. You basically tell the provider where the error icon should appear in relation to the control with the error and indicate the error text, as shown in Figure 35.6.

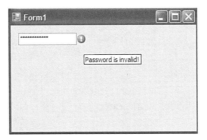

FIGURE 35.6   The ErrorProvider component in action.

The EventLog Component

The EventLog component provides a componentized wrapper around a specific event log. Using the Log and Source properties, you can indicate which log the component will use and the application name that will be given as the event source. You can use this component to write new entries to the event log or even monitor changes to that event log so that your code can respond when new entries are written to the specified log.

The FileSystemWatcher Component

The FileSystemWatcher is a monitoring component that allows your code to "listen" for specific changes to the file system. For example, you can monitor a directory and respond using an event handler when a new file is added to that directory. Although the FileSystemWatcher is an extremely powerful tool for monitoring disk-level activity, you should not use it when precise timing is required. In order to keep the overhead of this component low, it may not always inform your code immediately when a change occurs. In situations with very high load, it is possible that this component can be several seconds behind the actual activity.

The `HelpProvider` Component

The `HelpProvider` control is an extremely useful component that allows you to provide contextual help for individual controls by extending those controls in the same manner as the `ToolTip` and `ErrorProvider` controls. With a `HelpProvider` control present on your form, all controls on the form will have a `Help on helpProvider1` (or whatever the name of your help provider is) property that you can use to provide contextual help. You will also see additional properties such as `ShowHelp on xx`, `HelpKeyWord on xx`, `HelpNavigator on xx`, and `HelpString on xx` where xx is the name of the help provider component. Figure 35.7 shows an example of a simple help provider in action.

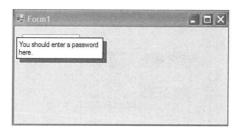

FIGURE 35.7   The `HelpProvider` component.

Using the Visual Studio 2005 Image Library

One of the most annoying things about previous versions of Visual Studio was that the graphics that came with it were extremely outdated. The library itself hadn't been updated since early on in Visual Basic 6's life, making the icons, bitmaps, and animations provided by Visual Studio .NET completely unusable in a modern application. With Visual Studio 2005, Microsoft has supplied a full library of extremely professional-looking bitmaps, icons, and animations that are current and fit well with Windows XP and Office style guidelines. To get this library, you can extract all of the files from the `\Program Files\Microsoft Visual Studio 8\Common7\VS2005ImageLibrary.zip` file that ships with Visual Studio 2005. Keep in mind that this file might not show up depending on the options you chose at installation.

The `ImageList` Component

This component is responsible for storing a list of images. `ImageList` components are used by other components for supplying a list of images such as the list of icons used in a `ListView` or a `TreeView` control. The designer is very easy to use and allows you to browse and preview images contained in the `ImageList`.

The `MessageQueue` Component

This component provides an encapsulation around interaction with a specific Microsoft Message Queues (MSMQ) Queue.

The `PerformanceCounter` Component

This component provides an interface to the Windows Management layer by allowing you access to a performance counter. You can both read existing values from the performance counter or write new ones or even create your own custom counter.

The `Process` Component

The process component provides access to process-level information and methods concerning a specific process. It is most often used to launch subapplications from within the main application.

The `SerialPort` Component

The .NET Framework 2.0 is the first version of the framework to have native support for serial communications, making the lives of a lot of developers working with embedded software and hardware developers much happier. This component provides access to a specific serial port, allowing you to read and write data to/from the port as well as respond to port-specific events.

The `ServiceController` Component

The `ServiceController` component provides access to a specific Windows Service, allowing you to start and stop that service. You can even control services on other machines provided the infrastructure and security environment supports such actions.

The `Timer` Component

The `Timer` component sets up an event that will fire at a specific time interval, allowing your code to execute on that time interval.

Components and Controls for Printing

Windows Forms 2.0 has full support for utilizing the rich printing infrastructure that is part of Windows. This section gives you an overview of the components and controls that belong to the "Printing" category in the designer Toolbox.

The `PageSetupDialog` Component

The `PageSetupDialog` is used to present the user with the familiar Page Setup preferences dialog. The results of this dialog are made available as properties on the component after the user confirms his or her selections.

The `PrintDialog` Component

The `PrintDialog` component is used to present the user with a dialog that prompts him to select a printer and other printing options such as page orientation, color, and so on.

The `PrintDocument` **Component**

The `PrintDocument` component provides a set of properties and methods that allow developers to send data directly to a printer without having to know the specifics of the printer. This component is used quite often by developers to print lists of data contained on currently displayed forms.

The `PrintPreviewControl` **Component**

The `PrintPreviewControl` is a trimmed-down version of the `PrintPreviewDialog`. This control displays only a preview of the document that is about to be printed as indicated by the `Document` property, which is of type `PrintDocument`.

The `PrintPreviewDialog` **Component**

The `PrintPreviewDialog` component is used to present the user with the full print preview dialog, including confirmation buttons that will print the preview, and so on.

Dialog Components

Windows has many dialogs that are part of the basic operating system. These dialogs prompt the user for extremely common information such as a choice of color, a file folder, a font, and so on. This section provides you with an overview of the stock dialog components available in Windows Forms 2.0. Dialogs are typically used when your application requires some explicit input from the user before it can continue.

The `ColorDialog` **Component**

The `ColorDialog` presents the user with a list of available colors. The user's color choice is then made available as the `Color` property. This dialog also allows the user to define custom colors.

The `FolderBrowserDialog` **Component**

This dialog presents the user with an interface that prompts the user to select a folder. The browser in this dialog allows the user to navigate throughout all configured partitions just as in the standard file explorer.

The `FontDialog` **Component**

This dialog prompts the user to select a font from the list of all installed fonts.

The `OpenFileDialog` **Component**

This dialog prompts the user to select a file using a browser interface. The file selected is available through the `FileName` property or the `FileNames` property if more than one file was selected.

The `SaveFileDialog` Component

This dialog prompts the user to select a path and a filename that will be used to save data within the current application.

Summary

This chapter provided a quick tour through all of the controls available in the Windows Forms 2.0 Toolbox. This tour included a description of what each control does and when you would normally use that control in a practical situation. In addition, controls that are new to Windows Forms 2.0 or have been greatly enhanced were highlighted.

This chapter didn't provide you with much in the way of code samples, but it did give you an idea of the tools that you now have available at your disposal. As you progress through the rest of the Windows Forms section of this book, you will see how the various tools and techniques you encounter can be applied to the controls discussed in this chapter. As an exercise, you might want to come back to this chapter after you learn new techniques and see how those techniques can be applied to the wide variety of controls discussed here.

CHAPTER 36

Advanced User Interface Programming

This chapter introduces you to some of the more advanced techniques that can make your Windows Forms application more appealing, better-looking, more robust, and even more aware of other cultures and languages. You will be introduced to GDI+, the 2D graphics library that is responsible for rendering graphics in Windows Forms and how to use GDI+ to create unusual interface elements such as shaped forms. You will see how to use visual inheritance to reuse the look and feel of an existing form on new and modified forms. Finally, this chapter provides an overview of globalization in Windows Forms applications.

Introduction to GDI+

GDI+ is the graphics library responsible for all graphics rendering within the .NET Framework. You can use GDI+ to draw lines and shapes, fill shapes with solid colors or gradients, perform simple animation, or even manipulate existing images found on disk or retrieved from the web.

All GDI+ rendering is done on a special GDI+ surface. These surfaces can be a Windows Form or the contained area within a control. The GDI+ surface is represented by the `Graphics` object in the `System.Drawing` namespace. When you are drawing lines and shapes or performing fill operations, they will all be done against a `Graphics` object.

You can create a `Graphics` object in one of three different ways:

- Obtain an instance of the `Graphics` class from the `PaintEventArgs` argument in the `Paint` event of a form or a control. This is fairly common when you are overriding the default paint routine of a form or a control.

- Use the `CreateGraphics` method of a form or a control to return an instance of the `Graphics` class that encapsulates the drawing surface represented by that form or control.

- Create an instance of `Graphics` from any object that inherits from the `Image` class. This technique is used quite often when using GDI+ to manipulate existing images.

Obtaining a Graphics Object

To obtain a reference to the `Graphics` object using `CreateGraphics`, create a new Windows Forms application and drag a button onto the default form. Then, set the event handler for that button's `Click` event to the following lines of code:

```
private void button1_Click(object sender, EventArgs e)
{

using (Graphics g = this.CreateGraphics())
{
    using (Pen p = new Pen(Color.Purple))
    {
        g.DrawLine(p, new Point(1, 1), new Point(this.Width, this.Height));
    }
}
}
```

This code will draw a line from the top left of the form to the bottom right of the form using a purple line. In order to draw *anything* in GDI+, you must have a pen. The pen defines the style of what you are drawing. You can either create a `Pen` instance based on a color as shown in the preceding code or you can create a `Pen` from a custom brush such as a `LinearGradientBrush` (discussed in the "Using a Gradient Brush" section). Figure 36.1 shows the line drawn by the preceding code.

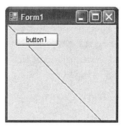

FIGURE 36.1   Drawing a line.

Creating a "Hello GDI+" Sample

In addition to drawing lines using GDI+, you can also draw text. The `Graphics` class contains a `DrawString` method that can be used to place text on a drawing surface such as a form or a control. When you draw the text, you must specify the text font, a brush to use when drawing the text (using custom brushes while drawing text can create some very interesting effects such as gradient-filled letters), and the location where the text will appear, as shown in the following code:

```
private void button2_Click(object sender, EventArgs e)
{
    string text = "Hello GDI+";
    using (Graphics g = this.CreateGraphics())
    {
        using (Font textFont = new Font("Agency FB", 18))
        {
            using (SolidBrush textBrush = new SolidBrush(Color.DarkRed))
            {
                StringFormat drawFormat = new StringFormat();
                g.DrawString(text, textFont, textBrush, 1.0f, 1.0f, drawFormat);
            }
        }
    }
}
```

After running this sample with the button1 that you created previously still in place, you get output that has a diagonal line on the form and some colored text in the top-left corner of the form, as shown in Figure 36.2.

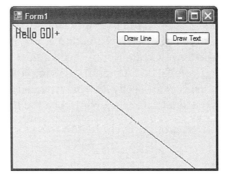

FIGURE 36.2   Drawing lines and text.

You might notice that anything you draw in response to a button click will quickly disappear if your form needs to repaint itself. This is because when the form repaints it doesn't know that it needs to draw the line or the text. An important lesson to learn in GDI+ programming is when you should use a Paint event and when you shouldn't. To see how this all fits together, add the following lines of code to the sample you've been working with:

```
protected override void OnPaint(PaintEventArgs e)
{
    base.OnPaint(e);
    using (Graphics g = this.CreateGraphics())
    {
        using (Font textFont = new Font("Arial", 18))
        {
            using (SolidBrush textBrush = new SolidBrush(Color.Black))
            {
                g.DrawString("Always Painted",
textFont, textBrush, 1.0f, (float)this.Height / 2);
            }
        }
    }
}
```

Now run the sample. You'll see that the phrase "Always Painted" shows up immediately. If you click the Draw Line and Draw Text buttons, you should see all of the graphics. Minimize the window and then restore it. The diagonal line and the "Hello GDI+" phrase have disappeared because the form repainted, erasing all previously rendered graphics. After the form repaint, using the OnPaint overridden method, the form redrew the "Always Painted" text. This gives the impression to the end user that the phrase "Always Painted" never disappeared.

Drawing and Filling Shapes

The next sample will show you how to use pens and solid brushes to create hollow and filled shapes using the Graphics class. Start by creating a new Windows Forms application. Add four buttons to the form: Create Hollow Rectangle, Create Filled Rectangle, Create Hollow Ellipse, and Create Filled Ellipse. In this sample the names of the buttons are left as button1 through button4 respectively. Finally, add a button labeled "Clear Image" to the bottom. Next, add a PictureBox control to the form.

The code in Listing 36.1 shows all of the event handlers for the various buttons, including the Clear Image button.

LISTING 36.1   Drawing and Filling Shapes

```
using System;
using System.Collections.Generic;
using System.ComponentModel;
using System.Data;
using System.Drawing;
using System.Text;
using System.Windows.Forms;
```

LISTING 36.1   Continued

```csharp
namespace GDIPlus2
{
public partial class Form1 : Form
{
public Form1()
{
    InitializeComponent();
}

// hollow rectangle
private void button1_Click(object sender, EventArgs e)
{
    using (Graphics g = pictureBox1.CreateGraphics())
    {
        using (Pen p = new Pen(Color.Red))
        {
            g.DrawRectangle(p, 1.0f, 1.0f,
pictureBox1.Width - 10, pictureBox1.Height - 10);
        }
    }
}

// clear image
private void button5_Click(object sender, EventArgs e)
{
    pictureBox1.Image = null;
}

// filled rectangle
private void button2_Click(object sender, EventArgs e)
{
    using (Graphics g = pictureBox1.CreateGraphics())
    {
        using (SolidBrush brush = new SolidBrush(Color.DarkOrchid))
        {
            g.FillRectangle(brush, 1.0f, 1.0f,
pictureBox1.Width - 10, pictureBox1.Height - 10);
        }
    }
}

// hollow ellipse
private void button3_Click(object sender, EventArgs e)
{
```

36

LISTING 36.1   Continued

```
    using (Graphics g = pictureBox1.CreateGraphics())
    {
        using (Pen p = new Pen(Color.DarkBlue))
        {
            g.DrawEllipse(p, 1.0f, 1.0f,
pictureBox1.Width - 10, pictureBox1.Height - 10);
        }

    }
}


// filled ellipse
private void button4_Click(object sender, EventArgs e)
{
    using (Graphics g = pictureBox1.CreateGraphics())
    {
        using (SolidBrush b = new SolidBrush(Color.Brown))
        {
            g.FillEllipse(b, 1.0f, 1.0f,
pictureBox1.Width - 10, pictureBox1.Height - 10);
        }
    }
}
}
}
```

Figure 36.3 shows this application in action. Notice that the order in which you click the drawing buttons has an impact on the type of image you see on the right. Each sequential drawing instruction will draw *on top of* the currently rendered surface. This means that if you draw a small circle and then draw a large square over the same area, the circle will disappear.

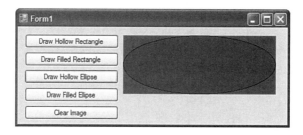

FIGURE 36.3   Drawing and filling shapes.

Remember that because these graphics were drawn in response to button clicks and not during the Paint event, they will disappear when the window is repainted.

Using a Gradient Brush

A *gradient* is a gradual transition from one color to another. This transition can also take place at any angle you choose, giving you an amazing number of choices when creating shading and color transition effects. Many user interface studies have shown that a subtle color transition for a control's background is far easier to look at than solid colors. This is why all of the toolbars in Office 2003 aren't solid backgrounds. They are actually vertical transitions from an aqua color to a light blue color.

The subtle application of gradient brushes to your application and your custom controls can do wonders for its look and feel. If used appropriately, they can make an ordinary application look far more professional.

To illustrate how to use gradient brushes, try rewriting the previous application. Everywhere that a SolidBrush was used, you can replace that code with the instantiation of a LinearGradientBrush. Listing 36.2 shows the new code that will replace solid fills with gradient fills.

LISTING 36.2   Hollow Shapes and Gradient Fills

```
using System;
using System.Collections.Generic;
using System.ComponentModel;
using System.Data;
using System.Drawing.Drawing2D;
using System.Drawing;
using System.Text;
using System.Windows.Forms;

namespace GDIPlus3
{
public partial class Form1 : Form
{
public Form1()
{
InitializeComponent();
}

private void button5_Click(object sender, EventArgs e)
{
pictureBox1.Image = null;
}

private void button1_Click(object sender, EventArgs e)
{
```

LISTING 36.2   Continued

```
using (Graphics g = pictureBox1.CreateGraphics())
{
    using (Pen p = new Pen(Color.Black))
    {
        g.DrawRectangle(p, 1.0f, 1.0f,
            pictureBox1.Width - 10, pictureBox1.Height - 10);
    }
}
}

private void button2_Click(object sender, EventArgs e)
{
using (Graphics g = pictureBox1.CreateGraphics())
{
    using (LinearGradientBrush lgb = new LinearGradientBrush(
        new Rectangle(1, 1, pictureBox1.Width - 10, pictureBox1.Height - 1),
        Color.Cyan, Color.Blue, 90))
    {
        g.FillRectangle(lgb, 1.0f, 1.0f, pictureBox1.Width - 10,
            pictureBox1.Height - 10);
    }
}
}

private void button3_Click(object sender, EventArgs e)
{
using (Graphics g = pictureBox1.CreateGraphics())
{
    using (Pen p = new Pen(Color.Black))
    {
        g.DrawEllipse(p, 1.0f, 1.0f,
            pictureBox1.Width - 10,
            pictureBox1.Height-10);
    }
}
}

private void button4_Click(object sender, EventArgs e)
{
using (Graphics g = pictureBox1.CreateGraphics())
{
    using (LinearGradientBrush lgb = new LinearGradientBrush(
        new Rectangle(1, 1, pictureBox1.Width - 10, pictureBox1.Height - 1),
```

LISTING 36.2   Continued

```
        Color.Orange, Color.Red, 90))
    {
        g.FillEllipse(lgb, 1.0f, 1.0f, pictureBox1.Width - 10,
            pictureBox1.Height - 10);
    }
}


}
}
}
```

Run the sample and see how the new filled shapes have gradually shifting colors in them to form the gradient effect as shown in Figure 36.4. Experiment with changing the gradient's angle (it is 90 degrees in Listing 36.2) and the start and end colors to see the variety of effects you can create.

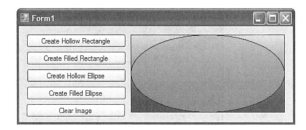

FIGURE 36.4   Gradient shape filling.

Creating Shaped Forms and Controls

The shape of a Windows Form doesn't necessarily have to be rectangular. Each form has a Region property that can be used to programmatically change the shape of a form using a GraphicsPath object. The GraphicsPath class is used to build and represent shapes. The full details of using this class to build highly complex shapes are beyond the scope of this section of the chapter, but you can find out more about this class using the online MSDN reference.

To create a form that has a customized region (shaped form), all you need to do is override the OnPaint method and change the Region property, as shown in the following code:

```
protected override void OnPaint(PaintEventArgs e)
{
    base.OnPaint(e);
    GraphicsPath shape = new GraphicsPath();
```

```
      shape.AddEllipse(0, 31, this.Width, this.Height-31);
      this.Region = new Region(shape);
}
```

This creates an ellipse that starts 31 pixels below the top of the window, completely hiding the original window's title bar from the new shape. Figure 36.5 shows a shaped form on top of the Visual Studio IDE. As you can see, areas of the window's original rectangle that fall outside the shape defined in the Region property end up being transparent.

FIGURE 36.5   A shaped Windows form.

Although it is extremely compelling to create a Windows Form that appears as an ellipse, there is also potential for creating nice user interfaces by modifying control shapes. For example, you can create pill-shaped buttons by taking a regular rectangle and rounding the edges within the Region property of the control. Quite a few applications have made use of triangular buttons to improve their look and feel.

Using Visual Inheritance

Visual inheritance is a tool that allows you to create a form that inherits from a parent form. The "visual" part of the inheritance refers to the fact that all of the control layout and property information from the parent form is provided to the child form. For example, if you wanted to create a single parent form that contained the company's logo and the company name on it that could then be inherited by all forms used by all applications within the company, visual inheritance would do the trick.

To see how this works, create a new Windows Forms application and rename the default Form1 form to parentForm. VS 2005 will prompt you to refactor that name throughout the solution; click OK to do this. Next, add a Panel to the form with a white background and set its Dock property to Top. You can then drag a PictureBox and a Label into this top area to create your fictitious company name and logo.

To create a form that visually inherits from the parent form, right-click the project and choose Add, Windows Form, Inherited Form. Call the new form ChildForm. Within the designer it will look very much like the parent form, except that on the child form you cannot modify the properties of any of the controls on the parent form. Figure 36.6 shows the parent form and child form in action.

FIGURE 36.6   Visual inheritance.

Visual inheritance is just standard .NET inheritance with full design-time support. As such, you can add a property on the parent form that can be modified by the child form. For example, you can create a Slogan property on the parent form that will change the text of the company's slogan:

```
public string Slogan
{
    get { return label2.Text; }
    set { label2.Text = value; }
}
```

And you can modify that slogan on the child form simply by changing the property value, as shown here:

```
public ChildForm()
{
    InitializeComponent();
    Slogan = "Our company is your company.";
}
```

Combining visual inheritance with other advanced GUI techniques such as using GDI+ as well as the power of the new data-binding features in Windows Forms 2.0 can create some amazing interfaces that were nearly impossible to create using previous versions of Windows Forms.

Globalizing Your User Interface

The first step to globalizing your Windows Forms user interface is in knowing how the globalization functionality works within the .NET Framework itself. You may remember from Chapter 12, "Assemblies and `AppDomains`," how satellite assemblies are used to locate culture-specific resources such as alternate text and images. In short, resource files are keyed with a culture name and when they are built, directories are created beneath the output directory and resource-only assemblies called "satellite" assemblies are created.

To see how all this works, start by creating an empty Windows Forms application. On the main form, find the `Localizable` property and change it to `true`. A panel and a label have been added to the main form just to have some controls to play with. In the Solution Explorer, double-click the `Form1.resx` file. You should see the resource editor in Figure 36.7. Each control stores its properties in a resource file.

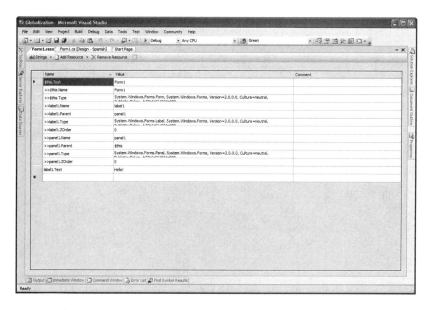

FIGURE 36.7   Editing form resource data.

Another property on the main form is the `Language` property, which starts off as `(default)`, meaning the neutral culture. You can select from all of the available cultures. When you change from the current language to a language that you haven't yet done any work for, Visual Studio 2005 copies all of the default language settings to the new language. So, if your label text is "Hello" in the default language and you switch the form's language to Spanish, the form will appear to stay the same. The designer will visually indicate that you are working on the Spanish-language version of the form, however. Change the "Hello" text in your label to "Hola" and then switch the language back and forth between (default) and Spanish. You will see that the label switches from "Hello" to "Hola."

It's really useful to be able to interactively set the properties of controls in different languages and switch back and forth between cultures, but that isn't the most beneficial aspect.

The fact that you can switch between languages in the designer combined with the fact that *all* user-set properties are stored in a resource file gives you the ability to make layout changes given the language. For example, if a particular label in one language is three times as long as the same label in a different language, you can make changes to the layout of the form to take this into account. You don't have to write any code that dynamically moves controls around at runtime to accommodate font sizes and string lengths.

In the sample included with this chapter, there is also a PictureBox on the form. While in the (default) culture, the American flag was loaded into the PictureBox. Then, the Spanish and Canadian flags were loaded in their respective cultures (Spanish/Spain and English/Canada). The code in Listing 36.3 shows how you can programmatically change the culture of the application to see what the culture-specific content looks like at runtime.

LISTING 36.3   Changing an Application's Culture

```
using System;
using System.Collections.Generic;
using System.ComponentModel;
using System.Data;
using System.Threading;
using System.Drawing;
using System.Globalization;
using System.Text;
using System.Windows.Forms;

namespace Globalization
{
public partial class Form1 : Form
{
    public Form1()
    {
        //CultureInfo ci = new CultureInfo("en-CA");
        CultureInfo ci = new CultureInfo("es-ES");
        Thread.CurrentThread.CurrentCulture = ci;
        Thread.CurrentThread.CurrentUICulture = ci;
```

LISTING 36.3   Continued

```
        InitializeComponent();
    }
}
}
```

Figure 36.8 shows the application running in Spanish, including the Spanish version of the greeting and the Spanish flag.

FIGURE 36.8   An application running in an alternative culture.

When you combine the power of strongly typed resource classes (explained in Chapter 12), the ability to have third parties supply both visual and textual translated content, and the powerful built-in support for Unicode language sets, you end up with what amounts to the most robust and powerful development environment for creating world-aware applications on the market today.

Summary

This chapter has provided you with a look at several advanced techniques that can be used to radically increase the power and beauty of your user interfaces. You learned how to use GDI+ to directly control 2D rendering such as drawing lines, shapes, and filling shapes with solid brushes or even complex brushes such as color gradients. The chapter then illustrated how to take the GDI+ basics already provided and apply them to creating forms and controls with irregular shapes. Finally, you saw how to use visual inheritance and globalization to further enhance the power and scalability of your Windows Forms applications.

CHAPTER 37

Data Binding with Windows Forms 2.0

Wen many of us were creating Windows applications with Visual Basic 6, the concept of data binding was often a controversial subject. Some people would never use automatic data binding whereas others would use nothing but. The idea behind data binding is simple: through some means (whether in design mode or at runtime), tell a control where it can find its source data and how to use that data when the control is being displayed. Unfortunately, the implementation of data binding often falls short of the idea. This was the case with Visual Basic 6; the default data-binding ability of the language was slow, inefficient, and often completely incompatible with the needs of the developer.

The .NET Framework and Windows Forms made extreme advances in the area of data binding, but even Windows Forms and .NET 1.1 could often create cumbersome and frustrating situations for developers. With .NET 2.0, data binding for Windows applications has undergone another radical overhaul. This chapter gets you started with using the built-in data binding mechanisms provided by Windows Forms 2.0.

Binding with Typed DataSets

As you saw in Chapter 20, "Strongly Typed DataSets," typed datasets are a feature provided by ADO.NET. They work by taking a schema that defines a set of relational data (tables, columns, foreign/primary keys, and so on) and turning that schema into a set of nested classes usable from within your application. Providing relational data exposed as a set of classes with strongly typed properties is a huge benefit to programmers working with relational data coming from any number of data sources including SQL Server or XML.

Using the Data Sources Window

When you're dealing with data-driven applications, the Data Sources window is probably one of the most powerful new features provided by the new Visual Studio. To get started, create a new Windows Application in C# (it doesn't matter what you call it). While looking at your main form, you may see a docked window called "Data Sources." If you don't, simply click the Data menu and then click Show Data Sources. You can also use the shortcut Shift+Alt+D. A sample of the Data Sources window is shown in Figure 37.1.

FIGURE 37.1   The Data Sources window.

This particular window shows that there are two data sources defined, both of them typed datasets. From this window, you can create new data sources as well as edit datasets with the designer or configure datasets with the Data Source Configuration Wizard as discussed in Chapter 20.

The Data Sources window shows all of the data sources configured for the current project. This means that if you have a typed DataSet, an Object DataSource, data obtained from SQL Server, or data obtained from an Access or OLE DB source, they will all show up in the Data Sources window. As you will find out later in this chapter, binding controls to data sources in this window is as easy as drag and drop.

Adding a DataSet to a Form

In previous versions of the .NET Framework, typed datasets were things that you could create on your own, and you could store them in your solution, but that was the extent of the built-in support. With Visual Studio 2005, typed datasets are an integral part of data binding.

To see how simple this really is, just create a new `DataSet` in your project. You can do this either through the Data Source Wizard in the Data Sources window, or you can right-click the project in Solution Explorer, choose Add Item, and select DataSet from the item templates list.

After your `DataSet` is configured to your liking, take a look at the Data Sources window. You will see that the typed `DataSet` you just created is listed there as a data source. Using the tree view, you can expand tables and columns and view the relevant properties of each aspect of the `DataSet`. If you highlight a `DataSet` in this window and click the Edit in Designer button, you will be taken to the dataset designer.

This sample contains a DataSet called `ContactsDataSet` with a single table called `Contacts`. This table has three columns: `FirstName`, `LastName`, and `ID`. The `ID` column is an `AutoIncrement` column that is also the primary key of the table.

Now all you have to do is open the Data Sources window and drag your newly created `DataSet` onto your form. When you let go of the mouse button, you will see that the following components have been added to the form:

- Your typed `DataSet` (in my case this was `ContactsDataSet`)—The typed `DataSet` actually appears at the bottom of the designer in the component tray as a full-fledged component.

- A `BindingSource` component

- A `BindingNavigator` component

- A `DataGridView` control

The `BindingSource` component is new to .NET 2.0 and provides a level of abstraction and encapsulation around the data source for a form. What this means is that the methods of the `BindingSource` component work the same regardless of where the underlying data is physically stored or how it is stored. It also publishes a set of events that allow the developer to hook into actions such as when a new item is added, when the current item is changed, and so on.

The `BindingNavigator` sits on top of a `BindingSource` and allows navigation through the items in the underlying source data. It contains the User Interface elements that are typically used in navigating a source of data including controls to move to the beginning of the source, move to the end, move to the next item, and move to the previous item, create a new item, delete the existing item, and save the current data.

As you can see, the task of setting up a typed `DataSet` to be bound on a form is really as simple as dragging and dropping. With a few clicks you have a form that can add, delete, and edit records within your own typed `DataSet`. Figure 37.2 shows an example of a form created with this simple drag-and-drop procedure. In Figure 37.2, I deleted the `DataGridView` and dragged two columns onto the form from the Data Sources window. These columns arrive on the form prebound to the underlying data.

FIGURE 37.2   The result of dragging a DataSet onto a form.

It is worth mentioning here that so far what you have created is a form that is manipulating the contents of an in-memory DataSet. Keep reading to find out how to store the contents of the UI-bound DataSet in a backing store such as SQL Server or Oracle.

Typed DataSet Binding Sample

The preceding section showed you that in a matter of seconds, you can drag a DataSet from your Data Sources window and onto a form designer and have something that both runs and compiles. However, something like this isn't very practical and will never appear like this in an application unmodified.

What you'll see in this section is how to take the ContactsDataSet from the preceding drag-and-drop example and create an application that reads and writes data from an XML file.

To start, create a new Windows Application called TypedDSBinding. Rename Form1.cs to mainForm.cs. Now add the ContactsDataSet to the project. You can either copy it from previous samples if you were following along, or just create the DataSet manually with a single table called Contacts and the three columns: ID, FirstName, and LastName.

Now just drag the Contacts table from your Data Sources window onto the blank main form. As you've seen already, a DataGridView, a BindingSource, and a BindingNavigator will all appear on your form. Delete the DataGridView and then drag the FirstName and LastName columns onto the form. Thankfully, the painfully slow work of creating a TextBox, creating a Label, and then binding them up is all done for you when you drag columns onto a form.

The first piece of code you're going to want to write is the code to load the data into your DataSet from the XML file. Double-click the main form to create a Form_Load event handler and enter the following code:

```
private void mainForm_Load(object sender, EventArgs e)
{
    if (File.Exists(@"..\..\Contacts.xml"))
    {
        contactsDataSet.ReadXml(@"..\..\Contacts.xml");
    }
}
```

Now you need to be able to save the list of contacts to disk when you're done. The first step is to single-click the button in the ToolStrip with the icon of a floppy disk. By default the Save button is disabled. Enable it, and then create a handler for the Click event as shown in the following code:

```
private void bindingNavigatorSaveItem_Click(object sender, EventArgs e)
{
    contactsDataSet.AcceptChanges();
    contactsDataSet.WriteXml(@"..\..\Contacts.xml");
}
```

Now when you run the application you will be able to create new contacts and edit existing ones, as well as delete contacts, and you didn't have to write any complex code—just a few lines of code to load and save a DataSet as an XML file.

Binding Caveats

One issue you may run into while working with automatically bound controls is that at times data you entered may seem as though it disappeared. This often happens when the data from the control is pushed back to the BindingSource. The changes from a control are only pushed to the BindingSource when the control's value changes. For most controls, the value doesn't technically change until the control *loses focus*. This means that for a value to "stick," you have to tab out of that control.

When you add new rows to a BindingSource, the row isn't actually going to be inserted until you *move the current position off that row*. This means that to add a new row, you need to add the row, enter the data, and then move back to a different record.

One way to make your UI work more intuitively in these scenarios is when the user clicks the Save button, you can programmatically tab them out of the current control and then manually commit the current row before saving by using a method like EndEdit on the BindingSource.

Introducing the BindingSource

To put it bluntly, the BindingSource component is your new best friend. In previous versions of .NET, one of the most frustrating things about data binding is that you could only do so much at design time. You had to wait until your application was running to see the real binding behavior. With the use of the `BindingSource` component, you can accurately model the binding behavior of all your controls at design time, even if you are binding to an object, a typed `DataSet`, an XML file, or even a Web Service.

Think of `BindingSource` as an intermediary or a connector between data bound controls and a data source. With the `BindingSource` in the middle, there no longer needs to be a tight coupling between the control and the data source, so we can bind controls to virtually any kind of data *at design time*. In addition to providing an encapsulation around a data source, it also provides standardized methods for starting, committing, and canceling edit operations.

Tables 37.1, 37.2, and 37.3 show some of the commonly used methods, properties, and events of the `BindingSource` class. It is important to get a good grasp of how this class works before continuing through the rest of this chapter because the `BindingSource` is used by many of the other components and classes discussed in this chapter.

TABLE 37.1   Commonly Used `BindingSource` Methods

Method	Description
Add	Adds an existing item to the underlying list
AddNew	Creates a new item and adds it to the underlying list
CancelEdit	Cancels the current editing operation
CancelNew	Disposes of a new item that hasn't yet been committed
Clear	Removes all items in the underlying list
Contains	Used to determine whether a given item exists in the associated data source
EndEdit	Commits pending changes to the data source
IndexOf	Returns the index of a specified item
Insert	Inserts an item into the list at a given position or index
MoveFirst	Sets the current position of the `BindingSource` to the beginning of the underlying list
MoveLast	Moves to the last item in the list
MoveNext	Moves to the next item
MovePrevious	Moves to the previous item
Remove	Removes an item from the list
RemoveAt	Removes an item from the list based on its position within the list
RemoveCurrent	Removes the current item from the list
ResetBindings	Tells all controls bound to this binding source to refresh their values
ResetCurrentItem	Refreshes all data-bound values of the current item
ResetItem	Tells all controls bound to the source to refresh their values associated with a given item
ResumeBinding	Resumes data binding
SuspendBinding	Suspends data binding; especially useful during form initialization routines

TABLE 37.2   Commonly Used BindingSource Properties

Property	Description
AllowNew	Indicates whether or not the BindingSource will allow new items to be created in the list. If AllowNew is true, the AddNew method can be used to create new items.
Count	Gets the number of items in the list.
Current	Gets the current item in the list.
DataMember	Gets or sets the name of the list within the DataSource to which the BindingSource is bound.
DataSource	Works like a .NET 1.1 DataSource property—indicates the source of data to which the BindingSource is bound.
Filter	Gets or sets a filter expression used to filter items in the list.
Item	Gets or sets the item at a specific index. C# can use array [ ] notation in place of this property.
List	Gets or sets the list to which the BindingSource is bound.
Position	Gets or sets the index of the current item within the underlying list data.
Sort	Gets or sets the column names used for sorting and the sort order.

TABLE 37.3   Commonly Used BindingSource Events

Event	Description
AddingNew	This event is fired before an item is added to the underlying list.
BindingComplete	This occurs when all bound controls have finished binding to this source. This is extremely useful for performing actions that can't be done while binding is still taking place.
CurrentChanged	This event is fired when the Current property is changed. Not to be confused with CurrentItemChanged.
CurrentItemChanged	This event is fired when the Current property changes, or any property on the current item changes.
DataError	This event is fired when a data exception is silently trapped. You can use this to inform your code of the error.
DataMemberChanged	Fired when the DataMember property changes.
DataSourceChanged	Fired when the DataSource property changes.
ListChanged	Fired either when the underlying list changes, or when one of the items in the list changes.
PositionChanged	Fired after the Position property has changed.

Rather than showing you specific examples of how the BindingSource works, you will see the BindingSource in action throughout the rest of the chapter as the different kinds of binding are explained in detail. Because the component acts as an intermediary between bound controls and the underlying data, you can't really see how it works unless you are trying to bind data, and examples of data binding are shown throughout the rest of the chapter.

Using the BindingNavigator

The BindingNavigator class was mentioned a few times in the section on binding with typed DataSets but never in much detail. This section provides you with in-depth coverage of the BindingNavigator and how to get the most out of this powerful new control.

BindingNavigator **Basics**

The first and foremost thing to remember about the BindingNavigator is that it is really nothing more than a tricked-out ToolStrip. It is basically a ToolStrip that comes preloaded with VCR-like buttons that provide a user interface for moving through and manipulating the items within a BindingSource. This means that if your design doesn't call for a navigation toolstrip, you can stop building at the BindingSource and leave this component out. However, if you want users to be able to click buttons to move forward, back, to the end, and to the front, as well as being able to add and remove items, this control is definitely what you need.

User-Triggered Binding Actions

The following is a list of the actions that users can perform by clicking the various built-in buttons supplied with the BindingNavigator. Keep in mind that if need be, you can add your own custom buttons to the BindingNavigator because at its core it is still just a ToolStrip.

Create New Item

The AddNewItem property on the BindingNavigator indicates the ToolStripItem that will cause an item to be added. When this ToolStripItem is clicked, the AddNew method of the underlying BindingSource will be called. You can either use the Click event on the ToolTripItem, or you can use the AddingNew event on the BindingSource to inject your own code into the new item creation process.

Delete Item

The DeleteItem property on the BindingNavigator indicates the ToolStripItem that will cause an item to be deleted.

Move First

The MoveFirstItem property on the BindingNavigator indicates the ToolStripItem that will set the position of the underlying BindingSource to the beginning of the list.

Move Last

The MoveLastItem property of the BindingNavigator indicates the ToolStripItem that, when clicked, will set the position of the underlying BindingSource to the last item in the list.

Move Previous

The MovePreviousItem property of the BindingNavigator indicates the ToolStripItem that, when clicked, will move the current item pointer up one index in the list.

Move Next

The `MoveNextItem` property of the `BindingNavigator` indicates the `ToolStripItem` that, when clicked, will move the current item pointer down one index in the list.

Save Data

There is no special property of the `BindingNavigator` that points to the "Save" `ToolStripItem`. This is because the code that is invoked to save data is entirely your creation—there is nothing in the `BindingSource` responsible for saving the data to disk or database.

To help you see what events you can trap and which properties are important in the chain of events, take a look at Table 37.4.

TABLE 37.4   Chain of Events Starting with User Action

User Action	BindingNavigator Property	ToolStripItem Event	BindingSource Event(s)
Click New	AddNewItem	Click	AddingNew
			ListChanged
			CurrentChanged
			CurrentItemChanged
			PositionChanged
			BindingComplete
Click "<<"	MoveFirstItem	Click	BindingComplete
			CurrentChanged
			CurrentItemChanged
			PositionChanged
Click "<"	MovePreviousItem	Click	BindingComplete
			CurrentChanged
			CurrentItemChanged
			PositionChanged
Click ">"	MoveNextItem	Click	BindingComplete
			CurrentChanged
			CurrentItemChanged
			PositionChanged
Click ">>"	MoveLastItem	Click	BindingComplete
			CurrentChanged
			CurrentItemChanged
			PositionChanged
Click "X"	DeleteItem	Click	CurrentChanged
			CurrentItemChanged
			ListChanged
Click Save	*None*	Click	CurrentChanged
			CurrentItemChanged
			ListChanged
			BindingComplete

37

Working with the `DataGridView`

The `DataGridView` is much like its predecessor in that it provides for a grid-like display of rows and columns of data from an underlying data source. That's where the similarity ends. If you have worked very much with .NET 1.0 and 1.1 `DataGrids`, you know that despite their power, you almost always ended up having to create cumbersome controls and templates and classes just to get the grid to do what you needed. The frustration of trying to shoehorn the `DataGrid` to fit into the design of your application is over. This section shows you how to create not only powerful and fast grids of data, but visually compelling ones as well.

`DataGridView` Basics

You've seen the most basic example of how to get a `DataGridView` up and running: drag a table from your Data Sources window onto a form and a `BindingNavigator`, `BindingSource`, and `DataGridView` will appear on the form. The `DataGridView` will automatically display all of the columns in the table, which is typically not the behavior you want.

Before getting into a basic example of binding with the `DataGridView`, you should have a quick look at some of the events, methods, and properties of this control. Table 37.5 lists the events, Table 37.6 lists the methods, and Table 37.7 lists the properties. By looking at this information, you may begin to see how to do some of the more complex things with the `DataGridView`. For a complete list of all events, and methods, and properties, see the MSDN documentation that came with your copy of Visual Studio 2005 or the online MSDN documentation at http://msdn.microsoft.com.

TABLE 37.5   Some of the Events Published by the `DataGridView`

Event	Description
`CancelRowEdit`	Event is fired when a row edit is cancelled.
`CellBeginEdit`	Occurs when the selected cell goes into edit mode.
`CellClick`	Occurs when a cell is clicked; includes any part of the cell such as the border.
`CellContentClick`	Occurs only when the cell's inner content is clicked.
`CellContentDoubleClick`	Occurs when the cell's inner content is double-clicked.
`CellDoubleClick`	Event is fired when a cell is double-clicked.
`CellEndEdit`	Occurs when the selected cell leaves edit mode.
`CellFormatting`	Event is fired when a cell needs to be formatted for rendering. Use this for custom cell formatting that is far easier than the old `DataGrid`.
`CellPainting`	Occurs when a cell needs to be painted.
`CellValueChanged`	Occurs when the value of a cell changes.
`DataBindingComplete`	Occurs when the data-binding operation for the control is complete.
`DefaultValuesNeeded`	This event is fired when the user enters the row for new records, requiring default values to appear.
`Scroll`	This event is fired when the user scrolls the control's view.

TABLE 37.5   Continued

Event	Description
SelectionChanged	Occurs when the user's current selection changes.
UserAddedRow	This event is fired when the user has *finished* adding a row to the `DataGridView`.
UserDeletedRow	This event is fired when the user has *finished* removing a row from the `DataGridView`.
UserDeletingRow	This event is fired when the user starts to delete a row from the `DataGridView`.

TABLE 37.6   Some of the Methods of `DataGridView`

Method	Description
BeginEdit	Places the currently selected cell into edit mode
CancelEdit	Cancels the editing of the currently selected cell
ClearSelection	Clears the current selection
CommitEdit	Commits changes pending in the current cell edit *without* stopping edit mode
EndEdit	Commits changes pending in the current cell and stops edit mode
HitTest	Returns hit test information based on X and Y coordinates including the Row and Column at the given coordinates
SelectAll	Selects all cells in the `DataGridView`
Sort	Sorts the `DataGridView`

TABLE 37.7   Some of the Properties of `DataGridView`

Property	Description
AllowUserToAddRows	A Boolean indicating whether the user can create new rows in the `DataGridView`
AllowUserToDeleteRows	Indicates whether the user can remove rows
AllowUserToOrderColumns	Indicates whether the user can change the order of columns
AllowUserToResizeColumns	Indicates whether the user can change the size of columns
AllowUserToResizeRows	Indicates whether the user can change the height of the rows
AlternatingRowsDefaultCellStyle	Gets or sets the default style of odd-numbered rows
AutoGenerateColumns	Indicates whether the `DataGridView` will automatically generate display columns for each data column
ColumnCount	Gets or sets the number of displayed columns
Columns	Gets the collection that contains all columns in the control
CurrentCell	Gets or sets the currently selected cell
CurrentRow	Gets the row in which the currently selected cell resides
DataMember	The name of the table or list within the data source to which the grid is bound
DataSource	The data source to which the grid is bound

TABLE 37.7   Continued

Property	Description
DefaultCellStyle	Defines the default style (such as foreground, background, font, and so on) for cells
EditMode	Indicates what user action should trigger edit mode
MultiSelect	Indicates whether the user can select more than one cell at a time
NewRowIndex	Gets the index that will be used for the next new row
ReadOnly	Indicates whether the grid is read-only
Rows	Accesses the collection of rows associated with the grid
VirtualMode	Indicates whether the developer has provided their own custom data management routines

As mentioned earlier, there are many more properties, methods, and events that provide the DataGridView with its power. In the rest of this section you will see a few of these properties in the context of some practical and common samples.

Using a ComboBox Column in a DataGridView

Those of you who have worked with the 1.1 version of the DataGrid know that there were quite a few limitations on its usefulness. For example, in a room full of developers, only the bravest (or most foolish, depending on who you ask) would volunteer to write the code to allow their DataGrid to support combo boxes, drop-down image lists, check boxes, and more. In fact, most people simply resorted to buying more powerful grids from component vendors.

That kind of custom grid programming is no longer a problem with the DataGridView. As you'll see in this and subsequent sections, the DataGridView was designed from the ground up to allow programmers to customize, tweak, and extend it.

The sample in this section involves creating a column in the DataGridView that uses a ComboBox. This model is used when the column in the underlying data source is a number or some other key into a lookup table (such as a state code, an order number, a color code, and so on). This sample literally took me five minutes to create.

To start off, create a new Windows Application (C# of course). For that new application create a new DataSet that looks like the DataSet shown in Figure 37.3.

After you have the ContactsDS dataset created, drag it onto the surface of the main form and then delete the BindingNavigator tool strip. Modify the columns list and edit the ContactTypeID column. Change the header text to "Contact Type." Then change the ColumnType property to DataGridViewComboBoxColumn. You should notice that a few new properties have appeared for this column under the Data category:

- DataSource—The data source that supplies the items for the ComboBox.

- DisplayMember—The name of the member on the list item that will be displayed in the ComboBox.

- `Items`—A collection that allows you to manually configure the list of items in the `ComboBox`.

- `ValueMember`—The name of the member on the list item that will be used as the current value of the selected item in the `ComboBox`.

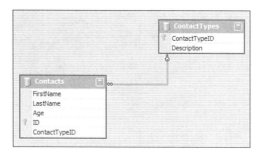

FIGURE 37.3   A contacts DataSet to illustrate a lookup column in a `DataGridView`.

For this sample, set `DataSource` to the `ContactTypes` table. You can browse to this table and it will create a component called `ContactTypesBindingSource` and bind to that. Set the `DisplayMember` to `Description` and `ValueMember` to `ContactTypeID`. You can even set `DisplayStyle` to `Nothing`, which will actually hide the drop-down button until the cell goes into edit mode (this makes the column appear as a regular text column until the user clicks into it).

That's it—you just created a column in a `DataGridView` that is an integer field that gets the list of available options from another table and displays that list in a `ComboBox`—and you *didn't have to write a single line of code*. This kind of task is brutal and painful in .NET 1.1 but really couldn't be simpler using the new `DataGridView` control.

To make the sample do something interesting, add the following lines of code to the `Form_Load` event to add a few contact types:

```
contactsDS.ContactTypes.AddContactTypesRow("Personal Contact");
contactsDS.ContactTypes.AddContactTypesRow("Business Contact");
```

Take a look at this application in action as shown in Figure 37.4. The Save Data button shown in Figure 37.4 is just a simple button that takes the data being managed by the application and stores it in an XML file that can then be read later.

Advanced Cell Customization

Another grid feature that often makes developers cringe is the notion of customizing the appearance of a cell such as its background color, font, and more. In this next example, which builds on the previous `ComboBox` example, you will see just how much you can do with the new `DataGridView` with very little effort on your part.

37

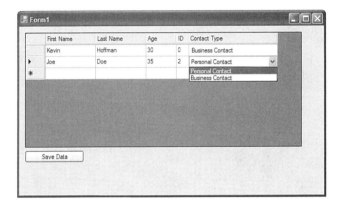

FIGURE 37.4   The ComboBox column in action.

If you ever tried to implement ledger-style coloring in a Windows Forms DataGrid, you know that it's not as easy as you like, especially if you know how easy it is to accomplish with the v1.1 ASP.NET DataGrid. You can now accomplish a ledger-style coloring in just a few seconds. In the DataGridView properties, edit the AlternatingRowsDefaultCellStyle property by clicking the ellipsis ("...") button. Set the background color to yellow and run the application. You should now have a ledger-style grid without writing any extra code.

Another task that normally frustrates programmers working with the old DataGrid is conditionally formatting a single cell. For this example, assume that you are required to change the background color of the "Age" cell to Aquamarine if the person in that row is 35 or older. For this, all you have to do is handle the CellFormatting event, as shown in the following code snippet:

```
private void contactsDataGridView_CellFormatting(
    object sender,
    DataGridViewCellFormattingEventArgs e)
{
    // return if the column being formatted isn't one we're interested in
        if (e.RowIndex < 0) return;
        if (e.ColumnIndex != contactsDataGridView.Columns["Age"].Index) return;
        if ((e.Value == null) ||
            (e.Value == DBNull.Value)) return;
        if (e.RowIndex == contactsDataGridView.NewRowIndex) return;

        int age = (int)e.Value;
          // we know this is the "Age" column, so this is a safe typecast to assume

        if (age >= 35)
          e.CellStyle.BackColor = Color.Aquamarine;
}
```

The CellFormatting event is called every time the cell needs to be formatted for output. This gives you the chance to change any of the properties of the cell to which you have access.

However, if you need to do something slightly more complicated, such as formatting that requires a Graphics object, you need to use the CellPainting event. Don't worry; using the CellPainting event is nowhere near as painful as modifying the Paint event of the old DataGrid.

In the code snippet that follows, you see an example of a CellPainting event handler that creates a gradient background for the LastName column:

```
private void contactsDataGridView_CellPainting(
object sender, DataGridViewCellPaintingEventArgs e)
{
  if (e.RowIndex < 0) return;
  if (e.ColumnIndex != contactsDataGridView.Columns["LastName"].Index) return;
  // if item is selected, use default painting
  if ((e.State & DataGridViewElementStates.Selected) ==
    DataGridViewElementStates.Selected)
    return;

  Rectangle rect = new Rectangle(e.CellBounds.X, e.CellBounds.Y,
                                 e.CellBounds.Width - 1, e.CellBounds.Height - 1);
  using (LinearGradientBrush lgb =
    new LinearGradientBrush(rect, Color.White, Color.LightCoral, 0f))
  {
    e.Graphics.FillRectangle(lgb, rect);
  }

  // if there's no value to draw, return
  if ((e.Value == null) || (e.Value == DBNull.Value)) return;

  using (Pen pen = new Pen(contactsDataGridView.GridColor))
  {
    e.Graphics.DrawRectangle(pen, e.CellBounds.X - 1, e.CellBounds.Y - 1,
      e.CellBounds.Width, e.CellBounds.Height);
  }
  // now draw the value
  StringFormat sf = new StringFormat();
  sf.LineAlignment = StringAlignment.Center;
  sf.Alignment = StringAlignment.Near;

  using (Brush valueBrush = new SolidBrush(e.CellStyle.ForeColor))
  {
```

37

```
    e.Graphics.DrawString(e.Value.ToString(),
e.CellStyle.Font, valueBrush, rect, sf);
  }

  e.Handled = true;
}
```

A little bit of GDI+ code was used in the preceding example to create the gradient and use a few brushes, but it's all pretty basic stuff. Using GDI+ in this manner requires that your application have a reference to `System.Drawing.Drawing2D`. The really important line of code is

```
e.Handled = true;
```

This tells the `DataGridView` that you have handled the painting for the cell in question. When `Handled` is true, the `DataGridView` will not render the default cell style painting. If you left `Handled` to `false`, all of the painting you did in this event handler would be over-written by the default cell style for that cell.

Figure 37.5 shows the new `DataGridView`, complete with the `ComboBox` column, the ledger style, and the gradient-background cell.

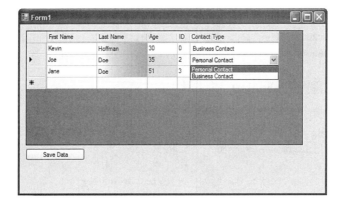

FIGURE 37.5   The `DataGridView` with advanced cell customization.

The `DataGridView` "Unbound"

Perhaps one of the most interesting features of the `DataGridView` is that you can actually use this control without binding it to any data. When you drag a `DataGridView` onto a form without specifying a data source, you can then use the Smart Tag or the `Columns` property to start adding unbound columns. To add an unbound column, all you have to do is specify the name of the column, the header text, and the cell's template (`TextBox`, `ComboBox`, `CheckBox`, `Image`, and so on). After you've done that, you're ready to programmatically add rows to the grid. You can do this in a couple of ways. The following few lines of code show a few of the different ways to get rows into the grid:

```
dataGridView1.Rows.Add(new object[] { "Kevin", "Hoffman" });
dataGridView1.Rows.Add();
dataGridView1.Rows.Add(9);
```

The first line of code adds a row and prepopulates the columns with values. The object array's indices must correspond to the column indices or the data might not show up properly. The second line simply adds a new, empty row. The third line adds nine empty rows to the end of the data in the grid.

After you have programmatically placed your own rows into the grid (or the user does it for you), all of the code you've seen in this chapter dealing with the DataGridView will also work on an unbound grid. This means that you can change the formatting and painting behavior of an unbound cell as well as create a look-up ComboBox column just as easily as if it was a bound control.

Data Binding with Objects

There are always discussions about whether it is better to use XML, typed datasets, or business objects when working with data within an application. Everyone has their own reasons, but I have always preferred business objects. With a business object, you are working in a completely object-oriented model and you have complete control over implementing the business rules directly within the business object.

The problem has traditionally been that Visual Studio wouldn't let you graphically hook up data-bound controls to business objects. You had to do this programmatically at runtime, which eliminated the RAD benefits of the visual designers. It was still better than manually loading the controls with data in for loops, but it wasn't ideal either.

With Windows Forms 2.0 and the new data-binding components, you now get the ability to *visually* bind your controls to actual business objects through the Visual Studio designers. This is a huge benefit to those of us who are die-hard business object fans. It also works out quite nicely if you're using a tool that maps business objects to your database (ORM tools, relational mappers, or even Microsoft's ObjectSpaces library).

Object Data-Binding Basics

To start with, all you need is a business object. To follow along, create a new Windows Application called ObjectBinding and then add to the solution a new class library called BusinessObjects. Then you can create any business object you like. I created a class called Contact with a first name and last name. These business objects need a default constructor, and public properties that will represent the columns of data when presented in a grid format.

Now you need to add a reference from the ObjectBinding project to the BusinessObjects project and build the solution. The reason for this is that when you use the Data Source

Wizard to add an Object Data Source, it browses compiled Assemblies, not source code files.

Open the Data Sources window and click the button to add a new data source. When prompted for the type of the data source you want, select Object and click Next. You will then see a dialog prompting you to select the assembly in which the business object class resides. Click the "+" sign to drill down into that assembly and locate the class that you want to use as a data source. Figure 37.6 shows the Data Source Wizard browsing to the Contact class.

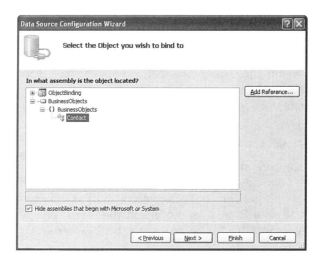

FIGURE 37.6   The Data Source Configuration Wizard selecting an Object Data Source.

Now you have a Data Source that is actually an object. After adding the new data source to the form, the form also now has a new BindingSource component on it called contactBindingSource (if your class is called Contact). You can use that BindingSource to gain access to the underlying objects.

Using the IEditableObject and INotifyPropertyChanged Interfaces

Now that you have seen just how easy it is for you to bind your controls to business objects, you can bring your game up another level by implementing a couple of interfaces that are designed to make your business objects even more compatible with data binding facilities.

Using the INotifyPropertyChanged Interface

When you drag a business object from the Data Sources window onto a form, what you end up with is mostly one-way binding. The class instance to which the control is bound will have its values changed whenever the control value changes. However, the control may not automatically know when the value on the object changes.

To ensure that your business object tells bound controls whenever a property changes, you can have your class implement the INotifyPropertyChanged interface. Any class that implements this interface is required to publish an event called PropertyChanged to which bound controls (or any other class that is aware of the interface) can subscribe. In the set accessor of your property, you can write a few lines of code to make use of the event, as shown in the following example:

```
public string MyProperty
{
    get
    {
        return myProp;
    }
    set
    {
        if (myProp != value)
        {
            PropertyChanged(this,
                new PropertyChangedEventArgs("MyProperty"));
        }
    }
}
```

Using the IEditableObject Interface

In addition to letting the user interface know when properties change, you can also allow your business objects to take part in simple commit-or-cancel edit operations. By implementing the IEditableObject interface, your class will expose the following methods:

- BeginEdit—Indicates that the user has begun an edit operation on your class

- CancelEdit—Indicates that the user cancelled the edit, informing your class to roll back the changes made since editing began

- EndEdit—Indicates that the user finished editing and would like to commit the changes

Listing 37.1 shows a Contact class that implements both the IEditableObject interface and the INotifyPropertyChanged interface.

LISTING 37.1   A Class That Implements IEditableObject and INotifyPropertyChanged

```
using System;
using System.ComponentModel;
using System.Collections.Generic;
using System.Text;
```

LISTING 37.1   Continued

```csharp
namespace BusinessObjects
{
  public class Contact : INotifyPropertyChanged, IEditableObject
  {
    struct contactData
    {
      internal int id;
      internal string firstName;
      internal string lastName;
    }

    private bool editing = false;
    private contactData currentContact;
    private contactData oldContact;

    public Contact()
    {
      currentContact = new contactData();
      currentContact.id = -1;
      currentContact.firstName = string.Empty;
      currentContact.lastName = string.Empty;
    }

    private void NotifyPropertyChanged(string propName)
    {
      PropertyChanged(this, new PropertyChangedEventArgs(propName));
    }

    public int ID
    {
      get
      {
        return currentContact.id;
      }
      set
      {
        if (currentContact.id != value)
        {
          currentContact.id = value;
          NotifyPropertyChanged("ID");
        }
      }
    }
  }
```

LISTING 37.1   Continued

```
public string FirstName
{
  get
  {
    return currentContact.firstName;
  }
  set
  {
    if (FirstName != value)
    {
      currentContact.firstName = value;
      NotifyPropertyChanged("FirstName");
    }
  }
}

public string LastName
{
  get
  {
    return currentContact.lastName;
  }
  set
  {
    if (currentContact.lastName != value)
    {
      currentContact.lastName = value;
      NotifyPropertyChanged("LastName");
    }
  }
}

#region INotifyPropertyChanged Members

public event PropertyChangedEventHandler PropertyChanged;

#endregion

#region IEditableObject Members

public void BeginEdit()
{
  if (!editing)
  {
```

37

LISTING 37.1   Continued

```
      editing = true;
      oldContact = currentContact;
    }
  }

  public void CancelEdit()
  {
    if (editing)
    {
      currentContact = oldContact;
      editing = false;
    }
  }

  public void EndEdit()
  {
    if (editing)
    {
      oldContact = new contactData();
      editing = false;
    }
  }


  #endregion
  }
}
```

Parent-Detail Binding

One of the things that hasn't yet been covered in this chapter is the parent-detail binding pattern. This is a common situation where the user navigates through rows in a parent table and each of those rows is the parent row for child rows in another table. The example most commonly used to illustrate this is when dealing with an Orders table and an OrderDetails table. While the user is browsing through the list of orders, a list of order items appears every time the user changes the current order.

Binding with a parent-child relationship is just as easy as binding to a regular data source. With a typed DataSet, you bind the parent control to the parent table, just as you normally would. Then, for the child view, you simply bind to the DataRelation (often named with an "FK_" prefix indicating that the data relation is a foreign key) that dictates the parent-child relationship. After you do this, the parent-child relationship will be reflected in the GUI.

As an exercise, take the information that you have learned throughout this chapter and try to build your own parent-detail data binding. You can use all of the data-binding techniques covered in this chapter to create the parent binding, and then when selecting a data source for the child records, simply select the data relation rather than the child table itself.

Summary

This chapter was all about data binding with Windows Forms 2.0. Not only has data binding become quicker and easier than before, but it is now more flexible and more efficient in many cases. In addition to getting an overview of data binding, you were also introduced to the `DataGrid`'s successor: the `DataGridView`. The `DataGridView` is an extremely flexible and extensible grid control that makes it easy to create compelling visual grids without having to resort to spending weeks creating custom columns or buying third-party grids. Finally, this chapter covered an extremely powerful new feature of Windows Forms 2.0: object binding. After reading this chapter, you should feel comfortable creating powerful, flexible, data-driven user interfaces in Windows Forms applications.

37

CHAPTER **38**

Developing Smart Clients

At last, there is a marked distinction between simple disconnected applications and the new breed of applications made possible by the .NET Framework: smart clients.

The phrase *smart client* is a broad term that may apply to many different types of applications depending on the person using the phrase. For the purposes of this chapter, the author is referring solely to a specific subset of applications that he considers the only true "smart clients." These applications have the following characteristics:

- Agile—An *agile* application is one that can operate properly under varying circumstances. Users should never run the application and end up in an environment where the application fails to work. For connected applications, this means that the application can work in both offline and online modes.

- Distributed client—A *distributed client* basically means that the ultimate back end of the client is not a simple file on disk, but a web service providing encapsulation for some remote data store.

- Responsive—*Responsive* applications are fast; users should never encounter a situation where they are sitting idle waiting for the application to finish doing something. This means that smart clients need to make heavy use of multithreading technologies to remain responsive while still operating on large data sets.

- Secure—A *secure* application knows the identity and privilege level of the user working within the application. These credentials may be stored remotely or may be validated locally. The bottom line is that a smart client will not allow a user to do something that the developers or administrators did not intend, including tampering and other malicious activity.

This chapter provides you with what you need to start building smart clients using Windows Forms 2.0. After you learn how to build these applications, you will learn how to deploy them in Chapter 39, "Application Deployment Using ClickOnce."

Practical Web Service Consumption

One failing that a lot of Internet and free samples have is that they do very little to convey how to use a technology in a practical, real-world scenario. Unless you happen to be writing an application that does nothing but display the phrase "Hello World" in 30 various and sundry ways, most "quick" samples don't do you much good.

For example, most web service samples all work against a single fixed URL. This means that when the web reference was added within Visual Studio, the sample never changed the URL of the web references. There aren't many development situations where the URL of a web service while being developed is the same as the production URL. In addition, there can often be multiple servers hosting the same service—how does the client application know the URL of the web service in these situations?

In previous versions of Windows Forms, the developer would typically place the URL for the web service in the `app.config` file and then programmatically retrieve that value and set the web service's `Url` property accordingly.

Thankfully, that tedious process is no longer required. Using the new application settings system, the URL of the web service is added to the `app.config` file automatically when you add the web reference.

To see how this works, create a new Windows Forms application and add a web reference to a web service. You will see that the web service's URL is placed in the `app.config` file as shown in the following code:

```
<applicationSettings>
<PracticalWSClient.Properties.Settings>
    <setting name="PracticalWSClient_PracticalWS_Service" serializeAs="String">
        <value>http://localhost/PracticalWebService/Service.asmx</value>
    </setting>
</PracticalWSClient.Properties.Settings>
</applicationSettings>
```

By storing the URL of the web service in a configuration file rather than leaving it hard-coded in the application itself, you can rapidly change the location of the web service and you can even allow end users to change the setting. The new application settings model is covered in the next section.

Obtaining a Web Service URL from UDDI

An alternative to storing the raw URL of the web service in an application configuration file is to retrieve the URL of the web service using Universal Description and Discovery Interface (UDDI). UDDI is itself a web service that exposes a catalog of directory nodes. These nodes can contain information ranging from business information about the service providers to an actual interface containing a URL to access the service.

By using UDDI, companies that produce smart clients can make a single change to a central UDDI record and all clients would then know about the new URL for the web service and adjust accordingly.

In addition to this centrally managed URL, companies can provide multiple URLs for redundancy. If the first URL fails to respond within a specific time period, a smart client can then move to the next URL in the directory and try to establish a connection with that web service.

UDDI information can either be published globally (see uddi.org) or it can be hosted within an organization using the new UDDI services that are a part of Windows Server 2003.

The UDDI SDK and creating and using tModels (the data structures that represent a stored model within a UDDI directory) are both beyond the scope of this chapter. For more information on UDDI see http://www.uddi.org or check out http://www.microsoft.com/windowsserver2003/technologies/idm/uddi/default.mspx for information on the Windows Server 2003 UDDI support.

Using the New Application Settings System

The new application settings system that is an integral part of all .NET Framework 2.0 applications dramatically increases the power of configuration files.

In previous versions of the .NET Framework, application configuration files were used to provide read-only information that could be used to feed data into the application at startup. The new application settings framework provides that same functionality, but also allows the developer to

- Visually create settings using a designer

- Programmatically read settings at User or Application scope

- Save settings to the local file system at User or Application scope

- Bind control properties (read *and* write) to User or Application scope configuration settings

You have already seen a little bit of the first item when you created a web reference. Right-click your Windows Forms project, select Properties, and then click the Settings tab. You will see the settings designer shown in Figure 38.1.

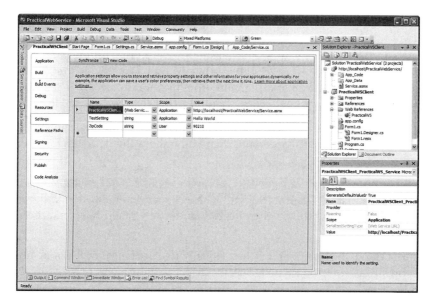

FIGURE 38.1   The settings designer.

This designer looks very much like the resource editor. To add a new setting, simply provide a name, a data type, and a scope (User or Application). In previous versions of the .NET Framework, the developer had to resort to writing tedious isolated storage code to store and retrieve user-scoped preferences and options.

When your application starts, all applicable settings are automatically loaded. This means that all application-scoped settings are loaded and all user-scoped settings for the current user are loaded. Controls that are bound to configuration file properties will load those properties from the configuration system whenever those values are needed.

The first time you use the Settings Designer class within Visual Studio, a `Settings` class is created for you. This class provides encapsulation around the settings in the designer, as well as strongly typed member access. Using this class, you can read and write settings and save those settings, as shown in the following code:

```
MessageBox.Show("Your zip code is " +
    Properties.Settings.Default.ZipCode);


Properties.Settings.Default.ZipCode = txtZipCode.Text;
Properties.Settings.Default.Save();
```

The `Default` property provides access to an instance of the class created by the designer. If you like, you can write your own C# code and extend this class by modifying the `Settings.cs` class that has been added to the Visual Studio solution.

One of the most powerful things you can do with the new application settings system is to bind control properties to configuration properties. To do this, create a new string property called `Greeting` and make sure it is scoped at the `User` level. Next, drag a `TextBox` onto the form and call it `txtGreeting`. In the `txtGreeting` properties panel, expand the `ApplicationSettings` group at the top and click the ellipsis button next to `PropertyBinding`. You will see a configuration setting property map dialog like the one in Figure 38.2.

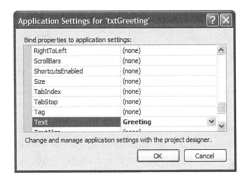

FIGURE 38.2   Configuration setting property map dialog.

This binding only handles reading the data from the configuration system when the application starts up. If the data changes, you have to call `Properties.Settings.Default.Save()` in your code to persist the change. The really powerful aspect of this new system is that the scoping is dealt with automatically. Without your having to write any additional code, your application can automatically differentiate between preferences set by any of the application's users as well as maintain application-wide settings.

Supporting Offline and Online Operation

Part of an application's agility comes from its ability to work properly under any circumstance. In today's mobile age, someone could be using an application on a laptop in a disconnected environment, bring the laptop to a coffee shop and connect wirelessly, and then bring the laptop home and connect to a wired LAN. A truly agile application needs to be able to work when the network is connected and when it is disconnected.

The first part of working in both connected and disconnected modes is making sure that your application makes a local cache of offline activity that can then be uploaded to the web service after the connection is restored. The format and storage medium of this offline cache will be up to you and will largely depend on the specifics of your application, so that won't be covered in detail here.

In order for your application to begin uploading data to the web service when a connection is restored, your application needs to know when a connection has been restored.

The new `System.Net.NetworkInformation` namespace provides developers with a handy utility class called `NetworkChange`. This class hosts events that are used to notify applications when changes in network status occur.

The first event is NetworkAvailabilityChanged. This event reports when there is a change in network availability. The network is considered "Available" when there is at least one network interface device that is considered "Up." If all network interfaces are down or otherwise having trouble, the network is not available.

This might seem like the ideal way to detect whether your user has network access to the web service. Unfortunately, this isn't entirely true. Here's the rub: If the user has multiple network interfaces, such as Wireless (Wi-Fi) access, a LAN card, a 1394 IEEE card (FireWire), or a VPN (Virtual Private Network) interface device, this can complicate things. What happens is that one of these devices will lose access, but other devices may remain "up," yet none are connected to a "real" network. In this case, the NetworkAvailabilityChanged event arguments will still report that the network is available, yet the client application cannot communicate with the web service.

To provide true connection detection, your code also needs to respond to the NetworkAddressChanged event, which is called whenever a network address is changed. Network addresses change when a device acquires a DHCP address (connect) and when a device disconnects or becomes disabled.

Listing 38.1 shows the source code for a form that sends messages to a list box when addresses change and when network availability changes. With this application running, experiment by turning off Wi-Fi hardware switches, disabling interfaces, enabling interfaces, and plugging and unplugging physical LAN cables. Make note of when the address change event is called compared to when the network availability event is called. For maximum effect, try this on a machine with a wireless card, a LAN card, and another network device like a VPN or a FireWire device.

LISTING 38.1   Monitoring Network Status

```
using System;
using System.Net;
using System.Net.NetworkInformation;
using System.Collections.Generic;
using System.ComponentModel;
using System.Data;
using System.Drawing;
using System.Text;
using System.Windows.Forms;

namespace Agile1
{
public partial class Form1 : Form
{
public Form1()
{
InitializeComponent();
System.Net.NetworkInformation.NetworkChange.NetworkAddressChanged +=
```

LISTING 38.1   Continued

```
    new NetworkAddressChangedEventHandler(NetworkChange_NetworkAddressChanged);
System.Net.NetworkInformation.NetworkChange.NetworkAvailabilityChanged +=
    new NetworkAvailabilityChangedEventHandler(
NetworkChange_NetworkAvailabilityChanged);
}

delegate void RespondDelegate();

void NetworkChange_NetworkAvailabilityChanged(object sender,
System.Net.NetworkInformation.NetworkAvailabilityEventArgs e)
{
RespondDelegate d =
    delegate()
    {
        lbLog.Items.Add(
            string.Format("Network availability changed. Net {0} available.",
            e.IsAvailable ? "is" : "is not"));
    };
this.Invoke(d);
}

void NetworkChange_NetworkAddressChanged(object sender, EventArgs e)
{
RespondDelegate d =
    delegate()
    {
        bool hasOneGateway = false;
        NetworkInterface[] nis = NetworkInterface.GetAllNetworkInterfaces();
        foreach (NetworkInterface ni in nis)
        {
            IPInterfaceProperties ipProps = ni.GetIPProperties();
            if (ipProps.GatewayAddresses.Count > 0)
                hasOneGateway = true;
        }
        if (hasOneGateway)
            lbLog.Items.Add("Network address changed (probably still online)");
        else
            lbLog.Items.Add("Network address changed (probably NOT online)");
    };
this.Invoke(d);
}
}
}
```

38

The code in the preceding listing uses the presence of at least one gateway address as a litmus test to guess whether a real network connection is present after the address change. It also makes handy use of anonymous methods to use the `Invoke()` method to forward the GUI-modifying code to the main UI thread. Figure 38.3 shows what happened when this program ran. The author had turned off his wireless card and then turned it back on, and then disabled every adapter on his machine, which finally produced a network availability event. Then he turned them all back on, which completed the test with a valid gateway.

FIGURE 38.3   Monitoring network availability and address changed events.

Authorizing and Authenticating Users

When working with ASP.NET applications, the authentication of a user can be extremely easy. Using Forms or Windows authentication, ASP.NET code can identify the current user simply by accessing the `User` property of a page. It isn't quite that simple when working with Windows Forms applications, especially smart clients.

When working with smart clients, many client applications use the back-end web service for user authentication by supplying user credentials over a secure connection to a web service. Users can also be authenticated against a local database or even an XML file. Regardless of the method of validating user credentials, most smart clients need to be able to prompt the user for their credentials, validate those credentials, and then shut the application down if the credential validation fails.

This section shows you how to create a reusable Windows Form that can be used to prompt users for credentials and even validate those credentials without knowledge of the underlying validation scheme or persistence medium.

To start, create a new Windows Forms project and add a new form to it called `LoginPrompt`. It should have a text box for the user name, a text box for the password, and a button labeled Login. The code in Listing 38.2 shows the code in `LoginPrompt.cs`.

LISTING 38.2   A Universal Login Dialog

```csharp
using System;
using System.Collections.Generic;
using System.ComponentModel;
using System.Data;
using System.Drawing;
using System.Text;
using System.Windows.Forms;

namespace Security
{
public delegate bool ValidateCredentialsDelegate(string userName, string password);

public partial class LoginPrompt : Form
{
    private ValidateCredentialsDelegate credValidator = null;
    private bool validationResult = false;

    public LoginPrompt()
    {
        InitializeComponent();
    }

    public LoginPrompt(ValidateCredentialsDelegate del)
    {
        InitializeComponent();
        credValidator = del;
    }

    private void btnLogin_Click(object sender, EventArgs e)
    {
        if (credValidator != null)
            validationResult = credValidator(txtUserName.Text, txtPassword.Text);
        this.DialogResult = DialogResult.OK;
        this.Close();
    }

    public bool ValidationResult
    {
        get { return validationResult; }
        set { validationResult = value; }
    }
}
}
```

To use this dialog, all you need to do is instantiate the dialog and supply a delegate that will be invoked to validate the user's name and password. The hardest part about using a login prompt is shutting the application down elegantly when the credential validation fails. To do this properly, you need to modify the `Program.cs` file that is created when you create your Windows Forms application, as shown in Listing 38.3.

LISTING 38.3　Using a Universal Login Dialog

```
using System;
using System.Collections.Generic;
using System.Windows.Forms;

namespace Security
{
static class Program
{
/// <summary>
/// The main entry point for the application.
/// </summary>
[STAThread]
static void Main()
{
    Application.EnableVisualStyles();
    Application.SetCompatibleTextRenderingDefault(false);
    Form1 mainForm = new Form1();
    mainForm.Visible = false;
    LoginPrompt lp =
new LoginPrompt(new ValidateCredentialsDelegate(ValidateCredentials));
    if (lp.ShowDialog() == DialogResult.OK)
    {
        if (lp.ValidationResult == true)
            Application.Run(mainForm);
    }
}

static bool ValidateCredentials(string userName, string password)
{
    return false;
}
}
}
```

Multithreaded Web Service Consumption

When a client application needs to make calls to a web service for data and other business operations, some of those operations and data retrievals can take a long time. Any number of factors can contribute to a web service call taking a long time to return, including data volume, processing cost on the server, or even server load and slow network connections.

Multithreaded web service consumption has changed slightly since the previous versions of the .NET Framework. In version 2.0 of the framework, you invoke an xxAsynch() method where xx is the name of the server-side method. When the asynchronous method completes, the xxCompleted event will be triggered. All you have to do is handle the xxCompleted event and you will be consuming the web service asynchronously.

To see how to consume a web service in a background thread so that the foreground thread (user interface) can continue uninterrupted, create a new Windows Forms application and add a web reference to any web service of your choice.

Next, add two buttons to your form: one to consume the service synchronously and one to consume the service asynchronously. The code in Listing 38.4 illustrates how to consume the service synchronously and asynchronously.

LISTING 38.4   Synchronous and Asynchronous Web Service Consumption

```
using System;
using System.Collections.Generic;
using System.ComponentModel;
using System.Data;
using System.Drawing;
using System.Text;
using System.Windows.Forms;

namespace ThreadedConsumer
{
public partial class Form1 : Form
{
    localhost.Service svc = null;

    public Form1()
    {
        InitializeComponent();
        svc = new localhost.Service();
        svc.SlowMethodCompleted +=
            new ThreadedConsumer.localhost.SlowMethodCompletedEventHandler(
svc_SlowMethodCompleted);
    }
```

LISTING 38.4   Continued

```
void svc_SlowMethodCompleted(object sender,
    ThreadedConsumer.localhost.SlowMethodCompletedEventArgs e)
{
    toolStripStatusLabel1.Text = "Asynch method completed.";
    MessageBox.Show(e.Result);
}

private void button2_Click(object sender, EventArgs e)
{
    MessageBox.Show(svc.SlowMethod());
}

private void button1_Click(object sender, EventArgs e)
{
    svc.SlowMethodAsync();
    toolStripStatusLabel1.Text = "Started Asynchronous method...";
}
}
}
```

Using the BackgroundWorker **Control**

Using asynchronous methods on a web service is just one way in which you can speed up your application and increase your application's reliability and availability, two key factors in creating a truly agile smart client. However, your application may want to do more than just make multithreaded single calls to a web service. Quite often, smart clients need to perform background tasks and report the status of that task to the user.

The BackgroundWorker component is an extremely handy tool that takes care of a lot of the tedious work that used to go into performing long-running tasks in the background and reporting progress to the foreground thread and user interface. By handling the BackgroundWorker component's three events, you can write code that executes in a background thread and you don't have to worry about the complexities of starting the thread or about using the Invoke() method to communicate with the UI thread. These events are

- DoWork—This event handler is invoked in a background thread. Whatever method you define for this event handler is the "work" method for the component. Within this method, you check the CancellationPending property to stop execution and call the ReportProgress method to indicate the percentage of the background task that has been completed.

- ProgressChanged—Use this event handler to respond to a change in the progress (percent complete) of the background task. This event handler is often used to modify the state of progress bars and other UI elements indicating progress.

- RunWorkerCompleted—Use this event handler to respond to the condition when the background task has completed.

To see this component in action, create a new Windows Forms application and add a StatusStrip control to the form. Using the interactive designer, you can add a progress bar to the StatusStrip control. Then you'll need a button to kick off the background process. Drag a BackgroundWorker onto the form. Next, double-click the blank spaces in the event handler boxes for all of the BackgroundWorker component's events. Listing 38.5 shows the code that makes it all work.

LISTING 38.5   Using the BackgroundWorker Component

```
using System;
using System.Collections.Generic;
using System.ComponentModel;
using System.Threading;
using System.Data;
using System.Drawing;
using System.Text;
using System.Windows.Forms;

namespace BgWorker
{
public partial class Form1 : Form
{
public Form1()
{
    InitializeComponent();
}

private void backgroundWorker1_DoWork(object sender, DoWorkEventArgs e)
{
    tsProgress.Value = 0;
    for (int i = 0; i < 100; i++)
    {
        if (backgroundWorker1.CancellationPending)
        {
            e.Cancel = true;
            return;
        }
        Thread.Sleep(100);
```

38

LISTING 38.5   Continued

```
        backgroundWorker1.ReportProgress(i);
    }
}

private void backgroundWorker1_ProgressChanged(
  object sender, ProgressChangedEventArgs e)
{
    tsProgress.Value = e.ProgressPercentage;
}

private void backgroundWorker1_RunWorkerCompleted(
  object sender, RunWorkerCompletedEventArgs e)
{
    if (e.Cancelled)
    {
        tsProgress.Value = 0;
        MessageBox.Show("Long-running task was cancelled.");
    }
    else
        MessageBox.Show("Long-running task completed.");
}

// launch background task
private void button1_Click(object sender, EventArgs e)
{
    backgroundWorker1.RunWorkerAsync();
}

// cancel background task
private void button2_Click(object sender, EventArgs e)
{
    backgroundWorker1.CancelAsync();
}
}
}
```

With the task in progress, your form might look something like the one shown in Figure 38.4.

FIGURE 38.4   Using the `BackgroundWorker` component.

Summary

Whether we developers like it or not, users are expecting more and more from our applications. When a platform like the .NET Framework comes along, it raises the bar for what users expect professional applications to do and how they should behave. The demand for agile applications that follow the IJW ("It Just Works") credo is at an all-time high.

To keep users pleased and to produce high-quality applications, developers need to know the techniques involved in building agile, scalable, powerful smart clients. This chapter provided you with samples of how you can create applications that detect the presence of the network, consume web services asynchronously, perform background tasks without interfering with the foreground UI, and present users with a login prompt upon entering the application. These tools and techniques, combined with all of the other information this book provides on Windows Forms programming, should help you create extremely powerful and compelling applications.

38

CHAPTER **39**

Deploying Applications Using ClickOnce

In the past, deploying Windows applications has often been a painful and arduous task. Previous versions of the .NET Framework made it easier to deploy Windows Forms applications because the .NET Framework's inherent architecture removed DLL versioning problems and allowed side-by-side execution. However, it was still more difficult to bundle and deploy Windows Forms applications than it was to simply give a customer the URL to an ASP.NET web application.

The goal of this chapter is to show you that the old adage "Windows is harder to deploy" no longer exists. Using ClickOnce technology, you can have the best of both worlds: The rich, highly interactive, high-performance environment of Windows Forms with the quick and painless deployment that used to be the sole domain of ASP.NET applications.

This chapter will progressively build a fairly large sample to illustrate the various principles of ClickOnce technology. It is recommended that you follow along with this sample as the chapter progresses, as true mastery of ClickOnce only comes from the actual development and maintenance of a ClickOnce application.

Introduction to ClickOnce

Before learning about ClickOnce and how it works, it is beneficial to learn the problems that it solves. In traditional software installation packages, there are several issues that can be difficult for developers to get around that make the entire development process take more time (and therefore cost more money). When a user receives a Windows

Installer package either from a CD or from a web download, that user must run that installation package to install the software. This often requires administrative privileges on the computer. After the software is installed, new versions, releases, updates, and patches often require that the previous version be completely removed before the new version can be installed. In addition, the new version is often a completely new package that contains the entire application rather than just the portions that have changed. Applications like many antivirus packages have built in their own custom update technology to allow the application to update itself once installed, but it still must be installed using a Windows Installer package that might require administrative privileges.

ClickOnce is a technology introduced with version 2.0 of the .NET Framework that provides a means by which developers can quickly and easily publish their applications. In addition to simplified deployment, ClickOnce allows applications to automatically receive updates from a central location that will only be downloaded as they are needed. Finally, ClickOnce also ensures that when a new version is placed in the publication location (which can be a network share or a location on the web), only the assemblies that are required are downloaded.

As you will see throughout the remainder of this chapter, security is taken care of by storing ClickOnce applications in an isolated per-user, per-application "sandbox" that prevents the application from interfering with other installed applications. ClickOnce applications don't inherently require administrative privileges, they don't require expensive and time-consuming uninstalls to make way for new releases, and they only download what they need. All of this functionality has been embedded directly into the .NET Framework and will dramatically increase your power to deploy and update your applications.

Although ClickOnce is an incredibly powerful new technology, it is also designed for applications that are running in a somewhat isolated environment. ClickOnce installations cannot make global changes for shared libraries. There are still a few scenarios in which you would want to use a Visual Studio Setup Project (Windows Installer) to deploy your application.

> **TIP**
>
> One scenario that is not often mentioned in documentation of ClickOnce applications is that you can use Windows Installer (Visual Studio 2005 "Setup" project) to deploy a ClickOnce application on a CD or download. After the user installs this application, the autoupdate functionality of ClickOnce can take effect. In other words, you can deploy a ClickOnce application using Windows Installer if you have complex initial setup requirements, but you still want to be able to "push" updates via the ClickOnce update mechanisms.

Table 39.1 shows a comparison of features between Windows Installer deployment and ClickOnce deployment to help you get an idea of when to use each technology. A more detailed version of this table is also available on MSDN.

TABLE 39.1   Feature Comparison: ClickOnce Versus Windows Installer

Feature	ClickOnce	Windows Installer
Automatic update	✓	✓ (requires additional code in the app)
Automatic rollback after installation	✓	
Download updates from the web	✓	
Affects shared components/other apps		✓
Permissions granted	Only necessary	Full trust
Permissions required	Internet/Intranet Zone	Administrator
Manifest (app and deploy) signing	✓	
Installation GUI	Y/N Prompt	Wizard
On-demand file install	✓	
Install shared files		✓
Install assemblies in GAC		✓
Install for multiple users		✓
Add shortcut to Start menu	✓	✓
Add shortcut to Startup		✓
Add application to Favorites	✓	✓
Register new file types/extensions		✓
Application install location	ClickOnce Cache	Program Files

What it all boils down to is that using ClickOnce to deploy your applications is extremely fast and flexible, provided your application doesn't need to make changes to global resources and settings. ClickOnce is *ideal* for deploying Smart Clients that typically have small footprints and provide a rich, interactive user interface that operates against a web service or relational database back end.

Publishing ClickOnce Applications

Writing complex code and dealing with enormous configuration files are not the hardest parts of using ClickOnce deployment. One of the most difficult tasks is in making the decisions that affect how your application is deployed and updated. This section takes you through the process of deciding how you want to publish your application including walking you through publishing a ClickOnce application.

You can publish your ClickOnce application in several ways. Each of these options is controlled through various options in the Publish Wizard that is used when you publish your application.

Deployment over the Web or Network Share

When you know that your customers will have network access to a single deployment location and the logistics burden of distributing a CD is too costly, deploying your application on the web or a network share is an excellent solution. Using this method, the user will navigate to a URL or to a network share and either click a link pointing to a deployment manifest (an XML file containing deployment data related to ClickOnce) or will double-click the deployment manifest file on the share. If the application requires additional security permissions, the user will be prompted to grant those permissions. A huge benefit to this model is that *only* the required permissions will be granted, unlike Windows Installer, which installs everything with full trust. After the application has been downloaded to the local user's ClickOnce cache, a shortcut to that application will be created on the user's Start menu and will appear in the Add/Remove Programs dialog in the Control Panel.

To enable web- or share-based deployment, simply type in a web URL or a file-share path when prompted for the publication location by the Publish Wizard.

Deployment on CD

If you need to get your application to users who cannot establish a network connection to the central deployment location or have low-bandwidth connections, you may decide to distribute the application on a CD. At other times you might want to distribute the application on a CD, such as when you don't want the application's original installation source to be available on the Internet.

Using the Publish Wizard, you can deploy the application to a CD or to a location that can then be used as an image with which to burn CDs. The end user then installs the application from the CD just like any other Windows application. A shortcut will be added to the user's Start menu and an entry will appear in the Add/Remove Programs dialog in the Control Panel. To use the CD/DVD deployment model within the Publish Wizard, you simply select a location on a disk that will be used for CD imaging when prompted for the publication location by the Publish Wizard.

Application Launched Directly from Web or Share

This model is what many people refer to as the "zero footprint" deployment model. When a user clicks the application link on the web or a network share, the application is installed into the user's ClickOnce cache just like the first (web) deployment model. However, when the application is done running, the application will be removed from the ClickOnce cache. This deployment model does not add an entry to the Add/Remove Programs dialog in the Control Panel, nor does it create a shortcut on the user's Start menu. To use this deployment model, select the "No, this application is only available online" option from the Publish Wizard. This deployment model is ideal for applications that are run from the web but are run infrequently, such as tax software that might only be run once per year. Applications with frequent updates that are activated more often by the user should use the web deployment model instead of the "zero footprint" web launch model.

Deploying a ClickOnce Application

Now that you have seen the various options available to you for deployment methods using ClickOnce, you can walk through the process of deploying your own ClickOnce application.

The first thing you need before you can deploy your application is, of course, an application. This sample uses an application called ClickOnce1. To add to the realism, a Windows Forms Control Library called FormLibrary was created and an AboutBox form was added to that library. Then a reference from ClickOnce1 to FormLibrary was added.

Add a menu strip to the main form in the ClickOnce1 application and make one of the menu options launch the About box as follows:

```
FormLibrary.AboutBox1 aBox = new FormLibrary.AboutBox1();
aBox.ShowDialog();
```

This is to illustrate how dependencies work within a ClickOnce application and to prove that referenced assemblies will indeed be downloaded during the installation process.

Make sure that both of your assemblies (ClickOnce1 and FormLibrary) have the same version number, 1.0.0.0. Also make sure that you supply some additional information in the AssemblyInfo.cs file like the publisher name, assembly title, and so on.

Because you will eventually want to test how the update feature works, add a few random controls to the main form so that you will have a visual comparison between future versions.

Before publication, this application looked like the one in Figure 39.1.

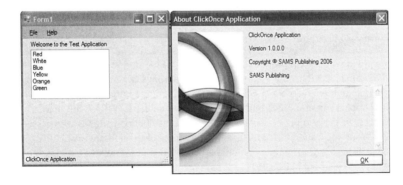

FIGURE 39.1   A sample ClickOnce application.

Now you're ready to publish the application. There are a couple of entry points that will launch the Publish Wizard, but this author recommends going into the Publish tab of the Project Properties editor. This gives you a quick overview of publication settings defaults before launching the wizard.

39

Before launching the wizard, click the Options button to see the various publication options that are available to you. Make sure you set the publisher name and the application name and the optional support URL. Also note the handy option, "For CD Installations, Automatically Start Setup When CD Is Inserted."

When you're done with the Options dialog, click the Prerequisites button. This dialog allows you to specify all of the prerequisites your application needs to run. The .NET Framework 2.0 Runtime is already selected. One very useful feature is that you can select "SQL Server 2005 Express Edition" and your application will never deploy without first installing SQL Express on the end user's machine. This is unbelievably useful for data-driven ClickOnce applications.

One last thing you should do before you publish your application is to decide whether you want to sign the ClickOnce manifests. By using Authenticode technology to digitally sign these XML files, you can attach verifiable proof of the authenticity of the publisher. For testing purposes you can leave this step off. However, in a commercial publication you *will* want to sign the application manifests as well as the application itself using strong naming. For this sample, the author clicked the Create Test Certificate button just to have a verifiable source with which to test.

> **NOTE**
>
> To use manifest signing, Visual Studio 2005 will be invoking the command-line utility `SignTool.exe`. This tool requires that CAPICOM 2.0 or higher be installed on your machine. To obtain this tool, go to
> http://www.microsoft.com/downloads/details.aspx?displaylang=en&FamilyID=860EE43A-A843-462F-ABB5-FF88EA5896F6. When you have the tool, you can place it in your `system32` directory and register it using the `regsvr32.exe` command-line utility.

> **CAUTION**
>
> Strong naming was used in previous versions of the .NET Framework to verify the authenticity of assemblies downloaded from the Internet or installed from CD. With the built-in ability to automatically update them, you are opening your application to a huge liability if you do not sign both your application assemblies and your ClickOnce manifests. Without this, hackers could obtain access to the distribution location and replace distribution contents with their own malicious files. Your application, not able to verify the source of the updates, would happily download the malicious code. The use of automated updates would allow this malicious code to rapidly travel to your entire installed client base before anyone knew what was happening.

Click the Publish Wizard button to launch the ClickOnce Publish Wizard. If you're satisfied with all of the options you have specified, you can simply click the Publish Now button to deploy immediately. The wizard will prompt you for the location (URL/file path) of the publication and the installation footprint options (online only or both online and offline).

Assuming everything worked well and the publishing was a success, you should be presented with a web page that looks like the one shown in Figure 39.2.

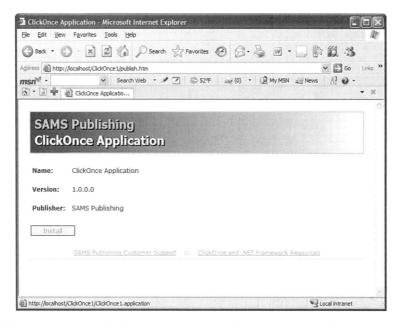

FIGURE 39.2   Application deployment page created by ClickOnce publication.

If you hold the mouse pointer over the Install button, you'll see that the link to the installation is actually a link to the application manifest file, `ClickOnce1.application`. The web deployment location looks like the one shown in Figure 39.3. As you can see, there is a central application manifest file that provides information about the application (as well as an Authenticode signature if the manifest was signed) and an application manifest for each individual version of the application.

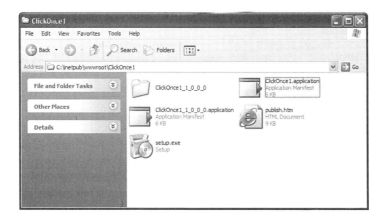

FIGURE 39.3   Initial publication of a ClickOnce application to the web.

To finish out the deployment of this application, click the Install button. You will see a progress dialog indicating that the application requirements are being validated. Then, if you used a test certificate or no certificate at all, you will see a warning indicating that the publisher cannot be verified. This is just a test, so click Install because you are the publisher. The installation process should be very quick for this application. When it's done, the application runs and you'll see the main form with all of the controls that you added to it.

If your sample has the same data as the one this sample has been developing, you will see that the Start menu now has a "SAMS Publishing" group that contains the following two shortcuts: "ClickOnce Application" and "ClickOnce Application Online Support." Note that the icon for the application in the Start menu is the same as the icon you defined in the application settings editor. The online support shortcut appears if you specify a Support URL in the Publish settings tab.

The last thing to do before moving on to the section on updating a ClickOnce application is to verify that the application shows up in the Add or Remove Programs dialog in the Control Panel.

When you launch the application a second time from the Start menu, the application requirements validation dialog will appear as the application checks the publication location for updates. As you'll see later in the chapter, you can programmatically override this behavior for a smoother and richer experience during this stage.

To satisfy your curiosity, shut down the IIS website that hosts the publication location and run the application again. The application will run just fine even though the deployment location is offline. If the deployment location is offline, the application behaves as though there are no new updates.

Updating ClickOnce Applications

After your application has been published and customers have downloaded it and are using it, new releases will always be necessary. Bug fixes need to make it out to clients as well as new releases that contain new functionality.

With previous versions of the .NET Framework, the basic model was to issue a new Windows Installer image. Customers would then have to obtain the new installer image and run that, which would completely remove the previous version of the application and then create a fresh installation containing the new version. Any dynamic update support within a .NET Framework application in previous versions was developed entirely by hand by developers or using the Automatic Update Application Building Block from Microsoft.

When you publish an application, you have the option of automatically incrementing the publish version with every publication. This can be a handy feature, but it can occasionally cause problems. The publish version is a completely arbitrary number that is *not directly related to any assembly version*. This means that you can publish version 2.0 of your application and you may still be using several version 1.0 assemblies. This is deliberate because a lot of companies follow this model and do not increase version numbers of assemblies unless the assembly changes. The separation of publish version and assembly version provides maximum flexibility for the developer.

To see the options available for ClickOnce updates, go to the Publish tab of the Project Settings editor and click the Updates button. The dialog box shown in Figure 39.4 shows the options available for automatic updates. If your application does automatically check for updates, it can check either before the application starts or it can check after. Delaying the update check until after startup allows for a faster start time for the application, but new updates will not be applied until the application is shut down and started again.

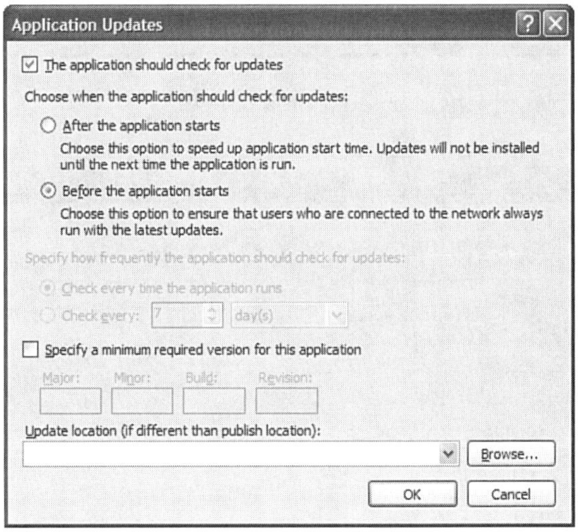

FIGURE 39.4   ClickOnce automatic update configuration.

To see how updates work with ClickOnce, make some changes to the main form that are easy to catch, such as changing the background color, removing controls, adding new ones, and so on. Then, increase the assembly version on both the ClickOnce1 and FormLibrary assemblies to version 2.0.0.0.

Then, without running the publication wizard, change the publish version to 2.0.0.0 and click the Publish Now button. After the publication takes place and the publication is verified, the destination directory hosted by IIS should look like the one shown in Figure 39.5.

Before downloading the new version of the application, the end user receives a confirmation prompt asking if she wants to download the new version, as shown in Figure 39.6.

After you have downloaded the new update, your application should show up with the appropriate version number (2.0.0.0) and any GUI changes that you made to the application will appear. Any change that you made, code or otherwise, is associated with that specific publish version of the application.

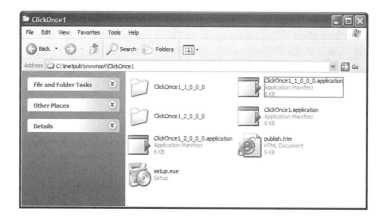

FIGURE 39.5   Multiple versions exposed for ClickOnce.

FIGURE 39.6   Download ClickOnce update dialog.

Although we developers don't like to admit it, patches sometimes have their own bugs. In fact, developers often encounter situations in which a patch causes problems worse than the ones for which the patch was intended. This isn't always the developer's fault—environmental factors such as the client system, configuration, and OS can often cause patches and updates to fail. If this happens, the user is far from helpless. If the user had installed using a Windows Installer package, he would have to uninstall the application and try to find a copy of the previous version. With ClickOnce, all the user has to do is click the Change/Remove button next to the ClickOnce application. The user will then be prompted if he wants to restore the application to its previous state or uninstall it. Restoring the application to its previous state can undo any damage caused by the last update, restoring the user to a known working condition until she can get help from support.

> **NOTE**
>
> Keep in mind that this system will only undo the most recent update to the application. If you upgrade that version, and then upgrade again, you will not be able to automatically go back two versions. In that case, you would have to uninstall and start over. Every time a user gets an update, they should make sure it works, and if not, immediately undo the update and contact the application vendor.

Programming with the `System.Deployment.Application` Namespace

In addition to all of the things that ClickOnce automates for you, there are also a lot of things that you can do manually. For instance, you can write code that will manually check for updates, code that initiates the download of an update, or even code that manually downloads an optional file like an image or an unreferenced assembly. You also have control over the updating GUI and can replace the standard update dialog procedure with your own code. All of this is made possible through the `System.Deployment.Application` namespace and the `System.Deployment.Application.ApplicationDeployment` class. This class provides the essential functionality that you need to exert maximum control over your application's ClickOnce update environment.

The `ApplicationDeployment` class contains several events that you can handle within your application. Some of them are

- `CheckForUpdateCompleted`—This event is fired when an asynchronous check for update availability is complete. Don't confuse this with the completion of an actual download.

- `CheckForUpdateProgressChanged`—To report progress information back to the user, this event is fired every time the progress of checking for an update changes. It uses the `DeploymentProgressChangedEventArgs` class to report progress. This class contains a property indicating the percentage completed, but also provides more detail in the form of the `BytesCompleted` and `BytesTotal` properties.

- `UpdateCompleted`—When an asynchronous download and installation of an update is finished, this event is fired to notify the user interface.

- `UpdateProgressChanged`—This event is fired whenever the progress changes on the download of an update.

To see how you can modify your application to replace the default update behavior with your own, it will take two steps. First, you will have to modify the code to support your new update mechanism and publish that revision out to the publication location. Then, you'll need to make another change so that you can watch your application download the new update.

The first step is to add an Update Now menu item to the form's main menu strip. Also add a progress bar to the status strip on the bottom of the form. If you didn't already have a status strip on your form, now would be a good time to add one. Next, modify your `Form1.cs` code to look like the code in Listing 39.1.

LISTING 39.1 Manually Performing Updates and Reporting Progress

```
using System;
using System.Collections.Generic;
using System.ComponentModel;
```

39

LISTING 39.1   Continued

```
using System.Data;
using System.Deployment.Application;
using System.Drawing;
using System.Text;
using System.Windows.Forms;

namespace ClickOnce1
{
public partial class Form1 : Form
{
private ApplicationDeployment ad = null;

public Form1()
{
    InitializeComponent();
    ad = ApplicationDeployment.CurrentDeployment;
    ad.CheckForUpdateCompleted +=
        new CheckForUpdateCompletedEventHandler(ad_CheckForUpdateCompleted);
    ad.UpdateProgressChanged +=
        new DeploymentProgressChangedEventHandler(ad_UpdateProgressChanged);
    ad.CheckForUpdateProgressChanged +=
        new DeploymentProgressChangedEventHandler(
ad_CheckForUpdateProgressChanged);
    ad.UpdateCompleted += new AsyncCompletedEventHandler(ad_UpdateCompleted);
    this.Text = "ClickOnce Application (v" + ad.CurrentVersion.ToString() + ")";
}

void ad_UpdateProgressChanged(object sender,
DeploymentProgressChangedEventArgs e)
{
    tsProgress.Value = e.ProgressPercentage;
}

void ad_CheckForUpdateProgressChanged(object sender,
DeploymentProgressChangedEventArgs e)
{
    tsProgress.Value = e.ProgressPercentage;
}

void ad_UpdateCompleted(object sender, AsyncCompletedEventArgs e)
{
    if (e.Error != null)
    {
```

LISTING 39.1   Continued

```
        MessageBox.Show("There was an error updating the application:\n" +
            e.Error.ToString());
        return;
    }

    if (MessageBox.Show("Update installed successfully. Restart application?",
        "Application Restart",
        MessageBoxButtons.YesNo) == DialogResult.Yes)
    {
        Application.Restart();
    }
}

void ad_CheckForUpdateCompleted(object sender,
  CheckForUpdateCompletedEventArgs e)
{
    if (e.Error != null)
    {
        MessageBox.Show("Failed to check for update: \n" + e.ToString());
        return;
    }
    if (e.UpdateAvailable)
    {
        tsLabel.Text = "Update Found!";
        tsProgress.Value = 0;
        if (e.IsUpdateRequired)
        {
            MessageBox.Show("A mandatory update is available.
            ➥Update will begin immediately.");
            ad.UpdateAsync();
        }
        else
        {
            if (MessageBox.Show("An optional update is available.
            ➥Would you like to download it now?",
                "Update Available", MessageBoxButtons.YesNo) == DialogResult.Yes)
            {
                ad.UpdateAsync();
            }
        }
    }
    else
    {
```

LISTING 39.1   Continued

```
        tsLabel.Text = "ClickOnce Application";
        tsProgress.Value = 0;
        MessageBox.Show("No new updates are available for this application.");
    }

}

private void aboutToolStripMenuItem_Click(object sender, EventArgs e)
{
    FormLibrary.AboutBox1 aBox = new FormLibrary.AboutBox1();
    aBox.ShowDialog();
}

private void updateNowToolStripMenuItem_Click(object sender, EventArgs e)
{
    // if this application is a clickonce app
    if (ApplicationDeployment.IsNetworkDeployed)
    {
        ad.CheckForUpdateAsync();
        tsLabel.Text = "Checking for Updates...";
        tsProgress.Value = 0;
    }
}
}
}
```

Build and then publish this application as version 2.1.0.1, making sure to change the automatic update checking from "Before" to "After." Run the application and make sure that the application updates to the right version. Then, make some minor change to your application and label that version 2.1.0.2. Publish this application and then run the application again. Instead of the default behavior and GUI for updating applications, you should be able to click the Update Now menu item. When checking for updates, you should see the new progress bar at the bottom in the status trip. When an optional update is available, a prompt like the one shown in Figure 39.7 appears. If you choose to download the update, the progress bar again reports progress, but this time it is reporting the download progress of the new update.

At this point you have created a new application, deployed that application with the click of a button, and created an automatic update framework that takes care of all of the details of downloading new versions, installing those versions, and even rolling them back when failures occur. In addition to that, you have just replaced the default behavior and UI of ClickOnce updating with your own interface and code.

FIGURE 39.7   Custom ClickOnce GUI.

Summary

Ease of deployment has almost always been a unique feature of web applications. In the past, when it came to deciding on what platform the next application would run, ASP.NET applications always won when the decision came down to ease of deployment.

This chapter illustrates that this is no longer the case. Using ClickOnce deployment, applications can be interactive and easy to deploy with a rich user interface and all the power of the .NET Framework underneath.

In this chapter you saw how to deploy a ClickOnce application and the various deployment options that are available to you as the developer of a ClickOnce application. After you have deployed that application, you need to be able to provide updates, patches, new releases, and so on. This chapter covered the mechanism for updating a ClickOnce application and the various methods by which ClickOnce applications can receive updates.

At this point you should be able to start working with ClickOnce applications and hopefully begin recommending Windows Forms 2.0 as a viable quick-deployment platform and putting an end to the vicious rumor that Windows Forms applications are cumbersome to deploy and maintain.

39

Using Enterprise Services

Enterprise Services is a suite of tools and functionality made available to enterprise applications through an operating system feature called COM+. COM+ is a component management system that provides tremendous power above and beyond the component features that the .NET Framework provides. COM+ provides a hosted environment for components that gives them abilities such as Just-in-Time activation, support for distributed transactions, object pooling, security, and even the ability for one component to subscribe to events published by another component.

This chapter assumes that you already have some basic familiarity with COM+, its purpose, and how it works. This chapter provides you with instructions on how to use C# 2005 to take advantage of the many features of COM+ Enterprise Services.

Registering Serviced Components

Before you get into the meat of writing code that takes advantage of the many services available through COM+, you need to be aware of the most basic of all COM+ tasks: registration. In order for a component to take part in COM+ transactions, be JIT-activated, exist within a pool, and so on, that component must be registered with COM+. You can either manually register your components or you can make use of special assembly-wide code attributes to automatically register the components. In order to test any of the code written in the remainder of this chapter, you will have to register the components.

Manual Registration

Manual registration of a serviced component involves using the `regsvcs.exe` command-line tool. This tool ships with the .NET Framework. For a complete reference on this tool, check out the MSDN documentation for it at http://msdn2.microsoft.com/en-us/library/04za0hca.aspx.

Before you can register your components, the assembly in which they reside needs to have a strong name. Strong-naming an assembly is as simple as checking the appropriate box in the Project Settings area.

To register all public classes within an assembly as serviced components within a COM+ application (a COM+ application is a collection of components that share similar properties and configuration), you can use the following syntax:

```
regsvcs /appname:TestApp MyComponents.dll
```

The `appname` parameter refers to the name of the COM+ application. If you are unfamiliar with the basic features of COM+ and how it works, consult the administrator's guide for your operating system.

Automatic Registration

Automatic registration can be much simpler than manually registering your components. Through the use of a special set of code attributes, you can embed COM+ information into your assembly. The first time the assembly is loaded and these attributes are found, the components contained in your assembly can be registered automatically before the first line of component code is executed. Table 40.1 contains a list of the attributes involved in automatic registration as well as the configuration that can take place during that configuration.

TABLE 40.1   Enterprise Services Assembly-Wide Attributes

Attribute	Description
ApplicationActivation	This attribute is used to indicate whether the COM+ application is activated in the client process (Library mode) or in the server host process (Server mode).
ApplicationID	This is used to provide a GUID for the COM+ application. If this attribute is left out, one will be automatically generated.
ApplicationName	Indicates the name of the COM+ application. Specifying this attribute will allow for automatic registration upon the invocation of a serviced component within the assembly.
ApplicationQueuing	Configures queued components.
ComVisible	In order for the components in this library to be registered with COM+, the ComVisible attribute must be set to true. Visual Studio defaults this attribute to false.

To see how automatic registration works, and to create the first serviced component in this chapter, start by creating a new console application called ComPlusHelloWorld. Add a new Class Library project to the solution called HelloLib.

In the class library, add a reference to the System.EnterpriseServices Assembly, delete Class1.cs, and add a new class called HelloWorldComponent.cs. The code for this class is shown in Listing 40.1.

LISTING 40.1   HelloWorldComponent

```
using System;
using System.Collections.Generic;
using System.Text;
using System.EnterpriseServices;

namespace HelloLib
{
public class HelloWorldComponent : ServicedComponent
{
    Public HelloWorldComponent()
    {
        // all COM+ components MUST
        // 1. be public
        // 2. be concrete (generics)
        // 3. have public constructor
    }
    public void HelloWorld()
    {
        Console.WriteLine("Hello world from within a COM+ component!");
    }
}
}
```

Add a strong name to this assembly and make sure that the ComVisible attribute in the AssemblyInfo.cs file is set to false. Also, add the following attributes to the AssemblyInfo.cs file:

```
[assembly: ApplicationActivation(ActivationOption.Library)]
[assembly: ApplicationName("Hello World Application")]
```

Now add a reference to the HelloLib project and the System.EnterpriseServices assembly from the ComPlusHelloWorld console application project. Modify Program.cs in the Console Application to contain the following code:

40

```
using System;
using System.Collections.Generic;
using System.Text;

namespace ComPlusHelloWorld
{
class Program
{
    static void Main(string[] args)
    {
        HelloLib.HelloWorldComponent hello =
            new HelloLib.HelloWorldComponent();
        hello.HelloWorld();

        Console.ReadLine();
    }
}
}
```

Note that nothing special needs to be done to create an instance of a serviced component other than adding a reference to the component's assembly.

Run the console application and you will see the "Hello World" message from the component. Then go into the Component Services administrative control panel to verify that a COM+ application was indeed created for your assembly. Figure 40.1 shows the Component Services control panel showing the new COM+ application.

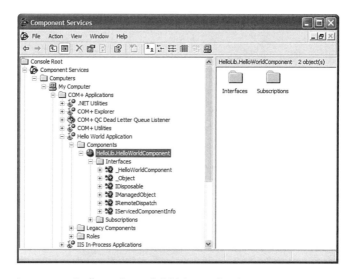

FIGURE 40.1   An automatically registered COM+ application.

Now that you know the mechanics of creating a serviced component, registering it, and utilizing it, you can continue through this chapter and learn how to make use of the various COM+ services.

Just-in-Time Activation and Pooling

In enterprise applications, many server resources often sit idle waiting for client requests. The problem arises from the fact that, in most circumstances, these resources are consuming precious space on the server whether they are idle or not. The Just-in-Time Activation service provides a way around the wasting of idle resources. An object that is JIT-activated will be activated just before a method is invoked. When the call is complete, it will be deactivated again. Even while the object is deactivated, clients with references to that object will still have valid references. This can create a performance increase for components that are called infrequently.

To create a component that is JIT-activated, you need to first create a class that inherits from System.EnterpriseServices.ServicedComponent. To do this, you need to add a reference to the System.EnterpriseServices assembly. A class that is JIT-activated looks like this:

```
[JustInTimeActivation]
public class MyJITClass : ServicedComponent
{
    // class implementation
}
```

The sequence of events for working with a JIT-activated object is as follows:

1. Client/consumer of the component creates an instance of the object.
2. Client invokes a method call on the component.
3. Component is activated.
4. Actual method is invoked.
5. Component is de-activated.

The concept of object pooling deals with another enterprise resource issue. Components within an enterprise application often have very high instantiation overhead. Their initial use often obtains things like database connections or even remote connections to other parts of the application via web services or remoting. Situations where it takes a long time to create objects but those objects are not used for very long are perfect for pooling.

An object pool is a store of preinstantiated objects. If 50 objects are sitting in a pool waiting for a client to make a request, those clients don't incur the heavy initial creation penalty. The following class will reside in an object pool:

```
[JustInTimeActivation]
[ObjectPooling(MinPoolSize=1, MaxPoolSize=30, CreationTimeout=1000)]
public class PooledObject : ServicedComponent
{
    public PooledObject() { }

    protected override void Activate()
    {
       // object is taken from pool to service a client request
    }

    protected override void Deactivate()
    {
       // object put back in pool
    }
}
```

Object pooling is one of the powerful features of COM+ and it alleviates some of the burden and cost of the initial instantiation of objects by storing a pool of preinstantiated components and making them available for immediate use.

Queued Components

Queued components provide an asynchronous client model for invoking methods on COM+ Serviced Components. Sometimes the client wants to make a method call on a COM+ component but then wants to go on about its business without worrying about how long it takes for the method to complete. This is where queued components help. If a serviced component is queued, the method calls to that component are stored in a Microsoft Message Queuing (MSMQ) queue. When the component has time, it will then process the messages in the queue. This gives your component the ability to perform long-running operations without halting the client application or without using multi-threaded programming. The use of MSMQ grants the transmission of messages a measure of reliability and durability. If the power on a server fails with messages still in the queue, they will be processed when the server starts up again.

To implement a component that receives method calls via a queue, you need to define an interface, mark that interface with the InterfaceQueueing attribute, and then define a class that inherits from ServicedComponent as well as implements the interface, as shown in the following code:

```
using System;
using System.IO;
using System.Collections.Generic;
using System.Text;
using System.EnterpriseServices;
using System.Windows.Forms;
```

```
namespace QueuedLibrary
{
[InterfaceQueuing]
public interface IQueuedComponent
{
void ProcessData(int numData);
}


public class SampleQueuedComponent : ServicedComponent, IQueuedComponent
{
public void ProcessData(int numData)
{
    MessageBox.Show("Data received from queue " +
numData.ToString(), "Data Received");
}
}
}
```

Obviously, in a production environment you won't want to be using the `MessageBox` method because there will rarely be a case where a queued method call will have any meaningful user interface.

Queued components must reside in server-side assemblies that have enabled queuing. The attributes used to accomplish this are as follows:

```
[assembly: ApplicationName("Queued Component Demo")]
[assembly: ApplicationQueuing(Enabled=true,
  QueueListenerEnabled=true, MaxListenerThreads=100)]
[assembly: ApplicationActivation(ActivationOption.Server)]
```

Again, you must provide any COM+ assembly with a strong name for it to be able to be imported into COM+. Because the queued components assembly must run as a server-activated object, it cannot take part in automatic registration; you must use the `regsvcs.exe` tool to register the COM+ application before a client can communicate with it.

To create a client that consumes a queued component, you need to make use of the `System.Runtime.InteropServices.Marshal` class. You use `Marshal.BindToMoniker` instead of new to create an instance of the object:

```
IQueuedComponent iqc = null;
try
{
    iqc =
        (IQueuedComponent)
        Marshal.BindToMoniker("queue:/new:QueuedLibrary.SampleQueuedComponent");
}
```

40

```
catch (Exception ex)
{
    MessageBox.Show(ex.ToString());
}
iqc.ProcessData(42);
// this needs to be done to release properly
Marshal.ReleaseComObject(iqc);
```

After invoking a method on a queued component, you should see a new message appear in a private queue, as shown in Figure 40.2.

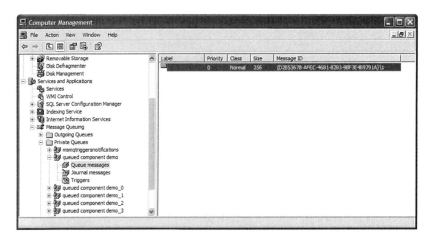

FIGURE 40.2   MSMQ containing a queued component message.

Either the message will be processed on its own, or you can force the message to be processed immediately by starting and stopping the COM+ application. After the message has been processed, it disappears and the method is invoked, as evidenced by the dialog box shown in Figure 40.3.

FIGURE 40.3   Dialog box displayed as a result of a queued component method call.

Role-Based Security

COM+ provides full support for role-based security. Roles can be added to a COM+ application that contain a list of authorized users or groups. The code within a COM+ application can then check to see if the calling user belongs to a specific role and act accordingly. This allows for method-call-level security against unauthorized use.

To see this in action, first you need to make sure that your COM+ application authenticates method calls. By default, this authentication is turned on, so you should only need to modify these settings if you previously turned them off.

Within your application, you can check to see if the calling client belongs to a specific role with the following line of code:

```
SecurityCallContext.CurrentCall.IsCallerInRole("My Role");
```

Before checking to see if a caller belongs to a certain role, you should make sure that security checking is enabled for the application:

```
if (SecurityCallContext.CurrentCall.IsSecurityEnabled) ...
```

If security checking is not enabled, the `IsCallerInRole` method won't do you any good. Also keep in mind that these roles are roles defined using the Component Services control panel—they are not Windows security groups, although you can include a Windows security group in a COM+ role.

Transactions

Transactions within a serviced component are controlled either with code inside a method call or with attributes. Transactions in COM+ work in a similar fashion as the new `System.Transactions` namespace in the .NET Framework. If a serviced component indicates that a transaction should commit, then if that component is the owner of the transaction, it will commit. However, if that component was invoked by another component, the component will only be allowed to "vote" as to the commit status of the parent transaction. This can all be configured through various options.

To control the transactional properties of a class through attributes, you use the `TransactionAttribute` class.

Table 40.2 contains a list of the properties that can be set for the `TransactionAttribute` class.

TABLE 40.2 TransactionAttribute Properties

Property	Description
Isolation	Controls the isolation level of the transaction: Any, ReadCommitted, ReadUncommitted, RepeatableRead, Serializable
Timeout	Controls the timeout period for the transaction
Value	Sets the transaction option through the TransactionOption enumeration: Disabled, NotSupported, Required, RequiresNew, Supported

The following code shows a class with the `TransactionAttribute` controlling transaction options for the component:

40

```
[Transaction(TransactionOption.Required,
  Isolation=TransactionIsolationLevel.Serializable,
  Timeout=20)]
public class TransactionalComponent: ServicedComponent
{
    // class implementation
}
```

Using the `ContextUtil` property of the `ServicedComponent` class, your component can
manually control its vote for transaction commit or rollback, as shown in the following
lines:

```
[Transaction(TransactionOption.Required,
  Isolation=TransactionIsolationLevel.Serializable,
  Timeout=20)]
public class TransactionalComponent: ServicedComponent
{
    public void TransactionalMethod()
    {
        ContextUtil.MyTransactionVote = TransactionVote.Commit;
        try
        {
          // perform work
        }
        catch
        {
          ContextUtil.MyTransactionVote = TransactionVote.Rollback;
        }
    }
}
```

This code will perform some task and if an exception occurs during the execution of that
task, the method will indicate that the transaction should be rolled back.

> **NOTE**
>
> Keep in mind that transactions only work with Compensating Resource Managers (CRM). What
> this boils down to is that not all work will be automatically rolled back if your component indi-
> cates a rollback. For example, if your transaction modified a database and modified a text file
> and then indicated a rollback, the database would roll back all changes made during the trans-
> action, but the text file would not. This is because files on disk aren't transactional. You need to
> be acutely aware of which resources you affect during a transaction to make sure they all roll
> back properly.

Shared Properties

Even though statelessness is a common goal and often a requirement for many enterprise applications, especially those making use of serviced components, sometimes state needs to be maintained.

A COM+ application can have its own state in the form of shared property groups and shared properties. This state is scoped for the entire COM+ application. This means that if the COM+ application is library-activated, the state is available to any code within the process that started the application. If the COM+ application is server-activated, the state is available to any client. In fact, in a server-activated COM+ application, clients can actually shut down and the state will be waiting for them when they start back up again (provided the server application hasn't restarted).

To see shared properties in action, this next sample will illustrate using shared properties to store the last assigned order number. If COM+ can maintain information like this in-memory, shared, and available to all COM+ components within an application, that can be a tremendous savings of time and resources by not requiring the components to make a connection to the database just to receive the last assigned order number.

You have already seen how to create and register these components, so that information won't be repeated here. Basically all you need to do is create a class library that has the following Enterprise Services attributes:

```
[assembly: ApplicationName("Shared Property Demonstration")]
[assembly: ApplicationActivation(ActivationOption.Server)]
```

Then, add a class called SharedPropComponent to the library and enter the code shown in Listing 40.2.

LISTING 40.2   A ServicedComponent That Makes Use of Shared Properties

```
using System;
using System.Collections.Generic;
using System.Text;
using System.EnterpriseServices;

namespace SharedPropLib
{
public class SharedPropComponent : ServicedComponent
{
public SharedPropComponent() { }

public int GetNextOrderNumber()
{
    bool groupExists;
    bool propExists;
    int lastOrderNumber;
```

40

LISTING 40.2   Continued

```
    PropertyLockMode propLock = PropertyLockMode.SetGet;
    PropertyReleaseMode propRelease = PropertyReleaseMode.Standard;

    SharedPropertyGroupManager spgm = new SharedPropertyGroupManager();
    SharedPropertyGroup spGroup = spgm.CreatePropertyGroup("Orders", ref propLock,
        ref propRelease, out groupExists);
    SharedProperty orderNumber =
spGroup.CreateProperty("OrderNumber", out propExists);

    if (!propExists)
        orderNumber.Value = 1;

    lastOrderNumber = (int)orderNumber.Value;
    orderNumber.Value = lastOrderNumber + 1;
    return lastOrderNumber;
}
}
}
```

This code uses a property group called `"Orders"`, and a property within that group called
`"OrderNumber"`. Remember that all of the code that accesses property groups is scoped to
the current COM+ application, so you don't need to waste an entire group segregating
your application from other COM+ applications manually. After registering the application manually using `regsvcs.exe` (because server-activated applications can't be registered
automatically), use the following code as a test harness for the new component:

```
using System;
using System.Collections.Generic;
using System.Text;

using SharedPropLib;

namespace SharedPropertyDemo
{
class Program
{
    static void Main(string[] args)
    {
        SharedPropComponent sProp = new SharedPropComponent();

        // obtain a couple order numbers
        for (int x = 0; x < 10; x++)
        {
```

```
        Console.WriteLine(sProp.GetNextOrderNumber().ToString());
    }

    Console.ReadLine();

  }
}
}
```

What you should expect to see is that the first time you run the application it will count from 1 to 10.

> **TIP**
>
> You might need to disable authentication checks on the application before this will work. Various development environments are often not configured to allow the developer's account to do things such as work with shared property groups. To disable security and authentication checks, use the Properties dialog for the COM+ application itself, not the component.

What's more interesting is that if you shut down the test harness application and then start it back up again, it will count from 11 to 20. The timeout is configurable; you can set the timeout period or leave the server application running indefinitely. If the COM+ server application has not shut down due to idle timeout, all of the information contained within the shared property groups and shared properties will remain intact, even though there isn't a single client consuming a component within the application.

Shared properties can be used for all kinds of things. If your application wants to maintain relatively transient state information but doesn't want to incur the overhead of using a database to do so, the COM+ shared property system is definitely the technology to use.

Loosely Coupled Events

Within a COM+ application, it is possible to have one component throw an event and have another component listen for and respond to that event. The event itself is decoupled from the components themselves and managed through the COM+ infrastructure, allowing for some pretty powerful techniques to be employed within your application.

Creating a loosely coupled event system involves the following tasks:

1. Create an event interface. This is an interface that will describe the features of the event.

2. Create an event component that implements the interface. The event component itself must be derived from `ServicedComponent` and implement the event interface.

3. Define an event sink. The event sink is essentially the listener component that will be passed to the event when the event is fired by the publisher.

4. Create a publisher that fires the event.

The event interface is quite simple; it's just an interface that defines the method required by the event:

```
using System;
using System.Collections.Generic;
using System.Text;

namespace LceDemoLibrary
{
    public interface IMessageEvent
    {
        void EventMessage(string message);
    }
}
```

Next, create the event class that implements the event interface. This class is just a simple serviced component:

```
using System;
using System.Collections.Generic;
using System.Text;
using System.EnterpriseServices;

namespace LceDemoLibrary
{
[EventClass]
public class MessageEvent : ServicedComponent, IMessageEvent
{
    #region IMessageEvent Members

    public void EventMessage(string message)
    {

    }

    #endregion
}
}
```

Note that there is no real implementation for the EventMessage event. This is deliberate as the real work comes from the event sink (the subscriber).

To create the event sink or subscriber class, add the following class to the class library:

```
using System;
using System.Collections.Generic;
using System.Text;
```

```
using System.EnterpriseServices;
using System.Windows.Forms;

namespace LceDemoLibrary
{
public class MessageEventSink : ServicedComponent, IMessageEvent
{

    #region IMessageEvent Members

    public void EventMessage(string message)
    {
        MessageBox.Show(message, "Event Sink Message");
    }

    #endregion
}
}
```

Note that the event sink component implements the same interface as the event component. This is done so that COM+ can tell which events can be subscribed to by which subscribers or sinks.

With this library built, register it manually using the regsvcs.exe tool. In order for it to work, you need to use the Component Services administration console to hook up the event subscription, and you can't do that until the COM+ application has been registered.

After the application has been registered, open the Component Services administration console and expand the newly registered application. Expand the component node for the LceDemoLibrary.MessageSink component, right-click the Subscriptions node, and choose New, then Subscription. Browse to select the MessageEvent class underneath the IMessageEvent interface and select to have the subscription enabled immediately.

Now create a test harness that looks something like this:

```
using System;
using System.Collections.Generic;
using System.Text;

using LceDemoLibrary;

namespace LceDemo
{
class Program
{
```

40

```
static void Main(string[] args)
{
    Console.WriteLine("Triggering Loosely Coupled Event.");

    MessageEvent me = new MessageEvent();
    me.EventMessage("Hello from the Console Application");
    Console.ReadLine();
}
}
}
```

When you run this application, the event is created and then COM+ will pass that event directly to the event sink you created by virtue of the subscription configured earlier. Without any delay, you should see the dialog box in Figure 40.4.

FIGURE 40.4   Dialog box as a result of loosely coupled event handling.

Loosely coupled events provide a wealth of power, flexibility, and reliability, which are the cornerstone features of COM+ Enterprise Services that no COM+ developer should forget about.

Summary

COM+ provides an extremely powerful suite of tools and services for enterprise applications that covers everything from JIT activation to object pooling, and data sharing to loosely coupled, reliable durable events. This chapter showed you how you can take advantage of the various COM+ services through managed code. The task of utilizing COM+ is extremely easy with code attributes and a few special classes available to COM+ components for things like security checking and voting on transaction outcomes. After completing this chapter, you should be ready to start using COM+ in your applications and making informed decisions about when COM+ makes sense to use in an enterprise application.

PART VII

Developing Enterprise and Distributed Applications

IN THIS PART

CHAPTER **41**

Remoting

Remoting is one of the core parts of the .NET Framework that enables code from one AppDomain to communicate with code in another AppDomain, enabling the creation of RPC-style distributed applications. This chapter provides you with an introduction to remoting and then gets right into configuring and coding with remoting. You will learn about the new Inter-Process Communication (IPC) channel as well as how to use object lifetime leases and even how the generics feature is completely supported within the remoting infrastructure.

This chapter is by no means a complete reference on remoting. It provides you with enough information to get started using remoting and following some best practices. If you want more information on remoting, one of the best sources of detail surrounding .NET remoting is *Advanced .NET Remoting, Second Edition* by Ingo Rammer and Mario Szpuszta, ISBN 1590594177 (Apress).

Overview of Remoting

Remoting is the system within the .NET Framework that enables developers to create distributed applications quickly and easily. Remoting provides a layer of abstraction that allows the developer to worry more about the content and design of a distributed system than about the mechanism by which the components communicate. The choice of transport layer (such as TCP/IP, Inter-Process Communication, and so on) has no significant impact on the use of the remoting classes. This means that remoting applications can communicate over TCP/IP or any other means without having to make significant changes to the application.

There are three aspects to any remoting system:

1. A remotable object—Any .NET object that will be transmitted between remoting endpoints

2. A remoting host—An application domain that has been configured to respond to requests for the object indicated in item #1

3. A remoting client—An application domain that initiates a request for the object indicated in item #1

Remoting works in an extremely simple way. A host application domain informs the remoting infrastructure that it is hosting an object on a specific URL using a specific channel (you'll see more on channels later in the chapter). A remoting client then requests that object by supplying the object's URL to the remoting infrastructure.

The remoting client then works with a proxy, much the same way COM interoperability works. Rather than your code communicating directly with the remote object, your code instead works with a proxy that exposes properties and methods with the same names and types as the remote object. Each member then forwards the request over the channel to a proxy on the other end. Figure 41.1 illustrates how the proxies fit in between the real objects involved.

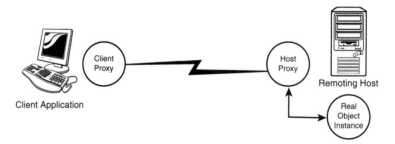

FIGURE 41.1   Remoting at a glance.

Data transfer between application domains is at the core of remoting's functionality. The management of remote object instances and the method of transferring data between application domains both warrant detailed discussion.

Introduction to the `MarshalByRefObject` Class

In Chapter 1, there is a discussion about the difference between value types and reference types. A *value type* is one in which the data is stored directly on the stack, whereas a *reference type* only maintains a pointer on the stack and the real data is contained within the managed heap.

A similar difference exists for objects transmitted via remoting. When you pass an object as a parameter to a remote method, that object can either be passed as a serialized copy, or it can be passed as a reference to the original. If your code passes an object by reference over remoting, the code on the other end of the channel can make changes to the object. Those changes will take place on the original object.

If you pass a standard object to a remoting host, that object will be serialized and a new copy of the object will be created by deserializing the object data. To pass an object reference without creating additional copies, you can use an object that is derived from the MarshalByRefObject class. When you use objects that derive from MarshalByRefObject, a proxy is created, like the one shown in Figure 41.1, that essentially forwards calls to the original object. This feature gives remoting quite a bit of power and flexibility.

You don't have to do anything special to make your class a MarshalByRefObject other than inheriting from it, as shown in the following code:

```
public class MyRemotableObject: MarshalByRefObject
{
    // class implementation
}
```

To ensure that your object is copied rather than used as a reference, simply ensure that it is serializable:

```
[Serializable()]
public class MyObjectToCopy
{
    // class implementation
}
```

Single Call Versus Singleton Objects

When using remoting, the client code requests an instance of a remote object using the remoting infrastructure. The instance that the client is using is not the same as the instance on the remote host.

When using remote objects, sometimes you want the object to be created long enough to perform a single task and then be disposed, and sometimes you want objects to remain, state intact, between method calls from a client.

The first type of object is called a *single call* object. Single call objects are instantiated at the request of a client and belong to only that client. After the client is done with the object's single call, the object is disposed of. This means that with a single remoting host, each client gets its own unique, temporary copy of that object, as shown in Figure 41.2.

Conversely, a *singleton* object is an object that is shared among all clients. After the object has been created, possibly by a client, it will then be shared by all clients by being retrieved as a reference. In this situation, when client A makes a change to data on the remote object, client B will see that change, as illustrated in Figure 41.3.

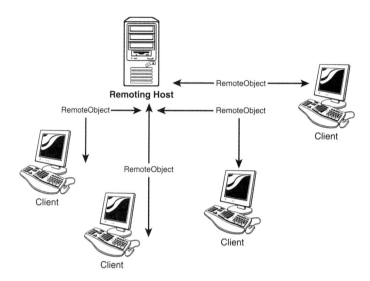

FIGURE 41.2   Single call objects in a remoting infrastructure.

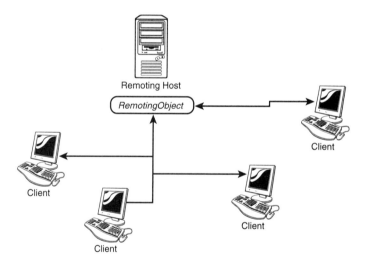

FIGURE 41.3   Singleton objects in a remoting infrastructure.

If you want to obtain a remote object instance that belongs solely to the client requesting it, a single call object is the right choice. However, if you want multiple clients to have access to the same remote object and its shared state, use a singleton object.

Working with Remoting Channels

Before you can create a working remoting sample, you need to be able to manipulate the remoting configuration. A remoting host needs to inform the remoting infrastructure of what objects it is hosting and the channel and URL at which the object can be found. A remoting client needs to tell the remoting infrastructure where it can find remote objects.

A remoting host provides the remoting infrastructure with information about an object being hosted by using code similar to the following:

```
RemotingConfiguration.RegisterWellKnownServiceType(
                typeof(HostedObject),
                "HostedObject.rem",
                WellKnownObjectMode.Singleton);
```

The `RemotingConfiguration` class is the main interface between your code and the remoting infrastructure. The remoting host uses the `RegisterWellKnownServiceType` method to indicate what type is being exposed remotely, as well as the well-known object mode and the object's URI. It is extremely common for the same application to host multiple objects. To distinguish one object from the other, a URI is assigned to each object. In the past, this URI has often been the object's type followed by `.rem` as a convention, but you can use any string you like. The object mode in the preceding line of code can either be single call or singleton.

Whereas the host, or server, must register a "service" type, a remoting client can either configure a client type using a configuration file, or it can just manually obtain a reference to the remote object by specifying its URI. The URI consists of the channel name, the machine address, and the object URI. For example, for an object hosted as `RemoteObject.rem` on the TCP channel at a machine called `LabServer12` on port 2020, the URI a client would use to obtain a reference to the object would be

```
tcp://labserver12:2020/RemoteObject.rem
```

The next two sections show you how to configure two different types of channels, IPC and TCP, as well as when each should be used. Using each of these channels, you will build and run a distributed system.

Using the IPC Channel

The Inter-Process Communication (IPC) channel is one that is used to communicate between components on the same machine. The IPC channel uses a mechanism very similar to named pipes, a means of Inter-Process Communication used before managed code. If you know that the remote objects with which your client code needs to communicate reside on the same physical machine, there is no faster and more efficient remoting channel to use than the IPC channel.

To start this sample, create a new console application called `SimpleRemoting`. This will also create a solution with the same name. Before doing anything to the console application, create a new class library called `SharedLibrary`. Inside the `SharedLibrary` project, add the following definition for the `ISharedObject` interface:

```
using System;
using System.Collections.Generic;
using System.Text;

namespace SharedLibrary
{
    public interface ISharedObject
    {
        void PrintMessage(string msg);
    }
}
```

There is a specific reason for this shared library. For a client to create an instance of a remotely hosted object, the client needs to be able to access the type information on the remote object. This means that, in most cases, the client needs a direct reference to the assembly containing the remote object. At first this doesn't seem like such a bad thing, but it creates a dependency that can cause a lot of problems in the long run. By creating an interface in an assembly that can be referenced by the client and the server, the client can work with any server that implements the interface, regardless of the concrete implementation. This also prevents the client from having to reference any of the assemblies on the remote side.

The remoting host application can then contain an implementation of the shared interface. Add a class called HostedObject to the SimpleRemoting console application project. Make sure to add a project reference from the console application project to the SharedLibrary project and a reference to the System.Runtime.Remoting assembly. The code for this class is shown in Listing 41.1.

LISTING 41.1   The HostedObject Class

```
using System;
using System.Collections.Generic;
using System.Text;

using SharedLibrary;

namespace SimpleRemoting
{
public class HostedObject : MarshalByRefObject, ISharedObject
{
public void PrintMessage(string msg)
{
    Console.WriteLine("Message Printed from AppDomain:   " +
        AppDomain.CurrentDomain.FriendlyName);
```

LISTING 41.1   Continued

```
    Console.WriteLine("Message: " + msg);
}
}
}
```

The PrintMessage method will display some text to the console output window. This text will contain the name of the application domain in which the HostObject class is running, as well as the message sent to it by the client application.

Next you need to set up the hosting environment for the HostedObject class. To do this, modify the Program.cs file of the SimpleRemoting project to look like the code shown in Listing 41.2.

LISTING 41.2   Program.cs for SimpleRemoting

```
using System;
using System.Runtime.Remoting;
using System.Runtime.Remoting.Channels;
using System.Runtime.Remoting.Channels.Ipc;
using System.Collections.Generic;
using System.Text;

namespace SimpleRemoting
{
class Program
{
static void Main(string[] args)
{
    IpcChannel ipc = new IpcChannel("sampleapp");
    ChannelServices.RegisterChannel(ipc, false);
    RemotingConfiguration.RegisterWellKnownServiceType(
        typeof(HostedObject),
        "HostedObject.rem",
        WellKnownObjectMode.Singleton);

    Console.WriteLine("Remoting host activated... Press enter to stop.");
    Console.ReadLine();
}
}
}
```

Because the IPC channel is restricted to working on a single machine and it functions the same way named pipes do, you specify a string name for the port instead of a number. In all remoting applications, the channel on which an object is hosted or consumed must be registered using ChannelServices.RegisterChannel. The false in that method call turns off remoting security checks. In a production application, you would probably want channel security to be enabled.

Now you need a client application. Add a new console application to the solution called RemotingClient. Add a project reference to the SharedLibrary project and a reference to the System.Runtime.Remoting assembly. Modify the Program.cs file so that the code looks like the code in Listing 41.3.

LISTING 41.3   Program.cs for RemotingClient

```
using System;
using System.Runtime.Remoting;
using System.Runtime.Remoting.Channels;
using System.Runtime.Remoting.Channels.Ipc;
using System.Collections.Generic;
using System.Text;

using SharedLibrary;

namespace RemotingClient
{
class Program
{
static void Main(string[] args)
{
    IpcChannel ipc = new IpcChannel("sampleapp_client");
    ChannelServices.RegisterChannel(ipc, false);

    ISharedObject sharedObj = (ISharedObject)
      Activator.GetObject(
typeof(ISharedObject), "ipc://sampleapp/HostedObject.rem");

    if (sharedObj == null)
    {
        Console.WriteLine("Failed to establish IPC link");
        return;
    }

    sharedObj.PrintMessage("Hello from AppDomain " +
AppDomain.CurrentDomain.FriendlyName);

    Console.ReadLine();


}
}
}
```

This code attempts to create an instance of the remote object. If a valid instance has been created, it calls the `PrintMessage` method of the remote object with a string that contains the friendly name of the client's application domain.

Build the solution and then run the `SimpleRemoting.exe` file. You will see the message indicating that the remote host has started. Now run the `RemotingClient.exe` application. In the window containing the output from `SimpleRemoting.exe`, you will see the following text:

```
Remoting host activated... Press enter to stop.
Message Printed from AppDomain:  SimpleRemoting.exe
Message: Hello from AppDomain RemotingClient.exe
```

There are two important things to note about the way this application ran:

- The output appeared within the `SimpleRemoting.exe` window.

- The application domain of the hosted object was `SimpleRemoting.exe`.

This is important because the `Singleton` object executed within the *host* application domain. This is often a reason for using remote objects: so that a client can gain access to something that ordinarily only the remote object could access, such as a database or other protected resource.

Using the TCP Channel

The TCP channel varies only slightly in its use from the IPC channel. The IPC channel uses a string name for its port, whereas the TCP channel uses a standard TCP port number to identify the port on which the channel is running. The sample in this section will show you how to work with the TCP channel as well as show you how to pass nonstandard .NET types (such as classes you created) back and forth between remoting endpoints.

To start off, create a new console application called `TcpRemoting`. A new solution will be created with the same name. Next, create a new class library called "Shared Library." This should look fairly similar to the IPC sample so far. Add a new class to the SharedLibrary project called `Customer`, as shown in the following code:

```
using System;
using System.Collections.Generic;
using System.Text;

namespace SharedLibrary
{
[Serializable()]
public class Customer
{
    public string ID;
    public string FirstName;
```

```
    public string LastName;
}
}
```

Note the presence of the SerializableAttribute class associated with the Customer class. Without this, or inheriting from MarshalByRefObject, a class instance cannot be transmitted between remoting endpoints. Now create the shared interface in a file called ISharedObject.cs:

```
using System;
using System.Collections.Generic;
using System.Text;

namespace SharedLibrary
{
    public interface ISharedObject
    {
        void ProcessCustomer(Customer cust);
        Customer GetCustomer(string ID);
    }
}
```

With the shared components in place, you can modify the Program.cs of the TcpRemoting project as shown in Listing 41.4.

LISTING 41.4   Program.cs for TcpRemoting

```
using System;
using System.Collections.Generic;
using System.Text;

using System.Runtime.Remoting;
using System.Runtime.Remoting.Channels;
using System.Runtime.Remoting.Channels.Tcp;

namespace TcpRemoting
{
class Program
{
    static void Main(string[] args)
    {
        TcpChannel tcp = new TcpChannel(8080);
        ChannelServices.RegisterChannel(tcp, false);

        RemotingConfiguration.RegisterWellKnownServiceType(
            typeof(SharedObject),
```

LISTING 41.4   Continued

```
            "SharedObject.rem",
            WellKnownObjectMode.Singleton);

        Console.WriteLine("Remoting host started. Press enter to stop.");
        Console.ReadLine();
    }
}
}
```

Now that the server is ready to go, you can change the Program.cs of the TcpClient project to match the code in Listing 41.5.

LISTING 41.5   Program.cs for TcpClient

```
using System;
using System.Collections.Generic;
using System.Text;

using SharedLibrary;

namespace TcpClient
{
class Program
{
static void Main(string[] args)
{
    ISharedObject sharedObj = (ISharedObject)
        Activator.GetObject(typeof(ISharedObject),
        "tcp://localhost:8080/SharedObject.rem");
    if (sharedObj == null)
    {
        Console.WriteLine("Failed to obtain remote reference.");
    }
    else
    {
        Customer cust = new Customer();
        cust.ID = "newcust001";
        cust.FirstName = "John";
        cust.LastName = "Customer";
        sharedObj.ProcessCustomer(cust);
        Customer retrievedCust = sharedObj.GetCustomer("newcust002");
        Console.WriteLine("Retrieved customer from remote location:  " +
```

LISTING 41.5   Continued

```
            retrievedCust.FirstName + " " + retrievedCust.LastName);
    }
    Console.ReadLine();


}
}
}
```

When you compile and run this application the same way you ran the IPC sample, the host console output will contain the phrase:

```
Remoting host started. Press enter to stop.
Processing customer newcust001
```

The client output will look like this:

```
Retrieved customer from remote location:  Auto Generated
```

The main thing to take away from these samples is that the choice of remoting channel is more a design decision than anything else because the task of using each channel varies only slightly with the specific channel. In addition, knowing where the code is executing and in which AppDomain the code executes can be extremely helpful when designing complex remoting solutions.

Working with Lifetime Leases

The garbage collector is responsible for disposing of objects that are no longer being used by active code within a .NET application. Remoted objects present a bit of a dilemma: Which garbage collector is responsible for disposing of the object, and how exactly does the GC know when a remoted object is no longer in use?

Some other distributed systems use what is known as "reference counting" to determine whether an object is ready for disposal. Reference counting over a network can create a lot of network traffic and overhead that only gets worse with the number of clients consuming a given remote object.

What the .NET Framework does is use a lifetime lease. When an MBR (MarshalByRefObject class instance) is created, it is given an initial lease. This lease determines how long the object can remain active without being accessed by clients. If the object's lease runs out, it will be disposed. The next time a remote client accesses a member of the MBR, that remote client will be provided with a new instance of the object.

This behavior can be unexpected and can often cause a lot of problems in production applications. In a testing environment, MBRs often live much longer than they do in production because the remote object is being accessed far more often than in a production environment. When this happens, it is easy for developers to assume that the MBR is always active and is maintaining state properly.

The most common way of customizing the lifetime lease behavior of an MBR is to override the InitializeLifetimeService method on the MarshalByRefObject class. This gives the developer the ability to either create an instance of an object that implements the ILease interface to modify the object's lease properties or to return a null, indicating that the object will live forever ("forever" in this case means until the application hosting the object shuts down).

Take a look at this implementation of InitializeLifetimeService:

```
public override object InitializeLifetimeService()
{
    ILease lease = (ILease)base.InitializeLifetimeService();
    if (lease.CurrentState == LeaseState.Initial)
    {
        lease.InitialLeaseTime = TimeSpan.FromMinutes(10);
        lease.SponsorshipTimeout = TimeSpan.FromMinutes(2);
        lease.RenewOnCallTime = TimeSpan.FromSeconds(10);
    }
    else if (lease.CurrentState == LeaseState.Renewing)
    {
        // lease has expired and is requesting to be renewed
        lease.Renew(TimeSpan.FromMinutes(1));
    }
    return lease;
}
```

In the preceding code, some default values are assigned to the lease when the lease is first being created. A lease is first created when the remoting object is first activated (either by client or server). If the lease has expired and is seeking renewal, the preceding code adds one more minute to the object's lifetime.

If your remote object is stateless and does not need to maintain the values of properties between requests, there is very little need to control the object's lifetime. However, if you have created a Singleton remote object that is maintaining state information such as a list of all connected clients, you might want to grant the object an infinite lifetime by overriding InitializeLifetimeService as follows:

```
public override object InitializeLifetimeService()
{
    return null;
}
```

Object lease management is one of those tasks that are often neglected when creating a remoting application. Awareness of lease lifetimes early in the development process can save you a lot of debugging and troubleshooting when it comes time to deploy the application in a production environment.

Remoting with Generics

Quite possibly one of the most powerful new features of remoting in the .NET Framework v2.0 is the support for generics. This chapter has illustrated that client code can create an instance of a remote object and manipulate that instance either as a serialized copy or as a reference to the remote object via the MarshalByRefObject class. What makes remoting even more powerful is that remote objects can make use of generics and still be fully supported on the client.

To illustrate how this works, you can rewrite the first IPC example in this chapter to work with generics. By now you should be pretty familiar with the mechanics of creating a remoting solution using the "Shared Library" pattern. The following code provides a generic interface for the shared library:

```
using System;
using System.Collections.Generic;
using System.Text;

namespace SharedLibrary
{
    public interface ISharedObject<T>
    {
        void PrintMessage(T msg);
    }
}
```

The data type of the message being sent to the remote object is now controlled by the generics type argument T. The following code shows the implementation of the shared interface in the server project:

```
using System;
using System.Collections.Generic;
using System.Text;

using SharedLibrary;

namespace IpcGenerics
{
public class SharedObjectImplementation<T>: MarshalByRefObject, ISharedObject<T>
{
public SharedObjectImplementation()
{
```

```
    Console.WriteLine("Shared Object instantiated: " + this.GetType().ToString());
}
#region ISharedObject<T> Members

public void PrintMessage(T msg)
{
    Console.WriteLine("Incoming Message: " + msg.ToString());
}


#endregion
}
}
```

Listings 41.6 and 41.7 show the Program.cs code for the server and client respectively.

LISTING 41.6   Program.cs for Generics IPC Sample Server

```
using System;
using System.Runtime.Remoting;
using System.Runtime.Remoting.Channels;
using System.Runtime.Remoting.Channels.Ipc;
using System.Collections.Generic;
using System.Text;

namespace IpcGenerics
{
class Program
{
static void Main(string[] args)
{
    // init channel
    IpcChannel ipc = new IpcChannel("Generics-Remoting");
    ChannelServices.RegisterChannel(ipc);

    RemotingConfiguration.RegisterWellKnownServiceType(
        typeof(SharedObjectImplementation<string>),
        "StringObject.rem",
        WellKnownObjectMode.SingleCall);

    RemotingConfiguration.RegisterWellKnownServiceType(
        typeof(SharedObjectImplementation<DateTime>),
        "DateObject.rem",
        WellKnownObjectMode.SingleCall);
```

LISTING 41.6 Continued

```
    Console.WriteLine("Multiple objects hosted on channel. Press enter to stop.");
    Console.ReadLine();
}
}
}
```

LISTING 41.7 Program.cs for IPC Generics Client Sample

```
using System;
using System.Runtime.Remoting;
using System.Collections.Generic;
using System.Text;

using SharedLibrary;

namespace IpcClient
{
class Program
{
static void Main(string[] args)
{
    ISharedObject<string> stringObject =
        (ISharedObject<string>)
        Activator.GetObject(typeof(ISharedObject<string>),
        "ipc://Generics-Remoting/StringObject.rem");

    ISharedObject<DateTime> dateObject =
        (ISharedObject<DateTime>)
        Activator.GetObject(typeof(ISharedObject<DateTime>),
        "ipc://Generics-Remoting/DateObject.rem");

    stringObject.PrintMessage("Hello from IPC client");
    dateObject.PrintMessage(DateTime.Now);

    Console.WriteLine("Remote messages sent.");
    Console.ReadLine();
}
}
}
```

Each concrete type (for example, ISharedObject<string> or ISharedObject<DateTime>)
gets its own URI and the client can then create instances of each of the remotely hosted

concrete types. When the application is put together and both sides are executed, the following is the output from the server console:

```
Multiple objects hosted on channel. Press enter to stop.
Shared Object instantiated: IpcGenerics.SharedObjectImplementation
➥`1[System.String]
Incoming Message: Hello from IPC client
Shared Object instantiated: IpcGenerics.SharedObjectImplementation
➥`1[System.DateTime]
Incoming Message: 1/29/2006 9:45:54 AM
```

In the .NET Framework 2.0, when you print the name of a generic type implementation, a `1 appears and then the name of the type argument is included in square brackets. So in the preceding output, you can see that `Generics.SharedObjectImplementation` is the generic class and `System.String` and `System.DateTime` are both type arguments.

Summary

This chapter provided you with a basic introduction to the world of distributed applications using remoting. Remoting allows developers to create applications that can consume objects remotely without having to do extra work to make the same code work over HTTP, TCP, and so on. Using the channels available within the remoting infrastructure, applications can expose objects to clients that could be on the same machine or halfway across the world, providing a framework to create some of the most powerful distributed applications available today.

Index

SYMBOLS

NUMBERS

A

AppendChild method, 92

AppendFormat method (StringBuilder class), 210

appending files (I/O), 81-82

application services (ASP.NET), configuring, 364

application settings system, 589-591

Application Start events, 326

application start times, improving, 212

application state, 325

   Application Start events, 326

   Application.Lock() method, 326

   Application.UnLock() method, 326

   usage example, 327-328

   web farms, 343

Application.Lock() method, 326

Application.UnLock() method, 326

ApplicationActivation attribute (Enterprise Services), 620

ApplicationDeployment class, 613

ApplicationID attribute (Enterprise Services), 620

ApplicationName attribute (Enterprise Services), 620

ApplicationName property, 414, 417, 428, 441

ApplicationQueuing attribute (Enterprise Services), 620

applications. *See also* smart clients

   ASP.NET

      building, 310

      debugging, 311

      deploying, 310

   multithreaded, writing, 123-128

   Windows Forms 2.0

      Console Applications, 522

      cultures, changing, 561-562

      Windows Applications, 522

array indexer notation, 33

Array of Arrays notation, 40

ArrayList collection, 43-45

arrays

   array indexer notation, 33

   collections, comparing to, 43

   declaring, 33

   defining, 33

   initializing, 34

   IntelliSense, opening, 34

   jagged arrays, 40-42

   multidimensional arrays, 37-41

   one-dimensional arrays, 34-36

   operations list, accessing, 34

   resizing, 43

artificial dependencies (software), 504

ASP.NET

   application services, configuring, 364

   applications

      building, 310

      debugging, 311

      deploying, 310

      state, 325-328, 343

   ASP.NET SQL Server Configuration Wizard, 364

   client callbacks, 315-319, 322

   compiler, 300

   controls

      hierarchies, 300

      overview of, 307-309

      state, 468-471

   data binding, 395-400

   Data Source Configuration Wizard, 396-397

   data sources, 396

   DataSource property, ViewState objects, 471

State Server providers

  out-of-process servers, 334-336

  Serializable classes, 334

  turning on/off, 333

  usage example, 335-336

  Web.conf files, modifying, 333-334

System.Diagnostics.Debug class, 311

System.Web.TraceContext class, 311

themes

  creating, 360

  customizing, 371-373

  editing, 362

  global themes, 363

  runtime errors, 361

  skins, 360

  skins, adding, 362-363

  theme-specific images, 364

  viewing, 362

usage example, 331

  event handling, 339-340

  HTTPSessionState class, methods list, 330

  HTTPSessionState class, properties list, 329-330

  managing, 329

  session IDs, 328

  Session objects, 332

  SQL Server Session State providers, 337-338

  storing, 329

  web farms, 343

user controls

  creating, 460-462

  pages, adding to, 460

  properties, 462

user profiles

  anonymous profiles, 368-371

  application services, configuring, 364

  customizing, 371-373

  profile providers, configuring, 365-366

  properties, 367-371

view state, 468-472

  Restoring, 341

  usage example, 342

  web farms, 344-345

  web configuration, 302

ASP.NET 1.1, GUI consistency, 348

aspnet regsql command-line tool, 337

assemblies

  creating, 158-160

  external, 159-160

  loading, 155

  manifests, 156-157

  multifiles, 156

  partially trusted callers, 186

  PIA (Primary InterOp Assembly), 171-174

  reflection, 158

  resources

    embedding, 160

    storing/retrieving, 160-163

  satellite, localization, 163-165

Assembly class, 158-159

Assembly Linker tool (AL.EXE), 158

asynchronous data access (ADO.NET), 241-242

asynchronous files, 85-86

asynchronous web service consumption, smart clients, 597-598

attributes

  custom (reflection), creating, 150-153

  instance members, 52

  static members, 52

How can we make this index more useful? Email us at indexes@samspublishing.com

HintAncestorNodes method, 457

HintNeighborhoodNodes method, 457

HitTest method, 573

HTML (hypertext markup language)

controls list (ASP.NET), 309

Master Pages, 356

HttpSessionState class

methods list, 330

properties list, 329-330

hub-and-spoke model, resource localization, 163

I

I/O (input/output), 77

file management

asynchronous files, 85-86

creating/appending files, 81-82

directories, 83-85

isolated storage, 86-88

reading existing files, 82-83

streams, 77

composition, 78

instantiating, 79-80

MemoryStream class, 78-81

Unicode, 80

ICallbackEventHandler interface, 315

identity

imperative security, enforcing via, 188-189

permissions, 183

IDs (session), 328

IEditableObject interface, 581-584

if/else statements, 17-19

Image Library (Visual Studio), 544

ImageList component (Windows Control Libraries), 544

imperative security (CAS), 185-189

implicit transactions (ADO.NET), 247-250

ImportNode method, 93

IndexOf method, 27, 44, 568

IndexOfAny method, 27

inheritance (classes)

multiple inheritance, 57

new keyword, 57

override keyword, 58

single inheritance, 57

usage example, 58-59

visual inheritance, 558-560

Initialization stage (ASP.NET page life cycle), 303

initialization vector (IV), 194

Initialize method, 35, 457

InitializeRequest method, 456

InnerText property, 92

InnerXml property, 92

INotifyPropertyChanged interface, 581-584

Insert method, 568

InsertAfter method, 92

InsertBefore method, 92

InsertCommand, 233

Install button (Publish Wizard), 609

Installer (Windows), ClickOnce versus, 604-605

InstallSqlState.sql script, 337

instance members, 52

instance methods (strings), 27-28

instantiating streams, 79-80

int aliases (.NET data types), 9

IntelliSense, opening arrays in, 34

J – K – L

multithreaded programming, 121-122

  synchronization

    Interlocked class, 133

    lock keyword, 129

    Monitor class, 132-133

    Mutex class, 130-132

    ReaderWriterLock class, 133-136

    reset events, 136-138

  ThreadPool class, 138-139

  writing applications, 123-128

multithreaded web service consumption, smart clients, 597-598

Mutex class, 130-132

N

Name property, 92

namespaces, 9

  System.IO, classes, 83

  System.Transactions, 245

    explicit transactions, 246-247

    implicit transactions, 247-250

navigation controls list (ASP.NET), 309

nested transaction scopes, 248-250

.NET classes, COM interoperability, 174-175

.NET data types

  aliases table, 9

  common types table, 8-9

  namespaces, 9

  reference types, 10

  shortcuts table, 9

  System.Boolean, 8

  System.Byte, 8

  System.Char, 8

  System.Decimal, 8

  System.Double, 8

  System.Int16, 9

  System.Int32, 9

  System.Int64, 9

  System.SByte, 9

  System.Single, 8

  System.String, 9

  System.UInt16, 9

  System.UInt32, 9

  System.UInt64, 9

  value types, 10

.NET Framework, 184

  CLR, 6-8

  COM objects, 6

  COM+ 2.0, 6

  Common Type System, 7

  evolution of, 6

  Forms 2.0 (Windows), 519

  regular expressions, 29-31

  StringBuilder, 29

  strings, 24

network shares, ClickOnce applications, 605-606

network status, monitoring (smart client example), 592-594

NetworkAddressChanged events, 592-593

NetworkAvailabilityChanged events, 592-593

new keyword, inheritance, 57

NewRowIndex property, 574

NGen.exe (Native Image Generator) tool, improving application start times, 212

NodeType property, 92

NOT (!) operators, 16

Notifylcon control (Windows Control Libraries), 535

Page PreInit event (ASP.NET page life cycle), 304

Page PreRender event (ASP.NET page life cycle), 304

Page Start stage (ASP.NET page life cycle), 303

Page Unload event (ASP.NET page life cycle), 304

PageSetupDialog component (Windows Control Libraries), 545

Panel control (Windows Control Libraries), 539

parameters (type)

    constraining, 67-69

    factory patterns, 68

    generics, 66-67

    naming, 67

ParentNode property, 92

partially trusted callers, assemblies, 186

Passport authentication, 409

PassportIdentity class, 409

PasswordAttemptWindow property, 414, 428

PasswordFormat property, 428

PasswordQuestion property, 430

PasswordRecovery control, 421

PasswordStrengthRegularExpression property, 414, 428

-pe option, Web.config files, 424-426

Peek method, 47

performance counters (ASP.NET), list of, 483-485

Performance Wizard, 212-213

PerformanceCounter component (Windows Control Libraries), 545

permissions, 182-184

persistent session state support (SQL Server), 337

PersonalizableAttribute class, creating connected Web Parts, 391

personalization providers, 378-379

PIA (Primary InterOp Assembly), 171-174

PictureBox control (Windows Control Libraries), 536

placeholders, creating in Master Pages, 350-351

Point3D UDT example, 285-287

polymorphism, example of, 60-61

pooling (COM+), 623

Position property, 569

PositionChanged event, 569

Postback Event Handling stage (ASP.NET page life cycle), 303

postbacks, 306

pre-emptive multitasking, 129

PrependChild method, 92

Prerequisites button (Publish Wizard), 608

PreviousSibling property, 92

Primary InterOp Assembly (PIA), 171-174

PrintDialog component (Windows Control Libraries), 545

PrintDocument component (Windows Control Libraries), 546

Printing section (Windows Control Libraries), 545-546

PrintPreviewControl component (Windows Control Libraries), 546

PrintPreviewDialog component (Windows Control Libraries), 546

private member visibility level, 56

private protected member visibility level, 56

Process component (Windows Control Libraries), 545

profile provider

    classes, 449

    configuring, 365-366, 455-456

public member visibility level, 56

public protected member visibility level, 56

public-key encryption, 194-195, 198-200

Publish Now button (ClickOnce), 611

Publish Wizard

ClickOnce applications, publishing to CD, 606

Create Test Certificate button, 608

Install button, 609

launching, 607-608

Options button, 608

Prerequisites button, 608

Q – R

queries, adding via typed DataSets, 272-273

Queue class, 73-74

Queue collection, 46

methods table, 47

usage example, 47-48

queued components (COM+), 624-626

RadioButton control (Windows Control Libraries), 536

RadioButtonList control, 399

Rank property, 35

RCW (Runtime Callable Wrapper), 170

ReaderWriterLock class, 133-136

reading files, existing (I/O), 82-83

ReadOnly property, 574

real dependencies (software), 504

RedirectFromLoginPage method, 411-412

RedirectToLoginPage method, 411

reference counting, 648

reference types

boxing/unboxing, 208-209

defining, 10, 207

referencing .NET-hosted COM objects, 175

reflection, 141-143

assemblies, 158

custom attributes, creating, 150-153

events, 148-150

generics, 145

MemberInfo class, 146-148

MethodInfo class, 143-146

System.Type class, methods/properties, 142

RegEx class, 30

registering

.NET-hosted COM objects, 175

COM+, 620-622

RegisterWellKnownServiceType method, remoting, 641

regular expressions, 29-31

ReleaseItemExclusive method, 456

remoting

aspects of, 638

channels, 641

IPC channels, 641-645

TCP channels, 645-648

generics, 650-653

lifetime leases, 648-649

MarshalByRefObject class, 639

overview of, 637

RegisterWellKnownServiceType method, 641

RemotingConfiguration class, 641

single call objects, 639

singleton objects, 639

RemotingConfiguration class, 641

U

How can we make this index more useful? Email us at indexes@samspublishing.com

WSDL (Web Services Description Language), 490, 495-498

WSE (Web Services Extensions), 512

X

XML (eXtensible Markup Language)

documents

display sample, 94-95

hierarchy levels, representation of, 95

Items.xml document, 93-94

reading/writing, 91-95

XSD validations, 100-101

XSLT transformations, 97-99

itemsTransform.xslt document, 97-98

DataTables, loading/saving, 238-240

DOM, 91

querying, XPath, 95-97

XML Schema home page, 264

XmlDataSource, 396

XmlDocument class, methods table, 92-93

XmlNode class, 91-94

XMLProvider C# Class Library

Membership provider, creating, 431-440

Profile provider, creating, 450-455

Role provider, creating/installing, 442-448

XOR (^) operators, 16. *See also* OR operators

XPath, 95-97

XSD (XML Schema Definition)

items.xsd document, 100-101

schemas, creating typed DataSets, 264-265

XSLT (XSL Transformation), 97-99

Y – Z

zones (Web Parts), 380

Your Guide to Computer Technology

www.informit.com